THE OXFORD HANDBOO(

PRESOCRATIC PHILOSOPHY

THE OXFORD HANDBOOK OF

PRESOCRATIC PHILOSOPHY

Edited by

PATRICIA CURD
AND DANIEL W. GRAHAM

OXFORD
UNIVERSITY PRESS

OXFORD

UNIVERSITY PRESS

Oxford University Press, Inc., publishes works that further
Oxford University's objective of excellence
in research, scholarship, and education.

Oxford   New York
Auckland   Cape Town   Dar es Salaam   Hong Kong   Karachi
Kuala Lumpur   Madrid   Melbourne   Mexico City   Nairobi
New Delhi   Shanghai   Taipei   Toronto

With offices in
Argentina   Austria   Brazil   Chile   Czech Republic   France   Greece
Guatemala   Hungary   Italy   Japan   Poland   Portugal   Singapore
South Korea   Switzerland   Thailand   Turkey   Ukraine   Vietnam

Published by Oxford University Press, Inc.
198 Madison Avenue, New York, New York 10016
www.oup.com

First issued as an Oxford University Press paperback, 2011

Oxford is a registered trademark of Oxford University Press

Library of Congress Cataloging-in-Publication Data

The Oxford handbook of presocratic philosophy / edited by Patricia Curd
and Daniel W. Graham.
p. cm.
Includes bibliographical references and index.
ISBN 978-0-19-514687-5; 978-0-19-983755-7 (pbk.)
1. Philosophy, Ancient.   2. Pre-Socratic philosophers.   I. Curd,
Patricia, 1949–   II. Graham, Daniel W.
B187.5O94   2008
182—dc22   2007011788

Printed in the United States of America
on acid-free paper

CONTENTS

....

ABBREVIATIONS

The following abbreviations have been used throughout.

DG   Diels, Hermann. *Doxographi Graeci*. Berlin, 1879. Reprint, Berlin: de Gruyter, 1965.

DK   Diels, Hermann. *Die Fragmente der Vorsokratiker*. Edited by Walther Kranz. 6th ed. 3 vols. Berlin: Weidmann, 1951.

HGP   Guthrie, W. K. C. *A History of Greek Philosophy*. 6 vols. Vol 1. *The Earlier Presocratics and the Pythagoreans*. Cambridge: Cambridge University Press, 1962. Vol. 2. *The Presocratic Tradition from Parmenides to Democritus*. Cambridge: Cambridge University Press, 1965.

KR   Kirk, G. S., and J. E. Raven. *The Presocratic Philosophers*. Cambridge: Cambridge University Press, 1957.

KRS   Kirk, G. S., J. E. Raven, and M. Schofield. *The Presocratic Philosophers*. 2nd ed. Cambridge: Cambridge University Press, 1983.

LSJ   Liddell, Henry George, and Robert Scott, eds. *A Greek-English Lexicon*. Revised by Henry Stuart Jones and Roderick McKenzie. Oxford: Clarendon Press, 1968.

PP   Barnes, Jonathan. *The Presocratic Philosophers*. Rev. ed. London: Routledge and Kegan Paul, 1982.

ZN   Zeller, Eduard. *Die Philosophie der Griechen in ihrer geschichtliche Entwicklung*. Edited by Wilhelm Nestle. 6th ed. Pt. 1. *Vorsokratische Philosophie*. 2 vols. Leipzig: O. R. Reisland, 1919–20.

Abbreviations for ancient works follow LSJ, although there are occasional expansions for ease of recognition.

The texts of the fragments and *testimonia* of the Presocratics follow DK, except where noted. Texts for the Commentators on Aristotle follow the editions of the Berlin Academy *Commentaria in Aristotelem Graeca* (Berlin: G. Reimer). The usual method of referring to the Presocratics has been followed. Each philosopher is assigned a number by DK; where the reference may be unclear, we have included the author number. "A" refers to the section of *testimonia* assigned to each philosopher by DK; "B" refers to the section of fragments accepted as authentic by DK.

Contributors

WALTER BURKERT is Professor Emeritus of classical philology at the University of Zürich. His research and publications concentrate on ancient Greek philosophy and religion, including oriental contacts and perspectives of anthropology. Among his publications are *Lore and Science in Ancient Pythagoreanism* (1972), *Homo Necans* (1983), *Greek Religion* (1985), *The Orientalizing Revolution* (1992), and *Babylon Memphis Persepolis: Eastern Contexts of Greek Culture* (2004)

PATRICIA CURD is Professor of Philosophy at Purdue University. She is the author of *The Legacy of Parmenides: Eleatic Monism and Later Presocratic Thought* (1998) and *Anaxagoras of Clazomenae: Fragments and Testimonia; A Text and Translation with Notes and Essays* (2007).

MICHAEL FREDE (1940–2007) taught at the University of California, Berkeley, and Princeton University and was Professor of the History of Philosophy at Oxford University and fellow of Keble College. After retirement from Oxford, he lived in Athens, Greece. He was the author, translator and commentator, editor, or co-editor of numerous books, including *Aristotle's Metaphysics Lambda* (Oxford, 2000) and *Rationality in Greek Thought* (Oxford, 1996).

MICHAEL GAGARIN is the James R. Dougherty, Jr. Centennial Professor of Classics at the University of Texas. He has written widely in the areas of Greek law, rhetoric, literature, and philosophy, including the volumes *Drakon and Early Athenian Homicide Law* (1981), *Early Greek Law* (1986), *Antiphon the Athenian: Oratory, Law and Justice in the Age of the Sophists* (2002), and *Writing Greek Law* (2008). He is currently preparing (together with Paula Perlman) an edition of the Laws of Crete (text, translation, commentary, and interpretative essays).

DANIEL W. GRAHAM is A. O. Smoot Professor of Philosophy at Brigham Young University. He is the author of *Explaining the Cosmos: The Ionian Tradition of Scientific Philosophy* (2006) and author, editor, or translator of five other volumes on ancient philosophy. He is currently preparing a bilingual edition of the Presocratic philosophers, *The Texts of Early Greek Philosophy,* for Cambridge University Press.

R. J. HANKINSON is Professor of Philosophy and Classics at the University of Texas at Austin. He has published more than fifty articles on many aspects of ancient philosophy and science; his books include *The Sceptics* (1995) and *Cause and Explanation in the Ancient Greek World* (1998).

CARL HUFFMAN is Edwin L. Minar Professor of Classics at DePauw University in Greencastle, Indiana. He has held a Guggenheim Fellowship and two fellowships from the National Endowment for the Humanities. He is the author of *Archytas of Tarentum: Pythagorean, Philosopher and Mathematician King* (2005) and *Philolaus of Croton: Pythagorean and Presocratic* (1993). He is currently working on an edition of the fragments of Aristoxenus of Tarentum, which deal with the history of philosophy.

ANDRÉ LAKS is Professor of Ancient Philosophy at the Université Paris-Sorbonne and member of the Institut Universitaire de France. He taught for a long time at the University Charles de Gaulle, Lille, France, and at Princeton University from 1990 to 1994. He has recently published a book on Plato's *Laws* (*Médiation et coercition. Pour une lecture des 'Lois' de Platon*, 2005); an essay on the emergence of negativity in archaic philosophy (*Le vide et la haine*, 2004); an introduction to the concept of Presocratic philosophy (*Introduction à la 'philosophie présocratique,'* 2006); and a collection of some of his articles on Aristotle, Theophrastus, and Presocratic philosophy (*Histoire, doxographie, vérité*, 2007). A second, revised and augmented version of his edition of Diogenes of Apollonia (1983) has just been published (2008). He is the coeditor, with Michel Narcy, of the journal *Philosophie antique*.

J. H. LESHER is Professor of Philosophy at the University of North Carolina at Chapel Hill. He is the author of *Xenophanes of Colophon* (1992), *The Greek Philosophers* (1998), *Plato's Symposium: Issues in Interpretation and Reception*, coedited with Debra Nails and Frisbee Sheffield (2006), and numerous articles on the Presocraticis, Plato, and Presocraticis Aristotle.

RICHARD D. MCKIRAHAN is E. C. Norton Professor of Classics and Professor of Philosophy at Pomona College, Claremont, California. He is the author of *Philosophy before Socrates* (1994) and *Principles and Proofs: Aristotle's Theory of Demonstrative Science* (1992), has translated texts by Simplicius and Philoponus for the Ancient Commentators on Aristotle series, and is the author of articles on ancient philosophy.

ALEXANDER P. D. MOURELATOS is Professor of Philosophy and Classics at The University of Texas at Austin, where he founded and for twenty-five years directed the Joint Classics–Philosophy Graduate Program in Ancient Philosophy. His publications in the areas of philosophy, classics, and linguistics include *The Route of Parmenides* (1970); he is preparing a book on Xenophanes.

JOHN PALMER is Associate Professor of Philosophy at the University of Florida. He is the author of *Plato's Reception of Parmenides* (1999) and a number of articles on early Greek philosophy and its reception.

OLIVER PRIMAVESI holds a Chair of Greek Language and Literature at the University of Munich, where he has founded, together with Christof Rapp, the *Munich School of Ancient Philosophy* (2010). He is the coauthor, with Alain Martin, of *L'Empédocle de Strasbourg* (1999), author of *Empedokles Physika I: Eine Rekonstruktion des zentralen Gedankengangs* (2008), and coeditor of *The Presocratics from the Latin Middle Ages to Hermann Diels* (2011).

T. M. ROBINSON is Professor Emeritus of Philosophy at the University of Toronto. He is the author of *Heraclitus: Fragments* (1987) and various articles on Heraclitus and Parmenides. He has served as President of the International Association for Greek Philosophy and of the International Plato Society, and is currently Honorary President of the International Association for Greek Philosophy.

DAVID T. RUNIA is Master of Queen's College at the University of Melbourne, Australia. Prior to this appointment he was Professor of Ancient and Medieval Philosophy at the University of Leiden. He is the coauthor (with Jaap Mansfeld) of *Aëtiana: The Method and Intellectual Context of a Doxographer* (1997) and numerous other studies on Philo of Alexandria and on Plato and the history of Platonism.

DAVID SEDLEY has taught since 1975 at the University of Cambridge, where he is Laurence Professor of Ancient Philosophy and a Fellow of Christ's College. His books include *The Hellenistic Philosophers,* coauthored with A. A. Long (1987), *Lucretius and the Transformation of Greek Wisdom* (1998), *Plato's Cratylus* (2003), *The Midwife of Platonism: Text and Subtext in Plato's Theaetetus* (2004), and *Creationism and Its Critics in Antiquity* (2007, from his 2004 Sather Lectures at the University of California, Berkeley). He works on the editing of philosophical papyri, and has also been editor of *Classical Quarterly* (1986–1992) and *Oxford Studies in Ancient Philosophy* (1998–2007).

PHILIP VAN DER EIJK is Professor of Greek at Newcastle University. He has published widely on ancient philosophy, medicine and science, comparative literature, and patristics. He is the author of *Medicine and Philosophy in Classical Antiquity* (2005), *Diocles of Carystus* (2000–2001), *Philoponus, On Aristotle On the Soul 1* (2005–6), and *Aristoteles, De insomniis, De divinatione per somnum* (1994). He has edited and coauthored *Ancient Histories of Medicine* (1999) and coedited *Ancient Medicine in Its Socio-Cultural Context* (1995).

STEPHEN A. WHITE is Professor of Classics and Philosophy at the University of Texas. He is the author of *Sovereign Virtue: Aristotle on the Relation between Happiness and Prosperity* (1992) and articles on Aristotle and later Greek philosophy, and coeditor with W. W. Fortenbaugh of *Lyco of Troas and Hieronymus of Rhodes: Text, Translation, and Discussion* (2004) and *Aristo of Ceos: Text, Translation, and Discussion* (2006). He is currently preparing a translation of Diogenes Laertius.

PAUL WOODRUFF is Darrell K. Royal Professor of Ethics and American Society and Inaugural Dean of Undergraduate Studies at the University of Texas, where he has chaired the Department of Philosophy and, since 1991, directed the Plan II Honors Program. He is the author of scholarly articles, translations from ancient Greek, and plays, poems, and opera libretti, including *Reverence: Renewing a Forgotten Virtue, First Democracy: The Challenge of an Ancient Idea,* and *The Necessity of Theater* (Oxford, 2008).

M. R. WRIGHT is Emeritus Professor of Classics at the University of Wales. She was previously a Fellow for the Center of Hellenic Studies and Senior Lecturer in Classics at Aberystwyth, Wales, and Reading, England; she was then at Lampeter (the first woman to hold a professorship and established chair there). She has written numerous articles and reviews in ancient philosophy, mainly on the Presocratics and Plato, and is the author of *Empedocles* (1981 and 1995), *The Presocratics* (1985), *Cicero on Stoic Good and Evil* (1991), *Cosmology in Antiquity* (1995) and editor of *Reason and Necessity* (2000). She devised one of the first online ancient Greek primers (www.wright.classics.com/mathos).

THE OXFORD HANDBOOK OF

PRESOCRATIC PHILOSOPHY

INTRODUCTION

1. ABOUT THIS VOLUME

This volume is concerned with the first philosophers and scientists in the Western tradition. Why what we call philosophy and science first emerged in the West in Greece during the sixth century BCE is a question that intrigued even the classical Greek philosophers (Aristotle makes some suggestions), but it is one that we cannot answer. The figures who are studied in this book, the Presocratic philosophers, would not have recognized themselves under either of those names. Certainly, they would not think of themselves as waiting for or prefiguring Socrates; and it is fairly clear that *philosophy*, as a name for the intellectual activity in which they were engaged, did not begin to be in common use until the time of Plato and Isocrates, after the period that concerns us. Why, then, is this a handbook of *Presocratic philosophy*? The name *Presocratic philosophers* serves as a useful label for picking out a group of thinkers in the Greek-speaking world of the sixth and fifth centuries BCE. Such labels are common in the history of philosophy—Augustine and Anselm certainly did not think of themselves as *medievals*, and neither Aquinas nor Hume would have claimed that they studied *epistemology*, although both certainly were concerned with what knowledge is and how and what human beings can know. In our case, the figures in this study were engaged with a range of problems and theories that later philosophers (who identified themselves as such) recognized as similar to their own, and as significant (though perhaps mistaken) forerunners of their own (presumably correct) views. Yet, for all that, the term "philosophy" can be misleading in the study of the Presocratics, for it can artificially narrow our perception of the range of topics and problems that occupied these men. They studied many things that are now outside the scope of academic philosophical inquiry. They studied the phenomena of the heavens and the earth. They had views about the nature of the cosmos (and whether there could be more than one cosmos), the stars, the weather, human thought and perception, disease and health, the natures of plants and animals (and their activities), respiration, the circulation of the blood, embryology, gods and piety, cities and individuals, and the possibilities and limits of human thought. They thought about motion and change, patterns of change and stability, mortality and immortality, ignorance and understanding.

This volume collects essays on the Presocratics that are aimed at both specialists and upper-level students of the field of Greek philosophy. One can approach early Greek philosophy through either particular figures of the period or thematic studies that cover broader time periods. Introductory texts, by necessity, must be fairly neutral and detached in their treatment of contentious issues. Our hope is that in this volume the reader will find evidence of the exciting field that is Presocratic studies: the editors have asked writers to take account of recent controversies and new interpretations of the Presocratics. We have encouraged the contributors to branch out and make new contributions to the field, to argue for their own views; thus the reader will find disagreements between authors and arguments both for and against certain interpretations. It is through the rigorous examination of new and provocative views that our understanding of these important philosophers will advance. It is hoped that in these essays, a reader can find some of the best and latest work on Presocratic thought, giving a picture of the state of Presocratic studies today and also setting problems for future scholarly work.

If the term "Presocratic philosopher" is a conventional designation established by scholars, it marks out a set of figures who do seem to merit special attention. So long as there is a tribe of philosophers in the West, they will look back to the first antecedents of their profession. And it seems that the Presocratics are the obvious candidates for founders of the movement. Rhetoricians have always recognized the subclass of sophists as the founders of their movement; in light of common interests sophists shared with the natural philosophers, they seem to merit inclusion in the larger group of Presocratic philosophers. In the same period, there were other gifted intellectuals who shared some interests with the Presocratics—historians such as Herodotus, playwrights such as Euripides, and politicians such as Pericles. Physicians, notably the Hippocratic writers, were especially influenced by Presocratic theories. Yet these were not in the same way theorists of nature, or of being, or of human society. In the Presocratics we find an intellectual movement with distinctive aims and methods, one that had a continuing influence on philosophical and scientific discussions in antiquity, and even in the modern world. Their achievement has always inspired awe among their students, and we still have much to learn from them.

Part of the difficulty of working with Presocratic material is the problem of our texts and the sources for them. No Presocratic text has survived complete and intact. We are almost entirely dependent on the vagaries of later ancient writers for what we know of these thinkers and their work. David Runia provides a short critical history of this, and discusses the latest developments in the study of the sources for the Presocratics. It is certain that they drew on the myths and traditions of the Greek world as well as Eastern myths and astronomical records. Walter Burkert's contribution shows just how complicated that influence was, yet the novelty of the early Greek mode of inquiry seems clear. Thales, Anaximander, and Anaximenes of Miletus proposed startlingly different explanations of the world around them, including complex theories to explain the phenomena of the heavens. A standard way of characterizing their new view is that they were the first who attempted to explain the natural world in terms of itself, using concepts that avoided supernatural causes, and this is certainly true, even though aspects of their language might suggest lingering aspects of a personified world picture, for example, Anaximander's claim that the things that are "give penalty and recompense to one another for their injustice, in accordance with the ordering of time" (12B1) or Thales' assertion that the lodestone has a soul (presumably because it moves iron, 11A22). It is commonly said of the early Presocratics that they were fundamentally materialist physicists, explaining the world around them in terms of some basic material stuff that undergoes alterations and changes while at the same time remaining (in some sense) the same and so underlying and being responsible for all physical phenomena. The three Milesians differ, on this view, primarily in their choice of basic stuff (water in the case of Thales, some mysterious "indefinite stuff" for Anaximander, and air for Anaximenes). This view of the Milesians goes back at least as far as Aristotle. In the 1990s, scholars began to challenge some of the traditional assumptions about the Milesians (and other early Presocratics), questioning the standard interpretation of their views and stressing the early Presocratic interest in astronomy. Stephen White, in his contribution, bases his account of the Milesians on their attempts at measurement and explanation of the regularities of astronomical phenomena, arguing that attending to the interactions among observation, measurement, and theory can help provide a richer understanding of the Milesian contribution to the development of both science and philosophy. Similarly, close attention to the meteorological theories of Xenophanes of Colophon has led to a greater appreciation of his role as a theoretical philosopher, and has led scholars to see him as more than a traveling poet with some interests in the vagaries of religious belief among human beings, and some suggestive remarks about knowledge. For instance, in claiming that the rainbow is by nature cloud colored in a certain way, Xenophanes uses a pattern of analysis and explanation that will stay with philosophy for a long time; in exhorting humans to engage in inquiry, he makes explicit the method of the Milesians and begins to test its efficacy. A. P. D. Mourelatos, in a discussion of Xenophanes' "cloud astro-physics" (the analysis and explanation of all heavenly and meteorological phenomena in terms of cloud), provides a view of this newer Xenophanes, who is now being recognized as an important philosopher-scientist in his own right and a crucial figure in the development of critical thought about human knowledge and its objects in the next generation of Presocratic thinkers.

Heraclitus of Ephesus, called the Riddler (by Timon of Phlius) and the Obscure (by Cicero), has hardly suffered from neglect. His views on change (or flux), on understanding the *logos* and the unity of opposites, on religious and ethical questions, and on the dunderheadedness of most ordinary people have been subjects of debate and ridicule since ancient times. Also since ancient times, commentators have had difficulty not only understanding Heraclitus, but also fitting him into certain pictures of the development of early Greek thought: is he a cosmologist who follows the Milesian line and adopts fire as the single substratum of all things? Is he primarily an ethicist with no real concern for scientific inquiry? The renewed interest in the Presocratics of the last few decades has not ignored Heraclitus, and some new and fruitful lines of inquiry are now being pursued. In his chapter on Heraclitus, Daniel Graham presents a unified Heraclitus who is a thoughtful critic of his predecessors, and keenly interested in the possibility of human understanding. This Heraclitus rejects the Milesian account of a single substance with systematic changes and transformations that guarantee the stability of the whole. He recognizes that his new views will be difficult to understand, but provides hints and lessons to allow his hearer or reader to grasp his philosophical account. Parmenides of Elea, too, has not been ignored by the scholarly community—a number of new interpretations of Parmenides have appeared in the last decade. Yet it can still be difficult to understand just how Parmenides reaches his conclusions: how are the parts of his long argument in fragment B8 connected with one another, and how do they function to further his claims that what-is is and must be and that what-is-not is not and cannot be? Richard McKirahan undertakes here a close analysis of fragment B8, teasing out the structure of the arguments, and showing what parts of the traditional and new interpretations of Parmenides those arguments do (or do not) support. He presents some surprising conclusions and opens up spaces for new interpretations.

Traditional histories of Presocratic philosophy have tended to see a double strand of interests developing, usually side by side without much interaction (at least until the time of Plato). First, there are the Milesians and their descendents among the *physiologoi*: Heraclitus (however uneasily he might fit the pattern), Parmenides (as critic of physical science), the pluralists and atomists (who persist in the study of the cosmos despite Parmenides' arguments). Second, there are Pythagoras and the Pythagoreans, who concentrated on formal or mathematical accounts of things, and were as committed to living a certain sort of life as to philosophical inquiry. This picture has been disputed recently: scholars have not only argued that Parmenides wished to reform rather than reject cosmological inquiry but also integrated the Pythagoreans more fully into a more expansive picture of Presocratic interests.[1] Recently, the Pythagoreans have received rather more attention, both in their own right and as part of the developing picture of Presocratic thought, than they received for much of the twentieth century. Thanks to these studies, a new and more complicated picture is emerging. Carl Huffman refines this picture in his chapter, critically examining Aristotle's claims about

Pythagorean influence on Plato, along with the related question of who among early Greek thinkers actually counts as a Pythagorean. Huffman provides a reminder that Aristotle's account of the history of earlier thought is always a history of just a part of the philosophy of his predecessors, and makes clear that the eagerness with which some present-day scholars find Pythagorean influence on later thought may be misplaced. Not only our view of the Pythagoreans has become more nuanced but also our understanding of post-Parmenidean thought. The fuller assimilation of the Pythagoreans into the story and a better appreciation of the influence of Parmenides have changed our view of later Presocratic thought. Patricia Curd, in her chapter on Anaxagoras of Clazomenae, undertakes to show the connections among the metaphysical, epistemological, and cosmological parts of Anaxagoras's theory. The discovery and publication of new material has also enhanced our understanding of Presocratic thought. A spectacular example is the new material[2] from Empedocles of Acragas that has become available. Oliver Primavesi considers how the new finds have affected our view of Empedocles, and suggests how interpretation of that material might help solve (or dissolve) some longstanding problems about the structure and content of Empedocles' writings.

Presocratic atomism was one of the most influential of the early theories: both Plato and Aristotle thought of it as a major competing theory, and it was an important source for post-Aristotelian Hellenistic theories (as was Heraclitus). It has been a commonplace that the atomism developed first by Leucippus of Abdera and then by Democritus of Abdera was a reaction to the Eleatic arguments of Zeno and Melissus, but the details of that influence have sometimes seemed rather hazy. Daniel Graham and David Sedley here bring them into sharper focus. The paucity of direct evidence and the welter of reports and responses in later philosophical treatments hampers all study of Presocratic atomism. Graham undertakes the task of recovering Leucippus, the first atomist, attempting to determine his own particular views, and to show how Eleatic arguments and theories affected atomism; not in the first place as a target to be undermined, but as a positive model that Leucippus used. Sedley also considers the Eleatic foundations of atomism, especially the question of the importance of Zeno and Melissus for Democritus. By concentrating on some of the less-studied aspects of atomism (through a close study of Aristotle's criticism of Democritus) and especially of the development of the concept of the unlimited into the notion of the infinite, he furthers our understanding of not only the development of early atomism but also the Eleatics Zeno and Melissus.

In the last part of the fifth century, we meet with figures who both carried on and marked a change in the Presocratic tradition. Diogenes of Apollonia developed a theory based on air. He has often been dismissed as a minor or eclectic thinker (eclecticism somehow being a mark of inferiority) who merely echoed (in an inferior way) Milesian views that Parmenides had discredited. André Laks challenged that view in a monograph published in 1983; here Laks takes up Diogenes again, investigating some of the reasons Diogenes has been unappreciated, and making a case for Diogenes' mind-based teleology as a significant philosophical contribution. The sophists, too, have suffered from the charge, which goes back to Plato, of not being "real" philosophers. By now, this view is largely discredited, yet as Paul Woodruff and Michael Gagarin show, important questions remain to be answered about the topics the sophists studied and taught, and their views, both positive and negative, about truth, religion, and convention.

While many studies focus on individual early Greek thinkers, we can perhaps best appreciate the Presocratic achievement by looking at their views synoptically: seeing how certain assumptions and questions were common to them. Five chapters in this volume consider the Presocratics from this vantage point. Philip van der Eijk explores the often overlooked but crucial connections between ancient Greek medicine and early Greek thought, emphasizing how porous the boundaries were between disciplines that we now see as quite different, and how the practitioners of medicine and philosophy understood, criticized, and influenced one another. M. R. Wright explores early Greeks' cosmological speculation, showing how they explored the possibility of a "theory of everything" and human understanding of the cosmos. R. J. Hankinson focuses on their explorations of the fundamental concepts of reasons and causation, and the problems of explanation, and argues, like Wright, that it is indeed reasonable to see in Presocratic thought the foundations of Western scientific explanation. J. H. Lesher explores Presocratic epistemology, arguing that these thinkers replace divine revelation as a warrant for knowledge with naturalistic accounts of how and what we humans can know; thus replacing earlier Greek pessimism about knowledge with a more optimistic outlook that allows for human discovery of the truth. Despite what may seem to be a rejection of traditional Greek notions of the gods and the piety due them, many of the Presocratics maintained a keen interest in what we would call religious belief, and that interest is the subject of the chapter by T. M. Robinson; not only Xenophanes but others of the Presocratics had important views on the relation between the human and divine, and in some, as in Empedocles, that relation could underlie their philosophical theories.

Both Plato and Aristotle saw the Presocratics as important sources and forerunners. Thinking about how they treated their early Greek predecessors can help us to see how Plato's and Aristotle's understanding of the Presocratics affected later accounts, which often are all we have to go on when we study them. As noted, our own view of the Presocratics is enormously complicated by the problems of sources and traditions for their work. Michael Frede sheds light on Aristotle's own understanding of philosophy, hence his views of his predecessors (which can help us understand some of the claims he made about the earlier thinkers). John Palmer deals with classical thinkers (including Plato and Aristotle) who interpreted, wrote about, and preserved the Presocratics, pointing out that just as we must read the Presocratics through the filters of Plato and Aristotle (and their successors and commentators), Plato and Aristotle were influenced by the already burgeoning tradition of historiography that developed in the late fifth and fourth centuries.

2. THE HISTORIOGRAPHY OF PRESOCRATIC PHILOSOPHY

When we study the great philosophers of the classical age, we read their writings (as in the case of Plato and Aristotle) or works depicting the philosopher and his methods (Socrates). But in the case of their philosophical predecessors, we have no intact philosophical works. We are forced to gather reports about them by informed sources (testimonies) and quotations of their words (fragments) taken from these sources. When we study these literary remains, we must take into account the biases of the ancient secondary sources; we are dependent on them to put the fragments in context, yet we recognize the possibility that they may distort the context or misconstrue the meaning of the passage. Despite the fact that the ancient secondary sources are much closer in time to the Presocratics, and share much of their social, historical, and linguistic environment, we find that these sources are often insensitive to differences that divide them from the earlier thinkers, hence they are apt to misunderstand the Presocratics in certain ways.

Modern scholarship consists of a twofold attempt to recover ancient thought: an effort to reconstruct the historical, social, linguistic, and intellectual context in which the Presocratics wrote, and an effort to reconstruct their theory in a systematic way so that the scattered remarks and doctrines attributed to them make philosophical sense. The first project falls primarily within the domain of the classicist, the second within that of the philosopher. In practice, however, scholars who work in the field must in large measure be, to use an Aristotelian term, "dualizers," competent in both fields. They must also be masters of detail, because the textual sources are so diverse; and capable of visionary imagination, because the gaps in the record require significant reconstruction.

The gap in time that separates the Presocratics from contemporary students is 2,600 years, at its greatest extent. But it is possible, in broad outlines, to trace the path by which the ancients' works come to us; and it is desirable to do so precisely to see what information is available, how it is understood, and what remains to be done. Before the beginning of this brief survey, however, I must make some preliminary observations about the subject of this study. In one sense, the Presocratics are a modern invention: modern scholars have given them a name, identified them as philosophers, and located them at the beginning of an ongoing intellectual tradition. In another sense, they are an ancient invention: Aristotle (among others) distinguished groups of *phusikoi* or *phusiologoi* (roughly: philosophers of nature) whom he saw as his own predecessors, and sophists, whom he saw as forerunners in ethical and political theory. Our views of the Presocratics are the product of a long tradition of interpretation that we should be aware of.

2.1. The Ancient Tradition

In recent years, scholars have begun to recognize that the study of the Presocratics began even during their own time. Hippias of Elis (a sophist) devoted a treatise to the early thinkers in which he seems to have organized their views in a systematic way. Similar schematic groupings of the Presocratics by Plato, Aristotle, and Isocrates suggest that they are working from a common source, most likely Hippias. Gorgias also organized the views of his predecessors in a schematic way for the sake of disagreeing with them. Hippias may have laid out his predecessors' views for the purpose of refuting them; Gorgias may simply have wished to show how every possible option had been canvassed in a futile attempt to explain phenomena that elude explanation.[3] Plato seems to have gotten his view of Heraclitus from an interpretation unique to the Heraclitean Cratylus. In all these cases, it appears that some preliminary classification and analysis was going on before Plato and Aristotle emerged as major philosophers indebted to the new style of philosophy derived from Socrates.

Plato imitated Socrates' conversational style of philosophy by composing dramatic dialogues in which Socrates is a prominent speaker. Plato presents Socrates as offering an alternative to sophistic methods, sometimes in discussions with sophists such as Protagoras and Gorgias. In later works, Plato shows an increasing interest in the natural and theoretical philosophers, depicting Cratylus, Parmenides, and Zeno as interlocutors (*Cratylus, Parmenides*), as well as having other characters examine their theories (e.g., theories of Heraclitus and Parmenides in the *Theaetetus* and *Sophist*, respectively). Plato thus sometimes has early thinkers appear *in propria persona*, and even when he has other characters discuss these thinkers' theories, he views them as contributing to an ongoing dialogue. Although his method mostly dispenses with a historical perspective on the Presocratics, he does recognize and for the first time articulate the principle of charity: the need to give an accurate and fair-minded account of a philosopher's theory (in a candid moment of self-criticism, *Tht.* 166a–b).

Whereas Plato presents philosophical theories—his own and others'—in dialogues, Aristotle develops them systematically in treatises. Aristotle recognizes a role for dialectic, or conversation-style treatment, in the preliminary examination of philosophical topics, which for him requires a survey of important opinions on a given topic. Thus the circumspect philosopher will collect the views of those who have already developed theories on a given topic, will consider the puzzles and problems they have confronted, and will develop a theory that will resolve those problems and show what insights are to be accepted and what errors avoided. Accordingly, at the beginning of his treatises Aristotle often surveys the views of

Presocratic philosophers as well as those of Plato and his contemporaries. For instance, Aristotle explores theories of soul in the *De Anima*, theories of change in the *Physics*, theories of elements in *On Generation and Corruption*, and theories of cause in *Metaphysics* 1. In all of these works, Aristotle organizes the opinions of Presocratic philosophers as being on one side or other of an issue that is under debate.[4] He does, in one notable case, describe a history of theoretical development, namely in the *Metaphysics* discussion of cause (which presents more of a history of ideas than a history of philosophy per se). In general, however, he (like Plato) is more interested in the synchronic presentation of arguments and positions than the diachronic development of theories. He occasionally shows an interest in the systematic coherence of a Presocratic's theory, but more often he focuses on whichever Presocratic doctrine connects with whatever topic he is examining. It appears that he prepared monographs, or perhaps preliminary notes, on several Presocratic figures, but these studies have not survived.

The great ancient sourcebook of Presocratic philosophy was the one Aristotle's follower and colleague Theophrastus prepared. His *Doctrines of the Natural Philosophers* or *Doctrines on Nature,* in 16 books, collected the opinions of the Presocratics (and others) on topics in natural philosophy (D.L. 5.48). The opinions were organized by topic rather than figure, and if Theophrastus's treatise *On Sense* is typical, were set in a critical exposition that aimed at refuting false doctrines and vindicating true ones. Too lengthy and detailed for practical use, the *Doctrines* was excerpted and digested into a shorter collection Diels called the *Vetusta Placita,* or *Early Doctrines,* in the first century BCE. But even before this work, there must have been an earlier collection, recently posited as the *Vetustissima Placita,* or *Earliest Doctrines.*[5] This work was available in the third century BCE and presumably became the basis of further digests of philosophical doctrines, in which later philosophers' views were attached to those of earlier philosophers. Various versions of this work may have circulated as textbooks or reference guides for students of philosophy. It is not clear that the editors or revisers of these books had any independent knowledge of the Presocratics, whose original works became increasingly scarce and, no doubt, difficult to understand.

In the Hellenistic period, some of the schools showed interest in the works of Presocratic philosophers. The Stoics accepted Heraclitus's physics of fire as being the forerunner of their own theory of nature. The Epicureans were atomists who could look to Leucippus and Democritus as their forebears (even if Epicurus himself preferred to downplay his debts to previous movements). Some skeptics found Xenophanes' views on knowledge congenial. Since, however, the documents of the Hellenistic schools themselves are scarce, we do not benefit much from their continued interest in the Presocratics.

Hellenistic writers developed a new genre in biography. After Aristotle's student Aristoxenus wrote some philosophical biographies, philosophers became popular subjects for biographical studies. Materials, however, on early philosophers were meager and often unreliable. In any case, biographers preferred anecdotes and bons mots to facts and arguments. The Peripatetic Sotion wrote his

Succession of the Philosophers in 13 books in the early second century BCE. He sought to establish links between one philosopher and another in an unbroken succession down to his time, as in the case of the heads of Hellenistic schools—never mind that before Plato's Academy there may have been no formal schools. Apollodorus of Athens wrote his *Chronicle* in verse in the second century BCE, dating important historical and also philosophical events from the fall of Troy to his own time. This work provided a historical framework for the history of philosophy, even if it was crudely schematic in some ways.

In the first century CE, an unknown scholar, Aëtius, compiled his *Placita* (Doctrines), based on the *Early Doctrines,* which extended the coverage down to the time of Posidonius (first century BCE). This work is the source of extant collections of doctrines in pseudo-Plutarch (the *Epitome*) and John Stobaeus (*Selections*). Aëtius's work, reconstructed in Diels's *Doxographi Graeci*, supplies much of the information we have about specific doctrines of Presocratic philosophers. Since its pedigree (though not all of its content) goes back to Theophrastus, we can rely on it as a source of information on Presocratic doctrines.[6]

At some point, the collections of doctrines that were originally organized topically in Theophrastus (and those who epitomized his work) were organized by author. We find this arrangement in the Christian bishop Hippolytus, who wrote in the early third century CE, accusing heretics of repeating Presocratic theories. About the same time, an otherwise unknown writer, Diogenes Laertius, wrote *The Lives of the Eminent Philosophers*, in ten books. Combining biography with doxography, he studies the philosophers from Thales down to the first century CE. He draws on over two hundred writers (many at second hand) to give us much valuable information about the philosophers—along with gossip, slanders, and misinformation.

Much philosophical research in late antiquity is carried out in commentaries on classical philosophers, especially on Aristotle, whose systematic treatises seemed to embody the best in philosophy and science, but needed learned explication to be intelligible to readers. We are especially indebted to Simplicius, a sixth-century commentator who worked in Athens until the Emperor Justinian closed the pagan schools, and then in Mesopotamia and Syria, before returning to Athens. Because works of Presocratic philosophers were scarce, he quotes extensively from books available to him the words of Parmenides, Anaxagoras, Empedocles, Zeno, Melissus, and Diogenes of Apollonia.

2.2. The Middle Ages and Renaissance

Barbarian invasions overwhelmed the Roman Empire, and eventually divided the eastern, Greek-speaking half of the empire from the western, Latin-speaking half. A successor empire continued in the East as what we call the Byzantine Empire, with its capital in Constantinople (Byzantium, renamed by the emperor Constantine). In the West, the Roman Empire collapsed. Since most educated Romans under the empire had been taught Greek as well as Latin, few Greek books had been trans-

lated into Latin. In the Middle Ages, few people in the western part of Europe had
any knowledge of Greek. Only a few works of Aristotle were translated into Latin,
by Boethius, and half a Platonic dialogue, the *Timaeus*, had been translated by
Chalcidius. Greek philosophy could be studied, if at all, mostly secondhand, in the
works of Lucretius, Cicero, Seneca, or Augustine.

Meanwhile, scholars in the East continued to study the works of Greek philosophy and literature in their native language. Many works of philosophy, science,
and medicine were translated into Syriac, and later into Arabic for the Arab con-
querors of the Middle East. Thus Aristotle and other Greek thinkers were studied
in Greek in what was left of the Byzantine Empire and in Arabic throughout
Muslim domains from the borders of India to Spain, at a time when they were not
available in western Europe.

As Europe recovered from foreign invasions in the twelfth century, scholars
became aware of books of ancient learning in Muslim countries. Works were
translated first from Arabic and then from Greek as scholars sought originals from
the Byzantine Empire. First the works of Aristotle were translated, then the works
of commentators on Aristotle. Diogenes Laertius was translated into Latin in the
twelfth century but later lost. Apparently the book of Anaxagoras was still available
in Sicily at this time, and copies of Empedocles' poem(s) may also have survived
into this period in Greece.[7] Aristotelian philosophy became the basis of university
teaching in the West, bringing with it an interest in all the things Aristotle had
studied.

In the Renaissance of the fifteenth and sixteenth centuries, Greek scholars were
welcomed to Italy to teach their language and share their books. Greek philosophy
and literature were translated into Latin at an increasing rate. The fall of Constantinople to the Turks in 1453 brought new Greek refugees and their books, but
put an end to the Byzantine patronage of Greek learning. Meanwhile, the invention
of the printing press meant that books could be mass produced, and careful
reproductions could avoid the errors copyists had made. Editions of Greek classics
were published, including the works of Plato, Aristotle, and Diogenes Laertius, as
well as Latin translations of them.

A great deal of energy and scholarship went into making editions. Aristotle was
published in a printed edition for the first time in 1495–98 by Aldus Manutius,
Plato in 1513 by the same and by Musurus, then in 1578 by Henricus Stephanus. The
Greek text of Diogenes Laertius was first published in 1533 by Hieronymus Froben
and Nicolaus Episocopian at Basel.

As yet the study of philosophy was rather a partisan and parochial affair: there
were schools of Platonists and Aristotelians, each defending their favorite philosopher from a traditional vantage point; Platonists read Plato through Neoplatonic
lenses, while Aristotelians read Aristotle through scholastic lenses. Although in
principle philosophers could distinguish doctrines of the ancient Greek philosophers from scientific knowledge, it came as a shock to philosophers when scientific
studies began to contradict the theories of Plato and Aristotle. Moreover, during
the time of the Protestant Reformation and the Catholic Counter-Reformation,

both Protestant and Catholic theologians tended to side with ancient philosophers against scientific innovations. In general, philosophers during this period rarely achieved a critical understanding of the ancient philosophers they read, much less of the Presocratics, whom they read at second hand through the works of Plato, Aristotle, Diogenes Laertius, and others.

2.3. The Modern Age

The seventeenth and eighteenth centuries saw important advances in understanding the Greek language and in preparing editions of classical authors. But historians tended to rehash Diogenes Laertius or just gather and translate testimonies, as in the case of Thomas Stanley's *History of Philosophy* (1655–62). In the eighteenth century, the first critical histories of philosophy were written. But it was in the nineteenth century that significant advances were made in writing the early history of philosophy. Hegel's historicism put a new emphasis on the historical dimension of philosophy. The notion that each age has its *Zeitgeist* and that one age becomes aware of ideas and theories unknown to earlier ages suggested a robust role for historical research in philosophy as in other studies. In Germany a new conception arose: *Altertumswissenschaft*, the science of antiquity, which envisioned a synthesis of archaeology, history, language study, and literature leading to a unified understanding of the classical world. At the new University of Berlin, Friedrich Schleiermacher translated Plato, encouraged Immanuel Bekker to edit Aristotle, and awakened interest in Presocratic philosophy with some of his writings. In the Netherlands, Simon Karsten edited the philosophical poets, Xenophanes, Parmenides, and Empedocles (1825–38). Jacob Bernays, who taught at the University of Bonn and at a Jewish seminary in Breslau, drew on newly discovered fragments of Heraclitus from Hippolytus in his important studies of that philosopher. He also traveled to England, where he influenced Ingram Bywater in his edition of Heraclitus.

In Germany, Eduard Zeller wrote a detailed and carefully researched history of Greek philosophy, *Die Philosophie der Griechen,* in three volumes (1844–52), which had many subsequent editions, down to Nestle's (ZN). Putting the schools of philosophy in their historical context, Zeller followed the development of philosophy in meticulous detail. Although he criticized Hegel's treatment of ancient philosophy, Zeller was deeply influenced by the Hegelian way of thinking: he saw grand abstractions emerging, coming into conflict, and being resolved. Zeller's Hegelian division of Greek philosophy into three periods is still with us: the Presocratic from Thales to the sophists, the classical from Socrates to Aristotle, and the Hellenistic from the early third century BCE until the end of the ancient world. Zeller was still deeply indebted to Aristotle for his organization and analysis of the philosophers, but he brought all the tools of modern scholarship to bear on the study of Greek philosophy. Drawing on traditional school designations, Zeller treats first the Ionians (the Milesians of the sixth century BCE plus Diogenes of Apollonia of the fifth), next the Pythagoreans, then the Eleatics (including Xenophanes); subsequently he groups together Heraclitus, Empedocles, the atomists, and Anaxagoras, in that order—without a real unifying principle. He treats the sophists in a final section. In his study, school associations count for more than chronology in understanding the Presocratics, and (despite his Hegelian leanings) no clear dialectic emerges among the several schools or individual players.

The greatest advance the study of the Presocratics in the nineteenth century was made by Hermann Diels, whose monumental work *Doxographi Graeci* (1879) studied and collected the doxographical sources of antiquity.[8] He identified Theophrastus as the main source, recognized the *Vetusta Placita*, reconstructed Aëtius's collection, and in general vindicated the ancient doxography as a valuable source of information (despite its severe limitations). Subsequent work has suggested modifications of Diels's work, but his overall conclusions have held up remarkably well through the years.[9] The sources Diels collected in his work became the basis of the testimonies in his later edition of the Presocratics.

The first general collection of Presocratic fragments was published in Paris in the Didot series: *Fragmenta philosophorum graecorum*, edited by F. W. A. Mullach (1883). This rather promiscuous volume contains not only fragments of the Presocratics, but those of later philosophers such as Timon of Phlius and Cleanthes, as well as the spurious writings of Ocellus of Lucania. Mullach also includes the pseudo-Aristotelian *On Melissus, Xenophanes, Gorgias*. He gives the Greek with Latin translation, and sometimes running commentary. What is missing compared to later editions of fragments is any systematic collection of testimonies.

In 1887 an important French study appeared: Paul Tannery examined the Presocratics in the context of scientific theory in *Pour l'Histoire de la Science Hellène*. Complaining that most studies focused on metaphysical development (in a time still dominated by Hegel), Tannery wished to concentrate on "special theses of a purely scientific character."[10] His most innovative—and controversial—interpretation was a reconstruction of a Pythagorean cosmological theory: he argued that both Parmenides and Zeno reacted to this in positing a monistic ontology. Moreover, Parmenides' cosmology in the *Doxa* was in broad outlines borrowed from the Pythagoreans. Tannery thus made a dialectical connection between the Pythagorean school and the Eleatic school, suggesting an ongoing debate that lasted at least into the mid–fifth century BCE. He also developed an influential account of Anaxagoras's theory, according to which the homoiomeries or stuffs that Aristotle describes as his elements are really not elemental, but are composed of a set of qualities arranged in certain proportions that determine the character of the stuff. Tannery appended French translations of the testimonies and fragments of the philosophers to the chapters in which he expounded them.

In 1892, the British scholar John Burnet published what would be the standard textbook in English on the Presocratics for over fifty years (in four editions). *Early Greek Philosophy* contained English translations of the fragments of the major philosophers, together with an explanation of their several systems. Burnet followed Tannery in his account of how Zeno was reacting to the Pythagoreans, and he adopted his interpretation of Anaxagoras's ontology with slight modifications.

Up until this time, sourcebooks had typically been written in Latin; now the Presocratics were available to the general public of the English-speaking world with a helpful exposition.

The twentieth century offered a major leap forward in sources with Hermann Diels's work *Die Fragmente der Vorsokratiker* (1903). Diels collected sources for each philosopher separately, assigning an A-section for testimonies and a B-section for fragments (where these were available). He organized the testimonies to give information about first the philosopher's life, then his writings, then his teachings. He supplied a German translation for the fragments, and in later editions he supplied a critical apparatus for the Greek and Latin text. For the first time, scholars could find all the known material on all the Presocratic thinkers in one place. Diels's sourcebook quickly became the standard work for research on the Presocratics. Diels had already made several editions of individual philosophers, and a collection of the poet-philosophers. The one somewhat odd feature of the *Vorsokratiker* is the fact that he includes works of philosophers working well into the fourth century, including one, Nausiphanes, who was probably younger than Aristotle. Diels considered the Pythagoreans and atomists of the fourth century still Presocratic, in the dialectical sense of not having been influenced by Socratic concerns; but in any case, he employed a very broad construal of Presocratic philosophy. He also included figures whose philosophical credentials were weak at best, such as Damon the musician and Polyclitus the sculptor, and some pre-Presocratics who provided background material. Diels's work went through four editions in his lifetime, and two posthumous editions under the direction of Walther Kranz, the last appearing in 1951–52. This work has remained the standard sourcebook, but it is now unfortunately dated, for want of improvements after more than a half century of ongoing scholarship.

Any arrangement of materials will affect how they are studied and thought of. Diels's division of source materials into testimonies and fragments brought with it advantages and disadvantages. Set off by themselves, the fragments could be read as major excerpts of the original philosopher, at least for those for whom extensive fragments existed. Moreover, the validity of interpretations embodied in the doxography could be checked against the words of the philosopher. On the other hand, for the most part the fragments appeared out of their original contexts, and clues to their meaning from the contexts might be disregarded. If, however, Diels had not separated the fragments, the words of the fragments would have been surrounded by commentary or extrinsic discussions that could mislead readers or at least distract them from the original statements of the philosopher. It is always an open question whether the ancient source of a quotation understands the statements he is quoting, and in many cases sources are clearly applying their quotations to problems and situations different from what the original author intended.[11] In any case, henceforth the fragments of the Presocratics would increasingly take precedence over testimonies about them.

One major accomplishment of the twentieth century was the emergence of Parmenides as the pivotal figure of philosophical development. Previously, philosophers tended to be viewed as members of school traditions (a view promoted by Hellenistic succession-histories inspired by the relatively well-organized schools of Hellenistic philosophy). Histories tended to stress common views within schools (Milesian, Pythagorean, Eleatic, Pluralist, atomist) and perhaps ongoing debates between schools, rather than dialectic development in the Presocratic tradition as a whole. One question was the relative priority of Heraclitus and Parmenides. Hegel saw being as dialectically prior to becoming, hence thought Parmenides must inevitably have preceded Heraclitus. But Bernays noticed what he thought were echoes of Heraclitean language in Parmenides, and suggested the reverse order. This view gradually won out, although by the mid–twentieth century many scholars came to doubt that there was evidence that either philosopher knew the other.[12] Guido Calogero's study of Parmenides and the Eleatics (*Studi sull'Eleatismo,* 1932) used logical and linguistic analysis on Parmenides' "is" and "is-not," in effect pioneering this kind of close study of Parmenides. In Harold Cherniss's work (to be discussed next) Parmenides is clearly the central figure of Presocratic debates; the rules for theorizing change significantly as a result of Parmenides' criticisms of earlier cosmologies.

As already pointed out, we are deeply indebted to Aristotle, Theophrastus, and the Peripatetic school for preserving the views of the Presocratic philosophers. But Aristotle and his followers also interpret the Presocratics, translating their theories into the language of Aristotelian physics and metaphysics, and criticizing them from their own standpoint. This is not of itself problematic: every generation must discuss previous generations in its own terms and from its own perspective. The problem arises when we take the interpretations of a later generation uncritically. Although modern interpreters had criticized and corrected some interpretations of the ancients, this had never been done systematically or self-consciously. One major attack on Aristotelian interpretation was made by William A. Heidel, the first American scholar to make significant contributions to Presocratic studies. Having studied with both Zeller and Diels in Germany, he developed independent views about the Presocratic tradition. In 1906 he published a long article ("Qualitative Change in Presocratic Philosophy") on Presocratic theories of matter, in which he criticized the Aristotelian interpretation of matter in the Presocratics. Aristotle saw the Milesians as monists who recognized only one kind of matter, for instance water or air. This single kind of matter could take on the appearance of other stuffs–for instance Anaximenes' air could turn into wind, cloud, water, and so on by condensation—but the other stuffs were only modifications of the one substance. Consequently, the only kind of change allowed was alteration (or perhaps change of quantity). Heidel argued that this account embodied a misunderstanding of Presocratic physics. The Milesians did not distinguish between substance and properties, viewing what Aristotle would call qualities (such as hot and cold) as powers existing in their own right and interacting with each other and other things.

Another American, Harold Cherniss, subjected Aristotle's criticisms of the Presocratics to his own critical scrutiny in an influential book (*Aristotle's Criticism of Presocratic Philosophy,* 1935). He found multiple sources of error in Aristotle's treatments of the Presocratics. He used the fragments of the Presocratics with his own reconstruction to show how Aristotle had misconstrued Presocratic theories. Since Cherniss's book was published, scholars have been cautious of Aristotelian interpretations of the Presocratics; they cannot be used as uncritical data for reconstructing Presocratic theory. There have been some attempts to rehabilitate Aristotle. As scholars have shown, Aristotle often does mark a transition between his exposition of a Presocratic theory and his criticism of it; and his expositions are often less loaded with presuppositions than his criticisms. Overall, however, Cherniss showed that modern reconstructions of the Presocratics could improve on and correct ancient ones. John McDiarmid ("Theophrastus on the Presocratic Causes") argued that Theophrastus tended to follow Aristotle uncritically in his study of Presocratic doctrines, and so helped to perpetuate erroneous interpretations. One groundbreaking study of the Presocratics, by Charles H. Kahn (*Anaximander and the Origins of Greek Cosmology*), critically examined the evidence in light of a careful reconstruction of the historical context; this work continues to offer a paradigm of Presocratic scholarship, establishing Anaximander rather than Thales as the originator of the cosmological tradition, and going beyond Aristotle's limited treatment of him.

In the early twentieth century, questions of religion took center stage for several scholars. F. M. Cornford, inspired by anthropological studies, traced the emergence of philosophy from religion (*From Religion to Philosophy*). He found two opposing traditions among the Presocratics, a scientific tradition exemplified by the Ionians, and a mystical tradition exemplified by the Italians. The former gave rise to scientific thinking, while the latter stressed religious experience. A Swiss scholar, Willy Theiler, argued in his dissertation (*Zur Geschichte der teleologischen Naturbetrachtung bis auf Aristoteles*, 1925) that the argument from design for God's existence could be traced back from Xenophon to Diogenes of Apollonia. This gave Diogenes, hitherto a minor figure, an important place in the history of ideas. In his Gifford Lectures of 1936 (*The Theology of the Early Greek Philosophers*), Werner Jaeger studied the theology of the Presocratics, finding a developing sense of the divine that culminated in the teleology of Anaxagoras and Diogenes. In *The Greeks and the Irrational* (his Sather Lectures), E. R. Dodds stressed the neglected irrational aspects of Greek culture and religion, following an anthropological approach that led from a "shame culture" in the Homeric poems to a "guilt culture" in later times. Gregory Vlastos ("Theology and Philosophy in Early Greek Thought") argued for a middle ground between the scientific view of the Presocratics in Burnet and a view of them as theologians in Jaeger; while they clearly admit of a religious dimension, he maintained, they do not address the gods of Greek cult.

At the end of his life, Cornford switched from his dichotomy of an Ionian scientific tradition versus a mystical Italian tradition to a sweeping criticism of the Ionians (*Principium Sapientiae*). The Ionians were not really scientific but were mere purveyors of dogmatic speculations, uninformed by empirical verification. It was really the physicians of the Hippocratic tradition who pioneered the scientific method with their careful observations. Vlastos (in his review of *Principium Sapientiae*) criticized this view on the grounds that no theories of early Greece were precise enough in their predictions to be corrected by experiment; and the Hippocratics, no less than the Ionians, produced unsubstantiated hypotheses about the world.

One other major shift in emphasis that occurred in the mid–twentieth century was a reevaluation of the role of the Pythagoreans in early thought. Erich Frank, in *Plato und die sogenannten Pythagoreer,* had already provided a skeptical challenge to claims that there was a well-developed Pythagorean theory in the sixth and even fifth centuries BCE, but his argument had little impact in a field dominated by Tannery, Burnet, and Cornford, followed by Raven, *Pythagoreans and Eleatics*, who saw the Pythagoreans as perhaps the leading movement of early Greek philosophy. Cherniss and Vlastos had already pointed out the lack of reliable evidence for these expansive views when Burkert carefully sifted the evidence in a masterful study (*Lore and Science in Ancient Pythagoreanism*). He showed that there was no secure early evidence identifying Pythagoras himself as a philosopher; he was, rather, a religious leader. On the other hand, Burkert distinguished between genuine and spurious fragments of Philolaus so as to rehabilitate this figure of the late fifth century as a genuine philosopher and cosmologist, who was the source of much of Aristotle's account of Pythagoreanism.[13] The result has been a wholesale devaluation of Pythagoras himself as a formative influence in Presocratic thought, and a skepticism about any unified Pythagorean doctrine. On the other hand, Philolaus has emerged as a major philosopher with connections to Ionian and Eleatic as well as Pythagorean influences. In this volume, Carl Huffman continues to undermine claims of Pythagorean influence with a rereading of Aristotle.[14]

Thus far, we have not said much about the philosophical currents that developed in Europe and beyond. As already shown, Hegelian analyses had an impact on views of the Presocratics in the nineteenth century. According to his widely accepted theory, there is a rational historical progression of concepts, which are embodied in the thought of each era. Thus the history of philosophy is an integral part of philosophical inquiry, and each era has a vital role to play in the onward march of self-knowledge. At the end of the nineteenth century, G. E. Moore and his student Bertrand Russell at Cambridge University led the so-called Revolt from Idealism, which brought a new style of philosophy to Great Britain. Rather than looking for a great system of philosophy emerging out of historical reflection, Moore and Russell taught philosophers to analyze concepts. Going back to David Hume, Russell saw statements as divided into sentences that were true by virtue of their meaning alone and those that were true (or false) by reference to the world. Increasingly, analytic philosophers stressed individual claims, rather than philosophical systems, and arguments for those claims. Symbolic logic became a powerful tool for evaluating arguments.

Meanwhile, on the Continent, Hegelian idealism was giving way to other methods of analysis. In Germany, Edmund Husserl pioneered phenomenological analysis, in which he bracketed experiences to study them as phenomena. His student Martin Heidegger increasingly focused on the metaphysical question of being, which he saw as inseparable from questions of human existence. Seeing a close connection between early Greek speculations and contemporary philosophical problems, Heidegger lectured on the Presocratics as predecessors to his own views. His work has inspired and continues to inspire study of the Presocratics in the Continental tradition.

At first, analytic philosophy does not seem to have had any significant effect on the study of Presocratic philosophy. And there was a danger that analytic philosophy might have a deleterious effect on all the history of philosophy. For whereas Hegelian idealism and the later Continental tradition had at least recognized an important historical dimension, analytic philosophy was ahistorical and could even become antihistorical. Russell's protégé Ludwig Wittgenstein had no interest in professional philosophy, and attempted in his *Tractatus Logico-Philosophicus* to lay out all the truths of philosophy in propositional form. Philosophers of the Vienna Circle, inspired by Wittgenstein, sought to develop philosophy as a critique of knowledge, especially of science, and to reject metaphysics as meaningless. For them, as well as for Wittgenstein, philosophy had no worthwhile history, and indeed not much future. After German military expansion brought the annexation of Austria, Nazi persecution scattered the philosophers of the Vienna Circle, mostly to Great Britain and the United States.

Refugees from Vienna brought a new excitement to the United States, hitherto little affected by analytic philosophy. During World War II, academic life was limited by the demands of training officer candidates. But soon after the war, leading analytic philosophers were hired at Cornell University, where Gregory Vlastos, who had previously taught in Canada and briefly studied with the classicist F. M. Cornford at Cambridge, imbibed the new method. Vlastos became a leading advocate and exemplar of analytic methods, applied to the problems of ancient Greek philosophy. Moving to Princeton University, he set up a joint program in classics and philosophy that became a model for American universities and that sent out its graduates to teach at leading universities. In England, G. E. L. Owen, a graduate of Oxford University, exemplified the same style of philosophy, combining the rigor of classical scholarship with the precision of analytic philosophy. He brought the new style of analytic philosophy to Cambridge University, long a center of Presocratic studies (Cornford had been there). G. S. Kirk and J. E. Raven provided an advanced textbook in *The Presocratic Philosophers* (1957). Another Cambridge scholar, W. K. C. Guthrie, wrote the authoritative six-volume *History of Greek Philosophy*, whose first two volumes (1962, 1965) provided an extensive study of the Presocratics. The interest of major philosophers such as Karl Popper and Wesley Salmon in the Anglo-American tradition put Presocratic studies in the mainstream of philosophy. A sort of benchmark of studies in the analytic style was reached with the publication of Jonathan Barnes's work *The Presocratic Philosophers* (1979, 1982), followed by the second edition of Kirk and Raven's work, with Malcolm Schofield rewriting several chapters (1983).

At a time when one might have anticipated an increased interest in Presocratic studies, there was in fact a flight to Hellenistic philosophy, which suddenly became the focus of much scholarly interest, attracting many of the scholars who had previously worked on the Presocratics. There have been important editions and monographs on individual philosophers in recent years, exciting work on the doxographical tradition, and some new discoveries of papyrus texts.[15] Yet much remains to be done in understanding the first philosophers and their legacy. We hope this volume will call attention to the valuable work of the last few years and contribute to a renewed interest in Presocratic studies.

NOTES

1. On Parmenides see Curd, *Legacy*, Graham, *Explaining the Cosmos*. On the Pythagoreans, see Burkert, Huffman, Kahn.

2. See Martin and Primavesi, *L'Empédocle de Strasbourg*; the Derveni Papyrus has also yielded new insights, and new sources of controversy. See Betegh, *The Derveni Papyrus*; Kouremenos et al., *The Derveni Papyrus*; and Janko, "The Derveni Papyrus (Diagoras of Melos, *Apopyrgizontes Logoi*?)"; "The Derveni Papyrus: An Interim Text"; "The Physicist as Hierophant."

3. See the chapters by David Runia and John Palmer here.

4. See esp. *Top.* 105b12, with Mansfeld, *Studies in the Historiography of Greek Philosophy*, 22.

5. Mansfeld, "Chrysippus and the *Placita.*"

6. On *DG* see Mansfeld and Runia, *Aëtiana*, and Runia's chapter here.

7. On Diogenes Laertius and Anaxagoras see Berschin, *Greek Letters and the Latin Middle Ages*, 232–33; on Empedocles see Primavesi, "Lecteurs antiques et byzantins d'Empédocle," 199–201, who shows that a manuscript may have been extant in the fifteenth century.

8. See Calder and Mansfeld, *Hermann Diels (1848–1922) et la Science de L'antiquité* on Diels's life and scholarship.

9. See now the reconsiderations of doxography in Mansfeld and Runia, *Aëtiana*, and the chapter by David Runia here.

10. Tannery, *Pour l'Histoire de la Science Hellène*, p. 11.

11. See Catherine Osborne, *Rethinking Early Greek Philosophy*, for a dissenting view on the usefulness and importance of contexts.

12. See Graham, "Heraclitus and Parmenides."

13. Huffman, *Philolaus of Croton*, has more fully explicated Philolaus in accordance with Burkert's insights.

14. It should be noted that optimistic views of early Pythagoreanism continue to be written, including Zhmud, *Wissenschaft, Philosophie und Religion im frühen Pythagoreismus*; Kahn, *Pythagoras and the Pythagoreans*; Riedweg, *Pythagoras: His Life, Teaching, and Influence.*

15. Most notably the Strasbourg Papyrus, with significant additions to Empedocles fragments (see Martin and Primavesi, *L'Empédocle de Strasbourg*); and the Derveni Papyrus, with an early philosophical commentary on an Orphic poem (see Laks and Most, *Studies on the Derveni Papyrus*; Betegh, *The Derveni Papyrus*).

BIBLIOGRAPHY

Berschin, Walter. *Greek Letters and the Latin Middle Ages: From Jerome to Nicholas of Cusa.* Washington, D.C.: Catholic University of America Press, 1980.

Betegh, Gábor. *The Derveni Papyrus: Cosmology, Theology, and Interpretation.* Cambridge: Cambridge University Press, 2004.

Burkert, Walter. *Lore and Science in Ancient Pythagoreanism.* 1962. Translated by E. L. Minar, Jr. Cambridge, Mass.: Harvard University Press, 1972.

Burnet, John. *Early Greek Philosophy.* 1892. 4th ed. London: Adam & Charles Black, 1930.

Calder, William M., III, and Jaap Mansfeld, eds. *Hermann Diels (1848–1922) et la Science de l'Antiquité.* Geneva: Fondation Hardt, 1999.

Calogero, Guido. *Studi sull'Eleatismo.* 1932. Florence: "La Nuova Italia" Editrice, 1977.

Cherniss, Harold. *Aristotle's Criticism of Presocratic Philosophy.* Baltimore: Johns Hopkins University Press, 1935.

Cornford, F. M. *From Religion to Philosophy.* London: Edward Arnold, 1912.

———. *Principium Sapientiae.* Cambridge: Cambridge University Press, 1952.

Curd, Patricia. *The Legacy of Parmenides.* Princeton: Princeton University Press, 1998.

Dodds, E. R. *The Greeks and the Irrational.* Berkeley: University of California Press, 1951.

Frank, Erich. *Plato und die sogenannten Pythagoreer: Ein Kapitel aus der Geschichte der griechischen Geistes.* Halle: Max Niemeyer, 1923.

Graham, Daniel W. "Heraclitus and Parmenides." In *Presocratic Philosophy: Essays in Honour of Alexander Mourelatos,* edited by Victor Caston and Daniel W. Graham, 27–44. Aldershot, England: Ashgate, 2002.

———. *Explaining the Cosmos.* Princeton: Princeton University Press, 2006.

Heidel, W. A. "Qualitative Change in Presocratic Philosophy." *Archiv für Geschichte der Philosophie* 19 (1906): 333–79.

Huffman, Carl A. *Philolaus of Croton.* Cambridge: Cambridge University Press, 1993.

Janko, Richard. "The Derveni Papyrus (Diagoras of Melos, *Apopyrgizontes Logoi?*): A New Translation." *Classical Philology* 96 (2001): 1–32.

———. "The Derveni Papyrus: An Interim Text," *Zeitschrift für Papyrologie und Epigraphik* 141 (2002): 1–62.

———. "The Physicist as Hierophant: Aristophanes, Socrates, and the Authorship of the Derveni Papyrus," *Zeitschrift für Papyrologie und Epigraphik* 118 (1997): 61–94.

Jaeger, Werner. *The Theology of the Early Greek Philosophers.* London: Oxford University Press, 1947.

Kahn, Charles H. *Anaximander and the Origins of Greek Cosmology.* New York: Columbia University Press, 1960.

———. *Pythagoras and the Pythagoreans.* Indianapolis: Hackett, 2001.

Kouremenos, Theokritos, George M. Parássoglou, and Kyriakos Tsantsanoglou, eds. *The Derveni Papyrus. Edited with Introduction and Commentary.* Studi e testi per il "Corpus dei papiri filosofici greci e latini," Vol. 13. Florence: 2006.

Laks, André, and Claire Louguet, eds. *Qu'est-ce que la philosophie présocratique?* Cahiers de Philologie, vol. 20. Villeneuve d'Ascq: Presses Universitaires du Septentrion, 2002.

Laks, André, and Glenn W. Most, eds. *Studies on the Derveni Papyrus.* Oxford: Clarendon Press, 1997.

Mansfeld, Jaap. "Chrysippus and the *Placita.*" *Phronesis* 34 (1989): 311–42.

———. *Studies in the Historiography of Greek Philosophy.* Assen: Van Gorcum, 1990.

Mansfeld, Jaap, and David T. Runia. *Aëtiana: The Method and Intellectual Context of a Doxographer.* Philosophia Antiqua, vol. 73. Leiden: E. J. Brill, 1997.

Martin, Alain, and Oliver Primavesi. *L'Empédocle de Strasbourg.* Berlin: de Gruyter, 1999.

McDiarmid, John B. "Theophrastus on the Presocratic Causes." *Harvard Studies in Classical Philology* 61 (1953): 85–156.

Osborne, Catherine. *Rethinking Early Greek Philosophy: Hippolytus of Rome and the Presocratics.* Ithaca, N.Y.: Cornell University Press, 1987.

Primavesi, Oliver. "Lecteurs antiques et byzantins d'Empédocle: De Zénon à Tzétzès." In Laks and Louguet, 183–204.

Raven, J. E. *Pythagoreans and Eleatics.* Cambridge: Cambridge University Press, 1948.

Riedweg, Christoph. *Pythagoras: His Life, Teaching, and Influence.* Translated by Steven Rendall. Ithaca, N.Y.: Cornell University Press, 2005.

Tannery, Paul. *Pour l'histoire de la science Hellène.* 1887. Edited by A. Dies. 2nd ed. Paris: Gauthiers-Villars, 1930.

Theiler, Willy. *Zur Geschichte der teleologischen Naturbetrachtung bis auf Aristoteles.* 1925. 2nd ed. Berlin: de Gruyter, 1965.

Vlastos, Gregory. Review of *Principium Sapientiae,* by F. M. Cornford. *Gnomon* 27 (1955): 65–76.

———. "Theology and Philosophy in Early Greek Thought." *Philosophical Quarterly* 2 (1952): 97–123.

Zhmud, Leonid. *Wissenschaft, Philosophie und Religion im frühen Pythagoreismus.* Berlin: Akademie Verlag, 1997.

PART I

BACKGROUND

CHAPTER 1

THE SOURCES FOR PRESOCRATIC PHILOSOPHY

DAVID T. RUNIA

BETWEEN about 2,600 and 2,400 years ago, a group of men lived whose thought formed the beginning of the discipline of philosophy as we now know it. All contemporary material records of these men have disappeared, with the possible exception of a piece of a statue and some likenesses on early coins and vases.[1] For our knowledge of these men we are wholly dependent on the literary tradition. Literary tradition involves transmission combined with interpretation. Everything we know about these men has been transmitted through the use of writing, in one way or another. Interpretation accompanies the process every step of the way. The very notion that these philosophers can be best understood as Presocratics is redolent with interpretative interventions. Although this view is not without ancient precedents, the driving force behind its dominance in the twentieth century was the great achievement of the German classical scholar Hermann Diels (1848–1922), which exercises authority to this day.

The aim of this contribution is to examine in broad outline what the sources for Presocratic philosophy are and how we need to deal with them. I will commence with the dominant legacy of Diels. Thereafter, I will examine various strands of transmission streamlined by Diels in more detail with a view to determining what we need to take into account when we exploit them. Finally, I shall reach some tentative conclusions on what should be the way forward in future research.

1. The Dielsian Legacy

As I write these words, it is exactly one hundred years since Diels published the first edition of *Die Fragmente der Vorsokratiker* (*FVS*).[2] During his lifetime, three more editions followed, the last appearing in the year of his death.[3] In 1934, his pupil Walther Kranz prepared a fifth edition. In 1951, after the interruption of World War II, the sixth and final edition was published.[4] Circumstances prevented a full revision. Changes were added as *Nachträge* (supplementary notes) to each of the three volumes. This edition, which has been reprinted numerous times, is still in use. Just as the Stephanus numbering of 1578 is used for all references to Plato's works, so all references to Presocratic philosophers have been standardized with reference to the Diels-Kranz edition of 1951.

There is, of course, no need to give a detailed description of how this edition works. It is to a greater or lesser degree familiar to all scholars working in the field. What is worth doing is to point out some of its features that can easily be taken for granted, but that in fact are vital for understanding what the work is trying to achieve.[5]

1. In a sense, the title of the work is a misnomer. It does not just contain the fragments of the Presocratics, if we understand fragment to mean a piece or extract from their original works. It contains much more. Diels wanted to give an all-around picture of the main evidence we have for every aspect of these men, not just their thought but also their lives and even to a limited extent their influence. But he did not aim for completeness either. The collection was first presented as a kind of reader for university courses. Later editions were fuller, but never aimed to give an exhaustive presentation of all the available evidence.

2. Another feature of the title is that it enshrines the concept of the "Presocratics." In recent years, moves have been afoot to speak of "early Greek philosophers" instead.[6] But as long as Diels's work remains the standard reference work, the old habit will die hard. There are obvious difficulties with this approach, notably the fact that some of the Presocratics (the most striking case is Democritus) postdate Socrates. But the concept does have a highly respectable ancient pedigree. Aristotle, in his survey of philosophy prior to his own, says that Socrates turned to ethics and neglected the world of nature (*Metaph.* 1.6, 987b2). Cicero says the same in more poetical language: Socrates was the first to call philosophy down from heaven and bring her into the homes of men (*Tusc.* 5.10). In his preface to the fifth edition, Kranz admits that the concept behind the book is somewhat odd (*merkwürdig*), yet he claims that the book does represent a unity: "Its unity lies in the fact that here a philosophy speaks to us which has not passed through the school of thought espoused by Socrates (and by Plato), i.e. not just the pre-Socratic, but also the non-Socratic old philosophy."[7] This what we might call "all except x" approach leads to a further difficulty in the book's conception. Clearly its main concern is the natural philosophy of the earliest Greek philosophers. But the contents are much broader. It also includes the prephilosophical cosmologists

(sec. 1–10) and the first generation of sophists (secs. 79–90), as well as surprising figures such as the poet Epicharmos (sec. 23) and the sculptor Polyclitus (sec. 40). The most difficult line of demarcation in its all-inclusive approach was between natural philosophers and the earliest medical scientists. Alcmaeon and Hippon are included (sec. 24, sec. 38), but very understandably, Hippocrates and his school are left to one side.

3. When we look at the collected "fragments" themselves, the main feature that leaps out at us is the division into the A-, B-, and C-sections. These are used for all the main philosophers, amounting to almost exactly half of all those included (44 out of 90). In the A-sections, the *testimonia* are given that pertain to the life, writings, and doctrines of the philosopher. Although more detailed subheadings are not used, it is apparent that in the presentation of doctrines a more or less fixed order is followed, approximately as follows: (1) first principles or metaphysical doctrines, cosmology (including astronomy and meteorology), (2) psychology and physiology (including epistemology), (3) zoology, (4) anthropology, (5) ethics. In the B-sections, Diels presents what he regards as the actual fragments, that is, those texts that can be determined to have been written by the philosophers themselves. Usually, almost no context is given for these fragments, which are set off from the text that surrounds them by the use of a different typeface. Only the fragments themselves are rather literally translated into German. If possible, Diels orders the fragments first by the work from which they were taken, and then by their position in that work. He is prepared to engage in interpretation in order to do this, but draws the line at Heraclitus, where all but the first two fragments are presented in alphabetical order of the later source. Dubious fragments are collected together at the end of the section. The C-sections, which occur only sporadically throughout the book (for 10 philosophers only), are brief and give some texts illustrating how later authors imitated the philosopher. No systematic attempt is made to document the *Nachleben* of the writers concerned, though of course much of this could be reconstructed from the huge variety of sources used to compile the A- and B-sections. It is evident that although the work exhibits fixed patterns of presentation, Diels and Kranz were concerned to adopt a flexible approach, enabling them to accommodate the great variety of authors they were dealing with. In an appendix I give a more detailed analysis of the organization of the work that shows this flexibility (sometimes approaching inconsistency) quite clearly.[8]

I have started off with Diels's *Fragmente der Vorsokratiker* because of the dominant position it has held for the past century in the study of early Greek philosophy. It represents the culmination of Diels's research, but its method can only be properly understood if we take into account that three monumental works which he produced earlier provided the foundations for the final work.

The first is the *Doxographi Graeci* (*DG*) published in 1879.[9] Its starting point is a number of writings, mainly from the imperial period and even later, in which the views (*doxai*) or opinions (*areskonta*) of earlier Greek philosophers, including numerous Presocratics, are presented. Using a daring neologism, Diels called the writers of such works "doxographers," that is, parallel in some way to biographers who wrote lives of famous thinkers. A quotation from Cicero prefaces the work: "tardi ingeni est rivulos consectari, fontes rerum non videre."[10] This sentence is the perfect motto for the method of *Quellenforschung* that swept all before it in nineteenth-century German classical scholarship. According to this approach, the analysis of derivative texts should allow one to penetrate to the sources, which, being at the origin, will be pure and undefiled. At the fount of the Greek philosophical tradition stood the Presocratics. Through use of the method of analysis of sources and witnesses, it will be possible to determine how valuable and reliable the traditions recording their views are. Diels's favorite analytical technique is the use of parallel columns.[11] If two writings share the same material, especially if the verbal resemblances are great, they will go back to a common source. In this way, an entire stemma of the transmission of these views could be reconstructed. His first move was to determine the nucleus of the later doxographic tradition. This is represented by the doxographer Aëtius, whose lost work is reconstructed in 170 pages of parallel columns drawn from the pseudo-Plutarchean *Placita* and Stobaeus, together with other witnesses added in an apparatus at the foot of the page. Aëtius's work consisted of five books: book 1 on first principles, book 2 on cosmology and astronomy, book 3 on metereology and geology, and books 4 and 5 on psychology, physiology, and zoology. It is no coincidence that this is basically the order of the A-fragments on doctrine in *FVS* (where the double columns disappear and texts are explicitly attributed to Aëtius as reconstructed in *DG*). Diels was convinced that further analysis, presented at great length in the labyrinthine *Prolegomena* to the editions of the texts, could demonstrate that this material primarily goes back to the Peripatetic school of Aristotle and Theophrastus, where research was first carried out on the early history of Greek philosophy. The actual nucleus of this tradition, Diels concluded, was the Theophrastean work entitled *Physikôn doxai*, in which the views of the early natural philosophers were first comprehensively recorded. In *FVS*, Diels makes a striking reference to this work when setting out the A-fragments illustrating the doctrine of Heraclitus.[12] The validity of the reports is thus established. They go back to the original source, which was able to draw on the original writings of the Presocratics, as well as other material now wholly obscured to our view.

The second work is his edition of Simplicius's *Commentary on Aristotle's Physics*, published in two volumes in 1882 and 1895.[13] Even though it was written at the beginning of the 6th century CE, it is the single most important source of actual literary fragments of the Presocratics we possess.[14] In the preface to the first volume, Diels announced his intention "to edit the remains of the philosophers before Socrates."[15]

The third work was a separate edition of the Greek philosophical poets, *Poetarum Philosophorum Fragmenta* (*PPF*), completed in 1899 and published in 1901.[16] In a sense, this can be seen as a trial run for the final work. Here we already find the division into A- and B-fragments, the former being divided into "Testimonies," "Lives," "Doctrines of the Poem" (or "Poems"), that is, parallel to *FVS*. Of course,

THE SOURCES FOR PRESOCRATIC PHILOSOPHY 31

the distinction between authentic words going back to the author and secondary reports is much easier to draw in the case of poetic fragments. This edition is both less and more complete than the final work. It contains only poets (not limited to the Presocratics), but it does try to give a complete list of all the sources for their fragments and *testimonia*, which the final work declines to do. Like the two previous works, it is written from beginning to end in learned Latin prose. The fact that *FVS* was presented in the vernacular, with German translations of the original fragments, certainly contributed to the undeserved neglect the earlier work has suffered. It was never reprinted. Copies are scarce, and it is seldom cited.

The main lines of development that led to the classic edition of the Presocratic fragments should now be clear. The Dielsian achievement is as staggering as its legacy is pervasive. In the section that follows I shall examine the various strands of transmission that have been woven into Diels's collection separately, taking into account developments in research that have taken place since his time. This will allow me not only to review the various important witnesses to the Presocratic writings, but also to proceed to some suggestions on how research might move forward in the twenty-first century.

2. The Strands of Transmission for the Presocratic Philosophers

2.1. Original Writings

The works of the Presocratic philosophers were not many in number or extensive in length.[17] Anaximander, Heraclitus, Parmenides, and Anaxagoras all wrote single short books. Democritus, the first copious writer, probably wrote more than all his predecessors combined, which in itself marks a turning point.[18] It does seem astonishing bad luck that not a single complete work survives. Simplicius informs us that by the end of antiquity, copies of Parmenides' poem were scarce.[19] But as late as the twelfth century, there were some copies of Empedocles' poems in Byzantium, and Oliver Primavesi inclines to the view that a copy of the *Purifications* may have reached Venice in 1424.[20] The only complete works in *FVS* are two speeches by Gorgias and the *Dissoi logoi*. The former are printed in large type, but not translated (82B11, 11a). The latter is the final text cited and is edited in minuscule print (90). Patently, these works do not correspond to Diels's conception of what was important in Presocratic philosophy.

Alas, it is not realistic to think that a complete work will still turn up, although one can always hope. The papyrus finds have been disappointing, as a perusal of the Florentine *Corpus dei papiri filosofici greci e latini* reveals.[21] Apparently not many Presocratic writings circulated in Egypt.[22] But, it must be said, the two most sensational finds of the last 50 years have been papyri: the Derveni roll found in Macedonia and the Strasbourg Empedoclean snippets.[23] They are very likely remnants of complete copies. The information they bring has been significant. At the same time, they forcibly remind us how far removed students of the Presocratics are from the luxury of complete works enjoyed in most other areas of ancient philosophy. Even the students of early Hellenistic philosophy are better off!

2.2. Plato

The first fully preserved source that gives us copious information on the philosophy of the Presocratics is Plato. Six of his dialogues are named after figures included in Diels's collection: the *Parmenides, Cratylus, Protagoras, Gorgias, Hippias Major, Hippias Minor*. Other Presocratics who figure more than incidentally in his writings are Heraclitus, Zeno, Empedocles, Anaxagoras, and various sophists such as Prodicus and Thrasymachus.

But Plato is a quirky witness. His writings are not historical treatises but purport to record sophisticated conversations with a philosophical bent. At first he was above all keen to place the example of Socrates' life and thought on the philosophical agenda. In the second half of his career he began to show more interest in his philosophical predecessors, but always with a view to furthering discussion and controversy. There are lots of idiosyncrasies, of which four brief examples can be given. (1) Why does the *Parmenides* focus exclusively on the questions of unity and plurality and hardly mention the doctrine of being? (2) How are the interpretations of Heraclitean philosophy in terms of *panta rhei* and *ouden menei* to be reconciled with the genuine fragments of the philosopher? (3) Why does Plato use fictional mouthpieces for his Pythagorean spokespersons? (4) Why does he never refer to Democritus by name, even though much of his natural philosophy is directed against him?[24] In short, history of philosophy is not what Plato is about, and he is a witness to be used with caution.

Yet Plato does provide us with information that allows some insight into the very beginnings of reflection on the development of philosophical thought. A number of texts introduce basic analytical schemas, such as the opposition between stability and motion, being and becoming, unity and plurality, which are linked both with the poets and earlier philosophers.[25] He himself develops this method when he speaks of a conflict between "idealists" and "materialists" as a battle of gods and giants, and refers to his own to be superseded position as being espoused by "friends of the forms."[26] Careful analysis of these texts—in combination with further evidence supplied by Aristotle—carried out by Bruno Snell, Jaap Mansfeld, and others has convincingly shown that the sophists Hippias and Gorgias initiated such schemas.[27] Hippias collected a large range of materials illustrating various topics from poets and prose-writers, both Greek and foreign, as he claims in the single surviving sentence of the work that remains (86B6). Its purpose was to collect and harmonize, making extensive use of lists and parallel thoughts and phrases. Gorgias, in contrast, is much more the rhetor and debater, emphasizing the oppositions between thinkers and the contradictions within their own works. Oddly enough, his *Encomium of Helen* contains a reflective passage on the power of *logos* (speech/reason) to put its mark on the soul. Such power is illustrated by the *logoi* of meteorologists (i.e., natural philosophers), who exchange the one opinion (*doxa*) for the other, and "the battles of philosophers which demonstrate how speed of insight renders the trust we have in opinion easily changeable" (82B11.13). The two patterns of harmonization and opposition, established by these early theoreticians and illustrated in Plato's dialogues, were to be of enormous influence in how the early history of Greek philosophy was treated and recorded.[28]

2.3. Aristotle and the Peripatos

The most important witness for our knowledge of the Presocratics is undoubtedly Aristotle. A glance at the Index of *FVS* will show how dependent Diels was (and we are) on the information Aristotle supplies. All the major treatises in the Aristotelian corpus, such as the *Physics, Metaphysics, On the Heaven, On the Soul,* and so on, are full of reports about and discussions of the doctrines of the early Greek philosophers. Some of the minor works are valuable, too, including writings that go back to the Peripatos rather than Aristotle himself, for example, the *Problemata* and the set of notes entitled *De Melisso Xenophane Gorgia*.[29] As already noted, the survey he gives of the development of philosophy prior to his own in the first book of the *Metaphysics* has been enormously influential, both on account of its schema of the beginning of philosophy in terms of the transition from *mythos* to *logos* and because of its trenchant analyses of the doctrines of the first philosophers as *phusiologoi* (philosophers of nature), which still color our views today.[30]

It is clear that Aristotle was well positioned to make this contribution. The lists of his writings indicate that he (possibly aided by collaborators) prepared himself by compiling works on the writings and thought of predecessors such as Alcmaeon, Xenophanes, Zeno, Melissus, Archytas, and other Pythagoreans, as well as producing two books on problems raised by Democritus.[31] Presumably these works contained excerpts, summaries, and analyses. The effort is impressive, but how fairly and conscientiously was it done? For decades controversy has raged on this issue in response to the challenge Cherniss posed in his classic study *Aristotle's Criticism of Presocratic Philosophy*.[32] If, as Cherniss claimed, Aristotle consistently distorted the views of the Presocratics because he analyzed them from the perspective of his own philosophy, what hope do we have of getting beyond him to the doctrines themselves? The controversy seems to have ebbed of late, because it is generally recognized that although Aristotle certainly does see the doctrines of his predecessors as leading up to his own views to a greater or a lesser extent, within the limits of his own method he is quite conscientious in making clear what the views were which he is responding to with his superior position.[33] But this conclusion does raise for us the further question: why did Aristotle think it so important to take his predecessors into account when working out his own philosophy? At least three answers can be given.

The first answer has to do with the method Aristotle uses for his research. Although in his *Analytics* he presents the ideal of demonstrative science, in which all conclusions are demonstrated by means of a sequence of proven propositions ultimately going back to first principles, in his own writings this method is hardly used. Instead, his procedure more closely resembles what he calls dialectical science,[34] for which the starting point is taken to be "reputable opinions" (*endoxa*) put forward by authoritative practitioners of the field in question. Through analysis of these views, sound starting points can be found for his own treatment of the topic. Alternatively, in the course of an investigation one can adduce opponents' views and refute them in order to clarify and advance one's own position. In the areas of physics and zoology, this role is often reserved for the atomistic and mechanistic thought of Democritus.

A second answer is related to Aristotle's larger view of how science and philosophy develop. There can be no doubt that he believes progress is possible and that it has occurred. It is implicit in his account in the first book of the *Metaphysics*. In an intriguing text in Cicero, he is reported to have rebuked the ancient philosophers for thinking that philosophy had been completed through their efforts, but at the same time he was convinced that in recent years such great progress had been made that it would soon attain its accomplishment.[35] It would seem that his view of cultural progress is teleological on an analogy with what happens in the natural realm. When one adds to this his recognition that the first steps are the most difficult and the most influential,[36] it is easy to see how he would have wanted to study the efforts of the first philosophers and analyze how they had influenced the direction of the quest for wisdom in ways he might have to correct.

To what extent, however, does Aristotle show an interest in the early philosophers that can be called historical or historiographical? This is the third answer that could be given to the question posed above. We know that Aristotle's school, the Peripatos, had some features that are reminiscent of a modern research institute, for example, the famous project to collect the constitutions of the Greek *poleis*. Is it not natural to assume that an interest in the history of Greek science and philosophy must have started in these surroundings? This is Diels's argument in the *Doxographi Graeci*. In a crucial passage, he claims that Aristotle instituted the interest in the history of philosophy but its main thrust came from his disciples Theophrastus and Eudemus, who were the leaders in the movement to record the discoveries and doctrines of the earlier scientists and philosophers.[37]

This view of Aristotle as giving the vital impulse that led to the history of philosophy leads us right into the middle of the present-day debate on the origin and method of ancient doxography. So before we can resolve the present question as to what led Aristotle to take an interest in his predecessors, we need first to change tack rather radically and examine what the main issues are relating to this postulated genre of writing about ancient philosophy that has proved so important for the study of the Presocratics.

2.4. Doxography

As shown earlier, the term "doxography" derives from the Latin *doxographus*, the neologism devised by Diels and bombarded into prominence through its use in the title of his first major scholarly work. It is now commonly used in studies devoted to the history of philosophy for any summary account of the views held by a philosopher.[38] But its original intent was much more specific. Diels used the term *doxographi* to refer to a group of authors whose works he edited in *Doxographi Graeci*. As noted, by far the most important of these writers was Aëtius, whose work could be reconstructed from the pseudo-Plutarchean *Placita*, Stobaeus, and the church father Theodoret. The other writings to be edited were fragments and excerpts from Arius Didymus, Theophrastus, Cicero, Philodemus, Hippolytus, the pseudo-Plutarchean *Stromateis*, Epiphanius, pseudo-Galen, and Hermias. Although these various documents and collections were quite diverse, what they had in common was that they all contained *doxai* or philosophical views that were somehow or other interconnected.

In general terms, *doxai* (Latin *opiniones*) or *areskonta* (Latin *placita*) can be described as brief statements of the views held by a philosopher on a particular subject. A single sentence or even a few words can often be enough. Remarkably, a *doxa* is very often devoid of any argument. This would seem to make it a most unsatisfactory vehicle for the presentation of a philosopher's viewpoint. After all, philosophers very often regard the arguments supporting a particular viewpoint as more important than the viewpoint itself. Consequently, if we are lucky enough to have plenty of writings or sources for a particular philosopher, as in the case of Plato and Aristotle, the views recorded in collections of *doxai* are almost laughably inadequate and in most cases hardly worth detailed examination. But this is emphatically not the situation we encounter for the philosophy of the Presocratics. There is so little information available that the doxographical tradition simply cannot be ignored.

Doxai are perhaps best regarded as little packets or sound-bites of doctrinal information. Because they are so compact, their organization is infinitely malleable and adaptable. They can be compared or contrasted, affirmed or denied, clustered or individualized, listed and ordered in a multitude of ways. The *Placita* of Aëtius are the best example. The work in its original form[39] must have contained some thousand *doxai* organized in about 130 chapters, which ranged from a single *doxa* (very rare) to groups of 20 or more. The techniques most used are the *diaeresis* (division), in which a number of differing *doxai* are listed, and the *diaphonia* (disagreement), in which contrasting views are opposed (the basic methods of Hippias and Gorgias are still recognizable!). An ancient reader who consulted the collection would thus obtain a highly compact overview of what philosophers thought on a wide range of issues to do with first principles and the natural world. One example out of many is the subject of the sea, how it was constituted, and why it is salty. Of the six *doxai* given, five belong to Presocratics.[40] Naturally, doxography of this kind does not just have to occur in a stand-alone work such as the

Aëtian *Placita*. *Doxai* are also most useful when giving a preliminary overview of a subject, such as we find in book 1 of Cicero's *De natural deorum*, where the Epicurean Velleius strings together a huge list of views on the subject of God in which the conflicting nature of the *doxai* is strongly emphasized.[41]

The goal Diels set himself was to analyze this tradition so that it could be mapped and the value of its information could be determined. To a degree, he was quite fortunate. A significant part of the tradition of the *Placita* could be reduced to a single author, the aforementioned Aëtius. Recently Jaap Mansfeld and myself have undertaken a detailed reexamination of the evidence for the tradition of the *Placita*.[42] The research is still in progress, but with regard to Diels's reconstruction it can already be concluded that much of his hypothesis can be confirmed. The figure of Aëtius remains shadowy, and it is often better, when referring to him, to cite the two witnesses pseudo-Plutarch and Stobaeus rather than Diels's half-baked and sometimes flawed reconstruction,[43] at least until a full reconstruction has been produced. There can be no doubt, however, that a fair amount of Aëtius's work can be reconstructed, and its structural rationale, involving the twin techniques of *diaeresis* and *diaphonia*, can be understood.[44]

The remainder of the elaborate chart Diels made of the doxographical tradition has yet to be fully evaluated. It was right to postulate that, anterior to Aëtius in the first century CE, there were traditions of *placita* in authors such as Varro and Cicero, and before them Chrysippus and Epicurus, that can be traced.[45] But in the light of the research carried out by Jaap Mansfeld, we may be certain that Diels's methodology is fundamentally flawed. Relying on the techniques of *Quellenforschung* and stemmatology, he tried to reduce the tradition to a single origin in the history of philosophy practiced in the Peripatos.[46] Increasingly it is being recognized that the method of doxography is highly flexible and adaptable, enabling it to be used in a diversity of quite different philosophical contexts. There is no single doxographical tradition, but rather a multiplicity of contexts and strategies in which *doxai* can be put to use.[47]

But even if this increased understanding is taken into account, much research remains to be done. What, for example, was the purpose of Aëtius's extensive collection of *doxai*? If the truth be told, we do not really know. It might have been a schoolbook, but in what educational context would it have been used? And what caused these *doxai* to be formulated much earlier in the tradition? To answer this question an important discovery made by Mansfeld may offer assistance. He was able to demonstrate that Diels, in his eagerness to promote the role of Theophrastus in the Peripatos, consistently overlooked how much of the *placita* material goes back to the writings of Aristotle. Links can be convincingly established between Aëtian *doxai* and texts found mainly in *De Caelo*, the *Meteorology*, and the psychological works. A connection can be made with Aristotle's method of the *endoxa* that has already been mentioned. For example, at the beginning of his treatise *De anima* he writes (1.2, 403b20–3): "For our study of soul it is necessary, when formulating the problems of which in our further advance we are to find the solutions, to summon the opinions [*doxai*] of our predecessors, so that we may profit by whatever is sound in their suggestions and avoid their errors." This passage can be seen as the ultimate origin of the doxographical material found in the first chapters of Aëtius book 4 on psychology (including many Presocratic *doxai*).[48] Mansfeld further noted that a number of standard *doxai* turned up in an unexpected location, the *Topica*, in which Aristotle undertakes to develop procedures of argument for every kind of inquiry, whether scientific or rhetorical. Moreover, he was also able to show that various kinds of questions asked in doxographies revealed links to the standard questions in Aristotelian theory of knowledge based on the categories, for example, does something exist? what is its nature? what is its quality? and so on. Boldly, Mansfeld then formulated the hypothesis that the origin of the doxographical method should not be sought primarily in an incipient interest in the history of philosophy, but rather in the use of the dialectical method in order to solve problems of a scientific or a philosophical kind. Citing *Topics* 1.14, 105a34–36, b12–25, Mansfeld claims that the passage[49]

> provides an indispensable insight into the origins of accumulations of *placita* in the Early Peripatos. One makes collections of problems about which several kinds of questions may be put, and one makes notes—which may include name-labels—listing the individual views that have been proposed on each aspect of the matter at issue.

The hypothesis has the great advantage of explaining why in much doxography, including Aëtius, it is the problem that is of primary importance, followed by various solutions, whereby the actual name of the philosopher holding the view is of secondary importance (hence the use of the term "name-label" attached to the *doxa*). Although sometimes chronology is taken into account when presenting the *doxai* (e.g., Thales may well come first), this is by no means always the case. Consistent with this insight, Mansfeld argued that Theophrastus's great collection of *doxai* in 18 books (of which the fragment *De sensibus* may have been a part) was called *Physikai doxai* (Opinions on physical questions) rather than *Physikôn doxai* (Opinions of the natural philosophers), as Diels surmised. The difference between the two titles is crucial: in the latter case it is the *doxai* that are primary, not the philosophers who developed them.[50]

Mansfeld's hypothesis, which amounts to the first significant revision of Diels's theory since its formulation in 1879, has been cautiously welcomed. Quite recently, however, it has come under strong attack by the Russian scholar Leonid Zhmud. He argues that Mansfeld and his Dutch colleagues (including myself) have been unnecessarily and ungraciously revisionist.[51] Diels was right in affirming that history of philosophy was at the origin of doxography and that the primary work for this enterprise, as far as the Presocratics were concerned, was Theophrastus's *Physikôn doxai* (*sic!*), which was parallel to the histories of theology and the various mathematical disciplines written by Eudemus. Zhmud is certainly quite misleading when he suggests that the "Dutch school" has shown little respect for Diels's achievement. This is patently not the case. We amply recognize how fundamental his research was and still remains. After more than a century, however, some scrutiny and criticism of its methodological underpinnings and theoretical assumptions is amply justified. Zhmud is right to point out how much is at stake when we decide whether primacy should be given to historiography or to dialectic when determining the origins of doxography. But his attempt to vindicate Diels's view that historiography was at the heart of the Theophrastean project suffers from an anachronistic conception of the notion of *historia* and is not supported by the limited evidence available for what Theophrastus was doing in his work on the Presocratics and Plato. The Dielsian hypothesis of the Theophrastean origin had been reassuring in this regard, for it appeared to provide a solid foundation for the extensive collections of A-fragments in *FVS*. Much of it, however, may have been an exercise in wishful thinking.

A final question needs to be briefly raised. What was the scope of ancient doxography? As already noted, Aëtius's collection basically covers the domain of physics (in the ancient sense), with the inclusion of first principles. There is little room for logic or epistemology, except when the latter is connected with psychology and physiology, as in the case of theories of perception. This concentration coheres well with many of the Presocratics' interests. Doxography for the domain of ethics was developed to some degree in the Hellenistic period, but apparently was never distilled into a collection that could compare with that of Aëtius.[52] The amount of doxography in Aristotle's various ethical works is rather limited, even though more than once he indicates the need to examine the *doxai* in this field of study.[53] Presumably, little material was available that offered opportunities for systematic analysis. A striking example of an ethical doxography that includes Presocratics is the list of views on the end or goal of life (*telos*) found in Clement of Alexandria *Stromateis* 2.128–130. It includes Anaxagoras, Heraclitus, Pythagoras, Democritus, Hecataeus, Apollodorus of Cyzike, and Nausiphanes.[54]

2.5. Biography and Other Related Genres

Just as Aëtius plays a central role in the doxographical tradition, so Diogenes Laertius is the chief focus for biographical information. Diels duly commenced each A-section of his fragment collection with the biographical notice found in Diogenes.[55] He is by no means an ideal source, but we have to work with what we have.

Diogenes' treatment of the Presocratics is rather variable, both in extent and quality. All the major authors are included. Thales receives a long section in book 1 in the context of the seven sages. The other Milesians are found at the beginning of book 2, followed by Anaxagoras, Archelaus, and then Socrates. The remaining Presocratics are all found in books 8 and 9, where extensive coverage is given to Pythagoras, Empedocles, Heraclitus, and Democritus, but others are treated much more cursorily. The clue to this patchy and scattered treatment lies in the macrostructure of Diogenes' work, which combines features from two difference genres of the ancient historiography of philosophy. Firstly (and less importantly), the method of the *Peri haireseôn* literature is followed.[56] This results in a disproportionate amount of attention being paid to the founder of a *hairesis* or "school," including in most cases a long doxographical section. For the Presocratics, the method explains the long sections on Thales and Pythagoras, but little else. They of course largely fell outside the scheme of "schools of thought" that was developed in later antiquity. Secondly (and more important), Diogenes bases the structure of his work on the conception of the *diadochê* (succession). This view of the history of philosophy does include the Presocratics to a significant degree, because Greek philosophy is thought to commence with two major lines of succession. The Ionian line begins with Thales, and embraces the philosophers treated in books 2–7, of whom only four by definition are Presocratics (since Socrates himself is the fifth).[57] The Italian line, commencing with Pythagoras, is treated in book 8. Book 9 then deals with the "dispersed" thinkers, which include Heraclitus, Xenophanes, the Eleatics, the atomists, and Protagoras. Diogenes here draws extensively on the so-called "successions literature," a Hellenistic genre associated with the innovative work of Sotion of Alexandria and Antisthenes of Rhodes. Unfortunately only fragments survive, mainly from Diogenes himself.[58]

It is worth emphasizing that Diogenes, though he probably wrote in the early to mid–third century CE, included no philosophers later than the Hellenistic period in his work.[59] Studies on him have made some advances in recent years, but much of his mystery remains. It is striking that, in the case of Pythagoras for example, none of the mystagogic emphasis found in Porphyry and Iamblichus is present.[60] Very likely Diogenes was working in a backwater, not up to date with the latest trends.[61] At a micro level, the information he provides is valuable but often strangely varied. The best way, in my view, to understand the mix is to use the notion, inaugurated by Delatte, of "rubrics" of information, some of which are present in every *bios*. These include the philosopher's origin/descent, his education and travels, his place in the succession or school, his character and way of life, the circumstances of his death, his chronology, his writings, his doctrines, relevant documents, people with the same name, and so on.[62] The key to this approach, as Mansfeld has well seen,[63] is the conviction that there must be a correspondence between a philosopher's life and his doctrine (and also, we might add, his speech). This concern is also in the foreground of much of the biographical material found outside Diogenes and assiduously collected by Diels and Kranz in their A-fragments.

It should be further noted that an account of doctrine is nestled in most of Diogenes' *bioi*. In contrast to what we find in Aëtius and similar sources, *doxai* are collected together for a single thinker and combined in a doctrinal cameo. In two cases, Heraclitus and Leucippus, a "general" and a "detailed" version even stand side by side.[64] The first book of Hippolytus's *Refutation of All Heresies* (probably contemporary with Diogenes) consists entirely of such potted "doxographies" of individual thinkers and is also organized by means of the successions principle.[65] Clearly there is both a link between Diogenes' method and that of Hippolytus, and between biography and doxography, but the exact details remain controversial and cannot be further discussed in this context.

Three other genres of ancient writings should be briefly taken into account in this context. The first, chronography, can be fairly narrowly defined. It is associated above all with the Hellenistic scholar Apollodorus, who wrote a famous chronographic work, the *Chronica*. Building on the earlier work of Eratosthenes, Apollodorus laid out a general chronology of Greek political and cultural history up to his own time.[66] There are indications, however, that his system, involving birth, death, and *akmê* (i.e., *floruit*), goes back to the sophists.[67] Evidence for it is found in Diogenes Laertius and Eusebius. It is important for the historical localization of the Presocratics.

The second genre, broadly labeled "gnomological literature," is much more diffuse. The titles for Diogenes' work found in some of the manuscripts is "Lives and maxims of those who gained fame in philosophy and the doctrines in each school of thought."[68] Here *gnômai* (maxims) are placed beside *bioi* (lives) and *areskonta* (doctrines). Various anecdotes containing pronouncements (*apophthegmata*) or pointed sayings (*chreiai*) are attributed to the Presocratics, though fewer than in the case of later figures.[69] Once again the chief purpose is to illustrate the unity of life and doctrine. The historical value of this material is of course questionable. In later antiquity, extensive collections were made of the maxims of early philosophers (who follow on from the earlier sages).[70] Residues of these collections are found in Stobaeus, most notably the huge collection attributed to Democritus, which form the bulk of his B-fragments in Diels-Kranz. It is likely that much of this material was drawn from ethical and political writings now lost.[71]

The third genre is even further removed from any kind of historicity. Letters are preserved attributed to Thales, Anaximenes, Pythagoras and his school, and Heraclitus (a small corpus of nine letters, including two purportedly addressed to him by King Darius). Diels and Kranz did not include these in their fragment collection. This genre, too, informs us mainly about the reception of the Presocratics in later times.[72]

2.6. The Hellenistic Period

In many respects, Hellenistic philosophy in the third to first centuries BCE led to a revival of approaches prominent in the Presocratic period, pursued now with greater sophistication and systematic rigor in the wake of the major advances made by philosophy in the fourth century. But for two reasons this helps us little in the question of sources. First, almost nothing of Hellenistic philosophy has survived from the third and second centuries. We cannot, therefore, find out anything about Heraclitus from the early Stoics, even though we know they consciously claimed his philosophical heritage.[73] Second, the philosopher whose works survive best, Epicurus, tried to maximize his originality and so distanced himself from his Presocratic antecedents in the atomist tradition. We learn less from him about his predecessors than from his first-century followers Philodemus and Lucretius. Cicero's philosophical and rhetorical writings are a rich source, but contain little that is independent of the doxographical tradition.[74]

2.7. The Imperial Period

One of the real conundrums of the study of ancient philosophy is the origin of a large number of pseudonymous Pythagorean works preserved mainly by Stobaeus. Some of these may possibly go back to the late fourth century and Hellenistic times.[75] Others, such as the work by Timaeus Locrus purporting to be the original source of Plato's *Timaeus*, certainly belong to the first century BCE.[76] Pythagoreanism as a philosophical movement was revived during that period. Its rise is indicative of new developments that were of great significance for the evaluation of Presocratic philosophers. Philosophy came to be seen normatively as a single tradition, what later came to be called the *philosophia perennis*. The earlier the philosophers, the closer they were to the source of primal wisdom. Later philosophers were technically more adept, but lacked the depth of their predecessors. The Presocratics most likely to be cited in this context were Pythagoras, Heraclitus, Parmenides, and Empedocles.[77] Very often their thought is forced into a (Neo)-platonizing mould, in which Empedoclean unity and Parmenidean being are interpreted in terms of the One and the Intelligible Cosmos respectively.[78] But without this development their works would not have been copied, and we would have to do without many of the B-fragments still extant.

In this context, pride of place must go to the enormously erudite Plutarch. The catalogue of his writings mentions 10 books of notes on Empedocles, a book on the question "what did Heraclitus think," another on Protagoras, and a title that suggests a study on Democritean first principles.[79] Plutarch likes to show off his cleverness. Many citations appear in convoluted contexts.[80] But the quotations can often be identified, and they are numerous: we are indebted to him for at least 17 Heraclitean aphorisms and 71 lines of Empedocles found nowhere else.[81] Plotinus stands in the same tradition, but is much more the philosopher, wanting to make allusions to and reinterpret the tradition rather than record and manipulate it. In comparison, the learning of the prolific Galen is less deep, but he contributes some valuable material on Democritus.

A quite different tradition is represented by Sextus Empiricus. He is the heir to the rich skeptical tradition that methodically pitted its radical epistemology against all the other "dogmatic" philosophies. Sextus's contribution to our knowledge of Xenophanes, Parmenides, Empedocles, and Democritus is quite outstanding, with his preservation of the prologue of Parmenides' poem as absolute highlight.[82] In some respects, Sextus stands quite close to the doxographical tradition, which, as shown, shared his love for *diaphôniai* and *antilogiai*.[83] The same can be said, but in a different respect, of Seneca, whose *Naturales quaestiones* contain much Presocratic material on metereology that cannot simply be reduced to Aristotle and the tradition of the *Placita*. Like all the writers mentioned in this section so far (except possibly Galen), he will have made at least some study of the original works.[84]

In the Judeo-Christian tradition, which starts with Philo of Alexandria in the first century CE, confrontation sets the tone, but it is occasionally mixed with admiration and surprising erudition; Clement of Alexandria was educated in the

Greek philosophical tradition, and his works (especially the *Stromateis*) contain a remarkable amount of unduplicated material.[85] Hippolytus is another highly significant source, whose offerings are embedded in a heresiological strategy that shares its method with the Neoplatonist appropriation of the major Presocratics mentioned earlier, but uses it for a quite different purpose.[86] Unfortunately, Eusebius appears not to have had any original Presocratic works available to him in his rich library at Caesarea, but his knowledge of the tradition of historiography of philosophy yields us a few valuable quotes.[87] After him it is mainly the doxographical tradition that continues to be recorded and exploited in Christian writers.[88]

2.8. The Commentators

The final stage of the transmission of Presocratic writings and doctrine in antiquity is represented by the teachers of philosophy in Athens and Alexandria from about 350 to 640.[89] Philosophically Platonism had triumphed, but the curriculum also included Aristotle, whose doctrine was harmonized with that of Plato. Most writings from this period are commentaries on Aristotle and Plato. The task of many of these works is to explain what is not directly comprehensible for students at not too advanced a level. The overall framework is Platonist, but the tradition is seen as unified, and so it is regarded as worthwhile to include the earlier thinkers within the scope of the commentaries. The commentaries on Plato by Proclus and others yield some material, but the commentaries on Aristotle are much richer. Outstanding in every respect is the contribution of the last of the Athenian professors of philosophy, Simplicius (c. 490–560). His commentaries on Aristotle's *Physics* and *De Caelo* contain an unsurpassed wealth of material on the Presocratics.

Commenting on the doctrine of Parmenides that "being" only has one meaning, discussed by Aristotle at *Physics* 1.3, 187a1–11, Simplicius does us the immense favor of quoting 52 lines of his poem at a stretch (28B8.1–52). His words of introduction deserve to be quoted (*in Ph.* 144.25–29):

> And in case I seem petty to anyone [in my criticisms], I would gladly write out in this commentary the verses of Parmenides that Being is one and that there is no plurality of beings, both on account of the conviction that they will give my words and on account of the rarity of the Parmenidean treatise. The words after the refutation of nonbeing read as follows.

Simplicius quotes fulsomely because he knows that the work he has in his possession is rare and as a pagan he is aware that pagan Hellenism is under threat. So, to rephrase a comment by Richard Sorabji, the distorting Neoplatonist context does not prevent the commentaries from being incomparable sources for Presocratic philosophy.[90] It is remarkable that so late an author is our only witness for virtually all the verbatim fragments of Zeno and Melissus, for most of those belonging to Anaxagoras and Diogenes of Apollonia, and for substantial quotations from the poems of Parmenides and Empedocles. Most remarkably of all, Simplicius quotes the only fragment we have of Anaximander, at second or even third hand.[91] Anaximander's book was by his time irretrievably lost. It would seem that the same was the case for Heraclitus's treatise and the works of the atomists, for none of these is cited directly. Without Simplicius, our knowledge of Presocratic philosophy would be disastrously impoverished.[92] If his commentaries on the *Metaphysics* and *Metereology* had survived, or if he had had access to more Presocratic writings, we might have been a lot better off than we are. Such are the vagaries of transmission.

3. SOME SUGGESTIONS ON THE WAY FORWARD

It is more than 50 years since the last revision of Diels's great fragment collection. Although, as shown, it has stood the test of time remarkably well, there are quite a few reasons that it would be well worth bringing it up to date in a new edition. The few newly discovered fragments could be added, as well as some Diels neglected to include. New editions of the texts cited could be used. The entire body of works cited could be translated, not just the B-fragments, in response to the regrettable fact that the level of expertise in the ancient languages Diels and Kranz assumed is no longer widespread, even sometimes in the case of professional scholars. An attempt could also be made to reorganize the A-fragments in the light of new developments in our understanding of the doxographical and biographical traditions.

Realistically, however, it is not very likely that this project will get off the ground. It would take a dedicated team years or even decades to complete. Moreover, the assumption that it is possible to contain the whole of Greek intellectual thought prior to Socrates and Plato in a single work has to be abandoned. Studies in science, medicine, rhetoric, literary theory, and other areas related to philosophy have been going their own way for some time. At most, it might be valuable to put together a volume with additions to Diels recording the developments of the past half century.[93]

For some 40 years now, scholars have been pursuing a different route. Studies have been devoted to individual thinkers. I am thinking particularly of editions and of detailed studies involving the editing and close reading of fragments. Fine early examples were Marcovich's Heraclitus (subsequently revised) and Luria's Democritus.[94] More recent are Sider's Anaxagoras, Laks's Diogenes of Apollonia, Coxon's Parmenides, Huffman's Philolaus and now Archytas.[95] The attitude adopted toward Diels varies. Huffman, for example, considers it too confusing to try to introduce a new numbering of the fragments, whereas Laks introduces a new system, including usefully an S-section for the *spuria*. The latter policy is to be preferred if we are ever to move beyond Diels. Confusion can be avoided through the use of concordances. New editions are being prepared of the Democritean and

Empedoclean remains.[96] Serge Mouraviev has undertaken the most spectacular project; his *Heraclitea* in five parts will run to more than ten volumes when it is completed.[97] The collection of fragments certainly does advance beyond Diels (as did the edition of Marcovich that preceded this one).[98] But one wonders whether this Herculean effort is not going too far.

These editions encounter a difficulty, which is basically no different from the one that Diels faced in his *FVS*. There is a significant divergence between the author-based interest of the modern historian and the practice of the ancient sources, which often have quite different purposes in mind when they relate the opinions and doctrines of Presocratic philosophers. As shown in this chapter, much of the information we possess goes back to ancient documents belonging to genres that are quite foreign to the practices of modern historiography. The indefatigable research of Jaap Mansfeld and his collaborators has made significant advances in this area.[99] Much further research remains to be done. One can safely predict that this research will be of enormous benefit to scholars working on individual Presocratics. It represents the most significant advance since Diels set his stamp on the field.

It is always tempting to imagine how rewarding it would be to have direct contact with an early Greek philosopher through his writings, without having to worry about the layers of tradition that interpose themselves between him and us. But this can be no more than a daydream. Diels was in fact much more aware of the importance of the tradition of reception than were many later scholars who based their work on his magnificent compendium. As I have tried to show here, the study of the Presocratics cannot be done without including the study of how later traditions received and read them, both in the ancient world and in the modern era. It is, in my view, not the least of its attractions.

APPENDIX: CHAPTER SUBHEADINGS IN *FVS*

Here I give an overview of the chapter sub-headings Diels uses in presenting the literary remains of the 90 philosophers and other thinkers in *FVS*. As noted (section 1), this overview gives a good insight into how flexibly Diels and Kranz adapted their basic scheme to the wide variety of material they collected. Each chapter is simply headed with a number and the name of the philosopher. After this heading, the variation occurs, as follows (my translations of the German original; the asterisked chapters have further subheadings).

A-Section

"Life and Writing(s)": 1, 2, 6, 7, 9, 23, 40, 87, 88
"Life": 3, 18 (exceptionally no use of A-, B-, C-sections in this chapter), 37, 69

"Writing": 4
"Life and Doctrine": 11, 12, 13, 21,* 22,* 24, 28,* 29,* 30,* 31,* 38, 47,* 59,* 60,*
    64,* 67, 68,* 70, 72, 73, 75, 80, 82, 84, 85, 86
"Doctrine": 18*
"Life, Writings, Doctrine": 36
"Life, Apophthegms, Writings, Doctrine": 44*

B-Section (including subheadings, but not book titles)

"Fragments with Ancient Authority": 1
"Alleged Fragment": 11
"Fragments": 2, 3, 4, 7, 9, 12, 13, 21, 22, 23, 24, 28, 29, 30, 31, 36, 37 (expanded
    heading), 38, 40, 44, 59, 64, 67, 68,* 69, 70, 72, 73, 75, 80, 82, 84, 85, 86,
    87,* 88 (divided into "Poetische" and "Prosaische")
"Authentic Fragments": 47
"Late Forgeries": 3
"Writings": 60*
"Inauthentic Writings": 47
"Inauthentic Material": 7, 31, 44, 59
"Inauthentic Fragments": 68
"Falsified Fragments": 30
"Falsifications": 60
"False Materials": 28, 38, 84
"Forgeries": 73
"Dubious Material": 9, 28, 31, 36, 44, 68, 84, 86
"Dubious Writings": 47
"Dubious Fragments": 21, 22 (expanded heading)
"Dubious Titles": 80
"Grammatical Material": 73
"From Unknown Writings": 80, 82, 84, 85, 86, 88 (prosaische)
"Lacking Good Evidence": 80, 82
"Inauthentic or Uncertain Fragments": 88
(No heading at all) 6

C-Section

"Dubious Material": 12
"Imitation": 21, 22, 68, 80, 82, 86
"Reminiscence": 31
(No title) 60
"Nachwirkung": 64
(No headings at all) 5, 8, 10, 14–17, 19, 20, 25–27, 32–35, 39, 42, 43, 45, 46, 48,
    49, 50–57, 61–63, 65, 66, 71, 74, 76–78, 81, 83, 89, 90
Idiosyncratic chapters: 58 (Pythagorean school); 79 (name and concept of
    sophists)

NOTES

My cordial thanks to Jaap Mansfeld (Utrecht) and Han Baltussen (Adelaide) for offering valuable advice on a draft version. Responsibility for errors and value judgments remains wholly mine.

1. For the fragment of a large archaic statue containing an inscription of Anaximander's name see Couprie, *Verordening van de Tijd*, back and front cover and p. vii. For numismatic and ceramic evidence see Schefold, *Die Bildnisse der antiken Dichter, Redner und Denker*, 107, 199; the coin images of Pythagoras date from nearly a century after his death; the vase portrait of Critias may be contemporary. Schefold's standard work gives a good overview of the depictions of Presocratic philosophers which have survived, but it should be noted that some of his identifications are quite speculative.

2. Berlin, 1903, in a single volume (610 pages).

3. In 1906 (when the move to two volumes was made), 1912, 1922 (in this edition the thinkers before Thales are placed at the beginning of the volume). The third index volume first appeared in 1910.

4. DK 1951–52. Unless otherwise indicated, references to Presocratics in this article will be to this edition.

5. The following section has been greatly aided by three recent discussions: Mansfeld, "Sources"; Burkert, "Diels' *Vorsokratiker*"; Leszl, "Problems Raised by an Edition and Translation of Democritus, with Comparisons with Other Presocratics."

6. For example, very consciously both in the title and in the editor's introductory essay in Long, *The Cambridge Companion to Early Greek Philosophy*.

7. Quoted in DK, 6th ed., vol. 1, p. viii (my translation).

8. On this variety in the C-sections see Laks, "Éditer l'influence?" 89–91.

9. *DG*; subsequently reprinted many times, but never revised or updated. On this work see further Mansfeld and Runia, *Aëtiana*, esp. 64–110; Mansfeld, "*Doxographi Graeci*."

10. *De oratore* 2.117: "It betrays a slow-witted mentality to pursue the streams, but not to see the sources of things."

11. On this and other philological techniques used by Diels see Mansfeld and Runia, *Aëtiana*, 111–20; Mansfeld, "Doxographical Studies."

12. Heading preceding 22A5, vol. 1: 145. It reads (translated): "Cf. the excerpts from Theophrastus's *Physikôn doxai* A 1, 7 (mediated) and 8–11 (unmediated)."

13. Diels, *Simplicii in Aristotelis Physicorum libros quattuor priores commentaria*; Diels, *Simplicii in Aristotelis Physicorum libros quattuor posteriores commentaria*.

14. The index at *FVS* 3.638–40 lists 93 B-fragments. See further in section 2 here.

15. Diels, *Simplicii in Aristotelis Physicorum libros quattuor priores commentaria*, p. ix, n. 2.

16. Diels, *Poetarum philosophorum fragmenta*. See the account of Burkert, "Diels' *Vorsokratiker*," 171–74.

17. In researching this section I have derived much benefit from a paper on a similar subject by Mansfeld, "Sources." See also the informative recent handbook by Mejer, *Überlieferung der Philosophie im Altertum*, covering the transmission of the whole of ancient philosophy.

18. As we know from the extensive catalogue preserved at D.L. 9.46–49.

19. See further section 2.8 here.

20. Primavesi, "Lecteurs antiques et byzantins d'Empédocle," 200–201.

21. See the five volumes published so far, *Corpus dei papyri filosofici greci e latini (CPF)*.

22. Best example is a papyrus of Antiphon the Sophist, published at 87B44, now republished as *CPF* no. 17.1–2. Note that the Heraclitean papyri recorded in *CPF* no. 57.1T–5T are not fragments of a copy of his book, but mainly doxographical references.

23. Kouremenos, Parássoglou, and Tsantsanoglou. *The Derveni Papyrus*; Martin and Primavesi, *L'Empédocle de Strasbourg*. Martin and Primavesi, *L'Empédocle de Strasbourg*.

24. This is a question already raised in antiquity; see D.L. 3.25.

25. Cf. *Cra.* 402a–c, *Tht.* 152d–e, *Smp.* 178a–b.

26. *Sph.* 242c–249e; friends of the forms at 248a.

27. Snell, "Die Nachrichten über die Lehren des Thales und die Anfänge der griechischen Philosophie- und Literaturgeschichte"; Mansfeld, "*Cratylus* 402a–c: Plato or Hippias?" and "Aristotle, Plato, and the Preplatonic Doxography and Chronography"; Patzer, *Der Sophist Hippias als Philosophiehistoriker*; Primavesi, "Lecteurs antiques et byzantins d'Empédocle," 192–93, respectively.

28. This point is well made by Mansfeld, "Sources," 26–28.

29. This work may well be as late as the first or second century CE, as suggested by Mansfeld, "*De Melisso, Xenophane, Gorgia.*"

30. The validity of the schema is extensively discussed in Buxton, *From Myth to Reason?*

31. See the list at D.L. 5.25–26.

32. Cherniss, *Aristotle's Criticism of Presocratic Philosophy.*

33. For some sound comments on this controversy see Altoff, "Aristoteles als Medizindoxograph," 62–64.

34. The difference between demonstrative and dialectical science is set out in *A.Pr.* 1.1, *Top.* 1.1. The crucial role of dialectic in Aristotle's philosophical method is now generally recognized; see for example Nussbaum, "Saving Aristotle's Appearances." Its relation to the doxographical method is explored by the monograph of Baltussen, *Theophrastus against the Presocratics and Plato.* For comments in relation to the history of philosophy and medicine see Altoff, "Aristoteles als Medizindoxograph," 60–62.

35. Cicero, *Tusc.* 3.69, regarded as *Protrepticus* fr. 8 in Ross, *Aristotelis fragmenta selecta*, but attributed by Düring to the *De philosophia*. A cyclical view of human cultural history is assumed at *Metaph.* 12.10 and *De phil.* fr. 8 Ross.

36. See the famous text about his discoveries in logic at *SE* 34, 183b15–36.

37. *DG* 102.

38. Some extreme examples of loose usage are given by Runia, "What Is Doxography?" 33–35. The entire article gives an overview of ancient doxography.

39. We probably still have about two-thirds of the original work.

40. Preserved in Ps.-Plut. *Plac.* 3.17. All five are taken up in *FVS*: Anaximand. A27, Anaxag. A90, Emped. A66, Antiph. B32, Metrod. A19.

41. *DND* 1.25–41, taken up by *DG* 531–50, together with the close parallel in *PHerc.* 1428, probably by Philodemus. It includes the *doxai* of 11 Presocratics. Other examples at Runia, "What Is Doxography?" 45.

42. Mansfeld and Runia, *Aëtiana*. Two more volumes are projected. Volume 2, focusing more directly on Aëtius' compendium, will be published in 2008.

43. See the double columns in *DG* rather than his practice in *FVS*, where only the Aëtian reconstruction is cited.

44. A number of chapters and longer sections of the work have already been subject to extensive analysis: see Mansfeld, "Doxography and Dialectic" (4.2–7); "Cosmic Distances" (2.31); "From Milky Way to Walo" (C3.1–6, 18); Runia, "Xenophanes on the Moon" (2.25); "A Difficult Chapter in Aëtius" (2.4); "Xenophanes or Theophrastus? An Aëtian *doxo-*

graphicum on the Sun" (2.20); and "What Is Doxography?" (1.23); Baltussen, "Plato in the *Placita* (Aëtius Book IV)" (4.8–23 on the Platonic *doxai* only).

45. Diels lumped these together in what he called the *Vetusta Placita*; see further Mansfeld and Runia, *Aëtiana*, 79–80. Much still needs to be further untangled here. Mansfeld, "Chrysippus and the *Placita*" has shown that the evidence of Chrysippus entails a *Vetustissima Placita*.

46. See above section 1 and nn. 10–11 here.

47. See the programmatic introduction to Mansfeld and Runia, *Aëtiana*, xiii–xxi.

48. Together with some anticipations in Pl. *Phd.* 96b. On this section see Mansfeld, "Doxography and Dialectic," 3210–212.

49. Mansfeld, "Doxography and Dialectic," 3202. These ideas are further developed in Mansfeld, "*Physikai doxai*," 63–66.

50. Mansfeld, "*Physikai doxai*," 63–66. On *De sensibus* and dialectic see further Baltussen, *Theophrastus Against the Presocratics and Plato*.

51. Zhmud, "Revising Doxography." A brief rejoinder has been published by Mansfeld, "Deconstructing Doxography."

52. The huge effort of Giusta, *I dossografi di etica*, to establish a kind of *Doxographi Graeci* in the area of ethics is generally regarded as a failure.

53. See the texts cited by Mansfeld, "Doxography and Dialectic," 3202. On his dialectical method in general in the *Ethics* see Barnes, "Aristotle and the Methods of Ethics."

54. Located in *FVS* at 59A57, 22A21, 68B4, 73A4, 74.3 (one of only three *testimonia* for Apollodorus), 75B3. The doxa on Pythagoras attributed to Heraclides Ponticus is not included.

55. This is the case for 19 Presocratic philosophers. Exceptions occur in the special cases of Pythagoras (not included) and Epicharmus (here Diels prefers to start with the *Suda*).

56. *Hairesis* is often translated "sect," but "school of thought" is preferable. Institutional continuity is not a necessary condition. On this literature see Mejer, *Diogenes Laertius and His Hellenistic Background*, 75–81; Runia, "What Is Doxography?" 41–42.

57. See 1.122, 8.1.

58. On this literature see Kienle, *Die Berichte über die Sukzessionen der Philosophen*; Mejer, *Diogenes Laertius and His Hellenistic Background*, 62–74, and *Überlieferung der Philosophie im Altertum*, 45–47. The fragments have been collected by Giannastasio Andria, *I frammenti delle "Successioni dei filosofi."*

59. The only exceptions are a list of skeptics at 9.116 and some of the later Stoics treated in the latter part of book 7 that has been lost.

60. As noted by Mansfeld, "Sources," 33.

61. Especially if his hometown was Nicaea, as suggested by 9.109. I do not think there are any real grounds for doubting this. The relatively strong emphasis on Pythagoras, Empedocles, and Heraclitus fits in well with first- to second-century preoccupations, i.e., he was not at the cutting edge of developments in ancient philosophy.

62. See Delatte, *La vie de Pythagore de Diogène Laërce*; a slightly different list at Hope, *The Book of Diogenes Laertius*, 145–68.

63. Mansfeld, *Prolegomena*, 179–91.

64. D.L. 9.7–12, 9.30–33.

65. Diels included it in *DG* 551–76. A similar approach is found on a smaller scale in Ps.-Plut. *Strom.* (*DG* 579–85).

66. See Mosshammer, *The Chronicle of Eusebius and the Greek Chronographic Tradition*; Dorandi's article on Apollodorus in Goulet, *Dictionnaire des philosophes antiques*, 271–74; Mejer, *Überlieferung der Philosophie im Altertum*, 41–42.

67. As investigated by Mansfeld, "Aristotle, Plato, and the Preplatonic Doxography."

68. See the edition of Marcovich, *Diogenes Laertius Vitae philosophorum*, 1.5: Λαερτίον Διογένους βίων καὶ γνωμῶν τῶν ἐν φιλοσοφίᾳ εὐδοκιμησάντων καὶ τῶν ἐν ἑκάστῃ αἱρέσει ἀρεσκόντων.

69. See esp. the *bioi* of Thales, Empedocles, Heraclitus. On such anecdotal material in Diogenes see Kindstrand, "Diogenes Laertius and the *chreia* Tradition." On the tradition in general see now Searby, *Aristotle in the Gnomological Tradition*. A vast collection of the ancient material is found in Robbins, *Ancient Quotes and Anecdotes*.

70. See further the overview of Gärtner, "Gnome"; in relation to philosophers, Wehrli, "Gnome, Anekdote, und Biographie."

71. See further Taylor, *The Atomists*, 223–25; on the collection attributed to "Democrates," J.-P. Flamand in Goulet, *Dictionnaire des philosophes antiques*, 2:644–47.

72. On the Ps.-Heraclitean collection see P. P. Fuentes González and J. L. López Cruces in the same work, 2:618–27; on fictional letter collections, Holzberg, *Der griechische Briefroman*.

73. Well demonstrated by the scanty remains in Mouraviev's exhaustive collection of material: Mouraviev, *Heraclitea* II.A.1, 186–201. As Jaap Mansfeld points out to me, however, their interest in Heraclitus did encourage later authors such as Clement to cite various Heraclitean texts.

74. Though Cicero is an important witness, he yields almost no B-fragments (an exception is the important text quoting Metrodorus, 70B1).

75. As argued by Thesleff, *The Pythagorean Texts of the Hellenistic Period*. See now Centrone, "Platonism and Pythagoreanism in the Early Empire," 567–75, who concludes (575): "the Pseudo-Pythagorean texts belong in substance to the Platonist tradition."

76. Baltes, *Timaios Lokros über die Natur des Kosmos und der Seele*. Close examination of the reformulation of Timaean doctrines shows links to Alexandria of the first century BCE.

77. See for example the fine analysis of the witnesses to Empedocles by Primavesi, "Lecteurs antiques et byzantins d'Empédocle," 184–91.

78. Examined in detail in the case of Hippolytus by Mansfeld, *Heresiography in Context*.

79. Lamprias catalogue, nos. 43, 205, 141, 145. See list in Sandbach, *Plutarch's Moralia in Sixteen Volumes*, Fragments, 3–29.

80. On the difficulties of reading Plutarch on earlier philosophers see Kidd, "Plutarch and His Stoic Contradictions."

81. As noted in Primavesi, "Lecteurs antiques et byzantins d'Empédocle," 189. Similarly erudite, but less philosophically informed, is the second-century author of the *Dinner Sophists*, Athenaeus; he is especially important for his extensive quotations of Xenophanes.

82. But note that the skeptic is not overly conscientious. Comparison with Simplicius's more accurate record reveals that Sextus's Parmenidean quotes are really patchworks; see Mansfeld, "Sources," 39.

83. See section 2.4 here.

84. On the complex relation to the *Placita* tradition see Mansfeld, "Sources," 31–32.

85. On Philo's extensive use of the doxographical tradition prior to Aëtius see now Runia, "Philo and Hellenistic Doxography." Of Diels's 126 Heraclitean B-fragments, 23

come from Clement. Clement stands fourth on Primavesi's list of contributors to the B-fragments of Empedocles, after Simplicius, Aristotle, and Plutarch, with 29 new lines.

86. Mansfeld's analysis, *Heresiography in Context* is methodologically superior to that of Osborne, *Rethinking Early Greek Philosophy*.

87. E.g. Protagoras at Eus. *PE* 14.3.7, Metrodorus at Eus. *PE* 14.3.10.

88. Notably in the work *Curatio affectionum Graecarum* (*Therapy for the Greek Diseases*) by Theodoret, Bishop of Cyrrhus (393–460), the third major source for our knowledge of Aëtius. On this work see Mansfeld and Runia, *Aëtiana*, 272–90.

89. This little-known period of ancient philosophy is coming into more prominence due to the splendid Ancient Commentators on Aristotle Project of Richard Sorabji based at King's College, London; see Sorabji, "The Ancient Commentators on Aristotle"; Vinzent, "'Oxbridge' in der ausgehende Spätantike," both with useful lists of protagonists.

90. See Sorabji, "The Ancient Commentators on Aristotle," 15, who writes: "The distorting Neoplatonist context does not prevent the commentaries from being incomparable guides to Aristotle." See now also D'Ancona, ed., *The Libraries of the Neoplatonists*.

91. Anaximand. B1. Simplicius derived his information from Theophrastus, possibly through the further intermediation of an earlier commentator such as Alexander of Aphrodisias.

92. The point well made by Mansfeld, "Sources," 38–39. On Simplicius's methods of citation see Baltussen, *Theophrastus against the Presocratics and Plato* and *Philosophy and Exegesis in Simplicius*.

93. As suggested by Jaap Mansfeld in a discussion on Diels's legacy at Vandœuvres. See Burkert "Diels' *Vorsokratiker*," 204. He also advocated a reprinting of the last edition that Diels did himself, DK 4th ed. (1922). The publication in three volumes of *Die Vorsokratiker*, edited by M. L. Gemelli Marciano, Düsseldorf: Artemis 2007–2008, will not replace Diels, despite the claims of the publisher on the dust jacket.

94. Marcovich, *Heraclitus*, and *Eraclito: Frammenti*; Luria, *Democritea*.

95. Sider, *The Fragments of Anaxagoras*; Laks, *Diogène d'Apollonie*; Coxon, *The Fragments of Parmenides*; Huffman, *Philolaus of Croton, Archytas of Tarentum*. A series of six major Presocratics has also been published by Toronto University Press, but their treatment is rather superficial. Earlier separate editions of various Presocratics were published in the Italian series Biblioteca di Studi Superiori. Note also the series Traditio Praesocratica recently announced by De Gruyter. The series aims "to document the transmission of early Greek philosophy" by means of a series of editions of individual philosophers. The first two volumes on the Milesians by G. Wöhrle have been announced to appear soon.

96. See Leszl, "Problems Raised by an Edition and Translation of Democritus, with Comparisons with Other Presocratics," 141 (two projected editions are mentioned); Primavesi, "Lecteurs antiques et byzantins d'Empédocle" (private communication).

97. The aim is to give a complete critical edition of the witnesses to Heraclitus's life and work and of the vestiges of his book. Part 1 is entitled *Prolegomena*, part 2 *Traditio*, part 3 *Recensio*, part 4 *Refectio* (i.e., reconstruction of his book), part 5 *Indices*.

98. Mouraviev, *Heraclitea*. The treatment of individual later authors as witnesses to the original work is outstanding. Mouraviev uses Latin for all the subject headings, which in comparison with Diels is a retrograde step (he does include French translations of the texts).

99. As recognized with varying degrees of acceptance by Lévy, "Doxographie et philosophie chez Ciceron"; Laks, "Du témoignage comme fragment"; Leszl, "Problems" (but wrongheadedly disputed by Zhmud, "Revising Doxography"; see above, n. 51).

BIBLIOGRAPHY

Altoff, J. "Aristoteles als Medizindoxograph." In *Ancient Histories of Medicine*, edited by P. J. van der Eijk, 57–94. Leiden: Brill, 1999.

Baltes, M. *Timaios Lokros über die Natur des Kosmos und der Seele.* Philosophia Antiqua, vol. 21. Leiden: Brill, 1972.

Baltussen, H. "Plato in the *Placita* (Aëtius Book IV): A Dielsian Blind Spot." *Philologus* 144 (2000): 227–38.

———. *Theophrastus against the Presocratics and Plato: Peripatetic Dialectic in the* De sensibus. Philosophia Antiqua, vol. 86. Leiden: Brill, 2000.

Barnes, Jonathan. "Aristotle and the Methods of Ethics." *Revue Internationale de Philosophie* 34 (1980): 490–511.

Burkert, Walter. "Diels' *Vorsokratiker*: Rückshau und Ausblick." In *Hermann Diels (1848–1922) et la science de l'antiquité*, edited by W. M. Calder III and Jaap Mansfeld, 169–97. Vandoeuvres-Geneva: Fondation Hardt, 1999.

Burkert, Walter, L. Gemelli Marciano, E. Matelli, and L. Orelli, eds. *Fragmentsammlungen philosophischer Texte der Antike.* Göttingen: Vandenhoeck & Ruprecht, 1998.

Buxton, R., ed. *From Myth to Reason? Studies in the Development of Greek Thought.* Oxford: Oxford University Press, 1999.

Centrone, B. "Platonism and Pythagoreanism in the Early Empire: Philo of Alexandria." In *The Cambridge History of Greek and Roman Political Thought*, edited by C. J. Rowe and M. Schofield, 559–84. Cambridge: Cambridge University Press, 2000.

Cherniss, Harold. *Aristotle's Criticism of Presocratic Philosophy.* Baltimore: Johns Hopkins University Press, 1935.

Corpus dei papiri filosofici greci e latini. 5 vols. Florence: Accademi Toscana di Scienze e Lettere "La Colombaria," 1989–.

Couprie, Dirk. *Verordening van de Tijd.* Dissertation: University of Amsterdam, 1989.

Coxon, A. H. *The Fragments of Parmenides.* Assen: Van Gorcum, 1986.

D'Ancona, C., ed. *The Libraries of the Neoplatonists.* Philosophia Antiqua 107. Leiden: Brill, 2007.

Delatte, A. *La vie de Pythagore de Diogène Laërce.* Brussels: Lamertin, 1922.

Diels, Hermann. *Poetarum philosophorum fragmenta.* Berlin: Weidmann, 1901.

———, ed. *Simplicii in Aristotelis Physicorum libros quattuor priores commentaria.* Commentaria in Aristotelem Graeca, vol. 9. Berlin: G. Reimer, 1882.

———, ed. *Simplicii in Aristotelis Physicorum libros quattuor posteriores commentaria.* Commentaria in Aristotelem Graeca, vol. 10. Berlin: G. Reimer, 1895.

Gärtner, H. A. "Gnome." In *Der neue Pauly*, 4:1108–16. Stuttgart: J. B. Metzler, 1998.

Giannastasio Andria, R. *I frammenti delle "Successioni dei filosofi."* Naples: Bibliopolis, 1989.

Giusta, M. *I dossografi di etica.* Pubblicazione della Facoltà di Lettere e Filosofia, vol. 15.3–4. Turin: Università di Torino, 1964–67.

Goulet, R., ed. *Dictionnaire des philosophes antiques.* 4 vols. and supplement. Paris: CNRS Éditions, 1989–.

Holzberg, N., ed. *Der griechische Briefroman: Gattungstypologie und Textanalyse.* Classica Monacensia, vol. 8. Tübingen: Gunter Narr, 1994.

Hope, R. *The Book of Diogenes Laertius: Its Spirit and Its Method.* New York: Columbia University Press, 1930.

Huffman, Carl A. *Philolaus of Croton.* Cambridge: Cambridge University Press, 1993.

————. *Archytas of Tarentum: Pythagorean, Philosopher and Mathematician King*. Cambridge: Cambridge University Press, 2005.

Kidd, Ian. "Plutarch and His Stoic Contradictions." In *Fragmentsammlungen philosophischer Texte der Antike*, edited by Walter Burkert, L. Gemelli Marciano, E. Matelli, and L. Orelli, 288–302. Göttingen: Vandenhoeck & Ruprecht, 1998.

Kienle, W. von. *Die Berichte über die Sukzessionen der Philosophen in der hellenistischen und spätantiken Literatur*. Dissertation: Berlin, 1961.

Kindstrand, J. F. "Diogenes Laertius and the *chreia* Tradition." *Elenchos* 7 (1986): 217–43.

Kouremenos, T., G. M. Parássoglou, and K. Tsantsanoglou. *The Derveni Papyrus. Edited with Introduction and Commentary*. Studi e testi per il Corpus dei papiri filosofici greci e latini 13. Florence: Olschki, 2006.

Laks, André. *Diogène d'Apollonie: La dernière cosmologie présocratique*. Lille: Presses Universitaires de Lille, 1983.

————. "Du témoinage comme fragment." In *Collecting Fragments*, edited by Glenn W. Most, 237–72. Göttingen: Vandenhoek & Ruprecht, 1997.

————. "Éditer l'influence? Remarques sur la section C du chapitre Diogène d'Apollonie dans les *Fragmente der Vorsokratiker* de Diels-Kranz." In *Fragmentsammlungen der philosophischer Texte der Antike*, edited by Walter Burkert, L. Gemelli Marciano, E. Matelli, and L. Orelli, 88–103. Göttingen: Vandenhoeck & Ruprecht, 1998.

Leszl, Walter. "Problems Raised by an Edition and Translation of Democritus, with Comparisons with Other Presocratics." In *Qu'est-ce que la philosophie présocratique?* edited by André Laks and Claire Louguet, 141–82. Lille: Presses Universitaires du Septentrion, 2002.

Lévy, C. "Doxographie et philosophie chez Ciceron." In *La concept de nature à Rome: La physique*, edited by C. Lévy, 109–23. Paris: Presses de l'École Normale superieure, 1996.

Long, A. A., ed. *The Cambridge Companion to Early Greek Philosophy*. Cambridge: Cambridge University Press, 1999.

Luria, Salomo. *Democritea*. Leningrad: Akademija Nauk S.S.S.R., 1970.

Mansfeld, Jaap. "Aristotle, Plato, and the Preplatonic Doxography and Chronography." In *Storiografia e dossografia nella filosofia antica*, edited by G. Cambiano, 1–59. Turin: Terrenia Stampatoria, 1986.

————. "Chrysippus and the *Placita*." *Phronesis* 34 (1989): 311–42.

————. "Cosmic Distances: Aëtius 2.31 Diels and Some Related Texts," *Phronesis* 45 (2000): 175–204.

————. "*Cratylus* 402a–c: Plato or Hippias?" In *Studi*, vol. 1 of *Atti del Symposium Heracliteum 1981*, edited by Livio Rossetti, 43–55. Rome: Ateneo, 1983.

————. "Deconstructing Doxography." *Philologus* 146 (2002): 277–86.

————. "*De Melisso, Xenophane, Gorgia*: Pyrrhonizing Aristotelianism." *Rheinisches Museum* 131 (1988): 239–76.

————. "Doxographical Studies: Quellenforschung, Tabular Presentation and Other Varieties of Comparativism." In *Fragmentsammlungen philosophischer Texte der Antike*, edited by Walter Burkert, L. Gemelli Marciano, E. Matelli, and L. Orelli, 16–40. Göttingen: Vandenhoeck & Ruprecht, 1998.

————. "*Doxographi Graeci*." In *Hermann Diels (1848–1922)*, edited by William M. Calder III and Jaap Mansfeld, 143–64. Vandoeuvres-Geneva: Fondation Hardt, 1999.

————. "Doxography and Dialectic: The Sitz Im Leben of the *Placita*." In *Aufstieg und Niedergang der Römischen Welt*, edited by W. Haase and H. Temporini, vol. 36, pt. 4, 3056–329. Berlin: De Gruyter, 1990.

————. "From Milky Way to Halo. Aristotle's *Metereologica*, Aëtius, and Passages in Seneca and the Scholia on Aratus." In *Philosophy and Doxography in the Imperial Age*, edited by A. Brancacci. Accademia Toscana di Scienze e Lettere "La Colombaria" Studi, vol. 228, 23–58. Florence: Olschki, 2005.

————. *Heresiography in Context: Hippolytus' Elenchos as a Source for Greek Philosophy.* Philosophia Antiqua, vol. 56. Leiden: E. J. Brill, 1992.

————. "*Physikai doxai* and *Problemata physika* from Aristotle to Aëtius (and Beyond)." In *Theophrastus: His Psychological, Doxographical and Scientific Writings*, Rutgers University Studies in the Classical Humanities, vol. 5, edited by W. W. Fortenbaugh and D. Gutas, 63–111. New Brunswick, N.J.: Rutgers University Press, 1992.

————. *Prolegomena: Questions to Be Settled before the Study of an Author, or a Text.* Philosophia Antiqua, vol. 61. Leiden: E. J. Brill, 1994.

————. "Sources." In *The Cambridge Companion to Early Greek Philosophy*, edited by A. A. Long, 22–44. Cambridge: Cambridge University Press, 1999.

————. *Studies in the Historiography of Greek Philosophy.* Assen: Van Gorcum, 1990.

Mansfeld, Jaap, and David T. Runia. *Aëtiana: The Method and Intellectual Context of a Doxographer, Vol. 1 The Sources.* Philosophia Antiqua, vol. 73. Leiden: E. J. Brill, 1997.

Marcovich, Miroslav. *Diogenes Laertius Vitae philosophorum.* 2 vols. Stuttgart: Teubner, 1999.

————. *Eraclito: Frammenti.* 1978. Rev. translation. Biblioteca, di Studi Superiori 64. Florence: La Nuova Italia, 1978.

————. *Heraclitus.* Mérida, Venezuela: University of the Andes Press, 1967.

Martin, Alain, and Oliver Primavesi. *L'Empédocle de Strasbourg.* Berlin: de Gruyter, 1999.

Mejer, Jørgen. *Diogenes Laertius and His Hellenistic Background.* Hermes Einzelschriften, vol. 40. Wiesbaden: Franz Steiner, 1978.

————. *Überlieferung der Philosophie im Altertum: Eine Einführung.* Historisk-filosofiske Meddelelser, vol. 80. Copenhagen: The Royal Danish Academy of Sciences and Letters, 2000.

Mosshammer, A. A. *The Chronicle of Eusebius and the Greek Chronographic Tradition.* Lewisburg, Pa., 1979.

Mouraviev, Serge. *Heraclitea: Édition critique complete des témoinages sur la vie et l'oeuvre d'Héraclite d'Éphèse et des vestiges de son livre et de sa pensée.* 5 parts, 9 vols. Saint Augustine: Academia Verlag, 1999–.

Nussbaum, Martha C. "Saving Aristotle's Appearances." In *Language and Logos*, edited by M. Schofield and M. C. Nussbaum, 267–93. Cambridge: Cambridge University Press, 1982.

Osborne, Catherine. *Rethinking Early Greek Philosophy: Hippolytus of Rome and the Presocratics.* Ithaca, N.Y.: Cornell University Press, 1987.

Patzer, Andreas. *Der Sophist Hippias als Philosophiehistoriker.* Freiburg: Karl Alber, 1986.

Primavesi, Oliver. "Lecteurs antiques et byzantins d'Empédocle: De Zénon à Tzétzès." In *Qu'est-ce que la philosophie présocratique?* edited by André Laks and Claire Louguet, 183–204. Lille: Presses Universitaires du Septentrion, 2002.

Robbins, V. K. *Ancient Quotes and Anecdotes.* Sonoma, Calif.: Polebridge Press, 1989.

Ross, W. D. *Aristotelis fragmenta selecta.* Oxford: Clarendon, 1955.

Runia, David T. "A Difficult Chapter in Aëtius Book II on Cosmology." In *Philosophy and Doxography in the Imperial Age*, edited by A. Brancacci. Accademia Toscana di Scienze e Lettere "La Colombaria" Studi, vol. 228, 1–22. Florence: Olschki, 2005.

————. "Philo and Hellenistic Doxography." In *Philo of Alexandria and Post-Aristotelian Philosophy* edited by F. Alesse. Studies on Philo of Alexandria, vol. 5, 13–52. Leiden: E. J. Brill, 2008.

————. "What Is Doxography?" In *Ancient Histories of Medicine*, edited by Philip J. van der Eijk. *Studies in Ancient Medicine*, vol. 20, 33–55. Leiden: E. J. Brill, 1999.

————. "Xenophanes on the Moon: A *doxographicum* in Aëtius." *Phronesis* 34 (1989): 245–69.

————. "Xenophanes or Theophrastus? An Aëtian *doxographicum* on the Sun." In *Theophrastus: His Psychological, Doxographical, and Scientific Writings*, edited by William W. Fortenbaugh and Dimitri Gutas, 112–40. New Brunswick, N.J.: Transaction, 1992.

Sandbach, F. H., ed. and trans. *Plutarch's Moralia in Sixteen Volumes*, vol. 15, Fragments, Cambridge Mass.: Harvard University Press, 1969. Loeb Classical Library, vol. 429.

Schefold, K. *Die Bildnisse der antiken Dichter, Redner und Denker.* Basel, 1997.

Searby, D. M. *Aristotle in the Gnomological Tradition.* Acta Universitatis Upsaliensis, vol. 19. Uppsala: Uppsala Universitet, 1998.

Sider, David. *The Fragments of Anaxagoras.* Meisenheim am Glan: Verlag Anton Hain, 1981.

Snell, Bruno. "Die Nachrichten über die Lehren des Thales und die Anfänge der griechischen Philosophie- und Literaturgeschichte." *Philologus* 96 (1944): 170–82.

Sorabji, Richard. "The Ancient Commentators on Aristotle." In *Aristotle Transformed: The Ancient Commentators and Their Influence*, 1–30. Ithaca, N.Y.: Cornell University Press, 1990.

Taylor, C. C. W. *The Atomists: Leucippus and Democritus.* Toronto: University of Toronto Press, 1999.

Thesleff, H. *The Pythagorean Texts of the Hellenistic Period.* Åbo, Finland: Åbo Akademi, 1965.

Vinzent, M. " 'Oxbridge' in der ausgehende Spätantike, oder: Ein Vergleich der Schulen von Athen und Alexandrien." *Zeitschrift für Antike und Christentum* 4 (2000): 49–82.

Wehrli, Fritz. "Gnome, Anekdote, und Biographie." *Museum Helveticum* 30 (1973): 193–206.

Wöhrle, Georg. *Anaximenes aus Milet: Die Fragmente zu seiner Lehre.* Stuttgart: Franz Steiner Verlag, 1993.

Zhmud, Leonid. "Revising Doxography: Hermann Diels and His Critics." *Philologus* 145 (2001): 219–43.

CHAPTER 2

PREHISTORY OF PRESOCRATIC PHILOSOPHY IN AN ORIENTALIZING CONTEXT

WALTER BURKERT

1. CONTEXTS OF HISTORY

Philosophy up to now is bound to a chain of tradition that starts with Greek texts about 2,400 years ago: the works of Plato and Aristotle have been studied continuously since then; they were transmitted to Persians and Arabs and back to Europe and are still found in every philosophical library. Plato, in turn, was not an absolute beginning; he read and criticized Heraclitus, Parmenides, Anaxagoras, Empedocles, Protagoras, and other sophists—we speak of "Presocratics" but should rather say "Preplatonics"; Aristotle read and criticized Plato and everything else he could find, up to Anaximander. Even if philosophy is anything but certain about its own identity, the very question "What is philosophy?" is inseparably bound to the Greek fundaments. Nobody has been able to reinvent philosophy because it has always been there.

There is no comparable tradition of books, texts, translations that goes beyond Anaximander, Heraclitus, Parmenides. As far as we see there are no direct translations at all in Greek literature before Hellenistic times. There is not one book from the classical epoch that could be termed the translation from one of the oriental languages, though the African Periplus of Hanno is a possible exception.[1] Whereas Latin literature began with translations and adaptations from the Greek, the Greek situation in the formative period must have been different. And still there was literature, highly developed literature, all around in the various "oriental" civilizations close to the Greeks. And the Greeks were anything but immune to oriental impacts.

In fact what we take to be the beginning of Greek philosophy had its start right in the epoch when the Eastern superpower hit the Greek world and established its rule over the most flourishing, advanced, and sophisticated part, the cities of Ionia. Thales of Miletus is linked to a solar eclipse that is linked to the conflict of Medes, Lydians, and post-Assyrian Babylonians, in 585 BCE;[2] Anaximander is said to have written his book, one of the earliest Greek prose books, just when King Cyrus the Persian conquered Sardis, capital of the Lydians, in 547 BCE;[3] Xenophanes left his home, Colophon in Asia Minor, "when the Mede arrived" (B22). Heraclitus stayed at Ephesus and kept connections to the sanctuary of Artemis there, where the construction of the first big marble temple of Greece had been started by Croesus, king of Lydia, and was to be completed under Persian rule; the main priest at the Artemision adopted a Persian title, Megabyxos.

But the establishment of Persian rule over the eastern Greeks was just the last act in a process of interactions that had been going on for a long time. After the breakdown of the so-called Bronze Age koinê, after the end of palaces and literacy, when a fragmented and unstable conglomerate of petty tribes and settlements had been left around the eastern Mediterranean, development, indeed progress had mainly come from three sources: the intensification of Mediterranean trade with Phoenician cities such as Tyre in the lead; the spreading of a simple writing system, the alphabet; and the formidable expansion of Assyria—military crisis at the heels of economic and cultural progress.

The Assyrian expansion reached the Mediterranean by the ninth century; it had its climax in the eighth and seventh centuries: Damascus was conquered about 800, Israel in 722, Cyprus about 700; Sidon was destroyed in 670; Egypt came under Assyrian domination 671–655. The main adversary in eastern Anatolia, Urartu, collapsed under a northern invasion by "Cimmerians" around 700; so did Phrygia. At that time, Gyges became king of Lydia, he established his rule over the main Greek cities of Anatolia, and he made an alliance with Assurbanipal, king of Assyria. This allowed him to open the King's Road from Ionia to Mesopotamia. Then Assyrian power came to a sudden fall through the combined assault of Babylonia and Iranian Medes in 612: Nineveh, the Assyrian capital, was destroyed.

The Greeks were at the margins of these events. Greeks had settled in Cyprus by the twelfth century at the latest; they had established trading posts in Syria by the ninth century. They succeeded in developing long-distance trade themselves in competition with the Phoenicians, from Syria to Etruria, with "colonies" in south-ern Italy and Sicily. At that time, Euboea was the dominant place for eastern as for western connections. There were some conflicts with Assyrians both in Syria and in Cilicia; by the eighth century, Greek kings in Cyprus paid tribute to Assyria. This still was not comparable to the catastrophes that befell the Arameans and Luwians of southern Anatolia, the Phoenician cities of Syria, Israel in Palestine, and Egypt. The Greeks were fortunate to be touched but not crushed by the eastern onslaught. They rather profited: eastern skills spread to the Mediterranean regions, probably in part through refugees. Greeks, being the most eastern of the westerners, could start their special career right then.[4]

By far the most important cultural transfer was alphabetic writing. There is no need to dwell on the advantages of the alphabet here, as against the old writing systems, be it hieroglyphic or cuneiform.[5] Nor will there be a discussion of the difference between consonantic writing, which Semites have kept to the present day, and the writing of vowels, which the Greeks introduced, largely by misunderstanding.[6] The success of the Greek alphabet is seen in the fact that it was rapidly taken over by the neighboring peoples, nearly at once by the Phrygians in the east and the Etruscans in the west, to be followed by Lydians and Lycians in Anatolia—the case of the Carians is more complex—and by Latini, Veneti, Iberi on the other side.

Greeks adopted the alphabet, as it seems, a little bit after 800 BCE.[7] There is a kind of explosion of writing in the second half of the eighth century. A linear writing system of Mycenaean type had survived at Cyprus. But then the Greeks decided to write "Phoenician," as they called it. They carefully learned and preserved the letters' names, *alpha*, *beta*, *gamma*, *delta*, which do not make sense in Greek, and they kept their immutable sequence, which our computers still respect; the letter forms, too, were practically identical at first. The place of transfer is unknown—Phoenicians or rather Arameans, Syria or Cyprus? Some still argue for a considerably earlier date, but direct evidence is lacking.

Together with the alphabet, the Greeks also adopted the writing tablet, which retained its Semitic name, *deltos*, and the leather scroll and the layout of books, with the characteristic *subscriptio* at the end instead of a title at the beginning.[8] Some form of book transmission from cuneiform to Phoenician and Greek must have occurred. But since the transition to alphabetic writing meant using perishable materials, wooden tablets and scrolls, and giving up clay tablets, direct evidence suddenly disappears. With closer contacts to Egypt after the seventh century, papyrus was to oust the leather scroll. The first Greek books we can presume to have existed were poetry—Hesiod, Homer, perhaps oracles. There are those two famous documents of verse writing from about 730 BCE, the "Dipylon jug" at Athens and the "Nestor cup" at Ischia.[9] Especially the Nestor cup, with its careful writing of verses in lines, hardly leaves doubt that books with Greek poetry existed by that time.[10] The first prose books, however, came much later, with Anaximander and Pherecydes in the sixth century.

This invites some reflections on the media of philosophizing, including the problem of orality versus literacy. For approximately the last 2,400 years, we have known philosophy in the form of the philosophical book; still, philosophical books always came and still come to life in discussion circles, in "schools of philosophy." Plato set the example with his Academy, and similar institutions existed with changing success down to the end of antiquity and were resuscitated in the universities and academies of Europe. We are less well informed about the situation before Plato. We are told that Anaximander's book was the first book in prose ever published[11]—in which context? We are told that Heraclitus dedicated his book to the temple of Artemis at Ephesus[12]—did this mean publication or seclusion? We see that practical handbooks on astronomy and geography began to circulate in the sixth century; a *Nautike Astrologia* was fathered on Thales;[13] Skylax of Karyanda, at the time of Darius, wrote a *periêgesis*;[14] Hecataeus wrote on geography and presented a map of the earth.[15] We also find genealogical handbooks written in prose, by Hecataeus of Miletus, Acusilaus of Argos, Pherecydes of Athens.[16] Both the astronomical-geographical and the genealogical handbooks are in a way modernizations of the works of Hesiod, *Theogony* with *Catalogues*, and the *Works and Days* ending in astronomy. Acusilaus had theogony precede his genealogy. From about the same time, say 500 BCE, we have another book that begins with the creation of the world and continues with the development of the tribes that constitute the people: *Bereshit*, the first book of the Bible, whose final redaction may belong to this very period. Greeks were not isolated.

So much for books; it is difficult to find serious evidence for philosophical schools before Plato, even if later doxography has constructed successions (*diadochai*). There are contradictory statements as to the sect of the Pythagoreans;[17] Heracliteans are mentioned in the fifth century, but we cannot decide whether they just accidentally read and imitated Heraclitus or had some connection and organization. Parmenides adopted Zeno, we are told.[18] This would be quite an old and ubiquitous model of the tradition of knowledge, especially secret knowledge, within a "family," be it craftsmen, seers, or poets.[19] The doctors of Kos all were Asclepiads.

In the oriental world, there were additional institutions for the tradition of knowledge: the temples that existed as economically independent and self-supporting units and that fed a *clerus* of priests; to these the schools of writing, "the house of tablets," was attached. Since the complicated old systems of writing, which continued to be used throughout the first millennium BCE, required a professional formation that lasted for years, the house of tablets would make up the basis for the self-consciousness of "the knowing ones": a wise man is a "Lord of tablets." Wisdom literature tends to appeal to kings and seeks profit from their authority, be it Solomon or another monarch.

The situation of the Greeks, compared to this, is characterized by a threefold defect: there are hardly temples as economically independent units to feed a *clerus*; there is no prestige of a house of tablets; and kings, too, have soon disappeared. Alphabetic writing is so easy to learn and to practice that no class distinction will emerge from elementary school; it was the sophists who invented higher education as a new form of class distinction. In fact, this will have been a decisive factor to turn deficit into progress: cultural knowledge became separated from dominating institutions and hierarchies, from the house of tablets, from temples and from kingship; it became movable, to be managed by the single individual. This became widespread with the economic and political changes of the time, which brought individual initiative of persons and groups to the fore. Thus even "wisdom" became the capital of the enterprising individual, in competition with his like.[20] Of course, the western Semites from Tarsus through Tyre to Jerusalem would have had the same chances, with similar economy and a similar writing system. How far they went, we hardly can assess. They were harassed, disturbed, and stopped by the devastating invasions of Assyrians and Babylonians recorded in history. The Greeks, living farthest east among the westerners, were close to the events but remained nearly unaffected. The Jews, in the midst of troubles, could preserve their own identity only by the strained decision to make scripture their highest authority, instead of using it as the tool of spiritual freedom.

The special luck of the Greeks at the fringes of the productive and dangerous East was repeated, in a striking and unforeseeable way, with the Persian empire: it had its expansion stopped right at the borderline that has since been called the frontier between Asia and Europe. Roughly one-third of the Greek population had come under Persian domination, and lost its cultural importance for centuries; but the rest unexpectedly succeeded in retaining liberty and hence developing a new self-consciousness in opposition to Asia. This was the advent of what has since been called "classical" civilization; it came to claim independence at all levels; this has decisively affected even cultural history in retrospect.

In fact, what we call early Greek philosophy is indebted to earlier traditions of literature in a twofold way: there had been, and continued to be, what we call wisdom literature, knowledge crystallized in forms of elaborate sentences; and there was cosmogonical myth, "stories of creation." Note that any school of writing needs convenient texts for exercise; and what makes the contents of a primer? Sayings and simple narratives—that is, wisdom literature and mythology. So this is one of the social settings for the literature with which we have to deal. This is not to forget that mythology was used in hymns and other ritual texts to celebrate the respective gods; thus the *Enuma Elish* has its place in the New Year festival of Babylon—with other versions for other residences. Anyway, both types appear, not by coincidence—and not without appeal to kings—in Hesiod's two works *Theogony*, including the catalogues, and *Works and Days*. These two works seem to be close to the date when Greeks first borrowed the alphabet and learned about the function and layout of book scrolls. This does not mean that Hesiod was the only gate of access. There is the cosmogonical passage in the *Iliad* that is close to *Enuma Elish*.[21] And the theogony of Orpheus, as it is now known from the Derveni Papyrus, seems to be a meeting-place of oriental motifs; much must have been there that we cannot identify. But we also see how a body of astronomical knowledge and mathematical techniques had been accumulating especially in the temple schools of Babylonia; it made significant progress right in the crucial epoch of the sixth to fifth centuries. It clearly affected the Greeks. See our names for the planets, or the laborious sexagesimal system we still use to measure circles and angles.

2. Epochs of Research

The thesis or suspicion that Greek philosophy was not an original invention of the Greeks, but copied from more ancient eastern prototypes, is not a modern one. It goes right back to Aristotle's book *On Philosophy* and to his pupils, who discussed *barbaros philosophia*; they took account, of course, of Egyptians, Chaldeans, Iranian *magoi* including Zoroaster, Indian gurus, and also the Jews.[22] Earlier than Aristotle is the association of Pythagoras with Egypt;[23] and probably also that of Democritus and the Magi.[24] The question of *barbaros philosophia* is the first theme to be discussed in Diogenes Laertius. The last head of the Neoplatonic Academy at Athens, Damascius, in his book on first principles, offers interpretations of the cosmogonies of the Babylonians, Magi, Phoenicians, and Egyptians, quoting from the book of Eudemus, Aristotle's well-known pupil, which contained, among other information, an exact paraphrase of the first lines of the Babylonian *Enuma Elish*. This is one of the very few cases where direct translation from an Eastern book can be ascertained.[25] Normally knowledge of Eastern languages did not exist, or was even concealed. The Hellenistic translation of the Hebrew Bible, the Septuagint, stands out as a singular achievement; it was hardly noticed outside Jewish circles.

The thesis about *barabaros philosophia* was appropriated by Jews and Christians, who argued that Moses had been living many centuries before Plato.[26] Hence they alleged that Plato had taken all essentials of his philosophy from Israel: What is Plato if not a Moses speaking Attic, Numenius wrote.[27] Quite unimportant, in these ancient discussions, was the global direction: no trace of an East-West or North-South conflict.

The scholarly history of philosophy as developed in the nineteenth century has resumed the discussion, with changing results. By then, India and China had been discovered as high cultures to be taken seriously. India in particular could impress with texts that seemed close to Greek philosophy even by force of linguistic cognateness. Yet what gained the field was the critical position of Eduard Zeller: in the introduction to his magnificent work *Die Philosophie der Griechen in ihrer geschichtlichen Entwicklung*,[28] first published in 1856, he presented a review of earlier propositions as to Chinese, Indian, and other precursors of Greek philosophy, and he ended with a negative result. Zeller's position and arguments have often been reelaborated and repeated down to the middle of the twentieth century.[29] Hence we might acquiesce in the idea that the origin of Greek philosophy is self-generated and purely Greek.

As a consequence, the radical change that occurred right at the time of Zeller's essay has often been overlooked: the emergence of original texts in oriental literatures, first Egyptian and Mesopotamian, later Hittite and Ugaritic. Up to then, not much more than the Old Testament had been known from pre-Greek antiquity, and philologists had no trouble showing that these texts had not been known to Greeks before the Hellenistic period. The Avesta had become known in 1771,[30] but remained a marginal curiosity. Yet the new "Ancient Near Eastern" texts have made a new epoch. By now neither Hebrew nor Greek, neither Moses nor Homer are the beginning of literature, but rather Pyramid texts and Sumerian myths. The problem of the context in which Greek philosophy evolved from the sixth to the fourth century BCE now appears within quite another horizon. Yet it was an outsider, William Ewart Gladstone, who, in 1890, referred to the parallel of Apsu and Tiamat in *Enuma Elish* with Oceanus and Tethys in the Iliad.[31] Some discussions evolved about "Babel and Bible," and also about Homer and Gilgamesh. Themes relevant to philosophy arose from the other, the Iranian side, after Zarathustra had become famous through Nietzsche. Richard Reitzenstein, with the help of H. H. Schaeder, came from Hellenistic syncretism to Iranian origins; Iranian and Indian parallels to Hesiod's Myth of the Ages were pointed out, while the Uppsala school developed the idea of a World-Giant and an Iranian "God Time," Zurvan/Zervan; both would make their appearance in Greek Orphism. Albrecht Goetze even discovered "Persische Weisheit in griechischem Gewande," comparing one chapter of the Hippocratic treatise *On Sevens* with Pahlavi texts. Religious history still seemed to be more provoked than philosophy. It was not until 1941 that Francis Macdonald Cornford, in a Cambridge lecture, presented a careful comparison between Hesiod and *Enuma Elish*; this was published in 1950.[32] By then the Hittite texts had appeared, with the striking parallel of the Kumarbi myth to Uranus-Cronus in Hesiod; Hittite is Indo-European, which helped to break the barrier against the "Semitic" world. In the wake of Hittite, Ugaritic, too, was easily accepted. Uvo Hölscher outlined the new perspectives in a fascinating article, "Anaximandros und der Anfang der Philosophie"; Hans Schwabl, in his Pauly-Wissowa article "Weltschöpfung," developed the whole panorama of cosmogonic myth; Martin West's commentaries on Hesiod are full of pertinent information and reflection, not to mention the sober and informative book of Peter Walcot.[33]

The opening of new horizons coincided with a change in the concept of philosophy: Rational ontology in the wake of Aristotle and scholasticism lost its appeal for moderns, for Aristotle and even Plato could be seen as initiating basic errors as against the origin and basis of philosophy; there was a fresh interest in the Presocratics, especially in Heraclitus and Parmenides, from Karl Reinhardt via Heidegger down to Gadamer, combined with an intense interest in myth.[34] Characteristic is the title of Olof Gigon's book of 1945: *Der Ursprung der griechischen Philosophie von Hesiod bis Parmenides*. This includes Hesiod in the "origin," which seems to come to a stop with Parmenides. In the same year however the Hittite texts about Kumarbi had been published,[35] which were bound to add a pre-Hesiodic station to the sequence—Olof Gigon did not like this at all. But the evidence is there.

Things became more quiet again in the following decades; yet the readiness to include the East in our picture of antiquity has risen steadily, with a growing distance from 19th century concepts of the classic. More virulent discussion has started from a side issue, with Martin Bernal's *Black Athena*.[36] Bernal accuses the Western, especially the German, tradition of excluding the Semitic Southeast out of racial prejudice; he finds the origins of most cultural achievements in Bronze

Age Egypt—which would keep clear of philosophy. His thesis, and the reactions provoked, indicate the growing insecurity of our white Western world. Attacks are being launched against the "dead white males," of whom the Greeks are the oldest and should be dead most of all. It is to be hoped that such debates should be an incentive to scholarship rather than a barrier in the name of political correctness.

3. NON-GREEK TEXT CORPORA

The various languages and civilizations close to archaic Greece, including their idiosyncratic writing systems, call for specialists, whose fields of competence are necessarily drifting apart. Some introductory orientation should be presented nonetheless, as follows.

Besides the Graeco-Roman "classics," just two ancient corpora of texts have survived by direct tradition, the sacred books of Israel, conventionally called the Hebrew Bible or the Old Testament, and the Iranian Avesta. Greek literature is easily accessible, including translations, commentaries, and lexica, even if the dates, for example for Hesiod and Homer, are still a matter of dispute. The Bible has seen most intensive study for centuries, both from the Jewish and the Christian side, with the result that the historical and literary evaluation and especially the date of the texts, or segments of texts, remains profoundly controversial. The Avesta has few specialists, beyond linguists, and the problem of dating is desperate. It is clear there are two linguistic strata, "old Avestan," which is mainly the "songs," the *gathas* of Zarathustra, and "recent Avestan," which is the bulk of liturgy (*yasna*), hymns (*yashts*), and a "law against evil spirits" (*videvdat*). What we know about Zarathustra is mainly the message of the *gathas*. But for his date there are still propositions from before 1000 BCE to the sixth century.[37] One is inclined to date the rest of the Avesta roughly to the epoch of the Achaemenid Persians, sixth to fourth century BCE, even if the final written form, in a special script designed for the purpose, may be as late as 400 CE. At that time, Zarathustra's religion had long become state religion in the Sassanid empire. After the fall of the Sassanid kingdom, in the ninth century, a series of books was produced by Zoroastrians in a middle Persian language, Pahlavi, which collect and elaborate the old traditions, making use also of parts of the Avesta that have been lost since. Specialists have been trying to find very old, even pre-Zarathustrian Iranian lore in these ninth-century books, even if this means a jump over more than 1,000 years.

As against such problems presented by religious continuity, the rediscoveries and decipherments that pertain to Mesopotamia, Anatolia, Syria, and Egypt lead to indisputable strata of the Bronze Age and the early Iron Age. Yet most often we have to deal with fragments, and problems of interpretation are bound to continue.

Egypt, in a climate without rain, had the special chance to preserve wooden tablets and especially papyrus leaves with written texts, besides the vast monumental heritage. There is a rich conglomerate of religious speculation, dealing especially with cosmogony and afterlife, continuing down from the "Pyramid texts." Single sanctuaries were developing their proper theology and mythology; thus "a monument of Memphitic theology" is to be found, or "the cosmogony of Hermopolis." What is striking from the Greek perspective is the primeval origin from water, with the cosmic "egg" in the beginning. This is not to overlook the vast corpus of mortuary texts and a significant body of wisdom literature.

Incredibly rich is cuneiform writing that survives in tens of thousands of clay tablets. It starts in the third millennium with the Sumerian language, but soon takes to the Semitic language, which is now usually called Akkadian, including Babylonian and Assyrian. Cuneiform Akkadian spread to Syria by the third, to Anatolia by the second millennium; it is the general medium of diplomacy in the late Bronze Age; it begins to lose out as against the alphabet in the first millennium, but continues to be fully used in Mesopotamia until the first century BCE.

As to cuneiform "literature" in a more special sense, there are mythological tales about gods and heroes in Sumerian, including specific acts of creation, mostly in the form of comparatively short songs; there are also sayings of wisdom and fables. Later Akkadian develops prestigious epics, such as *Atrahasis*, *Gilgamesh*, and *Enuma Elish*, the ceremonial cosmogony for Babylon. There are also elaborate wisdom texts, such as the *Babylonian Theodicy*. A separate category, no less important, are tablets of mathematics and astronomy.

Hittite texts are mainly represented by the archive of Boghazköy-Hattusa, the Hittite capital. They are dominated by the Akkadian tradition, but Hurrite makes its impact, too. There are rich collections of ritual texts and of hymns to the gods, but also mythological tales in epic form. Special fame goes with the tales of divine combat and succession, *Kingdom in Heavens, Ullikummi, Illuyankas*. A substantial and complicated wisdom text, the *Song of Liberation*, has recently become known as a Hurrite-Hittite bilingual.

At Ugarit, excavations have brought to light several archives of tablets, partly in Akkadian, partly in a special quasi-alphabetic script that was used especially for ritual-mythological texts. The language is close to Hebrew; there are coincidences even of certain sentences. Parallels to Greek mythology have been noticed from the start, as concerns conflicts of gods, dying gods, dragon fights, and war. There must be a warning, though, that the texts are few, short, and fragmented, and whole passages may remain unclear because of a consonant script that insufficiently indicates grammatical forms. Both cuneiform Hittite and Ugaritic disappeared with the breakdown of the Bronze Age, about 1200 BCE, though the traditions, even mythologies, persisted in Canaan as in Asia Minor.

Syria in general and the Phoenician cities in particular, in the midst of their remarkable Iron Age development, definitely turned to alphabetic writing and gave up clay tablets. Hence the written documentation comes to a sudden stop. No doubt there were books of all kinds in the Phoenician and Aramean languages, but practically nothing has survived; we remain dependent on Greek accounts, especially for Phoenician cosmogonic myth. Just one of the wisdom books has made an international career, the *Story of Achiqar*. It was originally written in Aramean, some fragments of which survive in the Elephantine papyri; it may have been known to Democritus and more probably to Theophrastus. A Greek version is to be found in the *Life of Aesop*. The complete text survives in Syriac and, after this, in Armenian and Arabic.[38]

4. MATHEMATICS AND ASTRONOMY

The use of numbers is prehistoric, as is the familiarity with the seasons of the year, the changing positions of the sun, the periods of the moon. The proof of cultural dependence will come from details that are not ubiquitous but idiosyncratic, such as the names of constellations and planets, or the sexagesimal system that is peculiar to Mesopotamia. This makes Mesopotamian influence on Greece a certainty. Homer has two names for the best known constellation in the northern sky, Bear or Wagon; the name Wagon is Akkadian, too. Figuring out the Small Bear, which includes the polar star, belonged to the *Nautikê Astrologia*, which was fathered on Thales; it is said by Callimachus to come from the Phoenicians.[39] In most other cases, it is impossible to catch the mode of transfer, the date, the kind of texts that were at work. There are more legends than facts in what the Greeks tell about Egyptian priests, Chaldaeans at Babylon, Magi, or even Pythagoras.

Calculating was part of the Mesopotamian school teaching. There developed the sexagesimal system in writing numbers, which allows divisions by 2, 3, 4, 5, and 6. There are number tables to facilitate further calculations, including squares and cubes. It is surprising to find the "Pythagorean theorem" routinely applied about 1,000 years before Pythagoras. There is even a tablet with "Pythagorean numbers," matching the equation $x^2 + y^2 = z^2$. Equations of the second degree are solved by arithmetic, too.[40] This is largely parallel to Euclid, book 2; one generally accepts direct influence, even if the logic of mathematics must yield parallel developments, and modern forms of writing with mathematical symbols can make the similarities seem more impressive than the original texts would.

The sexagesimal system has made its impact on weights and coins in Greece, where it carries a Semitic term with it, *mana*, Greek *mnea*, *mnâ*, "measure." A "mine" is the sixtieth part of a "load to carry," *talanton*. The other use of the sexagesimal system that has remained belongs to the circle: 360 degrees, subdivided into 60 minutes, 60 seconds; one degree approximates the sun's daily movement in the zodiac. The first clear Greek evidence for this is with Hypsicles in the third century BCE;[41] but probably it was used already by Eudoxus, in the first half of the 4th century.

Babylonian astronomy is not aboriginally old, in contrast to what the Greeks thought.[42] Ptolemy, in his *Syntaxis*, has dated observations of the "Chaldaeans" from 721 BCE, as had Hipparchus before him. Watching for heavenly omens, a kind of astrology had developed at an early epoch. Eclipses of the moon and of the sun were thought to be signs of disaster, and rituals were developed and used to evade the threats—so far, no idea of causal necessity, which was to dominate later Greek astrology. Observations, including eclipses, accumulated, and regularities were found. At least since the sixth century there are number tables that, through "zigzag functions," allow precise calculations of stellar and lunar movements and visibilities. This is a form of science in the full sense, though quite different from the later Greek methods, and without any physical hypothesis for explanation. It was recovered from the surviving tablets by Franz Xaver Kugler; the new account is due to Otto Neugebauer; it reached its climax only in Seleucid times.

An old and simple problem of practical astronomy is the correlation of the moon's phases and the solar year. Whereas Egyptians decided to dissociate the solar year totally from the moon—which the Julian calendar took over—everywhere else true lunar months were kept, with intercalary months to keep to the seasons of the year. At Babylon, an intercalary cycle of 19 years is found, and there is hardly doubt that Meton, who proposed such a cycle at Athens in 432 BCE, derived his idea and knowledge from the East.

More precise observation is needed to notice the inequality of the seasons—the summer half of the year, from equinox to equinox, is a few days longer than winter. Tradition has Thales already dealing with the problem. Babylonians developed two different systems of astronomical computation to cope with this inequality.

More specific discoveries in astronomy concern the planets and the establishment of their path through constellations of the fixed stars, which the Greeks were to call the zodiac. Greek knowledge had remained scanty for a long time, since the simple identification of the morning star and the evening star (Heosphoros/Phosphoros and Hesperos) as one planet was ascribed only to Ibycus, Pythagoras, or Parmenides;[43] whereas Babylonians had calculated periods of Venus by the time of Ammisaduqa in the seventeenth century BCE.[44] The narrow path in which the planets keep moving can be observed most easily as the "way of the Moon"; this is an Akkadian term. Further observation shows that the sun and the planets keep to the same "path"—the projection of the earth's ellipse. This circle is marked, in vague analogy to the 12 months of the year, by 12 constellations that are then transferred to purely mathematical constructs, "signs" of 30 degrees each. Greeks called this the "circle of animals," zodiakos, and say it was first described by Cleostratus of Tenedos, a pupil of Anaximander. Earlier attestations of the zodiac seemed to be lacking in Mesopotamia, but are now reported from seventh-century tablets.[45] The first cuneiform horoscopes come from the beginning of the fifth century.[46]

Our names of the planets, Mercury, Venus, Mars, Jupiter, are indirect copies of the Akkadian designations, via the Greeks, who had translated Nabu, Ishtar, Nergal, and Marduk. This was done in the epoch of Plato at the latest, possibly some decades earlier.[47]

The idea of a Great Year that we find in relation to the planets in Plato and Aristotle, and in unclear context in Heraclitus, is suspected to come from

Babylonian astronomy or even from Iranian speculation. There is no direct evidence for this, but for indirect indications in Berossus about the *saros* equaling 6,000 years.[48]

Babylonians used to speak of the "circle" of heaven and earth. One tablet has a circular plan of the earth,[49] which has often been compared to the alleged map of the earth presented by Anaximander and Hecataeus. Yet the concept of a "sphere" of heaven seems to be a purely Greek step, as is the explanation of eclipses and the insight and proof that our earth itself must be a sphere.

5. WISDOM LITERATURE

What we call "wisdom literature" is a genre of literature that is fully developed in Egyptian, Sumerian, Akkadian, Hurrian,[50] and last but not least the Hebrew Bible. Comparable are, among Greek texts, Hesiod's *Works and Days*, Theognis, and Phocylides, a shadowy poem *Chironos Hypothekai*, the tradition about the Seven Sages that takes prose form in an epoch about 600 BCE; all this could still be oral, at least in part. Prose books take up the tradition: the *Aphorisms* within the Hippocratic Corpus, works of Democritus, then the *Anonymus Iamblichi* (DK 89) and Isocrates' *Pros Demonikon*. Tradition continues to the *logia* of Jesus. As to Presocratics, Heraclitus may be included in the genre,[51] and Anaximander, too, who, according to Apollodorus, presented his "opinions" in "a summary exposition" (*kephalaiôdês*):[52] not a stream of rhetoric but single pronouncements of wisdom.

Wisdom literature takes sayings of many forms to constitute general rules, be it imperatives, statements, or even short stories; thus fables, animal and plant fables, belong to it.[53] There are highly developed literary forms, such as dialogues, both in Egypt, in Mesopotamia, and in *Job*. Sometimes a certain situation is evoked, with kings entering the scene: *The Instruction of King Amenemhet I for His Son Sesostris I*;[54] Or in Sumerian, *The Instructions of Shuruppak to His Son Ziusudra*—Ziusudra who was to survive the flood. In the Old Testament, we find "The proverbs of Solomon son of David, king of Israel," and also "Sayings of Lemuel king of Massa, which his mother taught him" (Prov. 31); compare "the Admonitions of Hesiod to his brother Perses," as Hesiod's *Works and Days* have been inscribed by moderns, or "Counsels of Chiron to Achilles," *Chironos Hypothekai*.[55] A more thrilling story is introduced in the Aramean text of Achiqar, which became known also to the Greeks.[56] Achiqar is slandered by his nephew and taken to jail by the king; when his innocence has been proved and he is released, he gets a chance to transmit his wisdom to the bad nephew by flogging, one blow, one counsel.

The sayings of wisdom seldom occur even in a tentative order or system. If there is causal reasoning, it just goes one step; this is not philosophical ethics. There may be sophisticated literary devices such as akrostichon;[57] there are elaborate antitheses and striking metaphors, but also riddles. "A capable wife is her husband's crown; one who disgraces him is like rot in his bones" (Prov. 12:4); Hesiod is simpler: "Nothing better than a wife a man has ever seized as booty, than a good one—but nothing is more horrible than a bad one" (*Op.* 702).

There are still recognizable intellectual achievements in wisdom literature that go beyond trivialities: there is an elaborate use of language, with analogies and antithesis; there is the hypothesis, which is anything but obvious, that it is helpful to have wisdom, that it pays to learn this from the wise men—an optimism of *logos*, one might say. There is also the postulate of generalization: the wise man's counsel is valid always and everywhere, beyond the moment—even if the counsel may be: guard the moment, *kairon gnôthi*.

Optimism of *logos* has its limits; it may touch the frontiers of cynicism: "Most people are bad"—this, too, is a saying of the Seven Sages.[58] And is it really true that "wisdom is more valuable than gold" (Prov. 23:14)? Does piety pay? The text of Job takes pains to preserve the thesis; the so-called Babylonian theodicy reads: "Those who neglect the god go the way of prosperity, while those who pray to the goddess are impoverished and dispossessed."[59]

Logos optimism still is prone to entail a form of morality that relies on reason, as against emotions; morality that extols rationality, moderation, self-control together with justice and piety, as against hot temper, drunkenness, and sexual dissolution. "Avarice is a grievous and incurable illness," Egyptians say; "Better bread with a happy heart than riches with trouble";[60] "Measure is best," the Seven Sages preach.[61] A verse of Homer that made a lasting impression on Greek readers is Odysseus's warning to the suitor Amphinomus: "Such is the insight [*noos*] of men on earth as the day which Zeus, the father of men and gods, brings on," unreliable and changeable from brightness to gloom. The wisdom of Odysseus is taken up by Archilochus (West 131/132) and criticized by Heraclitus (B17, B72). But long before Homer, an Akkadian text analyzed humanity's condition in a similar way: "Their insight changes like day and night: when starving they become like corpses, when replete they vie with their gods."[62] A proverb from the world of animals became prominent with the Cologne Archilochus: "The bitch, being hasty, gives birth to blind pups"; the same proverb appears in a text from Mari 1,000 years before Archilochus.[63] There are further parallels in fables.[64]

More important than coincidences of this kind is the tendency to extend wisdom to cosmic dimensions. The ethics of measure comes to dominate the outlines of cosmology: both forms of prephilosophy we are pursuing, wisdom and cosmogony, come in touch. "In wisdom the Lord founded the earth and by understanding he set the heavens in their place" (Prov. 3:19). Wisdom itself proclaims: "When he set the heavens in their place I was there, when he girdled the ocean with the horizon, when he fixed the canopy of clouds overhead . . . when he prescribed its limits to the sea . . . then I was at his side each day" (Prov. 8:27–30). Egyptians have Maat, Order, marching at the side of the sun god, Babylonians have Misharu, Just Order, in the same place and function.[65] "Helius will not transgress his boundaries," Heraclitus wrote, "or else the Erinyes, the helpers of Justice, will find him."[66] Anaximander has it that the things being altogether, *ta eonta*, "pay penalty and retribution to each other for their injustice according to the assessment of Time";[67] he probably is thinking of the order of day and year, which indeed cover shortage by excess and vice versa. The paradigm of cosmic order is a form of justice, be it that Maat or Misharu accompany the sun or that Erinyes are pursuing any transgression. Justice holds the alternating keys for day and night, Parmenides formulates;[68] "This world-order...always was and is and shall be: an ever-living fire, kindling in measures and going out in measures," according to Heraclitus.[69] Heraclitus evidently has arrived at a new dimension, still proceeding from the same basis of justice and "measure for measure" within the cosmic order.

And even the peculiarity of Heraclitus's wisdom is seen more clearly against the background of traditional wisdom literature. The beginning of Solomon's proverbs reads, with slight abbreviation: "The proverbs of Solomon son of David...by which...the simple will be endowed with shrewdness, and...if the wise man listens, he will increase his learning."[70] Contrast the beginning of Heraclitus's book: "Logos of Heraclitus, son of Bloson: Of this *logos*, which is always, men prove to be uncomprehending, both before they have heard it and when once they have heard it; for although all things come to pass in accordance with this logos, men behave as if ignorant."[71] Doesn't this sound like a parody of the normal and naive promise of wisdom that it should teach those who don't know and improve those who do know? No, says Heraclitus, men prove to be uncomprehending, even if they are in immediate touch with those things that are happening. This definitely goes beyond the statement that wisdom was there when limits were prescribed to the sea. But it presupposes the traditional approach.

6. COSMOGONY

There are many variants of tales about the beginning of the world. The paradigm, as it were, is set by the Babylonian text *Enuma Elish*, the epic of creation recited at the Babylonian New Year festival.[72] In Egypt we do not find one representative text but several groups of texts, fully developed or of rather allusive character, usually reflecting the position of one particular sanctuary: Heliopolis, Memphis, Hermopolis.[73] In Hittite, we have the Kumarbi text, which is especially close to Hesiod.[74] This is not to leave out the beginning of our Bible, which has cosmogony even in two different tales.[75]

Cosmogony is highly speculative, as has always been recognized. Still, the outward form of the narrative is naive: it is a typical just-so story—a term of scorn for anthropologists.[76] In the beginning there was...then came...and then—just so. First the world was not there, then heaven and earth appeared, and gods, and men, and their relation was set right, just so. Even the so-called first philosophers among the Greeks did not disdain this form of story: "Together were all the things,"

Anaxagoras started, "and as they were together nothing was explicit, because fog and brilliant haze held down everything."[77] How close this is to "and the earth was without form and void, with darkness over the face of the abyss" (Gen. 1:2).

One speculative achievement still is to be found in the concept of "beginning," one beginning from which everything is about to rise. The Bible begins with the famous words "In the beginning" (*bereshit*) (Gen. 1:1), and Hesiod sets out to sing "from the beginning" and asks "which came into being first of them all?" (*Th.* 115), whereas Anaximander brings in the concept of *archê*, according to the statement of Theophrastus.[78]

Further achievements of speculation are reversal and antithesis. If you start to tell the tale about the beginning of everything, you must first dismiss from your view everything, the whole world of ours, people and animals, houses and trees, mountains and sea, heaven and earth. Thus the typical start of cosmogonical myth is performed by subtraction: there is that great and resounding Not Yet. Thus *Enuma Elish* starts: "When above skies were not yet named, nor earth below pronounced by name . . . [when nobody] had formed pastures nor discovered reed-beds, when yet no gods were manifest, nor names pronounced, nor destinies decreed" . . .[79] An Egyptian Pyramid text says, "When heaven had not yet been constructed, when earth had not yet come into being, when nothing yet had been constructed"[80]—what then was there? "Darkness brooding over the face of the abyss," the Bible tells us;[81] a yawning gap, Hesiod has it, *chaos*;[82] Night, the theogony of Orpheus said;[83] the Infinite, Anaximander seems to have written. "Together were all things," we read in Anaxagoras.[84] The most frequent response is: there was water in the beginning. This is not limited to the ancient world; it is also reported from America.[85] The beginning is water, Thales is reported to have stated;[86] But long before Thales, the Egyptians developed water cosmogonies in diverse variants.[87] The *Enuma Elish*, too, has ground water and salt water, Apsu the begetter and Tiamat who bore them all as the first parents of everything. Surprisingly enough, this recurs in the midst of Homer's *Iliad* with Oceanus and Tethys, "begetting everything."[88]

Togetherness is bound to dissolve: differentiation must come out of the one beginning. Every cosmogonical tale is bound to proceed on these lines. The most grandiose idea is that heaven was lifted from earth at the second state of creation. Normal archaic language usually does not have a word for "world"; it enumerates the basic constituents, "heaven and earth." So the world qua "heaven and earth" came into being by separation. Even this idea is not a specialty of the ancient Mediterranean world; it has been found in Africa, Polynesia, and Japan.[89] Hittites and Hesiod have the violent myth of a castration of heaven, of cutting apart the primeval couple.[90] Egyptians have a more peaceful development, as Shu, "Air," just lifts the goddess of heaven—which is female in this case—Nut, from the earth,[91] Geb. According to Anaximander, a sphere of fire grew around the center, which apparently was a form of slime; the sphere then burst into pieces that formed into wheels, carrying openings of flames around the earth.[92] This still means separation of heaven and earth. It persists, in a new key, in Leucippus.[93]

For the further development, there are two narrative options, two models: one might be called biomorphic, the other technomorphic. The biomorphic model introduces couples of different sex, insemination, and birth; the technomorphic model presents a creator in the function of the clever craftsman. The biomorphic model gives rise to successive generations, with chances for a battle between Old and New; it suggests tales, hence it is mythical in a strong sense. The succession myth is found in *Enuma Elish*, the Hurrite-Hittite Kingship in Heaven, and in Hesiod.[94] It has a curious echo in Hippon: "Fire, generated by water, defeated the begetter's power and constituted the world."[95] It is tempting to call the biomorphic model the Greek one, the technomorphic model the biblical one. "In the beginning, the Lord created heaven and earth";[96] "and god made..." He carves Eve from a rib, and he even makes first garments from skins. Hesiod, by contrast, has fully opted for the biomorphic version. Things are more complicated, though, especially as there are combinations of both models, as in the *Enuma Elish*, and also in the Orphic cosmogony as known from the Derveni papyrus: both introduce some generations of gods with the conflicts of the succession myth, but at a certain stage they have the principal god planning his creation.

Creation is more rational: it gives the author the opportunity to describe objects in detail. Listen to the *Enuma Elish*: when Marduk has slain Tiamat, the primeval mother, the monster of the sea, "the Lord rested and inspected her corpse, he divided the monstrous shape and created marvels, he sliced her in half like a fish for drying, half of her he put up to roof the sky"—we get the separation of heaven and earth even here—

> as for the stars, he set up constellations . . . he made the crescent of the moon
> appear, entrusted night to it. . . . Go forth every month without fail in a corona,
> at the beginning of the month, to glow over the land, you shine with horns
> to mark out six days; on the seventh day the crown is half. The fifteenth
> day shall always be the midpoint, the half of each month. When Shamash
> (sun) looks at you from the horizon, gradually shed your visibility and begin
> to wane.[97]

This is not exciting, but quite correct. The Old Testament is much more cursory: Elohim said, "Let there be lights in the vault of heaven to separate day from night . . . and God made the two great lights, the greater to govern the day and the lesser to govern the night, and with them he made the stars."[98] Least precise is Hesiod: "Theia gave birth to great Helios and resplendent Selene, and also to Eos who shines for all on earth, overcome in love by Hyperion: and Eos, mated to Astraios, gave birth to the Morning Star, and to the brilliant Stars."[99] Nobody would say Hesiod is more rational than the orientals; he just gives names to the concepts of the divine—Theia—and "walking above," Hyperion; but it is just tautology to make Astraios father of the stars, and he is absolutely unsystematic in separating the morning star from the other stars.

The concept of "creator of the world" is explicitly rebuked by Heraclitus: "This world-order . . . no one of gods or men has made" (B30). Heraclitus seems to develop the biomorphic model into a phytomorphic one, the principle of growing according to inner laws as the plants do; the Greek word for such growing is *physis*, which later was translated into Latin as *natura*. The famous saying that "*physis* likes to be concealed" (B123) probably takes its start from this precise observation: if you dig up the earth to see the germ growing, you destroy the plant. Yet we see that hardly any of Heraclitus's successors could do without a creator: Parmenides introduces a female daimon who "governs everything" and creates divine powers such as Eros;[100] Anaxagoras gives a similar function to Nous, Mind, the leading power for all differentiation; Empedocles has Love construing organs and organisms in her workshop; it was only Democritus who, criticizing Anaxagoras, tried to exclude mind from the shaping of macrocosm and microcosm.[101] The reaction came with Plato and Aristotle; Plato's *Timaeus* finally established the term "creator," *dêmiourgos*, in Greek philosophy.

It has become a commonplace that it was the Greeks who marched all the way from *mythos* to *logos*.[102] More recently it has been observed that even the orientals— scholars of Assyria, for example—were already pursuing such a way. Take one of the texts that comes from the house of conjurer-priests at Assur, about 650 BCE:[103] there are three earths and of three heavens, the text says: "At the Upper Earth he established the souls of men, in the center; on Middle Earth, he made sit his father Ea, in the center" (Ea is subterranean water); "in Nether Earth, he included the 600 gods of the dead (Annunaki), in the center." This postulates three stories in our world, the earth on which we live, with water beneath, just as Thales has it, and farther down, as the lowest register, the nether world with its appropriate gods. Heaven, by correspondence, has three registers, too: the highest story belongs to the god Heaven, Anu, himself, together with three hundred heavenly gods; Middle Heaven, made of resplendent stone—perhaps amber—is the throne of Enlil, the ruling god; the lowest story, made of jasper, is the place of constellations: "he designed the constellations of the gods on that." According to Livingstone, these texts are "making existing theology accord more precisely with the facts of the natural world," with the natural cosmos in which we are living. The account still keeps to the form of cosmogonical myth: the god made that, and that, and that, just so. Yet the result is the existing cosmos, which could best be indicated by drawing a figure, instead of narrative.[104]

Three heavens recur in Anaximander; he seems to have even used the plural "heavens" (*ouranoi*), which is absolutely unusual in Greek language.[105] But he combined the three heavens with three categories of heavenly bodies—stars, moon, and sun—thus introducing "the *logos* of sizes and distances," as Eudemus, Aristotle's pupil, was to explain.[106] His sequence, in turn, evidently was influenced by Iranian lore, the ascent of souls to Stars, Moon, Sun, and Endless Lights.[107] Anaximenes brought the correction that the stars are more distant than the sun. Between the Assyrian priest and Anaximander—the text of Ezekiel gives a date of 593/2 BCE—there is Ezekiel's vision of Jahweh on his throne, fixed to a wheeled chariot of complicated construction, the wheels of which go to and fro; and the throne is of amber, as at Assur.[108]

Anaximenes said that the stars are fixed to a crystalline sky "like drawings,'"
zôgraphêmata: this almost sounds like a translation of the Assyrian text: Enlil
"designed" or "drew" the constellations on the heaven of Iaspis.[109] Another Akkadian text of astronomical content, *Enuma Anu Enlil*, has the same idea with a
more theological coloring: on heaven "the gods designed the stars in their own
likeness." Peter Kingsley has drawn attention to the fact that almost the same
expression recurs in the Platonic *Epinomis*: the constellations are "pictures of gods,
like divine images, fashioned by the gods themselves."[110]

A kind of dialogue seems to go on between Assur, Jerusalem, and Miletus. Let
us not forget that Anaximander, according to tradition, wrote just at the moment
when Sardis was conquered by the Persians;[111] whereas Gyges had kept regular
contacts with Nineveh more than a century before; and the brother of Alcaeus, a
mercenary, had gone to Nebuchadnezzar's Babylon.[112]

7. IRANIAN AFFINITIES

The Achaemenid Empire is no longer prehistory, but contemporary history of the
Presocratic movement. The eastern sources, though, become particularly evasive in
this period, while the Greek indications often present Graeco-Persian amalgams
that are difficult to analyze.

The word *magos* is clearly borrowed from Iranian, and thus incontrovertible
evidence for early Iranian influence in Greece. It has a double use or meaning in
Greek, discussed already in a book, *Magikos*, attributed to Aristotle:[113] the "authentic" *magoi* are said to be priests with a special theology and ritual, in contrast
to the "witch doctors' magic" (*goeteutike mageia*), the sense that was to prevail.
Magoi occur in Herodotus as a class of Median priests and the spokesmen of
Persian religion; *magoi* as charlatans and magicians are attested in the Hippocratic
treatise *On the Sacred Disease*, and also in Sophocles and Euripides.[114]

For the oldest testimony, one usually refers to Heraclitus[115] and overlooks the
older and in fact fundamental evidence,[116] the Behistun inscription of Darius.
Darius declares: "There was a man named Gaumata, a Magus, who lied and spoke: I
am Bardia."[117] Every time the name "Gaumata" recurs, the formula "the magus" is
added, as if to make it unforgettable. Evidently this was an Iranian term; the text
does not give an explanation. But it also says (sec. 70) that Darius sent the text into
all his lands to be read in public. In other words, this text was made known to all the
Greeks in every city of Asia Minor and on the adjacent islands, around 520 BCE.
Hence Greeks would remember the word *magos*, and if such a man appeared, he
would arouse attention at once. Note that we are moving here in a time from which
we have no other direct testimonies; there are more than 80 years down to Sophocles, Herodotus, and Hippocrates, and possibly more than 20 years to Heraclitus, who loses the position as earliest witness.

This does not bring any "teachings of the magi" to our knowledge. We are left with fascinating conjectures and hazardous reconstructions, in an amalgam of Greek and authentic Iranian. The two pieces of Iranian lore that were presented in the 1920s with remarkable effect, the *Myth of the Ages* and "persische Weisheit in griechischem Gewande," rely on Pahlavi evidence. The one specialist to take up the second item more recently, Duchesne-Guillemin, arrived at contradictory results;[118] while the Hippocratic treatise *On Sevens* has somehow been lost.[119] The *Myth of the Ages* constitutes a problem about the sources of Hesiod;[120] the Pahlavi texts as well as the Indian *yugas* that have been brought into the context are so many centuries later that it requires special faith to make them close to the putative original.

Similar uncertainties and controversies accompany the construction of a god Time, Zurvan, supreme god in some pre-Zoroastrian or para-Zoroastrian religion; it was claimed to have influenced Chronos in Phercydes and in the Orphic theogony,[121] but also the god Aion, Eternity, who makes his appearance at the threshold of late antiquity.[122] The Iranian evidence, in this case, has to be collected from Pahlavi, Syriac, Armenian, and Arabic sources—another challenge for deep diving into multifarious syncretistic and late materials.

A special connection of Heraclitus and Iran has often been assumed, with the complex of fire and cosmic order as connecting ideas.[123] But apart from Heraclitus's obscurity, there are no Iranian texts on which to base direct comparison; the Zoroastrian fire cult appears fully developed only in post-Achaemenid times.

There remain two religious ideas in which some Iranian impact has been surmised for a long time: celestial immortality and dualism, which introduces an adversary to God.[124]

The idea of an ascent of the soul to heaven, which is still popular in our own religion, does not belong to the older stratum that is common to Mesopotamia, Syria, Palestine, and Greece; we rather find a Land of No Return or a House of Hades as a dark and dreadful subterranean place with swamps and clay, far from the gods. In the religion of Zarathustra, by contrast, since the earliest documents there is the promise that the pious will ascend to God and rest with him for the future.[125] In Greece, the idea of soul or spirit, *psyche* or *pneuma*, going up to heaven after death is found from the fifth century BCE.

The classical document for the Mazdaic doctrine is the *Hadoxt Nask*, a text in the Avesta language: the dead, in the third night, will be met by his own "religion," *daena*, in form of a beautiful girl, who guides him in three steps, good thought, good speech, good deed, to the "lights without beginning" in the presence of Ahura Mazda.[126] In the Pahlavi writings, quoting lost parts of the Avesta, the three steps are specified as the stars, the moon, and the sun.[127] There may be pre-Zarathustrian elements: Immortality, *amrta-*, is an Indo-European concept; there is a heavenly paradise in the Veda.

The Greek evidence for such an idea of heavenly ascent is less specific, even if it was once termed a "Pythagorean revolution."[128] Most prominent is the Athenian epigram for the dead from Potidaea in 432 BCE.[129] What is striking is the closeness to Presocratic thought, with physical ideas about *aither*[130] and "going back to the origins";[131] this recurs in Hebrew Qohelet (3.21) but is suspected of being an interpolation there. Could there be an Iranian impulse? The Presocratic elements, the *aither*-concept and the return to origins, are not to be found in Zoroastrian religion. On the other hand, there are Greek antecedents, above all Heracles, who rises to Olympus.[132] In addition, there is Egyptian influence, which surely was at work in the field of funerary beliefs. Celestial immortality, though, is not at the center of Egyptian eschatology, but rather moving in the retinue of the sun through the nether world and "going forth by day." In this sense, the ascent of an *aither*-soul to heaven is closer to the Iranian paradigm. Transmigration, connected with Pythagoras and "Orpheus" and wrongly credited to the Egyptians by Herodotus, must ultimately derive from India—which was part of the Persian empire since Darius, too; we are left, and lost, in a melting pot of influences.

Herodotus has it that the Persians do not worship images in temples but sacrifice on the "highest of the mountains, calling the whole circle of the sky 'Zeus'"(1.131.2). Herodotus's report suspiciously agrees with theories of the Presocratic enlightenment, especially those of Diogenes of Apollonia and Democritus.[133] In the Avesta, Ahura Mazda clearly is distinct from heaven, even if he is dwelling in the House of Praise amid the endless lights. There may still have been some convergence of religious speculation between East and West.[134]

More interesting is the principle of dualism. It is clear from the *gathas* that Zarathustra, as a radical reformer, was fighting older forms of cult, such as cattle sacrifice and soma-drinking, and that he was inverting the traditional terminology so that the old Indo-European word for god, *deivos*, became the designation of the bad demons, *daevas*. To his supreme god, Ahura Mazda, he opposed an evil spirit, Angra Mainyu, and had every human involved in the battle between the two. An elaborate account of this is found in the Pahlavi *Bundahishn*—and much earlier in a modified form in Manichaeism—but it is in Greek texts from the fourth century BCE that we find the earliest attestations, Theopompus, Aristoxenus, Eudemus.[135] The question of the influence of Iranian dualism on Greek philosophy has concentrated on the question whether Plato's construct of a bad world-soul in the *Laws* is dependent on Zarathustra.[136] As for the Presocratics, it is Empedocles who is developing a kind of dualism, as he explains what is going on in nature by the antagonism of two principles or gods, Philia and Neikos, the one positive and sympathetic, the other absolutely negative, disastrous, hateful. And Empedocles makes the conflict a battle, regulated by predestined time, with Neikos "jumping up" to take the rule "in the fulfillment of time" (B30). This is a piece of mythology that seems to be unnecessary in the system; modern interpreters would prefer to have continuous interaction between the two principles, instead of the phases of a cycle and a sudden jump to power. Has it been motivated by the Zoroastrian myth, the attack of Angra Mainyu on Ahura Mazda? There are no contemporary Iranian texts or reliable Greek testimonies to substantiate a positive answer.[137] How much it would help in interpreting Empedocles is another question.

Still, classicists are probably prone to underestimate the presence of Persia within the Greek horizon, and to exclude oriental heritage by ignoring it. They should take the opportunity to see the evolution of Greek thought in the rich perspective of its intercultural background.

NOTES

1. *Geographi Graeci Minores* I.1–14.
2. Hdt. 1.74 = 11A5.
3. D.L. 2.2 = Apollodorus *FGrH* 244F29 = 12A1.
4. For details, see Burkert, *The Orientalizing Revolution*.
5. Suffice it to refer to Jeffery, *The Local Scripts of Archaic Greece*; Heubeck, *Archaeologia Homerica*; Burkert, *The Orientalizing Revolution*, 25–33; Woodard, *Greek Writing from Knossos to Homer*. There are few documents of alphabetic writing antedating 1200 BCE, and few for the next centuries; the vast diffusion seems to have happened since the tenth century. The alphabet, with the Aramean language, infiltrated the Assyrian empire and was to dominate the administration of the Persian empire.
6. Burkert, *The Orientalizing Revoution*, 26.
7. The oldest document so far, about 770 BCE, comes from Osteria dell'Osa near Gabii: Bietti Sestieri, *La necropoli laziale di Osteria dell'Osa*, 209–12; Peruzzi, Civiltà greca nel Lazio preromano; *Supplementum Epigraphicum Graecum* 48, 1266.
8. Wendel, *Die griechisch-römische Buchbeschreibung verglichen mit der des Vorderen Orients*.
9. Dipylon jug: IG I² 919; Jeffery, *The Local Scripts of Archaic Greece*, 76, no. 1; Hansen, *Carmina Epigraphica Graeca I*, no. 432; *Supplementum Epigraphicum Graecum* 48, 89; Nestor cup: Jeffery, *The Local Scripts of Archaic Greece*, 239, no. 1; Hansen, *Carmina Epigraphica Graeca I*, no. 454 (wrong date; read 725–720); *Supplementum Epigraphicum Graecum* 46, 1327.
10. These need not have been the texts of "Homer" we have, but rather some earlier versions of them, or some relatives of Hesiod. Oracles adopt the form of hexameters as the common Greek medium.
11. 12A7.
12. D.L. 9.6 = 22A1.
13. DK 11B1–2.
14. *Geographi Graeci Minores* I.15–96; see von Fritz, *Griechische Gschichtsschreibung* 1.52–54.
15. *FGrH* 1; his map: 1T12 = Anaximand. A6 DK.
16. *FGrH* 2; 3.
17. Burkert, *Lore and Science in Ancient Pythagoreanism*, 114–18.
18. D.L. 9.25 = 29A1.
19. Burkert, *The Orientalizing Revolution*, 41–46.
20. Lloyd, "On the 'Origins' of Science."
21. See text below at n. 31; 90.
22. Arist. *Peri philosophias* fr. 6 Rose; fr. 35 = D.L. 1.1, see 1.6–11 = Sotion fr. 36 Wehrli; Thphr. fr. 584a Fortenbaugh = Porph. *Abst.* 2.26.3; Clearchus fr. 6 Wehrli.

23. Hdt. 2.81.2; Isoc. *Bus.* 28.

24. D.L. 9.34 = 68A1; Suid. s.v. = 68A2; Philostr. *VS* 10 = 68A9; Ael. *VH* 4.20 = 68A16; Hippol. 1.13 = 68A40; Philostr. *VA* 1.2.

25. Dam. *Pr.* 123–25, 1.316–24 Ruelle = Eudem. fr. 150 Wehrli.

26. Tatian 31; 40; Clem.Al. *Strom.* 1.101; 1.165–82; 5.89.

27. Numen. fr. 8 Des Places; see Aristobulus in Clem.Al. *Strom* 1.150.1.

28. Zeller, *Philosophie der Griechen I*, 21–52.

29. Hopfner, *Orient und griechische Philosophie*; Mondolfo and Zeller, *La filosofia dei greci nel suo sviluppo storico*, 63–99.

30. Anquetil-Duperron, *Zend-Avesta.*

31. Gladstone, *Landmarks of Homeric Studies*, app.

32. Cornford, "A Ritual Basis for Hesiod's *Theogony.*"

33. Hölscher, "Anaximander und die Anfänge der Philosophie"; Hölscher, *Anfänglisches Fragen*; Schwabl, "Die griechischen Theogonien und der Orient," 39–56; West, *Hesiod, Theogony*; West, *Hesiod, Works and Days*; Walcot, *Hesiod and the Near East.*

34. Reinhardt, *Parmenides und die Geschichte der Griechischen Philosophie*; M. Heidegger, "Der Spruch des Anaximandros," in Heidegger, *Holzwege*, 296–343; Gadamer, *Um die Begriffswelt der Vorsokratiker.*

35. See oriental sources in the references list.

36. Bernal, *Black Athena*; see Lefkowitz and Rogers, *Black Athena Revisited*; Lefkowitz, *Not Out of Africa.*

37. See Gnoli, 1–26.

38. See oriental sources in the references list. Democrit. B299 (spurious?) = Clem.Al. *Strom.* 1.69; Thphr. D.L. 5.50, list of works no. 273, p. 40, Fortenbaugh. See also Burkert, *The Orientalizing Revolution*, 32–33, with n. 30; Luzzato, "Grecia e vicino oriente: tracce della 'Storia di Ahiqar' "; Luzzato, "Ancora sulla 'Storia di Ahiquar.' "

39. Call. fr. 191.54 f., see 11B1 DK.

40. See van der Waerden, *Science Awakening*, and in particular Neugebauer, "Zur Geschichte des pythagoräischen Lehrsatzes."

41. Hypsicles, *Greek Authors' Edition*, ed. V. de Falco, M. Krause, O. Neugebauer (Göttingen: Vandenhoeck & Ruprecht 1966), 36/47.

42. See van der Waerden, *Die Anfänge der Astronomie*; Neugebauer, *History of Ancient Mathematical Astronomy*; Pettinato, *La Scrittura Celeste.*

43. Ibyc. fr. 331 *Poetae Melici Graeci*; Pythagoras or Parmenides: D.L. 9.23; see Burkert, *Early Pythagoreanism*, 307.

44. Reiner and Pingree, *Enuma Anu Enlil Tablet 63*; see oriental sources in the references list.

45. See Panchenko, "Who Found the Zodiac?"

46. Rochberg-Halton, "Babylonian Horoscopes and Their Sources."

47. Burkert, *Ancient Pythagoreanism*, 299–301. Kronos/Saturnus as against Babylonian Ninurta, also called "star of the sun," is a special case.

48. Pl. *Ti.* 39d; Arist. fr. 5; Berossus *FGrH* 680F3, p. 374 f. Jacoby; van der Waerden, "Das grosse Jahr und die ewige Wiederkehr"; Panaino, "Riflessioni sul concetto di anno cosmico," 87–101.

49. West, *Early Greek Philosophy and the Orient*, pl. 5.

50. See West, *Hesiod, Works and Days*; Uehlinger, "Qohelet im Horizont mesopotamischer, levantinischer und ägyptischer Weisheitsliteratur der persischen und hellenistischen Zeit," 155–247. Hurrian wisdom literature has become accessible with the "Song of Liberation" (Neu, *Das hurritische Epos von der Freilassung*).

51. See text at n. 73.

52. D.L. 2.2 = 12A1 = *FGrH* 244F29, trans. KRS 100.

53. Fables are in evidence also in the Hurrite "Song of Liberation"; Neu, *Das hurritische Epos von der Freilassung,* see oriental soeurces in the references list.

54. Lichtheim, *Ancient Egyptian Literature,* 1:135, see oriental sources in the references list.

55. Schmid, *Geschichte der griechischen Literatur,* 1:287–88.

56. See text at n. 39.

57. Prov. 31:10; the "Babylonian theodicy": BWL (see oriental sources) 70–89.

58. Bias 10.3, DK sec. 6.1; "A man is money," Aristodamus at Alcaeus fr. 360 Voigt.

59. BWL 74 f.

60. Assmann, *Ma'at, Gerechtigkeit und Unsterblichkeit im alten Ägypten,* 88; teachings of Amenemope, Lichtheim, *Ancient Egyptian Literature,* 2:152.

61. Cleobulus 10.3, DK sec. 1.

62. *Od.* 18.136–37; BWL 40 f., 43, with an Akkadian commentary; Burkert, *The Orientalizing Revolution,* 118.

63. Archil. fr. 196a West; Moran, "An Assyriological Gloss," 17–19; Burkert, *The Orientalizing Revolution,* 122–23.

64. Burkert, *The Orientalizing Revolution,* 120–24; West, *The East Face of Helicon,* 82–83, 502–5.

65. Assmann, *Ma'at, Gerechtigkeit und Unsterblichkeit im alten Ägypten.*

66. Heraclit. B94.

67. Anaximand. B1.

68. Parm. B1.11–14.

69. Heraclit. B30.

70. Prov. 1:1–5.

71. Heraclit. B1.

72. See oriental sources in the references list.

73. Survey in AA.vv., *Sources Orientales: La naissance du monde,* see oriental sources in the references list).

74. See text at n. 36.

75. Gen. 1 and 2.4: "book of births" (*toledoth*) may be understood as a second title.

76. *Just So Stories for Little Children* is the title of a book by Rudyard Kipling (London, 1902); it was taken as a polemical concept by Ribichini, Rocchi, and Xella, *La questione delle influenze vicino-orientali sulla religione Greca,* 42, with reference to Sigmund Freud's *Totem and Taboo.*

77. Anaxag. B1.

78. Simp. *in Ph.* 24.15 = 12A9; Hippol. *Haer.* 1.6.2 = 12A11; for the controversial interpretation see KRS 108–9.

79. *Enuma Elish* 1.1–8.

80. Pyramid text 1040 a–d, see also 1466 b–d, AA. vv., *Sources Orientales: La naissance du monde* 46 (see oriental sources in the references list).

81. Gen. 1:2.

82. Hes. *Th.* 116; the sense of *chaos* was very controversial already in antiquity.

83. Ouranos Euphronides, Pap. Derveni col. 14; Arist. *Metaph.* 1071b27; Eudemus fr. 150 Wehrli.

84. Anaxag. B1.

85. Tedlock, *Popol Vuh,* 64.

86. Arist. *Metaph.* 983b20 = 11A12.

87. Hölscher, *Anfänglisches Fragen.*

88. Burkert, *The Orientalizing Revolution*, 91–93.

89. Staudacher, *Die Trennung von Himmel und Erde.*

90. ANET 120, Hoffner-Beckman 40 (see oriental sources in the references list); see West, *Hesiod, Theogony*, 20–22, 211–13; and see ANET 125, Hoffner-Beckman 59 for Ullikummi.

91. AA.vv., *Sources Orientales: La naissance du monde* (see oriental sources in the references list), 47 sec. 9.

92. Anaximand. A10; see also Leucippus A1 sec. 32.

93. 67A1.

94. See Steiner, "Der Sukzessionsmythgos in Hesiods Theogonie und ihren orientalischen Parallelen."

95. Hippol. *Haer.* 1.16 = 38A1.

96. Several inscriptions of Xerxes praise Ahura Mazda "who created heaven, who created earth, who created man."

97. *Enuma Elish* IV-V, pp. 254–55 Dalley (see oriental sources in the references list).

98. Gen. 1:14.

99. Hes. *Th.* 371–82.

100. Parm. B12–13.

101. Democr. A1 = D.L. 9.35.

102. But see the discussions in Buxton, *From Myth to Reason.*

103. Livingstone, *Mystical and Mythological Explanatory Works of Assyrian and Babylonian Scholars*, 78–91; see Burkert, "Orientalische und griechische Weltmodelle von Assur bis Anaximandros."

104. Livingstone, *Mystical and Mythological Explanatory Works of Assyrian and Babylonian Scholars*, 71; see Schibli, *Pherekydes of Syros*, 133, on Pherecydes: "Pherecydes, in short, meant to provide an alternative version to the *Theogony*; he probably felt his own version more consistently and accurately explained the origin of the world and the gods of myth."

105. It was partially misunderstood in doxography, Burkert, "Iranisches bei Anaximandros," 103.

106. Eudem. fr. 146 Wehrli; Burkert, *Ancient Pythagoreanism*, 308–10.

107. Burkert, "Iranisches bei Anaximandros"; West, *Early Greek Philosophy and the Orient.*

108. Ezek. 6; see West, *Early Greek Philosophy and the Orient*, 88–89; Kingsley, "Ezekiel by the Grand Canal".

109. See Kingsley, "Ezekiel by the Grand Canal."

110. Pl. *Epin.* 984a; Kingsley, "Meetings with Magi."

111. Anaximand. A1 = D.L. 2.2 = Apollodorus *FGrH* 244F29.

112. See Burkert, "'Königs-Ellen' bei Alkaios."

113. D.L. 1.8, see 1.1, Arist. fr. 32–36; Sotion fr. 36 Wehrli. *Magoi* as ritual experts occur in the Derveni Papyrus Col. 6, see Tsantsanoglou, "The First Columns of the Derveni Papyrus".

114. S. *OT* 387; E. *Hel.* 1396; see also Gorg. *Hel.* 10–11, 14; Pl. *Plt.* 280d.

115. B14; the word *magoi* is deleted as an interpolation by Marcovich and other editors.

116. Not treated in de Jong, *Traditions of the Magi.*

117. Behistun inscription (see oriental sources in the references list), secs. 11; 13; 14; 16; 52; 68; the word is preserved in Old Persian and transcribed in Akkadian (*magusu*)

and in Elamite (*makuis*). The word also occurs for certain priests in the Persepolis tablets, from the time of Darius: Koch, "Iranische Religion im achaimenidischen Zeitalter" 23–24. For later Greek evidence on *magoi* see Bidez and Cumont, *Les mages hellenisés*. There is a bilingual inscription from Cappadocia, first century CE, from a man who was *magos* for Mithras, KAI 265.

118. Duchesne-Guillemin, "Persische Weisheit in griechischem Gewande?" Duchesne-Guillemin, "D'Anaximandre à Empédocle," 47; see Momigliano, *Alien Wisdom*, 128–29.

119. Mansfeld, *The Pseudo-Hippocratic Tract Peri Hebdomadon Ch. 1–11 and Greek Philosophy*, dated it to the time of Posidonius, with the applause of W. Theiler; Mansfeld changed his opinion, too, and now thinks of a Jewish-Hellenistic forgery, *Mnemosyne* 42 (1989): 184–185.

120. Hesiod (*Op.* 106–7) seems to indicate that it is not his own invention. The next problem is whether the four metal ages in Daniel 7 are ultimately derived from Hesiod or from Hesiod's source, possibly an Aramaic text from the early Iron Age; see Burkert, "Apokalyptik im frühen Griechentum."

121. See Zaehner, *Zurvan*; West, *Early Greek Philosophy and the Orient*, 30–33.

122. Junker, "Über iranische Quellen der hellenistischen Aion-Vorstellung"; criticism in Nock, *Essays on Religion in the Ancient World*, 377–96; Brisson, "La figure de chronos dans la théogonie orphique et ses antécédents iraniens"; Zuntz, *Aion, Gott Des Römerreichs*, who tried to make Augustus the main "inventor" of Aion.

123. See Duchesne-Guillemin, "Heraclitus and Iran," 34–49; West, *Early Greek Philosophy and the Orient*, 165–202.

124. The more relevant problem is in how far these ideas have influenced Judaism; see, for a critical position, G. Ahn, in Kratz, *Religion*, 191–209.

125. Gatha-texts (see oriental sources in the references list): Yasna 31.7: "abodes of blessedness, filled with light," as the god gives immortality (21); 43.3: passage "from good to better," from corporeal to spiritual, to the place where god is dwelling; 45.11: "salvation and not-dying in his realm"; 51.15: the "house of praise, where the god went first, is promised to you."

126. Piras, *Hådoxt Nask* (see oriental sources in the references list). The passage is redescribed in the Pahlavi texts *Bundahishn* and *The Book of Adrai Viraz*.

127. See text at n. 101.

128. See Burkert, *Ancient Pythagoreanism*, 358–60. The main passages are Epich. 23B9, B22 = frs. 213, 254 Kassel-Austin; E. *Erechtheus* fr. 65.72 Austin; E. *Supp.* 532.

129. IG I³ 1179.6 = Hansen no. 10: *aither men psuchas hupedexato . . .*

130. Diog.Apoll. A19, 42: soul as "part of god."

131. A relevant passage of Euripides was taken to be a reflex of Anaxagoras by the ancients, E. fr. 839 = Anaxag. A112.

132. The mentioning of Heracles 'staying with the gods' *Od.* 11.602–3 was denounced as interpolation by the ancient critics; Hebe as his wife is now attested in iconography by about 600, see *LIMC*, s.v. Herakles no. 3331; Hyacinthus and Polyboea driving toward heaven on the throne of Amyclae, Paus. 3.19.4.

133. 64A8; 68B30.

134. Frahm, "Zwischen Tradition und Neuerung," 84–99, shows that priests in Achaemenid Uruk developed a prominent role of the god "Heaven" (Anu). The decree of Artaxerxes for Ezra (Ezra 7:12; genuine?) calls the god of the Jews "God of Heaven."

135. Theopompus 115F65 in Plu. *Is.* 46–47, 369d–370c; Aristox. fr.13 Wehrli in Hippol. *Haer.* 1.2.12 (see Kingsley, "The Greek Origin of the Sixth-Century Dating of Zoroaster," 245–56); Eudem. fr. 150 Wehrli; a passing allusion in Arist. *Metaph.* 1091b10.

136. Pl. *Lg.* 896 d–e, 906a; see Plu. *Procr.* 1014d; *Is.* 370e–f; see Kerschensteiner, *Platon und der Orient*, who is negative.

137. Philostratus has Empedocles, among others, meeting with *magoi*, *VA* 1.2; Gorgias said he had seen Empedocles performing magic, 82A3 = Emp. A1 sec. 59 = D.L. 8.59; see also Kingsley, "Meetings with Magi."

ORIENTAL SOURCES IN TRANSLATION

General

ANET J. B. Pritchard, ed. *Ancient Near Eastern Texts Relating to the Old Testament.* 3rd ed. Princeton: Princeton University Press, 1969.

AA.vv. *Sources Orientales I: La naissance du monde.* Paris: Éditions du Seuil, 1959.

TUAT O. Kaiser, ed. *Texte aus der Umwelt des Alten Testaments.* Gütersloh: Gerd Mohn, 1982–2001.

Mesopotamia

S. Dalley. *Myths from Mesopotamia.* Oxford: Oxford University Press, 1989.

B. R. Foster. *Before the Muses: An Anthology of Akkadian Literature.* 2 vols. 2nd ed. Bethesda: CDL Press, 1996.

J. Bottéro and S. N. Kramer. *Lorsque les dieux faisaient l' homme: Mythologie Mésopotamienne.* Paris: Gallimard, 1989.

W. G. Lambert and A. R. Millard. *Atra-hasis: The Babylonian story of the Flood.* Oxford: Clarendon Press, 1969.

A. Heidel. *The Gilgamesh Epic and Old Testament Parallels.* 2nd ed. Chicago: University of Chicago Press, 1949.

———. *Enuma Elish: The Babylonian Genesis.* 2nd ed. Chicago: University of Chicago Press, 1951.

A. R. George. *The Babylonian Gilgamesh Epic.* Oxford: Oxford University Press, 2003.

BWL = W. G. Lambert. *Babylonian Wisdom Literature.* Oxford: Clarendon Press, 1960.

D. D. Luckenbill. *Ancient Records of Assyria and Babylonia.* 2 vols. Chicago: University of Chicago Press, 1926.

O. Neugebauer. *Astronomical Cuneiform Texts.* 3 vols. Princeton: Lund Humphries, 1955.

O. Neugebauer and A. J. Sachs. *Mathematical Cuneiform Texts.* New Haven: American Oriental Society, 1945.

E. Reiner and D. Pingree. *Enuma Anu Enlil Tablet 63: The Venus Tablet of Ammisaduqa.* Malibu, Calif.: Undena, 1975.

———. *Enuma Anu Enlil, Tablets 50–51.* Malibu, Calif.: Undena, 1981.

H. Hunger and D. Pingree. *MULAPIN: An Anstronomical Compendium in Cuneiform.* Horn: F. Berger, 1989.

Egypt

M. Lichtheim. *Ancient Egyptian Literature*. 3 vols. Berkeley: University of California Press, 1973–80.
———. *Late Egyptian Wisdom Literature in the International Context*. Freiburg, 1983.
M. Clagett. *Ancient Egyptian Science. A Source Book I: Knowledge and Order*. Philadelphia: American Philosopical Society, 1989.

Hittites

H. A. Hoffner and G. M. Beckman. *Hittite Myths*. Atlanta: Scholars Press, 1990.
H. G. Gueterbock. *Kumarbi: Mythen vom churritischen Kronos*. Zürich: Europaverlag, 1946.
———. *The Song of Ullikummi*. New Haven: American Schools of Oriental Research, 1952.
H. Otten. *Mythen vom Gotte Kumarbi: Neue Fragmente*. Berlin: Akademie-Verlag, 1950.
E. Neu. *Das hurritische Epos von der Freilassung*. Vol. I. Wiesbaden: Harrassowitz, 1996.

Canaan

A. Caquot, M. Sznycer, and A. Herdner. *Textes ougaritiques* I: *Mythes et légendes*. Paris: Ed. du Cerf, 1974.
A. Caquot, J.-M. de Tarragon, and J.-L.Cunchillos. *Textes ougaritiques* II. Paris: Ed. du Cerf, 1989.
M. D. Coogan. *Stories from Ancient Canaan*. Philadelphia: Westminster Press, 1978.
C. de Moor. An *Anthology of Religious Texts from Ugarit*. Leiden: Brill, 1987.
KAI = H., Donner and W. Röllig. *Kanaanäische und aramäische Inschriften*. 3 vols. 2nd edn. Wiesbaden: Harrassowitz, 1966–69.
A. I. Baumgarten. *The Phoenician History of Philo of Byblos: A Commentary*. Leiden: Brill, 1981.
Ahiqar: F. C. Conybeare, J. Rendell Harris, and A. Smith Lewis. *The Story of Ahikar from the Aramaic, Syriac, Arabic, Armenian, Ethiopic, Old Turkish, Greek and Slavonic Versions*. 2nd edn. Cambridge, 1913; TUAT III 2, 320–47.

Persia

J. Darmesteter and L. H. Mills. *The Zend-Avesta*. 3 vols. Oxford: Clarendon Press, 1883–95
H. Humbach. *The Gathas of Zarathushtra and the Other Old Avestan Texts*. Vol. 1. Heidelberg: Winter, 1991.
M. Boyce. *Textual Sources for the Study of Zoroastrianism*. Totowa, N.J.: Barnes & Noble Books, 1984.
A. Piras, ed. *Hådoxt Nask. Il racconto Zoroastriano della sorte dell'anima*. Rome: Istituto Italiano per l'Africa e l'Oriente, 2000.

Behistun Inscription of Darius

F. H. Weissbach. *Die Keilinschriften der Achämeniden*. Leipzig: Hinrichs, 1911, 8–74 (three versions).
R. G. Kent. *Old Persian. Grammar, Texts, Lexicon*. 2nd ed. New Haven: American Oriental Society, 1953, 116–34. (Persian version.)
TUAT I 419–450. (All versions in German translation.)

BIBLIOGRAPHY

Anquetil Duperron, A. H. *Zend-Avesta. Ouvrage der Zoroastre*. Paris: Tillard, 1771.

Assmann, I. *Ma'at, Gerechtigkeit und Unsterblichkeit Im Alten Ägypten*. Munich, 1990.

Bernal, Martin. *Black Athena: The Afro-Asiatic Roots of Classical Civilization*. London: Free Association Books, 1987.

Bidez, Joseph, and Franz Cumont. *Les Mages hellenisés: Zoroastre, Ostanès et Hystaspe d'après la tradition grecque*. Paris: Belles Lettres, 1938.

Bidez, Joseph. *Eos ou Platon et l'Orient*. Bruxelles: Hayez, 1945.

Bietti Sestieri, A. M. *La necropoli laziale di Osteria dell'Osa*. Rome: Qasar, 1992.

Brisson, L. "La figure de Chronos dans la théogonie orphique et ses antécédents iraniens." In *Orphée et l'Orphism dans l'antiquité gréco-romaine*, edited by L. Brisson, nr. III. Aldershot, England: Ashgate, 1995.

Burkert, Walter. "Apokalyptik im frühen Griechentum: Impulse und Transformationen." In *Apocalypticism in the Mediterranean World and the Near East*, 235–54. Tübingen: Mohr, 1983.

———. *Babylon, Memphis, Persepolis: Eastern Contexts of Greek Culture*. Cambridge, Mass.: Harvard University Press, 2004.

———. "Iranisches bei Anaximandros." *Rheinisches Museum* 106 (1963): 97–134.

———. "Königs-Ellen' bei Alkaios." *Museum Helveticum* 53 (1996): 69–72.

———. *Lore and Science in Ancient Pythagoreanism*. 1962. Translated by E. L. Minar, Jr. Cambridge, Mass.: Harvard University Press, 1972.

———. "Orientalische und griechische Weltmodelle von Assur bis Anaximandros." *Wiener Studien* (1994): 179–86.

———. *The Orientalizing Revolution*. Cambridge: Cambridge University Press, 1992.

Buxton, R., ed. *From Myth to Reason? Studies in the Development of Greek Thought*. Oxford: Oxford University Press, 1999.

Cornford, F. M. "A Ritual Basis for Hesiod's *Theogony*." In *The Unwritten Philosophy and Other Essays*, 95–116. Cambridge: Cambridge University Press, 1950.

Dornseiff, Franz, "Hesiods Werke und Tage und das Alte Morgenland." *Philologus* 89 (1934) 397–415. Reprinted as *Kleine Schriften I. Antike und alter Orient*, Leipzig:Koehler & Amelang, 1956; 1959, 72–95.

Duchesne-Guillemin, Jacques. "D'Anaximandre à Empédocle: Contacts gréco-iraniens." In *Atti del convegno sul tema: La Persia e il mondo greco-romano, problemi attuali di scienza e di cultura 76*, 76:423–31. Rome: Accademia Nazionale dei Lincei, 1966.

———. "Heraclitus and Iran." *History of Religions* 3 (1963): 34–49.

———. "Persische Weisheit in griechischem Gewande?" *Harvard Theological Review* 49 (1956): 115–22.

———. *The Western Response to Zoroaster*. Oxford, 1958.

Eissfeldt, O. "Phönikische und griechische Kosmogonie." In *Éléments orientaux dans la religion grecque ancienne*, Paris: Presses Universitaires 1960, 1–18.

Frahm, E. "Zwischen Tradition und Neuerung. Babylonische Priestergelehrte im achämenidenzeitlichen Uruk." In Kratz, *Religion und Religionskontakte*, 74–106.

Frankfort, H. A., J. A.Wilson, and T. Jacobsen. *The Intellectual Adventure of Ancient Man*. Chicago: Chicago University Press, 1946; reprinted as *Before Philosophy*, Harmondsworth: Penguin Books, 1949.

Fritz, K. von. *Griechische Geschichtsschreibung I.* Berlin: De Gruyter, 1967.

Gadamer, H.-G. *Um die Begriffswelt der Vorsokratiker.* Darmstadt: Wissenschaftliche Buchgesellschaft, 1968.

Gigon, O. *Der Ursprung der griechischen Philosophie von Hesiod bis Parmenides.* Basel: Schwabe, 1945.

Gladstone, W. E. *Landmarks of Homeric Studies.* London: MacMillan, 1890.

Gnoli, G. *Zoroaster in History.* New York: Bibliotheca Persica Press, 2000.

Goetze, A. "Persische Weisheit in griechischem Gewande." *Zeitschrift für Indologie und Iranistik* 2, (1923): 60–98; 167–77.

Hansen, P. A., *Carmina Epigraphica Graeca Saeculorum VIII–V a. Chr. n..* Berlin: De Gruyter, 1983.

Heidegger, M. *Holzwege.* Frankfurt, 1950.

Heubeck, A. "Mythologische Vorstellungen des Alten Orients im archaischen Griechentum." *Gymnasium* 62 (1955): 508–25. Reprinted in E. Heitsch, ed., *Hesiod*, Darmstadt: Wissenschaftliche Buchgesellschaft, 1966, 545–70.

———. *Schrift.* Archaeologia Homerica III 10, Göttingen: Vandenhoeck & Ruprecht, 1979.

Hölscher, U. "Anaximander und der Anfang der Philosophie." *Hermes* 81 (1953): 257–277, 385–418; extended revision in: *Anfängliches Fragen*, 9–89.

———. *Anfänglisches Fragen.* Göttingen: Vandenhoek & Ruprecht, 1968.

Hopfner, Th. *Orient und Griechische Philosophy.* Leipzig: Hinrichs, 1925.

Jeffery, L. H. *The Local Scripts of Archaic Greece: A Study of the Origin of the Greek Alphabet and Its Development from the Eighth to the Fifth Centuries B.C.* Rev. ed. Oxford: Clarendon Press, 1990.

Jong, Albert de. *Traditions of the Magi: Zoroastrianism in Greek and Latin Literature.* Leiden: Brill, 1997.

Junker, H. "Über iranische Quellen der hellenistischen Aion-Vorstellung." *Vorträge der Bibliothek Warburg 1921/2* (1923): 125–78.

Kerschensteiner, Jula. *Platon und der Orient.* Stuttgart: Kohlhammer, 1945.

Kingsley, Peter. *Ancient Philosophy, Mystery, and Magic: Empedocles and the Pythagorean Tradition.* Oxford: Clarendon Press, 1995.

———. "Ezekiel by the Grand Canal: Between Jewish and Babylonian Tradition." *Journal of the Royal Asiatic Society* 3 (1992): 339–46.

———. "The Greek Origin of the Sixth Century Dating pf Zoroastter." *Bulletin of the School of Oriental and African Studies* 53 (1990): 245–65.

———. "Meetings with Magi: Iranian Themes among the Greeks, from Xanthus of Lydia to Plato's Academy." *Journal of the Royal Asiatic Society* 3.5 (1995): 173–209.

Koch, H. "Iranische Religion im achaimenidischen Zeitalter." In Kratz, *Religion und Religionskontakte*, 11–26.

Kratz, R. G., ed. *Religion und Religionskontakte im Zeitalter der Achämeniden.* Gütersloh: Kaiser, 2002.

Laks, André, and Glenn W. Most, eds. *Studies on the Derveni Papyrus.* Oxford: Clarendon Press, 1997.

Lefkowitz, Mary R. *Not Out of Africa: How Afrocentrism Became an Excuse for Teaching Myth as History.* New York: Basic Books, 1996.

Lefkowitz, Mary R., and Guy MacLean Rogers, eds. *Black Athena Revisited.* Chapel Hill: University of North Carolina Press, 1996.

Livingstone, A. *Mystical and Mythological Explanatory Works of Assyrian and Babylonian Scholars.* Oxford: Oxford University Press, 1984.

Lloyd, G. E. R. "On the 'Origins' of Science." *Proceedings of the British Academy* 105 (2000): 1–16.

Luzzato, M. J. "Grecia e Vicino Oriente: Tracce della 'Storia di Ahiqar'." *Quaderni di storia* 18 (1992): 5–84.

———. "Ancora sulla 'Storia di Ahiquar'." *Quaderni di storia* 39 (1994): 253–77.

Mansfeld, Jaap. *The Pseudo-Hippocratic Tract Peri Hebdomadon Ch. 1–11 and Greek Philosophy.* Assen: Van Gorcum, 1971.

Momigliano, Arnaldo. *Alien Wisdom: The Limits of Hellenization.* Cambridge: Cambridge University Press, 1975.

Mondolfo, Rodolfo, and Eduard Zeller. 1932. *La filosofia dei greci nel suo sviluppo storico.* 3rd ed. Florence; La Nuova Italia, 1951.

Moran, W. H. "An Assyriological Gloss in the New Archilochus Fragment." *Harvard Studies in Classical Philology* 82 (1978): 17–19.

Neugebauer, Otto. *A History of Ancient Mathematical Astronomy.* 3 vols. Berlin: Springer Verlag, 1975.

———. "Zur Geschichte des pythagoräischen Lehrsatzes." *Nachrichten der göttingischen Gelehrten Gesellschaft, Math.-Ph. Klasse* (1928): 45–48.

Nock, A. D. *Essays on Religion in the Ancient World.* Cambridge, Mass.: Harvard University Press, 1972.

Panaino, A. "Riflessioni sul concetto di anno cosmico." In Ribichini, Rocchi, and Xella, *La questione delle influenze vicino-orientali sulla religione greca*, 87–101.

Panchenko, Dmitri. "Who Found the Zodiac?" *Antike Naturwissenschaft und ihre Rezeption* 9 (1999): 33–44.

Peruzzi, E. *Civiltà greca nel Lazio preromano.* Florence: Olschi 1998.

Pettinato, G. *La Scrittura celeste: Origini dell'astrologia caldea in Mesopotamia.* Milan: Mondadori, 1998.

Reinhardt, K. *Parmenides und die Geschichte der griechischen Philosophie 1917.* Frankfurt: Klostermann, 1959.

Ribichini, S., M. Rocchi, and P. Xella. *La questione delle influenze vicino-orientali sulla religione greca.* Rome: Consiglio Nazionale delle Ricerche, 2001.

Rochberg-Halton, F. "Babylonian Horoscopes and Their Sources." *Orientalia* 58 (1989): 102–23.

Schibli, H. S. *Pherekydes of Syros.* Oxford: Clarendon Press, 1990.

Schmid, W. *Geschichte der griechischen Literatur.* Vol. I. Munich: Beck, 1929.

Schwabl, Hans. "Die Griechischen Theogonien und der Orient." In *Eléments Orientaux dans la Religion Grecque Ancienne*, edited by Université de Strasbourg, 39–56. Paris: Presses Universitaires de France, 1960.

Staudacher, W. *Die Trennung von Himmel und Erde.* Ph.D. diss., University of Tübingen, 1942.

Steiner, G. "Der Sukzessionsmythgos in Hesiods Theogonie und ihren orientalischen Parallelen." Ph. D. diss., University of Hamburg, 1959.

Tedlock, D. *Popol Vuh. The Mayan Book of the Dawn of Life.* New York: Simon & Schuster, 1985.

Tsantsanoglou, K. "The First Columns of the Derveni Papyrus and their Religious Significance." In Laks and Most, *Studies on the Derveni Papyrus*, 93–128.

Uehlinger, C. "Qohelet im Horizont mesopotamischer, levantinischer und ägyptischer Weisheitsliteratur der persischen und hellenistischen Zeit." In *Das Buch Kohelet*, edited by L. Schwienhorst-Schönberger, 155–247. Berlin: De Gruyter, 1997.

Waerden, B. L. van der. *Die Anfänge der Astronomie.* Groningen, 1966.

————. "Das grosse Jahr und die ewige Wiederkehr." *Hermes* 80 (1952): 129–55.

————. *Science Awakening*. New York: Oxford University Press, 1961.

Walcot, Peter. *Hesiod and the Near East*. Cardiff: Wales University Press, 1966.

Walker, C. B. F. *Astronomy before the Telescope*. New York: St. Martin's Press, 1997.

Wendel, C. *Die griechisch-römische Buchbeschreibung verglichen mit der des vorderen Orients*. Halle: Niemeyer, 1949.

West, M. L. *Early Greek Philosophy and the Orient*. Oxford: Clarendon Press, 1971.

————. *The East Face of Helicon: West Asiatic Elements in Greek Poetry and Myth*. Oxford: Clarendon Press, 1997.

————. *Hesiod, Theogony*. Oxford: Clarendon Press, 1966.

————. *Hesiod, Works and Days*. Oxford: Clarendon Press, 1978.

Woodard, Roger D. *Greek Writing from Knossos to Homer: A Linguistic Interpretation of the Origin of the Greek Alphabet and the Continuity of Ancient Greek Literacy*. Oxford: Oxford University Press, 1997.

Zaehner, R. C. *Zurvan: A Zoroastrian Dilemma*. Oxford: Clarendon Press, 1955.

Zunz, G. *Aion, Gott des Römerreichs*. Heidelberg: Abhandlungen Heidelberg 2, 1989.

PART II

FIGURES
AND MOVEMENTS

CHAPTER 3

MILESIAN MEASURES: TIME, SPACE, AND MATTER

STEPHEN A. WHITE

ANY ATTEMPT to trace the origin of Greek philosophy faces two complementary problems, each severe. One is the unfortunate fact that evidence for the early philosophers is woefully meager. Their own words are almost entirely lost, and most of the little information that does survive is plainly filtered and generally suspect. The other problem is conceptual: what to count as philosophy? Yet neither problem is insuperable. If we adjust the parameters, we may obtain results that, while necessarily provisional, are both likely and illuminating. Here I propose to reorient the search for origins in two ways, corresponding to our two problems. First, rather than trying to reconstruct vanished work directly, I shall focus on a crucial stage in its ancient reception, in particular, the efforts by Aristotle and his colleagues in the latter half of the fourth century to collect, analyze, and assess the evidence then available for earlier attempts to understand the natural world. The influence of their work, as widely recognized and frequently lamented, was substantial and often decisive, not only for the interpretation of earlier work but even for what information about it would survive. In effect, renouncing the quixotic goal of recovering archaic Greek ideas in their own right may enable us to reconstruct, and better appreciate, how those ideas appeared to some well-informed and astute critics who, if not always sympathetic, were much better placed to understand their predecessors than we shall ever be. If their efforts were roughly on the mark—a much-disputed question, which I can here only touch on in passing— then careful analysis of their accounts is probably the best we can do, absent substantial new finds, to trace the infancy of theoretical thought in Greece. The other shift in focus I shall make is from philosophy to science; or rather, since that would raise similar and equally contested conceptual questions, I shall focus on evidence for the interplay between observation, measurement, and explanation in the work of three sixth-century Milesians: Thales (c. 625–c. 548) on astronomical phenomena, Anaximander (c. 610–c. 545) on the structure and dimensions of the cosmos, and Anaximenes (c. 590–c. 525) on the transformations of material bodies, terrestrial and celestial alike. In short, I shall review reports of their attempts to measure and explain regularity in time, space, and matter.[1]

1. THALES AND THE MEASURES OF TIME

The problem of evidence is doubly acute for Thales. Not only is our information entirely indirect and mostly late; it is also very unlikely that he wrote any books in the first place. Ancient sources report two or three titles: a *Nautical Astronomy* in verse, and another work or two, either *On Solstice and Equinox* or *On Solstice* and *On Equinox*.[2] But the verse was more credibly ascribed to an otherwise unknown Phocus of Samos;[3] and Anaximander is credited with writing the first "summary exposition" of his ideas, reportedly the year after Thales died (D.L. 2.2; cf. A6–7).[4] Nonetheless, the absence of any texts by Thales is not the hopeless situation it might now appear. Even if he wrote nothing himself, it would be a mistake to dismiss the extant textual tradition. Much of its information, including some in very late writers, goes back to Aristotle and his junior colleagues Dicaearchus, Eudemus, and Theophrastus. Their research, though only occasionally cited by name, was clearly the main source of most later reports; and in the fields of astronomy and geometry, it is likely that all specific reports about Thales derive from Eudemus in particular.[5] The crucial questions are thus two: what sources did they use, and did those sources provide any reliable information about Thales?

On the first count, it is clear that Aristotle's colleagues had access to most of the earlier texts known to us, and a good deal more that was later lost and forgotten. In particular, it is clear that Theophrastus read works by both Anaximander and Anaximenes; and given the collaborative organization of the Lyceum, it is safe to assume that his colleagues had access to those writings as well.[6] On the second count, if either of those Milesians recorded anything about Thales, their direct testimony would make the Aristotelian tradition reasonably secure in turn. Unfortunately, there is no sure sign that either of them did cite their older compatriot.[7] But we are not therefore reduced to vague conjecture. Even if neither Milesian said anything about Thales, others writing soon after them certainly did. Eudemus, in his *Research in Astronomy*, apparently cited both Xenophanes and

Herodotus, and probably also Heraclitus and Democritus, for his own account of Thales as "the first astronomer" (fr. 144 = D.L. 1.23); and a passage in Herodotus (1.74) verifies the one citation we can still test.[8] Another likely source of information was Hecataeus (fl. 500), a fellow Milesian old enough to know at least Anaximenes personally and to hear firsthand reports about all three. His inquiries overlapped with theirs, and his geographical work depended heavily on Anaximander's (A6); his writings may also lie behind what we read about Thales in Herodotus, who knew the work of Hecataeus well.[9] To be sure, such early written reports relied largely on oral reports, which are inevitably prone to distortion. But in a heavily oral culture like sixth-century Miletus and Ionia, the oral traditions of a close-knit elite can be remarkably accurate, especially if tied to material objects. When reports about Thales were first recorded and how they reached Eudemus remain a mystery. But it is a mystery that once had answers, even if we can no longer recover them. The absence of any certain lines of transmission, moreover, is balanced by the wide range of plausible alternatives. It is therefore more fruitful to shift our inquiry to what Eudemus said about Thales.

Evidence for Thales' study of the sky falls into three chronological groups. The earliest are two reports in Herodotus (from the 440s or 430s), two passing mentions in Aristophanes (in 424 and 414), and two passages in Plato (from the 370s and 360s). The second group comes from Aristotle's school: an anecdote in his *Politics* and three citations of Eudemus's study of early astronomy in late sources. Much of the testimony in both groups centers on phenomena watched by traditional "horizontal astronomy": observation of the horizon, mainly at dawn and dusk. The same emphasis is evident in later texts, which name Thales for many more insights but rarely identify their sources. Taken together, the three sets of testimony record a dozen distinct but related claims. The result, when duly analyzed, is a broad, coherent, and largely credible picture of Thales as a pioneer in the reliable measurement of time who counted and correlated periodic astronomical cycles. An inventory of the phenomena studied will be useful here.[10]

1. Solar eclipses: Hdt. 1.74 (A5), Eudemus fr. 143 in Clem. *Strom.* 1.14.65 (A5), Eudemus fr. 144 in D.L. 1.23, Eudemus fr. 145 in Theon *Math.* 3.40 (A17), *POxy* 3710 (citing Aristarchus of Samos), Aët. 2.24.1 (A17a), Cicero *Div.* 1.112 (A5), Pliny *NH* 2.53 (A5), *Suda* (A2), *Sch. Rep.* 600A (A3), Eus. *Chron.* (A5).
2. Solstices: Eudemus frs. 144–45 (D.L. 1.23, A17), D.L. 1.24, *Suda* (A2), *Sch. Rep.* 600A (A3).
3. Equinoxes: D.L. 1.23, *Suda* (A2), Pliny *NH* 18.213 (A18).
4. Seasons: D.L. 1.27.
5. Days per year: D.L. 1.27.
6. Days per month: *POxy* 3710 (citing Aristarchus), D.L. 1.24.
7. A lunisolar ratio: D.L. 1.24, Apul. *Flor.* 18 (A19).[11]
8. Pleiades: Pliny *NH* 18.213 (A18).
9. Hyades: *Sch. Arat.* 172 (B2).
10. Ursa Minor: Callimachus fr. 191.54–5 (A3a), *Sch. Rep.* 600A (A3).

11. Nile floods: Hdt. 2.20, D.L. 1.37, Aët. 4.1.1 (A16).
12. Olive harvest: Arist. *Pol.* 1.11 (A10), Hieronymus of Rhodes fr. 47 in D.L. 1.26, Cicero *Div.* 1.111.

The evidence encompasses solar, lunar, stellar, and seasonal phenomena, and various relations among them. The most celebrated item and also the earliest attested is the first on the list, and though evidently accepted by Eudemus,[12] it is especially puzzling. If Thales predicted a solar eclipse, as Herodotus seems to claim, and if his success was not completely fortuitous, then he must have relied on a previously established pattern of events that enabled him to extrapolate from previously observed phenomena to future recurrences. Use of such a predictable pattern would presumably meet two basic conditions for any form of measurement: first, isolating some reasonably determinate observable parameters, and second, defining a uniform module to quantify those parameters. In this case, the phenomena were solar eclipses, or in the simpler language of Herodotus, occasions when "the day suddenly became night" (1.74); and the module would have been some sort of temporal interval between eclipses. If we could trust this story, it would be clear evidence that Thales surpassed his Greek contemporaries in measuring at least one temporal parameter, namely, the intervals between eclipses. But should we trust the story? Or rather, is there any evidence that Eudemus had reasonable grounds for trusting it?

Absent new evidence, scholars are unlikely ever to reach consensus on either question. Some dismiss the story outright. Others appeal to similar Near Eastern practices.[13] In particular, if Thales was familiar with something like the so-called Saros cycle used by Babylonian priests to calculate in advance the days on which an eclipse might occur, then he could at least predict that one might occur within a limited period of time—as Herodotus puts it, "by setting a limit of the year in which it did occur" (1.74). When one did occur within that period, his success, though still heavily dependent on luck, would naturally become famous. Such a prediction would involve a fairly sophisticated form of measuring time. But it is questionable whether even Eudemus knew of the Saros or similar methods, which are first attested for Greek traditions three centuries later.[14] Or perhaps modern doubts are misdirected, and the question to ask is not whether or how Thales could predict an eclipse, but what exactly he predicted. Before pursuing that question, however, we first need to consider some related evidence. Eudemus is cited as the authority for one other astronomical discovery by Thales. Diogenes Laertius, writing around 200 CE, mentions solar eclipses alongside the second item, solstices (fr. 144 = D.L. 1.23–24):

> According to some, he is thought to be the first to do astronomy and to foretell solar eclipses and solstices, as Eudemus says in his *Research in Astronomy*; whence both Xenophanes and Herodotus admire him, and Heraclitus and Democritus also attest to him.[15] Some, including Choerilus the poet, say he was also the first to say souls are immortal. He also first discovered the interval [*parodon*] from solstice to solstice.

Theon of Smyrna, a Platonist active half a century or more earlier, singles out the same two phenomena in a brief summary of material from Eudemus (fr. 145 = *Math.* 3.40, 198.14–19):

> Eudemus reports in his *Astronomies* that Oenopides first discovered the obliquity of the zodiacal circle and the cycle of the great year; Thales [first discovered] an eclipse of the sun and the interval between its solstices, that it is always unequal; Anaximander [first discovered] that the earth is aloft and lies at the middle of the cosmos.[16]

It is unlikely that either writer knew Eudemus's work directly. Diogenes cites it only here, and Theon names the Platonist Dercyllides (first century BCE or CE) as his source.[17] Both say he credited Thales with discoveries involving the same pair of phenomena, solar eclipses and solstices. But exactly what Eudemus thought he discovered in the first case is not at all clear. Diogenes describes both cases together as "foretelling," and Theon describes both as "discoveries." Which is right—or more faithful to Eudemus? Thales was certainly not the first to observe either event; and it is virtually certain that he did not correctly explain both. Even if he did so for eclipses, as some sources claim (*POxy* 3710.36–41, A3, A17a), the explanation of the solstices involves a model of celestial mechanics nowhere reliably ascribed to him. In fact, we can be confident that Eudemus did not claim that Thales proposed any mechanical explanation, since that would be inconsistent with Theon's summary, which credits Anaximander with the first geocentric orbital model. Yet both reports try to clarify what Thales discovered about the solstices, and their accounts are clear and consistent if taken as complementary. According to Diogenes, Thales established two temporal intervals, one from the summer to the winter solstice, and another back to the summer solstice. According to Theon, he found that these intervals are "always unequal," probably by assigning each interval an integral number of days. Both reports also imply that Eudemus considered his figures at least roughly accurate. In Thales' day, the interval from the summer to the winter solstice was shorter by about four and a half days, and the first attested figures, from Euctemon c. 430, record a difference of five days.[18] But whatever Thales supposed the difference to be, for him to find that the intervals differed at all would have required careful and sustained observation. Even if his results were inaccurate, or their accuracy influenced by luck, he was unlikely to accept such asymmetry without compelling evidence. Or is this scenario again a reason to distrust Eudemus?

Much of what the ancient sources say about Thales—some would say all—has the air of legend. But in this case, there is strong circumstantial evidence that Thales did what Eudemus claims. By Eudemus's time, Greek astronomy had developed a precise technical concept of the solstices in terms of the sun's annual motion along the circle of the ecliptic. But we should not assume that he attributed the same concept to Thales. On the contrary, he was alert to the primitive form of Thales' geometrical insights (frs. 133–35 = A11, 20), and he was certainly familiar with the archaic method of determining the solstices by watching the horizon, which remained the popular custom in his own day and for centuries afterward. That custom is also reflected in the Greek name for the solstices and echoed by the modern label "tropics": the sun's *tropai* or "turnings" were estimated by watching the daily progress of sunrise or sunset along the horizon to find when the sun reaches the northernmost and southernmost points on the horizon before "turning" back in the opposite direction.[19] But if Thales used the traditional methods of horizontal astronomy, how could he "discover" anything, as Eudemus claimed?

No results were very precise; all were measured only in days. Nor were any very accurate, at least initially. Dates for both solstices appear already in Hesiod, each as a round number of days before similar sightings of the star Arcturus rising or setting on the horizon at dawn or dusk: 60 days before its evening rising (the first day it is visible on the eastern horizon after sunset) for the winter solstice (*Op.* 564–67), and 50 days before its morning rising (the first day it is visible on the eastern horizon before sunrise) for summer (663–65). It is impossible to correlate any of these dates with a modern calendar, since we know nothing about their origin, either when or where any of the phenomena might have been observed. But according to similar data from the fifth and fourth centuries, the margin of error was considerable (10 or more days), as the round figures anyway suggest.[20] Nonetheless, Hesiod's dates are instructive. They confirm that Thales was not the first either to "discover" or to "predict" the solstices in the sense of being the first to assign them dates in a calendrical scheme. What Eudemus attributed to Thales must rather be a significant advance in accuracy or precision. Another report in Diogenes Laertius credits him with both in connection with items 4 and 5: "they say he both discovered the seasons of the year and divided it into 365 days" (1.27). Although Diogenes names no source, related evidence supports the presumption that his report again comes from Eudemus.[21] More to the point, Thales' measurement of the year is not only more accurate than any other estimate attested for sixth-century Greece (360 days is the next best recorded). It is also more precise, exact for an integral number of days.

Establishing temporal intervals between regularly recurring events is certainly a form of measurement. It also provides a reliable basis for prediction, provided of course that the events are genuinely periodic and the intervals accurately measured. So if Thales did "discover" the solstitial intervals, as Theon puts it, then he was clearly able to "predict the solstices" as Diogenes reports. Neither his discovery nor his predictions presuppose either an accurate method of observing the true solstices or any notion of orbital motion, the ecliptic, or any celestial mechanics at all. All Thales required was a method of calculating, in advance and roughly accurately from year to year, the dates of events that are regularly correlated with the true solstices, even if only loosely or tangentially. In particular, even if the apparent horizon for his observations differed dramatically from the true horizon, finding the "turning" points in the sun's annual progress along the apparent horizon would be sufficient, provided that his horizon remained relatively constant year after year. In fact, even if all of his dates were off by many days, most "predictions" based on them would still be reliable so long as the errors were systematic or constant. Likewise, recognition of a solar anomaly (as the inequality of the seasonal intervals was later named) did not require accurate determination of the true solstices, only consistently different intervals between the correlated phenomena. On the other hand, since Eudemus credited Thales with "discovering" that inequality, his dates were presumably accurate enough to identify correctly which of the two solstitial intervals was longer. In any case, how did Thales define his dates, whether accurately or not, for these and other astronomical phenomena?

The same report that credits Thales with determining the correct number of days in a year (item 5) also credits him with "discovering the seasons of the year" (item 4, in D.L. 1.27). The definite articles are doubly significant. They imply that he was the first to distinguish the four seasons later considered standard, but not attested before him; and since those seasons were defined as the periods between the solstices and equinoxes, it also implies that he was the first to specify days for the latter as well. How Thales did so is not explained in any extant text, and some scholars have found the claim hard to swallow.[22] But related testimony about his star-watching provides clues both to the methods he probably used and to the likely basis for Eudemus's reports. A report about a prominent cluster of stars in the Roman encyclopedist Pliny (60s or 70s CE) is the crucial link (items 3 and 8, in NH 18.213 = A18): "The morning setting of the Pleiades Hesiod recorded (in the Astronomy extant under his name) as occurring on the autumnal equinox, Thales on the twenty-fifth day after the equinox, Anaximander on the twenty-ninth, Euctemon <on the forty-fourth, Eudoxus> on the forty-eighth."[23]

The basis for these stellar dates was standard horizontal astronomy: observation of stars on the horizon at dawn and dusk. Whether the equinoxes were determined the same way is unclear: perhaps by the Hesiodic source, perhaps also by Thales, but probably not by Euctemon or Eudoxus. Nonetheless, the method of dating is the same in every case: the equinox is correlated with a stellar event and assigned a stellar date, expressed as an integral number of days before a stellar sighting. The Pleiades (item 8) were the single most important group of stars for traditional Greek calendars, because their rising and setting jointly bisected the year for practical purposes. In that regard, dates for solar phenomena were otiose. Yet solar dates do have greater explanatory value: not to signal agricultural chores or changes in weather or daylight, but to correlate the gradual seasonal changes with the celestial body whose annual cycle so obviously affects them.[24] The significance of equinoctial dates (item 3) should not be exaggerated. By itself, the correlation of solar events with stellar sightings does not presuppose any celestial mechanics. It only links the progress of the sun along the horizon to the length of the day and the cycle of the seasons. But that link does identify a causal factor for the seasonal changes, and since the correlation is regular, it offers a way to measure the solar or "tropical" year directly, by counting the days between equinoxes. Or rather, it would provide a direct measure if those could be determined independently of the stars. But that is very difficult solely by means of horizontal astronomy. Should Pliny's report therefore be dismissed?

Pliny does not identify his source for this information, and Eudemus is named nowhere in his work. But whatever his immediate source, the equinoctial dates he reports for Thales and the others evidently come from a collection of observational data compiled in the fourth century, since Eudoxus is the latest authority cited. Pliny names over a dozen Greek astronomers as his sources for Book 18 alone (*NH* 1.18). Many of them produced calendars integrating stellar and solar dates, including Meton, Euctemon, and Democritus in the fifth century, and Eudoxus and Callippus in the fourth. Those five also appear in extant reports from Eudemus, who clearly had studied their work closely.[25] Moreover, three extant calendars from the following centuries are "variorum" collections, and they incorporate data from the same five early authorities, even when their dates appear to conflict, as they do in this case.[26] If any of the earlier works did the same, then it may be the source for the two Milesians' dates. Or were their dates recorded in a systematic timetable of their own?

That either Thales or Anaximander compiled a comprehensive astronomical calendar is only a conjecture, but it rests on strong circumstantial evidence. Anaximander reportedly erected a "gnomon" in Sparta that indicated the solstices, the equinox, and the seasons (D.L. 2.1; cf. A2, A4).[27] How exactly it did so is nowhere explained. A gnomon is simply a vertical rod or marker situated to cast a shadow that tracks the movement of the sun through the day and over the year. Gnomons were typically fixed in a horizontal surface that was marked to indicate where the sun's shadow falls at various times of year. Given the continuing prominence of stellar dates, it would be strange if Anaximander's device did not indicate some of those as well, either by indicating where the sun's shadow would fall on those dates, or by providing a way to register the days between indicated dates, such as the rows of holes that gave later *parapegmata* their name. Moreover, any such system presupposes sustained observation, and not only in Sparta. It is therefore very likely that a prototype had been previously constructed in Miletus.[28] But unless Anaximander outlived Thales by more than the year or so reported by ancient chronographers, or they worked completely independently, his calendar had to incorporate intervals established (singly or jointly) by his older compatriot.[29] In any case, the textual transmission of Thales' stellar and solar dates could well go back to an astronomical calendar inscribed in stone or some other durable material, though perhaps one widely ascribed rather to his younger "friend," "student," and intellectual "heir," as Anaximander is regularly labeled.[30]

Evidence that Thales utilized traditional horizontal astronomy to track time through the year is relatively abundant and entirely consistent. An interest in precise observation is implied by a report (item 9) that he distinguished two stars in the Hyades, one northern and one southern (*Sch. Arat.* 172 = B2).[31] The constellation was widely considered an important seasonal weather sign, and in line with the popular interpretation of its name as "Rain-Maidens" (see *Sch. Arat.* 171, Cic. *ND* 2.111), its morning setting (the last day it is visible above the western horizon before sunrise) was supposed to signal the advent of the rainy season in the Aegean (see Hesiod *Op.* 615). But as the collective name implies, tradition assigned multiple stars to the Hyades, and some are so far apart that their risings and settings span many days. In fact, the constellation is better known now as the head of

Taurus, and the rising and setting of its several stars spans two to three weeks. The obvious reason for Thales to single out two of these stars was to refine earlier observations by establishing the interval between sightings of two readily visible but significantly distant stars. Finally, there is even reason to suppose that Eudemus made such claims himself. The now standard name of Taurus is first attested in Greek for Eudoxus in the mid–fourth century, and systematic observations of its several stars first for Callippus c. 330. But Eudoxus continued to record data for the Hyades under their traditional name, whereas Callippus evidently used only the new name, and he did so in the course of establishing a new astronomical calendar based on a zodiacal system that his contemporary Eudemus would have considered definitive. It is reasonable to assume that Eudemus discussed these important recent innovations, as he did Callippus's refinements of Eudoxus's celestial mechanics (frs. 148–49). In the latter case, he also recounted the relevant observational data and its fifth-century background (fr. 149). It would thus be fully in keeping with his attested practice if he also cited Thales in connection with Callippus's calendrical reforms, just as he included the Milesian background in his account of Oenopides' study of the ecliptic and its obliquity (fr. 145, quoted earlier).

Similar use of horizontal astronomy to measure predictable annual cycles underlies two other reports. One figures in an explanation for the annual flooding of the Nile reported by Herodotus (item 11), perhaps drawing on Hecataeus, whose account he also reports.[32] According to Herodotus, some of those "famous for wisdom" attributed the floods to seasonal winds from the north impeding the river's course (2.20); and though he fails to name Thales, late sources ascribe the explanation to the renowned "sage" (D.L. 1.37, Aët. 4.1.1). The winds in question are the so-called Etesian or "annual" northerlies, whose onset was traditionally tied to the summer solstice (Hesiod Op. 663–72), concurrent with the onset of the flood (Hdt. 2.19). They were also supposed to last 50 days (followed by stormy southern winds, Op. 673–77), which presumably served to explain why the flood lasted 100 days, since it took an equal number of days to subside (Hdt. 2.19). Hence the explanation attributed to Thales presupposes a periodic annual timetable that correlated solar and seasonal cycles and provided a framework for him to calculate the intervals between regularly recurring phenomena—in short, the same sort of astronomical calendar implicit in other reports from Eudemus.

The other report, a well-known anecdote in Aristotle (item 12), does not refer explicitly to solar or stellar dates, and it is often dismissed as popular legend. Historicity aside, there is little doubt that Eudemus was familiar with the story.[33] According to Aristotle, who recounts it to illustrate the principle of monopoly, Thales silenced critics of his "philosophical" pursuits by renting all the olive presses in the region one winter, then making a handsome profit by charging higher rates for their use when the harvest arrived (Pol. 1.11 1259a9–18). So summarized, the story has little obvious connection with philosophy, as Aristotle emphasizes in opposition to his anonymous sources for the legend (a3–9, a18–21). But he introduces the story with a puzzling detail, which was also part of the legend, that it was "by astronomy they say he recognized that an olive harvest was coming" (a10–11). It hardly takes a Thales, of course, to tell that olive trees bear fruit, and translators have long assumed that it was specifically a bumper crop that he was supposed to have used astro-meteorology to forecast. After all, olive growers had long used various seasonal signs, perhaps including stellar or solar intervals, to guide their cultivation. On the other hand, if Thales had a more precise and reliable astronomical timetable, he could outwit the owners of the presses on the terms for rent by estimating the time to harvest more precisely—hence the special significance of arranging the contract in winter, far in advance—and without the unsavory prospect of gouging the growers.[34]

One other report (item 10) provides an exception that may prove the rule. Not long after Eudemus, the learned poet Callimachus (writing c. 270 BCE) credits Thales with "measuring" the constellation "the little Wagon" (fr. 191.54–55), as Ursa Minor was commonly called. Since the claim appears elsewhere in the context of other claims made by Eudemus (A3), Callimachus probably knew it through Eudemus's work on early astronomy rather than the verses of the *Nautical Astronomy* ascribed to Phocus.[35] He adds that Phoenician navigators relied on the constellation; and the contemporary poet Aratus, who dressed Eudoxus's stellar catalogue in hexameters, explains that the smaller Bear is more reliable for navigation than the more readily visible Ursa Major because it turns in a smaller circle (*Phaen.* 26–44). In short, it is a circumpolar constellation, and in Mediterranean latitudes, it never sets. On the one hand, that makes it a striking exception to Thales' evident reliance on horizontal astronomy. On the other hand, it illustrates how closely most attention was focused on stars at the horizon.

A reasonably wide range of testimony indicates that Thales compiled some sort of timetable correlating solar and stellar phenomena. How he established dates for the solstices and equinoxes remains unclear. The best anyone could do in the sixth century was to situate them within a framework of stellar dates by counting the days between them and previously established stellar risings or settings, as Pliny reports, and as applied astronomy continued to do for centuries. But how Thales determined the day of any solar event in the first place we can only conjecture. Since interest in the solstices predates him, we might suppose that he first tried to establish their dates more precisely. But a problem recognized some time later makes that difficult to do accurately: the sun's position on the horizon changes very slowly at its northern and southern extremes, and for several days, it appears to remain stationary (Cleom. 1.4). By contrast, its position changes most rapidly—hence most visibly—at the equinoxes. If he first established dates for those, not by horizontal astronomy but by using some sort of gnomon, he could then assign artificial dates to the solstices by simply dividing the intervals between the two equinoxes. But that method would presumably eliminate the solar anomaly, which Eudemus claimed Thales discovered (fr. 145). On balance, then, it appears more likely—or so it would have appeared to Eudemus—that Thales began by establishing dates for the solstices, and that he did so by observing the horizon. The simplest method involves two steps: first defining points on the horizon where the sun is observed to reach its northernmost and southernmost limits; and then, for each solstice, singling out one of the days the sun was observed there, either the first, or perhaps more likely (since each marked a "turning" point in the sun's annual course) the last, or perhaps most likely (if the equinoxes were then determined the same way) one midway between the apparent first and last days. The result would inevitably be somewhat artificial, and almost certainly inaccurate for the true solstices. But it would be consistent with horizontal astronomy, and it would be sufficient to establish a solar anomaly, as well as the number of days in the tropical year (item 5) and the intervals that became the four conventional seasons (item 4).

Two remaining claims concerning the moon bring us back to solar eclipses. Immediately after reporting that Thales discovered the intervals between solstices, Diogenes Laertius credits him with two more "firsts" in astronomy (1.24), for both of which Eudemus is again the likely source. The first specifies a ratio of exactly 1 to 720 involving the moon and sun (item 7), though the text is too elliptical or corrupt to tell what the ratio relates: sizes, distances, circuits, or periods.[36] The second claims that Thales was "the first to call the last day of the month a thirtieth" (item 6). The lunar cycle was the main way of tracking time in archaic Greece, for civic and household affairs alike, and its mean period is roughly 29½ days. Although explicit testimony is lacking, it is reasonable to assume that the resulting problem of integrating months and days was widely recognized, even if only by officials charged with regulating the numerous local calendars. The point of Thales' proposal was presumably not to assign 30 days to every month, which would quickly wreak havoc on lunar calendars. Much more likely, since Diogenes implies that the proposal was widely adopted, Thales' aim was to regularize the monthly discrepancies by labeling the last day of every month the "thirtieth" no matter how many days passed between successive sightings of a new crescent, which custom counted as the first day of the month. The effect of his proposal was to establish a pattern of alternating "full" and "hollow" months, as the periods of 30 and 29 days came to be called, though the origin of that system and its labels is obscure.[37] The key point, however, is reasonably secure, that Thales introduced a method for tracking the lunar cycle more reliably by counting days rather than by watching each month for the new moon. The novelty in calling the last day a "thirtieth" apparently lay in his artificial extension of the label to cover the last day of every month, full and hollow alike. That violated the literal sense of the word, but it produced a more regular way to measure time. The substitution of a numerical figure for traditional labels like "day before" or "old and new" was also more perspicuous and marginally more precise.

The system of full and hollow months, while simplifying the task of tracking the phases of the moon, presupposes close observation of the new moon in particular. That in turn provides a secure link to horizontal astronomy, and a tantalizing clue to Thales' insight into solar eclipses. Both solar eclipses and lunar phases appear typically and most readily in the sky overhead. The moon, through most of its monthly cycle, is plainly visible in the sky for progressively longer and shorter portions of the night or day as it alternately waxes and wanes. Only when one cycle ends and another begins is attention necessarily focused exclusively on the horizon. As the old moon wanes, its crescent becomes too thin to discern as it rises ahead of the sun at dawn and sets before sunset; then, two or three days later, after the sun "passes" it, the first reappearance of its crescent on the western horizon after sunset marks the beginning of a new cycle. Accordingly, the first day of each month was called "new moon"—not the day when no moon is visible, as we say today, but the day when the new crescent was first discerned. Since the true conjunction of moon and sun occurs in the interval between sightings of the last and first crescents, these observations provide an obvious context for insight into solar eclipses. The interest in precisely this period shown by Thales' proposal for naming the last day of each month raises an intriguing possibility. Did Thales discover that solar eclipses occur only at the new moon? Or rather, is that what Eudemus claimed he discovered? A recently recovered papyrus written in the second century CE preserves part of a commentary on the *Odyssey* that contains a passage that strongly suggests he did (*POxy* 3710 col. 2.36–43):

> That eclipses occur at new moon Aristarchus of Samos makes clear when he writes, "And Thales said [AS1] the sun eclipses when the moon has come in front of it, . . . [AS2] the day on which it produces the eclipse, which some call the 'thirtieth,' others 'new moon.' "[38]

The commentator's report is prompted by mention of a feast in *Odyssey* 20.156, which ancient scholarship tied to both a new moon (see 19.307 with *Sch.*) and an eclipse (see 20.356–57 with *Sch.*). To explain the connection between these events, the commentator quotes the famous astronomer Aristarchus. A student of Strato (Aët. 1.15.5), he was active shortly after Eudemus, and he tackled nearly every astronomical problem Eudemus is reported to have addressed: solar eclipses (frs. 143–45) and correlations of the lunar and solar cycles (fr. 147), as seen here; observations to date the solstices (frs. 144–45) in 280 BCE (Ptol. *Alm.* 3.1); the sizes and distances of the sun and moon (fr. 146) in his extant work of that title; and the regularity of planetary motions (frs. 148–49) in his notorious heliocentric hypothesis (Archim. *Aren.* 1.4–5). He thus had excellent opportunity and motive to study Eudemus's work on earlier astronomy, and the evidence that he did so is about as strong as we could hope. The immediate source of his claim about Thales, then, is almost certainly Eudemus. But exactly what insight did Aristarchus follow Eudemus in ascribing to Thales?

The commentator purports to quote Aristarchus's own words. If true, that leaves little room for distortion and warrants taking his words strictly. So construed, what Aristarchus imputes to Thales is not a systematic explanation of solar eclipses but only what appears to be an inference, based on the correlation with new moon, that the proximate cause is the moon's interposition ("coming in front"). Two points deserve emphasis. First, the causal claim in AS1 is described very simply, without any technical terminology or allusions to celestial mechanics. For all Aristarchus says here, the sun and moon could be circulating bowls (cf. Heraclitus A12) or floating discs (cf. Anaximenes A7.4, A15) or apertures in fiery rings (cf. Anaximander A18, A21–22). Moreover, the further report in AS2, that

Thales recognized a regular correlation, is entirely credible. Eudemus may have had equally good—or bad—evidence for ascribing both claims to Thales, or he may have considered the causal claim secure and adduced the correlation only as a conjecture about its observational basis. But in the context of horizontal astronomy, the converse is more likely, that Thales—or others—first noticed that one or more eclipses occurred at new moon, and then inferred that they occurred only at new moon. Moreover, it is the correlation and not the causal claim that suits the reports of Thales "predicting" one or more eclipses. Knowing only that "the sun eclipses when the moon comes in front of it" would be useless for telling when an eclipse might occur, unless he could also predict when the moon might do so. Only if he considered the correlation of lunar and solar cycles regular could he isolate the days when an eclipse could or could not occur. But if he could do that, then he could thereby predict them, in the limited sense that he could forecast for any day in the not too distant future whether or not an eclipse was possible. In fact, the only limit on the range of his forecasts would be the reliability of his lunar calendar, which depended on the accuracy of his projections of the lunar cycle.[39]

According to Theon, Eudemus credited Thales with "first discovering a solar eclipse" (fr. 145). Although "discovery" suits both claims cited by Aristarchus, the singular "eclipse" points to a prediction, hence the correlation. According to Diogenes Laertius, Eudemus was the "first to predict solar eclipses" (fr. 144), and both the verb and the plural again favor the correlation. We can no longer be sure what Eudemus did ascribe to Thales. But the evidence now available makes a general correlation more likely than either a full explanation or a specific prediction. The most famous predictions of the era were oracular, and their logical form was typically conditional. In a famous case near the end of Thales' life, Delphi warned Croesus of Lydia that if he attacked the Persians, a great kingdom would be destroyed (Hdt. 1.53). The correlation of solar eclipses with the new moon has a very similar form: the sun eclipses when the moon is new; or more precisely, if the moon is new, a solar eclipse is possible. Such a claim made early in the sixth century and vindicated in 585 would readily inspire the story that Thales "foretold" an eclipse, especially one synchronized (accurately or not) with a famous battle. Thales could have based his claim on observation of previous eclipses; as many as nine were visible in Miletus over the preceding 25 years.[40] Alternatively, that eclipse may itself have been the decisive evidence for his claim. Noticing that it coincided with a new moon, he could simply infer a correlation, which oral reports would easily distort into a prediction and link to a famous battle. Either scenario suits Herodotus's story that he foretold "the year in which" an eclipse occurred (1.74). In either case, oral transmission would transform the date of Thales predicting a type of event into a prediction of a single dated event; and the basis for the amazing legend of his predicting that an eclipse would occur in the year one did occur would be his declaration in that year that eclipses occur only at the same predictable phase of the lunar cycle.[41]

My reconstruction of Thales' discovery is necessarily conjectural. But it has two distinct merits. First, it harmonizes the conflicting testimony, since a generalized correlation combines elements of both prediction and explanation. On one hand, the correlation is weakly predictive, since it defines a necessary condition that isolates a limited number of days—roughly 1 in 30, or a dozen or so a year— and conjoins them in a universal disjunction. On the other hand, the correlation opens the door to an explanation by isolating what turns out to be a crucial causal factor. But my proposal does more than restore sense to conflicting reports. It also ties an otherwise dubious legend to the traditional methods of horizontal astronomy evident in other testimony about Thales. No new method of observation, no influx of data from foreign sources, no novel cosmological model was necessary to discern the concurrence of solar eclipses and new moon, only habitual observation of the horizon at dawn and dusk.

The title of the poem that some ascribed to Thales is instructive. By the fourth century, when the title may have originated, "nautical astrology" referred specifically to the traditional lore of stellar cycles and intervals, in contrast to the systematic celestial mechanics called "mathematical astrology" (Arist. *APo.* 1.13 78b35–79a6). For Eudemus as well, Thales exemplified the kind of old-fashioned "astrology" described by Plato in *Republic* 7. Primarily a method for gauging time (and to a lesser extent direction), it was considered "useful not only for farming and sailing but also for military command" because it made one "better able to perceive seasons, months, and years" (527d; cf. 522c–e, 526d). Those temporal "symmetries"—the integrated measurement of "night and day, of days and months, of months and years, and of stars in relation both to those and themselves" (530a–b)—encapsulate what Thales "discovered," from the Hyades and Pleiades to solstices and eclipses. Cosmology awaited the next generation. It is probably no accident of fate that we have no firm evidence that Thales proposed any model of the cosmos. Aristotle's report that he claimed that the land (or earth) stays aloft like wood floating on water (A14 in *Cael.* 2.13; cf. A12 in *Metaph.* 1.3) has minimal implications for a celestial superstructure. By all reliable accounts, it was rather his "friend" and "heir" who first envisioned the world as a vast mechanical system centered on the earth and bounded by the sun—in short, the prototype of the classical solar system.

2. ANAXIMANDER AND THE DIMENSIONS OF SPACE

The impact of Thales' astronomical timetelling reverberates in Anaximander's sole surviving pronouncement, that the world operates "according to the order of time" (fr. 1 = Simp. *in Ph.* 24.20; cf. Anaximenes A11). The bewildering variety of changes occurring all around us, he claimed for the first time on record, follows regular patterns. Thales had also found new ways to calculate large linear dimensions, such as the distance of boats at sea (A20) and the height of pyramids in

Egypt (A21).[42] Anaximander extended his inquiry to the world itself. Building on the newly established celestial order of time, he ventured to articulate the physical structure of the entire cosmos, complete with linear dimensions for its most prominent visible parts.

A systematic model of the cosmos was evidently an innovation. Earlier accounts, though vividly detailed at points, are fundamentally incomplete. Implicit in Homer and Hesiod is a three-tier model consisting of a terrestrial platform encircled by the fresh waters of Ocean and situated between Ouranos overhead and Tartaros below. How the three tiers are connected, if indeed they are, is obscure, as are the shape and size of each. The picture is fuzzy in part because it has no definite scale or boundaries. The earth remains an indeterminate landmass, and topographical relations, whether local or regional, are almost completely ignored. Distances are rare and measured only in time.[43] By contrast, Anaximander proposed determinate boundaries for both terrestrial and celestial realms, and he defined a uniform linear scale to measure both the whole and its parts. The result was both more systematic and more exact and it was based on new observations. Not only did he refine Thales' astronomical timetable: witness the Pleiades (A20) and the gnomon (A1–2, A4); he also postulated distinct physical structures for each of the three celestial systems he and Thales studied.

Anaximander's cosmos contains four main bodies. At the center, stationary and shaped like a drum or segment of a stone column (A10, A11, A25), is the earth. Encircling it are three successively larger rings of fire shrouded in mist: the closest for the stars, then another for the moon, and the outermost for the sun (A10, A11, A18). These rings are like "chariot wheels" (A21, A22), with "vents" or "mouths" on their inner rims through which the enclosed fire emits a "pipe" or beam of light (A21, A22).[44] The phases of the moon result from the gradual blocking and unblocking of its vents, and eclipses occur when the solar or lunar vents are blocked abruptly (A11, A21, A22). Its simplicity and mundane imagery notwithstanding, the model has momentous implications. First, and probably most striking at the time, it is effectively comprehensive, encompassing all visible objects in the sky.[45] This is all the more striking in light of Anaximander's distinctive emphasis on the "unlimited" nature of the world and its contents, even if he meant not that it is infinitely extended but only indefinitely large—only that the region beyond the outer wheel of the sun has no determinate shape or size.[46] In any case, his solar system is evidently self-sufficient, not only internally self-sustaining (through cycles of evaporation and storms) but apparently also both self-destructive and self-regenerating, without any intervention by external forces.[47]

Anaximander's use of rings has dramatic implications for astronomy. Where all we see are luminous shapes moving across the sky, he postulated immense but invisible circular rings. The rationale for his postulate, though nowhere explicitly stated in our meager sources, is readily inferred: the rings provide a mechanical basis for the observed motions by holding the luminaries aloft in orbital cycles, keeping their distances from earth constant, and generating their apparent movements by revolving around the earth at the center. Further, these wheels precisely specify the form of the celestial motions, and more simply than cylinders or spheres would: the luminaries appear to spin around the earth like wheels around a common stationary hub. But if the celestial wheels characterize motion as well as shape—not only circles but revolutions—then the wheels may be narrow or broad, either thin rings or wide-rimmed cylinders. Or there may be both: narrow hoops for the sun and moon but an elongated pipe or tube for the panoply of stars.[48]

The rings also generate regular periodic motion. Circles are inherently uniform and regular. Circular motion around a stationary center is therefore spatially uniform: every point on a ring maintains the same distance not only from the center but also from every other point on the ring. That in turn provides a physical basis for temporal regularity. To observers stationed at the center, any point or segment on a ring that turns at constant angular velocity will also *appear* to move with constant linear velocity. Anaximander's hypothesis of geocentric rings thus provides a physical basis for the periodic cycles he and Thales established. On the additional hypothesis that each ring maintains a constant angular velocity, the apparent motions of the sun, moon, and stars are a mechanical consequence of their physical movement though space. In short, the model builds regularity into the very structure of the cosmos, and it does so on the basis of numerically quantified observational data—both for the first time on record.

Closely related to these structural regularities is a principle of equilibrium. Although we cannot be sure that Anaximander designed his system with this principle in view, its impact on later thought was lasting and profound. According to Aristotle, the earth "remains" at the center "because of similarity" (*Cael.* 2.13 295b11–16 = A26). Theophrastus evidently reported the same (Hippol. 1.6.3 = A11), and Eudemus probably did so as well (fr. 145).[49] Moving beyond Thales' simple analogy of wood floating on water, Anaximander ventured a bold hypothesis that dismisses traditional appeals to homely images in favor of an abstract principle of sufficient reason. Where others, assuming that an obviously large and heavy object like the earth would have to fall, wondered what prevents it from plunging downward, he effectively turned the question on its head. Adopting a cosmic perspective, he asked instead what would make it move in any one direction rather than another, if its surroundings are in every direction the same. The nub of his argument is not that the earth (or anything else) is naturally or inherently stationary and inert, hence moves only under the influence of external forces. Rather, without any assumptions about immobility or inertia, he appears to rely on the principle that any change in motion—at least in direction and perhaps also in speed—requires an initiating force or cause. Absent such forces, the cosmos is in *dynamic* equilibrium, and the earth remains at the center even if it otherwise has some inherent tendency to fall.[50] So construed, Anaximander's case turns primarily on the earth's position, not its shape or weight or any other feature. Moreover, it establishes only that the earth "stays" (*menei*) or "lies" (*keitai*) at the center of the solar system, not that it "stands" (*histatai*) there still and immobile. His theory is thus compatible with some terrestrial motion, though presumably nothing large or sudden enough for us to notice—except when we do notice movement, as in earthquakes. The equilibrium hypothesis, while duly hailed as a brilliant stroke of abstract reasoning, is in that regard also consistent with observation and responsive to new empirical data.

Anaximander's cosmos has both regularity and stability built into it. It also exhibits some striking symmetries, probably not coincidentally. According to Eudemus (fr. 146), he was the first to specify sizes and distances for the heavenly bodies (Simp. *In Cael.* 471.1–9 = A19), and other sources report specific figures. The figures vary slightly in one case, and their interpretation is controversial.[51] But discrepancies aside, the specification of spatial dimensions for the model was itself a major innovation. Unlike folklore and poetry, which measured large distances only in time, Anaximander proposed a uniform linear metric for the entire cosmos. Unfortunately, the sources do not make it entirely clear what dimensions are involved:

E1. "In shape the earth is cylindrical, and it has as much depth as a third would be to its breadth": [Plu.] *Strom.* 2 (A10).

E2. "The sun is equal to the earth": Aët. 2.21.1 (A21); cf. "not smaller": D.L. 2.1.

E3. The sun has a "circle 27 times larger than the earth": Hippol. 1.6.5 (A11), Aët. 2.21.1 (A21); or "28 times larger": Aët. 2.20.1 (A21).[52]

E4. The moon has a "circle 19 times larger than the earth": Aët. 2.25.1 (A22).

The first point to note is that all magnitudes are specified in terms of the earth (hence the label E). In particular, E2–4 take the earth as a basic module or unit of measure, not unlike the modern use of the earth's mean distance from the sun as a basic "astronomical unit" (AU). But E2–4 refer only vaguely to "the earth" without specifying which dimension is used, and that leaves unclear both what serves as Anaximander's AU and what it measures. What dimensions of the solar and lunar rings—radius, diameter, width, depth, circumference, area, or what—are multiples of what dimension of the earth?

Two of the earth's dimensions are given in E1, one in terms of the other: the depth of its cylindrical drum is expressed as a fraction of its breadth, not vice versa, its breadth as a multiple of its depth. Moreover, the Greek term for "breadth" (*platos*) implies that the dimension in question is the "flat" diameter of its cylinder's face or surface (cf. Hippol. 1.6.3 = A11). If the same dimension figures also in the other reports, then Anaximander's basic module or AU is not only linear, as we would anyway expect, but also rectilinear and specifically diametric. In fact, both magnitudes given in E1—"depth" as well as "breadth"—are clearly transverse, as the Greek term "diameter" (literally "measure across") would imply. Finally, the factor of 3 recurs for the sun in E3, and it would also recur for the moon in E4 if 19 were to a missing 18 as 28 is to 27 in E3. Is such symmetry a sign that E2–4 also refer to diameters? More generally, is there any indication that Anaximander's figures had any observational basis? Or is the apparent symmetry purely arbitrary?

Only E1 specifies any dimensions. All three other reports express ratios between pairs of objects: the earth and the sun in E2, or the earth and the celestial rings of the sun and moon in E3 and E4. Since the relevant dimension of the earth is its surface diameter, are the other terms in each case also diameters? In E2, "the sun" presumably refers to the shining disk visible in the daytime sky, not to the invisible ring or wheel that carries the disk around as it turns. For in Anaximander's system, the sun is simply the bright fire seen through a vent on the inner rim of the solar ring. But then the point of comparison in E2 must be the circular face, which is the only feature the two terms of the ratio share; and in that case, it seems safe to assume that the equality is primarily diametric. In short, E2 claims that the diameters of the earth's surface and the sun's visible disk are equal, hence each is 1 AU across. Of course, that implies equality also in radius, circumference, and area; but as in E1 as well, the focus is evidently on the diameters. Do E3 and E4 also specify ratios of diameters?

Both E1 and E2 take the earth's diameter as basic, and E2 relates that to the diameter of another continuous area, the disk of the solar vent. If Anaximander measured the rings the same way, then E3 and E4 relate the earth's diameter to the sun's and moon's diameters. But Eudemus credited Anaximander with "first discovering the theory of sizes and distances" (fr. 146 = A19).[53] If the figures in E3 and E4 are for diameters, then the distances must be either radii or segments of them. To find the distances, we first have to specify a terminus on earth from which to measure. If the distances are measured from the center of the earth, they are simply the radius R of each ring, or half their diameters D. But if the distances are measured from the edge of the earth, then a portion of the earth's diameter—from one-half, measured along the horizon (HD), to one-sixth, measured vertically (VD)—must first be subtracted. The results are problematic, as table 3.1 shows.

An obvious problem is that only integers are recorded, and no option preserves integral values for all four dimensions. The obvious solution is to eliminate fractional dimensions. In any case, the figures for vertical distance have little to commend them. Anaximander was thought (whether rightly or not) to know that the daily paths of the sun and moon through the sky lie "aslant" (A22, cf. A5), hence never reach verticality, which is true for Greece and would hold everywhere if the earth were flat, as he supposed it to be.[54] Moreover, determining distances at

Table 3.1 Celestial Magnitudes

	D	R	HD	VD
Solar ring	<u>28</u>	14	13.5	13 5/6
	<u>27</u>	13.5	13	13 1/3
Lunar ring	<u>19</u>	9.5	9	9 1/3
	18	9	8.5	8 5/6
Stellar ring	10	5	4.5	4 5/6
	9	4.5	4	4 1/3

D = diameter; R = radius; HD = horizontal distance from earth; VD = vertical distance from earth; all figures are AU ("astronomical unit" = surface diameter of the earth). Only the three figures underlined are attested (see items E3-4 in the text); other values of D are conjectural (but see note 47 here), and all other figures are functions of D.

any other angle than horizontal would generate unwieldy fractions or irrationals. Hence the only plausible alternative is distance along the horizon. That orientation also yields the only pairs of integral values. Despite his reported use of the gnomon, Anaximander's figures remain fully consistent with "horizontal astronomy." Horizontal distance is also the natural dimension to depict in a survey map or plan. But which pairs of integers are authentic? Distances measured from the middle of the earth: radius $R = 14$, 9, 5? Or distances measured horizontally from its edge: $HD = 13$, 9, 4?[55] Only one diameter in the first set is attested, and only once—the solar ring's: 28. In the second set, two diameters are attested, and one in two different sources—the solar ring's: 27; and the lunar ring's: 19. The latter is better attested. It is also more in line with horizontal astronomy, since the outer edge of the earth marks the only true horizon in Anaximander's cosmos.

The basis for Anaximander's figures is puzzling. There is general scholarly consensus that they had no significant empirical basis, and a variety of alternative sources has been canvassed, spanning folklore, technology, and myth, including Near Eastern cosmogony.[56] It is certainly possible that the figures are entirely artificial, determined by abstract considerations of symmetry. In the context of Thales' astronomy, however, the possibility of an observational basis deserves another look. In conceiving so revolutionary a system, Anaximander must have considered its key components carefully, and complete disregard for accuracy seems inconsistent both with his other attested efforts in astronomy (including ongoing observation of stars and solar points: A20 with Thales A18, quoted earlier) and with the increasing role of exact measurement in archaic society, from architecture to reforms of weights and other measures. The only plausible rationale for adopting arbitrary figures would be inability to do better. But are there any positive signs of an empirical basis for the transmitted figures?

Eudemus apparently thought there were. After citing his report about Anaximander's sizes and distances (fr. 146), Simplicius immediately adds that "the sizes and distances of the sun and moon have been determined until now by starting from a grasp of their eclipses, and it was likely that Anaximander as well discovered these points" (*in Cael.* 471.6–8). Simplicius clearly adds the further historical claim on Eudemus's authority, not his own.[57] At the very least, he evidently thought Anaximander situated the moon's ring inside the sun's because of its role in solar eclipses. But did he have any reason to suppose there was any empirical basis for the specific figures Anaximander proposed? An alternative interpretation of the relevant testimony raises an intriguing possibility, which circumstantial evidence suggests Eudemus might have ascribed to him, though whether rightly or wrongly is impossible to say.

Anaximander envisioned the visible surfaces of the earth, sun, and moon as similarly round and flat. That is presumably why he measured their "size" by the diameters of their surfaces. But rings have a very different structure. Whereas diameters traverse the surface of a disc, they span the gap between opposite sections of a ring, and it would be odd to include the gap in their size. Moreover, they are essentially invisible. Only their vents have measurable size, and the only other relevant dimension is their distance, specifically the distance of their vents. In short, the figures for Anaximander's rings are more naturally interpreted as radial. That would also explain why the figures were transmitted in the first place: Eudemus included them in his account of Anaximander as the first to specify distances. In that case, the figures for the outer ring would have a straightforward observational basis, if two plausible conjectures be granted. One is that Anaximander used a ratio of 10 to 3 for circles (i.e., their circumferences) and their diameters (i.e., $pi = 3\ 1/3$).[58] If he did, his figures yield the results in table 3.2.

My other conjecture is that Anaximander took the ratio of the sun's diameter to its average daytime path through the sky to be 1 to 90, or 1 to 180 for its average total daily path (i.e., 2 degrees). In that case, one of the two attested figures for the solar ring is a consequence of his two assumptions: if a segment of 1 AU occupies one-ninetieth of a semicircle, then the entire circle is 180 AU, its diameter is 54 AU (three-tenths of 180), and its radius is 27 AU. That would give one, but only one, of the three attested figures a direct empirical basis. But the other two figures can be derived from it in two simple steps, provided the outermost ring is the sun's. Anaximander had three sets of phenomena to explain. Once he established the radius of the outermost ring, it would be natural to specify the size of the two others by dividing the greatest radius in thirds; hence R is 18 AU for the moon and and 9 AU for the stars. The resulting symmetry would then be a function in part of his data: three equal intervals, each a multiple of 9, simply to incorporate all three sets of phenomena. The other step, which in practice would naturally come first, would be to allow for a margin of error, either by rounding off the observational data or by setting upper and lower bounds, or both. In short, the other two figures attested would be alternative radii for the solar and lunar rings. In particular, the apparently conflicting figures of 27 and 28 for the solar ring would both be authentic, for example, the first a result of rounding down measurements slightly over 90 AU for the semicircle of the horizon, and the second an integral figure for a corresponding upper bound. That the figure 90 AU also yields a radius that is itself

Table 3.2. Celestial Distances

	H	R	D	C
Solar ring	27	28	56	186 2/3
	26	27	54	180
Lunar ring	18	19	38	126 2/3
	17	18	36	120
Stellar ring	9	10	20	66 2/3
	8	9	18	60

H = shortest distance from true horizon (outer edge of the earth's surface) to a visible disc; R = inner radius of a ring; D = inner diameter of a ring; C = inner circumference of a ring; all figures are AU ("astronomical unit" = surface diameter of the earth). Only underlined figures are attested (see items E3-4 in the text).

a multiple of three, just as required by the three sets of phenomena, would lend it further weight, both as apparent confirmation of and as further evidence for the impressively intricate "order of time" revealed by horizontal astronomy. But is there any reason to think that Anaximander tried to measure the sun in terms of the horizon in the first place, or even that Eudemus supposed he did?

On this scenario, Anaximander had to establish two related variables: the size of the sun, and the ratio of its size to its path. How he obtained either figure, or even if he did, we do not know. He could have stipulated either or both arbitrarily, or found one by observation of shadows. But horizontal astronomy offers a crude but simple way to measure the second, by observing sunrise and sunset at an equinox. Then, and only then, the sun sets diametrically opposite where it rises. It is difficult to measure arcs in the sky, especially "slant" arcs at shifting inclinations or angles to the horizon (attested in A5, A22), without instruments more sophisticated than anything attested for the sixth century. But on Anaximander's flat earth, the true horizon is truly a circle, and any half of it is therefore equivalent to the arc of the sun's path on the equinox. That makes it relatively easy to relate the width of the sun to a semicircle of the horizon by measuring the apparent width of the sun at the horizon (when fully risen at either sunrise or sunset), and then using that width to measure a semicircle of the horizon. For example, if the disk of a cup or plate held at arm's length covers the rising sun, then the disk can be used to measure the horizon by counting how many diameters of the cup or plate it spans. The results are bound to be wildly inaccurate, not least because the atmosphere makes the sun appear notably larger on the horizon than in the sky. But error can be minimized by fixing a rigid pointer at the center of an artificial horizon, such as a wheel laid flat or a cylindrical column drum, and then turning the pointer along the horizon like a dial. In any case, the substantial error in Anaximander's figures makes such worries moot. All that matters for the present scenario is whether such a procedure could account for his errors, or whether Eudemus could reasonably suppose they did.

Aristarchus, in his extant treatise on the same topic, establishes the sizes and distances of the same two luminaries on the basis of six simple hypotheses. Most of these presuppose principles of geometry or spherical astronomy that Eudemus ascribed to later theorists, and the first is a factual claim he ascribed to Anaxagoras (fr. 145).[59] But the sixth hypothesis has puzzled scholars as woefully outdated. It posits that "the moon subtends one-fifteenth of a zodiacal sign," or in more familiar terms, it has an angular diameter of 2 degrees. Not only is the figure roughly four times too large; a much more accurate figure is ascribed to Aristarchus by Archimedes (*Aren.* 1.10). More important here, the formulation in terms of zodiacal signs (defined as 12 equal arcs on the ecliptic) probably goes back only to the later fourth century, and Eudemus probably counted it among recent scientific discoveries.[60] But the basic idea was probably much older, and he might well have had evidence that the putative fact had been discovered much earlier, but expressed in cruder terms. In the first place, Aristarchus's second hypothesis is that "the earth has the ratio of a point or center to the sphere of the moon"; that simply formalizes an assumption implicit in Anaximander's figures if, as table 3.2 suggests,

he measured distances not from the edge of the earth but from its center. Moreover, Eudemus credited Thales with knowing how to gauge the distance of boats at
sea by some sort of triangulation (fr. 134 = Procl. *in Euc.* 1.26 in A20), and though
his method remains obscure, it obviously involved observation and indirect
measurement of remote objects on the horizon. Further, the figures that result on
this scenario produce appealing symmetry at yet another level: the ratios of the
sun's disk to the whole solar ring (1/180) and to its semicircle (1/90) would differ
from the radii of the two interior rings (18 AU and 9 AU) by the striking factor of
10. Finally, even the discrepancy in the figures reported for the sun can be explained
as margins of error. Aristarchus himself attempts to establish only boundaries, not
exact measures; for example, the distance and the diameter of the sun are between
18 and 20 times greater than the moon's. In much the same way, Anaximander's
two figures for the radius of the sun's ring (27 and 28), and presumably likewise for
the moon (18 and 19) and stars (9 and 10), could represent lower and upper bounds
for the calculations based on his imprecise observations.

Anaximander's most glaring error raises another intriguing possibility. The
sequence of his rings, while mistaken, is not blatantly inconsistent with anything
readily apparent to the naked eye. The moon's frequent occultation of stars is
hardly decisive, since their tiny lights can be obscured by passing in front of its
bright disk as well as behind it.[61] Yet it still is surprising that he did not make
distance inversely proportional to readily perceptible features, notably light and
heat: the stars faintest and devoid of radiant heat because most remote, the sun
brightest and hottest because so near.[62] Did Anaximander contravene so simple a
solution for no reason? His cosmogony, reflecting the obvious tendency of flames
to rise, affords a partial explanation, that the outer ring encloses the most fire. But
stellar fire is not only fainter; it emits no perceptible heat at all. A simple conjecture, and one we have already encountered in another connection, provides a
rationale if conjoined with some familiar facts of ancient life. Obviously, all three
rings have to turn at roughly the same angular velocity, since their diurnal periods
are all roughly the same. Even the moon's is only marginally longer or slower. Its
changing position relative to the sun and stars shows that its ring turns one time
less every 29–30 days, since they outlap it once in every lunar cycle. Nonetheless, its
daily motion seems to the naked eye as slow as the sun's, and the difference is
discernible only over intervals of multiple days. Yet the moon is obviously much
brighter than the stars, and the sun both brighter and hotter than them all. On
earth, the only source of artificial light in antiquity was fire, hence illumination was
pervasively correlated with heat (though not vice versa). Moreover, both were
typically generated by friction.[63] If Anaximander's celestial wheels behaved like
terrestrial wheels, they would generate heat and light as they turn by rubbing
against the surrounding mist.[64] Then, on the hypothesis that heat and light are
proportional to linear velocity (by virtue of friction), it follows that the sizes and
distances of the rings differ, and that the sequence is the opposite of what the
apparent size and brightness of the luminaries might otherwise suggest. Given their
nearly equal angular velocities, the most distant ring has the greatest linear velocity,

the nearest the least, and the brightest and hottest luminary must be the most remote, as Anaximander postulates.

In the absence of fuller testimony, only reasonable conjecture is possible. But scanty evidence is no warrant for dismissing the little we have. Though obscure in detail and possibly inconsistent at points, the larger picture is clear. For the first time on record, Anaximander postulated a model of the entire cosmos—in particular, a solar system bounded not by a starry heaven but by a ring of solar fire. He also ventured the first estimate of its size and scale, and in doubly geocentric terms: the earth is centrally situated and its diameter is the basic module for measuring the rest. Those who inherited his new perspective soon corrected the sequence he proposed—already Anaximenes made the stars outermost (Aët. 2.11.1, cf. Hippol. 1.7.6)—and eventually the sizes and distances were calculated more precisely and accurately. But according to the testimony of Eudemus and Theophrastus, the first system of celestial mechanics was developed by the Milesians, and principally by Anaximander.

A final word about our sources. Only two reports on Anaximander are explicitly attributed to Eudemus, and in one, he claims that Anaximander was the first to discuss sizes and distances (fr. 146). The extant figures are preserved only in Aëtius and Hippolytus, whose reports depend mainly on Theophrastus. But some of these reports on astronomy probably came from Eudemus. To be sure, neither ever names him. But Hippolytus never cites Theophrastus as a source either, and Aëtius does so at most once.[65] A convergence of reports on two related questions also points to Eudemus. Four sources report that Anaximander's earth was centrally located: Aristotle *De caelo* 2.13 (A26), Eudemus fr. 145 (A26), Diogenes Laertius 2.1 (A1), *Suda* (A2).[66] Aëtius ascribes the same view to "the followers of Thales" (3.11.1). Similarly, both Aëtius 2.21.1 (A21) and Diogenes 2.1 (A1) refer to E2, Anaximander's claim that the sun is the same size as the earth. In Diogenes, that is the third of three astronomical claims, each elsewhere associated with Eudemus: on the earth (its location and shape), the moon (its light), and the sun (its size and substance).[67] Aëtius inverts the order, starting from the sun and proceeding inward, both when outlining the system (2.15.6 in A18) and when reporting on its components separately (2.20–9 in A21–22). But the inversion still points to Eudemus, since it reflects the tradition (exemplified by Aristotle's *De caelo*) of starting with the outermost heaven. In any case, Eudemus's *Research in Astronomy* is by far the likeliest source for astronomical details, including specific numerical values, even if his reports reached later sources via Theophrastus.[68] More to the point, if either of them had access to records of this data, as we have seen reason to believe they did, then it is very likely that the other did as well. Hence the distrust some scholars harbor for the testimony of Aristotle and his colleagues on doctrinal or conceptual points affords little basis for doubting their reports of numerical data.[69] On the contrary, the transmission of such data is itself a sign that they had access to textual records, notwithstanding the discrepancies found in the relatively recent manuscripts of our much later sources. In short, even if the figures in surviving texts are corrupt—some or all the product of scribal error—it remains virtually certain that Anaximander proposed not only a comprehensive model of the cosmos but also astronomical measures of its main dimensions.

3. ANAXIMENES AND THE MEASURES OF CHANGE

Anaximander's cosmology embraced not only the solar system above but everything under the sun as well. The only surviving excerpt from his writings, and probably the oldest remnant of Greek philosophical writing, is a tantalizing claim that change throughout the cosmos follows necessary and orderly cycles through time (fr. 1 = Simp. *in Ph.* 24.16–21).

> He says [M1a] it [i.e., the material principle of everything in the cosmos] is neither water nor any other of what are called elements, but [M1b] some different nature that is unlimited, out of which come to be all the heavens and the worlds [*kosmous*] in them; and [M2a] there is generation for things out of those into which destruction also occurs "according to what must; for [M2b] they return rightful requital to one another for their wrong according to the order of time," as he says in rather poetic words.

The context of Anaximander's words is lost, their precise scope uncertain, their sense and reference obscure, and interpretation therefore highly controversial.[70] But their central thrust is clear. His bold assertion of natural regularity, which Theophrastus admired enough to quote (fr. 226A; see note 6 here), dismisses the erratic world of traditional belief and posits in its place an orderly system of change within the newly delineated order of cosmic time and space. It is unfortunate that the excerpt fails to clarify the governing factors of necessity (*to chreôn*), "rightful requital" (*dikên kai tisin*), and "order of time" (*tên tou chronou taxin*) or to specify exactly what they govern. The latter question is especially problematic. The initial clauses, which are probably not Anaximander's own words but a paraphrase by Theophrastus or an even later summary of his account, specify first "the elements" like water, then "the heavens and the worlds in them"—first physical materials in M1a, then discrete physical objects or regions in M1b. But the subject "they" (*auta*) in M2b could refer instead to the source or sources of those items' generation and destruction: either the plural "those" in M2a (ἐξ ὧν . . . εἰς ταῦτα), or the single "unlimited nature" in M1a–b (φύσιν ἄπειρον ἐξ ἧς). Many scholars, following Aristotle (*Ph.* 1.4 187a20–1 in A9), favor still another candidate that is not mentioned explicitly here, and they make the subject of cyclic change "the opposites": pairs of dynamic qualities or powers like heat and cold, or related materials or processes like fire and ice or summer and winter.[71] But rather than pursue these questions, which may be insoluble, I shall focus instead on Anaximenes, whose theory, though barely better attested, is at least more clearly articulated. In any case, his theories have enough in common with Anaximander's to blur questions of attribution and origin.

Aristotle is the earliest extant author to name Anaximenes, and the fullest surviving reports of his theories derive from Theophrastus, whose doxographic account is summarized by Simplicius (S), Hippolytus (H), and pseudo-Plutarch (P).[72] It will be useful to have all three accounts before us.

> S[implicius]: Anaximenes son of Eurystratus, a Milesian and companion of Anaximander, also claims, as did he [Anaximander], that [1] the underlying nature is one and unlimited, though not indeterminate, as he did, but rather determinate, for he says that it is air; [2] it differs in things by looseness and compactness; and [3] by thinning it becomes fire, by compacting it becomes wind, then cloud, and compacting still more, then water, then earth, then stones; and that [4] the rest are made out of these. He, too, makes [5] motion everlasting, and [6] because of it, he claims, transformation as well occurs. (Simpl. *in Ph.* 24.26–25.1 = A5 = Thphr. fr. 226A)

> H[ippolytus]: Anaximenes, also [i.e., like Anaximander] himself a Milesian and son of Eurystratus, claimed [1] unlimited air is the principle out of which are generated what is becoming and has become and will be and gods and divine things, and the rest out of its offspring. And [he claimed] [2] the form of air is like this: when it is most even [*homalôtatos*], it is invisible but evident by being cold, hot, moist, and moving; and [3] it is always moving, for everything that transforms does not transform unless it moves; for [4] it appears different by compacting and thinning, for [5a] when it dissolves into the thinner, it becomes fire; and [5b] winds in turn are air compacting; and [5c] out of air is produced cloud by felting; and [5d] [when felted] still more,[73] water; and [5e] after compacting more, earth; and [5f] into the most compact, stones.[74] And [he claimed] [6] the earth is flat and riding on air, and [7] likewise sun, moon, and all the other stars are fiery and ride on the air because of flatness. (*Haer.* 1.7.1–4 = A7)

> P[lutarch]: They claim that Anaximenes said that [1] the principle of the universe is air, and [2] it is unlimited in size but determinate by the qualities it has [ταῖς περὶ αὐτὸν ποιότησιν], and [3] everything is generated according to its compaction and thinning in turn; in fact, [4] the motion exists from eternity. And [5] by the air getting felted, he says, the earth was generated first, very flat, which is why, quite reasonably, it rides on the air; and [6] the sun, the moon, and the rest of the stars have the origin of their generation out of earth. (*Strom.* 3 = A6) [75]

Some have argued that this account of change is largely a fabrication by Theophrastus in line with Aristotelian schemes. But as Daniel Graham has recently shown, Plato sketches a very similar account in *Timaeus* 49b–c, and traces of the account can be found in many earlier thinkers, all the way back to Heraclitus and Xenophanes.[76] In short, there are good grounds for trusting the accuracy of Theophrastus's report. What then is his account of Anaximenes' theory?

All three sources first single out air as somehow basic: "the underlying nature" (*tên hupokeimenên phusin*) in S, or "the principle" (*tên archên*) in H and P. S and H then list six forms that air "becomes" or "exhibits":[77] fire by "loosening" (*araioumenon*) or "dissolving" (*diachuthêi*), and five others by "compacting" (*puknoumenon*) or "felting" (*kata tên pilêsin*). This account of change, striking in its novelty and simplicity alike, rests on two key ideas: an ordered sequence of materials, and the twin processes of "compacting" and "thinning." The resulting theory, as standardly construed, can be outlined as follows.[78]

Theory of Change (TC)

1. There is a determinate series of materials, based on their relative "compaction."
2. The series encompasses seven distinct materials: fire, air, wind, cloud, water, earth, and stone (in order of increasing compaction).
3. Materials change into other materials due to increased or decreased compaction.

Anaximenes is also widely taken to advance another thesis, both more basic and more sophisticated: not only a theory of change but also a conception of matter. The conception combines two distinct principles and specifies a single material to play both roles: air is both (1) a material source or principle of generation (and perishing), and (2) a material substrate or principle of material constitution (cf. Arist. *Metaph.* A.3).

Material Monism (MM)

1. There is a single basic material or principle (*archê*) out of which everything (else) is generated and into which everything (else) perishes.
2. Everything (else) is made out of that basic material or principle.
3. The basic material or principle is air.

As Graham emphasizes, TC and MM are in principle logically independent: neither entails the other. In fact, TC as it stands seems to point away from MM to pluralism: seven distinct constitutive principles that simply transform into one another without any persisting factor or residue. The tension between MM and TC2 is especially acute: how is the air that TC2 makes one of seven coordinate materials related to the air that MM makes the single basic material constituting all seven materials alike? Plainly, much rides on TC2. If air is itself a distinct material on a par with the other six, then TC and MM are incompatible. But if air is somehow more basic than the others, then it does not belong in TC2. Only if that list is reduced to the six others as its derivatives—call this emended list TC2*—is TC compatible with MM. Air would then be an enduring basic nature underlying the six distinct materials in TC2*; conversely, those would simply be states or phases of a single basic stuff, all more or less compacted air. The crucial question, then, is whether air belongs in the series listed in TC2. Is air one among seven comparable materials, as current consensus has it, or rather a more basic material underlying all the others?[79]

The latter alternative has distinct advantages. Theoretically, it resolves the problematic status of air itself. Air no longer has to play the conflicting roles imposed by TC2 and MM2, thereby eliminating a radical equivocation over ordinary air in TC2 and its theoretically basic analogue in MM. For TC2, though consistent with the cosmogonic and generative roles assigned to air in MM1, is inconsistent with its constitutive role in MM2. If air is fully on a par with the six other materials, then it can play only a generative role; but if it plays a constitutive role, then it cannot be on a par with the others and must be removed from TC2. Monism also makes better sense historically, as a modest reformulation of Anaximander's tantalizing but frustratingly vague conception of "the unlimited." Specifying air as basic provides a more determinate account of the cosmic principle, and one that is similarly "unlimited" in a variety of ways. By contrast, the explicit pluralism of TC alone, without MM, seems to be a later innovation by Empedocles in response to Eleatic arguments. Finally, and decisively, air-monism has stronger textual support, at least in the restricted sense that it is what Theophrastus ascribed to Anaximenes. A closer look at S and H should make that clear.

In Simplicius, air is named only once, in the opening sentence of the summary (S1). Yet air is also the implicit grammatical subject of the following two sentences, including the series of changes in S3. Though not itself named in that series, air is what first "becomes fire by thinning" and what then becomes wind and the rest "by compacting"; by contrast, S3 does not claim that fire becomes air. The implication is significant. As the grammatical subject throughout, air is also portrayed as the logical subject of every transformation in the series. In short, air persists through each change, and it does so as a material substrate transformed into six distinct states or phases, from fire to stone. The same analysis is evident in Hippolytus, though his elliptical phrasing obscures the latter stages. His summary presents air as the logical subject in both cycles. In H5a, air is plainly the grammatical subject for the process of thinning into fire. In H5b, it is a predicate accusative for the reductionist claim that winds "are really [einai] compacting air"; and H5c names air—rather than winds, as the serial sequence would have it—in a similarly reductionist claim that cloud "is produced out of air."[80] The same status is implicit in the following stages: air is the unexpressed subject of an implied verb or participle in H5d (see n. 73), of an aorist participle in H5e (ἐπὶ πλεῖον πυκνωθέντα), and of either a superlative adjective or a participle in H5f (πυκνότατον or τὸ μάλιστα [sc. πυκνωθέν]). Conversely, air figures nowhere as a distinct state or stage. In H and S alike, it first becomes fire, then wind, then the rest; but nothing else ever turns into air. That corresponds to TC2*, not TC2. Granted, neither S3 nor H5 says that fire turns directly into wind. But neither account describes anything turning into anything else, except air into its six phases or forms: first into fire and then into wind, in both versions; and then into four other phases, explicitly in S3, and apparently also in H5, though indirect discourse and multiple ellipses leave the syntax there uncertain.

A close reading of S and H reveals that both depict air as the most basic material stuff. It is not simply a source of six other materials that are fully on a par with it. Rather, as the uniquely basic substrate "out of which" (according to H1 and H5c) everything is composed and formed, it occurs only in the six phases or forms that occupy various parts of the world around us. In short, air fits the bill of MM: "unlimited" and absolutely pervasive, it is the ultimate constituent of every object and region in the world. The same conception of air is evident also in P's severely truncated account, which follows the same sequence as S and H. P1 first specifies air as basic, as in S1 and H1. P2 notes that it is quantitatively similar to Anaximander's "unlimited" but different qualitatively, as in S1. And P3 briefly describes the process by which air is differentiated, as in S2 and H4. Unlike S3 and H5, P gives no examples of this process, and the abstract terminology in its claims may reflect an abbreviator's hand.[81] Nonetheless, P depicts air as a material substrate: first as the subject of distinct "qualities" (including but not limited to the distinctive properties of the six other materials) in P2, then in P3 as the persisting subject or substrate that undergoes cycles of compaction and thinning.

The theory of change summarized in all three sources involves a series of six distinct states or phases of air, as in TC2*. Both S and H specify a pair of "opposing" extremes, fire and stone, and four intermediate states, not including air. Other reports show Anaximenes exploiting the same series to explain further materials, invariably analyzed in terms either of these six or of air itself. Hail and snow, for example, he equated with more or less compacted forms of water descending from clouds (Hippol. 1.7.7, Aët. 3.4.1); the phrasing, or rather paraphrasing, suits either intermediate states of compaction or compounds of two sharply distinct states. Reports of his cosmogony exhibit the same scheme. The earth was formed out of compacted air (by "felting" in [Plu.] = A6), and the sun, moon, and stars consist of vapor emitted from the earth and ultimately "thinned" into fire (Hippol. 1.7.5, cf. Aët. 2.13.10, 2.20.2). According to MM, of course, all of these materials and bodies are, at bottom, still air in various states of compaction or thinning. But the absence of air from the series in TC2* invites a new question. What becomes of the ordinary air we breathe, which seems to fill so much of the vast regions above and around us? Does the elimination of air from TC2 eliminate ordinary air from the world in turn? Or does Anaximenes equivocate by assigning air two distinct roles after all?

The dilemma looks serious. Anaximenes either equivocates in TC2 or disregards obvious evidence against TC2*. But two related points blunt the second horn. First, the term hitherto translated as "air" (as *aêr* usually is) had a distinct sense in early Greek. In later usage, as in modern English, it refers to the diaphanous gas all around us. But in archaic usage, it refers to various forms of vapor, including many like mist and fog that are more or less opaque. "Air" in those forms resembles cloud more than air.[82] In Anaximander's cosmology, for example, an unspecified amount of "air" is opaque enough to conceal fire as bright as the sun's (A10, A11, A18). By contrast, the air we breathe is more like wind than such misty "air." The second point is that Anaximenes' "air" is in continual and everlasting motion (H3, P4, S5). That again makes it more like wind and cloud than the ordinary air we breathe. In fact, wind differs from ordinary air only by being in motion; wind is simply moving air. But since "air" is always moving, it is singularly ill suited to double as wind at rest, as if somehow immobilized by greater de-compaction.[83] Moreover, immobility would be a very odd feature for a state of basic air that, on TC2, stands between its two most volatile states, fire and wind. To be sure, on MM, everything is basic "air," even portions of earth and stone that appear immobile. But while the mobility of "air" temporarily decreases in those two most compacted states, all four other generic states—water, cloud, wind, and fire—are highly volatile. TC2* thus yields a significantly more coherent theory than does TC2.

On this interpretation, Anaximenes neither overlooked nor eliminated ordi-nary air. On the contrary, what we breathe is wind, which is simply basic air in a highly uncompacted state. Here again, diction favors TC2*. In a passage that purports to preserve some of his own words, Anaximenes observes that our breath is warm when exhaled through an open mouth, but cool when exhaled through pursed lips (fr. 1 in Plu. *Prim. frig.* 947f). The example is supposed to illustrate how compaction produces different perceptible properties in air. But the term used for our breath is "blowing" (*pnoê*), a term used mainly for wind in archaic Greek. And according to another report, probably from Theophrastus, the closely related term "breath" (*pneuma*), which was also widely used for wind in archaic Greek, was synonymous with "air" for Anaximenes (Aët. 1.3.4 = fr. 2).[84] In ordinary usage, then, the term he used to label his basic stuff apparently referred to moving vapor of any sort, transparent or opaque. In his theory of change, however, the basic stuff called "air" is a theoretical entity, nowhere found in a "pure" state. All we ever encounter or perceive is basic air in various states of compaction, because abso-lutely everything "is really" (note *ousa* in fr. 2 and *einai* in H5b) more or less compacted vapor. For Anaximenes, then, "air" is a technical term, albeit one based on traditional usage. It refers neither to the misty vapors traditionally so called (all forms of "cloud" in his theory) nor to the ordinary air later so called (the "wind" or "breath" in his series) but solely to the basic material constituent of everything.

Doubts may persist. If "air" is basic and hence distinct from the familiar stuff we breathe, why did Anaximenes specify anything at all? A plausible answer emerges from a critique in Plato that clearly alludes to Anaximenes' theory when posing a generalized version of the same question. After introducing his notorious notion of "a receptacle for all generation, like a nurse" (*Tim.* 49a), Plato promptly raises a "puzzle" (*prodiaporêthênai*, 49b2; cf. b7) by sketching a series of trans-formations that echoes Anaximenes at several points (49b7–c7).

> T[imaeus]: First, [1] what we now named water, when it compacts as we believe, we see becoming stones and earth, and [2] when it melts and separates in turn, [we see] this same thing [becoming] wind and air, and after air has ignited, [we see it becoming] fire; and again [3] after fire coalesces and goes out, [we see it] going back into the form of air, and again air, as it comes together and com-pacts, [we see becoming] cloud and mist, and out of these, as they get felted still more, [we see] water flowing, and out of water, earth and stones again—a cy-cle thus transmitting, as it appears, [the process of] generation into one another.

Plato describes three distinct sequences of transformation: first, water into two solid phases; then water into two airy phases, and then into fire; and finally a full cycle from fire down to stone. The first sequence, in T1, matches Anaximenes' account exactly, even in its mechanism of compaction. The following two sequences also follow him closely, though not without some discrepancies: T2 omits cloud and assigns air a phase of its own; and T3 omits wind but includes two kinds of cloud. Taken together, the three sequences therefore yield an ordered series of eight phases, including air. The series is readily reduced to seven by taking "cloud and mist" as a doublet for a single phase. On the same grounds, it can be further reduced to six by taking "wind and air" as another doublet. T2 and T3 each list exactly six terms, and the two doublets are not only symmetrical but balanced in turn by the pairing of earth and stones in T1. Plato, of course, felt no obligation to parrot Anaximenes exactly; witness the variety of terms he uses to describe the several transformations. Writing after the Empedoclean tetrad of elements became standard, he understandably puts air on the same level as the rest. Likewise, T1 and T2 jointly encompass only four changes, each between a pair of Empedoclean elements (solid, liquid, vapor, and fire).[85] Clearly, Plato's sketch of material transformations is eclectic. Nonetheless, its echoes of Anaximenes point to a series not of seven comparable materials, but rather of six forms or states of a single material.

Plato's point here is avowedly polemical. He sketches the model of change only to pose an objection to it, and to any similar theory. The model, he charges, provides no compelling reason to privilege any stage over the others. His target, in short, is material monism: why pick out air as basic, or water, or fire, or anything in particular?[86] Far better, he contends, to treat all alike as transitory qualifications "in" something else, which he here calls a "receptacle." As a material monist, Anaximenes is plainly liable to Plato's objection. But how well does it stick? Did he have any credible reasons for selecting "air" as the basic factor and not some other material? Or rather, is there any indication that Theophrastus thought he did?

Although the evidence is too meager to draw any firm conclusions, traces of a rationale can be discerned. One plausible consideration is symmetry, which would privilege either the extremes (fire or stone) or an intermediate state. The middle of the seven terms in TC2 would be cloud, not air. On TC2*, by contrast, the misty vapor traditionally called "air" would aptly fall between the two middle terms, cloud and water.[87] More to the point, the diverse forms of vapor found in ordinary experience exhibit a number of features important for its cosmic role. First and foremost is its sheer indeterminacy or lack of characteristic qualities: transparent forms of vapor are perceptible only indirectly via the effects of their movement, temperature, or other features (H4, P2).[88] Conversely, vapors display a wide range of other perceptible features: hot or cold (as steam or wintry mist) or anything in between (H2, fr. 1), arid or humid (as heat waves or fog) as well as temperate (H2 and Hippol. 1.7.7, A17), and imbued with diverse odors. Complementing this qualitative variability is an exceptional flexibility or elasticity: readily yielding to bodies in any of the six phases from stone to fire, rapidly filling vacated space, and permeating large openings and tiny pores alike.[89] Not only is vapor pervasive in the sense of surrounding everything else; it is also far and away the predominate material in Anaximenes' cosmos, occupying much of the atmosphere above us, and even the immense heavens, where the earth and celestial bodies "ride on it" (H6–7, P5–6). In fact, its magnitude is "unlimited" (S1, H1, P2), as in Anaximander's cosmos, and in two respects.[90] Coextensive with the entire universe, it has no permanent or impermeable boundaries, either externally, since nothing else bounds it, or internally, since its contents are in continual flux as the diverse materials it constitutes—its various states of compaction—change location, shape, quality, and even state. Finally, the ordinary air around us is the site for many large and impressive transformations, most notably the compaction and dissipation of clouds and "rain-clouds" (Hippol. 1.7.7, A17), the precipitation of rain, snow, and hail (Hippol. 1.7.7, A17), and the luminescence of fire in all its many forms, from sun and stars (H4, A14) to lightning and rainbows (Hippol. 1.7.8, A17–18) and even the mundane flames of hearth fires, torches, and lamps.

On MM, the perceptible features that make "air" suitable for its role as material substrate are peculiar only to some of its more volatile states, only what is strictly called "wind" or "cloud." But that otherwise awkward implication resolves a major problem. If the ordinary air around us is all more or less mobile "wind," then Anaximenes has a ready basis for his claim that his basic air is always moving: motion is then what an Aristotelian would call an essential property of basic air.[91] Yet now the converse problem looms: if basic air is always in motion, and everything "is really" basic air, why do some things appear so manifestly immobile? Why do rocks and logs, fields and mountains not drift and float or simply vaporize into thin air? A simple and obvious rejoinder, though nowhere attested, is that they remain immobile because of their greater compaction, a result either of centripetal forces in their own air, or of pressure exerted by other air around them. But rather than pursue these necessarily conjectural questions, we may turn to a larger question underlying them. Is there any evidence that Anaximenes proposed—according to Theophrastus, at least—the kind of reductionist explanations that materialism typically favors?

The clearest and most dramatic evidence of reduction is the way Anaximenes explained the differentiation of his single basic material. How does basic air change into its six generic forms or states? His solution, specified in TC1, was a bold and powerful innovation: simply by increasing or decreasing compaction.[92] Fire is simply "air" in its minimally compacted state, stone its maximally compacted state, and the rest more or less compacted in turn. In addition to a principle of material reduction, Anaximenes deployed a related principle of property reduction to explain other regular perceptible differences. As illustrated by his example of breath, air (or strictly speaking, "wind") from the same source feels cool when compacted, warm when not (fr. 1). Likewise, the least compacted state of basic air is plainly the hottest, and the more compacted states (from water to stone) normally cool or cold. In short, temperature is evidently also a function of compaction. How widely Anaximenes applied the second principle we have too little evidence to say with any confidence. A number of other correlations are fairly obvious, most notably weight (or heaviness, in Aristotelian terms), immobility, hardness or rigidity, and opacity, all of which are directly correlated with relatively high compaction, as is coolness, whereas the contrary qualities are correlated with decompaction (cf. Arist. *Ph.* 8.7 260b7–10). Other features are less straightforward but hardly less obvious. Luminosity and transparency, like heat, are inversely correlated: more so if less compacted.[93] Moisture or wetness is peculiar to the two intermediate states, and dryness perhaps to the extremes. Of course, portions of each material often exhibit contrary features; winds often feel cool or cold, and stone gets very hot in a Milesian summer. How Anaximenes handled these apparent counterexamples, or even whether he did, we are not told. Anaximander appealed to the separation and combination of materials, and Theophrastus may have distinguished a second mechanism. After describing how air "becomes" its six states by compacting and thinning, S and H add that everything else is made "out of these" in turn.[94] But no report specifies what these further transformations are, how they occur, or even whether they are somehow derivative—for example, "blendings" or qualitative "alterations" of the six primary materials. Reports consistently highlight the single factor of more or less compaction, or thinning.[95] Since Theophrastus had other terminology available, the absence of any clear reference to other processes or kinds of transformation makes conjecture especially risky.

A principle of object and event reduction is also well attested. Adopting a form of analysis evidently pioneered by his older compatriots, Anaximenes explained a number of prominent atmospheric and geological phenomena as effects of material processes. Like Anaximander, he explained thunder and lightning as an effect of cloudbursts: when wind enclosed within clouds bursts out, the violent "rupture" produces noise, and the contrasting translucency gleams, just as water flashes when cut by oars (Aët. 3.3.1–2 in A17). The attendant precipitation he also analyzed as forms of basic air (Aët. 3.4.1 in A17, Hippol. 1.7.7): just as clouds are compacted air, so water emerges as rain when the air is "thickened" more, as hail when the moisture solidifies as it falls, and as snow when it absorbs "something breathy" (*ti pneumatikon*). Apparently, rain and hail are simply more specific differentiations of "cloudy" or "watery" air due to compaction. But the analysis of snow appeals to mixture as well;[96] and so does his analysis of earthquakes. According to Aristotle, Anaximenes proposed two complex and complementary processes. Quakes result either from drought, when the ground compacts and contracts (due to losing its thinner moisture) until it collapses (*empiptontôn*), presumably into hollows created as it dries, or from heavy rains, which can soak and swell the ground (since water is thinner) until it falls apart (*diapiptein*), presumably above ground (*Mete.* 2.7 365b6–12 = A21; cf. Aët. 3.15.3).[97] The principal mechanism in both cases is clearly compaction, but its operation equally clearly presupposes processes of mixture and separation, as earth first "absorbs" (*brechomenên*) water and then releases it by "evaporation" or "exhalation." A final case of reduction deserves brief mention. Life itself is another "offspring" or outcome of thinly compacted air in the form of "breath" or wind, which constitutes and "sustains" or "governs" the human soul, just as it does the whole cosmos (B2, cf. A23). Air, in short, is the basis for animate and inanimate properties and processes alike.

To return finally to my main theme, what role does measurement play in Anaximenes' analysis of change? His theory involves measures in three crude but significant ways. First, by defining an ordered series of states of a single material, it establishes an ordinal scale. Since transformations occur always in the same sequence—wind compacts to water only via cloud, and vice versa—any state of air has a determinate place on the scale.[98] Moreover, the single scale he postulated is eminently suited for quantitative analysis, hence for a cardinal scale of uniform measures as well. Granted, no source even alludes to any module, to units or "degrees" of compaction. But the extant record is extremely meager, and its silence therefore underwhelming. If Anaximenes did envision the possibility of quantifying compaction, he must have been hard pressed to find a practical method for doing so. Such a scenario seems more likely for several reasons. First, our sources differentiate the series of phases in both quantitative and qualitative terms: not only *mâllon* and *malista* but also *pleion* in H5 (cf. Aët. 3.4.1). The quantitative phrasing may come from Theophrastus or later interpreters (note qualitative *mâllon* in *Tim.* 49c5). Or conversely, they may be responsible for introducing the qualitative perspective, in line with the Aristotelian conception of compaction as essentially qualitative.[99] Or both perspectives may be authentic. In any event, it is unsafe simply to assume that Anaximenes interpreted compaction as a purely qualitative feature, especially in the context of his older compatriots' well-attested efforts to quantify related phenomena. Moreover, even primitive concepts of compaction—and its opposite, decompaction or thinning—are patently analogous to density. From the operational perspective of ordinary practice, in fact, the two are effectively indistinguishable. The simplest and obvious way to estimate either was in terms of capacity or, as we might put it, volumetrically: How much air does a given space or volume contain? Solving such problems was part of daily life for many at the time, not only artisans of many sorts, from potters and metalworkers to builders and shipwrights, but also anyone involved in the many chores of collecting, storing, and preparing household goods, such as food and drink (forms of earth and water), clothing (including wool for felting), and building materials (both earth and stone).

In this connection, it is worth recalling also that the sixth century saw dramatic progress in the standardization of weights and measures, including volumes for agricultural produce and its ceramic containers, and weights for metal coinage and other precious commodities.[100] Moreover, a quantified model of change as a form of measured exchange is securely attested for Heraclitus in the following generation. His talk of "measures" (*metra*) may well be original (B30, B94, cf. B90, B100). But it is an attractive conjecture that he drew directly on Anaximenes, though perhaps only to deride such idle presumption. Given the Ephesian's well-attested disdain for similar Ionian inquiries (B40, B58), parody would well suit his enigmatic pronouncements that seawater is "half earth, half whirlwind" (B31)—perhaps mocking the "airy" tunnels of light postulated by Anaximander to explain sunlight (see note 44 here)—and that "death of fire is birth of air, death of air birth of water, and vice versa" (B76, cf. B30), as if anything could possibly survive transformations as dramatic as Anaximenes postulated for his air.[101]

The principle of material reduction implicit in MM and exemplified in TC clearly underwrites two forms of measurement: an ordinal scale encompassing the series of six material states of basic air in TC2*, and at least the possibility of a cardinal scale of compaction understood as a crude form of density. It is reasonably clear that Anaximenes recognized the first form. Whether he failed to envision the second, or simply saw no way to apply it—no way to measure compaction directly—our evidence is too meager to tell. But the principle of property reduction raises the possibility of a third form of measurement. If Anaximenes did correlate other perceptible properties with compaction, as a number of reports suggest, then he could have measured compaction indirectly in terms of its correlates. For example, if he recognized a correlation between compaction and temperature, then he could in principle measure either in terms of the other. Of course, in that particular case, there was no prospect ever in the ancient world of quantifying hot and cold with any accuracy. Nor was there much hope of utilizing the parameters of time and space already measured by his compatriots. Even if Anaximenes correlated motion or mobility with compaction, no matter how finely he could measure distances, he had no way to measure time precisely enough to determine velocities. Yet the key point still stands. Any strict correlation of features established a general proportionality, thereby opening up the theoretical possibility of quantifying some features directly and measuring others indirectly.

Large questions loom. How could Anaximenes account for either the origin or the stability of individual objects and systems, or the regularity of their movements and changes, not least the celestial cycles discerned by Thales and Anaximander? As storms and whirlwinds illustrate, destruction and combustion also result from moving air, and highly erratically. But those are essentially questions of detail, problems for further study, both observation and reasoned argument, not challenges to the framework of empirical inquiry and quantitative analysis the three Milesians evidently pioneered. We should not expect them to answer all the new questions they posed, or to answer them all correctly, let alone fully. As Xenophanes proudly proclaimed in their wake, mortals "find out better over time by searching" (fr. 18). Still, if we can trust Aristotle and his colleagues, a central achievement of the Milesians was to initiate the project of scientific inquiry that continues today. The search for measurable order and regularity in the world as a whole is evidently their legacy, and their discoveries—or inventions, in many cases—launched the first scientific revolution. Any others who made similar attempts before them have long since been forgotten, apparently eclipsed, as Theophrastus put it (fr. 225 = Simp. *in Ph.* 23.25–8), by the subsequent success of the Milesians—or at least by the written records they made of their work. Whether their efforts should also be deemed the opening chapter in the history of philosophy is a further question. In any event, it is in sixth-century Miletus that Greek science first emerges into the light of history.[102]

NOTES

1. Concise survey and analysis of the main evidence in KRS 76–162; spirited discussion in Barnes *PP* 3–56; also Panchenko, "Thales and the Origin of Theoretical Reasoning." The testimony of Aristotle and his colleagues has been severely criticized by Cherniss, *Aristotle's Criticism of Presocratic Philosophy*, and McDiarmid, "Theophrastus on the Presocratic Causes," for conceptual distortion; shifting the focus to scientific questions also helps defuse their critique; see Kahn, *Anaximander and the Origins of Greek Cosmology*, 11–24.

2. The citations are inconsistent. D.L. 1.23 reports "two works" but then appears to name only one: *On Solstice and Equinox* (the second could be *Equinoxes*, but a plural would be odd after the singular "solstice"), unless the other work is *Nautical Astronomy* (named previously). The *Suda* (θ 17 = A2) names only one: *On Equinox* (singular).

3. So D.L. 1.23; doubts about its authorship go back at least to Theophrastus (fr. 225 = Simp. *in Ph.* 23; cf. Plu. *Pyth. Or.* 403a), and works by minor writers are more likely to attract famous names than vice versa. In any case, the poem may still have recounted some of Thales' ideas, though probably without naming him. A report from Lobon of Argos (third century BCE) about "200 verses" and some practical maxims (D.L. 1.34–35) is unreliable, as is a reference to "many other" writings in the *Suda* (A2).

4. Technical writing in prose is first attested for the mid–sixth century; on the diverse but limited use of writing in archaic Greece, see Thomson, *Literacy and Orality in Ancient Greece*, and on early philosophical writing, Kahn, "Writing Philosophy."

5. Zhmud, "Eudemus' History of Mathematics," shows that Eudemus's *History of* [or *Research in*] *Geometry* is the probable source of all later reports about Greek mathematics before his time. A similar case could be made for Eudemus's *History of* [or *Research in*] *Astronomy*; see Mansfeld, "Cosmic Distances," 195–201. Remains of his work are collected in Wehrli, *Schule des Aristoteles*, vol. 8; on Aristotle's account of Thales, see Mansfeld, "Aristotle and Others on Thales."

6. See Zhmud, "The Historiographical Project of the Lyceum." Theophrastus is the likely source of a brief quotation from Anaximander and an accompanying comment on his diction (fr. 226 = Simp. *in Ph.* 24), and perhaps also of a comment on the style of Anaximenes (D.L. 2.3), to whose work he devoted a monograph (fr. 136 no. 27). A century later, Apollodorus of Athens could read Anaximander's work (fr. 29 = D.L. 2.2).

7. Their lives overlapped significantly, and reports of close geographic, chronological, and social ties provide a biographical basis for their very similar interests. By the time Thales died, the two others had both attained "recognition": Anaximander by 571/0 (Oly. 52.2 in Eus. *Chron.*), and Anaximenes by 548/7 (Oly. 58.1 in Hippol. 1.7.8 = 13A7; cf. D.L. 2.3 = A1, *Suda* α 1988 = A2), if not a decade earlier in 557/6 (Oly. 55.4 in Eus. *Chron.* = A3); cf. KRS 76, 100–01, 143–44. If these ancient dates are reliable, Anaximenes was active well before Thales died, and their three lives together span barely a century—two decades less than Socrates and Plato alone.

8. Xenophanes of nearby Colophon (c. 570–c. 470), besides "admiring" Thales' astronomy (D.L. 1.23), pursued many of the same questions as the Milesians; their younger contemporary (see Sotion fr. 28 in D.L. 9.18), he could well have studied with Anaximenes, as Theophrastus claimed (fr. 227D in D.L. 9.21); see Lesher, *Xenophanes of Colophon*, 120–24, 154. Heraclitus names several predecessors in extant fragments, most with scorn; but see fr. 39 on Bias and Hdt. 1.170. Democritus's reference to Thales probably occurred in his astronomical work (see frs. 11b–15b), subject of a monograph by Theophrastus (fr. 137 no. 33).

9. See Graham, "Philosophy on the Nile," 306–7. Likely later sources include Hippias (see A11 on Thales, fr. 12 in Eudemus fr. 133); and Diogenes of Apollonia (a Milesian colony reportedly founded by Anaximander: A3, cf, Hdt. 1.168), to whom Theophrastus devoted a monograph (fr. 137 no. 39, cf, *Sens.* 39–48).

10. The list is arranged thematically and includes only reports I consider credible, hence no claims about the material constitution of celestial bodies (A17a and Aët. 2.25.8), lunar light (A17b), or the earth's climatic zones (A13c).

11. Apuleius also alludes to items 2–6 ("solis annua reverticula; temporum ambitus; lunae nascentis incrementa, senescentis dispendia, delinquentis obstiticula") and 8–11 ("stellarum meatus; siderum obliqua curricula; ventorum flatus"). For evidence that he was familiar with Eudemus's work in some form, see White, "Eudemus the Naturalist," 208–14, and White, "Thales and the Stars," 16.

12. Eudemus's *Research in Astronomy* is cited for three reports about Thales, and solar eclipses figure in all three.

13. For a recent defense, with references to previous discussion, see Panchenko, "Thales' Prediction of a Solar Eclipse." The eclipse in question is securely dated to May 28, 585; see Stephenson and Fatoohi, "Thales' Prediction of a Solar Eclipse."

14. Geminus *Isag.* 18 outlines a related cycle (the *exeligmos* = 3 Saros-cycles); and Pliny *NH* 2.56 appears to cite it; cf. *Suda* σ 148. On the other hand, Aristotle refers to Babylonian data (*Cael.* 2.12, 292a7–9), his nephew Callisthenes reportedly had records sent back to Greece (Simp. *in Cael.* 2.12) following the city's peaceful submission to Alexander in late 331, and Eudemus was familiar at least with Babylonian theogony (fr. 150).

15. Two details, if they come from Eudemus and not D.L., would show he was alert to problems of evidence: the initial reservation "according to some" indicates a cautious handling of sources, and the following citations show an interest in textual support.

16. The title may be a product of haplography (*Astronomi<cal Research>es*: Ἀστρολογι<καῖς ἱστορί>αις), either in manuscripts of Theon or in prior transmission from Eudemus to Dercyllides to Theon. "Obliquity" (λόξωσιν is Diels's generally accepted emendation for "belting" (διάζωσιν); "interval" (πάροδον, not περίοδον as emended by Fabricius) is confirmed by D.L. 1.24 (see note 19 here); and "lies" (κεῖται for κ[ιν]εῖται) is an obvious correction (see note 49 here).

17. See Tannery, "Sur les fragments d'Eudème de Rhodes."

18. For the seventh century, see West, *Hesiod, Works and Days*, 381; for Euctemon's figures, which Eudemus knew (fr. 149 = Simp. *In Cael.* 2.12 497.15–22), see *Ars Eudoxi* 22–23 (*PPar* 1), which is confirmed by dates in Geminus *Isag.* app.

19. Whence also the term for "interval": the linear "path to" (*parodos)* each extreme, not a revolving "path around" or "period" (*periodos).*

20. For Hesiod's two intervals of 60 and 50 days, Euctemon's dates yield 70 and 71 days.

21. Eudemus discussed later figures for both the seasonal intervals (Euctemon's in fr. 149) and the year as a whole (fr. 145 = Oenopides A7, with A8–9), and he compared rival claims on other questions; see von Fritz, "Oinopides," 2262–64, Zhmud, "Eudemus' History of Mathematics," 275.

22. Emphatically by Dicks, "Solstices, Equinoxes, and the Presocratics"; but see Kahn, "On Early Greek Astronomy," and White, "Thales and the Stars."

23. The range of dates probably reflects multiple differences: latitude, observational methods, circumstances, and (due to precession of the equinoxes) era. For the supplement in the text (from A. Boeckh), see White, "Thales and the Stars," 10 n. 35.

24. Anaximenes recognized that the seasons occur "not because of any of these [i.e., the rising and setting of any stars] but because of the sun alone" (Aët. 2.19.1–2 = A14).

25. Democritus in fr. 75 (cf. fr. 54 and note 8 here), the rest in frs. 148–49.

26. A fragmentary stone *parapegma* or "timetable" (c. 100 BCE from Miletus); the appendix to Geminus *Isag.* (date uncertain, perhaps also from Rhodes); and Ptolemy's *Phaseis* (c. 150 CE). The text of the Milesian calendar (SB 456AD) is in Diels, "Parapegmenfragmente aus Milet"; see Hannah, "Euctemon's Parapegma," Taub, *Ancient Meteorology*, 20–37.

27. Eus. *PE* 10.14.11 (A4) lists the same three terms and adds "time-intervals" (*chronoi*). The "horoscopes" (*hôroskopia*) in D.L. 2.1, "horologues" (*hôrologia*) in *Suda* (A2), and "*hôrae*" in Eus. (A4) all refer to annual "seasons" (still the unmarked sense of the word even in classical usage), not daily "hours" (a marked sense, typically indicated by a genitive or adjective). Hence any device so named would include all four solar points (cf. Anaximenes A14a). That was a major advance on the "heliotrope" ascribed to Pherecydes (D.L. 1.119), which presumably indicated only the "tropes" or solstices.

28. The likeliest and most useful location for a durable gnomon was a sacred precinct, where the priests or officials charged with managing the local calendar could consult it easily, regularly, and with the requisite ritual sanction. In Miletus, that was either the urban Delphinion or the rural oracle of Apollo at nearby Didyma (where Callimachus pictures Thales seated in fr. 191.57 = A3a). The destruction of both sites after the Persians crushed the Ionian revolt at nearby Lade in 494 provides a rejoinder to the objection *e silentio* that no record of any gnomon in archaic Miletus survives. It may not be purely coincidental that the two earliest *parapegmata* (both c. 100 BCE) were found at Miletus; see note 26 here.

29. Both deaths were dated to Olympiad 58 = 548–45 (see note 7 here); for their use of a gnomon or similar device, see KRS 83, 103. On Thales' use of shadows to calculate the height of pyramids, see note 42 here.

30. Dedication either jointly or by a junior to his senior was customary. Two well-attested customs would interact here: compiling lists and recording achievements on sacred dedications; see Hedrick, "The Prehistory of Greek Chronography," and Hannah, "From Orality to Literacy," on star-calendars specifically.

31. See White, "Thales and the Stars," 8–10.

32. See Graham, "Philosophy on the Nile."

33. Retold by Hieronymus of Rhodes (fr. 47 = D.L. 1.26); see note 42 here. Eudemus evidently shared Aristotle's taste for the telling anecdote; see esp. fr. 54a, citing olive crops again, apparently from Democritus.

34. See White, "Thales and the Stars," 16.

35. See White, "Thales and the Stars," 7–8, and note 3 here.

36. Apuleius, who was probably familiar with Eudemus's work at least indirectly (see note 11 here), reports a discovery in similar terms (*Flor.* 18 = A19).

37. Introduction of a similar system in Athens was popularly ascribed to Solon (Plu. *Solon* 25, cf. Ar. *Clouds* 1178–91, D.L. 1.59), perhaps following Thales. But the ascription is questionable, not least because Athenians ascribed to Solon many reforms that postdate him—just as Thales was credited with various later discoveries.

38. Full text and instructive notes in Haslam, *Oxyrhynchus Papyri*, 53: 89–112; analysis of the astronomical background in Bowen and Goldstein, "Aristarchus, Thales, and Heraclitus on Solar Eclipses." A lacuna of c. 12 letters in line 40 obscures the connection between the two main claims. Haslam, followed by Bowen and Goldstein, proposes the supplement σημειουμέ[νης τῆι κρύψει]: "the day (of the eclipse) being indicated by the hiding" of the

moon at new moon. Burkert, "Heraclitus and the Moon," citing Hdt. 1.74 and adapting a proposal by Lebedev, "Aristarchus of Samos on Thales' Theory of Eclipses," proposes σημειούμε[νος τοὺς ὅρους]: "indicating [or inferring?] the limits of the day" of the eclipse.

39. See Aaboe, "Remarks on the Theoretical Treatment of Eclipses in Antiquity," for similar but more advanced Babylonian methods of computing conjunctions.

40. Hartner, "Eclipse Periods and Thales' Prediction," 66, eclipses no. 17–25. Most were only partial in Asia Minor, but one in 588 was nearly total. Totality, though helpful for discerning the explanation, is irrelevant to noticing the correlation, which any and every detectable eclipse would confirm.

41. See Graham, "La lumière de la lune," 357–58, for an analogous explanation of the story that Anaxagoras predicted a meteor's fall (D.L. 2.10, A11) as inspired by a striking confirmation of his theory that celestial bodies are rocks.

42. He used some sort of triangulation to calculate the distances; for attempts to reconstruct the procedure, see Heath, *From Thales to Euclid*, 1.131–33. The pyramids he gauged by measuring their shadows and his own (or that of a vertical rod); for analysis of the testimony, see Goulet, "Thalès et l'ombre des pyramides." The first report comes from Eudemus (fr. 134); the second probably does: D.L. 1.27 cites his fellow Rhodian Hieronymus (fr. 48), active a few decades after Eudemus.

43. A day's flight from Mount Olympus to Lemnos (*Il.* 1.590–94); 10 anvil-days (the distance an anvil would fall in 10 days) from sky to earth and from there to Tartarus (*Th.* 721–25). For the Homeric and Hesiodic cosmos, see Clay, "The World of Hesiod."

44. The details are obscure. Couprie, "*Prêstéros Aulos* Revisited" challenges the standard view of the vents as "nozzles" and proposes an explanatory analogy of a "beam or stream of lightning fire" (cf. Aët. 3.3.1 = A23); another possibility is "hurricane pipes" representing inverted funnels of light (see pp. 121–22 here).

45. Cf. "contain" (*periechein*) in Arist. *Ph.* 3.4 203b11 (A15). No additional wheels are attested for any planets (unless among the multiple rings for stars in A11.5 and A18), but Anaximander was presumably aware that some stars (morning and evening star already in Homer) "wander" out of step with the others (cf. Aët. 2.15.6 in A18).

46. A major crux already for Aristotle and Theophrastus; see A9a, A14–17, with discussion in *HGP* 1.83–87 and *PP* 28–37.

47. For the cosmogony, see A10–11, with *HGP* 1.89–101. It is unclear whether reports of "many worlds" refer to successive or concurrent worlds; the former option fits related testimony better (Thales A13b, Anaximenes A11), but for a defense of the latter, see McKirahan, "Anaximander's Infinite Worlds." A neglected possibility is that some reports mistake parts of the single world for separate worlds; thus, Aët. 2.1.8 (in A17) would refer to "equal distances" not between worlds but between sun, moon, and stars; see tables 3.1 and 3.2 here.

48. A helpful survey of attempts to visualize the system is in Couprie, "The Visualization of Anaximander's Astronomy."

49. See note 16 here. In the transmitted text of Theon, "the earth is aloft and moves around the center"; the second claim is a blatant error (see D.L. 2.1, A2, A11.3, A26), whatever its source (a scribe, Theon, Dercyllides, or earlier).

50. See *PP* 23–28, and Bodnár, "Atomic Independence and Indivisibility," but reservations in Furley, *Cosmic Problems* 14–26.

51. Analysis of the main problems and previous solutions in O'Brien, "Anaximander's Measurements."

52. It is puzzling that the same source records different figures in successive sections: Aët. 2.20, "On the sun's substance" and 2.21, "On the sun's size"; see note 55 here. The basis

for E3 in Hippolytus is emendation, to supplement a conjectured lacuna; the received text has "the sun's circle 27 times larger than the moon"; emendation would be unnecessary if Anaximander assigned 1 AU to all three bodies, not only sun and earth (as in E2) but moon as well.

53. As reported by Theon, Eudemus refers to the "theory" or "account" of sizes and distances (τὸν περὶ μεγεθῶν . . . λόγον), not their ratios (which would be τὸν τῶν μεγεθῶν . . . λόγον).

54. For defense of A5 and A22, as crediting Anaximander with recognizing that the paths of the sun and moon are "oblique" (but not with determining the angle of obliquity, which Eudemus fr. 145 ascribes to Oenopides), see Panchenko, "Who Found the Zodiac"; cf. the image of a rotating cap, usually worn tilted backward, in Anaximenes A7.6.

55. Or both sets of figures could be authentic, one for the inner rims of the rings and the other for their outer rims; see O'Brien, "Anaximander's Measurements." Though widely favored, this alternative raises awkward questions about the shape of the rings of fire and the (amorphous?) mist that envelops them, and about what lies beyond the solar ring; it also requires positing two parallel sets of diameters, when Eudemus evidently cited only one set of distances.

56. See Kahn, *Anaximander and the Origins of Greek Cosmology*, 91–98; Burkert, "Orientalische und griechische Weltmodelle von Assur bis Anaximandros"; Hahn, *Anaximander and the Architects*. But cf. Kahn, 96–97: "It is easy to imagine that he assigned them distances in some simple relationship to [Babylonian] observational data, just as his dimensions for the earth must have had some connection with known (or supposed) facts." Where Kahn proposes "Babylonian predecessors" for "data concerning the periods in which the various bodies return to the same relative position," I would substitute the horizontal astronomy of his Greek predecessors and contemporaries, most notably Thales.

57. Following his intermediary, Sosigenes; see Tannery, "Sur les fragments d'Eudème de Rhodes." It is sometimes objected that Anaximander could not possibly estimate sizes by eclipses since he attributed them to closing vents in the solar and lunar rings. But no extant testimony explains what blocks the vents, or specifies any cover formed by the surrounding mist. A solar eclipse could result not from the solar vent closing (clouded over by its own mist?) but rather from the lunar ring below it "blocking" its light when the lunar vent is also "blocked" by the periodic cycle of mist below it—hence only at new moon, as Thales proposed. Only such regular cycles would be consistent with the dynamic equilibrium Aristotle attributes to the entire system.

58. The approximation is not attested so far as I know. But neither is any other in Greek sources before Archimedes. The ratio of 3 to 1 is used in early Babylonian texts, and $(16/9)^2 = 256/81$ (roughly 19/6) in early Egypt; see Friberg, "Mathematik," 538, and Gillings, *Mathematics in the Time of the Pharaohs*, 139–46; cf. Neugebauer, *The Exact Sciences in Antiquity*, 46–47, 78. Apart from my indirect argument here, only general considerations of simplicity and symmetry favor the ratio 10 to 3.

59. According to the manuscripts of Theon, Eudemus credits Anaximenes with knowing that lunar light is reflected sunlight; but it is virtually certain that Eudemus referred rather to Anaxagoras (the error could be scribal, Theon's, or earlier; cf. note 16 here). See Panchenko, "Eudemus Fr. 145 Wehrli and the Ancient Theories of Lunar Light."

60. See Panchenko, "Who Found the Zodiac"; on the question of size, see Panchenko, "Aristarchus of Samos on the Apparent Sizes of the Sun and Moon."

61. Even when stars pass in front of the blocked portion of the lunar disc (representing the moon's dark side), its ambient light (evident in "earthglow") might still be supposed to outshine them.

62. By contrast, Anaximenes (Hippol. 1.7.6 = A7) and/or Anaxagoras (Hippol. 1.8.7 = A42) cited the great distance of the stars to explain why their heat is imperceptible.

63. Friction (literally "rubbing") is the only explanation for celestial light and heat countenanced by Aristotle (*Cael.* 2.7, *Mete.* 1.3, 341a12–36), who adopts it despite its apparent conflict with other claims he makes; see Thorp, "The Luminousness of the Quintessence."

64. See Anaximenes A6, Anaxagoras A82, and Hippol. 1.8.10.

65. Theophrastus's name occurs in a title cited by Hippol. 8.15.1, and Aëtius names him twice when citing his views (on happiness in 1 *pro.* 3, cf. fr. 479; on luck in 1.29.4, cf. fr. 503), and perhaps once as a source (2.20.3 on Xenophanes), though the reference may be a later interpolation; cf. parallel reports in Thphr. frs. 232 and 236, which name Theophrastus.

66. Eudemus appears to be the origin of the two later versions: both D.L. and the *Suda* use his term "lying" (not Aristotle's "staying") to describe the earth's location (see note 16 here); and D.L. echoes his focus in fr. 146 (A19) on the "order" (*taxis*) of the luminaries.

67. The more detailed reports in [Plu.] *Strom.* 2 (A10) and Hippol. 1.7.3–5 (A11) discuss the three bodies in the same sequence, apparently due to their focus (presumably from Theophrastus) on Anaximander's cosmogony.

68. Aristotle may also cite his work: in a cursory discussion of "the order" of the stars, which he, too, correlates with orbital velocity, Aristotle defers to "work on *astrologia*" (*Cael.* 2.10 291a29–32); and Simplicius, in commenting on that phrase, cites Eudemus fr. 146 (*in Cael.* 471.1–9). See Mansfeld, "Cosmic Distances," 195–201; Wehrli, *Schule des Aristoteles*, vol. 8, 120.

69. See note 1 here.

70. See Kahn, *Anaximander and the Origins of Greek Cosmology*, 166–96, KRS 105–22. The phrase about time is widely taken to be Anaximander's own words, mainly on the ground that it personifies time, as in Pherecydes' cosmogonic myth (fr. 1); see Kirk, "Some Problems in Anaximander," 32–37; Kahn, *Anaximander and the Origins of Greek Cosmology*, 170–72. But whether the genitive is subjective (an order exhibited *by* time) or objective (an order imposed *on* time), an impersonal conception coheres better with the rest of our evidence; and even if not authentic, the phrase accurately characterizes the impersonal scheme of regular and often periodic cycles of change established by the three Milesians.

71. See Simpl. *in Ph.* 24.21–25 (continuing the passage quoted above) and 150.22–24; so KRS 128–30, following Vlastos, "Equality and Justice in Early Greek Cosmologies," Kahn, *Anaximander and the Origins of Greek Cosmology*, 159–63, HGP 1.76–82.

72. See note 6 here. Plu. *Prim. frig.* 948a = fr. 1 cites Aristotle for a point made by Theophr. *Vent.* 20; cf. *Probl.* 26.48, 34.7 in a compilation drawing on work by many in the early Lyceum.

73. The adverb *mâllon* implies ellipse of a participle, either *piloumenon* (supplied from the noun in the preceding prepositional phrase), or more likely *puknoumenon* or *puknôthenta* (supplied from the previous clause and used in the following clause). The text is riddled with corruption and heavily emended by editors; I translate the text in DK.

74. A clause here omitted adds "hence the most important opposites in generation are hot and cold." Whether this goes back to Theophrastus or a later epitomizer, it is patently an inference (reflecting the later association of this pair of contrary features with the two extremes in Anaximenes' scheme), and belied by B1.

75. P is clearly a more truncated summary than H; both go on to sketch a cosmogony, which in each case differs significantly in detail from Anaximenes' general cosmology; see Graham, "A Testimony of Anaximenes in Plato."

76. Graham, "A Testimony of Anaximenes in Plato," and Graham, "A New Look at Anaximenes," answering doubts posed by Klowski, "Ist der Aer des Anaximenes als eine Substanz konzipiert?" and Wöhrle, *Anaximenes aus Milet*.

77. S refers only to becoming, and it is risky to trust the apparently indiscriminate use of φαίνεσθαι, γίνεσθαι, εἶναι and ἀποτελεῖσθαι in H4–5c.

78. I adapt the scheme in Graham, "A New Look at Anaximenes." The solecism "compaction" is meant to avoid potentially misleading connotations in modern notions of density or pressure; it has the added advantage of admitting both transitive and intransitive uses.

79. See Mourelatos, " 'X is Really Y.' "On TC2, all other materials are "allomorphs" or "allotropes" of air (as ice is of water); on TC2*, they are rather "aeromorphs" or "aerotropes" (forms of air-stuff, as both water and ice are forms of a more basic "hydrostuff") that are collectively co-extensive with air.

80. Hippol. 1.7.7 and Aët. 3.4.1 (A17) also analyze cloud, not as compacted wind (its neighbor in the sequence of materials), but as compacted *air*, hence more in line with TC2* than with TC2.

81. P5 refers to felting and the earth; some take this as a further case of change and argue that its divergence from S3 and H5 betrays the entire scheme as a later fabrication; see Wöhrle, *Anaximenes aus Milet*, 18–23. But the reference is clearly to "the Earth" (τὴν γῆν, with the definite article and called "flat"), not a material as in S3 and H5; hence it belongs not to TC but to cosmogony and cosmology, as the further parallel of P6 and H7 confirms; see Graham, "A New Look at Anaximenes."

82. See Kahn, *Anaximander and the Origins of Greek Cosmology*, 140–63. His analysis is challenged by Finkelberg, "Anaximander's Conception of the *apeiron*," 231–40, on some points cogently; but Finkelberg overlooks the solution offered by my next point, that "air" is *moving* vapor (cf. ἄημι).

83. By positing a specific form of air analogous to wind but differing from it only in being inert, TC2 faces an obvious and serious dilemma. On MM, it uses the same term for diametrically opposed forms of air, one ordinary and inert but the other basic and always moving. Or without MM, it ascribes opposite features—both moving and inert—to the same material phase or state.

84. See LSJ under πνοή and πνεῦμα. Further, *pnoê* designates wind still in Emped. fr. 111.4, as does *pneuma* in Anaximenes A7 (Hippol. 1.7.8; cf. Arist. *Mete.* 1.13 349a19), Anaximander A23, A27 (Arist. *Mete.* 2.3 352b8), Xenoph. A46, Emped. B111.5, and Pherecydes A8 in Eudemus fr. 150. Alt, "Zum Satz des Anaximenes über die Seele," establishes that fr. 2 goes back to Theophrastus; but against her further contention that it comes from Diogenes of Apollonia and was mistakenly "transferred" to Anaximenes in later accounts, see Wöhrle, *Anaximenes aus Milet*, 65–66.

85. The third sequence adds a fifth change between vapor and liquid, namely "cloud and mist."

86. Plato's objection may lie behind the reservations Aristotle evinces in reporting that "Anaximenes and Diogenes posit air *before* water and *most a principle* of the simple bodies" (*Metaph.* 1.3 984a5–7 = A4). The priority of air is both cosmogonic and cosmological: both temporal (MM1) and ontological (MM2).

87. As it does in Plato's series (T3). Aristotle likewise criticizes a theory that makes the basic material intermediate in the then standard tetrad of elements and differentiated specifically by compaction (*Cael.* 3.5 303b11–16, *GC* 2.5 332a20–2), and though he does not name any proponents, the theory closely resembles Anaximenes' as interpreted here. Incidentally, the six-term series of TC2* also eliminates two asymmetries in TC2's series of seven: (1) the archaic "misty air" would be intermediate, between cloud and water, rather

than next to fire at one extreme, and (2) the whole series falls neatly into two triads (resistant or not) and three pairs (luminous, moist, dry) rather than unequal groups (three airy terms, two solids, a liquid, and fire).

88. Even when not perceived directly, its presence can be readily inferred from fanning or rapid bodily movement, and dust and "motes" are visible drifting and floating even in the stillest air.

89. Cf. *penetrat* in Anaximander A28 (probably from Anaximenes: see note 94 here). Anaximenes' air is not entirely or invariably yielding: the earth "rides" steadily on air because its "broad and flat" surface enables it to float (H6, P5, cf. A20, including Arist. *Cael.* 2.13), as do some or all of the other cosmic bodies (H7, A15).

90. See note 46 here. Anaxagoras B1 similarly calls air and aether (for fire: A43, 70, 73, 84) "unlimited" and "in all things greatest in both number and size."

91. It thus appears that, contrary to Aristotle's general complaint in *Metaph.* A.3, Anaximenes did specify (according to Theophrastus) a moving or efficient cause, at least at the general cosmological level, namely, the ever-moving basic air that is also his universal material cause.

92. Reports refer repeatedly to a pair of opposite qualities and processes: both compacting and thinning. But it is far from certain that Anaximenes understood this opposition in the essentially dualist terms of Aristotelian contraries (see esp. *GC* 2.5) rather than a single factor that varies in degree—or more loosely, by more or less. If the latter, his single continuum would be more akin to modern theories than to most of his ancient heirs. The duality apparent in our sources may be the result of the way changes were normally described directionally as increases: cloud "compacts" into water (rather than decreasing in thinness), and water "thins" into cloud (rather than decreasing in compaction).

93. Visible features are also regularly (but only implicitly) correlated: the primary or sole source of light is air in its thinnest state; and its transmission decreases from transparency to opacity as compaction increases. See A18 on rainbows. Two sets of properties that Anaxagoras correlated, parallel with Anaximenes (thin, hot, dry vs. compact, cold, moist), include bright and dark (B15; cf. A70 = Thphr. *Sens.* 59).

94. H1: τὰ δὲ λοιπὰ ἐκ τῶν τούτου ἀπογόνων; S4: τὰ δὲ ἄλλα ἐκ τούτων. The use of ἐκ suggests a compositional analysis in terms of mixture; stones, for example, though inherently cool, might become hot by *absorbing* some of the thin—hence fiery and hot—air around them; cf. snow and earthquakes in the next paragraph.

95. See note 92 here.

96. See note 94 here.

97. Ammianus attributes the same account to Anaximander (17.7.12 = A28), either by mistake or because both Milesians shared the same account. Seneca attributes to Thales a much simpler ("inept") explanation: the earth is shaken by the water on which it floats (*NQ* 3.14 = A15).

98. The sole apparent exception, in P5–6, is cosmogonic and elliptical: the focus on celestial bodies rather than material phases explains the omission of any intermediate stages leading to the earth's compacted body and the thin and fiery bodies of the stars.

99. See note 92 here.

100. See Seaford, *Money and the Early Greek Mind*, 198–230, for speculations on deeper conceptual connections.

101. Fr. 76 is widely considered suspect for including air, which is not prominent in other extant evidence for Heraclitus; but see *HGP* 1.453, and the exception would be explicable if he meant to criticize Anaximenes.

102. See Panchenko, "Thales and the Origin of Theoretical Reasoning." I am grateful to Alex Mourelatos for probing comments.

BIBLIOGRAPHY

Aaboe, Asger. "Remarks on the Theoretical Treatment of Eclipses in Antiquity." *Journal for the History of Astronomy* 3 (1972): 105–18.

Alt, Karin. "Zum Satz des Anaximenes über die Seele: Untersuchung von Aetios *Peri archôn*." *Hermes* 101 (1973): 129–64.

Barnes, Jonathan. *The Presocratic Philosophers*. London: Routledge, 1979 (abbreviated *PP*).

Bodnár, István M. "Anavimander's Rings." *Classical Quarterly* 38 (1988): 49–51.

Bowen, Alan C., and Bernard R. Goldstein. "Aristarchus, Thales, and Heraclitus on Solar Eclipses: An Astronomical Commentary on P.Oxy. 53.3710 Cols. 2.33–3.19." *Physis* 31 (1994): 689–729.

Burkert, Walter. "Heraclitus and the Moon: The New Fragment *P.Oxy.* 3710." *Illinois Classical Studies* 18 (1993): 49–55.

———. "Orientalische und griechische Weltmodelle von Assur bis Anaximandros." *Wiener Studien* 107 (1994): 179–86.

Cherniss, Harold. *Aristotle's Criticism of Presocratic Philosophy*. Baltimore: Johns Hopkins University Press, 1935.

Clay, Diskin. "The World of Hesiod." *Ramus* 21 (1992): 131–55.

Couprie, Dirk L. "*Prêstêros aulos* Revisited." *Apeiron* 34 (2001): 195–204.

———. "The Visualization of Anaximander's Astronomy." *Apeiron* 28 (1995): 159–81.

Dicks, D. R. "Solstices, Equinoxes, and the Presocratics." *Journal of Hellenic Studies* 86 (1966): 26–40.

Diels, Hermann, and Albert Rehm. "Parapegmenfragmente aus Milet." *Sitzungsberichte der königlich Preussischen Akademie der Wissenschaft* 23 (1904): 92–111.

Finkelberg, Aryeh. "Anaximander's Conception of the *Apeiron*." *Phronesis* 38 (1993): 229–56.

Friberg, J. "Mathematik." In *Reallexikon der Assyriologie*, edited by E. Ebeling et al., 531–85. Berlin: de Gruyter, 1990.

Furley, David J. *Cosmic Problems*. Cambridge: Cambridge University Press, 1989.

Gillings, Richard. *Mathematics in the Time of the Pharaohs*. Cambridge, Mass.: MIT Press, 1972.

Goulet, Richard. "Thalès et l'ombre des pyramides." In *Epieikeia: Studia Graeca in Memoriam J. Lens Tuero*, edited by M. Alganza Rodán et al., 199–212. Granada, Spain: Athos-Pérgamos, 2000.

Graham, Daniel W. "La lumière de la lune dans la pensée grecque archaïque." In *Qu'est-ce que la philosophie présocratique?* edited by André Laks and Claire Louguet, 351–80. Lille: Presses Universitaires du Septentrion, 2002.

———. "A New Look at Anaximenes." *History of Philosophy Quarterly* 20 (2003): 1–20.

———. "Philosophy on the Nile: Herodotus and Ionian Research." *Apeiron* 36 (2003): 291–310.

———. "A Testimony of Anaximenes in Plato." *Classical Quarterly* 53 (2003): 327–37.

Hahn, Robert. *Anaximander and the Architects*. Albany: State University of New York Press, 2001.

Hannah, Robert. "Euctemon's Parapegma," In *Science and Mathematics in Ancient Greek Culture*, edited by Christopher Tuplin and Tracey Rihll, 112–32. Oxford: Oxford University Press, 2002.

————. "From Orality to Literacy? The Case of the Parapegma." In *Speaking Volumes: Orality and Literacy in the Greek Roman World*, edited by Janet Watson, 139–59. Leiden: Brill, 2001.

Hartner, Willy. "Eclipse Periods and Thales' Prediction of a Solar Eclipse: Historic Truth and Modern Myth." *Centaurus* 144 (1969): 60–71.

Haslam, Michael. *The Oxyrhynchus Papyri*, vol. 53, 1986.

Heath, Thomas. *From Thales to Euclid*. A History of Greek Mathematics, vol. 1. Oxford: Clarendon Press, 1921.

Hedrick, Charles W. "The Prehistory of Greek Chronography." In *Oikistes: Studies in Constitutions, Colonies, and Military Power in the Ancient World*, edited by Virginia B. Gorman and Eric W. Robinson, 13–32. Leiden: Brill, 2002.

Kahn, Charles H. *Anaximander and the Origins of Greek Cosmology*. New York: Columbia University Press, 1960.

————. "On Early Greek Astronomy." *Journal of Hellenic Studies* 90 (1970): 99–116.

————. "Writing Philosophy: Prose and Poetry from Thales to Plato." In *Written Texts and the Rise of Literate Culture in Ancient Greece*, edited by H. Yunis, 139–61. Cambridge, Mass.: Cambridge University Press, 2003.

Kirk, Geoffrey S. "Some Problems in Anaximander." *Classical Quarterly* 5 (1955): 21–38.

Klowski, Joachim. "Ist der Aer des Anaximenes als eine Substanz konzipiert?" *Hermes* 100 (1972): 131–42.

Lebedev, Andrei V. "Aristarchus of Samos on Thales' Theory of Eclipses." *Apeiron* 23 (1990): 77–85.

Lesher, James H. *Xenophanes of Colophon: Fragments*. Toronto: University of Toronto Press, 1992.

Mansfeld, Jaap. "Aristotle and Others on Thales, or the Beginnings of Natural Philosophy." *Mnemosyne* 38 (1985): 109–29.

————. "Cosmic Distances: Aëtius 2.31 Diels and Some Related Texts." *Phronesis* 45 (2000): 175–204.

McDiarmid, John B. "Theophrastus on the Presocratic Causes." *Harvard Studies in Classical Philology* 61 (1953): 85–156.

McKirahan, Richard D., Jr. "Anaximander's Infinite Worlds." In *Before Plato: Essays in Ancient Greek Philosophy*, edited by A. Preus, 49–65. Albany: State University of New York Press, 2001.

Mourelatos, Alexander P. D. " 'X is Really Y': Ionian Origins of a Thought Pattern." In *Ionian Philosophy*, edited by K. J. Boudouris, 280–90. Athens: International Association for Greek Philosophy, 1989.

Neugebauer, Otto. *The Exact Sciences in Antiquity*. 2nd ed. Providence, R.I.: Brown University Press, 1957.

O'Brien, Denis. "Anaximander's Measurements." *Classical Quarterly* 17 (1967): 423–32.

Panchenko, Dmitri. "Aristarchus of Samos on the Apparent Sizes of the Sun and Moon." *Antike Naturwissenschaft und ihre Rezeption* 11 (2001): 23–29.

————. "Eudemus Fr. 145 Wehrli and the Ancient Theories of Lunar Light." In *Eudemus of Rhodes*, edited by István M. Bódnar and W. W. Fortenbaugh, 323–36. New Brunswick, N.J.: Transaction, 2002.

————. "Thales and the Origin of Theoretical Reasoning." *Configurations* 3 (1993): 387–414.

————. "Thales' Prediction of a Solar Eclipse." *Journal of the History of Astronomy* 25 (1994): 277–88.

————. "Who Found the Zodiac?" *Antike Naturwissenschaft und ihre Rezeption* 9 (1999): 33–44.

Seaford, Richard. *Money and the Early Greek Mind.* Cambridge: Cambridge University Press, 2004.

Stephenson, F. Richard, and Louay J. Fatoohi. "Thales' Prediction of a Solar Eclipse." *Journal for the History of Astronomy* 28 (1997): 279–82.

Tannery, Paul. "Sur les fragments d'Eudème de Rhodes relatifs à l'histoire des mathématiques." *Annales de la Faculté des Lettres de Bordeaux* 45 (1882): 70–76.

Taub, Liba. *Ancient Meteorology.* London: Routledge, 2003.

Thomson, Rosalind. *Literacy and Orality in Ancient Greece.* Cambridge, Mass.: Cambridge University Press, 1992.

Thorp, John. "The Luminousness of the Quintessence." *Phoenix* 36 (1982): 104–23.

Vlastos, Gregory. "Equality and Justice in Early Greek Cosmologies." *Classical Philology* 42 (1947): 156–78.

von Fritz, Kurt. "Oinopides." *Real-Encyclopädie* 17 (1937): 2258–272.

Wehrli, Fritz. *Die Schule des Aristoteles,* vol. 8: *Eudemos von Rhodos.* Basel: Schwabe, 1955/1968.

West, Martin L. *Hesiod, Works and Days.* Oxford: Clarendon Press, 1978.

White, Stephen A. "Eudemus the Naturalist." In *Eudemus of Rhodes,* edited by István Bodnár and William W. Fortenbaugh, 207–41. New Brunswick, NJ: Transaction, 2002.

————. "Thales and the Stars." In *Presocratic Philosophy,* edited by Victor Caston and Daniel W. Graham, 3–18. Aldershot, England: Ashgate, 2002.

Wöhrle, Georg. *Anaximenes aus Milet: Die Fragmente zu seiner Lehre.* Stuttgart: Franz Steiner Verlag, 1993.

Zhmud, Leonid. "Eudemus' History of Mathematics." In *Eudemus of Rhodes,* edited by István Bodnár and William W. Fortenbaugh, 263–306. New Brunswick, N.J.: Transaction, 2002.

————. "The Historiographical Project of the Lyceum: The Peripatetic History of Science, Philosophy and Medicine." *Antike Naturwissenschaft und ihre Rezeption* 13 (2003): 109–26.

CHAPTER 4

THE CLOUD-ASTROPHYSICS OF XENOPHANES AND IONIAN MATERIAL MONISM

ALEXANDER P. D. MOURELATOS

"LOOK ALOFT!" cried Starbuck. "The St. Elmo's Lights (corpus sancti) corposants! the corposants!"

All the yard-arms were tipped with a pallid fire; and touched at each tri-pointed lightning-rod-end with three tapering white flames, each of the three tall masts was silently burning in that sulphurous air, like three gigantic wax tapers before an altar.... While this pallidness was burning aloft, few words were heard from the enchanted crew; who in one thick cluster stood on the forecastle, all their eyes gleaming in that pale phosphorescence, like a far away constellation of stars.... Starbuck caught sight of Stubb's face slowly beginning to glimmer into sight. Glancing upwards he cried: "See! see!" and once more the high tapering flames were beheld with what seemed redoubled supernaturalness in their pallor.

"The corposants have mercy on us all," cried Stubb again.

The phenomenon of St. Elmo's fire described in this passage from Melville's *Moby Dick*[1] was as familiar to the seafaring ancient Greeks as it was to the nineteenth-century whalers from Nantucket. Xenophanes of Colophon was almost certainly the first to have offered a naturalistic explanation of the phenomenon. I have started with a literary description so as to provide readers with a vivid image, considering that in these days of artificial lighting and of anti-static devices on air- and sea-craft St. Elmo's fire has become virtually unknown to us.[2] The modern explanation is that "[t]he phenomenon occurs when the atmosphere becomes charged and an electrical potential strong enough to cause a discharge is created between an object and the air around it," the resulting slow discharge taking the form of reddish or bluish specks of light or flares at the extremities of pointed objects.[3] The flaring does not actually burn—Melville's candles are all simile— the discharge of electricity is low enough to be harmless, but the discharge is often accompanied by a sizzling or crackling noise—*pace* Melville's "silently burning."

Xenophanes' account has been preserved in Aëtius, the doxographic compendium (1st or 2nd century CE) reconstructed by Hermann Diels late in the nineteenth century[4] mainly from two sources that show extensive parallelism: pseudo-Plutarch *Placita Philosophorum* or *Epitome of Physical Opinions* (hereafter *Epit.*, 2nd century CE);[5] and Ioannes Stobaeus' *Eclogae Physicae* or *Physical Extracts* (hereafter *Ecl.*, 5th century CE).[6] In the Stobaeus version,[7] which is also the one printed in the standard edition of the Presocratics, the report reads:

> Ξενοφάνης ... τοὺς δὲ ἐπὶ τῶν πλοίων φαινομένους οἷον ἀστέρας, οὕς καὶ Διοσκούρους καλοῦσί τινες, νεφέλια εἶναι κατὰ τὴν ποιὰν κίνησιν παραλάμποντα.

> Xenophanes, ... moreover, (says *or* holds) that those star-like apparitions on ships, which are indeed[8] called Dioskouroi by some, are cloudlets that glimmer because of a special agitation. (DKA39 Aëtius)[9]

The diminutive form *nephelia*, "tiny clouds, cloudlets,"[10] in this report could not be one Xenophanes had used since it does not fit his meter.[11] But that Xenophanes himself should have referred to St. Elmo's fire by the name of the divine twins of myth and traditional worship is in itself quite likely. The association between the Dioskouroi and St. Elmo's fire appears unmistakably as early as the seventh or sixth century BCE, in a fragment of a hymn to the Dioskouroi by the lyric poet Alcaeus.[12] We may safely assume, then, that the sailors of Xenophanes' day saw St. Elmo's fire as the luminous manifestation of beneficent intervention by the divine twins at a time of peril.[13] Xenophanes, the poet-philosopher of the Greek Enlightenment, would have wanted to deflate the pious sentiment with a naturalistic explanation.

1. WIDER CONTEXT OF NATURALISTIC EXPLANATION

This reconstruction of the core content of A39 receives strong support from a parallel in the fragments of Xenophanes' poetry—the two hexameter lines concerning the rainbow:

ἥν τ᾽ Ἶριν καλέουσι, νέφος καὶ τοῦτο πέφυκε,
πορφύρεον καὶ φοινίκεον καὶ χλωρὸν ἰδέσθαι.

What they call Iris [the rainbow goddess] that too is in reality a cloud: one that appears to the eye as purple, red, and green. (B32)

In this case the deflationary effect is conveyed immediately by the use of the prosaic term *nephos*.[14] Of special interest is the conjunctive expression *kai touto*, "that too," which indicates that the reductivist explanation was offered more than once by Xenophanes. The parallel between A39 and the rainbow fragment encourages the hypothesis that the thought-form "what they call X is really Y" may also have appeared, explicitly or implicitly, in Xenophanes' original remark concerning St. Elmo's fire.[15] And even though the phrase "star-like" is not distinctive enough to provide any clue of what Xenophanes himself may have said, the association between stars and St. Elmo's fire is quite natural (recall "like a far away constellation of stars" in the quotation from Melville). Moreover, there is evidence that the association between stars and the divine twins is part of the original mythic image of the Dioskouroi.[16] We may indulge, then, a conjecture of the form of the Xenophanean original behind A39—something of this order:

> Those star-like apparitions mariners call the Dioskouroi—they are in reality clouds: small ones that glow because of some agitation.

Taken together, and placed in the larger context of Xenophanes' hexameter fragments, B32 and the core content of A39 are naturally read as parts and specimens of Xenophanes' polemic against the anthropomorphic and anthropocentric gods of traditional piety:[17] those star-like apparitions on ships are purely natural occurrences, not a sign of benign intervention by the Dioskouroi; the rainbow is a mere cloud, not Zeus's portent of war or storm (Homer *Il.* 17.547–549). It appears, moreover, that this thrust of Xenophanes' polemic was reinforced with remarks concerning rain, wind, lightning, the sun, and the moon. The cause and source of rain is not Zeus; nor is Boreas or some other wind-god the cause of wind. For both there is the same "fount" (*pêgê*) and "generator" (*genetôr*), the vast sea with its mists, zephyrs, and breezes (B30). Likewise, thunderbolts are not Jovian missiles: at Aëtius 3.3.6 (DKA45) we read: "lightning bolts occur (*ginontai*) as clouds become luminescent (*lamprynomenôn*) because of motion (*kata tên kinêsin*)."[18] Another deflationary comment lies just below the surface of the one-line fragment B31: "The sun that soars above (*hyperiemenos*) and warms the earth." Our ancient source for this fragment detected in the participle *hyperiemenos*, "soaring," an etymologizing evocation of the personified sun of Homer, the divine Hyperion.[19] This perceptive gloss reveals Xenophanes' thought: "The sun does warm the earth; but not because the sun is the benign Hyperion."

Also enhanced and explained, when placed in this context of polemic, is a rather puzzling report from Aëtius 2.30.8 (from Stobaeus *Ecl.* only) concerning both sun and moon:

Xenophanes [held] that the sun contributes to (*chrêsimon einai pros*) the generation and governance of the world and of the living things in it, whereas the moon makes no contribution (*parelkein*). (A42)

This singling out of the moon for teleological disparagement might itself seem otiose if we fail to remind ourselves that mythical lore had invested the goddess of the moon with a panoply of powers—control of menstruation and pregnancy, of the growth of plants and animals, of disease and health, and more.[20] Take away the name "Hyperion," Xenophanes would seem to be saying, and the sun still has the power to cause changes by virtue of its heat; take away the personification of Selene and the lore that goes with it, and all you are left with is a weak, cold, causally inert light.

There is, however, yet another context in which these four pieces of evidence concerning Xenophanes' philosophy ought to be placed. It is important to note at the outset that Xenophanes did not limit himself to a polemic against traditional belief concerning the gods; he offered (B23–B26) his own positive, albeit speculative, proposal concerning the nature of the deity. Correspondingly, when he debunked the anthropocentrism implied in associating mysterious lights on ships with the Dioskouroi, the rainbow with Zeus, the sun's warmth with a beneficent Hyperion, or the moon with numinous powers, he did not limit himself to a purely phenomenological reduction—"Just what you see and feel: a cloud, a warm light, a cold light!"[21]—he provided a comprehensive speculative theory. Scope of the theory was the *metarsia* or *meteôra*, "things that appear in the skies." That scope defines, of course, *meteôrologia* in the ancient sense, which combines what we call "meteorology," "astronomy," and "astrophysics."

The full doxography for Xenophanes shows that B30, B31, B32, A39, A42, and A45 give us glimpses of that comprehensive physical theory.[22] Unfortunately, in many major accounts of the Presocratics, Xenophanes' natural philosophy is either passed over completely or is interpreted with astonishing lack of reader's charity.[23] Here I propose to present a sympathetic—avowedly reconstructive and speculative—reading of the theory. For I believe it is more than arguable that the theory is internally coherent, that it can be attractively connected to intelligent observation of celestial and atmospheric phenomena, that it also has significant systematic connections with other parts of Xenophanes' philosophy, and that it does not at all have the vices of stultifying empiricism some modern scholars have found in it. In short, my own estimate is that, by sixth-century standards, Xenophanes' physical doctrine is no less of a proto-scientific theory than are the corresponding accounts by his predecessors Anaximenes and Anaximander. Indeed, Xenophanes' doctrine of the *meteôra* is our best specimen of sixth-century scientific theory, inasmuch as it is only in this case that we are in a position to supplement evidence provided by ancient testimonia with the evidence of verbatim quotations.

It will be helpful from this point forward to observe a distinction between *meteôra* in the wider sense, which encompasses ordinary clouds as well, and the "astrophysical *meteôra*," the phrase I shall use to refer to the sun, the moon, stars (including, of course, planets), comets, and other effects of unusual luminescence in the skies. The present essay aims specifically to ascertain Xenophanes' doctrine of the nature and constitution of the astrophysical *meteôra*. But, before we narrow our focus to the theme of nature and constitution, a brief overview of the entirety of Xenophanes' cosmological and astrophysical doctrine is very much in order.[24]

2. BRIEF OVERVIEW OF XENOPHANES' NATURAL PHILOSOPHY

Xenophanes holds that there is just a single boundary in the universe; the one "seen by our feet" (B28), a vast undulating plane (corrugated by mountains and valleys; note *êeri prosplazon* at B28.2) that separates the realm of what is below and what is above. Below our feet, the earth extends infinitely or indefinitely (B28.2); and, given the emphasis on a single limit, the earth probably also extends infinitely or indefinitely in all directions of its surface as well.[25] Two cosmic stuffs, earth and water, are in a tide-like action-reaction of ebb and flow. Periodically, areas that were once under water, are uplifted; and after they dry up, fossils of marine life are exposed (A33[5]–[6]). At all times, water spreads over large areas of the earth and even penetrates to some significant depth below the earth's surface (B37). But the dominant domain of water is that of "above," viz., the vast region of air, winds, moisture, rains, snow, and ordinary clouds, which are all generated and sustained by water through an intuitively obvious process of evaporation and condensation (B30). The exact process whereby the astrophysical *meteôra* are constituted I shall discuss in some detail below. For the purposes of this overview, suffice it to say that water and processes of rarefaction-condensation play a major role, and that Xenophanes must surely have drawn on the theories both of Anaximenes and of Thales. Specifically in the case of the sun, we are told that eclipses occur when the sun passes over arid areas of earth that do not provide sufficient evaporation to sustain the luminary (A41).[26] By implication, both lunar eclipses and the monthly disappearance of the moon result from failure of evaporative support.

The single-boundary geometry of the Xenophanean cosmos rules out the possibility that stars, moon, or sun could pass "under" the earth in closed-curve orbits. On what I consider the most likely reconstruction of his cosmology,[27] the stars and constellations continuously twirl above our heads, the downward tilt of the celestial pole being an illusion that is caused either by mountains to the north or by our off-center position (far toward the south) as observers—or by both these factors.[28] By contrast, the sun and (presumably) the moon run on a straight line, from east to west, above the plane of the earth, the curved trajectory being an effect of perspective (41a). Both luminaries proceed westward indefinitely,[29] presumably till the next event of an eclipse, after which a new sun or moon is reconstituted (either overhead or somewhere beyond our horizon) from a fresh supply of evaporative material (41 and 41a).

It is perhaps this rectilinear model of the movement of the two luminaries, more so than any other feature in Xenophanes' natural philosophy, that has scandalized his modern detractors. For it is a clear implication of the model that there is no single sun or single moon but a plurality of each. Indeed, there is not just one single-file east-west series of successive suns and moons; rather there are many parallel such rows, many to our north, many to our south (41a).[30] This would presumably have served to explain facts known from the lore of travel to remote regions of the south or the north: the sun of the Ethiopians (deep Africa) is hotter and is generally higher in the sky than the sun known in and around the Mediterranean; the sun of the far north is not only much weaker than that of the Mediterranean region but is even reported to undergo eclipses (winter non-visibility) for as long as a month.

To avoid the rather jarring plurals "suns" and "moons," and adhering in this respect to the pattern of the ancient testimonia, I shall generally continue using the singular expressions in connection with Xenophanes; but it should henceforth be understood that the reference is to the sun or to the moon as a *type* of astrophysical *meteôron*, not as *tokens*, not as concrete individuals.

In sections 3–9 below, I canvass the evidence concerning the constitution of the astrophysical *meteôra*. I then offer an exploration, in sections 10–14, of simple observations that could be taken to provide support for an assimilation of all the astrophysical *meteôra* to clouds. Two of the concluding sections, 15 and 16, place Xenophanes' astrophysics in the context of sixth-century material monism; and I end with a coda, section 17, that takes note of some intriguing parallels to modern patterns of scientific explanation.

3. The Cloud-Astrophysics in the Testimonia

Let us now take a careful look at the Greek testimonia[31] concerning Xenophanes' conception of the constitution of the *meteôra*. For this survey of the relevant texts, I have omitted the evidence we have already considered—about the rainbow and about St. Elmo's fire. Also omitted are the few references, either in the testimonia or in fragments,[32] to clouds proper. For Xenophanes the latter function as *explanantia* (or as part of the germane explanantia) rather than as *explananda*. Accordingly, nothing distinctive about clouds proper is found in the source texts; ordinary intuitions are being assumed. Included, however, in the texts below is some material which, upon closer examination, may be judged *not* to represent Xenophanean doctrine.

(A) *The sun*
  • A32 pseudo-Plutarch *Strom.*: ἐκ μικρῶν καὶ πλειόνων πυριδίων [MSS read πυρίων] ἀθροίζεσθαι, "accumulates out of tiny and numerous flares/sparks."

- A32 pseudo-Plutarch *Strom.*: τὸν δὲ ἥλιον . . . καὶ τὰ ἄστρα ἐκ τῶν νεφῶν γίνεσθαι, "the sun and the stars come into being from the clouds."

- A33 Hippol. *Haer.*: ἐκ μικρῶν πυριδίων ἀθροιζομένων, "from tiny flares/sparks, as they accumulate."

- A40 Aëtius (pseudo-Plutarch *Epit.*; cf. *DG* 348): ἐκ πυριδίων τῶν συναθροιζομένων μὲν ἐκ τῆς ὑγρᾶς ἀναθυμιάσεως, συνα-θροιζόντων δὲ τὸν ἥλιον· ἢ νέφος πεπυρωμένον.[33] " . . . out of tiny flares/sparks that are gathered from the moist exhalation, and cumulatively form the sun; alternately, it is an ignited/incandescent cloud."

- Eusebius *PE* 15.23.2 (derived from pseudo-Plutarch *Epit.*): . . . ἐκ πυ-ριδίων τῶν φαινομένων συναθροιζομένων μὲν ἐκ τῆς ὑγρᾶς ἀναθυμιάσεως, συναθροιζόντων δὲ τὸν ἥλιον ἐκ νεφῶν πεπυ-ρωμένων. " . . . out of tiny flares/sparks that are, first (*men*), manifestly gathered from the moist exhalation, and then (*de*) cumulatively form the sun out of ignited/incandescent clouds."

- A40 Aëtius (Stob. *Ecl.*; *DG* 348–349): ἐκ νεφῶν πεπυρωμένων εἶναι . . . Θεόφραστος ἐν τοῖς Φυσικοῖς γέγραφεν ἐκ πυριδίων μὲν τῶν συναθροιζομένων <ἐκ> τῆς ὑγρᾶς ἀναθυμιάσεως, συνα-θροιζόντων δὲ τὸν ἥλιον. " . . . is [constituted] out of ignited/incandescent clouds . . . Theophrastus in his *Physics* writes [that it is constituted] out of tiny flares/sparks, which are gathered from the moist exhalation, and thus cumulatively form the sun."[34]

- Theodoretus (*DG* 348): καὶ μέντοι καὶ τὸν ἥλιον καὶ τὴν σελήνην ὁ Ξενοφάνης νέφη εἶναι πεπυρωμένα φησίν. "Xenophanes says even of the sun and of the moon that they are ignited/incandescent clouds."

(B) *The moon*[35]

- A43 Aëtius (both pseudo-Plutarch *Epit.* and Stobaeus *Ecl.*): νέφος εἶναι πεπιλημένον. " . . . is a compressed cloud." Two variant readings in *Epit.*: πεπυρωμένον, "ignited/incandescent"; and †πεπυρωλυ-μένον, "(?)ignited/incandescent/compressed(?)."

- Eusebius *PE* 15.26.2: νέφος εἶναι πεπιλημένον. " . . . is a compressed cloud."

- Pseudo-Galen *Phil. Hist.* (*DG* 627): εἶναι νέφος πεπυρωμένον. " . . . is an ignited/incandescent cloud."

- Ioannes Lydus (*DG* 356): νέφος εἶναι πεπυρωμένον. " . . . is an ig-nited/incandescent cloud."

- Theodoretus: "[sun and moon are] an ignited/incandescent cloud"; cf. above under (A).[36]

- A43 Aëtius (Stobaeus *Ecl.*, *DG* 358): . . . ἴδιον αὐτὴν ἔχειν φῶς. " . . .has its own light."

(C) *The stars*

- A32 pseudo-Plutarch *Strom.*: "come into being from the clouds"; see above under (A), second passage.
- A38 Aëtius: ἐκ νεφῶν μὲν πεπυρωμένων [sc. εἶναι or γεγενῆσθαι].[37] σβεννυμένους δὲ καθ' ἑκάστην ἡμέραν ἀναζωπυρεῖν νύκτωρ καθάπερ τοὺς ἄνθρακας. ". . . [are/have been constituted] out of ignited/incandescent clouds. They die down each day, and during the night they flare up again, just as coals do."
- Achilles *Intr. Arat.* (*DG* 343): ἐκ νεφῶν συνεστάναι ἐμπύρων καὶ σβέννυσθαι καὶ ἀνάπτεσθαι ὡσανεὶ ἄνθρακας. ". . . are/have been constituted out of ignited clouds, and they are extinguished and rekindled just as coals do."
- Theodoretus (*DG* 343): ἐκ νεφῶν μὲν λέγει πεπυρωμένων ξυνίστασθαι· σβεννυμένους δὲ μεθ' ἡμέραν νύκτωρ πάλιν ἀναζωπυρεῖσθαι καθάπερ τοὺς ἄνθρακας. ". . . he says, are constituted out of ignited/incandescent clouds. They die down by day, and by night they flare up again, just as coals do."

(D) *Other phenomena*

- A44 Aëtius: πάντα τὰ τοιαῦτα[38] νεφῶν πεπυρωμένων συστήματα ἢ κινήματα.[39] "All things of this sort [comets, shooting stars, and similar phenomena of unusual luminescence in the skies] are aggregations or movements of ignited/incandescent clouds."[40]
- A45 Aëtius (Stobaeus *Ecl.* only): ἀστραπὰς γίνεσθαι λαμπρυνομένων τῶν νεφῶν κατὰ τὴν κίνησιν. "Lightning occurs as clouds become luminescent when agitated."

I discuss each of the four groups of texts before I proceed to some general observations concerning Xenophanes' astrophysics. Because discussion of the texts in (D) will bear on the examination of texts in (B), the latter will be taken up last.

4. THE MEANING OF *PEPYRÔMENON/-A*

Prominent as a differentiating adjective for astrophysical *meteôra* in the testimonia is the perfect passive participle *pepyrômenon/-a*. There is no reason to question that this form (either as neuter nominative, or in the two other genders and in other cases, singular or plural) was used by Xenophanes: it can easily be worked into the prosody of his dactylic verse. Moreover, relatively early uses precisely of the perfect participle are indeed attested—in Plato, in Aristotle, and in one of the Hippocratic treatises.[41] In my translations in section 3, I have provisionally used both "ignited" and "incandescent"; but we must now choose and be more precise.

In the text from Achilles—see above at (C)—we also find the adjective *empyron*, "ignited," "afire," "aflame," used with reference to the stars. In all other testimonia, however, it is only *pepyrômenon/-a* that serves as the operative description of astrophysical *meteôra*. The term conveys the state or condition an object reaches after it is subjected to a process of active *pyroun*, "to fire, to apply high heat to" (expressed on the object's side by the passive *pyrousthai*). The paradigm case for the use of the perfect passive participle is in metallurgy: silver or gold is heated to the melting point, especially so it may be purged of impurities; iron is fired to the stage at which it becomes white-hot, incandescent.[42] This paradigm makes it possible for the participle to be used widely and frequently (indeed as widely and frequently as the finite forms of the verbs *pyroun/pyrousthai* are likewise used) in a metaphorical way: in medicine, to convey states of congestion, swelling, inflammation, or fever; in contexts of moral psychology, states of incitement, stimulation, stirring, agitation, or excitement. In both the literal and the metaphorical uses, the process of *pyroun/pyrousthai* involves stages or degrees, and one may therefore speak of something as being "more" or "very" or "less" *pepyrômenon*. By contrast, the concept "ignited/afire/aflame" has essentially a binary (on/off) logic, the relevant opposite being "quenched."[43] For reasons I have detailed elsewhere,[44] I am convinced that Achilles misrepresents Xenophanes when he foists upon him the mytho-poetic idea that sun, moon, and stars are "kindled in the east and quenched in the west."[45] I shall therefore put aside Achilles' testimony and concentrate on the texts in which *pepyrômenon* is the only term at issue.

It is important to stress that the object of (or the "patient" in) *pyroun/pyrousthai*, even in the non-metaphorical uses of the verb, does not necessarily become ignited or kindled; nor does the object necessarily either contain fire before the process of *pyrousthai* or come to possess portions of fire after the *pyrousthai*. Especially telling in this connection is a sentence from fragment 475 from the works of the Stoic Chrysippus:

> [I]n saying of iron, when it is white-hot (τὸν σίδηρον, ὅταν ᾖ πεπυρωμένος), that it is inflamed and fiery (αὐτὸν ἐξάπτεσθαί τε καὶ πυροῦσθαι), we do not do so in the same way in which we speak of things of which fire is the material ingredient (μὴ λέγειν ὁμοίως τοῖς, οἷς ὕλη τὸ πῦρ). (Alexander of Aphrodisias, *De mixtione* 226.34, Bruns)

Indeed, examination of all uses of the potentially synonymous terms *pyrinos*, *empyros*, *anêmmenos*, *pyrôdês*, and *pepyrômenos* in the entire body of ancient texts edited or reproduced in Diels's *Doxographi graeci* reveals that whereas the first three terms do convey the sense of "ignited, afire, aflame," the latter two (*pyrôdês*, *pepyrômenos*) are used with respect to situations in which the subject possesses certain "fiery" characteristics without necessarily (and almost always without) being on fire.[46]

Accordingly, for *pepyrômenon/-a* I shall henceforth use only the translation "incandescent." The nature of the process that makes astrophysical clouds glow like white-hot iron should be no mystery to students of early Greek philosophy. Undoubtedly what we have in Xenophanes is an adaptation of Anaximenes' doctrine of *pilêsis*, "compression": water vapors exuded from the *megas pontos*, "the vast deep sea," undergo a process of compression; the resulting tension and "inflammation" (and let us not forget in this connection the metaphorical sense "being excited" for *pyrousthai*) causes the astrophysical clouds to glow brightly.

Crucially significant about the Anaximenes background is that the rarefaction-condensation theory treats fire not as "principle" and cause but as effect. In Anaximenes fire is the state of maximal rarefaction of air (DK13A7). In Xenophanes, the cosmic stuff that is subject to *pilêsis*, "compression," is not air but water; fire and air are *explananda*. There are suggestive implications here for amplifying the comparison between Anaximenes and Xenophanes, but this had better be deferred to the end of this study.

5. THE SUN-CLOUD: DOES IT ARISE FROM FLARES/SPARKS?

Noticeable immediately is the dissonance between the reports that have the sun constituted "out of tiny flares/sparks" and those that state simply that the sun "is a *pepyrômenon* cloud." The dissonance may seem slight if we assume (mistakenly, as was shown above) that *pepyrômenon* is to be translated "fiery," "ignited," "aflame." In any event, there is a more fundamental discrepancy between the two reports.[47]

In the version in pseudo-Plutarch *Epit.*, the two formulations ("out of..." and "is...") are juxtaposed (albeit rather awkwardly, in an abrupt disjunction); but in Stobaeus, who is often more precise in his preservation of wording in Aëtius (the original doxographic treatise behind pseudo-Plutarch and Stobaeus) the igneous theory of the sun's constitution is attributed expressly not to Xenophanes but to Theophrastus. In the entire relevant passage in Stobaeus, the sentence which begins with the mention of Theophrastus appears very much like a separate self-contained lemma: there is no particle connecting it with the preceding four sentences on Xenophanes, the last three of which go beyond the topic of the nature of the sun to summarize Xenophanes' theory of solar eclipses.[48]

This discrepancy has attracted the attention of experts on the analysis of doxographic sources, who have arrayed themselves in opposite camps as they seek to account for it. To mention just the major and influential exponents on each side,[49] Hermann Diels, R. W. Sharples, and David Runia hold that in Aëtius both the "*pepyrômenon* cloud" formulation and the theory of igneous origins of the sun were attributed to Xenophanes, and that Stobaeus misled his readers by failing to state explicitly, "as Theophrastus in his *Physics* says about Xenophanes." By contrast, Peter Steinmetz and Jaap Mansfeld have held that the doctrine of Xenophanes is represented only by the "*pepyrômenon* cloud" formulation, plus, of course, the three sentences on eclipses. On their account of the discrepancy,

Aëtius had reported the igneous theory as one held by Theophrastus; Stobaeus reproduced accurately what was present in Aëtius; but pseudo-Plutarch ineptly conflated two distinct reports, thus falsely attributing both doctrines to Xenophanes.

There is inherent plausibility and simplicity in the Steinmetz-Mansfeld view; nonetheless, the final and perhaps decisive round in this controversy should be awarded to David Runia.[50] For he not only corrects some inadequacies and infelicities in Steinmetz's reconstruction; he also puts forward a highly sophisticated comparative analysis of differences in the overall thematic organization of pseudo-Plutarch *Epit.* and Stobaeus *Ecl.*, respectively; and this analysis provides impressive support for his side in the controversy. It should be noted, however, that Runia's focus was not on eliciting from the sources what Xenophanes' doctrine might have been but rather and strictly on determining what stood in Aëtius.[51] This still leaves open the issue as to how Xenophanes' doctrine may have been picked up in the philosophical idiom of later antiquity that is employed in doxographical sources.

To begin with, the collocation "wet exhalation" makes one think of its Aristotelian-Peripatetic complement, "dry exhalation." The two types are famously distinguished in Aristotle's *Meteorology*; and it is very likely that Aëtius employs Aristotelian-Peripatetic concepts in formulating the doctrines he summarizes. Xenophanes might not have said more about the process whereby the sun is generated beyond what is said generally about clouds at B30: the big sea is the generator and fount. Even so, the succession of doxographers would have found it natural and convenient to state this in the language of Aristotelian and post-Aristotelian physics and meteorology.

Next, it is important to note that the term *pyridia*, which I have so far translated "tiny flares, sparks," is certainly not one Xenophanes could have used.[52] For, unlike *pepyrômenon*, it does not, in any of its grammatical cases, fit his meter. A possibility—which, to my knowledge, has so far been overlooked—is that what appeared in Xenophanes were forms of the feminine noun *pyria* or *pyriê* (plural *pyriai*) "vapor bath" (see LSJ, s.v.). Intriguing in this regard is the passage in Herodotus IV.75 that describes a form of dry sauna practiced by the Scythians: "it produces vapor (*atmis*) in quantity which (*tosautên*) no Greek vapor-bath (*pyriê*) can exceed." If the latter were indeed the term Xenophanes had used, trace of it may be detectable, with just the slight corruption of accent (πυρίων rather than πυριῶν) in the MSS for A32, pseudo-Plutarch *Strom.* (see section 3, [A], above).

A clue as to how Aëtius understood the term is provided by the language of "being gathered" and "cumulatively form." The *men/de* syntax that is found in the three texts at issue shows that two distinct processes are envisaged: first, the *pyridia* "are gathered (*synathroizomenôn* is surely passive) out of the moist exhalation; then, having been brought to high concentration, they "cumulatively form" (note active *synathroizontôn*) the sun. The implication is that, prior to the exhalation, the *pyridia* are present in the water in a dispersed or diluted state; they are then sifted and brought together by the process of exhalation; and finally, when critical mass is reached, conflagration results, and the sun is formed. All this accords well enough with those ancient cosmologies that posit a fiery nature for celestial bodies but allow for water-fire transmutation.[53]

There is, however, a major thematic objection to attributing a fiery-sun doctrine to Xenophanes: it would spoil and unbalance his bipolar universe of two world stuffs, earth below, water above, and a mixture of earth and water at the interface of the two (i. e., at or near the earth's surface). Runia implicitly concedes the awkwardness of this consequence when he makes this comment à propos the parallel case of Xenophanes' moon: "[Xenophanes'] clouds must have consisted of more than one element (anachronistically speaking)."[54] Indeed, Xenophanes should have found no need to introduce fire as an astrophysical explanans. For, as is shown by the explanation of lightning in text A45 in (D) of section 3, above, fire-like effects can result directly from violent motion. This doctrine is not original with Xenophanes; both Anaximander and Anaximenes had already offered the same explanation (DK12A11[7], 13A7[8]). And Anaximenes had offered an intuitive analogy: oars, plunging into the sea and forcibly "tearing" it (*schizomenê*), as the oarsman pulls hard, produce a simmering foam (*parastilbei*) in the water (DK13A17).[55]

Granted that *pyridion* could not have been used by Xenophanes, and, furthermore, if we give due weight to the thematic objection just raised, we still need to ask ourselves: What theme or feature in Xenophanes' account might have prompted the doxographers to speak of *pyridia* "being gathered and cumulatively forming the sun"? We have already considered the simple and by no means implausible hypothesis that Xenophanes' own term was *pyriê/-ai*, "vapor bath." Another simple hypothesis, though less charitable vis-à-vis the doxographers, is that they understood *pyridion* as "flare," and that the latter term functioned for them in effect as equivalent to *nephelion paralampon*, "glowing cloudlet," the doxographers' phrase for Xenophanes' explanatory account of St. Elmo's fire. The story of "being gathered/accumulating out of the moist exhalation" would, accordingly, be sheer embellishment that drew on the Aristotelian and post-Aristotelian doctrine of transmutation of water into fire.

But a more charitable hypothesis is also possible, one that would detect traces of early Ionian cosmology in the doxographers' double process of "being gathered" and "accumulating." Again, Anaximenes comes to mind. The prior state of wide dispersal implied by *synathroizomenôn* may reflect rarefaction: the loose and relaxed state of water as vapor and mist. In *synathroizontôn* we have condensation, the compressed, congested, inflamed, and dynamically charged state that results in luminescence.

We converge here on the same conclusion that was reached in our examination of the semantics of *pepyrômenon/-a*: there is no reason to suppose that Xenophanes' sun is constituted of fire, or formed from firelets, or sparks. Like all other astrophysical *meteôra*, the sun comes to be from water vapor; and its blazing, effulgent properties result from the high degree of congestion —"inflammation," as we might aptly call it—of its watery nature.

6. THE STARS: CLOUDS STIRRED, NOT IGNITED

Issues corresponding to the ones raised about the sun come up in connection with Xenophanes' doctrine of the nature of stars. The report that stars are "incandescent clouds" is enhanced and supported by the simile of coals. The same Achilles who assumed that Xenophanes' sun is "ignited" every day at sunrise and extinguished at sunset also assumed that the simile of coals was intended to convey that stars are ignited at nightfall and extinguished at daybreak. Indeed, his use of the adjective *empyrôn*, "ignited, fiery"—as well as other details in the Achilles text that are omitted in (C), in section 3, above[56]—indicate that Achilles barely saw a simile; he took the language of kindling/extinguishing quite literally. But the adverbial prefix *ana-* in *anazôpyrein* suggests—and all the more so when, as in the Theodoretus text, it is reinforced by the adverb *palin*, "again," in *anazôpyreisthai*—that Xenophanes envisaged something quite different from what Achilles perceived. In the simile of coals the inverted bowl of the heavens is being likened to a brazier, the smoldering coals of which, after some stirring, flare up; subsequently they die down; later yet, they are revived, and so on.

I have argued elsewhere that this image of coals-in-a-brazier gives us the correct reading of the simile.[57] The key is precisely in the use of *anazôpyrein/ anazôpyreisthai*, "be revivified," "flare up." It is the stirring, the agitating, of the coals that makes them glow. By implication it is some agitation of the stellar clouds that makes them shine. We recall here what Xenophanes said about those cloudlets of St. Elmo's fire: they "glimmer because of a special agitation" (DKA39). This theme of motion naturally draws us to the texts of group (D), in which effects of luminescence broadly have their cause in coalescings, movement, agitation. So, then, what applies to these other phenomena and to St. Elmo's fire must surely also apply to the stars. As we saw in the case of the sun, fire or light is not the cause but the effect. What makes stars shine is not that they are aflame or that they draw fuel for burning. Stars are not coals. But like coals they glow when they are stirred.

7. OTHER PHENOMENA OF LUMINESCENCE IN THE SKIES

The report at A44 concerning Xenophanes' account of "Comets, shooting stars, and the like" implies reference to certain explanatory specifications: "aggregations (*systêmata*) or movements (*kinêmata*) of incandescent clouds." It is the specification of the degree and character of the "aggregation" and the "movement" that makes it possible to sort these phenomena into types and also to distinguish all of them from ordinary clouds. That Xenophanes should have used the nominalizations *systêma* or *kinêma* is out of the question: these are terms that belong to the vocabulary of later Greek philosophy. Behind these nominalizations, however, are the verbs *synistamai* and *kinoumai*.[58] The latter has an important and conspicuous use in Xenophanes: his one God "moves not at all" (*kinoumenos ouden*, B26); and it is quite plausible to suppose that *synistamai* might also have been deployed in Xenophanes' astrophysics. So, then, the nominalizations *systêmata* and *kinêmata* may reflect significant differentiae in Xenophanes' account of astrophysical clouds. The unifying "nature," the highest-level genus, is that of *cloud*, to be sure; and, when it comes to ordinary clouds, there is no need for differentiae other than those that would have been familiar from Anaximenes' theory, viz., shape, size, density. Astrophysical clouds, however, constitute a subaltern genus of "incandescent clouds." And, to do justice to the wide variation across this subaltern genus, we need to take into account not only the special ways in which these clouds "have come together" or "have been formed" (*synestêke*) but also the special ways in which the "inflammation" occurs and is maintained through motion (*kineisthai*).[59] This would entail reference to innumerable determinates of extent, force, and rhythm; and it would also entail specifying whether the agitating motion is primarily internal or external or a combination of the two.[60]

It is of major importance to appreciate the wide scope of the generalization in A44. The unusual and unpredictable phenomena observed in the night skies were distributed by the ancients over a plethora of types, with such descriptive names as "torches," "boards," "shields," "pillars," "daggers," "horse manes," "bearded ones," and even "goats."[61] In offering a single explanation, with the appropriate differentiae of aggregation and motion, for this motley array of phenomena, Xenophanes had made a significant stride toward the ultimate generalization that all the *meteôra* are clouds. It is striking that the Xenophanes lemma appears last in the Aëtius chapter "On Comets, etc.," and that it is only with respect to Xenophanes that the doxographer deploys the phrase "all things of this sort."[62]

8. The Lunar Cloud: Compressed and Incandescent

The manuscripts offer us three variants: we have *pepyrômenon* attested five times; *pepilêmenon* three times; and in one MS of *Epit.* we have the nonce word (or, what is more likely, non-word) *pepyrôlêmenon*.[63] Either of the first two forms could have been used by Xenophanes; they fit his meter. Diels, who preferred the second reading, astutely hypothesized that the strange third reading must be the result of a scribe's misguided attempt to capture the four-letter annotation *pilê* which some earlier reader or scribe—presumably more sophisticated or better informed—had placed directly above the four letters, *pyrô,* of *pepyrômenon.*[64] The supralineal annotation would, accordingly, have recorded either uncertainty as to which of two variant readings was correct or awareness that *both* participles should be applied to Xenophanes' moon.

But in our own recent past, in a brilliantly argued analysis of the sources and manuscript tradition for this particular lemma in Aëtius, David Runia ("Xenophanes on the Moon") reached a different conclusion: he found it certain that the reading in Aëtius was not *pepilêmenon* (the reading Diels preferred) but *pepyrômenon*; he also found cogent evidence to warrant the ruling that at pre-Aëtius stages of the doxographic tradition the two participles were being cited together: πεπυρωμένον πεπιλημένον—which is why both readings have good support in the sources (pp. 265–67).[65] The strange reading πεπυρωλημένον arose, then, not from misconstruing a supralineal notation but rather on this scenario: a scribe, having started with πεπυρω, skips over the first μένον and the πεπι of the second participle (πεπυ- and πεπι- being indistinguishable in post-classical Greek pronunciation) and puts down a conflation of the two separate words.

Runia's philological analysis—quite apart from its rigor and sensitivity—is also very compelling in the recognition it confers, and the emphasis it places, on the theme of "differentiation." He rightly emphasizes that, specifically in the case of the moon, we need the differentiae provided by each of the two participles that figure in our sources. But I believe Runia misses the correct nuance by translating *pepyrômenon* "ignited" (p. 269 and passim), which, as I pointed out earlier, leads him to the gratuitous and thematically vexing supposition that "[Xenophanes'] clouds must have consisted of more than one element" ("Xenophanes on the Moon," 267 n. 56).

Also missed by Runia—and likewise broadly missed in the literature on Xenophanes—is the precise nuance of *nephos pepilêmenon.* Runia translates "cloud that has undergone condensation" and draws the almost inevitable connection to the theory of Anaximenes (p. 267). But there is also a much more immediate and telling connection. A search of the Thesaurus Linguae Graecae databank for all of the different inflections of *nephos pepilêmenon* and *nephelê pepilêmenê*—excluding contexts that refer to Xenophanes, which have already been listed above—shows that either of these collocations is standard for "thick opaque cloud" and also for "thick opaque cloud with well-defined shape."[66] And even though the ancients do not appear to have developed anything like the Luke Howard scheme that has been the modern standard for classifying clouds, the two ancient collocations do have the flavor of nascent terminology. For they seem perfectly suited for what we call "cumulus clouds" or "heap clouds."

Here it is relevant to quote an observation P. J. Bicknell makes in his discussion of Xenophanes' cloud-astrophysics:

> Quite often the moon is visible during the day, and sometimes it is seen against a clear blue sky amongst small high cumulus clouds. On these occasions the greyish white colour of the lunar disc is exactly the same as that of the surrounding clouds.[67]

So, then, the moon in its constitution and shape is a special type of cumulus cloud. But it is even more compressed than an ordinary cloud. If an ordinary cumulus cloud is to shine with light, what is needed is that tearing, ripping action of a violent gust of wind—the cause, according to Ionian meteorology, of lightning. Yet even so, the luminescence in the latter case is fleetingly brief. By contrast, the steady compression of vapor within the moon produces waxing and waning luminescence over the period of the month of phases. The moon is both *pepilêmenon* and *pepyrômenon*, "compressed and incandescent." As Runia was right to stress, the second differentia is absolutely essential. Xenophanes not only did not believe that the moon gets its light from the sun, his cosmology makes it impossible for him to consider that more sophisticated explanation.[68] When the moon shines, the luminescence is "its own" (A43), and it results from internal compression and agitation.

9. "Is a Cloud," or "Comes from a Cloud"?

In the case of the sun, even in those reports that make no mention of a process of generation of the sun from "flares" or "sparks," we find two distinct formulations: "is [constituted] out of incandescent clouds"; "is an incandescent cloud." Let me refer to these formulations by the terms "generative" and "constitutive," respectively. The comments I have offered concerning stars, the moon, and phenomena of group (D), in section 3, seem already to tilt in favor of the constitutive formulation. Let me now strengthen this presumption with two arguments that draw on philosophical-thematic considerations.

The first argument is that "X is really a cloud" surpasses "X originated from a cloud" in explanatory import. It is not at all obvious what sort of facts might be explained by "X originated from a cloud"—a great variety of things emerge from clouds, including rain, ice, wind, and thunder. By contrast, "X is really a cloud" immediately provides an explanation of a fact of major importance and prominence, viz., that X remains suspended above the earth, that it does not fall—clouds do that.[69] It is relevant to recall here that Xenophanes was sufficiently intrigued by the question of the stability of the earth to have offered the radical explanation, "it stretches downward without limit" (B28; see Mourelatos, "La terre et les étoiles," 332–36). The similarly intriguing question of the suspended state of celestial objects was given a correspondingly straightforward answer: they are clouds.

The second argument is that the formulation "X is (really) a cloud" is strongly prompted by Xenophanes' project of demythologizing the phenomena in the skies. Ordinary mortals are mistaken in their beliefs concerning the *identity* and *nature* of what they see in the skies—the messenger of Zeus, the Dioskouroi who have come to the rescue, Hyperion, Selene with her torch of pale light. In countering beliefs of this type, a naturalist of the Greek Enlightenment may well have expatiated at length on the natural origins of the phenomenon at issue; but the logically decisive moment will have come when the traditional identity statement was confronted with, and was replaced by, the naturalist identity statement: "what you thought (or believed) is X is really (or is just/only/actually) Y." When a seemingly ominous glow would mysteriously appear at the top of a ship's mast, the first question the ancient sailor would have asked is "What is it?" The answer of traditional lore did provide some reassurance. To achieve a comparable effect of reassurance the naturalist account must have gone beyond "It originated from a cloud"; it must have put forward the competing reduction, "It is only a cloud."

10. INTUITIVE SUPPORT FOR XENOPHANES' THEORY: THE RAINBOW AND ITS CONGENERS

Let us now explore the case that could be made, on the basis of observations that are intuitively suggestive for any observer (ancient or modern) of the skies, for the assimilation of each of the following to clouds: the rainbow, the moon, the stars, the sun. In the comparisons and associations offered here and in the sections that follow, I shall draw freely on the modern nomenclature for clouds. As was noted earlier, the ancients did not develop anything comparable to the Howard system of classification we use today.[70] This cannot, however, be construed as evidence that the ancients had failed to notice types and varieties among clouds. To the contrary, Aratus' *Phainomena* and other texts and contexts of popular meteorology reveal a rich vocabulary of adjectives and similes used to describe differences among clouds.[71] In any event, my use of the modern vocabulary is only intended to provide succinct and familiar characterizations of the type of cloud that is at issue in one or another of the suggestive comparisons.

When the Greeks of pre-classical times spoke of *iris*, "the rainbow," they probably included under that term not only the familiar arc of colors that appears opposite the sun (or, more rarely, opposite the full moon) but also the various atmospheric phenomena we call "halos," "parhelia" ("mock suns," "sun dogs"), "coronae," and "cloud iridescence."[72] Such "rainbow-like" effects, as I shall collectively call them here, are fairly common,[73] even though rarely noticed by us today—we work indoors, and, when outdoors, our view of the sky is often obstructed, and our eyes tend to be turned to happenings on or near the ground. The full range of such phenomena must have been as familiar to the ancients as the rainbow proper. It is very telling in this regard that in Homer *iris* is said to be "a portent of war or of storm" (*Il.* 17.548–549). The latter disjunct applies questionably to the rainbow, which is rather a sign of the end of a storm; but it makes excellent sense with reference to solar or lunar halos.[74] On the assumption that

Xenophanes included rainbow-like effects under the term *iris*, the classification of *iris* as a cloud appears much more plausible. Rainbow-like effects give the appearance of being embedded in a cloud, whereas the rainbow appears detached from the clouds, and it may have patches of clear blue sky as background.

11. How to See the Moon as a Cloud

What sort of observations might have given rise to the idea that the moon is a cloud? I cited earlier Bicknell's very perceptive association of the moon with cumulus clouds. I would myself add that the association appears especially startling on the two-three days before or after half-moon (either first-to-second or third-to-fourth quarter), when an observer could easily overlook the gibbous moon, mistaking it for yet another oddly shaped cumulus cloud that happens to be in its vicinity. Moreover, the markedly irregular features that lie inside the lunar disk— and how Xenophanes would have scoffed at the anthropocentrism of those who saw a human face in the moon!—can be aptly compared to the hollows and tufts of cumulus clouds.[75] And when large masses of cumulus clouds are stacked up, row upon row, the underside of these clouds is strikingly flat and even; and many that have well-rounded tops have the appearance of the moon at half-moon—especially at waning half-moon, near moonset, by day, when the straight edge of the lunar half-disk is below and the rounded edge above.

Other phases of the moon invite comparisons with other cloud types. Most comparable to the full moon is the lenticular altocumulus: a somewhat flattened sphere which today's observers often describe as a flying saucer. Rare over flat terrain, these are seen often at or over the tops of mountains, a type of landscape that would have repeatedly come into Xenophanes' view as he traveled in Asia Minor, Greece proper, and Magna Graecia. Yet another association is that between the moon's thin crescent, either early in the first lunar quarter or late in the fourth quarter, and the hooks and sickle-blades that are characteristic of cirrus uncinus.

Strikingly compelling, is the moon-clouds association that is sometimes made by observers of a total lunar eclipse. During the period of totality (when, as we would put it, the moon has entered the umbra of the earth's shadow), the moon is reduced to a barely visible cloud-like patch. The comment "I should have thought it was a cloud" might quite naturally be—and sometimes actually is—uttered by observers at this stage; and the comment seems especially apt if clouds are present in the vicinity of the eclipsed moon.[76] Before and after totality, when the moon is passing between the umbra and the penumbra, the lunar disk not only has a weak reddish glow but it also appears irregular—rather like a cloud at dusk or dawn. When the thin luminous crescent reappears and begins to bulge as the moon exits the penumbra, one has the strong visual impression of the moon being re-born out of a cloud.

Specifically for Xenophanes, the association between the moon and clouds would be mediated even by certain aspects of lunar regularity: the elegant crescent of early waxing or late waning moon; and the elegant circle of full moon. With the rarest of exceptions, no cumulus or cirrus cloud can match this degree of geometric regularity. What does appear to match the moon's crescent is the rainbow's half circle; and what matches the circle of full moon is the ring of a solar or lunar halo. The rainbow and halos, accordingly, are evidence that cloud stuff can be a base and medium for the elegant geometry of the arc and the circle. Going beyond the phenomenological data, Xenophanes' theory might, in fact, imply that halos and coronae are rings of cloud stuff seen in the process of coalescing into, or replenishing, the disks of either of the luminaries.

12. Seeing the Stars as Clouds

For the connection between stars and clouds, two obvious links would be the Milky Way[77] and the aurora borealis[78]—both striking instances of luminous clouds in the night sky that are not, unlike clouds illuminated by lightning, just momentary occurrences. Doubtless, Xenophanes did not know of the Magellanic Clouds of the southern sky; but the intuitive use of the word "cloud" for these other galaxies (the use pre-dates the recognition that they *are* galaxies, and predates the use of the cloud-analogy by modern astrophysicists) shows the naturalness of describing a luminous patch in the night sky as a cloud.[79] Apart from galaxies, the many star clusters, such as the Pleiades or Hyades, provide a suggestive star-cloud link. For, surely, observers generally, and all the more so the many who have less than perfect eyesight, see such clusters as luminous hazy patches.[80] Moreover, it is relevant to note that when modern observers have the (relatively rare) opportunity to view the night sky in a region that is free of light pollution (away from towns and highways) an immense plethora of stars of smaller magnitude come to be discernible, which makes hazy star clusters seem ubiquitous and abundant. What is rare for us would have been the regular and only way of seeing the night sky for the ancients. And besides, inasmuch as the effect is enhanced for observers with less than perfect vision, the lack of eyeglass technology among the ancients would have been another factor serving greatly to strengthen and make widespread the perception that even in the absence of ordinary clouds and haze, the night sky is replete with stellar vapors.

Finally, an intriguing link is provided by the iconography of the Dioskouroi, the divinities the ancients associated with St. Elmo's fire. It appears that the Ionian Dioskouroi known to Xenophanes were in all likelihood divinities of astral origin.[81] In this instance Xenophanes was in a position not only to dispute popular belief but also to exploit the *endoxa* captured in it. The trinity of hypostases recognized in the tradition—the divine twins, St. Elmo's fire, stars—is adapted to his purposes by his substitution of "small clouds" for the first hypostasis. The substitution is not arbitrary. St. Elmo's fire can be seen both as points of light and as a more diffuse, nebulous glow. And so the phenomenon offers for Xenophanes compelling evidence that a star or small group of stars can also be a small cloud—evidence he can rightly claim as down-to-earth, almost palpable, given that stories abound of mariners attempting to touch St. Elmo's fire.[82]

13. SEEING THE SUN AS A CLOUD

The sun, being the source of light that so markedly changes the appearance of daytime clouds, might seem the least cloud-like of all celestial objects. Xenophanes may have reasoned by extrapolating along a line of augmentation: St. Elmo's fire is a luminous, somewhat diffuse, small cloud; a single star is a luminous cloud larger in size and doubtless more distant than St. Elmo's fire; a cluster of stars appears as a fuzzy glowing patch in the sky; a huge and pervasive cluster of clusters is that diffuse super-cloud we know as the Milky Way; a much more tightly wadded, densely compressed mass of cloud stuff constitutes the moon; and a yet denser, enormously more compressed, mass of cloud stuff constitutes the sun.

Not only St. Elmo's fire but also the rainbow are significantly intermediate cases in bringing off this assimilation of sun to cloud. The phenomenon of mock suns, as well as that of solar halos, with which mock suns are invariably associated, are both obviously relevant.[83] As was suggested earlier, solar halos could have been seen as rainbow-like rings closing in on the sun and reconstituting it after an eclipse. Moreover, the crescent phase, which can be thought to mediate the connection between rainbow and moon, might also have provided a conceptual link in the case of the sun. The reader may rebel at the implication that the sun undergoes phases. And yet at a time of total solar eclipse, the changes of shape undergone by the solar disk seem like a quick play of the phases of the moon—from full moon, through waning crescent, to new moon, to waxing crescent, and back to full moon. The parallel is also felt in the case of partial and annular eclipses, in spite of the absence of a counterpart to the new-moon phase.[84] Our astronomy textbooks often illustrate the sequence of a total solar eclipse with a series of time-lapse photographs whereby the solar disk, projected against a black background, appears to undergo lunar-like phases.[85]

Significantly, we have specific testimony that Xenophanes "had made mention of" (*paristorêken*) a total eclipse of the sun, one in which "the day came to appear like night" (A41).[86] Xenophanes had no inkling that solar eclipses are caused by the interposition of the lunar disk. He thought they are due to an episodic "quenching" of the sun because of a failure in the supply of vapor (A41a). Either his own observations of a total solar eclipse or anecdotal evidence he had concerning such phenomena would probably have included cognizance of another effect that should have interested him keenly. At the moment of totality, the corona of the sun becomes visible. To us this is an altogether different corona than the one that belongs with rainbow-like phenomena—an effect of solar physics, not of meteorology and optics.[87] To Xenophanes, on the other hand, the irregularly shaped nebulous glow around the eclipsed sun would have been yet another halo, yet another rainbow—a glimpse of the very process of rebirth of the sun from a luminous cloud. The phenomenon of an annular eclipse, had it come to his attention, would have similarly strengthened the association he perceived between the sun and rainbow-like phenomena.

14. The Argument from Resemblance and Augmentation

One may gain a stronger appreciation of the intuitive plausibility of Xenophanes' grand generalization by noticing how atmospheric and astronomical objects or phenomena can be arranged in certain series that involve not only perceptible affinities but also a certain pattern of progressivity or augmentation. The first series focuses on the first differentia,[88] that of coalescence or constitution (*synistasthai*), as this is reflected in cloud shape. Stars, inasmuch as they are points of light and have no shape, are not included in this first series. The principle of augmentation is that of increasing geometric regularity:

Stratus clouds
Detached clouds (e.g., fair weather cumulus, or bunched filaments or tufts of cirrus clouds)
Clouds that show marked geometric structure (e.g., altocumulus that show rolls or furrows, lenticular clouds)
Comets
Halos, coronae, and rainbows
The lunar disk—and its phases
The solar disk—and its "phases" at times of eclipse

The second series focuses on the second differentia, and specifically on the intensity and concentration of the agitation that results in luminescence. The progression is from more diffuse to more focused, concentrated luminescence.

St. Elmo's fire
Miscellaneous fiery apparitions in the night sky
Aurora borealis (?)
Milky Way (?)
Comets
Stars
The moon(s)
The sun(s)

These first two series select phenomena that perceptibly endure over more than a fleeting moment. But phenomena of fleeting duration might also have been taken to lend support to Xenophanes' grand generalization, as is suggested by this third series, in which the progression is again from diffuse to geometrically regular:

Clouds illuminated by (so-called) heat or sheet lightning[89]
Clouds illuminated by streak lightning, thunderbolts[90]
Fireballs
Shooting stars

Finally, the three series can be joined together into a single series in accordance with a principle of longevity, from short-lived to indefinitely enduring:

Clouds illuminated by (so-called) heat or sheet lightning
Clouds illuminated by streak lightning, thunderbolts
Fireballs
Shooting stars
St. Elmo's fire
Miscellaneous fiery apparitions in the night sky
Halos, coronae, and rainbows
Aurora borealis (?)
Ordinary clouds
The moon(s)
The sun(s)
Comets
Milky Way (?)
Stars and constellations

Very much worthy of note in these series is the crucial role played by St. Elmo's fire (shown above in bold). With the affinity of St. Elmo's fire with stars already recognized in popular belief,[91] the crackling noises of St. Elmo's fire are a feature that strengthens two further connections: directly, one between St. Elmo's fire and the two ostensibly similar phenomena of thunderbolts and fireballs; indirectly, one between the latter two and the stars.

15. WHAT IS THE EFFICIENT CAUSE?

Aristotle complained that there was "no single thing that Xenophanes clarified" (*outhen diesaphênisen*, Metaph. 1.5.986b22). As Mansfeld has shown ("Theophrastus and the Xenophanes Doxography," 309), the complaint is directed primarily against Xenophanes' supposed failure to be specific about material, formal, and efficient causes. The complaint seems hardly fair in the case of material causes for astrophysical phenomena. For, even from the few fragments and reports that have come down to us, it is clear that the material cause is water. With respect to formal causes, I shall shortly argue that there is some degree of recognition of this aspect of causality. The complaint does seem to be justified, however, in the cases of efficient causes. Not because Xenophanes did not cite any, but, to the contrary, because in Xenophanes' conspicuously dynamic cosmos there is a bewildering plethora of movers. The ebb and flow of the two world stuffs constantly shapes and re-shapes both the earth's contour and the distribution of water at or below the earth's surface. The deep sea drives the cycle of evaporation and condensation. Winds drive and shape clouds, sometimes forcing them to collide violently, at others ripping them apart, the effect in either case being lightning. The stellar clouds revolve about us; suns and moons proceed almost constantly (except for eclipses) from east to west; rainbows, halos, St. Elmo's fire appear and disappear; fireballs and shooting stars streak across the skies. What drives all these changes? And at a deeper level, what causes the internal agitation of the astrophysical *meteôra* that results in luminescence?

Xenophanes is certainly not unique among ancient cosmologists in having failed to give an account of specific, proximate, and intermediate causes. But (in this respect, again, like most other Greek cosmologists) he does offer a general account of ultimate and fundamental efficient causation. Amazingly this has generally been overlooked in modern accounts of his natural philosophy. And yet the relevant evidence stares us in the face. The way Xenophanes' single and supreme God acts on the universe is described in these words:

$$\text{ἀλλ' ἀπάνευθε πόνοιο νόου φρενὶ πάντα κραδαίνει.}$$

> ...but completely without toil he shakes all things by the thought of his mind. (B25)[92]

One could hardly think of a better Greek term than *kradainei* for all the varieties and levels of motion I have cited in the preceding paragraph. In particular, the term is wonderfully apt either for the "tearing" of clouds that produces lightning or for that "inflamed" internal jostling and quivering that makes the sun, the moon, the stars, and all cognate astrophysical *meteôra* emit light.

16. XENOPHANES AND IONIAN MATERIAL MONISM

According to the traditional account—shaped largely by Aristotle—the Ionians (Thales, Anaximander, Anaximenes, Heraclitus) held that "All things are M," offering different candidates for "M"—viz., water, or air, or fire, or the *apeiron*, the latter being conceived of as a characterless substratum. The traditional version typically interprets "All things are M" as a statement of material constitution, the relevant sense being either that all things are *out of* M stuff, or that they are *variant forms*—allotropes as it were—of M. The best evidence for Ionian material monism is certainly in the Anaximenes testimonia. It seems gratuitously skeptical to deny that Anaximenes should have made the claim "All things are air" and should have used the formula "This too is air." To be sure, used with reference to something other than either air itself or some close congener of it—such as haze or vapor—the formula "This is air" appears strained; we hear an effect of metonymy or perceive some incompleteness. Our intuition is that the subject at issue is in the *first instance* something else, e.g., a perfume, or a ball of wool, or a feather. So Anaximenes is logically bound to elaborate, which evidently he did in positing the mechanism of rarefaction-condensation. It is important to notice the two distinct steps in the logic here: the original "This is air"; and the trailing commentary that recounts the formative process and its result in "this." Xenophanes' formula, "This too is a cloud," has a certain important advantage over its Milesian counterpart: the formative process does not have to be mentioned separately; a cloud is necessarily the product of a process of rarefaction-condensation; it is necessarily a certain type of formation. So the difference between Xenophanes' cloud-astrophysics and Anaximenes' air-cosmology is not merely that between a more restricted and a more general theory; Xenophanes offers a more sophisticated version of the sort of project Anaximenes initiated. In opting to say "This too is a cloud," rather than "This too is air (or cloud-stuff)," Xenophanes was responding to an intuitively felt philosophical demand for tighter integration of stuff, formative process, and resulting formation.

Another attractive comparison between Xenophanes and Anaximenes that emerges from the present study focuses on the adaptation of the mechanics of rarefaction-condensation. Whereas in Anaximenes rarefaction-condensation applies to all four cosmic stuffs, with the consequence that earth is the extreme of condensation, in Xenophanes earth lies wholly outside the scheme. Aristotle wondered why none of the Ionian material monists picked earth as the base and principle for the generation of the other three stuffs (*Metaph.* 1.7.989a5–10). His answer, stated quite generally—so that it may also serve as a response to students of the Presocratics across the ages who have raised the same question—is that earth is not fine-textured enough to have the transformational versatility of the other three. This contrast in dynamic character between the earth and the other three may have motivated Xenophanes to detach earth from its cosmic congeners. And by setting up water as something wholly unlike earth, he was in a position to exploit the mechanics of condensation-rarefaction even more resourcefully than Anaximenes had managed. Water can be loosened up into vapor and thin air; but the latter can be compressed and concentrated in a variety of ways. Channeled in a stream, it becomes wind; gathered into a flock-like formation, it becomes an ordinary cloud; torn and agitated violently, it yields fire (lightning); more compressed than it is in an ordinary cloud, it glows, and thus yields the enormous variety of astrophysical clouds, from St. Elmo's fire and rainbow to the sun.

Of course, as in the case of Anaximenes, there will inevitably be some semantic strain when we attempt to state, in the context of Xenophanes' cloud-astrophysics, the claim of "vapor"-monism. Surely, one might want to protest, neither St. Elmo's fire nor the rainbow—let alone the sun and the moon—are "clouds" in the ordinary sense. There will have to be a trailing commentary on Xenophanes' claim too. But note how different the commentary will be in this case: What needs to be pointed out is that "cloud" is being used in a speculative analogy. The "is" takes the rainbow and maps it on to ordinary clouds. Those familiar clouds have a certain nature, a *physis*: they exhibit an astonishing variety of colors and hues; they have the ability to billow and to shrink; they can congeal into tight wads but also loosen up to the point of vanishing; they have the ability to assume a variety of shapes, sometimes strikingly geometrical ones; they can be quiescent or highly agitated; and with respect to any of the characteristics mentioned, they can either exhibit that characteristic steadily or undergo change at virtually any speed between languid and swift; and in stormy conditions they glow in flashes. All this is true of the nature of ordinary clouds, and it is precisely that nature that is being used as a model for exhibiting the nature of extraordinary clouds—St. Elmo's fire, rainbow, sun, moon, etc. The fact that clouds are made of vapor should not mislead us. Aristotle would have been loath to admit it, but actually Xenophanes' "This too is a cloud" qualifies no less as formal cause than it does as material cause.

17. A MODERN ANALOGUE: REDUCTIONS AND INTER-THEORETIC IDENTITY CLAIMS

Having started with a quotation from a modern novel, let me conclude with two allusions to modern science and philosophy. It is worth noting that Xenophanes' assimilation of astrophysical bodies to clouds survives in modern astronomy. As was noted earlier, some of the galaxies are known as "clouds"—e.g., the Magellanic clouds of the southern sky—and astronomers also speak of "clouds of interstellar matter" and of "nebulae." Much more to the point, however, is the continuity of the "X is really Y" pattern. Xenophanes' B32 is the prototype of a type of statement that serves to formulate important claims of scientific theories and of physicalist metaphysics. Stock examples in our own day are: "Lightning *is* a particularly massive electrical discharge"; "A table *is* a cloud of micro-particles"; "Mind *is* a neurophysiological process." The "is" used in such statements is now sometimes referred to as that of "inter-theoretic identity," inasmuch as it figures largely in the context of *reducing*[93] one theory that is more limited in its explanatory scope to another that is more powerful and more comprehensive.[94] Remarkably, after the lapse of two and a half millennia, the language of modern science and modern philosophy evinces the same fascination with meteorology and with meteorological modeling that is characteristic of Xenophanes. The cloud analogy is endemic in scientific language that reduces complex objects to ions, electrons, photons, and the like; and lightning, the cognate of St. Elmo's fire, is the modern philosopher's favorite subject for illustrations of inter-theoretic identity.

NOTES

A preliminary and short version of this study was published in K. J. Boudouris, ed., *Ionian Philosophy*, Studies in Greek Philosophy, 1 (Athens: International Association for Greek Philosophy, 1989), pp. 280–90. In its present version, the chapter is drawn from a larger project (in progress) on the natural philosophy of Xenophanes. I sincerely thank the many colleagues, students, and friends who have offered me comments on various parts of that larger project, and in particular, Alan Bowen, Victor Caston, David Furley, Jim Hankinson, Jim Lesher, Charles Kahn, Jaap Mansfeld, and Steve White. For assistance in checking proofs, many thanks to Alleyne Rogers, and also to Janice Chik and Olive Forbes.

Parts of this chapter have been presented in lecture version, and have received the benefit of discussion and criticism, at the following venues: the International Association for Greek Philosophy, First Conference, Samos 1988; the 12th Annual Workshop in Ancient Philosophy, Rice University, 1989; Carleton College; the University of Pennsylvania; the Center for Hellenic Studies; the Australian National University; University of Newcastle, New South Wales; Texas A & M University; Universität Bern, Switzerland; the University of Edinburgh, Scotland; DePauw University; Hellenic Philosophical Society, Athens, Greece; Université de Paris I—Panthéon Sorbonne; Florida State University; Southern Illinois University; Aarhus University, Denmark; and the Hungarian Philosophical Society and the Hungarian Classical Society, Joint Session, Eötvös University.

1. Chapter 119, "The Candles."

2. Another famous literary description of St. Elmo's fire is in Shakespeare's *Tempest* (act 1, scene 2, 196–201).

3. *The New Columbia Encyclopedia*, 4th ed., 1975, s. v. "Saint Elmo's fire"; cf. Heuer, *Thunder, Singing Sands, and Other Wonders*, 37–44.

4. See *DG* 267–444. The reconstruction has in large measure been vindicated (albeit with significant qualifications) by the searching analysis and review undertaken by Mansfeld and Runia, *Aëtiana: The Method and Intellectual Context of a Doxographer*; cf. Runia, "Xenophanes on the Moon," 248–50. The much more skeptical assay of Diels's reconstruction in Lebedev, "Neglected Fragments of Democritus and Metrodorus of Chios," and Lebedev, "Did the Doxographer Aëtius Ever Exist?" now appears unwarranted. Cf. Frede, "Aëtiana."

5. See Mau, *Plutarchi Moralia Vol. V, Fasc. 2, Pars 1*, 89. Cf. *DG* 347.

6. See Wachsmuth, *Ioannis Stobaei Anthologii libri duo priores*, 204. Cf. *DG* 347.

7. The version in pseudo-Plutarch differs only in omitting the parenthetic relative clause and in having "About the Stars Called Dioskouroi" appear as entry heading.

8. It would be pointless to translate the *kai* here by "also." No other name for the phenomenon is implied. The *kai* is emphatic; it might be rendered "notably."

9. References are, as standardly, to the B (fragments) or A (testimony) sections of DK. Where this is relevant for my argument, or if an A section contains citations from more than one source, I shall also give abbreviated references to source-authors.

10. I adopt the very apt translation "cloudlets" from Runia, "Xenophanes on the Moon," 266.

11. This was pointed out long ago by Diels in *DG* 220 n. 2.

12. Fr. 34 (Lobel and Page). See now Furley and Bremer, *Greek Hymns*, 1:166, 169–70; also 2:117–19. Before the publication of this fragment, it was thought that the connection between the Dioskouroi and St. Elmo's fire was not made till Roman times: so in *Paulys Realencyclopädie der classischen Altertumswissenschaft*, edited by G. Wissowa, s. v. "Dioskuren," vol. 5 (1905), col. 1097.

13. Another early mention of the Dioskouroi as saviors of mariners (but without as strong a suggestion of the effect of St. Elmo's fire as we have in Alcaeus) is in the second Homeric Hymn to the Dioskouroi, no. 33, which is assigned to the sixth or even seventh century BCE: see Athanassakis, *The Homeric Hymns*, 107; cf. Furley and Bremer, *Greek Hymns*, 1:169.

14. Epic diction would require the feminine form, *nephelê*, which has a strong flavor of animism: see Eisenstadt, "The Philosophy of Xenophanes of Colophon," 111–13.

15. The hypothesis could not be supported solely on the basis of the phrasing in A39: "which are indeed called Dioskouroi" may be entirely a doxographer's contribution. See above, n. 12.

16. In representations of the Dioskouroi (as the divine twins) in art or in coins, stars above or near their heads are very common. The earliest occurrences of the motif are dated to the second half of the fifth century. In literature, the first explicit statement of the astral connection is in Euripides (*Hel.* 137–40, 1495–1505). The association of the Dioskouroi with the constellation Gemini is, however, quite late—of Roman Imperial origin. See *Lexicon iconographicum*, s.v. "Dioskouroi," esp. pp. 567, 577, 587–88, 591–92, 610.

17. Cf. B11–B16.

18. Cf. Furley and Bremer, *Greek Hymns* 1:171 n. 28, 1:171 n. 28: "The same Xenophanes [same as the one who gave a naturalistic explanation of St. Elmo's fire] intelligently perceived that rapidly moving clouds were the cause of lightning. Exeunt Zeus & Sons!"

19. The source is the allegorist Heraclitus (not the philosopher), *Alleg. Hom.* 44.5. Cf. Heitsch, *Xenophanes*, 68; Eisenstadt, "The Philosophy of Xenophanes of Colophon," 108. For Homer's use of "Hyperion" as a name or attribute of the sun, see, e.g., *Il.* 19.398, *Od.* 1.8 and 24.

20. See Roscher, *Ausführliches Lexikon der griechischen und römischen Mythologie*, cols. 3147–3163, s.v. Mondgöttin. Although the association of Selene with Artemis or Hecate may not have yet been established by Xenophanes' time, the personified Moon appears in Hesiod *Th.* 371, and lunar influence on vegetation is implied in Sappho 96 (Lobel and Page, *Poetarum lesbiorum fragmenta*).

21. In what follows I correct a rather simplistic account of Xenophanes I gave in "The Real, Appearances, and Human Error in Early Greek Philosophy," 350: "Xenophanes in this instance [B32] is a hard-headed empiricist. . . ."

22. See Heitsch, *Xenophanes*, 60–75 and 159–72.

23. Here is Hermann Fränkel's estimate: "This theory seems singularly primitive and arbitrary, even for the time of its proponent. It is badly thought out and paltry (Fränkel, "Xenophanes' Empiricism and His Critique of Knowledge [B34]," 120). Again: "This is an extraordinary cosmology, daring and poverty-stricken at once. . . . [I]t is forced and unconvincing. . . . Everything is explained on the basis of everyday experience, and every effort is made to prevent any considerable widening of our ideas concerning the world about us" (Fränkel, *Early Greek Poetry and Philosophy*, 334). The tone was set in the nineteenth century by Eduard Zeller: "They are isolated observations and conjectures, sometimes

pregnant and suggestive, but sometimes of a rudimentary and child-like kind"; "[Xeno-phanes'] conception of the stars shows clearly how little the naturalistic treatment of phe-nomena suited his mental tendency" (Zeller, *A History of Greek Philosophy: From the Earliest Period to the Time of Socrates*, 567 and 578; cf. ZN 664, 677). Cf. von Fritz, "Xenophanes," col. 1559 (my translation): "[the evidence concerning Xenophanes' natural philosophy] does not give the impression that, in this field, he should count among the great and original of philosophers." Here is Guthrie's influential estimate: "Xenophanes is credited with other beliefs about the heavenly bodies which are strange indeed and scarcely comprehensi-ble.... If correctly reported, they suggest that Xenophanes did not take these matters very seriously, but was probably chiefly concerned to ridicule religious notions of the heavenly bodies" (*HGP* 1:390, 393). In a milder put-down, Xenophanes' theories are compared un-favorably with those of the Milesians (Hussey, *The Presocratics*, 33; Veikos, *I Prosokratikyí*, 91). A type of comment that is presented as charitable takes Xenophanes' cosmological pronouncements on celestial phenomena to have the force of humor and irony, in the spirit of his *Silloi* (Burnet, *Early Greek Philosophy*, 123; KRS, 174–175). Runia, who is rightly critical of the "opinion that Xenophanes' [natural philosophy] was little more than a satirical sketch," notes that this disparaging opinion is "widespread" ("Xenophanes on the Moon," 268).

24. In this overview, I adhere to the account offered in Lesher, *Xenophanes of Colo-phon*, 120–48, except for points with respect to which I specifically allude to interpretation offered by myself outside this present essay.

25. See Mourelatos, "La terre et les étoiles," 332–36.

26. But without the wholly unwarranted glossing in DK of *ekleipsin* as *dysin*, "sunset."

27. See Mourelatos, "La terre et les étoiles," 337–46.

28. This view is directly attested for Anaximenes (DK13A7); but I believe Xenophanes fully adopted it. See Mourelatos, "La terre et les étoiles," 347–48.

29. I do not agree with the alternative explication mentioned in Lesher, *Xenophanes of Colophon*, 218 n. 59, that the sun, after sunset, goes indefinitely "downward."

30. The ancient source, Aëtius, uses the technical term *klimata*, "inclinations of the celestial pole," i.e., latitudes. The term belongs to the context of a spherical-earth geog-raphy and astronomy. It could not have been a term used by Xenophanes; but it is perfectly apt to convey succinctly distinctions between regions "to the north" and regions "to the south"—distinctions that are implied by Xenophanes' doctrine.

31. We also have important indirect testimony from the Arabic tradition, in the form of a ninth-century Arabic version, by Qostā Ibn Lūqā, of pseudo-Plutarch *Epit.* The Arabic text has been edited, with German translation and notes, in Daiber, *Aëtius Arabus*. There is good reason to believe that the Greek text that was used for this Arabic translation reflects an earlier and better archetype than the one that lies behind the tradition of Greek manuscripts for pseudo-Plutarch *Epit.*: see Daiber, ibid., 325. But where there are signifi-cant differences between the Arabic translation and the Greek vulgate, "the question must often remain open," as Daiber puts it (326; my translation from the German), "whether the renderings that deviate from the Greek are due to translation error, or to intentional al-teration by the translator, or to a variant Greek source." In the case of Xenophanes, the German translation of Qostā's text shows significant differences in wording in almost every lemma. Since the uncertainties are compounded by my not knowing Arabic, I shall use Daiber's German translation of "Aëtius Arabus" only to corroborate evidence obtainable from analysis of the Greek sources.

32. For the system of references, see above, n. 9.

33. The reading ἢ νέφος πεπυρωμένον is in all the manuscripts of *Epit.* But in *DG* Diels prints the correction ἐκ νεφῶν πεπυρωμένων. I follow Mau, *Plutarchi Moralia Vol.*

V, Fasc. 2, Pars 1, 90, in adhering to the received reading, which has been confirmed by the Arabic translation: "Xenophanes glaubte, daß die Substanz der Sonne aus kleinen feurigen Körpern besteht, welche aus dem Dampf zusammentreten. Aus ihrer Ansammlung entstehen die Sonne oder glühende Wolken"; See Daiber, *Aëtius Arabus,* 155. The translator into Arabic evidently took the phrase ἢ νέφος πεπυρωμένον not as the start of an independent clause but rather, in accusative case, as disjunctive complement to συνα-θροιζόντων. The Arabic version would thus suggest that the Greek source read: συνα-θροιζόντων δὲ <ἢ> τὸν ἥλιον ἢ νέφος πεπυρωμένον, "cumulatively forming either the sun or an ignited/incandescent cloud."

34. It has long been thought that Θεόφραστος ἐν τοῖς Φυσικοῖς, κ.τ.λ., is a report *by* Theophrastus concerning Xenophanes. One would assume, accordingly, that a relative adverb such as *hôs,* "as," appeared before Theophrastus' name in the original doxographic source. See discussion immediately below.

35. I cite the texts as in DK and in Mau, *Plutarchi Moralia,* 94. See, however, Runia, "Xenophanes on the Moon," 251, and discussion below.

36. Several other Greek sources, including variant readings in pseudo-Plutarch *Epit.,* corroborate the attribution in the form in which it appears in Johannes Lydus, *nephos einai pepyrômenon:* see Runia, "Xenophanes on the Moon," 251–53, 265–67. There is also support from the Arabic translation: cf. "Xenophanes glaubte, daß der Mond eine glühende Wolke ist" (Daiber, *Aëtius Arabus,* 161).

37. Diels in DK inserts *ginesthai* after the "sc." But the section to which this report belongs in the doxography bears, in pseudo-Plutarch, the title Τίς ἡ οὐσία τῶν ἄστρων, and in Stobaeus, the title Περὶ οὐσίας ἄστρων. In most entries in this section the elided verb is εἶναι. The entry that immediately precedes the Xenophanes entry in Stobaeus reads: Ἀριστοτέλης ἐκ τοῦ πέμπτου σώματος γεγενῆσθαι τὰ ἄστρα. This is, presumably, Diels's basis for supplying *ginesthai.* In fact, it only justifies supplying the perfect form *gegenêsthai,* "to have come to be," the resultative-stative sense of which is very close to *einai,* after all. The occurrence of *synestanai* and *synistasthai* in Achilles and Theodoretus, respectively, corroborate the inference that the elided verb of A38 must be either *einai* or a stative equivalent of it. The Arabic translation, too, appears to involve a stative sense: cf. "Xenophanes glaubte, daß die Sterne aus Wolken bestehen," Daiber, *Aëtius Arabus,* 151.

38. The chapter heading indicates the scope of Xenophanes' two pronouns: Περὶ κομητῶν καὶ διᾳττόντων καὶ δοκίδων (pseudo-Plutarch; see Mau, *Plutarchi Moralia,* 50 n. and 101); Περὶ κομητῶν καὶ διᾳττόντων καὶ τῶν τοιούτων (Stobaeus; see Wachsmuth, *Ioannis Stobaei Anthologii libri duo priores,* 4, 227). In the Arabic translation of pseudo-Plutarch, the chapter heading is worded differently: cf. "Über die beschweiften Sterne [=κομῆται], das Herabstürzen der Sterne [=διᾴττοντες] und die längliche Röte, welche im Himmel erscheint, als ob sie eine Rute [=κίων] wäre"; Daiber, *Aëtius Arabus,* 169.

39. Slight variation in pseudo-Galen *Phil. Hist.* 75, which is derived from pseudo-Plutarch: σύστημα ἢ κίνημα (*DG* 630).

40. The Arabic translation has considerably different wording: cf. "Xenophanes glaubte, daß das Entstehen von all dem aus glühenden oder sich bewegenden Wolken erfolgt" (Daiber, *Aëtius Arabus,* 171).

41. I draw on a Thesaurus Linguae Graecae search, chronologically ordered, of all occurrences of the string *pepyrômen-.*

42. Out of the 666 instances of the string *pepyrômen-* in the Thesaurus Linguae Graecae database, the vast majority of applications of the participle modify nouns for metals, or involve the metaphorical uses referred to above. Overwhelmingly numerous in

CE centuries are uses in contexts of Christian ethics, catechism, and theology ("the searing arrows of sin," "the fire-purged words of the Lord," and the like).

43. Right in Diels's text of Aëtius, in the Chrysippus lemma of the chapter on lightning, we read: ὅταν δὲ ἄθρουν ἐκπέσῃ τὸ πνεῦμα καὶ ἧττον πεπυρωμένον, πρηστῆρα γίνεσθαι· ὅταν δ' ἔτι ἧττον ᾖ πεπυρωμένον τὸ πνεῦμα, τυφῶνα (Stobaeus *Ecl.*; *DG* 370b4–7; cf. Wachsmuth, *Ioannis Stobaei Anthologii libri duo priores*, 233).

44. Mourelatos, "La terre et les étoiles," 338–45.

45. This assumption vitiates, in my judgment, the otherwise intriguing theory espoused in Keyser, "Xenophanes' Sun on Trojan Ida," that Xenophanes' sun results from daily coalescence of bits of fire in a process analogous to what is hypothetically envisaged in Lucretius 5.660–65. As Runia points out (Runia, "Xenophanes or Theophrastus?" 117 n. 13 and 120 n. 35), the possible bearing of this Lucretius passage on Xenophanes was anticipated by Diels.

46. See the Index Verborum in *DG* s.vv. (for ἀνημμένος s.v. ἀνάπτειν, for πεπυρωμένον s.v. πυροῦν). Specifically in the case of πυροῦν/ -σθαι, of the seven passages listed, excluding the ones from Xenophanes that are at issue for us, the semantic environments indicate heating rather than burning: depending on degree of πυροῦσθαι of πνεῦμα, we get either a hurricane or a water-spout (*DG* 370b5–6); in the north we have cold and compaction, in the south, πυροῦσθαι (377a25–27); πνεῦμα πυρωθέν ... οὐκ ἐπικαῖον (an especially telling connection, 452.31–453.2); πυρούμενα are things subjected to firing, such as iron (521.19 and 22); πνεύματος πεπυρωμένου (admits but does not require the sense of burning, 367a5 and b5); blood as πυρούμενον, in a context that discusses πυρετός, "fever" (441a13); air undergoes πυροῦσθαι simply because of the piercing character of solar motion (it is pointed out that the sun itself is not πύρινος, 451).

47. The discrepancy has long been noted as problematic: see *DG* 217, 220, 348; KRS, 173–74. Cf. *HGP* 1:392; des Places, *Eusèbe de Césarée*, 364. See also n. 50 below.

48. See Wachsmuth, *Ioannis Stobaei Anthologii libri duo priores*, 207.

49. For a detailed account of the controversy, see Runia, "Xenophanes or Theophrastus?" 118–29.

50. In spite of his using for *pepyrômenon/-a* the translation "ignited," which I believe I have shown to be mistaken. See Runia, "Xenophanes or Theophrastus?" 120, 126; cf. Runia, "Xenophanes on the Moon."

51. Runia himself stresses this point: "[W]e cannot go back behind the doxographical texts with any certainty" ("Xenophanes or Theophrastus?" 126). "Certainty" is much too high a demand even for the circumscribed project Runia set for himself. The reader of the present essay will, no doubt, realize that what I am attempting is precisely the speculative project Runia eschews.

52. A search of the Thesaurus Linguae Graecae databank for *pyridion* (with short upsilon, as in *pyr*, "fire") belies Steinmetz's supposition, in *Die Physik des Theophrastos von Eresos*, 165, that *pyridion* is a "typical Theophrastean word." In fact, except for the doxographical contexts that are at issue here, there are no occurrences of the term either in the preserved works of Theophrastus or in fragments securely assigned to his works. In the entire TLG corpus, the term occurs nowhere else except in the testimonia for Xenophanes listed above in section 3 under (A). Not relevant, of course, are two occurrences in TLG of forms of *pyridion* that clearly derive from *pyros* with long upsilon, "wheat" (*pyridion* = "grain of wheat").

53. Keyser, accordingly, speculates that Xenophanes "must [have] used some other word or phrase for 'sparks' or 'bits of fire,'" say, *phlogos sperma* (Keyser, "Xenophanes' Sun on Trojan Ida," 309).

54. Runia, "Xenophanes on the Moon," 267 n. 56.

55. There is no need to suppose that Anaximenes had in mind only effects of phosphorescence by marine microorganisms. To be sure, the effect is greatly enhanced if there is such phosphorescence; but it is easily noticed either by day or by night simply when the sea is calm—the forcible stirring of the water, and the simmering foam that results, being caused only by the action of the oars.

56. For critical examination of these details, see Mourelatos, "La terre et les étoiles," 337–47.

57. See preceding note.

58. Diels points out that the nominalizations may be thought of as derived from νεφῶν πεπυρωμένων ἃ συνίσταται ἢ κινεῖται: DG 367a n.

59. The theme of "differentiation" in the various component theses of Xenophanes' theory of the meteôra is rightly stressed in Runia, "Xenophanes on the Moon," 266–67. Runia assumes, however, that the differentiation is only in terms of size or density.

60. There is immense complexity, doubtless, in the case of ordinary clouds as well. But the circumstances of motion are mainly external and obvious: it is largely the wind that drives and shapes ordinary clouds (cf. Xenophanes B30).

61. See Aristotle Mete. 1.4–7; Pliny HN 2.22–26; Seneca QNat. 1.1. Cf. Gilbert, Die meteorologischen Theorien des griechischen Altertums, 597–600, 656–57. Medieval and Renaissance manuals of meteorology augment the ancient typology. They take note of such types, among others, as "dancing goats," "the flying dragon," the ignis fatuus ("will-o'-the-wisp"): see Heninger, Handbook of Renaissance Meteorology, 91–101.

62. The lemma on Heracleides and the Peripatetics implies that they, too, had a comprehensive theory, but the emphatic panta that occurs in the Xenophanes lemma is missing.

63. See Runia, "Xenophanes on the Moon," 246–48, 251.

64. See ibid., 251–52.

65. And this reading is also supported by the Arabic translation of Epit.: see Daiber, Aëtius Arabus, 161.

66. Worth excerpting here are two ancient scholia on Aratus' Phainomena: ὁποία περὶ τὰς πεπιλημένας νεφέλας φαίνεται ἀμαύρωσις (ad 872); νεφέλαι πεπιλημέναι αἱ τὴν ἀορασίαν ποιοῦσαι (ad 1013). See Martin, Scholia in Aratum Vetera, 426–27, 484–85.

67. Bicknell, "A Note on Xenophanes' Astrophysics," 135–36.

68. See Mourelatos, "La terre et les étoiles," and "Xenophanes' Contribution to the Explanation of the Moon's Light."

69. Cf. Eisenstadt, "The Philosophy of Xenophanes of Colophon," 87.

70. See above, 148.

71. See Gilbert, Die meteorologischen Theorien des griechischen Altertums, 493 n. 2.

72. See Schaefer and Day, A Field Guide to the Atmosphere, 158–61, 168–72; cf. Holford, The Guinness Book of Weather Facts and Feats, 206–11; Gallant, Rainbows, Mirages, and Sundogs, 46–57. "Coronae" in the sense relevant here are, of course, to be distinguished from the "coronae" of modern astronomy, the super-charged gaseous envelopes beyond the chromosphere of the sun or of a star. Atmospheric coronae were not distinguished from halos till the nineteenth century.

73. "Systematic observations of halos for twenty two years (in the Netherlands) indicate the inner halo as the most frequent (in 209 days in a year at the average); the next are parhelia (71) and the tangential arcs to the inner halo (59)" (Encyclopedia Britannica, 14th ed., 1963, s. v. "Halo").

74. Cf. Baker, *An Introduction to Astronomy*, 17–18: "The impression that the appearance of a ring around the moon or sun gives warning of an approaching storm has some basis in the fact that the filmy clouds which form the halos are likely to fly ahead of storm clouds."

75. Bicknell, "A Note on Xenophanes' Astrophysics," 136, makes the suggestion, which I find less convincing, that the moon's features (its darker spots) were perceived by Xenophanes as holes that show the blue of the sky.

76. A newspaper column on the total lunar eclipse of August 16, 1989, quotes this remark by a non-scientist observer in Austin, Texas: "Earlier, it was kind of hazy. It seemed like a small cloud up there rather than the moon" (*Austin American-Statesman*, Aug. 17, 1989, p. A10).

77. It is surprising that the Milky Way is not mentioned in any of the testimonia concerning Xenophanes. That this phenomenon had figured in early Greek cosmologies is suggested by the prominence accorded to it in Parmenides' "Doxa": see DK 28B11, cf. 28A37, A43, A43a.

78. This phenomenon was known to Aristotle. See *Mete*. 1.5; cf. note just before 342a34 in Lee, *Aristotle: Meteorologica*, 36. Gilbert, *Die meteorologischen Theorien des griechischen Altertums*, 597, found it "impossible" that Aristotle should have referred to the aurora borealis, presumably on the grounds that Greece is too far south. But on two successive nights in March 1989, on the 13th and the 14th, the northern lights were seen in central and southern Texas (near 30° north latitude), almost 10 degrees farther south than Ionia and Southern Italy.

79. Americo Vespucci, writing to Lorenzo Pietro di Medici in 1503, describes the night sky of the southern hemisphere in these words: "Every night in that part of the sky innumerable vapors and glowing meteors fly about." Quoted from Popkin, *The Philosophy of the 16th and 17th Centuries*, 29.

80. This was very helpfully pointed out to me by Olive Forbes.

81. See above, n. 16.

82. See Heuer, *Thunder, Singing Sands, and Other Wonders*, 38.

83. See above, n. 72.

84. There is, of course, no gibbous phase in the case of either a solar or a lunar eclipse. The ancients, who may not—to the sad detriment of their eyesight—have had our scruples about staring at the sun at the time of an eclipse, would have sometimes seen the solar crescent directly; or they could have seen its image on the dappled shadow of trees of medium foliage, which is nature's equivalent for the cardboard-and-pinhole device we use to observe the solar crescent.

85. See Baker, *An Introduction to Astronomy*, 141, fig. 8.7; Snow, *The Dynamic Universe*, fig. 2.18.

86. Let us not dismiss the testimonium on the grounds that it goes on to add that Xenophanes had also spoken of a solar eclipse that lasted a whole month. Such a remark by him could well have been prompted by reports of protracted disappearance of the sun close to the time (before and after) of the winter solstice at regions of the extreme north.

87. See above, n. 72.

88. See above, n. 59.

89. The phenomenon listed here is that of a flashing cloud with no lightning streak or thunderbolt visible. Though English uses "lightning" both for the sudden glow in the clouds and for the thunderbolt, Greek uses κεραυνός for the latter but uses ἀστραπή or ἀστεροπή or στεροπή for the former. See, e.g., Pindar *Pyth*. 6.24, στεροπᾶν κεραυνῶν τε πρύτανιν [said of Zeus]; Aeschylus *Septem* 430, τὰς ἀστραπάς τε καὶ κεραυνίους

βολάς. Latin similarly distinguished between *fulguratio* (the luminous glow) and *fulmen* (the bolt). The distinction is observed in Modern Greek, too: αστραπή, αστραποφεγγιά versus κεραυνός, αστροπελέκι.

90. See preceding note.

91. See above, n. 16.

92. Translation as in Lesher, *Xenophanes of Colophon*, 32, 106; cf. Lesher's helpful comments on *kradainei*, p. 107. The interpreter who comes closest to appreciating this important connection between B25 and the cloud-astrophysics is Kelesidou, Ἡ φιλοσοφία τοῦ Ξενοφάνη [*I filosofía tou Ksenofáni*], 109. I do not myself find, however, the hints she detects of creative or procreative action or of providence ([my translation] "things that derive [*proerchontai*] from it [the divine *archê*] . . .; their transformation [*metaschêmatismos*] is regulated [*rhythmizetai*], in contrast with [what holds for] Ionian hylozoism"). Two pages earlier she entertains—but ultimately denies—the possibility that Xenophanes' God is a *dêmiourgos*, and that teleology plays a role in the Xenophanean cosmology (p. 101).

93. I am using the term in the technical sense that has been established in the philosophy of science. The verbal paradox of "reducing" something of smaller explanatory scope to something of greater explanatory scope can be mitigated by considering that the reduction typically takes us from large and middle-size objects to entities at the microscopic level.

94. See, for example, Churchland, *Matter and Consciousness*, 26–27, with references, on p. 35, to earlier literature. In cases in which the identity posited is one between a common-sense observable (lightning, table) and an object or structure postulated by theory (electrical discharge, cloud of micro-particles), the term "inter-theoretic identity" is still apt, inasmuch as it is now generally recognized that the conceptual framework of common sense is itself a proto-theory.

BIBLIOGRAPHY

See also Abbreviations, above, p. vii.

Athanassakis, A. N. *The Homeric Hymns: Translation, Introduction, and Notes*. Baltimore: Johns Hopkins University Press, 1970.

Baker, R. H. *An Introduction to Astronomy*. New York: D. Van Nostrand, 1952.

Bicknell, Peter. "A Note on Xenophanes' Astrophysics." *Acta Classica* 10 (1967): 135–36.

Burnet, John. *Early Greek Philosophy*. London: Adam & Charles Black, 1892. 4th ed. 1930.

Churchland, P. M. *Matter and Consciousness: A Contemporary Introduction to Philosophy*. Cambridge, Mass.: MIT Press, 1984.

Daiber, H. *Aëtius Arabus: Die Vorsokratiker in arabischen Überlieferung*. Wiesbaden: Franz Steiner Verlag, 1980.

des Places, É. *Eusèbe de Césarée: La préparation évangélique, livre I, intoduction, texte grec, traduction et annotation*. Paris: Les Éditions de Minuit, 1987.

Eisenstadt, M. "The Philosophy of Xenophanes of Colophon." Ph. D. diss., Texas at Austin, 1970.

Fränkel, H. *Early Greek Poetry and Philosophy*, trans. Moses Hadas and James Willis. New York: Harcourt Brace Jovanovitch, 1973.

———— "Xenophanes' Empiricism and His Critique of Knowledge (B34)," trans. M. R. Cosgrove. In *The Presocratics: A Collection of Critical Essays*, edited by A. P. D. Mourelatos, 118–31. Garden City, N.Y.: Anchor Press, 1974. Repr. Princeton: Princeton University Press, 1993.

Frede, M. "Aëtiana." *Phronesis* 44 (1999): 135–49.

Fritz, Kurt von. "Xenophanes." In *Paulys Realencyclopädie der classischen Altertums-wissenschaft*, edited by G. Wissowa. Ser. 2, vol. 9A.2 (1967): cols. 1541–62.

Furley, W. D., and J. D. Bremer. *Greek Hymns, 2 Vols.: Vol. 1 The Text in Translation; Vol. 2 Greek Texts and Commentary*. Tübingen: Mohr Siebeck, 2001.

Gallant, Roy A. *Rainbows, Mirages, and Sundogs: The Sky as a Source of Wonder*. New York: Macmillan, 1987.

Gilbert, Otto. *Die meteorologischen Theorien des griechischen Altertums*. Leipzig: B. G. Teubner, 1907.

Heitsch, E. *Xenophanes: Die Fragmente*. Munich: Artemis Verlag, 1983.

Heninger, S. K., Jr. *Handbook of Renaissance Meteorology*. Durham, N.C.: Duke University Press, 1960.

Heuer, K. *Thunder, Singing Sands, and Other Wonders: Sounds in the Atmosphere*. New York: Dodd, Mead, 1981.

Holford, I. *The Guinness Book of Weather Facts and Feats*. Enfield, Middlesex: Guinness Superlatives, 1977.

Hussey, Edward. *The Presocratics*. London: Duckworth, 1972.

Kelesidou, A. Ἡ φιλοσοφία τοῦ Ξενοφάνη [*I filosofía tou Ksenofáni*]. Athens: Academy of Athens, 1996.

Keyser, Paul T. "Xenophanes' Sun (Frr. A32, 33.3, 40 DK6) on Trojan Ida (Lucr. 5.660–5, D.S. 17.7.5–7, Mela 1.94–5)." *Mnemosyne* 45 (1992): 299–311.

Lebedev, Andrei. "Did the Doxographer Aëtius Ever Exist?" In *Philosophie et Culture: Actes Du XVIIe Congrès Mondial de Philosophie*, edited by V. Cauchy, 813–17. Montréal: Éditions du Beffroi/Éditions de Montmorency, 1988.

————. "Φύσις ταλαντεύουσα: Neglected Fragments of Democritus and Metrodorus of Chios." In *Vol. 2, Proceedings of the 1st International Congress on Democritus*. Xanthi: International Democritean Foundation, 1984.

Lee, H. D. P. *Aristotle: Meteorologica*. Cambridge, Mass.: Harvard University Press, 1952.

Lesher, James H. *Xenophanes of Colophon: Fragments*. Toronto: University of Toronto Press, 1992.

Lexicon iconographicum mythologiae classicae. 10 vols. [8 vols. in two parts; 2 index vols.]. Zurich: Artemis Verlag, 1981–99.

Lobel, E., and D. Page. *Poetarum lesbiorum fragmenta*. Oxford: Clarendon Press, 1955.

Mansfeld, Jaap. "Theophrastus and the Xenophanes Doxography." *Mnemosyne* 40 (1987): 286–312. Repr. with the original pagination in Jaap Mansfeld, *Studies in the Histor-iography of Greek Philosophy*. Assen: Van Gorcum, 1990.

Mansfeld, Jaap, and David T. Runia. *Aëtiana: The Method and Intellectual Context of a Doxographer*. Philosophia Antiqua, vol. 73. Leiden: E. J. Brill, 1997.

Martin, J. *Scholia in Aratum vetera*. Stuttgart: B. G. Teubner, 1974.

Mau, J. *Plutarchi Moralia Vol. V, Fasc. 2, Pars 1*. Leipzig: Teubner, 1971.

Mourelatos, Alexander P. D. "The Real, Appearances, and Human Error in Early Greek Philosophy." *The Review of Metaphysics* 19 (1965): 346–65.

————. "La terre et les étoiles dans la cosmologie de Xénophane." In *Qu'est-ce que la philosophie présocratique?* edited by André Laks and Claire Louguet, 331–50. Villeneuve d'Ascq: Presses Universitaires du Septentrion, 2002.

————. "Xenophanes' Contribution to the Explanation of the Moon's Light." *Philosophia* 32 (2002): 47–58.

Popkin, R. H., ed. *The Philosophy of the 16th and 17th Centuries*. New York: Free Press, 1966.

Roscher, W. H. *Ausführliches Lexikon der griechischen und römischen Mythologie*. Leipzig: Teubner, 1884–1924.

Runia, David T. "Xenophanes on the Moon: A *doxographicum* in Aëtius." *Phronesis* 34 (1989): 245–69.

————."Xenophanes or Theophrastus? An Aëtian *doxographicum* on the Sun." In *Theophrastus: His Psychological, Doxographical, and Scientific Writings*, edited by William W. Fortenbaugh and Dimitri Gutas, 112–40. New Brunswick, N.J.: Transaction, 1992.

Schaefer, V. J., and J. A. Day. *A Field Guide to the Atmosphere*. Boston: Houghton Mifflin, 1981.

Snow, T. P. *The Dynamic Universe: An Introduction to Astronomy*. St. Paul, Minnesota: West, 1985.

Steinmetz, Peter. *Die Physik des Theophrastos von Eresos*. Berlin: Verlag Dr. Max Gehlen, 1964.

Veikos, Th. [Βέϊκος, Θ.] Οἱ προσωκρατικοί [*I prosokratikyí*]. Athens: Zacharopoulos, 1988.

Wachsmuth, C. *Ioannis Stobaei Anthologii libri duo priores*. Berlin: Weidmann, 1884.

Zeller, Eduard. *A History of Greek Philosophy: From the Earliest Period to the Time of Socrates*, trans. S. F. Alleyne. 2 vols. London: Longmans, Green, 1881.

CHAPTER 5

HERACLITUS: FLUX, ORDER, AND KNOWLEDGE

DANIEL W. GRAHAM

WITH HERACLITUS a new type of thinker appears in archaic Greece. No longer satisfied with cosmological questions of the sort that drove the Milesians, he looks critically at the world, at society, and at how people know the world. He does not simply accept the framework of explanation developed by the Milesians, but questions it.

According to the Milesian framework, the world came to be by some sort of cosmic development. At one time there was a uniform state of water, or air, or the boundless (whatever that is). Then a process began by which different stuffs were separated out of the original stuff, and the several stuffs were sorted and arranged into layers of the sort that make up our world: earth below, water on the earth, air, and fiery heavenly bodies. To explain the world is to tell how it happened that the original undifferentiated stuff came to be our world. In telling that story, the cosmologist must describe the shape of the earth and the nature of its surroundings, must tell how living things arose from nonliving stuffs, and must account for the recurring phenomena of the world. The cosmologist must tell about the heavenly bodies: what their nature is, why they travel a daily path above the earth, participate in annual cycles, and yet continue to exist. The cosmologist must also describe the *meteôra*, the atmospheric phenomena such as clouds, winds, storms, rain, hail, lightning, and rainbows.

Though deeply influenced by Milesian speculation, Heraclitus does not imitate it. He promises to explain how things are in the beginning of his book. But he will not explain things in the straightforward didactic style of his predecessors. Nor will he advance a cosmogony. Nor will he focus on technical explanations and detailed accounts of the world. A reason for departing from the usual style of exposition is evident from his prefatory remarks: he thinks most people are incapable of understanding his message, even when it is explained to them. Whereas other natural philosophers have addressed themselves to a general audience (perhaps a limited one of educated individuals, but to that group generally), Heraclitus expresses his lack of faith in his audience from the outset. He will give us the truth, but we are not likely to benefit from it. The theme of human ignorance immediately signals a different emphasis from that of the Milesians: Heraclitus is not merely concerned with the way things are, but with how humans react to the world. The shift of emphasis leads some to say that Heraclitus is primarily concerned with the human condition.[1] That may be an overinterpretation.[2] But clearly he reflects on the human condition in his philosophizing, presumably for the first time in the philosophical tradition.

Heraclitus is famously obscure in his pronouncements and, as we shall see, ambiguous in his utterances. He is, according to Plato, Aristotle, the ancient sources in general, and many of his modern interpreters, a philosopher of change, for whom all things are in flux. Because all things are in flux, opposites are identical, and hence things have incompatible properties and contradictory statements are true.[3] But if this is so, as Plato and Aristotle recognize, then knowledge, communication, and finally philosophy itself are impossible. For there is no stable world to talk about, think about, or theorize about. Heraclitus's philosophy is for them a kind of *reductio ad absurdum* of the world. How then is knowledge possible? How can Heraclitus be saying anything at all? How can his philosophy be any more than a kind of misanthropic nihilism?

1. FLUX

Heraclitus's commitment to flux is visible in his statement about the world: "This world-order [*kosmos*], the same of all,[4] no god nor man did create, but it ever was and is and will be: everliving fire, kindling in measures and being quenched in measures" (B30). This passage contains the first recorded use of the term *kosmos* as meaning something like "the world."[5] Heraclitus recognizes it as a kind of order (an early meaning of *kosmos*), and identifies it with fire. This suggests the standard account of the early Ionian philosophers, according to which all things are a single substance, such as water (Thales) or air (Anaximenes). Yet fire is the least substantial of all things, so that it seems problematic to say that the world is fire, as if this were some stable substratum. In fact, some of the fire is kindling and some is being quenched, so that at least that part of fire is undergoing transition. The fire, he claims, is everliving; but that seems to result precisely from its changeableness. So in what sense can we say that there is a stable world?

Heraclitus tells us about the changes that fire, and other substances, undergo "the turnings of fire: first sea, and of sea half is earth, half fireburst" (B31a);[6] "[from earth] sea is liquefied and measured into the same proportion as it had before it became earth" (B31b). Giving concrete names to the stuffs, Heraclitus says that fire turns into water and water into earth. But half of the water turns back into fire. Thus we have the sequence fire, water, earth, with water being equally divided into a part that turns into fire and a part that turns into earth. Furthermore, there is a proportionate replacement, such that so much earth turns into so much water, while the equivalent amount of water turns back into the same amount of earth. Heraclitus recognizes a kind of law of conservation—not precisely conservation of mass, but at least of material equivalences. He does not tell us whether the proportions are of volumes, weights, or something else. But whatever they are, they are constant. If one unit of earth produces two units of water, then two units of water will produce one unit of earth. Consequently, Heraclitus seems to maintain that the world will always contain the same amounts of fire, water, and earth. To be sure, it will not be the same fire, water, and earth—for they are always changing places—but the same proportions and the same absolute amounts of each will be maintained.

Although we might have expected an account of change in which the world is radically fragmented, we find considerable continuity in Heraclitus's world. First, there is a regular order of changes: fire to water to earth. Second, there is a regular proportionality among the changes: the quantity of one stuff changes into a fixed and determinate quantity of the other stuff. Third, the changes are reversible: fire turns into water, water into fire; water turns into earth, earth into water. And fourth, so far as we can see, the sum total of changes in the world cancels out. For the loss of fire into water is made up for by the gain of fire coming out of water, and so on. In this world of constant change, there is a high degree of constancy, at least at a global level.

But there is perhaps one area where the flux is more radical than has often been realized. What precisely are the turnings (*tropai*) Heraclitus refers to in B31a? On the standard interpretation, which goes back to Aristotle, Heraclitus, like his Milesian predecessors, is a material monist: he believes that there is one and only one kind of matter in the world, and every stuff that appears different from that real and ultimate matter is merely a modification of it.[7] Thus, if the world is really composed of water, then air, fire, and so on will be merely manifestations of water in a different guise. If fire is the ultimate reality, then water and earth will just be manifestations of fire. But Heraclitus presents the turnings as equivalent and reversible. Can he really think that water is a kind of fire? Here a defender of the standard account could appeal to B30, which says that the world is everliving fire. What could be more explicit than that? The turnings, then, would have to be, as Aristotle would have it, alterations of fire that mask, but do not change, its true nature.

Passage B31 is not, then, conclusive for understanding the kind of change Heraclitus has in mind. But there are other passages that undermine the standard interpretation: "Fire lives the death of earth, and air lives the death of fire; water lives the death of air, and earth that of fire" (B76a); "To souls it is death to become water, to water death to become earth, but from earth water is born, and from water soul" (B36). The first fragment is somewhat suspect because it seems to presuppose the four elements made popular later by Empedocles (on the other hand air was already prominent in Anaximenes).[8] About the second there is no problem, however. Here soul occupies the place of fire, as it is associated in other contexts with fire, and we are told that the death of one stuff is the birth of the other and vice versa. The talk of birth and death is closely correlated with what Aristotle calls coming to be and perishing. If fire (that is, soul) dies into water, it perishes, ceases to exist. If that is the case, then water is not a manifestation of fire, but its successor and replacement. And it appears that all the stuffs are on equal terms: their relationships are reciprocal, their changes reversible. Stuff X is replaced by Y, Y is replaced by Z, Z is replaced by Y, Y is replaced by X. But no one is prior to the others nor does any one underlie or support the others. The *tropai* are instances of (unqualified) coming-to-be and perishing, not of alterations of some continuing substratum. This view seems to be supported by another statement: "Immortal mortals, mortal immortals: living the death of those, dying the life of these" (B62). The context is not clear, but the statement would apply to the elemental stuffs: they are immortal only by arising from each others' deaths. For instance, sea would always remain in the cosmos because of constant exchanges between its water and cosmic fire and earth. All in all, death and life are reciprocal processes that ensure the immortality of some entities.

If we now go back to B30, we see that Heraclitus's cosmos is actually *more* stable than that of any of his predecessors.[9] For they had generally held that the world comes to be from some antecedent state of uniformity, and gradually evolved to its present condition—and for at least some of them, it may perish later. But from what Heraclitus seems to say, his world always "was and is and will be," that is, continues in the same state without coming to be or perishing as a whole. It does so precisely because portions of the world are kindling and being quenched. In other words, the constant transformations of matter seem to maintain the overall stability of the totality. Ironically, Heraclitus's world is the most permanent of all, thanks to the ongoing renewal of its parts.

2. ORDER

There is, then, at least one thing that does not change in this world of change: the world itself. But what of common objects of everyday experience? Do they continue to exist in such a way that they can be known, or do they elude our grasp? The most important pieces of information about middle-sized objects seem to come from the so-called River Fragments, as follows.

ποταμοῖσι τοῖσιν αὐτοῖσιν ἐμβαίνουσιν ἕτερα καὶ ἕτερα ὕδατα ἐπιρρεῖ.

Potamoisi toisin autoisin embainousin hetera kai hetera hudata epirrei.

On those stepping into rivers staying the same, other and other waters flow. (B12)

Heraclitus, I believe, says that all things pass and nothing stays, and comparing existents to the flow of a river, he says you could not step twice into the same river. (Plato *Cratylus* 402a = A6)

Into the same rivers we step and do not step, we are and are not. (B49a)

It is not possible to step twice into the same river according to Heraclitus, or to come into contact twice with a mortal being in the same state. (B91a)

ποταμοῖς δὶς τοῖς αὐτοῖς οὐκ ἂν ἐμβαίης· ἕτερα γὰρ ἐπιρρεῖ ὕδατα.

You could not step twice into the same rivers; for other waters flow on. (Plutarch *Natural Questions* 912a, 40c[5] Marcovich, *Heraclitus*)

There has been a longstanding controversy over whether the second through the fourth statements (and others like them) provide the context and correct interpretation for the first, or whether they provide an erroneous reading of it.[10] Without going into the details of the argument, I would like to point out a certain redundancy in the statements. They all make use of some sort of analogy with a river, and they typically begin with the word for river(s) and talk about the water flowing in it. In Greek it is unnatural to put the word for river(s) first, since as in English the subject typically comes first. Thus there is a verbal presumption that the latter statements are somehow echoing the first. Furthermore, it has been shown decisively that the first statement is Heraclitean: it has a verbal complexity (to be discussed later) that could not reasonably come about by happenstance, or by paraphrase: information would be lost that could not be recovered.[11] The first question should then be to see what B12 has to say, and then to compare its message with the messages of the echoes in other statements.

The nine words of the fragment fall into two groups: *potamoisi toisin autoisin embainousin* and *hetera kai hetera hudata epirrei*: "rivers the-same those-entering-in" (all in the dative case) and "other and other waters flow on." The first all have the same endings (dative plural masculine) and hence all rhyme; three of the second group begin and end with the same sounds. Indeed, the first four make babbling river-sounds, while the last five seem to make rushing sounds as they pick up speed with pronunciation.[12] The words are very close to poetry in their richness of texture and their evocative power. Semantically, there is one major opposition: between "the same" in the first phrase and "other" (two times) in the second: as in many Heraclitean sayings, opposites play an important role in B12. On the most obvious (but, we shall see later, not the only) reading, the sentence means: "On those who enter into the same rivers, other and other waters flow." In other words, different waters flow over people who pass through the same rivers. This could, of course, be a commonplace observation: when you ford a stream, different waters flow around you. But all ancient interpreters understand the statement as being rich with metaphysical significance. So what is the point? If we take our clue from the main opposition in the sentence, the key contrast is between the sameness of the rivers and the difference of the waters. Is this a contradiction? No, for rivers and water are not identical, hence they are (logically) capable of bearing contrary properties. But Heraclitus seems to be calling our attention to the very fact that these properties are contrary.

If we are looking for connections rather than contradictions, the most obvious sense in which same rivers and different water connect is that the same rivers are composed of ever different waters. That is: the Cayster River, for instance, just is a succession of waters flowing down from a source to the sea. It is the very essence of this river, and any river, to be composed of moving waters that are renewed constantly. Should the waters cease to flow, we would have either a dry riverbed or a stagnant pond, not a river. Thus the river owes its very existence to the ongoing exchange of waters, or in other words, the changing waters are constitutive of the river. In the words of another illustrious theorist of identity, David Hume: "[A]s the nature of a river consists in the motion and change of parts; tho' in less than four and twenty hours these be totally alter'd; this hinders not the river from continuing the same during several ages."[13] If we now compare this initial message to the interpretation of Plato in A6, we find him saying that one cannot step twice into the same river. But Heraclitus does not say that in his own words: even if one cannot step twice into the same *water*, one can step twice into the same *river*, for that the river is the same is *given*.[14] Heraclitus's point is rather that different things (here: material components) can make up the same things (structures). Rivers, in fact, are long-lasting organizational states of transitory waters. The structure supervenes on the matter and outlasts it, attaining at least a relative permanence through its channeling of the ephemeral matter.

Plato (perhaps influenced by Cratylus)[15] takes Heraclitus's point to be that because the waters are changing, everything is changing; Heraclitus's message seems to be that because the waters are constantly changing, the river is (at least relatively) constant. Ancient comments on Plato's flux doctrine all seem to go back to similar reactions to B12. Even Plato's observation that for Heraclitus, *panta rhei*, "All things are in flux," seems to presuppose the one use of the term we find in Heraclitus's fragments, *epirrei* in B12. Indeed, we can see in Plutarch's rendition, which closely imitates the second half of B12 in its second half, that the Platonic phrase is just a stand-in for the first half of B12. Heraclitus made no separate statement saying that all things are in flux: that is Plato's interpretation of B12. Plato is right to see metaphysical and cosmic significance for the passage "comparing existents to the flow of a river," but he does not see how Heraclitus builds stability on a foundation of change. (Perhaps if he did, he would be unimpressed, since he holds that constancy must be *prior* to change in some fundamental sense.) If the river is a symbol of natural processes as a whole, then we learn from Heraclitus that in some sense everything (all elemental matter) is flowing; but it does not follow that all things (middle-sized objects, substances in Aristotle's terminology) are constantly changing (in their nature and presence to us). To the contrary, the river shows us how an exchange of matter can be precisely what gives life to an organized object.

Besides the flux doctrine, Heraclitus is famous for the coincidence of opposites. Opposites are, in some sense, the same. If their being the same implies their being *identical*, we shall find that we cannot stop contradictories from being true at the same time, and hence even if Heraclitus manages to avoid the incoherence of the flux doctrine (as understood by Plato and Aristotle), he may still fail to provide a coherent theory and a knowable world. Heraclitus's most explicit statement of his doctrine of opposites is this: "As the same thing in us[16] is living and dead, waking and sleeping, young and old. For these things having changed around are those, and those in turn having changed around are these" (B88). It has recently been claimed that these words reveal Heraclitus's identification of opposites.[17] But they do nothing of the sort. The second sentence tells us that the opposites are the same because one opposite changes to another and vice versa. We have seen this point already in Heraclitus's claim that living and dead are reciprocal processes. Another fragment provides an adequate gloss: "Cold things warm up, the hot cools off, wet becomes dry, dry becomes wet" (B126). What is cold becomes hot and vice versa. How is this an identity? It seems to be a straightforward claim that change occurs between opposites. But, it could be replied, if this is all Heraclitus means, how can he say that the opposites are the same? Yet his point seems to be not that they are identical (if they were identical, there would *be* no change, for change takes place between opposites), but that given that x is now F, now G (the opposite of F), F and G are part of a larger whole. They are stages in a process of transition (*tropê?*) such that one goes from having one to having the other—and back again. They are equivalent or, to be more precise, *transformationally equivalent* properties. If we alter F, we get G; if we alter G, we get F; and we always have either F or G (or perhaps an intermediate stage).

From Heraclitus's perspective, what is important is not what stage we are in (that is variable), but what larger pattern is exhibited in the reciprocal changes we undergo (that is invariant through change). The cosmos itself is such a pattern. Perhaps life is too (in a process longer than the individual human lifespan). From the larger perspective, even matter is variable, as we have seen. Thus: "All things are an exchange for fire and fire for all things, as goods for gold and gold for goods" (B90). Fire is transformationally equivalent to every other kind of thing (type of matter) as gold provides an equivalent purchase-value for goods. Fire is not identical to other kinds of matter, any more than gold is identical to grain, but the several stuffs are, nevertheless, interchangeable in the city marketplace, or in the cosmic emporium. Indeed, the cosmos is a grand economic market of supply and demand, where transactions are performed and debts are paid as fire changes into water and water into earth and vice versa.

What is crucial in both the doctrine of flux and the unity of opposites is the lawlike relationships that obtain between opposites. Some opposites are equivalent or comparable stages of a cycle; others are hierarchically arranged so that change sustains stability and stability governs change. In either case, opposites are different sides of the same coin: they are interdependent realities.

3. KNOWLEDGE

To return to Plato's problem: how can we have knowledge of a world that is constantly changing? We have seen that not everything in the world is constantly changing. The world itself is a permanent arrangement. And middle-sized objects such as rivers are at least relatively permanent. Yet even so, we could ask how it is possible to have reliable knowledge when the material basis of the world is in constant flux. It would help us to answer Heraclitus's views on knowledge if we could classify him using modern distinctions: is he an empiricist who says knowledge comes ultimately from sense experience, a rationalist who says knowledge comes from reason or innate ideas or structures, or perhaps a mystic who believes in some kind of extrarational illumination? There are interpreters who have held each of these views.[18]

Heraclitus provides a general introduction to his theory, including reflections on knowledge, in the prologue to his book:

> Of this Word's being forever do men prove to be uncomprehending, both before
> they hear and once they have heard it. For although all things happen according to
> this Word they are like the inexperienced experiencing words and deeds such
> as I explain when I distinguish each thing according to its nature and show how it
> is. Other men are unaware of what they do when they are awake just as they
> are forgetful of what they do when they are asleep. (B1)

Heraclitus identifies a "Word" or *logos* that is incomprehensible to most, though Heraclitus will explicate it plainly to us—perhaps in vain. The obstacle Heraclitus seems to see to human understanding is not particularly the fluidity of the world and its materials, but people's inability to grasp an underlying message. People are like sleepwalkers who hear and see but do not comprehend. They seem to have experiences without becoming experienced.

As commentators often stress, Heraclitus seems to welcome experience as a source, perhaps *the* source, of knowledge, but with reservations: "The things of which there is sight, hearing, experience, I prefer" (B55); "The eyes are more accurate witnesses than the ears" (B101a). But it is not enough to use the senses: "Having heard without comprehension they are like the deaf; this saying bears witness to them: present they are absent" (B34); "Poor witnesses for men are the eyes and ears of those who have barbarian souls" (B107). Nor is it enough to gather information from others: "Learning many things [*polymathiê*] does not teach understanding. Else it would have taught Hesiod and Pythagoras, as well as Xenophanes and Hecataeus" (B40). Four reputed wise men of Heraclitus's generation or a century before fail to qualify as genuinely wise. They depend uncritically on traditional information from religious lore (Hesiod and Pythagoras), custom and faith (Xenophanes), or historical, geographical, and genealogical inquiry (Hecataeus).[19] As Heraclitus departs from a straightforward pursuit of cosmology, he also departs from a simple acceptance of information from the senses, or from research more generally. He does not seem to see the problem of *change* as the source of trouble for epistemology; rather there is some difficulty in getting the individual to go from using the senses and gathering information to seeing the ultimate significance of experience, and the underlying message in the information. As Heraclitus puts it rather explicitly, "Many do not understand such things as they encounter, nor do they learn by their experience, but they think they do" (B17).

It appears, then, that experience is necessary for knowledge, but not sufficient. It is not enough simply to go out and experience the world. Rather, one must have some key by which to discern the meaning of experience. One hint is that found in B107, quoted earlier: the eyes and ears are no good for someone who has a barbarian soul. A barbarian is a non-Greek-speaker, one who does not understand the language (that is, Greek, the only language worth knowing). If a barbarian slave, for instance, observes a conversation among Greeks, he will not comprehend its significance, even though he sees and hears.[20] Similarly, if we experience nature without knowing the language of nature, we will not grasp the import of what we experience. Like sleepwalkers with our eyes open, we may be able to avoid bumping into objects around us, but we will not appreciate our situation or the significance of our surroundings. We will not understand how things work or how we should interact meaningfully with them.

But if I do not know the language of nature, how do I learn it? Here we enter into the intriguing world of signs. Heraclitus is famous for the complexity of his messages; we have already seen one example: the river fragment B12. A great many of his sayings involve elaborate syntactical and semantic relationships: parallels, contrasts, analogies, puns and wordplays, double-entendres. There have been many valuable studies of Heraclitus's verbal techniques.[21] Without doubt he is a master of language. More important, it is agreed that Heraclitus does not use his techniques merely to show off on the one hand or merely to confuse the reader on the other, but that his style is a manifestation of his conception of the world. He views nature as part of a "logos-textured world"[22] in which our experiences are laden with meaning. But the layers of meaning are hidden. Our encounters with Heraclitus's text are much like our encounters with the world: the superficial meaning conceals a deeper structure and reality.

To take one example: "A road up and down is one and the same" (B60). The structure of the Heraclitean expression is even simpler, and more paradoxical than the translation: "road up down one and the same." The road that goes uphill (in one direction) also goes downhill (in the other direction). The word *hodos* means both "road" and "route": it is false that the route, the vector, from the bottom of the hill to the top is identical to that from the top to the bottom. Yet there is only one road that conducts travelers both ways. The fact that it goes uphill is inseparable from the fact that it goes downhill. For it to be a road at all, it must in fact go in two opposite directions. Furthermore, the directions *anô katô* are used of a Greek racecourse to denote the directions "out" and "back."[23] If we focus on this sense, the message is that the lap out is the same as the lap back. In one sense, of course they are not identical; yet they form alternate legs of a single circular course. And the concrete racecourse and the event of the race itself are made up of both stages. Furthermore, the images of the road and the racecourse have many potential applications—as did that of the river. Every day the farmer goes out to his field in the morning and back at night. The merchant comes into town in the morning and leaves in the evening. Earth turns into water and then fire (road up) and vice versa (road down). The cosmos is everliving fire, kindling in measures (road up) and being quenched in measures (road down). The cosmos is a grand contest (a war) in which some are revealed as gods (road up), some as men (road down), some of the latter as slaves (road down), some as freemen (road up) (B53). Life is like a road . . . nature is like a road . . . the cosmos is like a road. One is reminded of levels of meaning in medieval interpretation: literal, ethical, anagogic. In Heraclitus there are no standard levels of interpretation, but there are potentially many applications.

If we turn back to Heraclitus's introductory remarks (B1), we see that even in his first sentence the word "forever" is ambiguous: does it go with the preceding or the following words?[24] (Aristotle complained of the difficulty in parsing the first sentence of Heraclitus; he saw the problem but missed the point.)[25] Heraclitus continues by pointing out that ordinary listeners "are like the inexperienced experiencing words and deeds such as I explain"—implying that an encounter with his words is, or should be, an *experience*. This gives us the connection between word and world: a philosophical presentation of experience is itself an experience, and it should be interpreted accordingly. When we see this, we may recognize Heraclitean sayings as imitations of experience in the *logos*-textured world. They are preliminary exercises that allow us to encounter the world in a meaningful way, at second hand of course, and prepare us to encounter the world for ourselves firsthand. We come to see relationships hidden in the world, in particular (as with the road) to see that contrary relationships are unified in a single reality.

Heraclitus likes to find oppositions in everyday realities, like the road. In another image, or pair of images, he calls attention to the opposing forces in apparently static objects: "They do not understand how being at variance with itself it agrees: back-turning[26] structure as of a bow or a lyre" (B51). The bow and the lyre are useful instruments precisely by embodying a tension between contrary forces. Without the opposition between string and wood, the bow would not be able to shoot, the lyre to play. But in the tension there is the unifying structure (*harmoniê*) of the bow or the attunement of the lyre. Moreover, Heraclitus joins in his image two very different kinds of instrument: one of war and one of peace, though both are associated with Apollo. Thus again the same principle joins opposing realms.

Heraclitus exploits a number of techniques in creating verbal experiences, some of which have been studied and well explained, others of which perhaps wait a fuller exposition. One I will focus on is at least not fully appreciated: syntactic ambiguity. In perhaps its simplest form, one word, like "forever" in B1, can be construed with two different phrases, consisting of the words before or after it. Another simple case consists of three words: *êthos anthrôpôi daimôn* (The character of man is his destiny) (B119). The three words are, roughly, "character[27] for-man destiny." The second word can attach to either the first or the third. In this case there is no real contrast of meaning, however we construe the second word, for the character of man is the destiny of man. But the fact that the second word stands between the two and can attach to either makes it a kind of verbal glue that joins the first and third words together. We find out that character is destiny because the two apparently different concepts are held together in a unity by their subject. In B1, "Of this Word's being forever do men prove to be uncomprehending," the word "forever" can go with either the preceding or the following words; either the Word is forever or men's incomprehension is forever. But since it can go with either, it provides a kind of verbal glue between the two: it is forever the case that the Word is and that men fail to comprehend it.

The sentence that is syntactically ambiguous is interesting precisely because it can be construed one way or another, but not both ways at the same time. The case is similar to that explored by Wittgenstein with an optical illusion known as the duck-rabbit.[28] A line drawing in the shape of a circle with an elongated salient can be "seen" as either a duck (with a bill) or a rabbit (with ears)—though not as both at the same time. There is a "gestalt-switch" that can turn our conception from one to the other; yet we cannot see both pictures at the same time. The image, then, is unstable for us, but by reflection we can know perfectly well that there is only one line drawing before our eyes with two interpretations. The interpretations are, as it were, two perspectives of the same object, two aspects of one thing. That there should be two aspects of one thing goes well with Heraclitus's themes. He criticizes his predecessor Hesiod precisely for his failure to see the unity in diverse things: "The teacher of the multitude is Hesiod; they believe he has the greatest knowledge—who did not understand day and night: for they are one" (B57). Hesiod had depicted Day and Night as gods that live in the same house but never occupy it at the same time; Heraclitus complains that there is a single reality of which day and night are but contrasting manifestations. In general: "Wisdom is one thing: to know the will that steers all things through all" (B41). Although this statement suggests an active power operating in the world, it is compatible with there being connections between opposite powers.

Let us return now to the river fragment. The first four words, we recall, looked and sounded alike: *potamoisi toisin autoisin embainousin.* Grammatically or morphologically they are alike in being masculine dative plurals. This phrase, too, conceals a syntactic ambiguity, indeed one very like those in B1 and B119: the words *toisin autoisin,* "the same," can be construed with either the preceding or the succeeding word. The most natural reading, "on those going into *the same rivers,*" which was adopted by ancient readers, gives us the interpretation examined earlier. But does the alternative reading make sense? "*On the same (people) going into rivers, other and other waters flow.*" This is perfectly comprehensible.[29] It is a less obvious reading because the pronoun "the same" needs a substantive to attach to. But so does the participle "going into," and we can fill in the substantive by assuming it is masculine and refers to people; if "people" is understood with the participle it can equally be understood with the pronoun preceding it. Now it may at this point appear that we are stretching a point to make the sentence syntactically ambiguous; surely, one might object, the first readings is perfectly intelligible, and philosophically important—why add more? But notice that it took a good deal of trouble to arrange the four words in question so that they might possibly be taken as ambiguous. Almost any change would render them unambiguous. For instance, it is odd that Heraclitus begins with the noun "rivers," when the normal word order would make the subject of the sentence, "waters," come first. Further, why did Heraclitus pluralize everything? It would be more natural to discuss a single river; and if "river" were in the singular, *potamôi*, the pronoun *ho autos* would have to agree with either that or the following participle, but not both. Furthermore, if the noun and the participle were separated by another word or phrase, there would be no syntactical ambiguity: the pronoun would naturally attach to whichever word it was closest to. Finally, it took a good deal of trouble to arrange the rest of the sentence so that both "rivers" and "those entering" were in the dative case rather than some other case. Thus any of a dozen changes, in number, case, word order, juxtaposition, would have avoided the ambiguity. But we find the pronoun sandwiched between a noun and a participle, in the same case and number, located in emphatic position at the beginning of the sentence, and we must suppose Heraclitus wanted all these accidents to come together in a bizarre unity.

What is the message of the second reading? Different waters flow onto those who enter into the rivers. Does this mean that the people who ford the rivers never stay the same? No, the people in question are explicitly said to be *the same* people: again we have the central contrast between the different waters and the same subjects. This time it is the individuals who cross the rivers who are contrasted with the waters. Symbolically, they remain the same even though they encounter continually different waters. What are the waters? Presumably they stand for *to peri-echon*, the surroundings, the environment, the changing situations that the individual confronts in experience. The individual stays the same even though conditions around him are ever changing. And, if we take a hint from the first reading, perhaps the individual stays the same precisely *because* he confronts ever different situations. It is the opportunity to react to the changing current of life that allows the individual to become a unified person, that constitutes the individual as a person. We see then that experience is constitutive for Heraclitus. Furthermore, the flux of experience—which reflects the flux of matter in the world—is quite real, but does not entail the impossibility of knowledge. On the contrary, it is the unified response to changing information that seems to constitute the person and, accordingly, to afford the opportunity for knowledge—for those who have eyes to see and ears to hear.

When we look at the river fragment as a whole, we see the same duality we saw with other fragments that express syntactic ambiguity. We see a structural similarity: the ambiguous term stands between two other terms, with either of which it can be construed, as *anthropôi* with *êthos* or *daimôn*. As a bridge between the two terms, it binds them into an unexpected unity. Since we can construe the phrase as AB, C, or A, BC, where B bonds with either extreme term, A = C. In this case, the rivers and the people who enter into them are somehow alike: they are constituted by the changing waters, yet each remains the same precisely because of its relationship to the waters. In one sense, the ancient interpretation is right: people are like rivers. But not because they are ever changing. They get their stability from the fact that they are higher-level realities that arise out of or supervene on or respond to the changing matter.

The river fragment is not only a statement, it is an experience. We find one meaning, which is incomplete. We find another, which construes the same elements differently. We find that there is an alternation between two equally valid, but mutually exclusive readings. Yet each makes sense in its own right, and the overall message of both is the same: that higher-level realities remain the same through changes. The words themselves are unstable, as unstable as an optical illusion such as the duck-rabbit. Yet there is a higher-level unity of theme in the words, as in the optical illusion. We learn, presumably, to look for hidden meanings and for unifying features of everyday experience. The statement is an exercise in experience that sharpens our understandings in preparation for confronting sense experience. What it gives us is *insight* into the world and its complexity. Insight, of course, is an elusive kind of cognition: understanding comes suddenly, as we say, "in a flash of insight," without any obvious contribution on our own part. It is precisely the sort of cognition that seems spontaneous and undirected, though it may clarify and organize a large segment of our experience for us. The closest equivalent in Greek is *nous*, or uncontracted in Heraclitus's Ionic tongue, *noos*. To return to a fragment already quoted: "Learning many things does not teach *noos*. Else it would have taught Hesiod and Pythagoras, as well as Xenophanes and Hecataeus" (B40). We can acquire a large stockpile of facts without ever attaining to the unifying understanding that marks wisdom. We can be reservoirs of information without being philosophers, encyclopedias of knowledge without being wise. In order to attain wisdom we must have the kind of understanding that organizes information: "Listening not to me but to the Word[30] it is wise to agree that all things are one" (B50); "Wisdom is one thing: to know the will that steers all things through all" (B41). With *noos* we see how all things are related to each other, and recognize the process by which things are interrelated. This cannot come merely by having experiences of the world, but only by reorganizing our experience so as to see the connections in it. It can come to us only suddenly.[31]

There are two extreme views about Heraclitus's logic and epistemology that interpreters sometimes emphasize. One is that Heraclitus is hostile, or at least averse, to logic and normal forms of logical inference. A similar view holds that for him knowledge is "mystical."[32] Indeed, Heraclitus's alleged hostility to logic can provide evidence for his mystical orientation. At the other extreme is the view that Heraclitus us both receptive to deductive logic (hence rational)[33] and dependent on sense experience for his sources of knowledge (an empiricist).[34] Numerous other interpretations are, of course, possible, but it will be convenient to use these versions as landmarks for an interpretation.[35]

It should be evident by now that Heraclitus does not think sense experience is sufficient in itself to "teach *noos*," any more than is information gathering. It has been shown that Heraclitus does use inference patterns and at least simple arguments in the extant fragments: it is surely false to claim that he is averse to deductive logic.[36] Thus he seems to accept experience as a major source of knowledge, and logic as a means of organizing truths. But there is still something missing between experience and logic on the one hand and *noos* on the other. We see him communicating with his audience not, primarily, through extended arguments or appeals to ordinary experience. Rather, he organizes his ideas into verbal representations, *logoi*, that stand for complex relationships capable of being grasped. The relationships are recognized suddenly (if at all), like the gestalts of the duck-rabbit. We perceive suddenly the complexity of the representation, and also its unity. We gain insight, *noos*.

This is a classic case of representing the world *inductively* rather than deductively.[37] We examine a concrete situation that is pregnant with meaning. We grasp the meaning, for instance that the duck and the rabbit are two aspects of a single representation. Under Heraclitus's tutelage, we recognize that the road up and down is one and the same, those going into rivers and the rivers themselves are the same in the face of ever-changing waters. The concrete case becomes a stand-in for a general truth. Life, or experience in general, is like a river, or like a road. Heraclitus fashions concrete descriptions of the world to function as emblems of general patterns. The image of the road, as we have seen, can suggest to us patterns of daily activity, human life and death, biological life and death, material change, cosmic process, athletic competition, human competition, cosmic opposition, and, no doubt, much more. Heraclitus does not begin from some alleged general truths and then deduce implications from it, nor does he present applications. He begins with a concrete situation that embodies or depicts the truth, lets us "discover" it, and leaves it to us to determine its range of applications. We go from specific to general, from concrete to abstract.

The kind of interpretation a Heraclitean puzzle calls for is intuitive and immediate: we do not grasp the unity of the river fragment or the road fragment deductively or methodically. Yet there is a kind of mental exercise involved, and a kind of synthetic understanding called for, of the same kind that might be called for in solving riddles and puzzles of various kinds. In terms of modern physiological distinctions, he is challenging our right brain, not our left. But there is nothing mysterious or mystical about the puzzles Heraclitus sets before us. They admit of intelligent solution and rational explication after the fact. On the other hand, they go far beyond what one might call ordinary sense experience, requiring complex manipulation of symbolic representations to sort out puns, syntactic ambiguities, allusions, and so on. Heraclitus's *logoi* are thus neither irrational nor empirical. They are exercises in intuition, in right-brain logic, in synthetic intelligence.[38] In this realm, Heraclitus cannot provide an extended argument for inferences, but he can sharpen our perceptions by providing complex symbols requiring the activity of our creative intelligence. He can invite us to make inductive leaps in place of deductive inferences.

And here we can see that Heraclitus's logic is at least not hostile to our own. For, as Plato would see later, the descent of logical deduction can only follow the ascent of induction, and specification can only follow generalization. We must ascend through hypotheses to first principles or axioms.[39] Plato's own picture of ascending and descending moments brings us back to a point from which we began: the road up and down is one and the same. Heraclitus is as committed to logic and rationality as Plato and Aristotle. But he challenges us in the stage where we are weakest: the upward journey to universal truths.

If this account is correct, Heraclitus is not an empiricist in epistemology, nor is he a rationalist in the usual sense. In logic he is not an advocate of deductive logic, nor is he an antirational mystic in quest of esoteric truth. While he holds that truth is all around us, he does not think it is easy to recognize. Philosophical understanding, the only kind of knowledge worth having, results from seeing the significance of everyday experiences—making unusual connections between ordinary events and objects. To do this is to have insight, an intuitive cognition. The student can train his intuition, and intuition is not, after all, irrational: it belongs to the inductive stage of understanding, which is presupposed by the deductive; it requires an integration of various disparate elements into a harmonious whole. The *logos*, the Message, is imprinted on the *kosmos*, the world-order. When we are awakened by philosophy, we can read the message in the events and objects of the world. We must read the book of the world by learning to parse its most humble statements. When we can do that, we may find the pattern of the whole reflected in its most mundane manifestations (whether artificial or natural): a road, a bow, a river.

What then is Heraclitus's overall theory of knowledge? As we have seen, he is not an empiricist. Nor is he a rationalist who believes in innate ideas or recollection of transcendent concepts. He believes the world is an ordered whole. It is ordered both spatially and temporally, as a river is a spatial structure made up of other and other waters, for its fires are constantly kindling and being quenched by measures. What we can know is not the changeable components or the transitory stages but the ongoing structure. In this Heraclitus has much in common with Aristotle and his distinction of substances into matter and form. The world is knowable, say both Heraclitus and Aristotle, because it is a structured whole, and structures are inherently knowable. How are they knowable? Heraclitus (and Aristotle) would answer: by virtue of a shared structure.[40] The *logos* is structure, or at least a manifestation of structure, and souls share in *logos*,[41] as does the medium of communication, language. The soul can recognize structure because it is itself a structured whole. There is a kind of isomorphism between the knower and the known inasmuch as they share a structure. Heraclitus's striking juxtaposition of the river (object of knowledge) and the wader (knower) suggests a common structure and a common temporal perseverance through environmental or metabolic or even cognitive change.

In one sense, the problem of knowledge Heraclitus confronts is very different from Plato's: Plato is concerned with perceptual accuracy in a temporally unstable world, while Heraclitus is concerned with grasping the overall pattern of connectedness. For Heraclitus an error in perception is not significant, so long as we appreciate the overall situation. For Plato it is an indictment of all our cognitive pretensions in the world of sensation. Plato holds that any cognitive success we have points beyond the immediate perceptual situation to a world of transcendent beings that make perception possible. Heraclitus, by contrast, holds that the objects we encounter in perception are complex signs revealing an inherent structure that is shared by the subject and the object. There is an ongoing flux like the flow of a river. But that flux is channeled by an in-dwelling order. We are at every moment immersed in the current, and constituted as subjects by its presence.

Heraclitus's theory is much closer to those of Plato and Aristotle than the latter philosophers recognize. Like them, Heraclitus sees the world as manifesting a higher order supervening on the flux of elements. Like them, he sees knowledge arising through an interaction between stable structures and changing components, and he sees the possibility of knowledge as grounded in the parallel structures of thought and the world. Like them, finally, he sees a harmony of contraries as integral to experience and to life itself. Unfortunately, Heraclitus was right in anticipating that most of his readers would misunderstand him, that they would respond to their encounters with his verbal experiences as though they were inexperienced. Yet the verbal techniques that made him inaccessible to his ancient critics have made him accessible to modern scholarship, so that we can appreciate at last how for him out of conflict is born the fairest harmony.

NOTES

1. "His real subject is not the physical world but the human condition, the condition of mortality" Kahn, *The Art and Thought of Heraclitus*, 23; Kahn, "A New Look at Heraclitus," 194; Rivier, "L'homme et l'exprience humaine dans les fragments d'Hraclite"; Dilcher, *Studies in Heraclitus*. For the view of Heraclitus as cosmologist, see Vlastos, "On Heraclitus"; Kirk, *Heraclitus*.

2. The newly identified fragments from the Oxyrhynchus Papyri show that Heraclitus had technical interests in observational astronomy: *P.Oxy.* LIII 3710 ii (c) 43–47 and iii. 7–11 with West, "A New Fragment of Heraclitus."

3. Pl. *Tht.* 152d–e, Arist. *Metaph.* 1010a7–15. This view is reaffirmed by Barnes, *PP*, chap. 4.

4. I accept this phrase, which some editors delete, e.g. Kirk, *Heraclitus*, 308–10; but it is defended by Vlastos, "On Heraclitus"; Kerschensteiner, *Kosmos*, 99–102; Marcovich, *Heraclitus*, 268–70.

5. Kirk, *Heraclitus*, 311–14, with criticisms in Vlastos, "On Heraclitus"; see Kahn, *Anaximander and the Origins of Greek Cosmology*, 219–30; Kerschensteiner, *Kosmos*, 97–99.

6. *Prêstêr*: A fiery meteorological event associated with storms: Arist. *Mete.* 371a15–17, Plin. *HN* 2.133.

7. Arist. *Metaph.* 983b6–13, 984a5–8, reaffirmed by Barnes, *PP*, chap. 4, and most commentators before him.

8. See Kahn, *The Art and Thought of Heraclitus* on the passage.

9. Only Xenophanes had a cosmology without a cosmogony; but even he seems to admit plural *kosmoi*, states of organization that are nonidentical: Hippol. *Haer.* 1.14.6 = A33; D.L. 9.19 = A1.

10. The line I will be pursuing here originates with Reinhardt, *Parmenides und die Geschichte der griechischen Philosophie*; see Reinhardt, "Heraklits Lehre Vom Feuer"; it is followed by Kirk, *Heraclitus*, 369, and Marcovich, *Heraclitus*, 206. According to this view, B12 is the most important or (better) the only river fragments, and it does not license the inference to a universal flux. Wiggins, "Heraclitus' Conceptions of Flux," 24, rightly points out that a flux of all continuants is compatible with cosmic order, so long as that order is lawlike. I would add that we still need some restriction of the kind of flux so as to rule out Plato's changes from one kind of reality to another. Tarán, "Heraclitus," has recently criticized the Reinhardt-Kirk-Marcovich view; I address his arguments elsewhere. Earlier critics include Vlastos, "On Heraclitus"; Mondolfo, "I frammenti de fiume"; Popper, "Kirk on Heraclitus"; Guthrie, *HGP* vol. 1, chap. 7; Emlyn-Jones, "Heraclitus and the Unity of Opposites"; Stokes, *One and Many in Presocratic Philosophy*, chap. 4; *PP*, chap. 4. See discussion in Graham, "Heraclitus' Criticism of Ionian Philosophy."

11. See esp. Kahn, *The Art and Thought of Heraclitus*, 167: "This is the only statement on the river whose wording is unmistakably Heraclitean." Some scholars wish to keep the following sentence from the context (Eusebius's *Preparation for the Gospel* 15.20.2–3, citing Arius Didymus discussing Cleanthes on Zeno of Citium and Heraclitus): "And souls too are nourished by moist exhalations." See Rivier, *Un emploi archaïque de l'analogie chez Héraclite et Thucydide*, 17-23; Bollack and Wismann, *Héraclite*; Conche, *Héraclite*, Mouraviev, *Heraclitea*, on T261. (Rivier also wishes to excise the word *embainousin* from the fragment; he treats it as disturbing the equilibrium of the sentence—looking to find a certain pattern in the sentence and failing to see another one.) Against the second sentence, see Tarán, "Heraclitus," 25–29; Dilcher, *Studies in Heraclitus*, 178–83; there are further philological problems I cannot go into here.

12. These points come from Kahn, *The Art and Thought of Heraclitus*, 167.

13. *Treatise* 1.4.6, p. 258 Selby-Bigge. Here Hume is concerned with conventional assessments of identity more than the strict identity which he denies to sensible objects.

14. As Marcovich, *Heraclitus*, points out, Plato may be reading the present tense of *embainousin* as iterative rather than progressive.

15. Pl. *Cra.* 402a; Aristotle reports that Plato heard and was influenced by Cratylus's lectures, *Metaph.* 987a32–b1.

16. The phrase "τ'ἔνι" is rejected by some editors, but defended by Marcovich, *Heraclitus*, 218.

17. *PP*, 72–73.

18. See Pritzl, "On the Way to Wisdom in Heraclitus," 303-4, for references; he seems to overlook Barnes's interpretation of Heraclitus as an empiricist, or at least heavily dependent on empirical evidence, e.g. *PP* 67, 78.

19. Heidel, "Hecataeus and Xenophanes," discusses Heraclitus's relationship to two of these figures.

20. Nussbaum, "*Psyche* in Heraclitus," 3–5, 9–15, and Lesher, "Heraclitus' Epistemological Vocabulary," rightly discuss the significance of language as connected thought, not mere words, for Heraclitus's understanding. Yet there is much more Heraclitus sees in language than just parsing sentences, as will become evident.

21. E.g., Fränkel, "A Thought Pattern in Heraclitus"; Kahn, "A New Look at Heraclitus"; Hölscher, *Anfängliches Fragen*, 136; Robb, *Language and Thought in Early Greek Philosophy*.

22. The phrase is from Mourelatos, "Heraclitus, Parmenides, and the Naive Metaphysics of Things."

23. See Lebedev, "The Cosmos as a Stadium."

24. Kahn, *The Art and Thought of Heraclitus*, 93–95; contrast Tarán, "The First Fragment of Heraclitus," who is still trying to disambiguate the sentence (no reference to Kahn).

25. Arist. *Rh.* 1407b11–18.

26. Reading *palintropos* rather than *palintonos*. Correctly defended by Vlastos, "On Heraclitus," 348–49.

27. More literally, the *daimôn* is a guardian spirit.

28. *Philosophical Investigations* 194.

29. Defended by Kahn, *The Art and Thought of Heraclitus*, 167. To the contrary, Robinson, *Heraclitus*, 84, "the point (*pace* Kahn) seems trivial, and hardly part of [Heraclitus'] intention." But the point is a substantial one, both philologically and philosophically, as I shall try to show.

30. Modern editors follow Bernays and Bergk in reading *logos* for the MS-reading *dogmat(os)*.

31. The classic study on *noos* is Fritz, "*Noos* and Noein in the Homeric Poems"; Fritz, "*Noos, Noein,* and Their Derivatives in Pre-Socratic Philosophy." Lesher, "Perceiving and Knowing in the *Iliad* and *Odyssey,*" proposes corrections.

32. Cornford, *From Religion to Philosophy*, 184; Vlastos, review of Ramnoux, 542.

33. The "rules for the interpretation of sense experience" of Hussey, "Epistemology and Meaning in Heraclitus," 35, suggest this line.

34. *PP*, chap. 4, esp. 67, 78.

35. For a balanced and helpful assessment, see Lesher, "The Emergence of Philosophical Interest in Cognition," 11–23.

36. Barnes, "Aphorism and Argument." Granger, "Argumentation and Heraclitus' Book," sees Heraclitus's book as having a minimum of argumentation.

37. It is perhaps not an accident that Aristotle's discussion of induction in *APo.* 2.19 concerns *nous*.

38. Thus I do not agree with Rankin, "Limits on Perception and Cognition in Heraclitus' Fragments," who concludes that "Heraclitus does not seem to rule out entirely our possible capacity for intuitions ... to which our [human] limitations do not seem *prima facie* to entitle us," resulting in a "contradiction" (252). On my view, we are perfectly capable of achieving valid insights into the nature of things, according to Heraclitus. On the other hand, such insight does not require "a reflective dividing and rejoining of what holds of a thing's nature expressed in names in relation to its immediately perceived active

life" (Pritzl, "On the Way to Wisdom in Heraclitus," 315); it does not require reflective analysis at all, though it may be sharpened by reflection and give rise to deepened reflection on the nature of reality.

39. Pl. *R.* 509d–511e.

40. See Modrak, *Aristotle's Theory of Language and Meaning*, on Aristotle's episte-mology.

41. B1, B2, B50, B113, B115.

BIBLIOGRAPHY

Barnes, Jonathan. "Aphorism and Argument." In *Language and Thought in Early Greek Philosophy*, edited by Kevin Robb, 91–109. La Salle, Ill.: Hegeler Institute, 1983.

Bollack, Jean, and Heinz Wismann. *Héraclite: Ou la séparation.* Paris: Éditions de Minuit, 1972.

Conche, Marcel. *Héraclite: Fragments.* Paris: Presses Universitaires de France, 1986.

Cornford, F. M. *From Religion to Philosophy.* London: Edward Arnold, 1912.

Dilcher, Roman. *Studies in Heraclitus.* Spudasmata: Studien zur klassischen Philologie under ihren Grenzgebieten, vol. 56. Hildesheim: Georg Olms, 1995.

Emlyn-Jones, C. J. "Heraclitus and the Unity of Opposites." *Phronesis* 21 (1976): 89–114.

Fränkel, Hermann. "A Thought Pattern in Heraclitus." *American Journal of Philology* 59 (1938): 3098–337.

Fritz, Kurt von. "*Noos* and Noein in the Homeric Poems." *Classical Philology* 38 (1943): 79–93.

———. "*Noos, Noein,* and Their Derivatives in Pre-Socratic Philosophy (Excluding Anaxagoras)." *Classical Philology* 40 (1945–46): 223–42; 41:12–34.

Graham, Daniel W. "Heraclitus' Criticism of Ionian Philosophy." *Oxford Studies in Ancient Philosophy* 15 (1997): 1–50.

Granger, Herbert. "Argumentation and Heraclitus' Book." *Oxford Studies in Ancient Philosophy* 26 (2004): 1–17.

Heidel, W. A. "Hecataeus and Xenophanes." *American Journal of Philology* 64 (1943): 257–77.

Hölscher, Uvo. *Anfänglisches Fragen.* Göttingen: Vandenhoek & Ruprecht, 1968.

Hussey, Edward. "Epistemology and Meaning in Heraclitus." In *Language and Logos*, edited by Malcolm Schofield and Martha Craven Nussbaum, 33–59. Cambridge: Cambridge University Press, 1982.

Kahn, Charles H. *Anaximander and the Origins of Greek Cosmology.* New York: Columbia University Press, 1960.

———. *The Art and Thought of Heraclitus.* Cambridge: Cambridge University Press, 1979.

———. "A New Look at Heraclitus." *American Philosophical Quarterly* 1 (1964): 189–203.

Kerschensteiner, Jula. *Kosmos: Quellenkritische Untersuchungen zu den Vorsokratikern.* Munich: C. H. Beck, 1962.

Kirk, G. S. *Heraclitus: The Cosmic Fragments.* Cambridge: Cambridge University Press, 1954.

Lebedev, Andrei. "The Cosmos as a Stadium: Agonistic Metaphors in Heraclitus." *Phronesis* 30 (1985): 131–50.

Lesher, James H. "The Emergence of Philosophical Interest in Cognition." *Oxford Studies in Ancient Philosophy* 12 (1994): 1–34.

———. "Heraclitus' Epistemological Vocabulary." *Hermes* 111 (1983): 155–70.

———. "Perceiving and Knowing in the *Iliad* and *Odyssey*." *Phronesis* 26 (1981): 2–24.

Marcovich, Miroslav. *Heraclitus.* Mérida, Venezuela: University of the Andes Press, 1967.

Modrak, Deborah K. W. *Aristotle's Theory of Language and Meaning.* Cambridge: Cambridge University Press, 2001.

Mondolfo, Rudolfo. "I frammenti de fiume e il flusso universale in Eraclito." *Revista Critica di Storia della Filosofia* 15 (1960): 3–13.

Mourelatos, Alexander P. D. "Heraclitus, Parmenides, and the Naive Metaphysics of Things." In *Exegesis and Argument*, edited by E. N. Lee, A. P. D. Mourelatos, and R. Rorty, 16–48. Assen: Van Gorcum, 1973.

Mouraviev, Serge. *Heraclitea.* 10 vols. 1. Saint Augustine: Academia Verlag, 1999–.

Nussbaum, Martha C. "*Psyche* in Heraclitus." *Phronesis* 17 (1972): 1–16; 153–70.

Popper, Karl R. "Kirk on Heraclitus, and on Fire as the Cause of Balance." *Mind* 72 (1963): 386–92.

Pritzl, Kurt. "On the Way to Wisdom in Heraclitus." *Phoenix* 39 (1985): 303–16.

Rankin, David. "Limits on Perception and Cognition in Heraclitus' Fragments." *Elenchos* 16 (1995): 241–52.

Reinhardt, Karl. "Heraklits Lehre vom Feuer." *Hermes* 77 (1942): 1–27.

———. *Parmenides und die Geschichte der griechischen Philosophie.* Bonn: Friedrich Cohen, 1916.

Rivier, André. *Un emploi archaïque de l'analogie chez Héraclite et Thucydide.* Lausanne: F. Rouge, 1952.

———. "L'homme et l'exprience humaine dans les fragments d'Héraclite." *Museum Helveticum* 13 (1956): 143–64.

Robb, Kevin, ed. *Language and Thought in Early Greek Philosophy.* La Salle, Ill.: Hegeler Institute, 1983.

Robinson, Thomas M. *Heraclitus.* Toronto: University of Toronto Press, 1987.

Stokes, Michael C. *One and Many in Presocratic Philosophy.* Washington, D.C.: Center for Hellenic Studies, 1971.

Tarán, Leonardo. "The First Fragment of Heraclitus." *Illinois Classical Studies* 11 (1986): 1–15.

———. "Heraclitus: The River Fragments and Their Implications." *Elenchos* 20 (1999): 9–52.

Vlastos, Gregory. Review of "Héraclite: Ou l'homme entre les choses et les mots," by C. Ramnoux. *Philosophical Review* 71 (1962): 538–42.

———. "On Heraclitus." *American Journal of Philology* 76 (1955): 337–78.

West, M. L. "A New Fragment of Heraclitus." *Zeitschrift für Papyrologie und Epigraphik* 67 (1987): 16.

Wiggins, David. "Heraclitus' Conceptions of Flux, Fire and Material Persistence." In *Language and Logos: Studies Presented to G. E. L. Owen*, edited by M. Schofield and M. C. Nussbaum, 1–32. Cambridge: Cambridge University Press, 1982.

CHAPTER 6

SIGNS AND ARGUMENTS IN PARMENIDES B8

RICHARD MCKIRAHAN

DAVID SEDLEY recently complained[1] that despite the enormous amount of work on Parmenides in the past generation, the details of Parmenides' arguments have received insufficient attention.[2] It is universally recognized that Parmenides' introduction of argument into philosophy was a move of paramount importance. It is also recognized that the arguments of fragment B8 are closely related. At the beginning of B8, Parmenides asserts that what-is[3] has several attributes; he offers a series of proofs that what-is indeed has those attributes. Some[4] hold that the proofs form a deductive chain in which the conclusion of one argument or series of arguments forms a premise of the next. Others[5] hold that the series of inferences is so tightly connected that their conclusions are logically equivalent, a feature supposedly announced in B5: "For me it is the same where I am to begin from: for that is where I will arrive back again." In fact, close study of the fragments reveals that neither claim is correct. Here I offer a new translation of B8, lines 2–51, with an analysis of the arguments, their structure, their success, and their importance.[6]

I begin with a caution. Many of Parmenides' arguments are hard to make out: even on the best arrangement of the available sentences and clauses they are incomplete. Since Parmenides lived before canons of deductive inference had been formalized, he may not have thought that there is need to supply what we regard as missing premises. The interpreter's job is not to aim for formal validity, but to attempt a reconstruction of Parmenides' train of thought, showing how he might have supposed that the conclusion follows from premises he gives. This is a matter of sensitivity and sympathy as much as of logic, depending on how we understand other arguments of his as well, and requires willingness to give him the benefit of the doubt—up to a certain point.

1. THE PROJECT AND THE PRESUPPOSITIONS

1.1. B8.2–6: The Project

Fragment B8 is notable for its programmatic remarks (8.2–6) and for its summary statements of results proved (8.13–18, 8.21, and, with qualifications,[7] 8.39–41). Several important matters depend on our interpretation of these passages. Does Parmenides complete the program he sets out? How do the arguments go? What premises are taken as already established prior to B8? What premises depend on arguments within B8? How are the various claims that B8 proves related to one another? Do the summaries actually summarize results already proved? On the answers to these questions depend our assessments both of Parmenides' achievement in constructing individual arguments and of his success in creating a theory whose theses are systematically related through links of deductive inferences.

> 8.2 ταύτηι δ' ἐπὶ σήματ' ἔασι
> 8.3 πολλὰ μάλ', ὡς ἀγένητον ἐὸν καὶ ἀνώλεθρόν ἐστιν,
> 8.4 οὖλον μουνογενές[8] τε καὶ ἀτρεμὲς ἠδὲ τέλειον.
>   On this [road] there are signs[9]
>   very many, that what-is is ungenerated and imperishable,
>   whole, unique,[10] steadfast, and complete.
> 8.5 οὐδέ ποτ' ἦν οὐδ' ἔσται, ἐπεὶ νῦν ἔστιν ὁμοῦ πᾶν,
> 8.6 ἕν, συνεχές
>   Nor was it ever, nor will it be, since it is now, all together,
>   one, holding together.[11]

Lines 8.2–6 contains two lists of attributes together with an argument ("since" in 8.5). The first list consists of ἀγένητον ("ungenerated"), ἀνώλεθρον ("imperishable"), οὖλον ("whole"), μουνογενές ("unique"), ἀτρεμές ("steadfast"), and τέλειον ("complete"); the second list consists of οὐδέ ποτ' ἦν ("nor was it ever"), οὐδ' ἔσται ("nor will it be"), νῦν ἔστιν ("is now"), ὁμοῦ πᾶν ("all together"), ἕν ("one"), and συνεχές ("holding together"). In addition, there are the attributes "motionless" and "unchanging," which seem on the face of it to be argued for in the sequel (8.26–31, 8.38–41).

I divide these attributes into six groups.

Group A: ungenerated, imperishable
Group B: whole, complete, all together, holding together
Group C: never was, will not be, is now
Group D: changeless, motionless
Group E: steadfast
Group F: unique, one

I proceed by going through the text, beginning with 8.6–33, which contains Parmenides' treatment of the attributes in groups A and B. I take up 8.5–6 (group C) after 8.34–41, since only then are we in a position to understand the argument for the attributes of group C. Members of group D are mentioned in several places (8.26, 8.38, 8.41, and possibly 8.29–30); I treat them as they occur, and again in a separate section after group C. There is no argument for the single member of group E. However, "steadfast" seems to mean no more than either "changeless" or "complete," and so it belongs with either group B or group D.[12] Finally, after discussing the final section of the Way of Truth, 8.42–51, I take up group F, for which I find no argument in the text.

1.2. The Presuppositions

Arguments for the attributes depend on theses assumed or established in the earlier part of Parmenides' poem. In B2, Parmenides declares that there are only two "roads of investigation . . . to be thought of" (2.2). One of these is constituted of "is" (2.3), the other of "is not" (2.5).[13] He eliminates the second road, on the ground that "you cannot know what-is-not (for it cannot be accomplished) nor can you declare it" (2.7–8), which leaves only the first road as a candidate for genuineness. That it is genuine may be a consequence of the assertion "the same thing both can be thought of and can be" (B3), which may mean that anything that can be thought of *is*; or, what is perhaps more likely, its genuineness is guaranteed by its very nature—the fact that it is constituted of "is." In B6[14] Parmenides mentions a third road, which he associates with two-headed, helpless mortals with wandering minds, in which what-is "is thought both to be and not to be the same and not the same" (6.8–9). This third candidate is rejected because it can never be the case that things that are not are (7.1).[15] The fragments that precede B8, then, consider three candidate roads, establish that one of them is legitimate, and eliminate the other two as illegitimate. By the time we arrive at B8, we are left in the situation where

> 8.1 μόνος δ' ἔτι μῦθος ὁδοῖο
> 8.2 λείπεται ὡς ἔστιν.
>
> Just one story of a road
> is still left: "is."

The sentence identifies the starting point of the remainder of the Way of Truth, 8.3–51, whose task is to explicate this assertion; it does not say anything about the road's content. The explication establishes that what-is (anything that is) has a number of attributes, and when we understand what they are, that it has them, and why it has them, we understand its nature as a thing that is. Hence, understanding what "what-is is" means is also the goal of the remainder of the Way of Truth.[16]

Much of the work of 8.3–51 relies on the following claims, which Parmenides has asserted or argued for in the preceding fragments.

2.7–8: You cannot know what-is-not nor can you declare it.

οὔτε γὰρ ἂν γνοίης τό γε μὴ ἐὸν (οὐ γὰρ ἀνυστόν) / οὔτε φράσαις.

6.1–2: It is right both to say and to think that it is what-is: for it is the case that it is, but nothing is not.

χρὴ τὸ λέγειν τε νοεῖν τ' ἐὸν ἔμμεναι· ἔστι γὰρ εἶναι, / μηδὲν δ' οὐκ ἔστιν

6.4–5, 8–9: [I hold you back] from that [road] on which mortals, knowing nothing, wander . . . by whom it (namely, what-is) is thought both to be and not to be the same and not the same.

αὐτὰρ ἔπειτ' ἀπὸ τῆς, ἣν δὴ βροτοὶ εἰδότες οὐδὲν / πλάττονται . . .
οἷς τὸ πέλειν τε καὶ οὐκ εἶναι ταὐτὸν νενόμισται / κοὐ ταὐτόν.

7.1: For in no way may this ever be defeated, so that things that are not are.[17]

οὐ γὰρ μήποτε τοῦτο δαμῆι, εἶναι μὴ ἐόντα.

2. B8.6–33: GROUPS A AND B

The attributes of groups A and B are directly argued for in B8.6–33. The arguments in those lines depend on the rejection of the second and third roads of inquiry (both that of "is not" along with the road of confused mortals), and the acceptance of the first road of inquiry, the road of "is" (B2, B6, B7, 8.1–2). The grounds for the rejection are given at 2.7–8: "you cannot know what-is-not (for it cannot be accomplished), nor can you declare it."[18] From this Parmenides concludes that it is impossible to say or think that anything that is is not, and consequently impossible to say or think that there is anything true of what-is that entails that what-is is not.

2.1. B8.6–21: Group A ("Ungenerated" and "Imperishable")

Group A is treated at 8.6–21 in a barrage of arguments in support of the attribute "ungenerated." There is no argument for "imperishable," but at 8.14 and 8.21 Parmenides claims to have established that result as well; he must think that some or all of the arguments for "ungenerated" can be adapted to prove "imperishable" as well. The arguments consider several analyses of generation, all involving generation from what-is-not. There is notably no argument against the possibility of generation from what-is (in particular, generation of something that is from something else that is). Lines 8.6–9 argue that what-is cannot be generated from what-is-not because what-is-not cannot be said or thought; 8.9–10 argues that there is no reason for what-is to be generated out of nothing (namely, out of what-is-not) earlier or later; 8.12–13 that there can be no generation from what-is-not because what-is-not cannot generate anything; 8.19–20 that there can be no generation in the future. Lines 8.13–18 announce the result and emphasize that it is based on the radical distinction between "is" and "is not" and the impossibility of thinking or expressing the latter. Line 8.21 also announces the result, as does 8.26–28.

> 8.6 τίνα γὰρ γένναν διζήσεαι αὐτοῦ;
> 8.7 πῆι πόθεν αὐξηθέν; οὐδ ἐκ μὴ ἐόντος ἐάσσω
> 8.8 φάσθαι σ' οὐδὲ νοεῖν οὐ γὰρ φατὸν οὐδὲ νοητόν
> 8.9 ἐστιν ὅπως οὐκ ἔστι.

> For what birth will you investigate for it?
> How and from what did it grow? I will allow you neither to say nor to think
> "from what-is-not": for "is not" is not
> to be said or thought.

The passage begins with three questions. If we take growth as equivalent to "birth,"[19] then the second and third questions—"How did it grow?" and "From what did it grow?"—can be taken as referring to necessary conditions for birth (the subject of the first question) to occur: generation is a process ("how") that requires a source[20] ("from what"). Only the third question is answered here: not from what-is-not. And the answer is justified by the move already used to eliminate the second road (2.7–8). ("Not to be said or thought" is equivalent to "you cannot know or declare.") The remaining (second) question is given one answer in 8.9–10, but another answer already follows from the unspeakable and unthinkable nature of what-is-not: "How?" "In no way!"

The following lines (8.9–10) make it reasonably certain that Parmenides uses "growth" as synonymous with "birth."

> 8.9 τί δ' ἄν μιν καὶ χρέος ὦρσεν
> 8.10 ὕστερον ἢ πρόσθεν, τοῦ μηδενὸς ἀρξάμενον, φῦν;

> What need would have roused it,
> later or earlier, to grow, having begun from nothing?

The words translated "later or earlier" can just as well mean "later rather than earlier." The argument makes a good point on either version: either "at no time is there a reason for it to grow" (here, clearly with the sense "come to be") or "there is no reason for it to come to be at any time rather than any other time." The second version is more sophisticated, involving a principle of indifference, but that is no reason to suppose that Parmenides intended the second rather than the first. This argument is in the form of a (rhetorical) question, the expected answer being something like "in such circumstances (that is, in circumstances where nothing is), nothing, or no event, could ever cause generation to occur," hence it does not occur.

> 8.11 οὕτως ἢ πάμπαν πελέναι χρεών ἐστιν ἢ οὐχί.

> In this way it is right for it either fully to be or not.

This line (whose beginning is frequently rendered "thus it is right") is usually taken to mark a conclusion, with οὕτως ("thus") meaning "therefore" and χρεών ("right") meaning "necessary." On this rendering, 8.11 means that it follows from a previous claim (presumably, that there is no generation from what-is-not) that what-is is fully (as opposed to incompletely). But there are difficulties. In the first place, πάμπαν πελέναι ("fully to be") does not seem plausible as a paraphrase of "ungenerated" or "ungenerated and imperishable." Instead, it is naturally read as meaning the same as τέλειον ("complete"). Now the attribute "complete" is not discussed at length until 8.22, and we find there that being complete is not the same as being ungenerated and imperishable.[21] It is hard to imagine why Parmenides might have thought that the fact that what-is is not generated from what-is-not entails that what-is is completely. Furthermore, the two passages that summarize these results (8.13, 8.21) declare only that generation and perishing have been eliminated, saying nothing about completeness. Therefore, if "fully to be" has the meaning required for this interpretation, the line is not wanted here. In fact, it makes no sense in the present context.

Yet οὕτως need not be a conjunction meaning "therefore." Its primary use is as an adverb, meaning "in this way," "in this manner," and so: "so," "this is how." The line makes good sense if we take it not as stating a consequence of the preceding argument but as remarking that the point just made will be relevant to the later discussion of the attribute "complete." What does οὕτως modify? The most plausible choice is found in this very line: "either to be or not (be)"; "in this way" thus means "being ungenerated," as the context demands. Line 8.11 means: "it is right for it either [a] fully to be in this way [namely, without being subject to generation] or [b] fully not to be in this way," where "it is right" means something like "these are the only possibilities." That is, the only two possibilities are (a) that it fully is without being subject to generation (i.e., it is/was not generated), and (b) that it fully is not without being subject to generation (i.e., it is not and it cannot undergo generation): it cannot not be now and be generated in the future. (These are only formal possibilities: the second of these alternatives has already been rejected, as 8.15–18 is about to remind us.) We will learn that being "complete" involves more than simply not suffering generation (or not perishing), but the argument so far justifies the claim that what-is "fully is" in *this* way.

8.12 οὐδέ ποτ' ἐκ μὴ ἐόντος ἐφήσει πίστιος ἰσχὺς

8.13a γίγνεσθαί τι παρ' αὐτό·

Nor will the force of conviction ever impel anything to come to be beside it from what-is-not.

I find it most plausible to take παρά to mean "beside" in the sense of "in addition to" and αὐτό ("it") to refer to what-is-not.[22] This gives another argument against generation: what-is-not cannot generate anything so as to yield not only the generator (namely, what-is-not) but also something that has come to be.[23]

8.13b τοῦ εἵνεκεν οὔτε γενέσθαι
8.14 οὔτ' ὄλλυσθαι ἀνῆκε Δίκη χαλάσασα πέδησιν,
8.15 ἀλλ' ἔχει· ἡ δὲ κρίσις περὶ τούτων ἐν τῷδ' ἔστιν·
8.16 ἔστιν ἢ οὐκ ἔστιν· κέκριται δ' οὖν, ὥσπερ ἀνάγκη,
8.17 τὴν μὲν ἐᾶν ἀνόητον ἀνώνυμον (οὐ γὰρ ἀληθής
8.18 ἔστιν ὁδός), τὴν δ' ὥστε πέλειν καὶ ἐτήτυμον εἶναι.

For this reason neither coming to be
nor perishing did Justice allow, loosening her shackles,
but she [Justice] holds it. And the decision about these things is in this:
is or is not; and it has been decided, as is necessary,
to leave the one [road] unthought and unnamed (for it is not a real
    road), so that the other [road] is and is genuine.

This section contains no argument; summarizing the results so far, it announces that they apply to perishing as well as to generation, introduces the image of Justice holding what-is bound in fetters, and offers a stark version of the choice facing us in our journey to understand the nature of what-is: "is or is not,"[24] the latter of which is immediately declared to be inadmissible.

8.19 πῶς δ' ἂν ἔπειτα πέλοι τὸ ἐόν;[25] πῶς δ' ἄν κε γένοιτο;
8.20 εἰ γὰρ ἔγεντ', οὐκ ἔστ(ι), οὐδ' εἴ ποτε μέλλει ἔσεσθαι.

But how can what-is be hereafter? How can it come to be?
For if it came to be, it is not, not even if it is sometime going to be.

These lines are usually taken to assert that what-is cannot exist in the past or the future, 8.20 being understood to mean "if it came to be (in the past) it is not (now), nor (is it now) if it is ever to be in the future." And this in turn is taken to support the view that what-is exists timelessly. This interpretation is ingenious but un-convincing. First, an argument against past and future existence does not belong in the middle of a series of proofs that what-is is ungenerated and imperishable. Second, such an argument is unneeded after the proof in 8.5–6 that what-is never was and will not be. And third, as an argument against past and future existence it is obscure and maladroit.

More straightforwardly, this is an argument against generation in the future. I take "hereafter" with "how can it come to be" as well as with "be"; otherwise it is hard to see why the second question would arise at all, generation of what-is having already been eliminated by the arguments at 8.6. Fragment B8.19, then, asks how what-is can be or come to be in the future. The material to answer the second question and to provide a partial answer to the first is supplied in 8.20.

In 8.20, I understand ἔπειτα ("hereafter") with εἰ γὰρ ἔγεντ' ("for if it came to be") as well: if something were to come to be in the future, it is not (now). And I take the last half of the line closely with the preceding, not (as in the usual rendering given earlier) as the protasis of a separate sentence: even if as the result of generation later than now it is going to be in the future, it still follows that it is not (now). So, since coming to be at a given time entails not being before that time, anything that will come to be in the future is not now. This answers the second question of 8.19: what-is (now) cannot come to be (in the future). The (partial) answer to the first question, then, is that a thing that is—that is, what is (now)—cannot be in the future as the result of coming to be in the future. On this interpretation, 8.19–20 neither denies nor confirms that what is now can continue to be in the future. Rather, the lines complement an earlier argument. Fragment B8.5–6[26] says that what is now cannot be in the future, leaving the possibility that something that is not now might come to be in the future. This is what these lines show to be impossible.

The discussion of group A concludes with another summary of results.

8.21 τὼς γένεσις μὲν ἀπέσβεσται καὶ ἄπυστος ὄλεθρος.

Thus generation has been extinguished and perishing cannot be investigated.[27]

2.2. B8.22–25: Group B ("Whole," "Complete," "All Together" and "Holding Together")

The discussion of group B occupies 8.22–25. The passage's arguments are based on the principle that what-is is "all alike," "not at all more or less in any respect," and "is all full of what-is," in short, what-is fully is.[28] By this Parmenides means that what-is is not infected[29] in any way by "is not" (in particular, none of its attributes are infected by "is not"), which would cause it to be less in some way, which would mean that it was lacking, and hence would lack everything (8.33): instead of being what-is, it would turn out to be what-is-not. The series of arguments in 8.22–25 and 8.29–33 are proofs that what-is is whole, complete, all together, and holding together. These turn out to be more or less equivalent to one another and to "fully is."

> 8.22 οὐδὲ διαιρετόν ἐστιν, ἐπεὶ πᾶν ἐστιν ὁμοῖον,[30]
> 8.23 οὐδέ τι τῆι μᾶλλον, τό κεν εἴργοι μιν συνέχεσθαι,
> 8.24 οὐδέ τι χειρότερον, πᾶν δ' ἔμπλεόν ἐστιν ἐόντος.
> 8.25 τῶι ξυνεχὲς πᾶν ἐστιν· ἐὸν γὰρ ἐόντι πελάζει.

Nor is it divisible,[31] since it is all alike,
and not at all more in any respect (which would keep it from
    holding together)
or at all inferior, but it is all full of what-is.[32]
Therefore it is all holding together;[33] for what-is draws near to what-is.

I take πᾶν ("all") and ὁμοῖον ("alike") in the second half of 8.22 to be adverbs.[34] The claim is not that what-is has the attribute of being all alike or that all of it has the attribute of being alike, but that what-is is in a certain way, namely, all alike, which can be paraphrased as "entirely and uniformly." (See πάμπαν πελέναι ["fully to be"] in 8.11.) Fragment B8.23–24 expresses this claim in different ways: it is all alike in that it is not at all more or inferior[35] (which seems to mean no more than "less") in any respect, and it is all full of what-is. The second half of 8.23 gives a reason for its not being "at all more": if it were at all more, it could not hold together (likewise, we may conclude, it could not hold together if it were at all less). Fragment B8.23–24 ("neither more nor less, therefore holds together") rephrases 8.22 ("is all alike, therefore is indivisible"). "Holds together" is approximately equivalent to the attribute "all together."[36]

    The context strongly suggests that πᾶν δ' ἔμπλεόν ἐστιν ἐόντος ("it is all full of what-is") (8.24) is either equivalent to or closely related to πᾶν ἐστιν ὁμοῖον ("it is all alike") (8.22). I take πᾶν ("all") adverbially in both lines (also in the phrase ξυνεχὲς πᾶν ἐστιν ["it is all holding together"] in 8.25), so that ἔμπλεόν ἐστιν ἐόντος ("full of what-is") is equivalent to, or specifies, ὁμοῖον ("alike"). What-is is alike in that it is chock-full of—what? The obvious answer is that ἐόντος refers straightforwardly to what-is, and that Parmenides is saying that what-is is full of what-is—that is, full of itself. This may sound odd, but there is nothing else for it to be full of, and it can hardly be full of what-is-not! In any case, after saying just before that it is in no way more or less (which might seem to leave open the possibility that it uniformly is in some middling degree) Parmenides here specifies that it fully is: it is completely full (not at all empty), as is required by the elimination of "is not" in any way.

    "What-is draws near to what-is" (8.25) must be figurative; if taken literally, "draws near" would imply that there is a time when what-is is not near to what-is, that what-is reaches its permanent state through a temporal process, an absurdity that this passage is meant to eliminate. I take it as repeating the implication of 8.23, that what-is "holds together."

This passage contains a number of claims connected by the inferential conjunctions "since," "therefore," "for." Thus it apparently contains one or more arguments for one or more theses about what-is. The claims are (1) "not divisible," (2) "all alike," (3) "not at all more in any respect or at all inferior," (4) "holds together," (5) "all full of what-is," (6) "all holding together," and (7) "draws near to what-is." The inferential conjunctions indicate that (1) follows from (2) and perhaps (3). Also, (6) is a consequence of (7), quite likely also of (1) along with some additional attributes of what-is.[37] But there is more. Claims (2) and (3) are probably different ways of expressing the same idea: something that is all alike is no more or less in any respect, and vice versa. Claim (4) seems to be presented as a consequence of (3): if it were any more or less, then it would not hold together, "which would prevent" being tantamount to "if . . . then . . . not." Claim (5) is a stronger claim than (3): if something is completely full, then no part of it is more or less full than another, but the converse is not generally true. I take the conjunction "but" (δ') closely with the preceding negatives (οὐδέ), so that the claim "not at all more or at all inferior but all full of what-is" is understood along the lines of "not poor but very rich."[38] Further, (4) and (6) are closely related linguistically and probably make the same claim, the former stating that it "holds together" (the verb is συνέχεσθαι), the latter that it is "holding together" or "held together" (ξυνεχές, an adjective cognate with the verb in form and meaning).[39] Claims (4) and (7) seem to amount to the same assertion (as was pointed out earlier); they also seem no different from (1). If what-is draws near and holds together, it is not divided; if it draws near and holds together indissolubly, it is not divisible. And vice versa.

Putting this together, we have the following picture. Claim (5) entails (3) but not vice versa. Claims (2) and (3) are equivalent, as are (1), (4), (6), and (7). Further, (2) (and therefore [3]) entails (1) (and therefore also [4], [6], and [7]). This makes (2) and (3) dependent on (5) and the other attributes dependent on them. Since (5), "all full of what-is," apparently means the same as "fully is," it follows that the properties proved in this passage depend on the "full being" of what-is. This is an important point. The emphatic statement "In this way it is right either fully to be or not" (8.11) clearly implies that what-is fully is, but until now we know no more about what being fully amounts to than we did at 8.11, which only reveals that being fully includes being ungenerated. It must include more if the argument in this passage is to succeed.

It is simplest and most reasonable to understand the claim that what-is fully is as asserting that what-is is. It is. In no way (for example, in no place, at no time, in no degree, in no respect, in no manner) is it the case that what-is is not. A way to express this simple but pregnant claim is to say that what-is fully is. This claim does not appear in the list of "signs," and there is no argument for it. These would be obstacles if this were a new claim about what-is, but they are in fact confirmation that the claim is synonymous with the well-established principle that what-is is.

Fragment B8.25 explicitly asserts that what-is is "holding together," and presents it as the consequence of another attribute, "draws near." Of the remaining attributes in group B, "all together" seems virtually the same as "holds together" and "draws near," on the safe supposition that Parmenides is not thinking of "drawing near" as a temporal process. "Whole" and "complete" seem to be the same, and both can be taken to mean either that what-is contains all of it that there is, or that none of it is missing. On both ways of understanding this pair of attributes, the fact that what-is holds together entails that what-is is whole and complete: all of it draws together, so none of it is missing, and what draws together is all of it that there is.

So the four attributes of Group B amount to the same thing. But then the discussion earlier suggests that "indivisible," "holds together," and "draws near" ([1], [4], and [7]) do, too, since they are equivalent to one another and to (6) "holding together" as well. Further, I think that (5) "all full of what-is," which is the basic premise of the argument in 8.22–25, is equivalent to (6) "all holding together," one of the final conclusions of the argument. "Holding together" and "full" are metaphors referring to the invariance of what-is. In fact all seven of the attributes (1) through (7) as well as the remaining attributes of group B are various ways of capturing the nature of this invariance. Thus, it makes best sense to regard the passage not as a rather obscurely structured argument, but rather as a clarification: it presents a number of essential attributes of what-is.

I do not claim that the various descriptions in play here are strictly synonymous or that Parmenides regarded them as such, or even that they are all logically equivalent or that Parmenides thought them to be. I take them as different ways of expressing the same idea, which leaves open that they may emphasize different aspects of it. For example, "whole" and "all together" are not synonyms, and do not as a rule entail one another. In the case at hand, Parmenides is discussing what-is and is fleshing out what it is like. These expressions all attempt to relate the nature of the same state of affairs: that what-is is. "Is complete," "is all together," and so on are all essential redescriptions of "is." From now on, I shall call the relation that these attributes have to one another in the Parmenidean context notional equivalence, and I shall call the attributes notionally equivalent.

2.3. B8.26–28: Group A (Further Consequences)

8.26 αὐτὰρ ἀκίνητον μεγάλων ἐν πείρασι δεσμῶν
8.27 ἔστιν ἄναρχον ἄπαυστον, ἐπεὶ γένεσις καὶ ὄλεθρος
8.28 τῆλε μάλ᾽ ἐπλάχθησαν, ἀπῶσε δὲ πίστις ἀληθής.

But motionless in the limits of great bonds
it is, without starting or ceasing, since generation and perishing
have wandered far far away; true conviction repelled them.

This short passage seems to introduce an important new attribute of what-is, that it is motionless;[40] and indeed the motionlessness of what-is (along with its uniqueness and changelessness) has been a hallmark of interpretations of Parmenides from Plato to the present. But whether or not Parmenides believed that what-is is without motion, that claim is not made here. Instead, we have something quite different: an argument for consequences of the fact that what-is is ungenerated and imperishable, the results obtained in 8.6–21.

There is no explicit argument here against motion. The immediate sequel, 8.27–28, goes on to draw two further consequences of its being ungenerated and imperishable, that it is without beginning (which would entail that it was generated) or end (which would entail that it is perishable)—attributes that have nothing to do with the absence of motion, or with the attributes of group B. In this context, an undefended assertion that what-is is motionless is an embarrassment.

Note, however, that "motionless" goes closely with the remainder of the first line (8.26) and not so closely with the next.[41] In fact, 8.27–28 is a self-contained argument. In context, then, "motionless" has to do with the limits of great bonds rather than with the absence of generation and perishing. The bonds are associated with Justice (8.14) and Necessity (8.30–31), which indicates force or constraint[42] rather than what we now think of as logical necessity. Where we think of what is necessary as that which cannot be otherwise, it is natural to think of something that is held in bonds as being unable to move—it cannot go anywhere but must stay put, which here means in particular that it cannot cease to be and be fully. This, I suggest, is the point of the word "motionless" in 8.26. It is notionally equivalent to the attributes listed in group B, and it expresses the fixed, limited, and bounded nature of what-is, whatever that might turn out to involve. On this interpretation, it remains an open question whether Parmenides believed that what-is is literally motionless or changeless, and if so, whether he provides an argument for the claim.[43]

2.4. B8.29–31: Group B (Further Consequences)

8.29 ταὐτόν τ’ ἐν ταὐτῶι τε μένον καθ’ ἑαυτό τε κεῖται
8.30 χοὔτως ἔμπεδον αὖθι μένει· κρατερὴ γὰρ ’Ανάγκη
8.31 πείρατος ἐν δεσμοῖσιν ἔχει, τό μιν ἀμφὶς ἐέργει,

Remaining the same and in the same and by itself it lies
and so remains there fixed; for mighty Necessity
holds it in bonds of a limit that holds it back on all sides.

These lines carry forward the image of "the limits of great bonds." In 8.26, the bonds kept it "motionless." Here they keep it "fixed" (ἔμπεδον carries a range of meanings that includes "firm-set," "steady," "sure," and "continual"), where "fixed" covers the three attributes listed in 8.29. Fragment B8.29 has been taken to assert that what-is is changeless ("remaining the same"), motionless ("in the same [place]") and unique ("by itself")[44]—three hallmarks of most interpretations of Parmenides. Yet Parmenides introduces these strong and varied claims abruptly, without a scrap of proof;[45] we are in the same unhappy situation as with the unexplained appearance of "motionless" at 8.26. Fortunately, the same kind of solution is available, since it is possible to read 8.29 as redescribing attributes already proved to belong to what-is—specifically, redescribing them in ways that accord with the language of limit, bonds, and constraint. Thus, "the same and in the same" are implications of "fully is": it does not change in respect of being fully. It remains the same as itself and remains in the same condition of being fully. The verbs "remains" and "lies" support this interpretation: what-is fully is and cannot cease to be that way. "By itself" (καθ' ἑαυτό) is amenable to the same treatment. It can mean "on its own," thus "alone," "solitary," but it can also mean "independent" (which is closer to the way Plato uses it of the Forms),[46] and this is a reasonable description of something that fully is and cannot cease to be that way. Nothing else can affect it, at least with regard to its being fully.

2.5. B8.32–33: Group B (Supplementary Argument)

8.32 οὕνεκεν οὐκ ἀτελεύτητον τὸ ἐὸν θέμις εἶναι
8.33 ἔστι γὰρ οὐκ ἐπιδευές· ἐὸν δ' ἂν παντὸς ἐδεῖτο.

For this reason it is right for what-is to be not incomplete;
for it is not lacking; otherwise, what-is would be in want of everything.

This is a further argument for the attributes "whole" and "complete" (τέλειον) (8.4), equivalent to "not incomplete" (οὐκ ἀτελεύτητον). What-is is not incomplete "for this reason," that is, because what-is is held "in the bonds of a limit which holds it back on all sides" (8.31), which amounts to saying that what-is fully is and consequently has the attributes catalogued in 8.29–30.[47] The argument is as follows: not incomplete because not lacking; not lacking because if lacking it would lack everything. The first of these propositions can be regarded as a tautology. The second depends on the radical difference between what-is and what-is-not, the lack of a middle ground (or mediating subject) between the two (6.4–9), the unavailability of what-is-not as a subject for attributes (hence picturesquely described as in want of everything), and the result that what-is fully is. If what-is were incomplete, it would not fully be, hence it would not be what-is, hence it would be what-is-not, hence it would be in want of everything.

The attributes of group B ("whole," "complete," "all together," and "holding together") prove to be different ways of expressing the idea that what-is fully is. They are immediate consequences of the radical rejection of "is not," with the result that only "is" remains as a possible starting point of investigation (see 8.1–2).

Further, on the proposed interpretation, group B is the background for the attributes treated in 8.29–33. The image of bonds and limits recurs with increasing prominence as the cause or guarantee of the certainty of these attributes and of the attributes of group B as well. We see more clearly than before that the binding, limiting necessity is rooted in the fact that these attributes are not so much consequences of "is" as explications of it.

It is worthwhile drawing attention to the fact that the arguments for the attributes of group B do not employ the results of the previous section, 8.6–21 (namely, "ungenerated and imperishable") as premises. The premises of 8.22–25 are "what-is is all alike," "what-is is no more or less in any respect," and "what-is draws near to what-is," which depend on the further premise "what-is is all full of what-is," which restates the earlier thesis "what-is fully is," which is a restatement of the fundamental Parmenidean principle that what-is is.

3. B8.34–51: Introduction

The argument for the attributes of what-is ends at this point. In the last 18 lines of the Way of Truth (down to 8.51), Parmenides first (8.34–41) explores implications of the earlier claim that "you cannot know what-is-not . . . nor can you declare it" (2.7–8): if you can know and/or declare something, it is not what-is-not, and therefore (there being no alternative) it is what-is. Then (8.42–49) he presses the metaphor of limit further, delivering his difficult message in still other ways; but it is the message already delivered at 8.33: "it is not lacking; otherwise, what-is would be in want of everything." Finally (8.50–51) he announces that his treatment of the nature of what-is has reached its end.

3.1. B8.34–41: What Can Be Thought or Spoken Of

Lines 8.34–38 argue that what-is is the only possible object of thought or language, and 8.38–41 draws the conclusion that no matter what mortals may suppose they are thinking about or can think about, what they are actually thinking about and what they actually can think about is what-is. What-is is the subject of their thoughts, even those thoughts that attribute prohibited terms such as generation and perishing.

> 8.34 ταὐτὸν δ' ἐστὶ νοεῖν τε καὶ οὕνεκεν ἔστι νόημα.
> 8.35 οὐ γὰρ ἄνευ τοῦ ἐόντος, ἐν ὧι πεφατισμένον ἐστίν,
> 8.36 εὑρήσεις τὸ νοεῖν· οὐδὲν γὰρ <ἢ>[48] ἔστιν ἢ ἔσται
> 8.37 ἄλλο πάρεξ τοῦ ἐόντος, ἐπεὶ τό γε Μοῖρ' ἐπέδησεν
> 8.38 οὖλον ἀκίνητόν τ' ἔμεναι

What is to be thought of is the same as that on account of which
   the thought is.
For not without what-is, on which it depends, having been
   solemnly pronounced,
will you find thinking; for nothing else either is or will be
except what-is, since precisely this is what Fate shackled
to be whole and motionless.

Several renderings of both parts of 8.34 are possible; in each case the different
translations reflect two different ways of interpreting the passage. The phrase ἐστὶ
νοεῖν can mean (a) "thinking is" (Owen, Sedley); and also (b) "is to be thought"
(Mourelatos), "is there to be thought" (KRS), "is for thinking" (Curd), "is to be
thought of."[49] The phrase οὕνεκεν ἔστι νόημα can mean (1) "the thought that it
is" (Owen), or "a thought that it is" (Barnes); and also (2) "why there is thought"
(KRS), "wherefore is the thinking" (Mourelatos), or "that on account of which the
(or a) thought is."[50] A widely accepted interpretation adopts versions of (a) and
(1), on which "thinking" and "the thought that it is" are the grammatical subjects
and "the same" is the predicate: "thinking is identical with the thought that it
is"[51]—that is, the thought that it is is the only possible thought.

I favor (b) and (2) on philological grounds. Meaning (b) has the advantage over
(a) that it construes νοεῖν in the way that most interpreters (including myself)
understand 2.2. Like 8.34, that line[52] contains an infinitive of the verb νοεῖν, which
there means "to be thought of," which amounts to "are available for thinking of,"
and so: "can be thought of." The word νοεῖν is a transitive verb, so that "are there for
thinking of" means "are there (for someone) to think of." I also favor (2) over (1),
since it takes οὕνεκεν ("on account of which") in the same "causal" sense as it has
just earlier in 8.32, where it was translated "for this reason."[53] Meanings (b) and (2)
give the sense: "what is to be thought of is the same as that on account of which the
thought is." It is worth noting that the word οὕνεκεν ("on account of which") can
have both a "final" as well as a "causal" force, meaning either "that for the sake of
which" as well as "that which caused." It is attractive to take the word as having both
senses here.[54] Line 8.34 says, then, that what is to be thought of both prompts
whatever thought is in question and in addition is the object of that thought. The
minimal fact about what-is is that what-is is, and the minimal thought that what-is
can prompt is the thought that what-is is.

Line 8.34, then, makes a powerful identity claim. The first member of the
identity, "what is to be thought of," implies only that what-is is something we may
think of, not that it is the only thing we may think of, which would imply that if we
think of anything, we must be thinking of what-is. The second, "that on account of
which the thought is," implies that what-is both prompts every thought, even the
minimal thought that what-is is, and—as the object of thought in the sense that
thought is directed toward it—is the only thing that thought can think of. Only
what causes thought can be the object of thought, and the first part seems to say
that what-is is available to be an object of thought. We may supply that nothing

other than what-is is so available (since nothing other than what-is is). The conclusion, then, is that only what-is can be thought of. The following lines (8.35–38) offer an argument for this claim.[55]

Lines 8.35–38 contain a series of inferential particles ("for" [γάρ] twice and "since" [ἐπεί] once) that indicate that the train of thought is as follows: (1) what-is is whole and motionless;[56] therefore, (2) nothing else than what-is either is[57] or will be;[58] therefore, (3) you will not find thinking without what-is, on which it depends, having been solemnly pronounced;[59] therefore, (4) what is to be thought of is the same as that on account of which thought is. Here is the argument.

(1) What-is is whole and motionless, that is, as we saw earlier,[60] what-is fully is and cannot cease to be fully. For anything different from what-is, it is not the case that it fully is and that it cannot cease to be fully. But then, anything different from what-is is lacking, and therefore it lacks everything (by 8.32–33) and so is not (or: and so is what-is-not). Therefore, (2) nothing else than what-is can be.[61] Further, thinking depends on its subject matter (an independent tacit premise). So, since what-is is all there is, what-is is the only possible subject matter of thought; consequently, thinking depends on what-is. Therefore, (3) thinking never occurs without what-is, both in that there is no thinking at all if what-is is not and in that thinking depends in several ways on what-is. The ways in which thinking depends on what-is include that what-is is both the cause and the object or topic of any thought as well as of any verbal expression, and this justifies claim (4).[62]

> 8.38 τῶι πάντ' ὀνόμασται,[63]
> 8.39 ὅσσα βροτοὶ κατέθεντο πεποιθότες εἶναι ἀληθῆ,
> 8.40 γίγνεσθαί τε καὶ ὄλλυσθαι, εἶναί τε καὶ οὐχί,
> 8.41 καὶ τόπον ἀλλάσσειν διά τε χρόα φανὸν ἀμείβειν.

> Therefore it has been named all things
> that mortals, persuaded that they are real, have posited
> both to be generated and to perish, both to be and not,
> and to change place and alter bright color.

Some see this passage as denying the reality of generation, perishing, motion, and change; the attributes in 8.40–41 are taken to have been eliminated by the previous arguments in B8. This interpretation is not without problems. First, it is not true that all of the attributes mentioned in 8.40–41 have been eliminated by argument. To be sure, the list includes some things that have been eliminated, notably the first pair, "to be generated and to perish." But the same cannot be said for the second pair, "both to be and not" (i.e., "both to be and not to be"). The latter ("not to be") has quite clearly been eliminated, but the former has equally clearly not.[64] And there has been no argument against "changing place" or "altering bright color." Proponents of this interpretation find these attributes denied in the prior assertions that what-is is motionless (8.26, 8.38), but in my view the word is there used in a figurative, not a literal sense; in any case no argument is given for it. Of course the possibility remains that the inadmissibility of these attributes is implied by something else that is proved in 8.5–38.[65] In any case, the alternative interpretation I am proposing does not rest on this point.

This passage does not explicitly deny the reality of anything. Rather, it asserts a consequence of the previous lines (8.34–38), which argued that what-is is the only thing that can be thought of and expressed in language. The consequence is that no matter what mortals may suppose they are thinking of or talking about whenever they think or talk—whenever they say, for example, that something is generated or perishes or is or is not or changes place or color—in fact they are talking about what-is. This view is supported by the choice of the word ὀνόμασται ("has been named"), which seems better suited to describing the subject terms than the predicates in the thoughts and statements envisaged. If I think that my brother is changing place, the previous passage gives a reason to suppose that the subject of this thought, "my brother," is being used as a name of (an expression denoting) what-is (something that is). But it does not so well support the idea that "changing place" is also being used a name of what-is. Thus, the passage does not settle the question whether or not there is anything wrong with the thought that my brother is changing place; it simply says that if I say that my brother is changing place I am actually talking about what-is, and it is not excluding the possibility that my brother is a thing that is. The same holds if I say that my brother was born (i.e., was generated). The predicate has been shown to involve an impossibility, but to ascribe the unacceptable predicate to something does not by itself imply that that thing, my brother in this case, is unacceptable; nor does it exclude that my brother is.[66]

4. Groups C, D, and E

We are now in a position to discuss three of the remaining groups of attributes: groups C, D, and E.

4.1. B8.5–6: Group C ("Was Not," "Will Not Be" and "Is Now")

8.5 οὐδέ ποτ' ἦν οὐδ' ἔσται, ἐπεὶ νῦν ἔστιν ὁμοῦ πᾶν,
8.6 ἕν, συνεχές·

Nor was it ever, nor will it be, since it is now, all together, one, holding together:

These lines contain an argument for the attributes "was not" and "will not be," with "since" (ἐπεί) marking the premise. It is not clear how far Parmenides intends the force of "since" to extend—the premise clearly includes "is now"; does it also include "all together," "one," and "holding together"? Further, at the point where these lines are presented it is not at all clear how the attributes "is now," "all together," "one," and "holding together" are related to the attributes listed previously in 8.3–4 ("ungenerated," "imperishable," whole," "unique," "steadfast," and "complete"). Is each of the attributes catalogued in this passage identical to or implied by one or more of those in the previous list, or are they (some or all of them) new attributes? The interpretation of the following lines (particularly down to 8.25) offered earlier provides answers to these questions, as follows. "All together" and "holding together" are notionally equivalent with one another and with "whole," and "complete" in that they are all ways of expressing that what-is fully is.[67] "One" (8.6) is notionally equivalent with "unique" (8.4).

No argument is given for "is now," but that attribute is a consequence of the previously established thesis that "what-is is."[68] If challenged, Parmenides might justify it as follows: if it is true of anything that it is not now, then it is not; therefore, if it were true of what-is that it is not now, then what-is is not. But it is not true that what-is is not. Therefore, it is not true that what-is is not now. Therefore, what-is is now.

It is usually supposed that the sole premise for "nor was it ever, nor will it be" is "it is now." If this is so, then either the argument is noticeably fallacious or it understands "is now" in an unusual way, since normally "is now" is not incompatible with "was" or "will be." Yet, there are cases where this does not hold. One is where something comes into being and we are referring to it at the first instant of its existence. It is now, but prior to now it was not. An analogous claim holds for the last instant of existence for something that perishes. Such cases, of course, do not do anything to establish that the fact that something is now entails in general that it was not previously nor will be in the future. There are some rather special types of cases where something's being the case now is incompatible with its being in the past or future. One is where we are speaking (instantaneously) of the present instant, or of something that is only at the present instant. ("It is now precisely π seconds after noon on 23 January 1934.") If this is true now, then it follows that it was not true before now and will not be true in the future. But Parmenides has given us no (other) indication that what-is is instantaneous, so in order for this interpretation to stand, we need to supply a strong claim about what-is that we have no (other) reason to believe. Another case where statements in the past and future tenses do not apply but statements in the present tense do is that of timeless truths. Typical examples are propositions in mathematics and logical truths. Some might also put scientific laws into this category. For example, $2 + 2$ is 4, but that does not mean that $2 + 2$ was or will be 4. Here the present tense is not used in contrast to past and future. An influential interpretation of this passage supposes that Parmenides is using "is" in this way in this passage (also in 8.19–20): these two passages show Parmenides discovering the timeless present.[69] This interpretation, in various versions (including that what-is exists in an eternal present, and that the present in which it exists does not have eternal duration at all, but is only a single temporal point), has become dominant in the past generation, even though it has been subject to serious objections, including the fact that "it is very unclear how he hoped to ground this conclusion in the arguments of [8.5–21]"[70] and "punctual existence . . . is not announced in the prospectus [i.e., the list of "signs"]; it is not stated in [8.21]; it is not used to infer any of the other properties of [what-is]; it is, superficially at least, contradicted by [8.29–30], which appear to speak of a stable and enduring entity."[71]

In fact, one version of the timeless-present interpretation is undermined in one of the two passages on which it is based. Parmenides uses the language of the "tensed is," not of the "tenseless is" when he insists that what-is "is *now.*" We would not make the point that 2 + 2 is 4 is timelessly true by saying that 2 + 2 was never 4 in the past nor will it ever be 4 in the future on the grounds that it is 4 *now.* In order for that explanation to work, we would have to say more about what we mean by "now" in such contexts. In particular, we would have to explain that we are not using it in its normal way, as contrasting with past and future. Without such an explanation, the claim would be self-defeating. And it is apparent that Parmenides does not provide any such explanation. This is a serious objection to the view that the present in which it exists is a single temporal point.[72]

In view of these difficulties, another approach to this problem is needed. Suppose that the premise of the argument is not just "it is now" but "it is now, all together, one, holding together." On this reading, the claim that what-is never was and will not be follows not from the fact that what-is is now, but from the fact that it is now and has the further attributes of being all together, one, and holding together. If the attribute in question is a consequence of this stronger premise (stronger, that is, than the premise asserting simply that what-is is now), then this interpretation will be preferable to the former ones, in that it does not require us to suppose that what-is possesses an attribute (instantaneous or timeless existence) that Parmenides never explicitly mentions.

There is a way to understand the argument along these lines: Parmenides objects to the past and future because they are not. Past-tense statements involve reference to a time that is not any longer, and future-tense statements involve reference to a time that is not yet. The objection, then, to saying that what-is was or will be is not that its being now is incompatible with its having been in the past or with its being in the future, but that the very notions of past and future involve what-is-not in a way that rules them out for a reason analogous to that given in one of the arguments against generation (8.6–9): they cannot coherently be said or thought any more than generation can. It is true that what-is is now—and this is important for Parmenides to mention, since simply denying that what-is was or will be might otherwise be thought to suggest that it is not at all. But what rules out the possibility that what-is was or will be is not just or even primarily the fact that it is now, but rather the fact that it is all together, one, and holding together, in other words, that it fully is, lacking nothing, in no way involved with "is not." The point is not that being now implies not being in the past or in the future, but that being in the past or in the future is inadmissible because of the "fullness" of the being of what-is.

A further advantage of this way of taking the argument is that it makes sense of the conjunction "since" (ἐπεί). Normally when "since" introduces a premise, the proposition or propositions it governs are presupposed to be true. It is acceptable to say "Since Spot is a dog, if all dogs are cats then Spot is also a cat," but not acceptable to say "Since all dogs are cats and Spot is a dog, Spot is also a cat." One exception to this rule is found in cases where what follows "since" is equivalent to or an obvious consequence of claims already accepted as true. (For example, "My daughter got all As on her report card. Since she is a good student, she should have no trouble in her new school.") A second kind of exception is formed by cases where the premise that follows has been previously asserted to be true or is otherwise known to be a belief of the speaker, whether or not it is in fact true. For example, "I hold that all dogs are cats. So, since all dogs are cats and Spot is a dog, it follows that Spot is also a cat." This is acceptable because when we hear it, even though we do not accept that all dogs are cats, we in effect relativize the claim introduced by "since" to the beliefs of the speaker: we accept that a person who believes that all dogs are cats will reasonably consider himself justified to believe that Spot is a cat.

In the case of the argument at 8.5–6, what follows "since" is a compound assertion, that what-is has four attributes—"now," "all together," "one," and "holding together"—none of which has yet been proved true of what-is or has even been previously mentioned. In view of the consideration introduced in the previous paragraph, it would be odd to introduce four new attributes of what-is in a "since" clause; this is a problem for all interpretations of Parmenides. But since the materials for the proof of "is now" are at hand and since the proof is trivial, this attribute is legitimately introduced into the "since" clause as belonging to the first class of exceptions mentioned earlier. On the interpretations offered in this essay, "all together" and "holding together" are notionally equivalent, and also notionally equivalent to "whole" and "complete,"[73] mentioned in 8.4 in the first list of attributes, and "one" is notionally equivalent to "unique,"[74] also mentioned in 8.4. In fact, they have been asserted to hold of what-is: "On this road there are signs very many, that what-is is ungenerated and imperishable, whole, unique, steadfast, and complete." The attributes thus belong to the second class of exceptions. The difficulty has vanished.

4.2. Group D ("Changeless" and "Motionless")

This interpretation of 8.5–6 has important consequences for the interpretation of 8.40–41 and in general for the question whether what-is can move or change. To make this clear, it will be necessary to go back to the list of attributes found at 8.40–41: "both to be generated and to perish, both to be and not, and to change place and alter bright color." As mentioned, the list includes some things that have been explicitly eliminated in the previous discussion, but other attributes that have not been, in particular "to be."

On one way of reading these lines, they mention some attributes that mortals typically ascribe to things they talk about, some of which have been eliminated and others that are legitimate. On the other hand, this passage talks about the views of mortals, which harks back to B6, which describes mortals as believing that "it both is and is not the same and not the same" (6.8–9). If we suppose that this is the view alluded to in 8.40, then we can see Parmenides objecting to thinking and asserting a thing "both to be and not to be" in whatever way mortals believe that "things that are not are." On this interpretation, the list so far includes only illegitimate attributes.[75]

An obstacle to this view is that "to change place" and "altering bright color" have not been explicitly eliminated or even discussed. This is apparent for the latter attribute, which is standardly (and correctly, I think) taken to exemplify qualitative change, or simply change in general. Most find the former attribute referred to at 8.26 and 8.38 ("motionless") and 8.29–30 ("remaining the same and in the same . . . remains there fixed"); in discussing those passages I interpreted them as not referring to motion in the sense of motion from place to place.

However, the fact that these items appear in the list at 8.40–41 does not entail that they are illegitimate, or, in particular, that they require reference to "is not," but only that they are among the attributes that mortals ascribe to things. In fact, it is harder to make out how these changes involve "is not" than it is for the other items on the list. Generation of what-is, for example, is eliminated, on the grounds that if what-is is generated, then prior to its generation it is not. And what-is is complete because if it were incomplete it would not fully be, which means that it is infected by what-is-not. But if, say, what-is is blue or spherical or two meters across or in the Lyceum, it is not clear that it is infected by what-is-not. We might say that some things have shapes, but it is impossible for anything to have more than one shape, let alone all possible shapes; so to be fully will require such a thing only to have some shape or another. And similarly for colors, sizes, weights, locations, and other kinds of attributes that apply to physical objects. Changing place or color will be a matter of changing from one condition of being fully to another.

And in fact, 8.41 does not say "to occupy a place and to be brightly colored," but "to *change* place and *alter* bright color." Motion and change are not simply a matter of coming to have and ceasing to have particular locations and qualities. They take place over time. To say that something has changed place or color is to make a statement about the past as well as about the present; to say that something is changing place or color is to make a statement about the future, not only about the present. It is to state or imply that the thing undergoing change in the past was or in the future will be different from how it is now; this is essential to the nature of change. But if, as 8.5 asserts, what is now was not and will not be, and if this is the case for the reason proposed earlier, it follows that if something that is is now blue or in the Agora, it is illegitimate to suppose that it previously was, or will be in the future, red or on the Acropolis. The problem is not with the attributes, but with the nature of change. It follows, then, that changes in place and in quality are eliminated. Other kinds of changes are eliminated for the same reason, that they involve past and/or future. It follows, then, that despite the absence of explicit arguments for these claims, what-is cannot move or change in any way. This does not imply that what-is cannot be blue or in the Agora—that is a separate question whose answer will depend on whether something that fully is can have those attributes.

4.3. Group E ("Steadfast")

The single attribute of group E, ἀτρεμές (literally "not trembling"), which I render "steadfast," is standardly taken to mean "unchanging" or "unmoving," and is thought to be unpacked in 8.41 in terms of changing place and changing color. On this view, it is established along with the attributes of group D. However, the word can also have the meanings "calm," "steadfast," and "firm," and so can be used more broadly than simply to signify the absence of change and physical motion. With these meanings it can be taken as another way of expressing the requirement that what-is fully is and cannot cease to be fully. It can readily be taken as pointing to the effects of the limits that constrain the nature of what-is. (Recall that one of these effects is that "it remains there fixed" [ἔμπεδον; 8.30], which is virtually synonymous with "steadfast.") On this reading, "steadfast" belongs with the attributes in group B. On either interpretation, it is established by arguments already given.

5. B8.42–51 Spatial Metaphors

I will set out the final passage before taking up the final group of attributes.

> 8.42 αὐτὰρ ἐπεὶ πεῖρας πύματον, τετελεσμένον ἐστὶ
> 8.43 πάντοθεν,[90] εὐκύκλου σφαίρης ἐναλίγκιον ὄγκωι,
> 8.44 μεσσόθεν ἰσοπαλὲς πάντηι· τὸ γὰρ οὔτε τι μεῖζον
> 8.45 οὔτε τι βαιότερον πελέναι χρεόν ἐστι τῆι ἢ τῆι.
> 8.46 οὔτε γὰρ οὐκ ἐὸν ἔστι, τό κεν παύοι μιν ἱκνεῖσθαι
> 8.47 εἰς ὁμόν, οὔτ' ἐὸν ἔστιν ὅπως εἴη κεν ἐόντος
> 8.48 τῆι μᾶλλον τῆι δ' ἧσσον, ἐπεὶ πᾶν ἐστιν ἄσυλον.
> 8.49 οἷ γὰρ πάντοθεν ἶσον, ὁμῶς ἐν πείρασι κύρει.

> But since the limit is ultimate, it [i.e., what-is] is complete
> from all directions, like the bulk of a well-rounded sphere
> equally matched[77] from the middle on all sides; for it is right
> for it to be not in any way greater or any lesser[78] than in another.
> For neither is it the case that what-is-not is—which would stop
>   it from reaching

the same[79]—nor is there any way in which what-is[80] would in one
    way be more than what-is
and in another way less, since it is all inviolable;
    for equal to itself from all directions, it meets with its limits uniformly.

The passage argues that what-is "is complete from all directions, like the bulk of a
well-rounded sphere equally matched from the middle on all sides" (8.42–44). The
inferential conjunction "since" (ἐπεί) marks this claim as a consequence of the
premise "the limit is ultimate" (8.42). The remainder of the passage (8.44–49) is
connected to the preceding by the particle "for" (γάρ) (8.44) and includes several
other inferential particles: "for" (γάρ) twice again (8.46, 8.49) and "since" (ἐπεί)
once more (8.48).

    I begin by outlining the argument using numbers to label sections marked by
inferential particles.

1. since the limit of what-is is ultimate.
2. (a) what-is is complete from all directions, (b) like the bulk of a well-
   rounded sphere equally matched from the middle on all sides.
3. for it is right for what-is to be not in any way greater or any lesser than
   in another.
4. For (a) neither is it the case that what-is-not is—(b) which would stop
   it from reaching the same—(c) nor is there any way in which what-is
   would in one way be more than what-is and in another way less.
5. since what-is is all inviolable.
6. (a) for what-is is equal to itself from all directions, (b) what-is meets with
   its limits uniformly.

The inferential particles indicate that the argument proceeds from the top down
and from the bottom up: Parmenides argues that (1) → (2) [or (2.a)], and
(6) → (5) → (4) → (3) → (2) [or (2b)]. Note, though, that (2), (3), (4), and (6) are
compound claims, and even if we count "not in any way greater or lesser than in
another" in (3) and "not any way . . . more . . . and in another less" in (4) as single
claims, (2), (4), and (6) still contain more than one assertion. (I have labeled these
assertions with letters.)

    Broadly speaking, there are two ways to construe the passage. One is to sup-
pose that it has a single conclusion, stated in (2), and that there are two separate
arguments for the conclusion: (1), and the stretch from (3) through (6). The other
is to suppose that there are two arguments and two conclusions. The two conclusions are (2a) and (2b); (2a) is a consequence of (1), and (2b) is a consequence of
(3) through (6).

    I favor the second construal. On my interpretation of Parmenides' conception
of Necessity, bonds, and limits,[81] it is not hard to understand that he would hold
that (1) is true and that (2a) follows from (1),[82] but much harder to see how he
might have thought that (2b), with its talk of spatial extension, follows from (1),
since until now there has been no good reason to think that the limits associated

with what-is are spatial limits in anything but a metaphorical sense.[83] On the other hand, sections (3) through (6) contain a great deal of spatial language, and it is easy enough to suppose that Parmenides believed that they entail (2b). It will be necessary to consider the passage in detail in order to confirm this interpretation.

Various connections can be discerned among these claims. Conclusion (2b) reasonably follows from (3): if something is not in any way greater or lesser than in another, it does resemble the bulk of a sphere in being evenly matched in all directions. Further, (3) can be seen as meant to follow directly from (4c): what is no way more or less is not in any way greater or lesser. But if that was Parmenides' intention, what are we to do with (4a) and (4b)? I believe that they constitute an independent argument for (3), and that Parmenides gives us two separate arguments for that thesis, as follows: argument I (4.a) → (4.b) → (3) and argument II (6a) → (6.b) → (5) → (4.c) → (3).

Argument I begins with the well established claim (4a) that what-is-not is not, and then asserts counterfactually that if it were the case that what-is-not is, then what-is would not extend to its limit uniformly. Therefore there is no impediment from this quarter to prevent what-is from extending to its limit uniformly. It is reasonable to suppose that Parmenides thought that (3) follows; the fact that it extends to its limit uniformly entails that it is not in any way greater or lesser than in another.

Argument II begins with the claim (6.a) that what-is is equal to itself "from all directions" (πάντοθεν). This is not the sort of claim Parmenides would introduce without justification, and the obvious place to look is a few lines earlier in 8.43,[84] where the same word occurs. If we take the earlier assertion in which it occurs as the grounds for (6.a), as I think we are meant to, then there are two possibilities, depending on whether we construe "from all directions" with the preceding or with the following words, that is, as part of (2a) or of (2b). If we take it with the following words, so that (6a) follows from (2b), then Parmenides' argument is circular. For (2b) is both a premise for (6a) and a consequence of (3). Thus, the claim that justifies the initial premise (6a) of argument II, turns out to be both a premise and a result that the conclusion of argument II entails and on account of which argument II was constructed in the first place. The same consideration tells against the first construal of 8.42–49, on which the passage has a single conclusion, that is, (2), and that there are two separate arguments for it, one of which is sections (3) through (6).

These are strong objections to taking "from all directions" as part of (2b). On the other hand, if we take it with the preceding words as part of (2a), we have a nicely structured argument. It begins (8.42) with the argument (1)–(2a). Conclusion (2a) then justifies the initial premise (6a) of the second argument, which then proceeds to prove (2b).

The move from (2a) to (6a) is important, since it is here that spatial language is introduced. As I interpret the passage,[85] the many clear instances of what I am calling spatial language (πάντοθεν: "from all directions," μέσσοθεν: "from the middle," πάντηι: "on all sides," ἱκνεῖσθαι: "reach") are metaphorical.[86] They are a natural continuation of the notion of πέρας ("limit"), whose earliest occurrences (even in philosophical contexts) have to do with spatial limits,[87] but which soon enough is used of limits and ends of other, nonspatial, kinds.[88] I take τετε-λεσμένον πάντοθεν ("complete from all directions") as notionally equivalent to τέλειος ("complete"), which is notionally equivalent to "fully is."

If we take the spatial images literally, the argument contains many gaps. How does the fact that what-is is complete from all directions (2a) entail that it is equal to itself from all directions (6a)? How does its being equal to itself from all directions guarantee that it meets with its limits uniformly (6b)? How does that fact establish that it is all inviolable (5)? How does its inviolability entail that it cannot be more here and less there (4c)? How does that claim imply that it is right for what-is to be not in any way greater or any lesser than in another (3)? And how does that result entail that it is equally matched from the middle on all sides (2b)? We can perhaps find reasonable answers to the last two of these questions, but the first four are difficult to answer on the basis of the material at hand in Parmenides' poem.

On the other hand, the spatial metaphor enables Parmenides to make a number of suggestive points. What-is fully is, in the sense that it is whole, complete all together, and holding together.[89] And what-is is limited, which means that it is permanently bound to have those attributes. "Complete from all directions" (2a) emphasizes that it fully is ("complete") and bound to be so ("from all directions"). "Equal to itself from all directions" (6a) amounts to the same thing, but empha-sizes the uniformity of what-is, as does "meets with its limits uniformly" (6b). "Inviolable" (5) is a way of saying that it cannot be stripped of any of its attributes, or be forced to have any that it does not have. "Not in one way more and in another way less" (4c) and "not in any way greater or lesser than in another" (3) also describe its uniformity in different ways. Even if these claims repeat what we already have been told, they are not without rhetorical purpose, since the repetition will tend to drive this important point home.

The fundamental importance of the point is underlined by the fact that these multiple repetitions occur at the very end of Parmenides' treatment of the first road (excepting the coda at 8.50–51). Having demonstrated that what-is is the only thing that can be thought or expressed, and that at least some of the attributes that mortals believe to hold of things cannot be thought or expressed either, and having based much of the discussion on the principle that what-is fully is, Par-menides has every reason to conclude his treatment of what-is by stressing the importance of this claim and expressing it in a number of different ways that will catch his audience's attention and perhaps lead them to understand his difficult point more clearly.

Parmenides compares what-is to the bulk of a ball or sphere. It is significant that he does not say that what-is is a sphere, or even like a sphere; it is compared to the "bulk" of a sphere, which proves to be an unexpectedly elusive notion. It is neither the mass (in the sense, approximately, of weight) of the sphere, nor its size, nor any other physical quantity. It has to do with the sphere's shape, but it does not mean "shape" or "surface." "Physical extension" comes close, "physical" to suggest that it is not an abstract geometrical notion, and "extension" instead of "size" to avoid the temptation to think of it as a definite amount.

Does he mean to claim that what-is is, in fact, spherical? There is no general agreement. The dispute is in essence a disagreement over the extent to which Parmenides uses language figuratively. If Persuasion (*Peithô*: 2.4) and Truth (or Reality) (*Alêtheiê*: 2.4), Justice (*Dikê*: 8.14), Necessity (or Constraint) (*Anankê*: 8.30) and Fate (*Moira*: 8.37)[90] are not meant to refer literally to personages, and if the pervasive language of roads (complete with signs) and traveling is not meant literally either; if need cannot literally rouse something to grow (8.9–10) and the force of conviction cannot literally rouse anything (8.12), it is natural to suppose that Parmenides is not talking literally when he speaks of Justice relaxing her shackles (8.14), of Necessity holding what-is in the bonds of a limit (8.30–31), and of Fate shackling what-is (8.37–38). It is equally natural to suppose that the language of shackles, bonds, and limits (in the passages just identified and elsewhere: 8.26, 8.42, and 8.49) is not meant literally either. It has been noticed[91] that the image of the bonds becomes "more plastic and concrete" as B8 progresses; first there is just a vague reference to Justice and her shackles (8.14), then the bonds are associated with a limit that holds it back on all sides (or all around: ἀμφίς) (8.31), and finally the limit becomes an outer limit, and is represented as the boundary of a sphere (8.42–43). The (by now) spatial imagery is furthered by more spatial language, such as the translations "here and there" (8.45, 8.48) and "larger and smaller" (8.44–45), which are possible, though I have not adopted them. Those like myself who do not believe that Parmenides intended the description of what-is as spherical give a nonliteral interpretation to all these passages. Those who believe the opposite[92] take some (but not all) of this material literally. I am inclined to view the language of limits, bonds, and shackles as a metaphor that is pressed to do some philosophical work. As the text advances from 8.14 to 8.48, we find the metaphor being put to use in ever more specific and detailed ways in order to suggest further things to say about the subject at hand, namely, what-is.[93]

6. Group F ("Unique," "One")

I find no explicit argument for either of these attributes in B8.[94] If Parmenides held that what-is is unique and one, then either he did so without offering an argument for these claims or he supposed that they are consequences of attributes he does argue for. It is necessary to say at the outset that, supposing that "unique" and "one" mean the same thing, the claim that what-is is unique and one can be taken in two different ways: (a) there is only one thing that is, and (b) whatever is (that is, each thing that is) is one thing. Melissus was a monist in sense (a), and the prevailing opinion is that Parmenides was as well. This view is firmly attested as early as Plato, who tells us that Zeno defended Parmenides' thesis that "the all is one" by putting up arguments to show that it is not many, and elsewhere reports that Parmenides believed that all things are one.[95]

But when Parmenides talks about what-is (*eon* or *to eon*), there is no suggestion that there is only one such thing. Like "what-is-not" (*to mê eon* [2.7] and *mê eonta* [7.1]), which serves as a "dummy subject" corresponding to the verbal expression "is not" (*ouk estin*), "what-is" (*to eon*) despite its being singular, not plural, simply means "whatever is," "anything that is," that is to say, anything that qualifies as a legitimate subject of "is." But if this is all "what-is" means, then we can make good sense of (b). "What-is is one" means that each thing that is (however many such things there may be) is one thing—no more and no less. And this may mean no more than that it has the attributes of group B: that it is whole, complete, all together, and holding together, as Parmenides explicitly argues. In short, if it were more than one thing it would not be holding together, thus failing to have one of the attributes of what-is, and if it were less than one thing it would not be at all. In the words of one of the editors of this book, "Anything that is must be one, but there may be more than one such thing."[96] This consideration leaves room for interpretation (b).

It might be objected that there is no mention of the attributes "unique" and "one" in the passage that argues for the attributes in group B (8.22–25). But this objection is by no means difficult to meet. For only one of the four attributes in group B—"holding together"—is actually mentioned in 8.22–25. The other three, "whole," "complete," and "all together," are notionally equivalent to or follow from the attributes actually mentioned there.[97] And on this interpretation, the same holds for the attributes "one" and "unique" as well. Further, recall that 8.22 begins "nor is it divisible [or, divided], since it is all alike"; if something is indivisible or undivided, there is an obvious sense in which it is not many, but one. This is a positive reason in favor of putting "one" and "unique" together with group B.

Further, consider the alternative. If we do not suppose that they are covered by the arguments at 8.22–25, then they remain the only two out of all the attributes found in the lists at 8.2–6 not to be established by argument. Moreover, if we suppose that "unique" and "one" mean the same attribute, then Parmenides has given that attribute particular emphasis by putting it on both lists. If he considers the attribute especially important, it would be very odd for him to have constructed arguments for all the rest of the listed attributes and not to have proved this remaining one as well. The alternative view avoids this embarrassment by understanding these remaining attribute(s) in a way that is philosophically acceptable (in fact, as making a more reasonable although less exciting claim than the traditional way of taking them), that makes good sense of the Greek, and that enables them to be proved by a stretch of argument that establishes other attributes from the original lists as well.

That does not mean that we should lightly reject the interpretation that Parmenides was a "numerical monist"—that he held that there is only one thing. After all, this is certainly a possible way to understand the claim that what-is is one and unique—perhaps the easiest and most natural way. He may have been such a monist even if he did not argue for the view. And he might have thought that numerical monism is implied by some of the attributes he does prove. For example, he might have supposed that if there were two distinct things (call them A and B), then A would not be B and B would not be A; hence neither would "fully be," and so both would be infected with "is not" and so would be ruled out.

Compare the similar situation with the attribute "blue," discussed earlier (section 4.3). Just as something's being blue entails that it is not red, but its not being red does not entail that it is infected by "is not," neither does A's not being B entail that A is infected by "is not." Just as it is impossible for a thing to have all possible colors or to be in all possible places, it is impossible for one thing to be all things. So instead of saying that something that has one color is lacking because it doesn't have all colors (i.e., because it fails to satisfy an impossible demand) or instead of saying that colors do not exist because red is not blue and blue is not red (i.e., because the principle on which colors and other such attributes are eliminated is unreasonable), and likewise instead of saying that one thing is lacking because it is not everything else, it is more reasonable to allow there to be a number of ways of "fully being," for example, having one color *or another*, or being one thing *or another*. This alternative approach may strike us as more reasonable; it certainly allows a more generous ontology. But however philosophically attractive it may seem, there is no assurance that Parmenides recognized its existence, or that even if it were drawn to his attention he would have accepted it.

On balance, I find interpretation (b) both the more philosophically defensible position and the one that better fits the text and better accords with my understanding of Parmenides' strategy to establish the attributes of what-is by argument; but I also think that those considerations do not settle the historical question of what Parmenides actually thought.

7. CONSEQUENCES OF THE ANALYSIS
OF THE ARGUMENTS

8.50 ἐν τῶι σοι παύω πιστὸν λόγον ἠδὲ νόημα
8.51 ἀμφὶς ἀληθείης.

At this point, I want you to know,[98] I end my reliable account
    and thought about truth.

Since Parmenides' account ends here, it is time to take stock and reach an overall assessment of his program and arguments. Has he achieved the goals he announced in the opening lines of B8? If so, how successfully has he achieved them? And then a final question: what does Parmenides actually achieve in his arguments?

First, then, does Parmenides complete his program? Does he succeed in proving or otherwise establishing all 12 of the attributes listed in 8.2–6 (plus "changeless" and "motionless"), which I divided into groups A–F? He deals with group A in 8.6–21, where he gives four arguments that what-is is ungenerated, and announces that he has also proved that it is imperishable, presumably because arguments against perishing can be supplied that are parallel to one or more of those against generation. The four attributes of group B turn out to be different ways of saying the same thing: that what-is fully is. They are established in 8.22–25. Group C is established in 8.5–6 on the basis of a compound premise ("since it is now, all together, one, holding together"), which contains one element ("is now") that is not proved at all (although it follows from theses established prior to B8) and three elements that are notionally equivalent to the attributes of group B, and so are established in 8.22–25. There is no argument for the attributes of group D, but they follow from those of group C: there is no past or future, so there is no change or motion. The single attribute of group E can be interpreted as notionally equivalent either to "motionless," in which case it is established along with group D, or to "holding together," in which case it is established along with group B. That there is no argument for the attributes of group F can be interpreted in two ways. On the traditional interpretation, according to which these attributes assert that there is only one thing that is—which is a claim that does not follow from any of the other attributes of what-is—these attributes are asserted without proof. On the alternative interpretation, according to which these attributes assert that anything that is (whether there be one or more) is a single, unique thing, these attributes follow from the same arguments that establish group B. The result of this summary discussion is that on certain interpretations, 8.6–51 establishes (or at least gives grounds to establish) each of the attributes mentioned in the programmatic section 8.2–6.

Second, how systematic is his approach? Do the arguments form a deductive system, for example, in which the conclusion of one proof is used as the premise for another? Of the two attributes of group A, one ("ungenerated") is established by four independent arguments, and the other ("imperishable") is announced as having been proved (8.13–14, 8.21) but is not stated to have been proved either as a consequence of "ungenerated" or by parallel arguments. These arguments are all based in various ways on previously established claims about what-is and about what-is-not. The first (8.6–9) depends on the claim that "is not" is not to be said or thought (2.7–8). The second (8.9–10) seems to depend on consequences of the counterfactual hypothetical supposition that nothing is. The third (8.12–13) depends on the view that what-is-not cannot generate anything in addition to itself. The fourth argument, which is directed against generation in the future, depends on the conclusion of the previous three arguments, that there is no generation from what-is-not. In 8.27–28, the attributes of group A are explicitly made the premises in a proof of two further attributes of what-is: "without starting" and "without ceasing."

The proof of the attributes of group B does not employ "ungenerated" and "imperishable" in its premises. Rather, its basic premise, "what-is is all full of what-is," can be justified by reference not to the attributes of group A, but rather to the claim that "what-is fully is," which depends on the principle "what-is is," which has been established earlier in the poem. Group C contains one attribute ("is now") that is unproved but whose proof can easily be supplied from things already established about "what-is" and "what-is-not." Group C also contains two attributes ("never was," "will not be") that are proved in 8.5–6. On the interpretation offered, their proof depends in part on attributes proved elsewhere, and to this extent it depends on another proof. There are no explicit arguments for the attributes in groups D and E, although Parmenides provides materials from which proofs for those attributes can be constructed. The same holds for the attributes in group F, on the view that they assert that each thing-that-is is one. However, on the standard interpretation—that they assert that there is only one thing—there is no argument for them at all.

My analysis of the claims and arguments of 8.3–51 points to the following answer to the question of systematicity. When allowance is made for terms that are notionally equivalent, the 14 attributes reduce to only eight or nine: "ungenerated"; "imperishable"; "whole" (with its notional equivalents "complete," "all together," "holding together," and possibly "unique" and "one"); "one" (and its notional equivalent "unique," if those attributes are not taken as notional equivalents of "whole"); "never was"; "will not be"; "is now"; "changeless"; and "motionless." "Steadfast" is notionally equivalent to either "whole" or "changeless" or "motionless." "Ungenerated," "imperishable," and "is now" follow from already known properties of what-is and what-is-not. The treatment of "whole" and its notional equivalents (8.22–25) can be made out to be a deductive proof, but is better taken as an exposition of different ways of understanding the nature of what-is. "Never was" and "will not be" follow from "is now" together with the attributes of group B, which expound the fact that what-is "fully is." "Changeless" and "motionless" (though Parmenides does not make the argument) follow from "never was" and "will not be." "Steadfast" is covered either in the treatment of "whole" and its notional equivalents, or in that of "changeless" and "motionless." The conclusion of this summary is that Parmenides does indeed employ the practice of using previously proved results in proofs of subsequent claims, but not nearly to the degree that is sometimes believed.[99]

The question here is whether Parmenides' arguments are sound, and if not sound, to what extent are they valid. This depends on the interpretation of each argument in turn, and I have no wish to repeat what I have already said. Since the arguments all go back in one way or another to claims about what-is and what-is-not that have been established prior to B8, whether the arguments in B8 are sound depends on matters that fall outside the scope of this essay, and I will not pursue the question further.

As to their validity, I offer three general remarks: (1) we need to decide what to count as arguments; some passages that contain inferential particles (especially 8.22–25) are better seen as repetitions and rephrasings of a point already established, the intent being to explicate a difficult concept rather than to prove that it possesses additional attributes. As for the arguments that do establish additional attributes, (2) they are not formally valid, but (3) in every case we can see how Parmenides might reasonably have supposed that they prove their conclusions. From the formal point of view, they contain two notable failures that contribute to our difficulty in understanding them: they skip over steps in the argument, and they force us to work hard in order to interpret premises and conclusions in ways that make sense and also that link them with the "signs" listed in 8.3–6 and with claims elsewhere in the argumentative passages. Parmenides' use of notionally equivalent terms is another source of difficulty. Even the need to invoke such a concept is an indication of the lack of consistency in usage of key terms in his premises, and once the license is granted to invoke the concept, its application in particular cases requires a good deal of sensitivity and sympathy from the interpreter.

On the other hand, I have tried to show that in every case the arguments can be understood in ways that do not do violence to the text and yet go through. If they do not "go through" according to the strict standards of logic as we know it, I think they do "go through" well enough if we relax the standards to the customary level in ordinary discussion. In the introduction to this essay I said that interpreting Parmenides' arguments is a matter of sensitivity and sympathy as much as of logic, and I stick by this claim. I also said that to do justice to what he says requires that we be willing to give him the benefit of the doubt—up to, but not beyond, a certain point. I hope that I have made a good case that we do not need to go beyond that point in order to count his arguments reasonably cogent.[100]

8. Parmenides' Achievement

As I said at the beginning, when we arrive at B8, we are left in the situation where "Just one story of a road is still left: 'is' " (8.1–2), but where all we know about that road is that it is the only road left and that in some sense it is constituted by "is." This result is still desperately in need of clarification. The final question I will take up, then, is what additional knowledge we gain about what-is in the remainder of the Way of Truth, that is, in 8.3–51, the text that has been the subject of this study. At face value, we learn a good deal more, to judge by the 14 attributes that make up groups A through F. Not only is it true of what-is that it is, but it is also ungenerated, imperishable, unique, and so on. Parmenides not only asserts that what-is has these attributes; he sets out to establish that it has them, and in doing so he tells us still more about it, including that it is motionless and limited.[101] But several of the attributes are notionally equivalent to one another; there are only eight or nine separate ones.[102] If Parmenides has succeeded in proving that anything that is has these properties, he will have established some strong and unexpected results. But what do these properties amount to?

All the arguments against generation and perishing (8.6–20) construe generation as generation of what-is out of what-is-not and perishing as perishing of what-is into what-is-not; there is nothing against the generation of what-is out of what-is or the perishing of what-is into what-is, that is, nothing against one thing becoming another.[103] It appears that Parmenides' claim holds only if we construe "generation" and "perishing" to mean generation out of and perishing into *what-is-not*. In fact, it is a plausible claim to make on this construal of generation and perishing. Yet this is not what we normally mean when we say that something comes to be or ceases to be. When an animal or an artifact comes to be, we do not suppose that it comes to be out of nothing, only that the individual animal or artifact did not exist before, which does not mean that it did not come to be out of ingredients that were there before and that could be changed or combined to become the new entity in question. On this showing, then, Parmenides has proved something true, but perhaps not very striking.

"Changeless" and "motionless" might merit an even more discouraging reply. Parmenides does not put up any arguments against change and motion. In order to do so, he would have to show that changes from having one quality (say) or from occupying one location to having another quality or occupying another location involve what-is-not. But he says nothing to prove this point, and there are perfectly natural ways of understanding such changes that do not involve reference to what-is-not. Red is not blue, and the Agora is not the Acropolis, but both colors and locations *are*, and nothing has been offered as a proof that the fact that red is not blue entails that red is not. This logical howler has frequently enough been attributed to Parmenides, but only as a way of making his arguments go through; there is no basis for it in the text. The change from one color or place to another is reasonably understood as a change from having one attribute to having another attribute, and there is no need to suppose that either attribute is involved in the kind of unthinkable and unexpressible kind of "not being" that Parmenides rejects.

There is no argument for "is now," but it follows easily enough from what has already been established. "Never was" and "will not be" are another pair of strong claims for which the argument is obscure. On the interpretation I have proposed, they follow from the fact that what-is is now and fully is, the latter of which means that it is not involved in any way with what-is-not. In particular, it does not have any predicates that involve what-is-not. And "was" and "will be" are predicates of that sort; hence what-is never was and never will be.

This pair of results is the key to the others. If something never was and never will be, it cannot have attributes that involve any time other than now. But change and motion imply a plurality of times, as do generation and perishing. In this way, Parmenides has provided the material to prove (though not the actual proofs) that what-is (something that is) is not only ungenerated and imperishable in the sense of being generated out of or perishing into what-is (something else that is) but also changeless and motionless. Substantial claims indeed.[104]

NOTES

1. Sedley, "Parmenides and Melissus," 113. Sedley's complaint applies to antiquity as well.

2. Jonathan Barnes is a notable exception to this tendency. I am indebted to his analysis in *PP*, chaps. 9–11.

3. So far as possible, I translate *to eon* by "what-is"; I avoid "being." The expression denotes anything that is (see note 18 here).

4. Notably KR 268.

5. Owen, "Eleatic Questions."

6. In some places my discussion depends on interpretations of B2, B6, and B7 that are not presented here for want of space. I sketch my justification for controversial views in the notes.

7. See section 3.1 here.

8. I follow most recent editors (as opposed to DK) in adopting this reading of the beginning of 8.4.

9. It is the general opinion that the "signs" are the attributes listed in these lines. But Parmenides does not say that there are many signs, including "ungenerated," "imperishable," etc. Rather he says that there are many signs that what-is is ungenerated, imperishable, etc. The claim makes better sense if we understand the "signs" to be the arguments that indicate (we should say prove) that what-is has the attributes in question.

10. μουνογενές is frequently (following Mourelatos, *The Route of Parmenides*, 113–14) translated "of a single kind," that is to say, uniform. In effect, it is put in group C. However, Mourelatos cites no other passages where the word has this meaning; he cites μονοειδής as meaning "of a single form" in Plato, but it must be noted that the word in question occurs in Plato with the meaning "unique" three times (*Ti.* 31b3 and 92c9 and *Criti.* 113d2) and never with the meaning "of a single form." In its only additional occurrence in Plato, it means "single" (*Laws* 691e1). It occurs just twice more in fifth-century Greek, and it means "only born," which amounts to "only" or "unique" (Herodotus 2.79.11, 7.222.1). The authors of the testimonia on Parmenides seem to understand the word to mean "unique" (Proclus *in Plat. Parm.* 708.33; Simp. *in Ph.* 144.18). For Parmenides, what-is is not "only born" (deriving the -γενές in μουνογενές from γίγνεσθαι, "become, be born") because being ungenerated it is not born at all. But it is "unique of its kind" (deriving -γενές from γένος, "kind"). (This matter is treated in Barnes, "Parmenides and the Eleatic One," 8-9.) "Unique of its kind" amounts (in a typical context) to "unique": "She is my unique daughter" is a simpler way of saying no more and no less than "My daughter is unique of her kind, the kind in question being the kind consisting of my daughters." Those who hold that Parmenides believed that what-is is unique in the sense that there is only one entity find support for this view in the claim that what-is is unique of its kind: there is only one kind available (*to eon* as opposed to *to mê eon*, the latter of which does not qualify as a genuine kind). Those who hold that Parmenides was not a numerical monist can easily interpret the claim as meaning that each thing that is is unique of its kind, and that there are as many kinds as there are entities.

11. My main reason for resisting the usual translation of συνεχές as "continuous" is that it conceals the relation between the adjective (8.25) and the corresponding verb, συνέχεσθαι, (8.23), which is crucial for the argument of the passage. See further note 39 here.

12. I discuss this issue briefly after dealing with group D.

13. These translations are unusual: the descriptions of the two roads are standardly translated "it is" and "it is not." The differences are important, but I do not have the space to argue for my preferred rendition here. See Laks, *La vide et la haine*, 9-10.

14. I pass over the difficult lines 6.1-2, which have been thought (prominently by Owen, "Eleatic Questions") to contain an argument for the claim of 2.7-8 and so to be of fundamental importance to Parmenides' overall program. See note 18 here.

15. Some (e.g., Cordero, "Les Deux Chemins de Parménide dans les Fragments 6 et 7") have argued that the third road collapses into the second; I disagree. While the second road declares "what is not is not," the third declares that "what-is is and is not the same and not the same." And while the second road is rejected because "is not" cannot be known or declared, the third is rejected because "it can never be the case that things that are not are." See also note 17 here.

16. I offer this as one viable way to understand the claim in B5 "for me it is the same where I am to begin from: for that is where I will arrive back again." The starting point and the end point are identical: "is." For another suggestion, see note 55 here.

17. The syntax of this line is difficult and has been interpreted in different ways. I have given what I take to be the point of 7.1. I follow Coxon's interpretation (Coxon, *The Fragments of Parmenides*, 290), on which "this" probably refers to something that came shortly before the start of B7, which may have been to the effect that what-is is or that only what-is is. Parmenides then rejects the third road on the grounds that it somehow involves not only the claim that what-is is but also the claim that what-is is not. The latter claim is unacceptable, since "is not" has already been rejected. In effect, the road of mortals is fatally infected with "is not."

18. Parmenides argues here that the second road of investigation, "is not," cannot be pursued, on the grounds that you cannot succeed in knowing or declaring what-is-not. The minimal complete thought characteristic of the first road is *eon* (or *to eon*) *estin* ("what-is is"), with "what-is" being a blank subject with no definite reference: anything that is, whatever it may turn out to be and however it may be appropriate to describe it or refer to it. Likewise for the second road: the blank subject of *ouk estin* ("is not") is *to mê eon* (or *mê eon*) ("what-is-not"), and the minimal complete thought characteristic of the second road is *to mê eon ouk estin* ("what-is-not is not"). The argument is not a refutation of "is not" as such. Nor is it a refutation of "what-is-not is not" in the sense of proving that that claim or thought is false. Instead Parmenides undermines "what-is-not is not" as a possible claim or thought. Since what-is-not cannot be known or declared, then a fortiori no claim *about* what-is-not can be known or declared (for instance, that it is not). Therefore, not even the theoretically minimum thought or assertion about the second road is coherent; no one can manage to think (much less know) it or declare it. On Owen's view ("Eleatic Questions"), the second road is eliminated not at 2.7-8 but at 6.1-2, which establishes the subject of "is" to be not the blank subject I am proposing but whatever can be spoken and thought of. In my view, the second part of 6.1 (ἔστι γὰρ εἶναι: "for it is the case that it is," which Owen translates "for it is possible for it to be") repeats the content of the first road (2.3), while the first part of 6.2 (μηδὲν δ' οὐκ ἔστιν: "but nothing is not," which Owen translates "but it is not possible for nothing to be") repeats the content of the second road (2.5), with the appropriate "minimal" subjects

SIGNS AND ARGUMENTS IN PARMENIDES B8   223

supplied. Given these premises, it follows that it is false (and therefore not right) to think that what-is-not is or that what-is is not, but true (right) to do what the first part of line 6.1 says: "it is right both to say and to think that it [namely, the subject of "is"] is what-is." The importance of 6.1-2 thus consists in the introduction of minimal subjects for "is" and "is not" together with the associated truisms that what-is is and what-is-not (namely, nothing) is not. This prepares the way for the discussion of the first road in B8, exploring the nature of what-is.

19. If we take growth and birth to be different, then the situation is different. We must either suppose that the question "what birth" is not answered at all or that its answer is the same as the answer to the question "From what did it grow?"—"not from what-is-not." But see what follows here.

20. "From what" can be taken in various ways (see Barnes, "Parmenides and the Eleatic One," 39–40). I find "from what source" the most plausible way of taking it here, not in the sense of asking what was the agent that generated it, or the event that caused it, or the stuff from which it was made (which is the closest of Barnes's senses to what I have in mind) but what *turned into* it, as hydrogen and oxygen turn into water or a seed turns into a tree.

21. See discussion of "fully be" in section 2.2 here.

22. An attractive alternative is to take αὐτό ("it") to refer to what-is. The claim then will be that what-is cannot grow by gaining additions from what-is-not (Mourelatos, *The Route of Parmenides*; Curd, *The Legacy of Parmenides*, 78).

23. The text is emended by some (including Tarán, *Parmenides*, and PP, 185-90) to read ἐκ τοῦ ἐόντος ("from what-is") instead of ἐκ μὴ ἐόντος ("from what-is-not").

24. ἔστιν ἢ οὐκ ἔστιν, usually translated "it is or it is not." For the omission of the pronoun "it," see note 13 here.

25. I follow many recent editors in accepting this reading is place of ἔπειτ' ἀπόλοιτο ἐόν (DK).

26. Discussed in section 4.1 here.

27. ἄπυστος, like its cognate παναπευθής (2.6), is related to the verb πυνθάνεσθαι, "to learn, find out, inquire." In B2, Parmenides refers to two "roads of investigation (ὁδοὶ διζήσεως)" (2.2), one of which he rejects on the grounds that it is "a track entirely unable to be investigated" (παναπευθέα ἀταρπόν). I take ἄπυστος in the present line similarly: perishing cannot be investigated because, like generation, it requires reference to what-is-not, requiring us to follow that "track entirely unable to be investigated."

28. I will use the expression "fully is" to describe the way in which what-is *is*. I use it as shorthand for the notionally equivalent Parmenidean descriptions "all alike," "not at all more or less in any respect," and "all full of what-is." For the idea of notional equivalence, see below in this section.

29. See note 17 here.

30. I agree with Coxon, *The Fragments of Parmenides*, 67, 203, and Barnes, PP, 178, in punctuating with a comma instead of a semicolon (with DK).

31. διαίρετος means both "divisible" and "divided." Either rendering is acceptable here. I have a slight preference for "divisible" because it agrees slightly better with my understanding of the claim "what-is draws near to what-is" (8.25).

32. ἔμπλεον ἐόντος. I avoid the common translation "full of being." Parmenides does not use ἐόν in this sense (as an abstract noun); elsewhere it means "what-is" or "a thing that is." It would be consistent with the present interpretation of "all alike" (8.22) to take ἔμπλεον adverbially ("it is fully"), but it seems necessary to take the following word, ἐόντος ("of being"), as the genitive complement of ἔμπλεον, which then must be an

adjective ("full"). The word order tells against taking ἐόντος with πᾶν: "*all of what-is* is full (or, is fully)"; as does the adverbial use of πᾶν elsewhere in this section.

33. For the translation "holding together," see note 39 here, and for the meaning, see below in this section.

34. If "alike" is taken as an adjective, it will presumably mean "homogeneous, qualitatively uniform," a substantial claim unlike anything that has gone before and unjustified by the preceding. This is a good reason not to take it this way.

35. Here the words are unquestionably adverbs: μᾶλλον, χειρότερον.

36. The translation given for these two attributes makes them seem virtually identical, something not apparent from the Greek (συνέχεσθαι and ὁμοῦ πᾶν).

37. It depends on how we take "therefore" (τῶι). It probably (though not certainly) indicates that "holding together" follows from something already said. If so, then two questions arise: from which of the things already said does it follow, and what role does the final clause, "for what-is draws near to what-is" (i.e., attribute [7]) play? As to the first question, one option is to say that it follows from the initial claim, (1) "not divisible," and understand claims (2)–(5) as premises used in the proof of (1); another is to say that it follows from (1) together with one or more of (2)–(5). As to the second, one option is to take (7) as equivalent to (1) (or [1] and whatever other of attributes (2)–(5) are used as premises for [6]). Another is to take it as a premise that in conjunction with (1) (or one or more of [2]–[5]) entails (6). A third is to take it as a premise that is different from the preceding premises and that by itself entails (6). In this case, there are two possibilities. On one of them, (1)–(5) have nothing to do with the argument for (6); (6) is a consequence simply of (7). On the other, there are two arguments for (6): (6) follows both from (1) (and one or more of [2]–[5]) and also from (7) in two independent arguments. There are other ways of putting the premises together as well; I have mentioned only those that strike me as most plausible.

38. On this reading we take the particle δέ as a strong adversative, which typically occurs after a preceding negative clause (Denniston, *Greek Particles*, 167).

39. συνεχές is usually translated "continuous," which raises the question in what way is what-is continuous. Three possible answers are that it is continuous in extent (spatially continuous), that it is continuous in time, and that it is continuous both spatially and temporally. But these meanings are unwarranted in Parmenides' argument that what-is is συνεχές in this passage. Moreover, translating the word as "continuous" fails to capture the close connection between this attribute and the claim that what-is "holds together" (the verb is συνέχεσθαι), which I take to be important for the argument. Hence "holding together," an adjectival phrase corresponding to the meaning of the verb. This rendering has a disadvantage. In 8.23, the verbal form must be translated in a way ("keeps it from holding together") that makes it hard to distinguish from the adjectival form that comes just two lines later.

40. κίνησις and ἀκίνητος can refer to both change in place and other kinds of changes. I adopt the standard translation "motionless" because it is better suited than "changeless" to express the result of being held "in the limits of great bonds." The image of being motionless within bonds will cash out into both motionless in place and changeless in other respects, and Parmenides mentions both of these attributes at 8.41.

41. Translators commonly take "motionless" as a predicate adjective, punctuating with a comma after "it is" (8.27), so that the sentence reads "But it is motionless . . . without starting and ceasing, since generation and perishing have wandered far away." There are three ways of construing the argument here. On the first, motionless is a consequence

of the absence of generation and perishing; this is a non sequitur. On the second, the consequence of the absence of generation and perishing is the lack of starting and ceasing (which is a reasonable inference), and "motionless" is taken to be equivalent to "without starting and ceasing" (a major blunder, since if "without starting and ceasing" is to follow from the absence of generation and perishing, they must be taken to refer to starting and ceasing *to be*, not starting and ceasing *to move*). On the third, the consequence of the absence of generation and perishing is again the lack of starting and ceasing, starting and ceasing mean starting and ceasing *to be*, and there is no argument at all for "motionless." The same observations apply if we adopt the translation "changeless."

42. Mourelatos, *The Route of Parmenides*, 25–28. On p. 160 he identifies Necessity with Fate, Justice, and Persuasion. He translates the word in question, ἀνάγκη, not as "Necessity" but as "Constraint."

43. For discussion of whether what-is is motionless in this sense, see section 4.2 here.

44. This is approximately Coxon's view, *The Fragments of Parmenides*, 207.

45. Coxon finds the proof in 8.32–33 (*The Fragments of Parmenides*, 208); I disagree. For my interpretation of those lines see what follows.

46. For example at *Phaedo* 78d5–6.

47. My translation of the second half of 8.33 is unconventional, the most common view being that ἐόν has conditional force: "if it were," so that the claim is that if what-is were (lacking), it would be in want of everything. But Parmenides standardly uses ἐόν and τὸ ἐόν to mean "what-is," most recently in the previous line. The violent shift in meaning is unexpected and unparalleled. "Otherwise" represents an omitted protasis ("if it were lacking"), which can be inferred from what precedes. The correction I am offering is of a grammatical point; the sense of the passage is unaffected. For omission of a protasis that can be supplied from the context, in cases where we have the potential indicative with ἄν in an independent sentence, see Smyth, *Greek Grammar*, 2349.

48. I adopt DK's text, which contains the supplement ἤ. The line is quoted twice by Simplicius, once as οὐδὲν γὰρ ἔστιν ἢ ἔσται, and once as οὐδ' εἰ χρόνος ἔστιν ἢ ἔσται. Neither version can be Parmenides' original wording, since both are unmetrical. Coxon, *The Fragments of Parmenides*, 210-11, prefers the second version, which he makes metrical by changing οὐδ' εἰ χρόνος to οὐδὲ χρόνος. For the translation, see note 57 here.

49. Sedley, "Parmenides and Melissus"; Mourelatos, *The Route of Parmenides*; Curd, *The Legacy of Parmenides*.

50. Owen, "Eleatic Questions"; Barnes, "Parmenides and the Eleatic One"; Mourelatos, *The Route of Parmenides*.

51. Owen, "Eleatic Questions."

52. αἵπερ ὁδοὶ μοῦναι διζήσιός εἰσι νοῆσαι: "the roads of investigation which are the only ones to be thought of." νοῆσαι is the aorist infinitive of νοεῖν.

53. The principal difference between (1) and (2) is the interpretation of οὕνεκεν. The word can mean both (as in [1]) "that" (used to introduce an indirect statement) and (as in [2]) "on account of which" in the sense either of "for the sake of which" or "because of which": the goal of the thought or what caused the thought. On (b) and (1), 8.34 asserts that the thought that it is is the only thing that can be thought.

54. I follow Mourelatos' interpretation here (*The Route of Parmenides*, 166-69).

55. This interpretation suggests a way to understand Parmenides' assertion "for me it is the same where I am to begin from: for that is where I will arrive back again" (B5). What-is is the starting point of any thought (or statement), since it is the cause of the thought, in

the sense that it prompts the thought. But it is also the end point of any thought, since it is what the thought is about. Thus the starting point and the end point of all thought, and of all discourse as well, is what-is. For another interpretation, see note 16 here.

56. The pairing of "whole" with "motionless" agrees with the proposed interpretation of 8.29–31. "Whole" means the same as "fully is," and the thought is that what-is is metaphorically motionless in that it is fully and cannot change so as to be any more or less. For further discussion of "motionless," see section 4.2 here.

57. On the alternative version of the text adopted by Coxon, *The Fragments of Parmenides*, and Sedley, "Parmenides and Melissus", the translation goes "nor is it the case that time is or will be." This version does not fit so well into the sequence of the argument. In particular, it is hard to understand how it entails (3).

58. If the claim "nothing else either is or will be except what-is" entailed that what-is will be, these words would be inconsistent with 8.5. However, other readings are available, for example: (a) what-is is, and it is neither now true nor will it be true in the future that anything else is; (b) what-is is, nothing else than what-is is, and nothing else will ever be generated; (c) what-is is, anything other than what-is is not, it is not now nor will it ever be true that what-is-not is; and (d) only what-is is, this fact cannot be otherwise, and so it will never be otherwise.

59. I generally follow Mourelatos' interpretation of ἐν ὧι πεφατισμένον ἐστίν (*The Route of Parmenides*, 170–72). The antecedent of ὧι ("which") is τοῦ ἐόντος ("what-is"). The participle πεφατισμένον ("having been solemnly pronounced") modifies τὸ νοεῖν ("thinking"), which is the subject of ἐστίν. ἐστίν ἐν means "depends on." Parmenides is stressing that thought and language (see "pronounced") depend on what-is, in effect that language, thought, and reality are directly reflected in one another.

60. Section 2.3 here.

61. See note 58 here for suggestions as to how this inference might go through.

62. The argument on the basis of which the second road of inquiry was refuted (2.7–8) depends on the premise "You cannot know what-is-not (for it cannot be accomplished) nor can you declare it," which is an immediate consequence of (4). But (4) depends on (1), which in turn depends on the result "what-is fully is," which is in turn based on the rejection of "is not." Is Parmenides guilty of arguing in a circle? Only if we see him as basing the earlier argument on this one, and the text certainly gives no sign of that. It would be more generous to say that at 2.7–8 he took the premise to be evident in its own right, and here he explicates it with the help of interim results. We now know much more about what-is than we knew then. In particular, we now know that what-is fully is, and we have derived the additional apparatus that makes it possible to construct this argument.

63. I follow most recent editors in reading ὀνόμασται ("has been named") rather than ὄνομ' ἔσται ("will be a name" with DK). Both readings have manuscript support. (For discussion, see Mourelatos, *The Route of Parmenides*, 180, and especially 181 n. 37 and 182 n. 41; and Coxon, who prefers the alternative reading; *The Fragments of Parmenides*, 211.) On the latter reading, the claim "therefore, all things that mortals have established will be a name" is taken to mean "... will prove to be mere names" (though there is nothing in the Greek to justify the qualification "mere"), and "mere names" to mean "not real." Another possible way of adopting the latter reading is to take τῶι as a dative of possession: "all things that mortals have established will be its name." This makes for an interesting claim, but I doubt that Parmenides would have introduced the topic without any conjunction or connecting particle—the role that τῶι has if it is taken to mean "therefore" as at 8.25.

64. However, the possibility that anything can both be and not be has been rejected at 7.1, so there is an obvious defense of the claim that only illegitimate attributes are men-

tioned at 8.40–41, one of the illegitimate attributes being "both is and is not." I can see no convincing grounds to decide between these interpretations of "both to be and not," and my interpretation of this passage is compatible with both.

65. For further discussion, see section 4.2 here.

66. To those who suppose that the passage denies the reality of the kinds of attributes listed at 8.40–41 and by extension the reality of the subjects to which they are ascribed, I have two remarks. First, that even if their view ends up with the same result as emerges from the interpretation I propose, it is a less attractive interpretation, since it takes a more difficult route to get there (as indicated by the objections raised earlier). And second, on their view the passage denies the reality of certain things, but this is false. It does not say that anything it mentions is unreal, nonexistent, or otherwise inadmissible; it simply lists some things that mortals attribute to the subjects they suppose they think and speak of.

67. The same may be true for "steadfast." See section 4.3 here.

68. 2.7–8 and 6.1–2.

69. Owen, "Plato and Parmenides on the Timeless Present."

70. KRS 250 n.1.

71. *PP*, 194.

72. Also *PP*, 192.

73. See section 2.2 here.

74. For a reason to suppose that "one" and "unique" are notionally equivalent with the attributes of group B, see section oo here.

75. My interpretation of 8.38–41 is neutral between these two ways of taking "to be and not" (see note 64 here). This does not imply that my interpretation of the Way of Truth as a whole is neutral on the question whether what-is can change place and alter bright color.

76. It is controversial whether to punctuate after τετελεσμένον ἐστί or after πάντοθεν ("on all sides"). Most recent editors place the comma after the latter, while Mourelatos (*The Route of Parmenides*, 123 n. 24) follows Diels, *Parmenides Lehrgedicht*, 38, in placing the comma after the former. My analysis of the argumentative structure of the passage (see later) requires it to go after the latter.

77. ἰσοπαλές ("equally matched") describes what-is, not the sphere. Translators frequently render the word by "equally balanced" (or "equally poised"), but in the only passage LSJ cites for this meaning (from the historian Ctesias), what is called "equally balanced" is a battle, which agrees well with the primary meanings, "equal in the struggle," "well matched," used to describe armies that have fought to a draw. This is no warrant for interpreting the word as referring to a state of equilibrium or equipoise.

78. μεῖζον and βαιότερον can be either adjectives or adverbs. In keeping with my interpretation of πᾶν ὁμοῖον in 8.22 (see section oo here), I take them as adverbs modifying "be" (πελέναι). If this is right, they do not indicate anything about the size of what-is, but have to do with its way of being: in all possible ways it is no more and no less. This makes the claim coordinate with the adverbs μᾶλλον and ἧττον ("more" and "less") in 8.48.

79. ὁμόν is frequently translated "its like." The interpretation given is that there are no gaps in what-is that will prevent your progress from one point of what-is to another (*PP*, 202). This could be construed as an argument against void. But the connection with the comparison of what-is with a sphere becomes remote. Also note the shift of subject from "what-is" to "you" (see "your"). (How can "what-is" progress from one point to another?) On the translation I have offered, "the same" (following Mourelatos, *The Route of Parmenides*, 123 n. 24), these difficulties do not arise. What is "the same" is the uniform limit; what is not prevented from reaching the limit is the subject, what-is; and there is no need to think in terms of progress from one place to another: "reaches" just means "extends to."

Lines 8.46–47 can be taken as an argument against void on this translation, too. It depends on how literally we interpret the comparison of what-is to the bulk of a sphere, in particular whether we think that what-is, like a sphere, has spatial extension.

80. I construe as follows (with Mourelatos, *The Route of Parmenides*, 123): οὔτ' ἔστιν ὅπως ἐὸν εἴη κεν ἐόντος τῆι μᾶλλον τῆι δ' ἧσσον. Some keep the construction of οὔτ' ἐὸν ἔστιν the same as that of οὔτε γὰρ οὐκ ἐὸν ἔστι (8.46): "nor is it the case that what-is is in such a way that (ὅπως = οὔτως ὥστε)" (see KRS 253; *PP*, 179).

81. See section 2.3 here.

82. See section 2.5 here for the proposal that (2a) amounts to "fully is and bound to be so."

83. See section 2.3 here on 8.26 and section 2.4 here on 8.30–31.

84. Here and in the next sentence I refrain from saying what I believe and what my translation indicates, that "from all directions" is part of (2a). The issue is disputed (see note 85 here), and my argument for the interpretation I prefer, which I am about to give, does not presuppose that my interpretation, or my translation, is correct.

85. Contrary to Sedley's "unashamedly spatial reading" of Parmenides ("Parmenides and Melissus," especially 117, 121–22).

86. Others might wish to include in addition μεῖζον ("greater," which can also be translated "larger"), βαιότερον ("lesser," which can also be translated "smaller"), τῆι ἢ τῆι ("in one way or another," which can also be translated "here or there"), τῆι μᾶλλον τῆι δ' ἧσσον ("in one way more and in another way less," which can also be translated "more here or less there"). See note 78 here.

87. See Kahn, *Anaximander and the Origins of Greek Cosmology*, 231–32.

88. LSJ cites a line in the *Persians* (632) by Parmenides' contemporary Aeschylus that contains the phrase θρήνων πέρας ("limit of lamenting"). See here for Mourelatos's discussion of this kind of ("speculative") metaphor.

89. See section 2.2 here.

90. This list is made up of the words capitalized in DK. Other editors do not always agree.

91. Mourelatos, *The Route of Parmenides*, 128–29.

92. Most recently Sedley, "Parmenides and Melissus," 121–22.

93. For a brief discussion of this use of metaphor, which he calls "speculative metaphor," see Mourelatos, *The Route of Parmenides*, 36–38 with references to Black.

94. *PP*, 205-7, refutes the view that 8.36–37 contains such an argument when it claims "for nothing else either is or will be / except what-is." I previously held that 8.22–25 can be taken so as to entail the uniqueness of what-is (McKirahan, *Philosophy before Socrates*, 169), on the grounds that anything that is fully has all possible attributes; but if there were two or more distinct things, each of them would have at least one attribute that none of the others did. I am no longer persuaded by this reasoning, partly because I doubt that that is the correct interpretation of "is fully" and partly for reasons given in section 4.2 here.

95. Plato, *Prm.* 128a–b, *Tht.* 180e, 183e.

96. {Curd, *The Legacy of Parmenides*, xxi}.

97. See section 2.2 here.

98. This clause represents the ethical dative σοι.

99. This result contradicts the interpretations mentioned earlier, in my introductory remarks.

100. My assessment of some of the arguments is more positive than that of *PP*.

101. The ancient tradition beginning at least as early as Aristotle (*Metaph.* 986b10–21) prominently associated these two attributes with Parmenides.

102. See section 7 here.

103. Also, nothing against several things becoming one (as when boards and nails become a bed), or against one thing becoming several (as when we disassemble a bed), or against other more complicated cases of this sort.

104. This diagnosis of the arguments and overall train of thought in B8 prescribes the following remedy of these unwelcome results: refute the arguments against "never was" and "will not be." The arguments for the remaining results will unravel if we succeed. To do so might require examining the notions of "is" and "is now" to see whether there is some way in which what-is-not can be. This is exactly the approach Plato took in his alleged attack on Father Parmenides in the *Sophist* (*Soph.* 241d).

BIBLIOGRAPHY

Barnes, Jonathan. "Parmenides and the Eleatic One." *Archiv für Geschichte der Philosophie* 61 (1979): 1–21.

Cordero, Nestor-Luis. "Les deux chemins de Parménide dans les fragments 6 et 7." *Phronesis* 24 (1979): 1–32.

Coxon, A. H. *The Fragments of Parmenides*. Assen: Van Gorcum, 1986.

Curd, Patricia. *The Legacy of Parmenides*. Princeton, N.J.: Princeton University Press, 1998.

Diels, Hermann. *Parmenides Lehrgedicht*. Berlin: Georg Reimer, 1897.

Kahn, Charles H. *Anaximander and the Origins of Greek Cosmology*. New York: Columbia University Press, 1960.

Laks, André. *La vide et la haine: Eléments pour une histoire archaïque de la négativité*. Paris: Presses Universitaires de France, 2004.

McKirahan, Richard D., Jr. *Philosophy before Socrates*. Indianapolis: Hackett, 1994.

Mourelatos, Alexander P. D. *The Route of Parmenides*. New Haven, Conn.: Yale University Press, 1970.

Owen, G. E. L. "Eleatic Questions." *Classical Quarterly*, n.s., 10 (1960): 84–102.

———. "Plato and Parmenides on the Timeless Present." *Monist* 50 (1966): 317–40.

Sedley, David. "Parmenides and Melissus." In *The Cambridge Companion to Early Greek Philosphy*, edited by A. A. Long, 113–33. Cambridge: Cambridge University Press, 1999.

Smyth, Herbert Weir. *Greek Grammar*. Edited by Gordon M. Messing. Cambridge, Mass.: Harvard University Press, 1956.

Tarán, Leonardo. *Parmenides*. Princeton, N.J.: Princeton University Press, 1965.

CHAPTER 7

ANAXAGORAS AND THE THEORY OF EVERYTHING

PATRICIA CURD

ANAXAGORAS OF Clazomenae proposed a theory of everything. Like other Presocratics, Anaxagoras addressed topics that we would today place outside the sphere of philosophical inquiry: not only did he explore metaphysics and the nature of human understanding but he also offered explanations in physics, meteorology, astronomy, physiology, and biology. His aim seems to have been to explain as completely as possible the world in which human beings live, and our knowledge of that world; thus he seeks to investigate our universe from top to bottom. This essay explores Anaxagoras's world from its basic foundations through the structure of the world we live in to the heavens and the cosmos as a whole. Although the fragmentary nature of the evidence and the problems of sources make it difficult to be sure that a rendering of a Presocratic philosopher's views is correct (so that any account will, of necessity, be a rational reconstruction), with careful use of fragments, *testimonia*, and other sources we can begin to understand the views of an early Greek thinker. So a second project is to show how one can build up a coherent and plausible interpretation of an early Greek thinker from incomplete evidence.

1. Background Assumptions

Anaxagoras was active in the middle third of the fifth century BCE: later than Parmenides and earlier than Plato.[1] This would make him roughly contemporary with Empedocles, and a little older than Democritus, Philolaus, and Diogenes of Apollonia. His time in Athens surely overlapped with the life of Socrates (born 470 BCE), but we have no evidence that they met. The two kinds of influence on Anaxagoras's thought can be called the scientific and the metatheoretical. The first stems from the tradition of inquiry and explanation that originates with the Milesian school of scientific thought; this accounts for the breadth of Anaxagoras's interests, and motivates his search for a unified theory of everything. The Milesians treat the physical world as a single coherent system that can be explained by the ultimate principles of nature, without recourse to the supernatural. Here, Anaximenes is an important predecessor (a number of ancient commentators mention similarities between the details of Anaxagoras's cosmological system and that of Anaximenes). Similarly, certain aspects of the medical tradition also seem relevant to the Anaxagorean theory of mixture and separation.[2]

The metatheoretical influence stems from Parmenides' logical and metaphysical investigations. While the Milesians inquired into the phenomena of the sensible world, they did not emphasize the philosophical questions that can be generated by such inquiry (for instance, questions about the nature and possibility of knowledge, the metaphysical foundations of a secure explanation, or the theoretical requirements for a successful cosmological argument). Such metatheoretical questions can perhaps be found in Xenophanes and Heraclitus, but it is in Parmenides that they receive their fullest treatment before Plato and Aristotle. Thus, we can regard Anaxagoras as attempting to provide natural explanations in the Milesian style for physical, meteorological, and cosmological phenomena that also meet Parmenides' philosophical requirements for a metaphysically basic entity (which he refers to as what-is) and for a successful explanation of phenomena.[3]

Parmenides' arguments concerning the nature of what-is restrict genuine being to something that neither comes to be nor passes away, which must be a strictly unified whole of a single kind, and which is unalterable in its nature. One way to understand Parmenides is to think of him as establishing formal philosophical criteria for an essence or nature. These metaphysical criteria also function as epistemological criteria. Only a nature or essence that meets his criteria is genuinely knowable: such a thing is the proper object of thought and inquiry, as he puts it in 28B2, B3, and B8.[4] Such a nature is the only appropriate starting point for successful inquiry into the natural world. According to Parmenides, earlier naturalistic attempts to explain the world reported by the senses founder because they begin with entities that are not genuinely real. Thus, these purported explanations cannot give us knowledge or certainty, as opposed to uncertain opinion. Parmenides holds out the hope that a cosmology that is grounded in the appropriate sort of entity can be successful, and can yield the sort of explanation sought by the

Milesians. Parmenides' arguments require that all the fundamental entities in a theory be genuinely real, though it need not be the case that there is only numerically one such entity. Thinkers after Parmenides, such as Anaxagoras and Empedocles, recognized the strengths of Parmenides' arguments about basic entities and tried to construct cosmological systems consistent with his criteria.[5] Anaxagoras faces the problem of explaining all natural phenomena without violating the metaphysical principles that Parmenides has demonstrated by argument. Anaxagoras establishes the Eleatic credentials of his view in a number of ways. The constituents of the universe are eternal (B1); there is no such thing as absolute coming-to-be or passing-away; instead there is mixture and separation of the things that are (B17). Mixture preserves the character of ingredients. Further, there is no lower limit on smallness of the ingredients in the mixture; thus progressive separation out of the mixture until there is a pure expanse of an ingredient is impossible (B3), nor can any ingredient be divided away until there is none of it left (B6).

Much recent scholarly attention has been focused on these two aspects of Anaxagoras's view.[6] We can call them the principle of everything-in-everything and the principle of unlimited largeness and smallness. Anaxagoras's claims that everything is in everything (B6, B11: "in everything there is a share of everything," B12) and that each thing is that which predominates (B12: "each one is and was most manifestly those things of which there are the most in it") are perplexing. If all things contain all things, at whatever level of inspection (B6), how can we determine what it is for there to be, say, gold or flesh, and how can we coherently speak of a predominance of gold (in this ring) or flesh (in this dog's paw)?[7] A related problem, bearing on the correct interpretation of the everything-in-everything principle, is that of how we should conceive of Anaxagoras's stuffs. Is the structure particulate, with "large" and "small" referring to particle size, or is there some other way to think of stuffs and measures of large and small? There have been advocates for and against a particulate view. Following recent scholarship, I have argued that Anaxagoras's basic entities are not particulate in structure.[8] Their mixture and interpenetration is not a matter of particle size, nor is the extraction of some gold from this gold a matter of extracting particles. *Large* and *small* do not refer to masses of stuffs or particle size. Rather, Anaxagoras's mixture of all the stuffs is a mass of ingredients that flow into one another (as do watercolor pigments or oil paints). They blend with one another; yet the mixture may not be uniform. Differing densities of ingredients in various parts of the mixture could give rise to different perceptual experiences, even though all things are in all things at all times. Anaxagoras needs the everything-in-everything principle to satisfy the Eleatic principle of no coming-to-be and no passing-away. This understanding of everything-in-everything allows him to acknowledge that principle while, at the same time, allowing for the diverse experiences that human beings have of the world. An ingredient can be said to be large if its density in a particular region of the mix is high compared to the densities of almost everything else in that region. (I say "almost everything else" because more than one characteristic may be perceptible, so that *this* clod of earth is colder, darker, and heavier than *that* clod.) Something is said to be small if it is submerged into the background mix in such a way that it is barely perceptible or entirely imperceptible, at least to whoever is perceiving it now. An ingredient could be both large (perceptible) and small (imperceptible), depending on the mix and on the perceiver. (My dog and I have different olfactory capacities, so the biscuit that seems bland to me is a symphony of smells to her.)[9]

The two principles, everything-in-everything and unlimited smallness and largeness, are explicitly connected with the rejection of the reality what-is-not and denials that coming-to-be and passing-away are real. See for instance, B3: "Nor of the small is there a smallest, but always a smaller (for what-is cannot not be)[10] — but also of the large there is always a larger." They ensure that the fundamental entities of Anaxagoras's theory (the ingredients of the original mixture) are metaphysically basic in the appropriate way. In addition, as we shall see (in section 4), each fundamental ingredient in the original mixture has a nature or essence known by cosmic Mind (*Nous*). Thus the Eleatic requirement that what is metaphysically basic also be epistemologically fundamental is satisfied. Given Anaxagoras's metaphysical and epistemological commitments, the everything-in-everything principle and the principle of unlimited largeness and smallness imply that his theory of everything must begin (in analysis, as there can be no temporal beginning of the things that are) with the existence of basic entities that cannot change in their natures, which are knowable, and which serve to explain everything else in the *kosmos*.

2. Ingredients and Natural Artifacts

Anaxagoras's metaphysical analysis underlies his cosmogonical account of the changes in the mixture that produce the world that human beings experience. In fragment B1, he says:

> All things were together, unlimited both in amount and in smallness, for the small, too, was unlimited. And because all things were together, nothing was evident on account of smallness; for air and aether covered all things, both unlimited, for these are the greatest among all things both in amount and in largeness. (B1)

Simplicius, the source for this fragment, tells us that it occurs near the beginning of Anaxagoras's book. It describes an undifferentiated combination of all things, before motion is introduced into Anaxagoras's system. It is important to note that this state of unlimited mixture is the original state: the things (whatever they are) that are in this mix neither came to be, nor will they pass away. They are the basic entities. At some point, Mind (*Nous*) causes the mixture to begin to rotate (B12), and the rotation, spreading out through the mass, causes the mass of ingredients to shift, disassociate, and reassociate. These rearrangements of basic ingredients account for the apparently changing objects and events that we perceive in our world:

> The Greeks do not think correctly about coming-to-be and passing-away; for no thing comes to be or passes away, but is mixed together and separated from the things that are. And thus they would be correct to call coming-to-be mixing-together and passing-away separating-apart. (B17)

Here Anaxagoras both reaffirms his allegiance to the Eleatic principles that reject coming-to-be and passing-away as unreal, and offers an explanation of apparent phenomena of generation and corruption. There are no such processes, but we are led to believe that such things happen through our observations of mixtures and separations that ultimately depend upon the rotation of the cosmic mass of ingredients. These ingredients are "the things that are," and only they are real. So, to make sense of Anaxagoras' system, we must determine what the list of Anaxagorean ingredients includes. One option would be to accept as an ingredient in the original mixture everything that appears, has appeared, or will appear in the sensible world. This would give us a very long and wide-ranging list for the contents of the original mix: planets and stars, clouds and rain, people and plants, bread and houses, and so on.[11] Another would be to attempt to find a system of reduction, such that Anaxagoras is committed to the basic reality of only a single class or kind of entity; in most such interpretations, these are the opposites.[12] Though both interpretations have had scholarly supporters, neither of these options fits particularly well with the texts.

Anaxagoras himself gives hints about the range of real things. In various fragments he lists opposites (the hot and the cold, the wet and the dry, the dark, the heavy, and so on), natural elemental stuffs (earth, water, air, fire), and parts of animals (flesh, hair; B10).[13]

> B1: When all things were together "aer and aether pervaded all things" because both were unlimited.
>
> B2: Air and aether separate out of the surrounding multitude.
>
> B4a: "Many things are present in all the things being mixed"; in addition, there are "seeds of all things."
>
> B4b: "The mixture of all things prevented [discrimination of characteristics]: of the moist and the dry and the hot and the cold and the bright and the dark, there being much earth present and seeds unlimited in amount."
>
> B8: "The things in the one *kosmos* have not been separated from each other, nor have they been cut off with an axe, neither the hot from the cold nor the cold from the hot."
>
> B10: "For how could hair come from not-hair, and how could flesh come from not-flesh?"
>
> B12: The stars, sun, moon, air, and aether are produced by separation because of the rotation of the original mixture; there is also mention of the

separation from each other of rare and dense, cold and warm, dark and
bright, and moist and dry.

B15: "The dense and the moist and the cold and the dark came together here
where the earth is now; the rare and the warm and the dry <and the
bright> moved out into the far reaches of the aether."

B16: A discussion of the progress by compaction from clouds to water to
earth to stones. Stones are said to be compacted from earth by cold.

It is difficult to read these texts as supporting claims that the original mixture
contains all the things that will ever appear in the world, or that all the other things
in the world can be reduced to opposites.[14] This suggests that the original mixture
contained fewer items than the expansive view requires and more items than the
reductionist "opposites" interpretation will allow. Nevertheless, the texts indicate
that Anaxagoras recognizes an important difference among the items we perceive
in the world. What we perceive are human beings; lemon, olive, and pine trees;
mountain ranges and rivers; buildings, loaves of bread, wheels of cheese; dogs, cats,
and horses; trout, squid, oysters; and so on. We could, perhaps remove the
buildings, loaves of bread, and wheels of cheese from this list, since they are
obviously artifacts resulting from human activity. It would be surprising indeed if
they appeared on Anaxagoras's list of metaphysically basic entities. Yet it is perhaps
equally surprising that natural items such as dogs, lemon trees, and rivers are also
missing. Natural features and plants and animals do not appear in the fragments
among the items being separated off from the original mixture. To be sure, B4a and
4b mention seeds, but what these are and how they function in the theory is unclear
(more of this later). B16 considers the formation of stones, earth, and clouds:
"From these, as they are being separated out, earth is compacted; for water is
separated off from the clouds, and earth from the water, and from the earth stones
are compacted by the cold, and these stones move farther out than the water."[15]

Although a reductionist account cannot be accepted in its strongest form (the
"opposites only" view), Anaxagoras gives no evidence that he thinks that artifacts,
or even accidental mixtures of natural ingredients, belong to the original mix.[16]
Perhaps most surprising, he denies that human beings and other living things are
metaphysically basic. Living things are most obviously members of the class of
things that come to be and pass away; yet B17 makes clear that no real thing can be
either generated or destroyed. Anything subject to coming-to-be and passing-away
(such as a lemon tree) is merely a temporary mixture of the basic real things, and
dependent for its being on the arrangement of those ingredients that constitute it.
The importance of this text for determining the range of real things in Anaxagoras's system has often been overlooked by the expansive theorists. Anaxagoras's
theory of real ingredients in the original mixture has the consequence that living
creatures (both plants and animals) are what we might oxymoronically call
"natural artifacts." While the idea of a natural artifact may seem strange to us, the
literal unreality of biological individuals (plants and animals) and of natural features of the world of perception was common to the theories of Parmenides,

Empedocles, the atomists, and Plato.[17] The reductionist theory recognizes this, but fails to see that for Anaxagoras, all the material ingredients of natural entities need to be included among the real things.[18] Allowing for a broad list of original ingredients as well as making room for natural artifacts allows Anaxagoras's theory to meet the metaphysical requirements imposed by the Eleatic arguments, while at the same time accounting for the phenomena of human experience.

The ordinary objects of our experience, the phenomena, are produced from the original mixture by the processes of separation and mixture. Because Anaxagoras's mixture is a plenum and there is (apparently) no void, each occurrence of separation is itself mixture; it is a remixture of the ingredients as they are separated and rearranged by the motion of the rotating mass of the stuffs and opposites.[19] This picture of the production of the phenomenal world immediately raises two questions. First, what causes the first motion and hence the initial breaking up of the mass of ingredients? Second, how can the mere mechanical arrangement and rearrangement of ingredients account for the variety and repeated structure of the objects of the sensible world that we perceive? Anaxagoras's answer to the first question is clear: cosmic *Nous* or Mind is the agent responsible for initiating the motion of the mixture, and so is the cause of the formation of the cosmos. The answer to the second question is less clear, but it is possible (and, I suggest, probable) that *Nous* is also responsible for the structure and repeatability of the objects in the world.

Nous initiates a rotation. The rotary motion spreads out, causing a breaking up and separating (rather like a winnowing) of the mass of ingredients. B13 explains:

> When *Nous* began to move [things], there was separation out [*apekrineto*] from everything that was being moved, and whatever *Nous* moved, all this was separated apart [*diekrithē*]; and as things were being moved and separated apart [*diekrinomenôn*], the revolution made them separate apart [*diakrinesthai*] even more.

In fragment B12, Anaxagoras asserts that *Nous* determines and controls the swirling motion of the ingredients, and he indicates that the motion begins in a single spot and moves outward:

> And *Nous* controlled the whole revolution, so that it started to revolve in the beginning. First it began to revolve from a small region, but it is revolving yet more, and it will revolve still more. . . . Whatever sorts of things were going to be, indeed whatever sorts were and now are not, and as many as are now and whatever will be, all these *Nous* set in order. And *Nous* also ordered this revolution, in which the things being separated out now revolve, the stars and the sun and the moon and the air and the aether. This revolution made the separation out. The dense is separated out from the rare, and the warm from the cold, and the bright from the dark, and the dry from the moist.

In B15 and B16 Anaxagoras explains that like ingredients group together to form the earth and the other aspects of the heavens, while at the same time, the actions of the ingredients on one another, combined with the continued revolutions, produce meteorological phenomena.[20]

While we may well be prepared to accept that the vortical motions of the ingredients can account for cosmos formation and meteorological occurrences such as winds, clouds, rains, and so on, it is not at all obvious how the rotary movement of ingredients could produce the systematic systems of separation and mixture followed by further separation and mixture that would be needed to produce plants, animals, and the rest of the objects and activities that constitute the biological world. The problem of the lack of structure and repeatability in Presocratic systems was a common complaint in Aristotle's criticism of earlier thought, and it is implicit in Socrates' criticisms of Anaxagoras and the other natural philosophers in Plato's *Phaedo*.[21] Given the intensity of criticism from Plato and Aristotle, it might be reasonable to suppose that Anaxagoras was either unaware of the difficulty or unable to solve it. Yet the fragments contain two tantalizing pieces of evidence that suggest a solution. In two passages (B4a and B12) Anaxagoras uses an intriguing phrase: "as many as have soul." These are the only two occurrences of *soul* (*psychê*) in the extant fragments. The presence of *psychê*, the life force, is necessary for a living thing, a biological entity. In B12, we find Anaxagoras asserting that "*Nous* has control over all things that have soul, both the larger and the smaller." In B12 Anaxagoras also asserts that *Nous* controls the revolution, and sets all things in order. The things that have soul are surely part of "all things." So, why should Anaxagoras put special stress on *Nous*'s control of ensouled things? One reason is fairly obvious: among the things that have soul are human beings, and our capacity for thought and practical activity, feeble though it may be in comparison with cosmic *Nous*, is *nous* too. Yet, although the link between the directing cosmic mind and the activity of human minds is certainly intended in this passage, that cannot be all there is to it. Thinking is an activity of soul, but the capacities of soul are not exhausted by rational powers. Other living things, too, have soul. So, perhaps, we should look for another connection between *Nous* and soul in Anaxagoras's theory.

The second mention of soul in the fragments is in B4a; because we have no helpful context for the fragment, we cannot be sure about the larger aim of Anaxagoras's assertion.[22] Simplicius's evidence suggests that the passage may have come fairly early in Anaxagoras's exposition; at any rate, Anaxagoras is discussing the consequences of the "everything-in-everything" principle and the separation off that results from the motion of the mass of ingredients:

> Since these things are so, it is right to think that there are many different things present in everything that is being combined, and seeds of all things, having all sorts of forms, colors, and flavors, that humans and also the other animals were compounded, as many as have soul.

Separation is also mixture; mixture is the process that accounts for what appears to us as coming-to-be (B17); thus the continued movements of the ingredients will eventually produce sensible objects by mixture. In addition, for living things ("as many as have soul") the process for apparent coming-to-be is compounding (equivalent to the mixture of B17). In the passage from B4a, Anaxagoras notes that "it is right to think that" anything that is combined will contain all (sorts of) things, including seeds. The conjunction of seeds with the reference to the compounding of living things that have soul might suggest that seeds are to be considered as the biological starting points for ensouled animals.[23] The second reference to seeds, in B4b, further supports that claim: there, Anaxagoras says that before there was any separation out, the original mix contained all things, and he provides a representative list:

> Before there was separation out, because all things were together, there was not even any color evident; for the mixture of all things prevented it, of the wet and the dry and of the hot and the cold and of the bright and the dark, and there was much earth present and seeds unlimited in number, in no way similar to one another. For no one of the others is similar to another. Since these things are so, it is right to think that all things were present in the whole.

Here again we have seeds mentioned, and in a context that also suggests biological starting points for living things. If this is so, we have three sorts of things connected with one another in the fragments: *nous* with souled entities, and souled entities with seeds. This provides a hint that the seeds are the mechanism by which *Nous* governs the growth and structure of animals and other living things, including plants and human beings. The testimonia provide intriguing evidence for the Anaxagorean view of plants. In A116, Plutarch reports that "the Platonists, the Anaxagoreans, and the Democriteans suppose that a plant is an earth-bound animal," while in A117, the pseudo-Aristotelian treatise on plants reports that "Anaxagoras and Empedocles say that plants are moved by desire and they also assert that they sense and can be made sad and happy. Anaxagoras said that they are animals and feel joy and sadness, taking the fall of their leaves as evidence. . . . Anaxagoras and Democritus and Empedocles used to say that plants have intellect and intelligence;" and "Anaxagoras said that a plant has respiration." The testimonia lead us to think that, for Anaxagoras, the soul capacities that are governed by *Nous* do not differ in type, but only in degree from one kind of living thing to another. This is consistent with the claim in B12 that "all *Nous* is alike, both the greater and the smaller" (and note the reference to the earlier claim in B12 that "*Nous* has control over all things that have soul, both the greater and the smaller").

If these (admittedly speculative) claims are correct, then *Nous* plays a larger causal role in Anaxagoras's theory than his ancient objectors allowed. For it is the primary mover of the ingredients of the universe, and as such it is the general cause of all cosmological and meteorological objects and events; in addition, *Nous* is the specific cause of order and structure in living things, as the soul that directs the individual's growth and development, and as the seat of sensation, emotion, and thought.

3. WORLDS HERE AND ELSEWHERE

At some time of its own choosing, *Nous* sets in motion the mass of the ingredients. The original motion begins, as we have seen, in a small area. The rotation then spreads outward through the mixture. Both the fragments and the testimonia report the increasing speed and widening area of the rotation, along with the power of the whirl as it moves through the mass of material (B9, B12, B13, A12, A71, A88). This whirling motion is the cause of all that occurs in the physical world: it causes the separation and remixture of the ingredients; it produces the cosmos, through the winnowing motion that moves heavy and dense materials to the center to form our Earth and light and rare materials to the outer edges of the whirl to produce the air, fire, and aether that form the heavens. The whirling motion mixes the materials that form the stars and other heavenly bodies, and governs their motions. The same whirl is responsible for the bodies between the earth and the moon, snatching stones from the surface of the earth and igniting them by the force and velocity of the rotation (A12, A71). This is surely the source of the claim that the sun is a burning stone or flaming iron, part of the evidence that Anaxagoras was an impious atheist. The force of the moving ingredients causes earthquakes, lightning, and thunder, as well as the motions of comets.[24]

Anaxagoras's scientific theorizing was prodigious and influential. Hippolytus (A42) says that Anaxagoras was the first to explain eclipses and the phases of the moon, and Anaxagoras offered plausible explanations for various meteorological phenomena: hail, thunder, lightning, comets, and meteors. Perhaps because he was a resident in Athens, he is often mentioned as having an effect on the views of Euripides and Pericles. His physical views were clearly well known; Archelaus was reportedly his pupil, and it may well have been Archelaus whom Socrates heard reading from the work of Anaxagoras. As Plato reveals in both the *Apology* and the *Phaedo*, Anaxagoras's views were notorious in Athens.

Although many of Anaxagoras's scientific theories (and their influence) are known to us only through the testimonia, there is a curious and rather mysterious claim in the fragments: the existence of worlds "elsewhere." The evidence is in fragment B4a:

> Since these things are so, it is right to think that there are many different things present in everything that is being combined, and seeds of all things, having all sorts of forms, colors, and flavors, that humans and also the other animals were compounded, as many as have soul. Also that there are cities that have been constructed by humans and works made, just as with us, and that there are a sun and a moon and other heavenly bodies for them, just as with us, and the earth grows many different things for them, the most valuable of which they gather together into their household and use. I have said this about the separation out, because there would be separation out not only for us but also elsewhere.

Where is the "elsewhere" where there is a sun and a moon "just as with us?" Anaxagoras may have meant only that conditions are the same on all parts of the

Earth.[25] Yet, as Simplicius, the source of the fragment, argues, if Anaxagoras means to refer to other places on our Earth, it is odd that he does not say "the sun, the moon, and the other heavenly bodies." Simplicius adds that he thinks the question of just what Anaxagoras did mean is worth investigation. Other interpretations have been suggested: perhaps Anaxagoras refers to worlds beyond our own ken in the mass of ingredients; perhaps he is not referring to any other real worlds at all, but simply performing a thought experiment to show that the action of *Nous* on the original mixture could not have failed to produce a world-system; perhaps, applying the everything-in-everything principle, Anaxagoras means to suggest an infinite nest of world-systems within any compounded thing.[26] While there are supporters for each of these views, neither the thought experiment account nor Simplicius's interpretation stand up to argument.[27]

There are good reasons to think that the multiple-worlds view, properly understood, is correct.[28] I shall defend it by discussing the world-within-worlds interpretation, which, though admittedly strange, seems the best alternative to the multiple-worlds view. The nested-worlds account gains its strength from three considerations, but these reasons are not conclusive. First, Anaxagoras is committed (in B6) to a principle of unlimited smallness (in Schofield's words, "size is not a measure of complexity," so there can be microscopic worlds as complex as our own in any bit of stuff including a drop of my blood, or in the flesh of a dog's paw. Second, it makes little sense to think that *Nous*, the supreme intellect and master of the cosmos, should go on duplicating worlds indefinitely: why should *Nous* make a series of identical worlds? Third, and finally, the doxographic tradition puts Anaxagoras in the group of thinkers who suppose that there is only one world (a—or indefinitely many—world[s] inside our own does not, apparently, violate this principle). In response, we might begin by noting that B4a claims that "there would be separation out not only for us but also elsewhere." "Elsewhere" is not the most perspicuous term to use if Anaxagoras means "inside us." Next, while it is true that Anaxagoras is committed to a principle of indefinite smallness, that smallness applies to the densities of ingredients. Separation and combination indeed apply at all levels, but there is nothing in B4a to suggest that this notion of smallness is at work in the fragment. Nor was there any earlier discussion of smallness and the possible complexity of the small to support what is clearly the most surprising claim that this interpretation would have the fragment make.[29] B4a relies on the everything-in-everything principle, but there is no evidence anywhere that this principle applies to anything but ingredients (the stuffs and the opposites).

With respect to the question of why *Nous* should produce an indefinite number of parallel worlds, it is worth noting that Anaxagoras does not say that the multiple separations produce exactly the same world orders. He merely notes that the process of separation would result in a sun and a moon as with us, and that the same sorts of creatures and activities would be produced. All that this commits Anaxagoras to is the claim that similar ingredients undergoing similar processes will have similar consequences: heavier materials will stay at the center of a whirl, lighter and rarer ingredients will continue to move to the outer reaches of the whirling mass, rocks will be snatched up by the whirl and ignited so as to produce such heavenly bodies as the stars, seeds will produce animals, human beings will settle cities. The main question is whether more than one whirl can occur in the mass of ingredients once it is set in motion by *Nous*. If we examine the evidence of such whirling masses as whirlpools in streams or oceans, the turning masses of clouds in a storm system, or the stars in a mass of heavenly bodies, there is no reason to suppose that Anaxagoras would reject the thought that the first rotation could have developed side whirls and eddies, once it began expanding through the mass of ingredients. Each of these subsidiary whirls is itself moved by the impetus of the original rotation, and so is caused by *Nous*. Yet in each whirl, the particular ratio of ingredients might well produce world-systems that are similar to our own while differing in certain nonessential ways. The edge of any whirl is not the end of the cosmos—there is always a further mass of ingredients waiting to be set in motion, and so a new set of side eddies and rotations can always occur.

Finally, although the doxographers assert that for Anaxagoras there is only a single universe, none notes what would have been a most startling proposition: there is a series of universes embedded in our own. In addition, Aristotle, who was interested in the question of whether there could be more than one universe, makes no claim either way about Anaxagoras's position on the one or many universes question. So, the doxography evidence is moot. It is worth noting, though, that the system that I suggest here does not constitute a multitude of universes. There is but a single universe: the mass of original ingredients. What occurs is a system of world orders within the whole, each system similarly produced by the rotation of the mass of stuffs and opposites that constitute the original entities of Anaxagoras's world. A further advantage of the multiple world-systems with a single universe view is that it gives Anaxagoras a consistent and economical mechanism for the production of each world, and for the course of cosmogonical events in each. It is the rotation begun by *Nous* that does the work. That rotary motion begins the separation out, places the earth at the center, allows for the character and motions of the stars and planets, produces the motions of clouds, and also the moving air under the earth that causes earthquakes. The action of *Nous* in beginning the rotation indeed fabricates our world, and the regular rotation of the mass of ingredients ensures that "there would be separation out not only for us but also elsewhere."

4. Nous and Understanding the World

Anaxagoras claims that *Nous* is the first motive cause of the separations and mixtures that form the cosmos. It is possible that *Nous* serves as the organizing principle of ensouled and hence living things through the agency of seeds. What remains to be explored is the capacities of *Nous* as a knower and cognizer. What does cosmic *Nous* know? Finally, as we (and all living things) possess *nous*, how do our capacities for knowing and understanding compare with those of cosmic *Nous*?

Fragment B12, the longest remaining passage from Anaxagoras, discusses the character and powers of *Nous*. Here are the opening lines:

> The other things have a share of [*moiran*] everything, but *Nous* is unlimited and self-ruling and has been mixed with no thing, but is alone itself by itself. For if it were not by itself, but had been mixed with anything else, then it would partake of all things, if it had been mixed with anything (for there is a share of everything in everything just as I have said before); the things mixed together with it would thwart it, so that it would control none of the things in the way that it in fact does, being alone by itself. It is the finest of all things and the purest, and indeed it maintains all discernment [*gnêmê*] about everything and has the greatest strength. *Nous* has control over all things that have soul, both the larger and the smaller. And *Nous* controlled the whole revolution, so that it started to revolve in the beginning. First it began to revolve from a small region, but it is revolving yet more, and it will revolve still more. And *Nous* knew [*egnô*] them all: the things that are being mixed together, the things that are being separated out, and the things that are being separated apart. Whatever sorts of things were going to be, indeed whatever sorts were and now are not, and as many as are now and whatever will be, all these *Nous* set in order. And *Nous* also ordered this revolution, in which the things being separated out now revolve, the stars and the sun and the moon and the air and the aether.

The passage begins by contrasting *Nous* with all the other basic ingredients: it is altogether unlike them in character and nature; further, unlike all the other things it is not *mixed with* anything, although B11 says it is *in* some things. Anaxagoras then specifies the positive characteristics of *Nous*: it is the purest and finest of all things and it is independent of all the ingredients (I take this to mean that it is not a material entity); it has all discernment and knowledge about all the things that are in the mixture and how they will combine and recombine to produce all the contents of the sensible world; it began, controls, and orders the revolution that produced separation, and thus the mixture and the breaking up of mixtures that humans take to be coming-to-be and passing-away. Central to this role is the claim that *Nous* knew all things, for it is this that allows *Nous* to be the ordering and controlling principle.[30]

That *Nous* plays this role is clear from the testimonia. While Plato's Socrates complained that Anaxagoras failed to provide teleological explanations of natural phenomena, Aristotle commends Anaxagoras for claiming that *Nous* operates in the natural world as well as in ensouled things:

> When someone said that *Nous* is present—in nature just as it is in animals—as the cause of the cosmos and of all its order, he appeared as a sober man among the random chatterers who preceded him. We know that Anaxagoras clearly held

these views, but Hermotimus of Clazomenae gets the credit for holding them earlier. (*Metaph.* 1.3.984b15; A58)

Aristotle's comment here suggests that Anaxagoras's account of the role of *Nous* was teleological in some sense, although perhaps not in the way Socrates would have demanded. B12 indicates that *Nous* understands and grasps the natures of each of the ingredients (the stuffs and opposites) in the original mix. Although Anaxagoras makes clear that no thing is entirely separable in actuality, he also implies that *Nous* is capable of grasping these natures, thus guaranteeing that what is metaphysically basic is also epistemologically basic (just as Parmenides' arguments demand). According to Anaxagoras, it is *Nous*'s knowledge that allows it to be the ordering principle and to direct the revolutions whose separating action produces the natural world. A problem here is that Anaxagoras himself seems not to have made clear how much of the rotary motion that drives the cosmos is purely mechanical (once it is put into motion by *Nous*) and how much of the development of the world can be attributed to actions of *Nous* itself. Neither the fragments nor the testimonia suggest that there is much room for decision-making by *Nous*, once the original rotation is begun.[31] Nevertheless, it seems clear from B12 that *Nous* knows the natures of the ingredients before the rotation begins: the rotation is not a process by which *Nous* comes to know; rather it is a process of world-making that *Nous* understands and begins in order that it take place. Fragment B12 stresses the power and control that *Nous* has and exercises. Separate from the ingredients (it is not in the world as an ingredient of the original mixture), *Nous* is a nonmaterial and intelligent force of the entire cosmos. As present in some things (as B11 says), *Nous* also acts as the local individual controlling force for those things that have soul: differing degrees of *nous*—the larger and the smaller—would account for the different capacities of living things.

The epistemological connection between *Nous* and the ingredients also allows for the intelligibility of the world. Because *Nous* grasps the natures of the ingredients, and because, as B12 claims, "All *Nous* is alike, both the greater and the smaller," *nous* in us (smaller *nous*) at least has the possibility of coming to understand the world around us. We do not have the complete, direct intellectual grasp that *Nous* itself does, because in us *nous* is present in a way that prevents it from fully actualizing its capacity to know: in ensouled beings it is contaminated by ingredients and opposites in a manner that can sometimes thwart its power. In us *nous* is unable always to grasp directly but must begin with sense-perception, which can be misleading (see B21). Yet we are capable of coming to know through the proper use of our senses. As Anaxagoras says, "appearances are a glimpse of the unseen" (B21a). Using our senses and our reasoning capacity, we can work out how things are (or must be)—perhaps as Anaxagoras himself was able to do, relying on evidence to construct a theory that explains and saves the phenomena. The claims of B12 suggest that our experience of our own understanding and decision making is a glimpse of the activities of pure cosmic *Nous*.

NOTES

1. There is much uncertainty about the dating of Anaxagoras's life and works (see Mansfeld, "The Chronology of Anaxagoras' Athenian Period and the Date of His Trial," for a good account of the controversy). Anaxagoras came from Clazomenae on the west coast of what is now Turkey; he was in Athens around the midcentury, and was a friend of Pericles. He was tried for impiety and exiled from Athens (see testimonia in 59 A1, A17, A18, A20, A35). Aristotle's comments in Book 1 of his *Metaphysics* (A43) show that Anaxagoras and Empedocles were close contemporaries, with Anaxagoras the elder of the two.

2. For the Milesians and the medical tradition, see the contributions by White and van der Eijk in this volume. In much of the doxographical tradition, Anaxagoras is linked with Anaximenes (see A1, A2, A3, A7, A41, A42, and A48). These reports often say that Anaximenes was the teacher of Anaxagoras, which is impossible on chronological grounds; in A65, A85, A88, and A93, Anaximenes and Anaxagoras are reported as sharing views. Runia (in this volume) discusses the problems of interpreting the doxographical evidence about the Presocratics.

3. Fuller discussion of the relevance of Parmenides' arguments can be found in Furley, "Anaxagoras in Response to Parmenides," Furley, "Anaxagoras, Plato, and the Naming of Parts," Furth, "A 'Philosophical Hero',", and Curd, *Anaxagoras.*

4. See Mourelatos, *The Route of Parmenides.* I discussed the Parmenidean questions in some detail in Curd, *The Legacy of Parmenides.* A close analysis of Parmenides' arguments is given in McKirahan's essay in this volume. Although there are points of disagreement between us, both my analysis and McKirahan's differ from traditional accounts of Parmenides as can be found in Gallop, *Parmenides of Elea*, Kirk, Raven, and Schofield, *The Presocratic Philosophers*, and Sedley, "Parmenides and Melissus."

5. We need not claim that later philosophers were primarily concerned to answer Parmenides, or that the point of their cosmological inquiry was to show, in the face of Parmenides' criticisms of earlier thinkers, that cosmology is even possible. Rather, understanding Parmenides' arguments about what is metaphysically and epistemologically basic, later Presocratic theories function within a Parmenidean framework. Whether or not the atomists also follow this pattern is controversial. Plato and Aristotle also recognized the strengths of Parmenides' arguments: see Plato's *Parmenides* and *Sophist*, and Aristotle on the principles of change in *Physics* 1 (where he agrees that there can be no change from or into what is not *simpliciter*; rather change is always from and into what is not in some qualified way). This view of Parmenides is challenged by Osborne in "Was there an Eleatic Revolution in Philosophy?"

6. Another topic that has much engaged scholars is the so-called principle of homoiomereity in Anaxagoras. Following discussions in Aristotle, Simplicius claimed that Anaxagoras counted "the homoiomerous parts" (things whose parts are like the whole) as elements. This account seems at odds with the everything-in-everything principle. Recent scholarship has tended to reject the idea that Anaxagoras himself used the term "homoiomerous" or thought of his ingredients in that way. See Graham, "The Postulates of Anaxagoras," and Curd, *Anaxagoras*, for discussion.

7. Clear statements of the problem can be found in Vlastos, "The Physical Theory of Anaxagoras"; Schofield, *An Essay on Anaxagoras*; and especially Strang, "The Physical Theory of Anaxagoras." Helpful discussions may be found in Peck, "Anaxagoras and the Parts." For contemporary analysis of the Anaxagorean problem, see Matthews, "On the Idea of There Being Something of Everything in Everything," a response by Sisko,

"Anaxagoras and Recursive Refinement," and rejoinder by Matthews, "Anaxagoras Re-Defended."

8. Particulate: Lucretius (A44), *HGP*, Kerferd, "Anaxagoras and the Concept of Matter Before Aristotle," Sorabji, *Matter, Space, and Motion*, Lewis, "Anaxagoras and the Seeds of a Physical Theory"; against the particulate view: *PP*; Schofield, *An Essay on Anaxagoras*, contains a full and careful discussion of the matter and a strong argument in favor of the nonparticulate account. I consider the arguments for and against, and defend my interpretation in Curd, *The Legacy of Parmenides* (chap. 4) and *Anaxagoras* (essay 3, "Everything in Everything").

9. On this interpretation of *large* and *small*, I follow Inwood, "Anaxagoras and Infinite Divisibility," and Furth, "A 'Philosophical Hero.'" Sometimes Anaxagoras uses the terms "large" and "small" in their ordinary sense of size, but the specialized sense also occurs.

10. The text of B3 is difficult. For a discussion of the apparent difficulties of the text as printed, see Schofield, *An Essay on Anaxagoras*, 156–57 n. 15. I here accept the text as printed in DK. This is apparently the reading in all the manuscripts (at least there are no variants in the apparatus to DK, in Diels's edition of Simplicius's *Commentary* on book 1 of the *Physics*, or in Schaubach's text of Anaxagoras). This is an unusual construction, and I leave it as written. Defenders of the manuscript text (with various translations and interpretations) include Lanza, *Anassagora*, *HGP*, Jöhrens, *Die Fragmente des Anaxagoras*, Raven (KRS), Stokes, "On Anaxagoras," Wright, *The Presocratics*. Zeller suggested eliding τὸ μὴ into τομῇ; adding μὴ gives τὸ γὰρ ἐὸν οὐκ ἔστι τομῇ <μὴ> οὐκ εἶναι, accepted by Sider in *The Fragments of Anaxagoras* and translated by him: "For that which is cannot be cut away to nothing."

11. The expansive view can be found in *PP*, Furth, "A 'Philosophical Hero,'" Mourelatos, "Quality, Structure, and Emergence in Later Pre-Socratic Philosophy."

12. The reductionist view can be found in Tannery, "La théorie de la matière d' Anaxagore," Schofield, *An Essay on Anaxagoras*, Inwood, "Anaxagoras and Infinite Divisibility, and now in Sedley, *Creationism.*"

13. See Graham, "Was Anaxagoras a Reductionist?" and Curd, *The Legacy of Parmenides*, chap. 4, for discussions of the lists Anaxagoras provides.

14. Schofield argues for the opposites or reductionist position in *An Essay on Anaxagoras*. The opposites view must reject B10 as authentic (as does Schofield, "Doxographica Anaxagorea") and also explain away the references in B1, B2, B4a and B4b. Further discussion and arguments against the reductionist view can be found in Graham, "Was Anaxagoras a Reductionist?" Sedley defends the reductionist view in *Creationism* (pp. 26–30). See also Warren.

15. It is not clear that we should read B16 as describing a cosmological separation (such as occurs in B13) from the original state described in B1 and B2; a number of commentators have taken it as a meteorological account, describing the phenomena between the surface of the earth and heavens. See *PP*, Graham, "Was Anaxagoras a Reductionist?" Curd, *Anaxagoras*, Stokes, "On Anaxagoras," Sider, *The Fragments of Anaxagoras*.

16. In B4a, Anaxagoras indicates that houses and other artifacts are produced by persons.

17. I am assuming that Parmenides would countenance what I have elsewhere called "rational cosmology." Nothing about the interpretation of Anaxagoras offered here depends on accepting this nonrestrictive interpretation of Parmenides' attitude to cosmology.

18. The problem of the structure of living things will be discussed later.

19. I say "apparently" here because there is no direct discussion of void in the fragments. B3 suggests that there can be no what-is-not (although the direct claim is only that

what-is cannot not be). The testimonia claim that Anaxagoras did not allow for void (Hippolytus in A42; Lucretius in A44; and Aristotle in A50 A68, and A115; along with pseudo-Aristotle in A50).

20. Recall that for the Greeks, meteorology is the study of any event or phenomenon between the surface of the earth and the lunar regions.

21. A classic statement of the problem is to be found in Mourelatos, "Quality, Structure, and Emergence in Later Presocratic Philosophy."

22. Simplicius nowhere quotes B4 continuously; for DK, Diels constructed it from passages where various quotations overlap. Fränkel (see Jöhrens, *Die Fragmente des Anaxagoras*, 38, and Fränkel, *Wege und Formen*, 287), argued that the whole passage came from three quotes that do not belong together. Following him, commentators now usually divide DK's text into two parts, B4a (the first 12 lines of B4 as it appears in DK) and B4b (the rest of the fragment).

23. This account of seeds as biological starting points follows Furley's interpretation. A number of scholars have read the mention of seeds as epexegetical: the opposites are "the seeds of all things" (see Vlastos, "The Physical Theory of Anaxagoras," and Inwood, "Anaxagoras and Infinite Divisibility"). Yet leaving biological seeds out of the original mixture opens a gap in Anaxagoras's theory: he would then have no account of the production of living things from the ingredients.

24. Clear and helpful discussions of Anaxagoras's views can be found in Tigner, "Stars, Unseen Bodies and the Extent of the Earth in Anaxagoras' Cosmogony."

25. That some ancient scholars took this to be Anaxagoras's meaning is suggested by Simplicius's rejection of that interpretation. Among modern scholars, Cornford, "Innumerable Worlds in Presocratic Philosophy," *HGP*, McKirahan, *Philosophy before Socrates*, adopt this view (with varying degrees of enthusiasm); a variation of this view is that Anaxagoras meant the moon (Zeller, *Die Philosophie der Griechen*) or the moon and other planets in our heaven (Jöhrens, *Die Fragmente des Anaxagoras*). Simplicius himself offered a Neoplatonist account involving multiple levels of separation.

26. The other-worlds-in-the-universe view: Burnet, *Early Greek Philosophy*, PP, Gigon, "Zu Anaxagoras," Sedley. The thought experiment: Fränkel, *Wege und Formen*, Vlastos, "One World or Many in Anaxagoras?" Furley, "Anaxagoras in Response to Parmenides," Schofield, *An Essay on Anaxagoras*, Sider, *The Fragments of Anaxagoras*. Worlds within worlds: Leon, "The Homoiomeries of Anaxagoras," Strang, "On Anaxagoras," Mansfeld, "Anaxagoras' Other World," Schofield, "Anaxagoras' Other World Revisited," Waterfield, *The First Philosophers*.

27. Schofield has argued that the thought experiment interpretation founders on textual problems: on that view, "it is right to think" must have two different meanings in B4a, both "we really must think x" and "we must counterfactually suppose y." In addition, why should Anaxagoras say that separation would have happened elsewhere, if the point of the passage is to show that things cannot have been otherwise than they are here? (Schofield's arguments may be found in his "Anaxagoras' Other World Revisited.") Further discussion of the thought experiment interpretation may be found in Louguet, "Note sur le fragment B4a d'Anaxagore." Simplicius's interpretation has been accepted as a nonstarter, since it is embedded in Simplicius's own Neoplatonist worldview. The other-places-on-earth interpretation, according to Vlastos ("One World or Many in Anaxagoras?"), fails because the other separation that Anaxagoras mentions should be cosmogonical—it should produce another world, not merely refer to another view of our world.

28. The arguments I give here are condensed from the fuller discussions of all these interpretations in essay 5, "Anaxagorean Science," in *Anaxagoras*.

29. Further, on this interpretation, "large" and "small" would have *always* to refer to size rather than to density or degree of submergence in the mixture, as I have argued that they do.

30. Discussions of the character of *Nous* can be found in Laks, "Mind's Crisis," De-Filippo, "Reply to André Laks on Anaxagoras' NOUS," Lesher, "Mind's Knowledge and Powers of Control in Anaxagoras DK B12," Menn, *Plato on God as "Nous,"* and Curd, *The Legacy of Parmenides*, and *Anaxagoras*.

31. See Laks, "Mind's Crisis," and Lesher, "Mind's Knowledge and Powers of Control in Anaxagoras DK B12," on this problem. Plato (through Socrates in the *Phaedo*, at 97b8-c2) claims that *Nous* is merely a motive cause. Aristotle found this a difficulty in Anaxagoras's theory (see his comment at *Metaph.* 1.4.985a18: "Anaxagoras uses *Nous* as a *deus ex machina* in world making, and he drags it in whenever he is puzzled about the reason why something is as it is necessarily, but in other cases he makes the causes of what happens everything except *Nous*").

BIBLIOGRAPHY

Burnet, J. *Early Greek Philosophy*. 4th edition. London: Adam and Charles Black, 1930.

Cornford, F. M. "Anaxagoras's Theory of Matter." *Classical Quarterly* 24 (1930) 14–30; 83–95. Reprinted in Furley and Allen, 2:275-322. All references here are to the latter.

———. "Innumerable Worlds in Presocratic Philosophy." *Classical Quarterly* 28 (1934) 1–16.

Curd, P. *Anaxagoras of Clazomenae: Fragments and Testimonia; A Text and Translation with Notes and Essays*. Toronto: University of Toronto Press, 2007.

———. *The Legacy of Parmenides: Eleatic Monism and Later Presocratic Thought*. Princeton, N.J.: Princeton University Press, 1998.

DeFillipo, J. G. "Reply to André Laks on Anaxagoras' NOUS." *Southern Journal of Philosophy* 31, supp. vol. (1993): 39–48.

Fränkel, H. *Wege und Formen*, 3rd ed. Munich: C. H. Beck, 1969.

Furley, D. J. "Anaxagoras, Plato, and the Naming of Parts." In *Presocratic Philosophy: Essays in Honor of A. P. D. Mourelatos*, edited by V. Caston and D. Graham, 119–26. Aldershot, England: Ashgate, 2002.

———. "Anaxagoras in Response to Parmenides." In *Cosmic Problems*, 47–65. Cambridge: Cambridge University Press, 1989.

Furley, D. J., and R. E. Allen, eds. *Studies in Presocratic Philosophy*, 2 vols. London: Routledge and Kegan Paul, vol. 1, 1970, vol. 2, 1975.

Furth, M. "A 'Philosophical Hero?' Anaxagoras and the Eleatics." *Oxford Studies in Ancient Philosophy* 9 (1991): 95–129.

Gallop, D. *Parmenides of Elea: Fragments*. Toronto: University of Toronto Press, 1984.

Gigon, O. "Zu Anaxagoras." *Philologus* 91 (1936/7) 1–41.

Graham, D. "The Postulates of Anaxagoras." *Apeiron* 27 (1994): 77–121.

———. "Was Anaxagoras a Reductionist?" *Ancient Philosophy* 24 (2004): 1–18.

Inwood, B. "Anaxagoras and Infinite Divisibility." *Illinois Classical Studies* 11 (1986): 17–33.

Jöhrens, O. *Die Fragmente des Anaxagoras*. Bochum-Langendreer: Druck, Heinrich Pöppinghaus, 1939.

Kerferd, G. B. "Anaxagoras and the Concept of Matter before Aristotle." *Bulletin of the John Rylands Library* 52 (1969): 129–43. Reprinted in *The Pre-socratics*, edited by A. P. D. Mourelatos, 489–503. Garden City, N.Y.: Doubleday, 1974. All references here are to the latter.

Laks, A. "Mind's Crisis: On Anaxagoras's NOUS." *Southern Journal of Philosophy* 31 (1993) Supplementary Volume, 19–38.

Laks, A., and C. Louguet, eds. *Qu'est-ce que la philosophie présocratique?* Villeneuve d'Ascq: Presses Universitaires du Septentrion, 2002.

Lanza, D. *Anassagora: Testimonianze e frammenti*. Florence: La Nuova Italia, 1966.

Lesher, J. H. "Mind's Knowledge and Powers of Control in Anaxagoras DK B12," *Phronesis* 40 (1995): 125–42.

Leon, P. "The Homoiomeries of Anaxagoras." *Classical Quarterly* 21 (1927): 133–41.

Lewis, E. "Anaxagoras and the Seeds of a Physical Theory." *Apeiron* 33 (2000): 1–23.

Lloyd, G. E. R. *Polarity and Analogy*. Cambridge: Cambridge University Press, 1966.

Louguet, C. "Note sur le fragment B4a d'Anaxagore: Pourquoi les autres mondes doivent-ils être semblables au notre?" In *Qu'est-ce que la philosophie présocratique?* edited by A. Laks and C. Louguet, 497–530. Lille: Presses Universitaires du Septentrion, 2002.

Mansfeld, J. "Anaxagoras' Other World." *Phronesis* 25 (1980): 1–4.

———. "The Chronology of Anaxagoras' Athenian Period and the Date of his Trial." Pt. 1: "The Length and Dating of the Athenian Period." *Mnemosyne* 32 (1979) 39–69; reprinted (with pt. 2, "The Plot against Pericles and his Associates," *Mnemosyne* 33 [1980]: 84–95) in *Studies in the Historiography of Greek Philosophy*, 264–306. Assen: Van Gorcum, 1990. All references here are to the latter version.

Matthews, G. B. "Anaxagoras Re-defended." *Ancient Philosophy* 25 (2005): 245–46.

———. "On the Idea of There Being Something of Everything in Everything." *Analysis* 62 (2002): 1–4.

McKirahan, R. *Philosophy before Socrates*. Indianapolis: Hackett, 1994.

Menn, S. *Plato on God as* Nous. Carbondale: Southern Illinois University Press, 1995.

Mourelatos, A. P. D., ed. *The Pre-Socratics*. Princeton, NJ: Princeton University Press, 1993.

———. "Quality, Structure, and Emergence in Later Presocratic Philosophy." In *Proceedings of the Boston Area Colloquium in Ancient Philosophy*, vol. 2, edited by J. Cleary, 127–194. Lanham, Md.: University Press of America, 1987.

———. *The Route of Parmenides*. New Haven, Conn.: Yale University Press, 1971.

Osborne, C. "Was there an Eleatic Revolution in Philosophy?" In *Rethinking Revolutions Through Ancient Greece*, edited by S. Goldhill and R. Osborne, 218–245. Cambridge: Cambridge University Press, 2006.

Peck, A. L. "Anaxagoras and the Parts." *Classical Quarterly* 20 (1926): 57–71.

———. "Anaxagoras: Predication as a Problem in Physics." *Classical Quarterly* 25 (1931): 27–37; 112–20.

Schofield, M. "Anaxagoras' Other World Revisited." In *Polyhistor: Studies in the History and Historiography of Ancient Philosophy*, edited by K. Algra, P. Van der Horst, and D. T. Runia, 3–20. Leiden: Brill, 1996.

———. "Doxographica Anaxagorea." *Hermes* 103 (1975): 1–24.

———. *An Essay on Anaxagoras*. Cambridge: Cambridge University Press, 1980.

———. Review of P. Curd, *Anaxagoras of Clazomenae, Notre Dame Philosophical Review* 2008. (March 26). <http://ndpr.nd.edu/review.cfm?id=12746>

Sedley, D. *Creationism and Its Critics in Antiquity*. Berkeley: University of California Press, 2007.

————. "Parmenides and Melissus." In *The Cambridge Companion to Early Greek Philosophy*, edited by A.A. Long, 113–33. Cambridge: Cambridge University Press, 1999.

Sider, D. *The Fragments of Anaxagoras: Edited with an Introduction and Commentary*. 2nd ed. Sankt Augustin, Germany: Academia Verlag, 2005.

Sisko, J. E. "Anaxagoras and Recursive Refinement." *Ancient Philosophy* 25 (2005): 239–45.

Sorabji, R. *Matter, Space, and Motion: Theories in Antiquity and their Sequel*. Ithaca, N.Y.: Cornell University Press, 1988.

Stokes, M. C. "On Anaxagoras." Pt. 1. "Anaxagoras' Theory of Matter." Pt. 2. "The Order of Cosmogony." *Archiv für Geschichte der Philosophie* 47 (1965): 1–19; 217–50, respectively.

Strang, C. "The Physical Theory of Anaxagoras." *Archiv für Geschichte der Philosophie* 45 (1963): 101–18. Reprinted in D. Furley and R. E. Allen, eds., *Studies in Presocratic Philosophy*, 2:361–80. All references here are to the latter version.

Tannery, P. "La théorie de la matière d'Anaxagore." *Revue Philosophique* 22 (1886): 255–74.

Tigner, S. S. "Stars, Unseen Bodies, and the Extent of the Earth in Anaxagoras's Cosmogony: Three Problems and their Simultaneous Solution." In *Arktouros: Hellenic Studies Presented to Bernard M.W. Knox*, edited by G. W. Bowersock, W. Burkert, and M. C. J. Putnam, 330–35. Berlin: de Gruyter, 1979.

Vlastos, G. "One World or Many in Anaxagoras?" In D. Furley and R.E. Allen, eds. *Studies in Presocratic Philosophy*, 2:354–60.

————. "The Physical Theory of Anaxagoras." *Philosophical Review* 59 (1950): 31–57. Reprinted in G. Vlastos, *The Presocratics*, vol. 1 of *Studies in Greek Philosophy*, edited by D. Graham, 303–27. Princeton, N.J.: Princeton University Press, 1995.

Warren, J."Anaxagoras on Perception, Pleasure, and Pain," *Oxford Studies in Ancient Philosophy* 33 (2007): 19–54.

————. *Presocratics*. Stocksfield, UK: Acumen, 2007.

Waterfield, R. *The First Philosophers*. Oxford: Oxford University Press, 2000.

Wright, M. R. *The Presocratics*. Bristol: The Bristol Classical Press, 1985.

CHAPTER 8

EMPEDOCLES: PHYSICAL AND MYTHICAL DIVINITY

OLIVER PRIMAVESI

1. NEW EVIDENCE AND OLD PROBLEMS

Our textual knowledge about the philosophical poetry of Empedocles[1] has been significantly improved by several recent findings. For the first time, fragments of direct transmission, that is, from an ancient papyrus scroll containing a poem of Empedocles, have been identified.[2] New *testimonia* of crucial importance have been discovered.[3] Two Empedoclean quotations, preserved, respectively, by a carbonized papyrus and by the lower script of a palimpsest manuscript, could be read in a reliable way by means of new techniques of photography.[4] Finally, the artificial fog surrounding the Hellenistic catalogue of Empedocles' works[5] has been dispelled: the original form of the catalogue—as reconstructed from the summary offered by Diogenes Laertius[6] in conjunction with a lacunose version of the full text preserved in the *Suda*[7]—mentions *two* poems of *different size*, that is, *Peri physeos* (3,000 lines in at least three books) and *Katharmoi* (2,000 lines in two books).[8]

Diogenes Laertius lists both *Peri physeos* and the *Katharmoi* and attributes 5,000 lines to both titles taken together, whereas the *Suda* in its transmitted form mentions only *Peri physeos tōn ontōn* and links this title with the book-number 2 and the line-number 2,000. The version of the *Suda* is incompatible with *two* other witnesses: Apart from the discrepancy between the *Suda* (one poem-title; 2,000 lines) and Diogenes Laertius (two poem-titles; 5,000 lines) there is a further discrepancy between the *Suda* (two books for *Peri physeos*)[9] and Tzetzes (a *third* book of the *Physika*).[10] According to Occam's razor,[11] we must explain both discrepancies, if possible, by one and the same mistake. The obvious explanation is that a scribe has left out in the text of the *Suda* not only the title *Katharmoi* but also, immediately before that title, the book- and line-numbers for *Peri physeos*, and that he jumped from the title *Peri physeos* directly to a book-number (2) and a line-number (2,000) that refer, in fact, to the *Katharmoi*.[12] The line-number for *Peri physeos* can be reconstructed by subtracting the preserved line-number 2,000 from the total of 5,000 attested by Diogenes Laertius.[13]

The contribution of the new factual knowledge to the longstanding problems of Empedoclean scholarship remains to be assessed.

A basic account of the teachings of Empedocles would distinguish between two main components. On the one hand, we have a "Presocratic" physics, including a theory of principles, a cosmology, and a biology. On the other hand, there is a mythical law (B115), clearly inspired by Orphic or Pythagorean legends,[14] which imposes on guilty gods (called *daimones*) a punishment consisting in their transmigration through a series of mortal beings, and which is somehow linked to an advocacy of vegetarianism.[15]

The first known attempt at making philosophical sense of Empedocles' mythical law was made by Plutarch: according to him, the punishment of the guilty gods (*daimones*) by transmigration is meant to *allegorize* the imprisonment of incorporeal *souls* in a series of mortal bodies:[16] the guilty gods (*daimones*) of Empedocles stand, as it were, for the immaterial souls of the Platonic tradition. Within the framework of Middle-Platonism, Plutarch's decoding of the Empedoclean myth looks, of course, fairly natural. Within the attested fragments of Empedoclean poetry, however, the notion of individual transmigratory "souls" is entirely absent, as Wilamowitz pointed out in 1929.[17]

Furthermore, Plutarch's interpretation does not offer anything like a solution to the central difficulty in interpreting Empedocles, namely, to the difficulty of reconciling Empedocles' physical theory with the assumption of *any* kind of personal transmigratory entity—be it guilty gods or fallen souls.

In modern times, there have been two main strategies in dealing with this difficulty:

1. Divorce: separating the transmigratory *daimones* and the physical theory by dividing them up among the two different poem-titles attested for Empedocles (*Katharmoi* and *Physika*), and assuming that Empedocles' philosophical tenets underwent a radical change during his lifetime.[18]
2. Compromise: Providing the myth of transmigration with (unattested) chemical formulae so as to make it compatible with the physical system to a certain extent,[19] or mitigating the determinism of the physical system by

means of (unattested) ethical saving clauses so as to leave a space for the moral responsibility so strongly urged by the mythical law.[20]

Both strategies are unsatisfactory, since the first does not account for the obvious parallelism between mythical law and physical system, whereas the second plays down the undeniable tensions between the two. Therefore, a third option should be examined, which has sometimes been hinted at, but never been fully exploited: interpreting the Empedoclean account of the transmigratory *daimones* as a mythological mirror,[21] not of the Platonic theory of the soul (as Plutarch did) but of Empedocles' physical theory itself.[22] This option should not be confused with the interpretation favored by the Neoplatonists, according to which there would be an allegorical one-way street: the Neoplatonists presupposed Plutarch's equation of Empedocles' guilty gods with Platonic souls and then came to regard Empedocles' whole physical system as an allegory of the Neoplatonic theory of the soul.[23]

The purpose of this chapter is to show that Empedocles has the habit of referring to divine entities of his physical system both in a physical and in a mythological way and that his uses of the word *daimon* form part of this twofold language.[24]

2. Physical and Mythological References to the "Long-Lived Gods"

2.1. Introduction: The Cosmic Cycle and Its Timetable

2.1.1. *The Structure of the Cycle*

For Empedocles the history of the world is a twofold story, a *cycle*[25] dominated by an alternation of two movements: (1) from many to one, and (2) from one to many.[26] The movement from many to one takes place under the rule of Love (Philotes); the movement from one to many takes place under the rule of Strife (Neikos).[27] The substrate of these two movements are the four elements fire, water, earth, and air.[28]

Movement (1) starts from a state of complete separation of the four elements and leads to a state of their complete unity. It is described as a centrifugal expansion of Love—starting at the center of the universe—which causes the gradual unification of the four elements by means of a zoogony:[29] Love is gradually pushing Strife back toward the periphery,[30] and wherever Strife has left, Love creates living beings by mixing the four elements.[31]

During the state of total unity, the four elements in their entirety form one single living being, the Sphairos. The Sphairos is at rest;[32] Strife is excluded.[33] Although the Sphairos is capable of emotions,[34] his anthropomorphic representation is explicitly rejected:[35] the Sphairos is ball-shaped,[36] as his name indicates.

Movement (2) starts with the destruction of the Sphairos[37] and leads back to the state of complete separation of the four elements. The separative activity of Strife enables the four elements to exercise their innate tendency toward homogeneity:[38] at first, air and fire (or, rather, a mixture of air and fire)[39] are set free, then earth discharges water.[40] It is a much-disputed question whether during the movement toward complete separation there is a (second) zoogony.[41] The main evidence in favor of a separate zoogony under the rule of Strife is, apart from B17.3–5 as emended by Panzerbieter,[42] the report on the four zoogonical stages given by Aëtius in A72. This *testimonium* shows that the transition from the first to the second stage is due to increasing unification, whereas the transition from the third to the fourth stage is due to increasing separation:[43]

> Empedocles says that the *first* generations of animals and plants were not at all whole, but were disjointed with parts not grown together; and the *second* generations were like dream images, with the parts growing together; the *third* were whole-natured; the *fourth* were no longer produced from homoeomerous substances like earth and water, but at this stage they were produced by each other, since in some of them the nourishment was condensed, while in others the beauty of the women kindled the movement of the semen, too.

It should be emphasized that the assumption of a zoogony during the phase of increasing separation would by no means imply that living beings are actually *created* by Strife: they could be created by Love, who is still resisting Strife, although her ability to do so is gradually declining.

During the state of complete separation, there are four homogeneous masses characterized by Plutarch as a radical anticipation of the Aristotelian and Stoic doctrine of separate natural places for the elements:[44] the center is occupied by the terrestrial globe, which is surrounded by the three spherical layers of water, air, and fire. According to Plutarch, the four separate masses are in motion; this is to a certain extent confirmed by B35, which shows that at least Love and Strife are moving until the very end of the state of total separation.

2.1.2. *The New Timetable of the Cycle*

It was suggested by O'Brien, *Empedocles' Cosmic Cycle*, that the life span of the Sphairos takes one-half of the cycle, whereas the remaining half is divided up equally among the movement toward complete separation (2) and the movement toward complete unification (1). By consequence, the state of complete separation between movement (2) and movement (1) would have to be instantaneous.[45] However, the recently discovered Florentine scholia on Aristotle on Empedocles presuppose a very different timetable:[46]

- According to scholia *b* and *c*, Love's rule, which is restricted to the movement toward complete unification, lasts for 60 time-units (*chronoi*). Between the end of the movement toward complete unification and the beginning of the movement toward complete separation, there is a time of rest for Love, too.[47]
- "Whenever," says Aristotle, "Empedocles has brought the entirety of existing things, except Strife, together into one, he maintains that each element once more comes-to-be out of the One."[48] According to scholia *f* and *g*, the first of the two achievements mentioned by Aristotle, that is, the formation of the Sphairos, is accomplished at the end point of Love's rule,[49] whereas the second achievement, that is, the formation of the four elements by means of a process of separation, will be accomplished *100 time-units later*,[50] and since this achievement will, according to scholium *g*, coincide *with the end point of Strife's rule*,[51] the scholium clearly identifies the formation of the four elements as mentioned by Aristotle with the formation of the pure elementary masses.[52] Strife's rule is restricted to the movement (2) toward full separation in the same way as Love's rule is restricted to the movement (1) toward full unification, and between the end point of Love's rule and the corresponding end point of Strife's rule there is an interval of 100 time-units.
- According to scholia *d* and *e*, Strife's rule and Love's rule alternate in intervals of 10,000 (years).[53] This interval is obviously equivalent to the interval of 100 time-units mentioned in scholium *g*. The equivalence yields two conclusions. First, one "time-unit" (*chronos*) equals 100 years. Second, whereas the scholia *d* and *e* state the law on the interval between Love's rule and Strife's rule in general terms, the correct application of that law is illustrated by scholium *g*: the interval of 10,000 years mentioned in scholia *d* and *e* will not obtain between the end of one period of rule and the beginning of the other, but rather between the end point of Love's rule and the end point of Strife's rule (and similarly between the starting point of Love's rule and the starting point of Strife's rule).[54] Furthermore, the general law is symmetrical, in that it describes not only the temporal relationship between Love's rule and the following rule of Strife but also that between Strife's rule and the following rule of Love.

With this in hand, we can proceed to a new reconstruction of the cosmic cycle.

- Between the starting point of Love's rule (destruction of the four pure masses) and the starting point of Strife's rule (destruction of the Sphairos) there is an interval of 100 time-units. Since the first 60 time-units of this interval are allotted to Love's rule, 40 time-units will be left over for the life span of the Sphairos.
- Between the end point of Love's rule (coming-to-be of the Sphairos) and the end point of Strife's rule (coming-to-be of the four pure masses) there is an

interval of 100 time-units. Since the first 40 time-units of this interval are allotted to the Sphairos, 60 time-units will remain for the rule of Strife, that is, for the movement toward full separation.

• Between the starting point of Strife's rule (destruction of the *Sphairos*) and the starting point of Love's rule (destruction of the four pure masses) there is an interval of 100 time-units. Since the first 60 time-units of this interval are allotted to Strife's rule, 40 time-units will be left over for the life span of the four pure masses.

Thus, we arrive at the following timetable of the cosmic cycle (to be read clockwise):

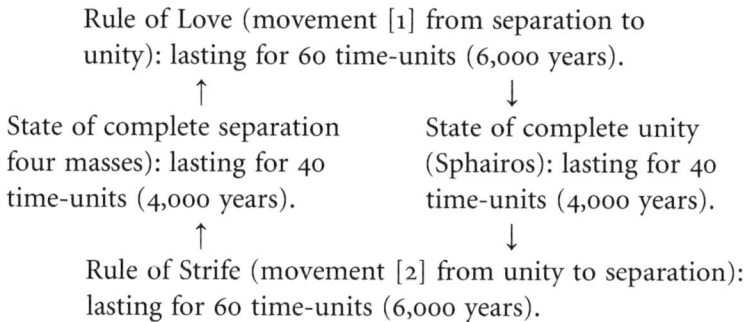

Rule of Love (movement [1] from separation to unity): lasting for 60 time-units (6,000 years).

↑   ↓

State of complete separation   State of complete unity
four masses): lasting for 40   (Sphairos): lasting for 40
time-units (4,000 years).   time-units (4,000 years).

↑   ↓

Rule of Strife (movement [2] from unity to separation): lasting for 60 time-units (6,000 years).

The decisive difference between this timetable and the scheme suggested by O'Brien is that according to O'Brien, the four pure masses would exist only for a moment's time, whereas according to the timetable presupposed by the scholia, the life span of the four pure masses is the same length as the life span of the Sphairos. This has considerable implications for the theological meaning of the cosmic cycle, as we will see in the following paragraph.

2.2. The Five Long-Lived Gods of the Cosmic Cycle

Among the fragments of Empedocles' poem *On Nature*, there are two passages where *long-lived gods* appear in a list of all beings[55] that are made from the four elements during the history of the world:

1. *Physika* 1.267–72
[But in Love] we come together to form a single ordered whole,
[Whereas in Hatred, in turn, it grew apart,] so as to be many out of one,
From which come all beings that were, all that are, and all that will be hereafter:
Trees sprang up, and men and women,
And beasts, and birds, and fish nurtured in water,
And even long-lived gods, unrivaled in their prerogatives.[56]
2. B21.7–12
In Anger they have different forms and are all apart,
But in Love they come together and are desired by one another.

For from these come all beings that were, all that are, and that will be:
Trees sprang up, and men and women
And beasts, and birds, and fish nurtured in water,
And even long-lived gods, unrivaled in their prerogatives.[57]

Who are these long-lived gods? The preceding items of the list clearly belong to the physical universe: trees, men and women, beasts, birds, and fish. This strongly suggests that the long-lived gods will form part of the physical universe as well: what we need, then, is a set of divine beings who consist of the four elements and are long-lived, but not eternal: they must come to be and pass away naturally during the cosmic cycle. One divine being fulfilling these conditions comes to mind immediately: the Sphairos, who is explicitly called a *god* in B31.[58] He is not *eternal*, since he comes to be at the end of movement (1) and passes away at the beginning of movement (2), but he is, of course, *long-lived*: his life span amounts to 4,000 years, according to the Florentine scholia.

And yet, the Sphairos will not suffice, since according to our list, a *plurality* of long-lived gods springs forth from the four elements. Therefore, we have to take into account the opposite period of the cosmic cycle as well: the life span of the four separate, homogeneous masses of earth, water, air, and fire.

The *divinity* of these masses is beyond doubt: it is precisely by entering the state of uncompromised chemical purity that the elements learn to be immortal (*athanata*), that is, divine, whereas later in the cycle they will again form mortal compounds (*thneta*);[59] this seems to imply that the four elements as such do not count as gods in the full sense: only the four pure masses do.[60]

It is equally clear that the four pure masses spring forth *from the four elements*. It is true that they do so not by mixture, as all the other items of the list do, but by separation and purification. This, however, is no objection against numbering the four masses among the physical gods of our list, since the list as such is not more closely linked to the movement of global unification than to the movement of global separation: it is only in version (b) (B21.7–12) that the list comes immediately after a reference to the increasing unification under Love, whereas in version (a) (*Physika* 1. 267–72) the list is introduced by a reference to the increasing separation under Strife.

But what about the *longevity* of the four masses? It is at this point of our argument that the new timetable of the cosmic cycle makes an important difference. According to this timetable, the four pure masses are not instantaneous, as suggested by O'Brien, *Empedocles' Cosmic Cycle*, but they exist for 4,000 years, (as the Sphairos does, too). Thus, they fully deserve the epithet "long-lived." We may add that without a reference to both the Sphairos and the four divine masses, our list of "*all* beings that were, *all* that are, and *all* that will be hereafter" would be remarkably deficient. Since the divine Sphairos and the divine four masses are neither trees, nor men and women, nor beasts, nor birds, nor fish, they must be the long-lived gods. We will now see that Empedocles refers to these five gods not only in a physical but also in a mythological way.

2.3. Mythical Names of the Five Long-Lived Gods

2.3.1. *Mythical Names of the Four Pure Masses*

In B6 the names of four more or less traditional gods—Zeus, Here, Aidoneus (Hades), and Nestis[61]—are introduced as designations of the "roots" (*rhizomata*) of everything there is. It is beyond doubt that these four names must refer, in one way or another, to the four Empedoclean elements.[62] On the other hand, the divine names clearly indicate that the four "roots" count as *divine beings*. Now we have already seen that according to B35.14, only the four pure masses under total separation enjoy the full status of divine beings, whereas the four elements as such do not. We must conclude that the four divine roots of B6 are the four pure masses under total separation.[63] Empedocles calls them "roots" because he regards them as the source and starting point of each revolution of the cycle.[64]

But why does Empedocles designate the four divine masses by means of four traditional divine names? Surely these names cannot be taken literally in the sense that, for example, one of the pure masses is in every respect identical with the anthropomorphic Olympian Zeus as portrayed by Homer. The obvious answer is that Empedocles is drawing on a method of decoding the Homeric gods that had been current in the Greek West since the sixth century BCE:[65] according to this method, attested already for Theagenes of Rhegium, *the Homeric gods represent the basic entities of the physical universe*, like elementary qualities or the elements themselves.[66] Thus, the traditional anthropomorphic design of these gods is redefined as a mere surface under which a deeper, physical level of meaning has been hiding all the time.

This method was introduced as a defense of Homeric poetry against the philosophical criticisms marshaled by Xenophanes and others. Xenophanes denounced the traditional stories on the gods as mere *plasmata* ("fictions")[67] precisely because of the anthropomorphic character of these gods,[68] which he tried to replace by the abstract monotheism of his own theological poetry;[69] in doing so, he had sharpened an alternative introduced already in the proem of Hesiod's *Theogony*: the "alternative between elaborating the text of the world... 'Homerically' and doing so 'Hesiodically,'"[70] that is, either by telling mythical fictions or by disclosing theological truth.

Seen against this background, Empedocles' procedure can be described as follows: he combines, within one and the same poem, the two established poetical modes of referring to the divine, that is, both the mythological and the philosophical one, so that they are mirrored in each other. The philosophical purpose of this mirroring function will be elucidated at the end of this chapter.

2.3.2. A Mythical Name of the Sphairos?

Unlike the case of the four pure masses, a mythical name of the remaining long-lived god, that is, the Sphairos, has not been preserved within the surviving fragments themselves. But the introductory comment of Ammonius on B134[71] presupposes that Empedocles designated the Sphairos quite unambiguously as Apollo:[72]

διὰ ταῦτα δὲ ὁ Ἀκραγαντῖνος σοφός, ἐπιρραπίσας τοὺς περὶ θεῶν ὡς
ἀνθροποειδῶν ὄντων παρὰ τοῖς ποιηταῖς λεγομένους μύθους, ἐπήγαγε—
[a] προηγουμένως μὲν περὶ Ἀπόλλωνος, περὶ οὗ ἦν αὐτῶι προσεχῶς ὁ λόγος,
[b] κατὰ δὲ τὸν αὐτὸν τρόπον καὶ περὶ τοῦ θείου παντὸς ἀποφαινόμενος—
"οὐδὲ γὰρ ἀνδρομέηι κεφαλῆι κατὰ γυῖα κέκασται,
οὐ μὲν ἀπαὶ νώτοιο δύο κλάδοι ἀΐσσονται,
οὐ πόδες, οὐ θοὰ γοῦν(α), οὐ μήδεα λαχνήεντα,
ἀλλὰ φρὴν ἱερὴ καὶ ἀθέσφατος ἔπλετο μοῦνον,
φροντίσι κόσμον ἅπαντα καταΐσσουσα θοῆισιν."

> (That is why the wise man of Acragas, in his criticism of the stories of allegedly anthropomorphic gods told by the poets, inferred (epēgage)—
>   [a] in the first instance about Apollo (with whom his argument was primarily concerned),
>   [b] but speaking in the same way about the divine in general, too—:

For no human head is fitted to his limbs,
No two branches spring from his back,
No feet, no swift legs, no hairy genitals:
He was merely a mind, holy and wonderful,
Rushing with rapid thought over the whole kosmos.)

The similarity between the Empedoclean lines (B134) quoted here by Ammonius and the description of the Sphairos in B29[73] is so close that B134 must be referring to the Sphairos, too.[74] As for the last line, *kosmos* does not, in Empedocles, designate our sad world of ephemeral plurality, but a harmonious blend of the four elements[75] and, in particular, the Sphairos. Thus, the "rapid thought" of a clearly nonanthropomorphic being must be the mental activity of the Sphairos, his "rejoicing" in himself.[76]

For a correct interpretation of the introductory remark of Ammonius, two points of syntax are essential.

1. The syntactical object of the main predicate "he inferred" (epēgage) is the quotation of B134 at the end of the passage.[77]
2. The two parenthetical qualifications that come immediately after the predicate "he inferred"—(a) on Apollo and (b) on the divine in general— are *both* subordinate to this predicate, simply because no other predicate is available.

Since both qualifications are subordinate to the predicate "he inferred", and since the object of "he inferred" are the five lines of B134, *both* qualifications must explain what Empedocles does in inferring B134.[78] Thus, B134 may hold for the divine (*to theion*) in general, too, but "in the first instance" (*prohegoumenos*) B134 is about Apollo, and it is Apollo with whom the argument of B134 is "immediately" (*prosechos*) concerned.[79]

Since B134 is about the Sphairos and since, according to Ammonius, B134 refers in the first instance and immediately to Apollo, we must conclude that Empedocles, according to Ammonius, designated the Sphairos as Apollo. The careful qualifications of Ammonius are unambiguous: this is not an interpretation ventured by Ammonius; this is what he found, in so many words, in his source. If we can trust that source, Empedocles has introduced "Apollo" as a mythical name of the Sphairos.[80]

We do not know the source of Ammonius, but we shall see that this mythical name would make excellent sense. For the time being, the presence of mythological references to the long-lived gods of the cosmic cycle is sufficiently established by the evidence of B6 alone. It remains to be seen whether the coexistence of and the relationship between physical and mythological references to divine entities shed light on the problem from which we started, namely, on the relationship between Empedocles' physical theory and his account of the daimon's crime and punishment.

3. DAIMON

3.1. The Meaning of *daimon* in Epic Poetry

In Greek epic poetry, *daimon* designates either, as in Homer, "one of the (Olympian) gods"—this meaning is preserved, for example, by Empedocles' immediate predecessor Parmenides[81]—or, especially in Hesiod, "one of the deceased members of the golden race, who act as guardians in later ages":[82]

> Homer calls the gods *daimones* like this[83] either because they are knowledgeable [*daëmones*][84]—for they have experience and knowledge of all things[85]—or because they are arbitrators [*diatetai*] and controllers of men, as Alcman the lyric poet says:[86] "[alone?] he shook the lots and made the distributions [*daimonai*],"[87] that is, their apportionments or shares. But Hesiod[88] calls *daimones* the deceased members of the golden race whose lifetime was the reign of Cronus, saying that "they are *daimones* . . . guardians of mortal men."

To this traditional assessment we must add that in Homer, *daimon* designates more often than not an Olympian god whose identity is *veiled* to those who experience his power.[89]

It seems prima facie very unlikely that the meaning of *daimon* in Empedocles' epic poetry should differ radically from the usage of Homer, Hesiod, and Parmenides.[90]

3.2. A Physical Reference to *Daimones* in Empedocles

Among the two Empedoclean fragments in which the word *daimon* occurs, one is quoted by Simplicius from a clearly physical context, that is, from a description of the second of the four zoogonical stages attested by Aëtius.[91] *Daimones* are involved, when the isolated limbs that had appeared at the first zoogonical stage are uniting at the second stage (B59):[92]

> but when daimon mingled more with daimon,
> these (isolated limbs) fell together as each happened
> and many other (beings) in addition to these were continuously born.

Who are these *daimones*? Within the physical universe, and at this point of the cosmic cycle, there are three possibilities: (a) the two forces of Love and Strife;[93] (b) the isolated limbs; (c) the four elements, contained in the isolated limbs.[94]

It is unconvincing to equate the *daimones* with Love and Strife, since between Love and Strife there is not mixture, but conflict; and while "conflict" is a possible meaning of the Greek verb "they mixed" (*emisgeto*) in the first line of B59, it would be very misleading to use the verb with this meaning in a description of increasing *mixture*, and it would be implausible to deduce an increasing unification of limbs from an increasing conflict between Love and Strife.[95]

It is equally unconvincing to equate the *daimones* with the isolated limbs involved in the process described in B 59. It is true that it could be said of the isolated limbs that, at the second zoogonical stage, "they mingled more with each other." But if the *daimones* were the isolated limbs, the process described in the first line of B59 would be the same as the process described in the second line. Thus, there would be no material difference between the protasis and the first part of the apodosis, which seems quite unlikely.

The only remaining possibility is to equate the *daimones* with the four elements. This terminology can perhaps be justified on the following lines: As long as the elements are being combined to a multitude of short-lived beings, they are neither completely pure, as they were under total separation, nor completely united, as they will be within the *Sphairos*.[96] Thus, the state of the elements during their transition from full separation to full unity (and, for that matter, during their way back from full unity to full separation) appears to be deficient on both counts. They seem to be addressed as *daimones* as long as their divinity is blurred, i.e., during the two transitional 6,000-year-periods of the cosmic cycle, whereas during the two 4,000-year-periods they form *long-lived gods*.

For further confirmation of this result we will have to look at the way in which Empedocles employs the notion of a *daimon* within the mythcal context of B115.

3.3. The Mythical Law

3.3.1. *Crime and Punishment of the Guilty Daimon*

In B115 and related texts, the Empedoclean speaker discloses a mythical law ordained by an oracle of Necessity; the law concerns guilt and punishment of the guilty daimon. The crime for which the daimon is punished seems to be bloodshed, although this interpretation presupposes a (plausible) textual conjecture in B115.3.[97] The admission of perjury as a further crime or further aspect of the crime rests on the authenticity of B115.4, which is a linguistically somewhat dubious adaptation of a Hesiodic line.[98]

The guilty daimon is expelled from a state of bliss[99] for 30,000 seasons,[100] during which, far away from the communion of the other blessed ones,[101] he passes through a series of painful incarnations into mortal beings.[102] At the end of B115, the Empedoclean speaker discloses that he himself is a guilty daimon.[103] After punishment and purification, the guilty daimon is entitled to return to his former abode[104] and to rejoin the communion of the other immortals.[105] So we get what Charles Kahn has aptly designated the "cycle of the daimon":[106]

1: All gods belong to the community of the blessed ones.
2: Whenever one of them commits a certain crime (bloodshed?),
   he is sent off into exile.
3: The guilty daimon is punished and purified by a series of incarnations.
4: The expiated daimon returns to the blessed ones.
1': All gods belong to the community of the blessed ones.

The basic meaning of *daimon* in that context is clearly the Homeric one, since a member of a community of blessed ones (B115.6: *makares*) and immortals (B147: *athanatoi*) is clearly a "god." And yet Empedocles uses the word *daimon* with reference to the period of exile only: in analogy with what we have observed concerning the physical use of *daimon*, we may venture the hypothesis that within the mythical law a daimon is an Olympian god *in exile*: The "cycle of the daimon" would then be the "cycle of the guilty god."

These preliminary reflections are confirmed by the fact that the cycle of the daimon is clearly modeled on *one specific Olympian god*: Apollo. According to two sources that were almost certainly known to Empedocles—the Pythagorean legend and the Hesiodic *Catalogue of Women*—it is Apollo who actually experienced what the Empedoclean law prescribes. First, there is the legend of Pythagoras, according to which Pythagoras is an incarnation of the Hyperborean Apollo.[107] The series of incarnations from Apollo to Pythagoras is attested in several versions, among which the sequence Apollo–Euphorbus–Pythagoras is probably the earliest.[108]

Since the Empedoclean account of a series of incarnations is clearly based on the legend of Pythagoras,[109] the obvious paradigm for his account of a divine being (daimon) subject to incarnations is Apollo.[110]

As soon as Apollo's mortal incarnations are identified as the paradigm of the "cycle of the guilty god," we observe striking parallels between that cycle and the myth told about Apollo in the Hesiodic *Catalogue of Women*[111] and alluded to by Aeschylus:[112] Asclepius, Apollo's son by Coronis, had used his healing powers to restore the dead to life, and for this had been blasted to death by the thunderbolt of Zeus, forged by the Cyclopes. Apollo in revenge killed the Cyclopes, and was sentenced by Zeus to a term of penance as serf to a mortal, Admetus. After that, he returns to the other Olympians. Thus, Empedocles' "cycle of the guilty god" shares with the Pythagorean legend the feature of an Olympian god who passes through a series of incarnations, and with the Hesiodic myth the feature of an Olympian who is sent into an earthly exile as a punishment for bloodshed. In both cases, the god in question is Apollo.

We may conclude that within the law disclosed in B115, *daimon* refers to a guilty (Olympian) god subject to a punishment that is modeled on the myth of Apollo's exile.[113] In order to determine the relationship between this concept of *daimon* and the physical *daimones* of B59, I will now compare the "cycle of the guilty god" and the cosmic cycle as a whole.

3.3.2. The Cycle of the Guilty God and the Cosmic Cycle

The cycle of the guilty god and the cosmic cycle have in common a regular alternation of ideal divine states and deficient intermediary states of *daimones*. The common regularity is underlined by the fact that both the punishment of the guilty god *and*, on the physical side, the interval between Love's seizure of power and Strife's seizure of power are regulated by a timetable or law that is guaranteed by one or more "broad oath(s)."[114]

And yet there is a conspicuous difference between the two cycles. The cycle of the guilty god seems to contain just *one* ideal state: the happy communion of all immortal gods. In the cosmic cycle, on the other hand, *two* ideal states are involved: both the rule of the divine Sphairos and the rule of the four divine masses. There is, however, clear evidence to the effect that the physical counterpart of the happy state of the god within the community of the blessed ones is not the rule of the four divine masses but only the rule of the Sphairos:

1. Both the punishment of the guilty god *and*, on the physical side, the destruction of the Sphairos are dominated or brought about by Strife (Neikos).[115] This implies that it is the lifetime of the *Sphairos* that corresponds to the god's happy state as a member of the community of the blessed ones.

2. The same conclusion is suggested by the fact that the designation of the Sphairos as "Apollo" (attested by Ammonius) obviously refers to the state of Apollo's uncompromised divinity, not to his exile. The correspondence

between Sphairos and uncompromised divinity will apply to the guilty god
in general, since Apollo is, as we have seen, the paradigm for the guilty god.

This means that in order to bring out the parallelism suggested by Empedocles, we
have to choose the Sphairos as a starting point on the physical side.[116] We may say,
then, that the rule of the Sphairos corresponds to the happy state of the god within
the community of the blessed ones, the destruction of the Sphairos to his crime and
departure, the movement toward complete separation to his punishment, and the
movement toward complete unity to his return.

The function of the mythical cycle of the guilty god seems to be, in the first
place, to mirror the contrast between the blurred divinity of the elements during
the periods of transition and the full divinity of the *Sphairos*. There is, however, one
fragment which suggests that the full divinity of the four pure masses, too, is
accounted for by the myth of the guilty god.

3.3.3. *The Exclusion of the Daimon from the Houses of Zeus and Hades*

The fragment B142 is transmitted by a Herculanean Papyrus[117] containing a work
(probably by Demetrius Laco)[118] on textual and exegetical difficulties in Epicurus.
The two Empedoclean lines are quoted in column 40 of the papyrus. Already
Diels[119] was able to offer a satisfactory text of the first line, whereas the reading of
the second line has been greatly improved, on the basis of fresh autopsy, by Puglia
1988[120] and even more so, by employing new techniques of photography, by
Martin. The text of B142 as read by Martin runs as follows.[121]

> Neither the covered halls of aegis-bearing Zeus
> nor the solid roof of Hades do anywhere receive him...

We may note immediately that among the preserved fragments of Empedocles the
fragment B6, quoted earlier, is the only other text where both Zeus and Hades
(Aidoneus) are mentioned together:

> Hear first the four roots of all things:
> bright Zeus and life-bringing Hera and Aidoneus
> and Nestis, whose tears are the source of mortal streams.

The mythical divine names in B6 stand for the four divine masses of the elements
under total separation, as we have already seen. Since two of the four divine names,
that is, Zeus and Hades, reappear in B142, it seems plausible that in B142, too, the
divine names refer to the pure masses. In B142, the compactness of the four elements under total separation is appropriately mirrored by the fact that not just the
names of the long-lived gods are mentioned, as in B6, but their solid dwellings:
"*covered* halls" and a "*solid* roof."

As for the identity of the excluded person, Diels suggested[122] identifying this
person with the daimon of B115:[123]

Perhaps the prophet was referring to the fate of the guilty ghost who could not find redemption either in fire or in air or on earth, as long as he did not, by way of penance and purgation, swear off his sins.

This is particularly plausible since, according to the mythical account given in B115, the daimon receives a hostile treatment by the four regions of the visible world that correspond to the four elements:[124]

> For the force of air pursues him into sea,
> and sea spits him out onto earth's surface, earth casts him into the rays
> of blazing sun, and sun into the eddies of air;
> one takes him from another, and all abhor him.

But whereas B115 contains a description of the hostile mood in which the guilty god is received by air, sea, earth, and sun, according to B142 the guilty god is *not* received by the gods who correspond to the divine masses under total separation.

Therefore, B115 and B142 seem to mirror the state of the elements (= *daimones*) during the periods of transition in two different ways. In B115.9–12 Empedocles alludes to the antagonism between two *contemporaneous* formations of the elements, that is, between those bits which are under the influence of Love (forming short-lived combinations) and those under the influence of Strife (forming the incomplete cosmic masses of our world). In B142, on the other hand, he illustrates the contrast between two *subsequent* states of the elements, that is, their being *daimones* involved in short-lived combinations and their being four divine masses (= long-lived gods) during total separation.[125] We may conclude that the myth of the guilty god contains an allusion to the divinity of the four pure masses, too.[126]

3.3.4. *The Mythical Nature of the Cycle of the Guilty God*

The exclusion of the daimon from the houses of Zeus and Hades (B142) clearly belongs to the same mythological level of expression as the mythical names of the four divine masses in B6. The same holds at least for certain aspects of the sequence of crime and punishment as described in B115: the daimon during his membership to the communion of the blessed ones[127] cannot be strictly identical with the Sphairos, since the Sphairos is, for lack of possible victims, unable to commit a crime such as bloodshed.[128] Furthermore, the communion of the blessed ones seems to enjoy a continuity that has no exact counterpart in the cosmic cycle: the daimon, during his wanderings, is "far away from the blessed ones,"[129] which implies that the blessed ones are still *somewhere*.[130] Therefore, we must ascribe basic features of the cycle of the guilty god to the mythological level.

On the basis of what has been shown in paragraphs 3.3.2 and 3.3.3, the correspondences between the cosmic cycle and the mythical cycle of the guilty god may be set out as follows.

Cosmic cycle	Punishment and redemption of the guilty god
Rule of the divine Sphairos	Happy state of the god (e.g., Apollo) who belongs to the community of the blessed ones.
Destruction of the Sphairos	Whenever one of the gods (e.g., Apollo) commits a certain crime [bloodshed?], he is sent off into exile.
Increasing separation of the elements (= *daimones*) under the rule of Strife; the living mixtures produced by Love are more and more fragmentary.	The guilty *daimon* is punished and purified by a descending series of incarnations.
Rule of the four divine masses (*rhizomata* = long-lived gods). No living mixtures are being produced at all.	He is not received in the houses of Zeus and Hades.
Gradual unification of the elements (= *daimones*) under the rule of Love; the living mixtures produced by Love are more and more complete.	The expiated *daimon* returns to the blessed ones via an ascending series of incarnations.
Rule of the Sphairos	Happy state of the god who again belongs to the community of the blessed ones.

3.3.5. *The Status of Personal Reincarnation: Physics or Myth?*

The coexistence, and interaction, of a physical and a mythical level of expression in Empedocles can, by now, be regarded as firmly established. But the demarcation-line between these two levels remains problematic: Is the concept of personal reincarnation restricted to the myth of the guilty god, or does it form part of the physical system, too?

Taken as a piece of positive doctrine, the kind of *personal* continuity through many generations implied in the concept of reincarnation cannot easily be accounted for in terms of Empedocles' physical theory, according to which living beings are just temporary compounds of the four elements.[131] In particular, there is no evidence, within the fragments and *testimonia* concerning Empedocles' physical system, for anything like a biochemical carrier of the personal continuity implied in transmigration. The two attempts at identifying such a thing do not carry conviction.

F. M. Cornford, taking for granted Plutarch's equation of the Empedoclean daimon with the soul, ascribed to Empedocles' physical system the notion of a soul pictured "as a portion of Love, contaminated, in the impure embodied state, with a portion of Strife." At the same time he suggested, rather hesitatingly, identifying the soul "with the numerical proportion, ratio, or harmonia of the elements, considered as an organizing principle capable of passing from one compound to another, and holding them together."[132]

J. Barnes attributed to Empedocles a theory of transmigratory *daimones* that are compounded "of all stuffs," that is, of all four elements. The fact that the fallen *daimones* have to put on mortal forms as their punishment would not imply that before their fall they were wholly bodiless. In their original state Empedocles would conceive them, according to Barnes, not as human in form, but nevertheless as tightly knit elemental compounds.[133]

Both scholars frankly admit the inherent implausibility of the construction they ascribe to Empedocles.[134] That being so and in the absence of any ancient evidence for either construction, it seems more prudent not to press the concept of reincarnation into a physical system that is obviously not suited to accommodate it. Are we entitled, then, to confine the notion of personal transmigration strictly to the mythological level?

4. The Function of Myth in Empedocles: Physics and Ethics

Empedocles seems to justify his famous ban on killing animals by alluding to the concept of personal reincarnation.[135] Since the revolutionary prohibition of animal sacrifice[136] is obviously of the utmost importance for Empedocles, it can, of course, not be based on a mere allegory. The question, then, is whether the physical counterpart of the myth, that is, Empedocles' cosmic cycle, provides a sufficient reason for Empedocles' ethical commandments even *without* the assumption of personal reincarnation. If our answer to this question were simply negative, we would have to accept Eduard Zeller's verdict against the interpretation of reincarnation as a mere symbol.[137] Now it is certainly true that the physical counterpart of the reincarnation myth *as conceived by Zeller*—"the animatedness of nature," "the development of life step by step"[138]—would be unsuitable to provide a basis for Empedoclean ethics. But Zeller obviously failed to take the theological dimension of Empedoclean physics seriously: All living beings created during the periods of transition are akin to each other in that they partake in the same four *daimones* (= elements in exile); all of these living beings are attempts of Love to restore the divine *Sphairos*.

We know, thanks to another recent discovery, that the universal kinship was expressly stated within the physical theory. This is shown by Fragment B20, the original text of which has been revealed by the Strasbourg papyrus (*ensemble c*):[139]

> 0 to devise works of change,
> 1 on the one hand in the case of the glorious bulk of human limbs:
> 2 at one time, through love, *we* all *come together* into one:
> 3 we parts that have acquired a body, at the height of flourishing life;
> 4 while at another time, again, torn asunder by baneful contentions
> 5 they [i.e., the parts] wander each one apart on the brink of life.

6 the same holds, on the other hand, for shrubs and water-dwelling
  fishes,

7 and for beasts whose bodies are in the mountains and for birds moving
  with their wings

Lines 2–3 state that Love makes parts (*guia*) that have already found a body unite
still further, whereas according to lines 4–5 Strife cuts these parts asunder.

The language of line 3 has reminded Denis O'Brien of the process attested by
A72 for Empedocles' second zoogonical stage and described in B59: formerly
isolated limbs are forming a body.[140] But this reading is hardly compatible with
the information supplied by Simplicius in the context of his quotation: According to Simplicius, B20 refers to the interaction of Love and Strife *as it can be
observed in our world*.[141] What can be observed in our world is that Love makes
human bodies (which consist of the four elements) come together in sexual acts,
whereas after death Strife makes these bodies decompose into the elements. So the
fragment seems to be about the observable contrast between making love and
death.

In lines 2–3, there used to be a textual problem: according to the indirect
tradition, the whole phrase seemed to lack a main verb in the indicative, since there
was only a participle and a subordinate relative clause.[142] Several conjectures had
been proposed.[143] This problem has been solved by *ensemble c* of the Strasbourg
papyrus in a surprising way: instead of the "parts coming together" (that is, the
participle *sunerchomen*') the papyrus offers "*we* all, the parts, *are coming together*"
(i.e., the indicative *sunerchometh*').[144] The new variant of the papyrus is confirmed
by two further examples of "our" coming together toward the One, which occur in
ensemble a of the papyrus.[145] More than one ancient reader has replaced the bold
indicative by the participle (*sunerchomen*') known from other Empedoclean lines
(where the participle fits the syntax).[146] But the price to be paid for this *lectio
facilior* is the syntactical problem just mentioned.

In the light of what has been said in this chapter, the difficulty of "we, the parts,
are coming together" is only apparent. Empedocles speaks in the name of the
elements in order to express the basic kinship of all living mixtures created during
the cosmic cycle.

This universal kinship makes the killing of one living being by another appear
no less horrible than does the myth of reincarnation: killing another living being
means to repeat, on a smaller scale, the destruction of the divine One by Strife.
Thus, ascribing the account of personal reincarnation to the mythological level
does *not* deprive Empedoclean ethics of its physical foundation.

This point, too, has been reinforced by the Strasbourg papyrus.[147] In *ensemble
d* of the papyrus appears the famous exclamation in which the speaker wishes he
had never killed and eaten an animal: "Alas that the pitiless day did not first destroy
me, before I contrived with my claws terrible deeds for the sake of food!"[148] The
papyrus has put this exclamation into its context, which had been unknown before:
this context is clearly physical. In particular, five lines following soon after the

exclamation describe an event known from B62: the third zoogonical stage, in which whole-natured forms of life are brought upward to the surface of the earth by the rising fire.[149] *Ensemble d* confirms that the prohibition of animal sacrifice was firmly rooted in the physical theory. And yet the mythological account of the incarnations of the guilty god is more than a *biblia pauperum*, it is certainly not intended merely for the large audience of the exoteric *Katharmoi*. The mythical law mirrors the physical theory in a way that brings out its impact from a human perspective; it shows the ethical implications of the physical theory by *evaluating* the different stages of the cosmic cycle. Empedocles' ethics is grounded in his physical theology *as elucidated by the myth of the guilty god.*

NOTES

Earlier versions of this chapter were read to audiences in Munich, Pisa ("Apollo and Other Gods"), and Berlin. This version has profited from the discussions on these earlier occasions; my special thanks go to Glenn Most (Pisa), Peter Strohschneider (Munich), to whom I owe the title, and André Laks (Lille), especially for the following remark ("Some Thoughts about Empedoclean Cycles," 265): "I take it that Empedocles presents us with two distinct, though related stories": this article may be read as an extended commentary on this remark. In addition, this version draws on the results of fresh textual research (PHerc. 1012, Florentine scholia, Suda manuscripts) that could not be taken into account earlier.

1. Empedocles will be quoted as far as possible from DK. The translations of Empedoclean fragments will be based on Barnes, *Early Greek Philosophy.*

2. The Strasbourg fragments from an ancient papyrus manuscript of Empedocles' *Physika* were published by Martin and Primavesi, *L'Empédocle de Strasbourg;* they are included in Inwood, *The Poem of Empedocles.* One of the results has been the textual emendation of several quotations already known before; see Primavesi, "Editing Empedocles." For the interpretation of the new material see Trepanier, "Empedocles on the Ultimate Symmetry of the World"; for fresh suggestions on the text see Janko, "Empedocles, *On Nature* I 233–364" and Primavesi, "Empedokles *Physika* I."

3. The Florentine scholia on Empedocles' cosmic cycle were made known by Rashed, "La chronographie du système d'Empédocle." This *proecdosis* of the paleographically difficult material was based on a microfilm only; therefore, it could not be entirely accurate. For an improved text based on the Florentine manuscript itself and provided with photographs see Primavesi, "Empedokles in Florentiner Aristoteles-Scholien."

4. The quotation of B142, contained in a carbonized papyrus from Herculaneum, was republished by Martin, "Empédocle, fr. 142 D.-K."; for metrical analysis and interpretation see Primavesi, "Die Häuser von Zeus und Hades." The quotation of Fr. 152 Wright, coming from the second book of Empedocles' *Katharmoi* and preserved by a Vienna palimpsest, was republished by Primavesi and Alpers, "Empedokles im Wiener Herodian-Palimpsest."

5. On the author of that catalogue (Lobon of Argos) and on his reliability see now the fundamental study of Garulli, *Il Περὶ ποιητῶν di Lobone di Argo.*

6. Diogenes Laertius 8. 77 (1.622.1–3 Marcovich).

7. *Suda* ε 1002 (2.258.19–21 Adler).

8. Primavesi, "Zur Überlieferung und Bedeutung des empedokleischen Titels Καθαρμοί."

9. Horna was simply wrong in asserting that in a *codex Marcianus* of the *Suda* the book-number is *four* and that the book-number *three* printed in the *editio princeps* of the *Suda* was based on manuscript evidence, too. In fact, the book-number *two* is the only reading transmitted by the *Suda* manuscripts, and the book-number *three* given in the *editio princeps* is an (admirable) emendation without any support in *Suda*-manuscripts. For both points see Primavesi, "Die Suda über die Werke des Empedokles."

10. According to Tzetzes B134 forms part of the theological argument unfolded by means of the third book of the *Physika*, see Leone, *Tzetzae Historiae* p. 276 (Chil. 7, Hist. 143, ll. 514–15): Ἐμπεδοκλῆς τῶι τρίτωι τε τῶν Φυσικῶν δεικνύων, / τίς ἡ οὐσία τοῦ θεοῦ, κατ' ἔπος οὕτω λέγει. The authenticity of this ascription has been convincingly defended by Zuntz, *Persephone*, 214–18.

11. "Pluralitas non est ponenda sine necessitate." See Gál and Brown, *Venerabilis inceptoris Guillelmi de Ockham scriptum in librum primum sententiarum (ordinatio)*, 74, 22–23.

12. A second book of the *Katharmoi* is attested by Herodianus; see the reedition of fr. 152 Wright by Primavesi and Alpers, "Empedokles im Wiener Herodian-Palimpsest."

13. Zuntz, "De Empedoclis librorum numero coniectura."

14. For Orphic influences in Empedocles see Riedweg, "Orphisches bei Empedokles;" for the Orphic myth of Dionysus Zagreus see Holzhausen, "Pindar und die Orphik."

15. This distinction is often linked to the question whether Empedocles' teachings came in two separate works, "On Nature" and "Purifications" (see, e.g., Kingsley, "Empedocles' Two Poems") or whether the two attested work-titles refer to one and the same poem (see, e.g., Osborne, "Empedocles Recycled"). While thinking that the evidence points clearly in the direction of two separate poems, I have formed the impression that the philosophical importance of this question is usually overestimated.

16. *De esu* 1.7, 996b–c: οὐ χεῖρον δ' ἴσως καὶ προανακρούσασθαι καὶ προαναφωνῆσαι τὰ τοῦ Ἐμπεδοκλέους· . . . ἀλληγορεῖ γὰρ ἐνταῦθα τὰς ψυχάς, ὅτι φόνων καὶ βρώσεως σαρκῶν καὶ ἀλληλοφαγίας δίκην τίνουσαι σώμασι θνητοῖς ἐνδέδενται.

17. Wilamowitz, "Die Καθαρμοί des Empedokles," 658–59 (= 517–18). In B138, *psuchē* serves as a metaphor for "blood"; in this context, it clearly does not refer to an immaterial "soul" but rather to "life." There is no other instance of *psuchē* within the attested fragments.

18. Diels, "Über die Gedichte des Empedokles," 405 (= 136): "Wir dürfen demnach annehmen, dass der schreiende Dualismus, der uns bisher in den Anschauungen des Akragantiners entgegentrat, wenigstens in seinen auffallendsten Erscheinungen erklärt wird durch die Verschiedenheit der beiden Hauptschriften." Similarly Wilamowitz, "Die Καθαρμοί des Empedokles," 661.

19. Cornford, "Mystery Religions and Pre-Socratic Philosophy," 569; *PP* 499–501. I will come back to these suggestions toward the end of this article.

20. Osborne, "Sin and Moral Responsibility in Empedocles' Cosmic Cycle," 295: "So is the physical cycle determined and mechanical or not? I want to suggest not. I want to suggest that the phases of the physical cycle are a result of free actions, on the part of agents who act voluntarily."

21. Sturz, *Empedocles Agrigentinus*, 484: "non proprie accipi posse metempsychosin Empedocleam"; 481: "tota enim ratio videtur esse poetica et allegorica." van der Ben, *The Proem of Empedocles' Peri Physios*, 57: "the story or narrative apparently is meant to be taken as symbolic"; see 95–96 n. 101.

22. Bignone, *Empedocle*, 279 (under the assumption that the account of the trans-migrating *daimones* belongs to the Katharmoi): "Il poema lustrale è dunque, anzi che una ritrattazione, una grande allegoria del poema della natura. In questo la fisica è al centro come oggetto principale e sempre presente: dell'anima mistica appena è un accenno vago; nel poema lustrale invece la storia dell'anima mistica è il soggetto, ma lo sfondo è lo stesso universo che il fisico ha ideato, col suo ciclo, le sue leggi, le sue forze, la sua comunità di esseri."

23. See e.g. Syrianus, *in Metaph.* 187.20–24 Kroll, who regards the alternation of One and Many as mere words veiling Empedocles' whole theology (=ῥήματα προβεβλημένα τῆς ὅλης αὐτοῦ θεολογίας). For a different interpretation of these words, however, see O'Brien, *Pour interpréter Empédocle*, 80, "le début de toute sa théologie." Simplicius, *in Cael.* 530.12–13, on the supposedly alternate rules of Love and Strife: τοῦ Ἐμπεδοκλέους ὡς ποιητοῦ μυθικώτερον παρὰ μέρος τὴν ἐπικράτειαν αὐτῶν λέγοντος. See O'Brien, *Pour interpréter Empédocle*, 73–90. This Platonizing interpretation is already exploited by Hippolytus, *Haer.* 7.29.14–24. The presence of a Platonizing interpretation of Empedocles in Hippolytus has been traced back by Diels, "Über die Gedichte des Empedokles," 399 (followed by O'Brien, *Pour interpréter Empédocle*, 210 n. 3) to Plutarch's great monograph on Empedocles, which Hippolytus actually quotes at *Haer.* 5.20.5; the doubts of Hershbell have been answered by O'Brien, *Pour interpréter Empédocle*, 95–97. Burkert, "Plotin, Plutarch und die platonisierende Interpretation von Heraklit und Empedokles," 140–142, thinks of a more complicated development—a view that seems now to be shared by O'Brien, *Empedocles' Cosmic Cycle*, 93–94.

24. I have taken a first step in this direction in "La daimonologia della fisica Empe-doclea."

25. B26.1; B26.12.

26. B17.1–2. The scope of the Empedoclean cycle of unification and separation (B17.1–2, 16–17; B26.5–12) must not be restricted to the realm of biology, as suggested by Hölscher, "Weltzeiten und Lebenszyklus," and van der Ben, *The Proem of Empedocles' Peri Physios*: Plato and Aristotle agree for once with each other that Empedocles' cycle implies a regular alternation of universal unity and universal plurality: Pl. *Sph.* 242e: αἱ δὲ μαλακώτεραι [*scilicet* Μοῦσαι, that is Empedocles] . . . τοτὲ μὲν ἓν εἶναί φασι τὸ πᾶν καὶ φίλον ὑπ' Ἀφροδίτης, τοτὲ δὲ πολλὰ καὶ πολέμιον αὐτὸ αὑτῷ διὰ νεῖκός τι. Arist. *Ph.* 8.1, 250b 26–29: ἢ ὡς Ἐμπεδοκλῆς ἐν μέρει κινεῖσθαι καὶ πάλιν ἠρεμεῖν, κινεῖσθαι μὲν ὅταν ἡ φιλία ἐκ πολλῶν ποιῇ τὸ ἓν ἢ τὸ νεῖκος πολλὰ ἐξ ἑνός, ἠρεμεῖν δ' ἐν τοῖς μεταξὺ χρόνοις; to be read in conjunction with 252a19–21: διόπερ βέλτιον ὡς Ἐμπεδοκλῆς, κἂν εἴ τις ἕτερος εἴρηκεν οὕτως ἔχειν, ἐν μέρει <u>τὸ πᾶν</u> ἠρεμεῖν καὶ κινεῖσθαι πάλιν. See O'Brien, "Empedocles Revisited," 460–61.

27. B17.7–8.

28. B17.18: πῦρ καὶ ὕδωρ καὶ γαῖα καὶ ἠέρος ἄπλετον ὕψος, quoted by Simplicius from the first book of the *Physika*.

29. B35.3b–6: ἐπεὶ Νεῖκος τ' ἀνυπέρβατα βένθε' ἵκηται / δίνης, ἐν δὲ μέσηι Φιλότης στροφάλιγγι γένηται, / ἐν τῆι δὴ τάδε πάντα συνέρχεται ἓν μόνον εἶναι, / οὐκ ἄφαρ, ἀλλὰ θελημὰ συνιστάμεν' ἄλλοθεν ἄλλα. The text of line 3b is based on the close parallel in *P.Strasb.* 1665–66 a (ii) 18 as emended by Apostolos L. Pierris during a colloquium on Empedocles in summer 2003. For another, more complicated attempt at emendation see Primavesi and Patzer, "Die übertiefe Tiefe (Empedokles B35, 3–5 und Physika I, 288–290)."

30. B35.8–13: πολλὰ δ' ἄμεικτ' ἔστηκε κεραιομένοισιν ἐναλλάξ, / ὅσσ' ἔτι Νεῖκος ἔρυκε μετάρσιον· οὐ γὰρ ἀμεμφέως / τῶν πᾶν ἐξέστηκεν ἐπ' ἔσχατα

τέρματα κύκλου, / ἀλλὰ τὰ μέν τ᾿ ἐνέμιμνε μελέων τὰ δέ τ᾿ ἐξεβεβήκει. / ὅσσον δ᾿ αἰὲν ὑπεκπροθέοι, τόσον αἰὲν ἐπήιει / ἠπιόφρων Φιλότητος ἀμεμφέος ἄμβροτος ὁρμή.

31. B35.14–17: αἶψα δὲ θνήτ᾿ ἐφύοντο, τὰ πρὶν μάθον ἀθάνατ᾿ εἶναι, / ζωρά τε τὰ πρὶν ἄκρητα διαλλάξαντα κελεύθους. / τῶν δέ τε μισγομένων χεῖτ᾿ ἔθνεα μυρία θνητῶν, / παντοίαις ἰδέηισιν ἀρηρότα, θαῦμα ἰδέσθαι.

32. O'Brien, *Empedocles' Cosmic Cycle*, 4–45; O'Brien, "Empedocles Revisited," 405–16. The most important text is Simplicius, *in Ph.* 1183.28–1184.1 = Eudem. fr. 110 Wehrli: Εὔδημος δὲ τὴν <u>ἀκινησίαν</u> ἐν τῇ τῆς Φιλίας ἐπικρατείᾳ κατὰ τὸν Σφαῖρον ἐκδέχεται, ἐπειδὰν ἅπαντα συγκριθῇ, "ἔνθ᾿ οὔτ᾿ ἠελίοιο διείδεται ὠκέα γυῖα" (Emp. B27.3–4), ἀλλ᾿, ὥς φησιν, "οὕτως Ἁρμονίης πυκινῷ κρυφῷ ἐστήρικται / Σφαῖρος κυκλοτερὴς μονίη περιγηθέι γαίων" (Emp. B27.3–4). Stein, *Empedoclis Agrigentini Fragmenta*, suggested combining the three lines quoted by Eudemus with the two lines quoted by Plutarch, *De facie* 12, 926E as referring to the full separation of the elements (= fr. 26a Bignone), but this is unconvincing; see Bignone, *Empedocle*, 599–604.

33. B27a: οὐ στάσις οὐδέ τε δῆρις ἀναίσιμος ἐν μελέεσσιν, which is—*pace* Wright, *Empedocles*, 255–56—better taken as referring to the Sphairos than as referring to the wise man; see B109.3.

34. B27.4: Σφαῖρος κυκλοτερὴς μονίηι περιγηέι <u>γαίων</u>.

35. B29: οὐ γὰρ ἀπὸ νώτοιο δύο κλάδοι ἀίσσονται, / οὐ πόδες, οὐ θοὰ γοῦν(α), οὐ μήδεα γεννήεντα, / ἀλλὰ σφαῖρος ἔην καὶ <πάντοθεν> ἶσος ἑαυτῶι.

36. B27.4 / B28.2: Σφαῖρος κυκλοτερής.

37. Simp. *in Ph.* 1184.2–4 = Eudem. fr. 110 Wehrli: ἀρξαμένου δὲ πάλιν τοῦ Νείκους ἐπικρατεῖν τότε πάλιν κίνησις ἐν τῷ Σφαίρῳ γίνεται· (Emp. B31) "πάντα γὰρ ἐξείης πελεμίζετο γυῖα θεοῖο." Emp. B30: αὐτὰρ ἐπεὶ μέγα Νεῖκος ἐνὶμμελέεσσιν <u>ἐθρέφθη</u> / ἐς τιμάς τ᾿ ἀνόρουσε τελειομένοιο χρόνοιο, / ὅς σφιν ἀμοιβαῖος πλατέος παρ᾿ ἐλήλαται ὅρκου.

38. A37.

39. O'Brien, *Empedocles' Cosmic Cycle*, 287–300.

40. A49. On the Philonian passage, which is transmitted only in an Armenian translation, see Kingsley, "Empedocles in Armenian." The separation of water is illustrated by B55: γῆς ἱδρῶτα θάλασσαν.

41. For an outline of this debate see Martin and Primavesi, *L'Empédocle de Strasbourg*, 75–82.

42. Panzerbieter, *Beiträge zur Kritik und Erklärung des Empedokles*, 8.

43. *DG* 430a21–431a5: Ἐμπεδοκλῆς τὰς πρώτας γενέσεις τῶν ζῴων καὶ φυτῶν μηδαμῶς ὁλοκλήρους γενέσθαι, ἀσυμφυέσι δὲ τοῖς μορίοις διεζευγμένας, τὰς δὲ δευτέρας συμφυομένων τῶν μερῶν εἰδωλοφανεῖς, τὰς δὲ τρίτας τῶν ὁλοφυῶν [Karsten, *Empedoclis Agrigentini Carminum Reliquiae*: ἀλληλοφυῶν MSS], τὰς δὲ τετάρτας οὐκέτι ἐκ τῶν ὁμοίων οἷον ἐκ γῆς καὶ ὕδατος, ἀλλὰ δι᾿ ἀλλήλων ἤδη, τοῖς μὲν πυκνωθείσης τῆς τροφῆς, τοῖς δὲ καὶ τῆς εὐμορφίας τῶν γυναικῶν ἐπερεθισμὸν τοῦ σπερματικοῦ κινήματος ἐμποιησάσης.

44. Plu. *De facie* 12, 926d–927d.

45. O'Brien, *Empedocles' Cosmic Cycle*, 1: "There are thus two great alternations in the life of the world. First there is the major alternation between one and many, rest and movement. Secondly there is the minor alternation within the period of movement and plurality. This is the alternation between the world of increasing Strife which leads away from the Sphrere, and the world of increasing Love which leads back to the Sphere." And: "Both alternations were made of equal parts, of halves. Increasing Love lasted for as long as

increasing Strife. The Sphere lasted for as long as the world of plurality and movement" (57). This hypothesis is based on an interpretation of Arist. *Ph.* 8, 1, which I have
shown to be possible but not cogent: "The Structure of Empedocles' Cosmic Cycle,"
248–53.

46. The text of the scholia will be quoted from Primavesi, "Empedokles in Florentiner
Aristoteles-Scholien." The information contained in them might be based on an inspection
of the original Empedoclean text, since such texts seem to have been available in Byzantium
at least until 1204 CE; see Primavesi, "Lecteurs antiques," 200–201.

47. Scholium *b* (Primavesi, "Empedokles in Florentiner Aristoteles-Scholien," 31):
παυομένης γὰρ καὶ τῆς φιλίας μετὰ τοὺς ξ' χρόνους, οὐκ εὐθὺς ἤρξατο ποιεῖν
ἀπόσπασιν τὸ νεῖκος, ἀλλ' ἠρέμει. Scholium *c* (Primavesi, "Empedokles in Florentiner
Aristoteles-Scholien," 32): οὐκ εὐθὺς μετὰ τὴν παρέλευσιν τῶν ξ' χρόνων ἐν οἷς
ἐκράτησεν ἡ φιλία γενέσθαι διάσπασιν.

48. Arist. *GC* 1.1, 315a 6–8 ὅταν εἰς ἓν συναγάγῃ (*scilicet* ὁ Ἐμπεδοκλῆς) τὴν
ἅπασαν φύσιν πλὴν τοῦ νείκους, ἐκ τοῦ ἑνὸς γίγνεσθαι πάλιν ἕκαστον (*scilicet*
στοιχεῖόν φησιν). The inconsistency here criticized by Aristotle is that Empedocles
maintains that the elements are eternal *and* that they pass away when the Sphairos comes to
be in order to be reborn after the destruction of the Sphairos; see Joachim, *Aristotle on
Coming-to-Be and Passing-Away*, 68–69: "Assuming that in the 'Sphere' all things are fused
into a unity, Aristotle urges that, when Love begins to go out and Strife to come in, the
elements come into being as distinct things." Hence, ἕκαστον in Aristotle's phrase
must stand for ἕκαστον στοιχεῖον, a point I ignore in Primavesi, "Empedokles in
Florentiner Aristoteles-Scholien."

49. Scholium *f* (Primavesi, "Empedokles in Florentiner Aristoteles-Scholien," 36):
σφαῖρον – ἵνα γένηται ὁ διανοητὸς κόσμος τῆς φιλίας ἐπικρατησάσης. Taken by
itself, the aorist participle ἐπικρατησάσης could refer as well to the *starting point* of Love's
activity. But the two relevant contexts—both in Aristotle (ὅταν εἰς ἓν <u>συναγάγῃ</u> τὴν
ἅπασαν φύσιν) and in the scholium itself (σφαῖρον – ἵνα <u>γένηται</u> ὁ διανοητὸς
κόσμος)—show that it is not the whole development *toward* full unification that is at stake
here (as suggested by Primavesi, "Empedokles in Florentiner Aristoteles-Scholien," 36) but
only the precise point of time at which the Sphairos comes to be. At that point of time,
however, Love's rule is *over* according to scholium *c*; therefore, τῆς φιλίας ἐπικρατησάσης (scholium *f*) is equivalent to μετὰ τὴν παρέλευσιν τῶν ξ' χρόνων ἐν οἷς
ἐκράτησεν ἡ φιλία (scholium *c*).

50. Scholium *g* (Primavesi, "Empedokles in Florentiner Aristoteles-Scholien," 37):
διακρίσει, μετὰ ρ' χρόνους – νείκους ἐπικρατήσαντος – σύμπαν. The temporal point
of reference for μετὰ ρ' χρόνους is not to be sought within the scholium itself, but in the
Aristotelian passage interpreted by the scholium: "after 100 time-units" clarifies the
temporal relationship between the accomplishment of the Sphairos and the coming-to-be
of the four elements.

51. The meaning of νείκους ἐπικρατήσαντος in scholium *g* is determined by the
parallel expression τῆς φιλίας ἐπικρατησάσης in scholium *f*, which clearly refers to the
end point of Love's rule. Accordingly, νείκους ἐπικρατήσαντος in scholium *g* must refer
to the end point of Strife's rule. The edition of scholium *g* in Rashed, "La chronographie du
système d'Empédocle," 242, is misleading: Rashed prints ἐπικρατοῦντος instead of
ἐπικρατήσαντος (which blurs the all-important correspondence with ἐπικρατησάσης
in scholium *f*); he refers μετὰ ρ' χρόνους to ἐπικρ., although the layout of the scholium
clearly shows that it belongs with διακρίσει; and he omits σύμπαν (which shows that the

rule of Strife was a universal one) altogether. For the correct readings see the photograph in Primavesi, "Empedokles in Florentiner Aristoteles-Scholien," 37.

52. The interpretation presupposed by scholium *g* must be motivated by unambiguous independent evidence on Empedocles, since it runs counter to Aristotle's argument: the coming-to-be (and passing-away) of the four divine masses is easily compatible with the eternity of the four elements in general.

53. Scholia *d–e* (Primavesi, "Empedokles in Florentiner Aristoteles-Scholien," 33): πρὸς /ι' – κρατεῖν τὸ νεῖκος καὶ τὴν φιλίαν. For the reading /ι' and its meaning (10,000) see Primavesi, "Empedokles in Florentiner Aristoteles-Scholien," 33–36.

54. It is to the fixed interval between the starting points of the two periods of rule that Empedocles himself refers in B30: αὐτὰρ ἐπεὶ μέγα Νεῖκος ἐνὶμμελέεσσιν ἐθρέφθη / ἐς τιμάς τ' ἀνόρουσε τελειομένοιο χρόνοιο, / ὅς σφιν ἀμοιβαῖος πλατέος παρ' ἐλήλαται ὅρκου.

55. For other lists, not including the long-lived gods, see Martin and Primavesi, *L'Empédocle de Strasbourg*, 185–86.

56. Lines 267–72 = P.Strasb. a(i) 6 – a(ii) 2: ['Αλλ' ἐν μὲν Φιλότητι συνερχό]μεθ' εἰς ἕνα κόσμον, / [ἐν δὲ ᾽Εχθρηι γε πάλιν διέφυ πλέ]ον' ἐξ ἑνὸς εἶναι, / ἐξ ὧν πάνθ' ὅσα τ' ἦν ὅσα τ' ἐσθ' ὅσα τ' ἔσσετ' ὀπίσσω· / δένδρεά τ' ἐβλάστησε καὶ ἀνέρες ἠδὲ γυναῖκες, / θῆρές τ' οἰωνοί τε καὶ ὑδατοθρ[έμμονες ἰχθῦς, / καί τε θεοὶ δολιχαίωνες τιμῆισι φέριστοι. Lines 269–72a are quoted by Arist. *Metaph.* B4, 1000a32.

57. Simplicius, *in Phys.* 33.12–17 Diels and *in Phys.* 159.19–24 Diels: ἐν δὲ Κότῳ διάμορφα καὶ ἄνδιχα πάντα πέλονται, / σὺν δ' ἔβη ἐν Φιλότητι καὶ ἀλλήλοισι ποθεῖται. / ἐκ τούτων γὰρ πάνθ' ὅσα τ' ἦν ὅσα τ' ἔστι καὶ ἔσται, / δένδρεά τ' ἐβλάστησε καὶ ἀνέρες ἠδὲ γυναῖκες, / θῆρές τ' οἰωνοί τε καὶ ὑδατοθρέμμονες ἰχθῦς, / καί τε θεοὶ δολιχαίωνες τιμῆσι φέριστοι.

58. B31: πάντα γὰρ ἐξείης πελεμίζετο γυῖα θεοῖο.

59. B35.14 αἶψα δὲ θνήτ' ἐφύοντο, τὰ πρὶν μάθον ἀθάνατ' εἶναι.

60. It is this period of the elements' divine power to which B17.29 refers: "When it is their turn, they (that is, the four elements) are in power as time revolves (ἐν δὲ μέρει κρατέουσι περιπλομένοιο χρόνοιο)"; see also B26.1.

61. B6: τέσσαρα γὰρ πάντων ῥιζώματα πρῶτον ἄκουε· / Ζεὺς ἀργὴς ῾Ηρη τε φερέσβιος ἠδ' ᾽Αιδωνεύς / Νῆστίς θ', ἣ δακρύοις τέγγει κρούνωμα βρότειον, quoted by Tzetzes from the first book of the *Physika*; see Hermann, *Tzetzae Exegesis in Iliadem*, p. 53.23. On Nestis see Kingsley, *Ancient Philosophy, Mystery, and Magic*, 348–58.

62. Which deity stands for which element, is another and more difficult question; see Kingsley, *Ancient Philosophy, Mystery, and Magic*, 13–68, with the criticisms offered by Picot, "L'Empédocle magique de P. Kingsley."

63. On the mythological level, B128 looks back to a time when Zeus did not yet exist or at least was not yet king.

64. It is a mistake, then, to apply the designation "roots" to the four elements as such, or to call the elements "gods" without further qualification, as Aristotle does: *GC* 2.6, 333b21–22: θεοὶ δὲ καὶ ταῦτα (*scilicet* τὰ στοιχεῖα).

65. Ford, *The Origins of Criticism*, 67–89.

66. DK 51–52 (no. 8 text 2); Lanata, *Poetica pre-platonica*, 106–11 (no. 14 text 3).

67. DK 128 (no. 21 B1.21–24).

68. DK 132–33 (no. 21 B11, B12, B14, B15, B16).

69. DK 135 (no. 21 B23, B24, B25, B26).

70. Kannicht, *The Ancient Quarrel Between Philosophy and Poetry*, 16, commenting on Hes. *Th.* 27–28: ἴδμεν ψεύδεα πολλὰ λέγειν ἐτύμοισιν ὁμοῖα / ἴδμεν δ᾽, εὖτ᾽ ἐθέλωμεν, ἀληθέα γηρύσασθαι.

71. Ascribed by Tzetzes to the theological argument unfolded by means of the third book of the *Physika*; see note 10 here.

72. Ammon. *in Int.* (= CAG 4.5), 249.3–5.

73. B29, quoted in note 35 here.

74. Jaeger, *The Theology of the Early Greek Philosophers*, 162 (unlike Bignone, *Empedocle*, 642), follows Dümmler, "Zur orphischen Kosmologie," 151, in referring B134 to the Sphairos: "Empedocles was obviously following directly in Xenophanes' footsteps when he described the god Sphairos as 'a holy and unutterable Mind, darting through the whole cosmos with its swift thoughts [Emp. B134].' " Similarly Kranz, *Empedokles*, 48 (under the assumption that B134 belongs to the Καθαρμοί), designates B134 as "die Verse, welche damals [that is, in the Katharmoi] die Erscheinung des Sphairosgottes der menschlichen Gestalt entgegenstellten."

75. See B26.5 (ἄλλοτε μὲν Φιλότητι συνερχόμεν᾽ εἰς ἕνα κόσμον), and *P.Strasb.* a(i) 6 (...συνερχό]μεθ᾽ εἰς ἕνα κόσμον) with Martin and Primavesi, *L'Empédocle de Strasbourg*, 182–83, where, however, the implications for B134 are still overlooked.

76. B27.4 and B28.2.

77. To that extent Zuntz, *Griechische philosophische Hymnen*, 16, is right: "Das Empedokles-Zitat ist das grammatische Objekt zu dem weit vorher stehenden Hauptverb ἐπήγαγε."

78. Here Zuntz, *Griechische philosophische Hymnen*, 18–20, goes astray: according to Zuntz, only qualification (b) (on the divine in general) would refer to the quotation of B134, whereas qualification (a) (on Apollo) would allude to the dubious hymn to Apollo that, according to Aristotle F70 Rose[3], was composed by Empedocles but burnt immediately after his death by his sister. Zuntz's interpretation is clearly ruled out by the syntax of the passage.

79. Wilamowitz, "Die Καθαρμοί des Empedokles," 644 (= 498): "Es muß entschieden daran festgehalten werden, daß die Verse dem Apollon gelten; die Ausdehnung auf den Gottesbegriff überhaupt konnte Ammonios hineinlegen, wenn nicht etwa der Gott, mit dem Pythagoras nah verbunden war, für ihn [that is, Empedocles] ὁ θεός, der einzige wahre Gott war; wenn Emp. ihn so aller mythischen Körperlichkeit entkleidete, kam auf den Namen wenig an, um so bedeutsamer, daß er ihn behielt."

80. Dümmler, "Zur orphischen Kosmologie," 151: "Empedokles kann etwa gesagt haben Apollon ist nicht, wie ihr ihn euch vorstellt, sondern ist die Welt in ihrer vollkommensten Form, der Sphairos oder die Weltvernunft." And: "Empedokles kann aber auch ebenso, wie er den Elementen Götternamen gab, den Sphairos wegen der in ihm herrschenden Harmonie Apollon genannt haben" (n. 4).

81. Parmenides B1.2–3 (where ὁδόν . . . δαίμονος seems to refer to the daily path of the Sun) and B12.3 (where δαίμων designates a goddess responsible for the procreation of living beings on a cosmic scale).

82. Schol. D ad Il. 1.222 (Van Thiel, 31–32): οὕτως δαίμονας [καλεῖ ὁ Ὅμηρος] τοὺς θεούς, ἤτοι ὅτι δαήμονες — ἔμπειροι γὰρ καὶ ἴδριες πάντων αὐτοί εἰσιν — ἢ ὅτι διαιτηταί εἰσι καὶ διοικηταὶ τῶν ἀνθρώπων. ZYQXA | ᾽Αλκμὰν ὁ λυρικός φησιν, ᾽†οιεθεν πάλοις ἔπαλλεν, δαίμονάς (δαιμονάς Nauck) τ᾽ ἐδάσσατο᾽, τοὺς μερισμούς, τὰς (διαιτήσεις) αὐτῶν. Ἡσίοδος δὲ δαίμονάς φησι τοὺς ἐκ τοῦ ζῆν μεταστάντας, ὄντας δὲ ἐπὶ τῆς Κρόνου βασιλείας, τοῦ χρυσοῦ γένους, λέγων αὐτοὺς δαίμονας

φύλακας θνητῶν ἀνθρώπων. ZYQAR. The translation of the first part is based on Campbell, *Greek Lyric II*, 441.

83. That is, as in *Iliad* 1.222.

84. See Pl. *Cra.* 398b.

85. This parenthetical explanation recurs in the Epimerismi to *Iliad* A; see Dyck, *Epimerismi Homerici qui ad Iliadis librum A pertinent*, 188.5–6.

86. *Poetae Melici Graeci*, 65.

87. δαιμονάς τ' ἐδάσσατο Nauck δαίμονάς τ' ἐδάσσατο MSS.

88. *Op.* 122–23.

89. Mader, "δαίμων," 198–99, on δαίμων in epic poetry: " 'Schicksalszuteiler'; da dieses eine Hauptfunktion der Götter, = θεός, überwiegend im Sinne von ein Gott, unbekannt, welcher (1a), aber auch Bezeichnung bestimmter Götter im Singular, und der (olympischen) Götter im Plural (1b); als 'Schicksalszuteiler' den Moiren usw. nahestehend: (Todes)Schicksal, Tod (3); ferner: δαίμονες als besondere Gruppe unterhalb der eigentlichen Götter: Schutzgeister, (nach dem Tod) erhöhte Menschen (2); nur bei Hesiod, doch wie auch die erst spät (Platon usw...) persönlich zugeordneten Schutzgeister eventuell schon bei Homer vorausgesetzt."

90. This is not to deny that in other contexts *daimon* may be taken as referring to "soul"; see Pap. Derv., col. 6, lines 3–4, as supplemented in Betegh, *The Derveni papyrus*,14.

91. A72; already quoted.

92. B59: αὐτὰρ ἐπεὶ κατὰ μεῖζον ἐμίσγετο δαίμονι δαίμων, /ταῦτά τε συμπίπτεσκον, ὅπῃ συνέκυρσεν ἕκαστα, /ἄλλα τε πρὸς τοῖς πολλὰ διηνεκῆ ἐξεγένοντο. See the introductory remark of Simpl. *in Cael.* 587.18–19: 'μουνομελῆ' ἔτι τὰ γυῖα ἀπὸ τῆς τοῦ Νείκους διακρίσεως ὄντα ἐπλανᾶτο τῆς πρὸς ἄλληλα μίξεως ἐφιέμενα.

93. Diels, *Poetarum philosophorum fragmenta*, 129, "Concordia Discordiae (Simpl.); illa in extrema recesserat, nunc longius progressa manus conserit cum aemula."

94. Diels, *Poetarum philosophorum fragmenta*, 129 "vulgo elementa intellegunt." ZN 987: "die Elemente"; Wright, *Empedocles*, 212.

95. O'Brien, *Empedocles' Cosmic Cycle*, 326–27.

96. Van der Ben, *The Proem of Empedocles' Peri Physios*, 31–32, misleadingly describes the restoration of the Sphairos by Love as "destruction of its [that is, Love's] own work."

97. εὖτέ τις ἀμπλακίῃσι φόνῳ φίλα γυῖα μιήνῃ Stephanus 1572; φόβῳ(ι) φίλα γυῖα μιν Plutarch MSS. The line having dropped out in Hippolytus, it is wrong to ascribe, as the editors of Plutarch constantly do, the emended version of the text to Hippolytus. The conjecture φόνωι...μιήνηι is, however, supported by *De esu* 1.7, 996b–c where Plutarch traces back the Empedoclean "allegory on the soul" (that is, our mythical law on guilt and punishment of the daimones) to the Orphic myth according to which mankind has inherited from the Titans the guilt of having killed the young Dionysus.

98. B115.4 as transmitted in Hippolytus: ὃς καὶ [—] ἐπίορκον ἁμαρτήσας ἐπομό<σ> σηι. This line is modeled on Hesiod, *Th.* 793: ὅς κεν τῆς ἐπίορκον ἀπολλείψας ἐπομόσσηι (τῆς—indicating the source of the ἀπολείβειν—Koechly and Solmsen; τὴν MSS). It cannot be by accident that the two deficiencies of the Empedoclean line (metrical: the orphaned *elementum longum* of the second foot; morphological: the wrong aorist ἁμαρτήσας instead of ἁμαρτών) are both clearly due to omission or replacement of precisely those elements in Hesiod that did not suit the Empedoclean context, since they refer to the Styx. If Hippolytus's series of Empedoclean quotations goes back directly or indirectly to Plutarch's great monograph on Empedocles, the Hesiodic line may

have been inserted in the Empedoclean context as a marginal supplement by Plutarch. The nature of this typically learned montage would have been misunderstood by Hippolytus (or his immediate source); hence the misguided attempt to adapt the line.

99. B119: ἐξ οἵης τιμῆς τε καὶ ὅσσου μήκεος ὄλβου.

100. B115.6: τρίς ... μυρίας ὥρας.

101. B115.6: ἀπὸ μακάρων.

102. B115.7–8: φυομένους παντοῖα διὰ χρόνου εἴδεα θνητῶν / ἀργαλέας βιότοιο μεταλλάσσοντα κελεύθους.

103. B115.13; for the identification as such it does not matter whether we read, on the basis of Hippolytus, τῶν καὶ ἐγὼ (νῦν) εἰμί, or, with Plutarch, τὴν καὶ ἐγὼ νῦν εἰμι.

104. Plu. *De Is. et Osir.* 361c.

105. B147: ἀθανάτοις ἄλλοισιν ὁμέστιοι, αὐτοτράπεζοι / ἐόντες, ἀνδρείων ἀχέων ἀπόκληροι, ἀτειρεῖς. This fragment is quoted by Clement, who informs us that it refers to the state μετὰ τὴν ἐνθένδε ἀπαλλαγήν.

106. Kahn, "Religion and Natural Philosophy in Empedocles' Doctrine of the Soul," 18.

107. Arist. fr. 191 Rose[3] (Ael. VH 2.26; p. 29.29–30.2 Dilts; D.L. 8.11; I. 578.18–20 Marcovich; Iamb., VP 140; p. 29.11–14 Deubner); Burkert, *Lore and Science in Early Pythagoreanism*, 141–44.

108. Heraclid. Pont. fr. 89 Wehrli; Kerényi, *Pythagoras und Orpheus*, 18–19; Burkert, *Lore and Science*, 138–41.

109. B129 refers to Pythagoras, according to the historian Timaeus; see Jacoby, *Die Fragmente der Griechischen Historiker*, 566 F 14 and Burkert, *Lore and Science*, 137–38.

110. Prometheus is punished, too, but his crime was not bloodshed, and a series of incarnations does not play any role in the myth of Prometheus. The Titans, on the other hand, attempt to kill Dionysus, and their ashes are subject to reincarnation, according to the Orphic myth of Dionysus Zagreus, but they did not belong to the community of the blessed ones even before their crime.

111. (Ps.)Hes., fr. 51–52 and 54 a–c Merkelbach/West; see text and translation in Dräger, *Untersuchungen zu den Frauenkatalogen Hesiods*, 106–12. On the problem of authorship, and on the reconstruction as proposed by Wilamowitz, *Isyllos von Epidauros*, 57–77, see Lesky, *Alkestis, der Mythus und das Drama*, 43–54, West, *The Hesiodic Catalogue of Women*, 69–72, and Dräger, *Untersuchungen zu den Frauenkatalogen Hesiods*.

112. A. *Supp.* 214. This line has been referred to Apollo's serfdom in Pherae since Plut. *Def. orac.* 15, 417e–f, where it is quoted as an example of "exiles and servitudes of the gods"; see further Sandin, *Aeschylus' Supplices*, 136.

113. Inasmuch as the divinity of the daimon is temporarily infringed, the Empedoclean usage may be said to anticipate the hierarchy attested by Pl. *Smp.* 202d–e: πᾶν τὸ δαιμόνιον μεταξύ ἐστι θεοῦ τε καὶ θνητοῦ. On the later meanings of *daímon* see, e.g., ter Vrugt-Lentz, "Geister (Dämonen) B.II."; Zintzen, "Geister (Dämonen) B.III.c."; Burkert, *Greek Religion*, 179–81.

114. B115.1–2: ἔστιν Ἀνάγκης χρῆμα, θεῶν ψήφισμα παλαιόν, / ἀίδιον, πλατέεσσι κατεσφρηγισμένον ὅρκοις. B30.2–3, quoted in n. 37 here.

115. According to B115.14, the wandering daimon is "trusting in mad Strife": Νείκεϊ μαινομένωι πίσυνος.

116. It is true that in the exposition of the physical theory it is, as we have seen, the four pure masses (*rhizomata*) that serve as starting point and end point for the description of the cycle (B17.1–2, 16–17; B26.5–12). But because of the repetitive nature of the cycle it does not matter, in principle, with which point of the cycle the description starts off.

117. PHerc 1012, edited in Puglia, *Demetrio Lacone*.

118. Crönert, "Kolotes und Menedemos," 100–25.

119. Diels, "Über ein Fragment des Empedokles."

120. Puglia, *Demetrio Lacone*, 167–68, Τὸν δ' οὔτ' ἄρ τε Διὸς | τέγεοι δόμοι αἰγ[ιόχοιο] / [οὔ] | τε.[. . ..]Ο Ἀΐδου δέ[χεται..] | Κ[..]ΗΣ τέγος [..]Δ[. . ..].

121. Martin, "Empédocle, fr. 142 D.-K.," 51: Τὸν δ' οὔτ' ἄρ τε Διὸς | τέγεοι δόμοι αἰγ[ιόχοιο] / [οὔ]| τε τί π]ηι Ἀΐδου δέ[χεται πυ]κι[νὸ]ν στέγος [ ]δ[ ]. For a defense of the hiatus between πηι and Ἀιδου see Primavesi, *Die Häuser von Zeus und Hades*, 56–58.

122. Diels, "Über ein Fragment des Empedokles," followed by van der Ben, *The Proem of Empedocles' Peri Physios*, and Bollack, *Empédocle, Les purifications*.

123. Diels, "Über ein Fragment des Empedokles," 1071 = 156,"Vielleicht sprach der Prophet von dem Schicksale des frevelnden Geistes, der weder im Feuer, noch in der Luft, noch auf Erden zur seligen Ruhe käme, wenn er nicht durch Busse und Läuterung seine Sünden abschwöre."

124. B115.9–12: αἰθέριον μὲν γάρ σφε μένος πόντονδε διώκει, / πόντος δ' ἐς χθονὸς οὖδας ἀπέπτυσε, γαῖα δ' ἐς αὐγὰς / ἠελίου φαέθοντος, ὁ δ' αἰθέρος ἔμβαλε δίναις· / ἄλλος δ' ἐξ ἄλλου δέχεται, στυγέουσι δὲ πάντες.

125. The epithet of Zeus in B142, "aegis-bearing," illustrates quite well the intransigent opposition of the compact elemental mass in question (fire according to the ancient tradition) to the coming-to-be of living mixtures (represented by the incarnations of the daimon), since the function of the divine aegis is to frighten off and destroy enemy mortals; see *Od.* 22.297–98: δὴ τότ' Ἀθηναίη φθισίμβροτον αἰγίδ' ἀνέσχεν / ὑψόθεν ἐξ ὀροφῆς· τῶν δὲ φρένες ἐπτοίηθεν.

126. It may be noted in passing that Gallavotti, *Empedocle*, 224, regarded B142 as a piece of negative theology about Apollo without perceiving the physical reference in "Zeus" and "Hades": "Il senso è che Apollo non abita l'Olimpo, e tanto meno l'Ades: non dobbiamo figurarci la divinità secondo i miti antropomorfici, accetti alla comune δόξα degli uomini."

127. B147.1: ἀθανάτοις ἄλλοισιν ὁμέστιοι, αὐτοτράπεζοι.

128. See Kahn, "Religion and Natural Philosophy in Empedocles' Doctrine of the Soul," 25–26: "Neither the common hearths and feasting of the daimons nor the possibility that they may be guilty of perjury and bloodshed is compatible with the view that they are to be fused into a single Deity, as the elements seem to be fused within the cosmic Sphere."

129. B115.6: ἀπὸ μακάρων.

130. This eternity is a common feature of the blessed communion and the *kosmos noetos* of later Platonism, which could explain the predilection of the Platonizing tradition for the Empedoclean myth as opposed to his physical theory. See Hippol. *Haer.* 7.29.17: μάκαρας καλῶν τοὺς συνηγμένους ὑπὸ τῆς φιλίας ἀπὸ τῶν πολλῶν εἰς τὴν ἑνότητα τοῦ κόσμου τοῦ νοητοῦ.

131. B8.3–4: ἀλλὰ μόνον μίξις τε διάλλαξίς τε μιγέντων / ἔστι.

132. Cornford, "Mystery Religions and Pre-socratic Philosophy," 569. Similarly O'Brien, *Empedocles' Cosmic Cycle*, 325–36, tentatively followed by Martin and Primavesi, *L'Empédocle de Strasbourg*, 83–86.

133. *PP* 500.

134. Cornford, "Mystery Religions and Pre-socratic Philosophy," 569: "To the modern mind the confusion and inconsistency of such a complex image is so patent that we can only by a strong effort hold its components together." *PP* 501: "The account is doubtless

implausible: Empedocles does not tell us how to identify a daimôn, or how to trace a daemonic substance from one mortal form to another; and if it is possible to think of ways in which this hypothesis might become scientifically testable, it is hard to think of a way which would not also lead to speedy refutation. But that is only to say what everyone believes: that transmigration does not happen."

135. See B137; in B136, however, the reference to reincarnation is not clear.

136. Burkert, *Lore and Science*, 182: "Animal sacrifice was the focal point of the traditional religion, that is of the official cult of the polis, and to renounce it would have been more than religious reform. It would have meant a complete overturn of traditional ways."

137. ZN 1006: "Ebensowenig werden wir die Seelenwanderung bei ihm als bloßes Symbol für die Lebendigkeit der Natur und die stufenweise Entwicklung des Naturlebens auffassen dürfen. Er selbst hat nun einmal diese Lehre in ihrem buchstäblichen Sinn mit der größten Feierlichkeit und Bestimmtheit vorgetragen, und sittliche Vorschriften darauf gegründet, die uns vielleicht sehr unwesentlich scheinen mögen, die aber für ihn unleugbar eine hohe Wichtigkeit haben."

138. ZN 1006: "die Lebendigkeit der Natur," "die stufenweise Entwicklung des Naturlebens."

139. *P. Strasb. Ensemble c:* [. . . ἔργα δι]άκτορα μη[τίσασθαι,] / [τοῦτο μὲν ἂν βροτέων] μελέων ἀρι[δείκετον ὄγκον·] / [ἄλλοτε μὲν Φιλότητι συν]ερχόμεθ᾽ ε[ἰς ἓν ἅπαντα] / [γυῖα, τὰ σῶμα λέλογχε βίου θη]λοῦντος [ἐν ἀκμῆι·] / [ἄλλοτε δ᾽ αὖτε κακῆισι διατμηθέντ᾽ Ἐρίδεσσι,] / [πλάζεται ἄνδιχ᾽ ἕκαστα περὶ] ῥη[γμῖνι βίοιο·] / [ὣς δ᾽ αὔτως θάμνοισι καὶ ἰχ]θύ[σιν ὑδρομελάθροις] / [θηρσί τ᾽ ὀρειμελέεσσιν ἰδὲ πτ]ερο[βάμοσι κύμβαις].

140. O'Brien, *Empedocles' Cosmic Cycle*, 227.

141. Simplicius Phys. 1124.9–11 Diels.

142. B20.2–3, as quoted by Simplicius: ἄλλοτε μὲν Φιλότητι συνερχόμεν᾽ εἰς ἓν ἅπαντα / γυῖα, τὰ σῶμα λέλογχε, βίου θαλέθοντος ἐν ἀκμῆι.

143. Karsten, *Empedoclis Agrigentini Carminum Reliquiae*, 134, replaced θαλέθοντος in B20.3 by θαλέθουσιν; Panzerbieter, *Beiträge zur Kritik und Erklärung des Empedokles*, 29, changed συνερχόμεν᾽ in B20.2 to συνέρχεται; Holwerda, "Zu Empedokles Fr. 20 D.-K.," 320, suggested writing ἁπαντᾶι instead of ἅπαντα in B20.2.

144. *P. Strasb.* c 3–4 (= B20.2–3); see note 140 here. An alternative syntactical interpretation of γυῖα has been suggested by Janko, "Empedocles, *On Nature* I 233–364," 19: "at one time we unite in Love *with all / the limbs* that bodies have when life is blossoming."

145. *P. Strasb.* a (i) 6: συνερχό]μεθ᾽ εἰς ἕνα κόσμον. *P. Strasb.* a (ii) 17: μεσάτους (*scilicet* τόπους) τ᾽ [. . . ε]ρχομεθ᾽ ἐν μ[όνον εἶναι]. The latter passage is very lacunose; for an attempt at reconstruction based on the speculative equation of the Empedoclean *daimones* with particles of love see Martin and Primavesi, *L'Empédocle de Strasbourg*, 211–14. One of the problems with this reconstruction is that it has to refer the formula ἓν μ[όνον εἶναι] to the retreat of Love alone toward the center of the universe, whereas in a (ii) 20, that is, three lines later, the formula clearly refers to the all-embracing One of the cosmic cycle, as it does in B35.3. See further Primavesi, "Empedokles *Physika* I."

146. This "correction" has taken place not only in the indirect tradition as represented by the quotation by Simplicius, but also in the papyrus itself, where a second hand has written a -ν- above the -θ-. Algra and Mansfeld, "Three Thêtas in the 'Empédocle de Strasbourg,'" have suggested that συνερχόμεν᾽ was the original reading in B20.2, which would have been taken to be a mistake (that is, the wrong active indicative *συνέρχομεν)

by someone who did not understand the elision, and who accordingly replaced it by the morphologically correct middle indicative συνερχόμεθ'. But someone unable to understand the elided form συνερχόμεν' would probably not replace it by the equally elided form συνερχόμεθ'.

147. Edited in Martin and Primavesi, *L'Empédocle de Strasbourg*.

148. *P. Strasb.* d 5–6 (= B 139 DK): [Οἴ]μοι ὅτ(ι)' οὐ πρόσθεν με δι[ώλεσε νη]λεὲς ἦμαρ, [πρὶν] χηλαῖς [σχέ]τλι' ἔργα βορ[ᾶς πέρι μητ]ίσα[σθαι]. The text of the papyrus is free from the faults of the quotation in Porphyry; see Primavesi, "Editing Empedocles," 81–83.

149. *P. Strasb.* d 10–14.

BIBLIOGRAPHY

Algra, Keimpe, and Jaap Mansfeld. "Three Thêtas in the 'Empédocle de Strasbourg." *Mnemosyne*, ser. 4, 54 (2001): 78–81.

Barnes, Jonathan. *Early Greek Philosophy*. Harmondsworth, England: Penguin, 1987.

Ben, N. van der. *The Proem of Empedocles' Peri Physios: Towards a New Edition of all the Fragments*. Amsterdam: B. R. Grüner, 1975.

Betegh, Gábor. *The Derveni papyrus: Cosmology, Theology and Interpretation*. Cambridge: Cambridge University Press, 2004.

Bignone, Ettore. *Empedocle: Studio Critico*. Turin: Bocca, 1916.

Bollack, Jean. *Empédocle, Les purifications: Un projet de paix universelle*. Paris: Éditions du Seuil, 2003.

———. "Empedokles von Agrigent." *Der Neue Pauly. Enzyklopädie der Antike*, 3: 1011–15. Stuttgart, 1997.

Burkert, Walter. *Greek Religion*. Cambridge, Mass.: Harvard University Press, 1985.

———. *Lore and Science in Ancient Pythagoreanism*. Translated by E. L. Minar, Jr. Cambridge, Mass.: Harvard University Press, 1972.

———. "Plotin, Plutarch und die platonisierende Interpretation von Heraklit und Empedokles." In *Kephalaion: Studies in Greek Philosophy and Its Continuation Offered to Professor C. J. de Vogel*, 137–46. Assen: Van Gorcum, 1975.

Campbell, D. A. *Greek Lyric II: Anacreon, Anacreontea, Choral Lyric from Olympus to Alcman*. Cambridge, Mass.: Harvard University Press, 1988.

Cornford, F. M. "Mystery Religions and Pre-socratic Philosophy." In *Cambridge Ancient History*, edited by J. B. Bury, S. A. Cook, and F. E. Adcock, vol. 1, pt. 4: 522–78. Cambridge: Cambridge University Press, 1926.

Crönert, W. "Kolotes und Menedemos: Texte und Untersuchungen zur Philosophen- und Literaturgeschichte." *Studien zur Palaeographie und Papyruskunde* 6 (1906): 100–25.

Diels, Hermann. *Poetarum philosophorum fragmenta*. Berlin: Weidmann, 1901.

———. "Über die Gedichte des Empedokles." *Sitzungberichte der Preussischen Akademie der Wissenschaften* (1898): 396–415. Reprinted in *Kleine Schriften zur Geschichte der Antiken Philosophie*, edited by Walter Burkert, 127–46. Darmstadt: Wissenschaftliche Buchgesellschaft, 1969.

————. "Über ein Fragment des Empedokles." *Sitzungsberichte der Preussischen Akademie der Wissenschaften* (1897): 1062–73. Reprinted in *Kleine Schriften zur Geschichte der Antiken Philosophie*, edited by Walter Burkert, 147–58. Darmstadt: Wissenschaftliche Buchgesellschaft, 1969.

Dräger, P. *Untersuchungen zu den Frauenkatalogen Hesiods*. Stuttgart: Steiner, 1997.

Dümmler, F. "Zur orphischen Kosmologie." *Archiv für Geschichte der Philosophie* 7 (1894): 147–53.

Dyck, A., ed. *Epimerismi Homerici qui ad Iliadis librum A pertinent*. Sammlung griechischer und lateinischer Grammatiker, vol. 5.1. Berlin: de Gruyter, 1983.

Ford, A. *The Origins of Criticism: Literary Culture and Poetic Theory in Classical Greece*. Princeton, N.J.: Princeton University Press, 2002.

Gallavotti, C. *Empedocle: Poema fisico e lustrale*. Scrittori Greci e Latini. Milan: Mondadori, 1975.

Garulli, V. *Il Περὶ ποιητῶν di Lobone di Argo*. Eikasmos: Quaderni Bolognesi di Filologia Classica, Studi 10. Bologna: Pàtron, 2004.

Gemelli Marciano, Laura. Review of *L'Empédocle de Strasbourg*, by Alain Martin and Oliver Primavesi. *Gnomon* 72 (2000): 389–400.

Hermann, Gottfried. *Draconis Stratonicensis Liber de metris poeticis. Joannis Tzetzae Exegesis in Homeri Iliadem* primum edidit et indices addidit. Lipsiae: Weigel, 1812.

Hershbell, J. P. "Hippolytus' Elenchos as a Source for Empedocles Re-Examined." *Phronesis* 18 (1973): 97–114, 187–203.

Hölscher, Uvo. "Weltzeiten und Lebenszyklus: Eine Nachprüfung der Empedokles-Doxographie." *Hermes* 93 (1965): 7–33. Reprinted, with modifications, in Uvo Hölscher, *Anfängliches Fragen*, 173–212. Heidelberg: Vandenhoeck & Ruprecht, 1968.

Holwerda, D. "Zu Empedokles Fr. 20 D.-K." *Mnemosyne* 50 (1997): 320–21.

Holzhausen, J. "Pindar und die Orphik: Zur Frg. 133 Snell/Maehler." *Hermes* 132 (2004): 20–36.

Horna, C. "Empedocleum." *Wiener Studien* 48 (1930): 3–11.

Inwood, Brad. *The Poem of Empedocles*. Toronto: University of Toronto Press, 1992. 2nd ed., 2001.

Jacoby, Felix. *Die Fragmente der Griechischen Historiker (F Gr Hist)*. Dritter Teil. Geschichte von Staedten und Voelkern. B. Nr. 297–607, Leiden: E.J. Brill 1950.

Jaeger, Werner. *The Theology of the Early Greek Philosophers*. The Gifford Lectures. Oxford: Clarendon Press, 1947.

Janko, Richard. "Empedocles, *On Nature* I 233–364: A New Reconstruction of *P. Strasb. gr.* Inv. 1665–6." *Zeitschrift für Papyrologie und Epigraphik* 150 (2004): 1–26.

Joachim, H. *Aristotle on Coming-to-Be and Passing-Away*. A Revised Text with Introduction and Commentary. Oxford: Clarendon Press, 1922.

Kahn, Charles H. "Religion and Natural Philosophy in Empedocles' Doctrine of the Soul." *Archiv für Geschichte der Philosophie* 42 (1960): 3–35. Reprinted with retractations in *The Pre-Socratics: A Collection of Critical Essays*, edited by Alexander P. D. Mourelatos. Modern Studies in Philosophy 21, 426–56. Garden City, N.Y.: Doubleday, 1974.

Kannicht, R. *The Ancient Quarrel between Philosophy and Poetry: Aspects of the Greek Conception of Literature*. Fifth Broadhead Memorial Lecture 1986. Christchurch, New Zealand: University of Canterbury Press, 1988.

Karsten, Simon. *Empedoclis Agrigentini Carminum Reliquiae*. Philosophorum Graecorum veterum praesertim qui ante Platonem floruerunt operum reliquiae 2. Amsterdam: Müller, 1838.

Kerényi, K. *Pythagoras und Orpheus*. Präludien zu einer zukünftigen Geschichte der Orphik und des Pythagoreismus. Albae Vigiliae, Neue Folge 9. Zürich: Rhein-Verlag, 1950.

Kingsley, Peter. *Ancient Philosophy, Mystery, and Magic: Empedocles and the Pythagorean Tradition*. Oxford: Clarendon Press, 1995.

———. "Empedocles in Armenian." *Revue des Études Arméniennes* 24 (1993): 47–57.

———. "Empedocles' Two Poems." *Hermes* 124 (1996): 108–11.

Kranz, Walther. *Empedokles: Antike Gestalt und romantische Neuschöpfung*. Zürich: Artemis-Verlag, 1949.

Laks, André. "Some Thoughts about Empedoclean Cosmic and Demonic Cycles." In *The Empedoclean Κόσμος: Structure, Process and the Question of Cyclicity*, edited by Apostolos L. Pierris, 265–82. Patras: Institute for Philosophical Research, 2005.

Lanata, Giuliana. *Poetica pre-platonica: Testimonianze e frammenti*. Biblioteca di Studi Superiori 43. Florence: La Nuova Italia, 1963.

Leone, Petrus Aloisius M. *Ioannis Tzetzae Historiae*. Pubblicazioni dell'Istituto di Filologia Classica. Università degli Studi di Napoli. I. Napoli: Libreria Scientifica Editrice, 1968.

Lesky, Albin. *Alkestis, der Mythus und das Drama*. Sitzungsberichte der Akademie der Wissenschaften in Wien, Philosophisch-historische Klasse, 203/2. Vienna: Hölder-Pichler-Tempsky, 1925.

Mader, B. δαίμων. *Lexikon des frühgriechischen Epos*, 2:198–200. Göttingen: Vandenhoeck & Ruprecht, 1991.

Martin, Alain. "Empédocle, fr. 142 D.-K.: Nouveau regard sur un papyrus d'Herculaneum." *Cronache Ercolanesi*, 33 (2003): 43–52, 2003.

Martin, Alain, and Oliver Primavesi. *L'Empédocle de Strasbourg*. Berlin: de Gruyter, 1999.

O'Brien, Denis. "Empedocles: The Wandering Daimon and the Two Poems." *Aevum Antiquum*, n.s., 1 (2001): 79–179.

———. *Empedocles' Cosmic Cycle*. Cambridge: Cambridge University Press, 1969.

———. "Empedocles Revisited." *Ancient Philosophy* 15 (1995): 403–70.

———. *Pour interpréter Empédocle*. Leiden: E. J. Brill, 1981.

Osborne, Catherine. "Empedocles Recycled." *Classical Quarterly* 37 (1987): 24–50.

———. "Sin and Moral Responsibility in Empedocles' Cosmic Cycle." In *The Empedoclean Κόσμος: Structure, Process and the Question of Cyclicity*, edited by Apostolos L. Pierris, 283–308. Patras: Institute for Philosophical Research, 2005.

Panzerbieter, F. *Beiträge zur Kritik und Erklärung des Empedokles*. Meiningen: F. W. Gadow & Sohn, 1844.

Picot, J.-C. "L'Empédocle magique de P. Kingsley." *Revue de Philosophie Ancienne* 18 (2000): 25–86.

Pierris, Apostolos L. *The Empedoclean Κόσμος: Structure, Process and the Question of Cyclicity*. Patras: Institute for Philosophical Research, 2005.

Primavesi, Oliver. "Apollo and Other Gods in Empedocles." In *La costruzione del discorso filosofico nell'età dei Presocratici*, edited by Maria Michela Sassi, 51–77. Pisa: Edizioni della Normale, 2006.

———. "La daimonologia della fisica Empedoclea," *Aevum Antiquum*, n.s., 1 (2001): 3–68.

———. "Editing Empedocles: Some Longstanding Problems Reconsidered in the Light of the Strasburg Papyrus." *In Fragmentsammlungen philosophischer Texte in der Antike: Le raccolte dei frammenti di filosofi antichi: Atti del Seminario Internazionale*, edited by W. Burkert, L. Gemelli Marciano, E. Matelli, and L. Orelli, 62–88. Göttingen: Vandenhoeck & Ruprecht, 1998.

———. "Empedokles in Florentiner Aristoteles-Scholien." *Zeitschrift für Papyrologie und Epigraphik* 157 (2006): 27–40.

———. "Empedokles *Physika* I: Eine Rekonstruktion des zentralen Gedankengangs." Archiv für Papyrusforschung, Beiheft 22. Berlin: de Gruyter, 2008.

———. "Die Häuser von Zeus und Hades: Zu Text und Deutung von Empedokles B 142 D.-K." *Cronache Ercolanesi* 33 (2003): 53–68.

———. "Lecteurs antiques et byzantins d'Empédocle: De Zénon à Tzétzès." In *Qu'est-ce que la Philosophie Présocratique?*, edited by A. Laks and C. Louguet, Cahiers de Philologie, vol. 20, 183–204. Villeneuve d'Ascq: Presses Universitaires du Septentrion, 2002.

———. "Neues zur aristotelischen Vorsokratiker-Doxographie." In *Antike Naturwissenschaft und ihre Rezeption*, edited by K. Döring, B. Herzhoff, and G. Wöhrle, 25–41. Trier: Wissenschaftlicher Verlag, 1998.

———. "Die Suda über die Werke des Empedokles." *Zeitschrift für Papyrologie und Epigraphik*, 158 (2006): 61–75.

———. "The Structure of Empedocles' Cosmic Cycle: Aristotle and the Byzantine Anonymous." In *The Empedoclean Κόσμος: Structure, Process and the Question of Cyclicity*, edited by Apostolos L. Pierris, 245–64. Patras: Institute for Philosophical Research, 2005.

———. "Zur Überlieferung und Bedeutung des empedokleischen Titels "Καθαρμοί." In *Katharsis vor Aristoteles: Zum kulturellen Hintergrund des Tragödien-Satzes*, edited by Martin Vöhler and Bernd Seidensticker, 183–225. Berlin: de Gruyter, 2007.

Primavesi, Oliver, and Andreas Patzer. "Die übertiefe Tiefe (Empedokles B35, 3–5 und *Physika* I, 288-290)." *Zeitschrift für Papyrologie und Epigraphik* 135 (2001): 1–10.

Puglia, E. *Demetrio Lacone: Aporie testuali ed esegetiche in Epicuro*. La Scuola Di Epicuro, vol. 8. Naples: Bibliopolis, 1988.

Rashed, Marwan. "La chronographie du système d'Empédocle: Documents byzantins inédits." *Aevum Antiquum*, n.s., 1 (2001): 237–59.

Riedweg, Christoph. "Orphisches bei Empedokles." *Antike und Abendland* 41 (1995): 1–27.

Ruocco, E. "Daimon, sphairos, ananke: Psicologia e teologia in Empedocle." In *Forme del sapere nei presocratici*, edited by A. Capizzi and G. Casertano, 187–222. Rome: Dell'Ateneo, 1987.

Sandin, P. *Aeschylus' Supplices: Introduction and Commentary on vv. 1–523*. Göteborg: Serviceenheten, Repro, 2003.

Stein, Heinrich. *Empedoclis Agrigentini Fragmenta*. Bonn: Marcus, 1852.

Sturz, F. W. *Empedocles Agrigentinus*. 2 vols. Leipzig: G. Sturz, 1805.

Thiel, H. v. *Scholia D in Iliadem secundum codices manu scriptos*. (19.07.2006), <http://kups.ub.uni-koeln.de/volltexte/2006/1810/>. 2006.

Trepanier, Simon. "Empedocles on the Ultimate Symmetry of the World." *Oxford Studies in Ancient Philosophy* 24 (2003): 1–57.

ter Vrugt-Lentz, J. "Geister (Dämonen) B.II.: Vorhellenistisches Griechenland." *Reallexikon für Antike und Christentum* 9 (1976): 598–615. Stuttgart: Hiersemann, 1976.

van der Ben, N. *The Proem of Empedocles' Peri Physios: Towards a New Edition of All the Fragments*. Amsterdam: Grüner, 1975.

West, M. L. *The Hesiodic Catalogue of Women*. Oxford: Clarendon Press, 1985.

Wilamowitz-Moellendorff, Ulrich von. *Isyllos von Epidauros*. Berlin: Weidmann, 1886.

———. "Die Καθαρμοί des Empedokles." *Sitzungsberichte der preussischen Akademie der Wissenschaften*, 27 (1929): 626–62. Reprinted in *Kleine Schriften*, 1.473–521. Berlin: Weidmann, 1935.

Wright, M. R. *Empedocles: The Extant Fragments*. New Haven, Conn.: Yale University Press, 1981.

Zintzen, C. "Geister (Dämonen) B.III.c.: Hellenistische und kaiserzeitliche Philosophie."
In *Reallexikon für Antike und Christentum*, 9: 640–68. Stuttgart: Hiersemann, 1976.
Zuntz, Günther. "De Empedoclis librorum numero coniectura." *Mnemosyne*, ser. 4, 18
(1965): 365.
———. *Persephone: Three Essays on Religion and Thought in Magna Graecia*. Oxford:
Clarendon Press, 1971.
———. *Griechische philosophische Hymnen*, edited by H. Cancik und L. Käppel. Studien
und Texte zu Antike und Christentum 35. Tübingen: Mohr Siebeck, 2005.

CHAPTER 9

TWO PROBLEMS IN PYTHAGOREANISM

CARL HUFFMAN

THERE HAVE been a number of surveys of ancient Pythagoreanism in recent years (e.g., Huffman, "The Pythagorean Tradition"; Kahn, *Pythagoras and the Pythagoreans*), so there seems little point to providing another one here. Instead, I will address two more focused but still central questions: (1) Did Aristotle really think that Plato derived most of his philosophy from the Pythagoreans? and (2) Who counts as a Pythagorean?

1

Two of the central issues in the study of early Pythagoreanism are (1) the extent and nature of the influence of the Pythagoreans on Plato, and (2) the nature of Aristotle's account of fifth-century Pythagoreanism. These two questions come together in a crucial sentence in the first book of Aristotle's *Metaphysics* (987a29–31; hereafter "Sentence P"). Sentence P has had enormous influence on scholarly accounts of the relationship between Plato and the Pythagoreans. It is almost universally taken to say that "Plato's philosophy followed them [i.e., the Pythagoreans] in most respects," suggesting a massive and fundamental debt to the Pythagoreans on Plato's part.[1] In the immediately following passage of the *Metaphysics*, however, Aristotle ascribes the origin of Plato's central metaphysical doctrines not to the influence of the Pythagoreans but to his contact with two people: the Heraclitean, Cratylus, and Socrates (987a32–987b10). This same account of the origin of Plato's theory of forms, with no mention of the Pythagoreans, is repeated later in book 13 of the *Metaphysics* (1078b12–30). As we shall see shortly, Aristotle does go on in *Metaphysics* 1 to make pointed comparisons between Plato and the Pythagoreans, but this is only after he has explained the origin of Plato's central metaphysical theory, the theory of forms, without any appeal to the Pythagoreans. Aristotle's own behavior in this passage of the *Metaphysics* should thus make us suspicious of a reading of Sentence P that has Aristotle say that Plato followed the Pythagoreans in most things.

Modern scholarship on Plato mirrors this apparent tension in the text of *Metaphysics* 1. Scholars will duly refer to Sentence P as suggesting important Pythagorean influence, but when Plato's views are discussed, Pythagoreanism is not an important part of that discussion. The recent *Cambridge Companion to Plato* has some 492 pages of text, yet only a total of one or two of those pages have anything substantive to say about Plato and the Pythagoreans; the only paragraph that focuses specifically on Plato's relation to the Pythagoreans is a discussion of precisely Sentence P.[2] Of the 12 references to the Pythagoreans in the index, most are mere mentions of "the mathematical work of the Pythagoreans" or the "Orphic-Pythagorean conglomerate." Clearly many modern scholars think it is possible to understand Plato with little mention of the Pythagoreans, which is puzzling, if Aristotle thought that Plato owed most of his philosophy to the Pythagoreans.

There can be no doubt that the Pythagoreans did indeed influence Plato in a number of ways. This influence can best be seen if we leave Aristotle aside for the moment and compare what we find in the Platonic dialogues with what we know of early Pythagoreanism from other sources. Kahn shows effectively that there are two main clusters of ideas with which Plato works and that can be plausibly regarded as Pythagorean in origin: (1) the attempt to explain the nature of things in mathematical terms, and (2) the conception of the soul as immortal and hence potentially divine.[3] The second cluster of ideas is particularly prominent in the *Phaedo* and in several of the Platonic myths such as those that end the *Republic* and *Gorgias*. The first cluster of ideas in their specifically Pythagorean form is not as widespread in Plato's dialogues as is sometimes assumed. Not all of Plato's discussions of mathematics are dependent on the Pythagoreans, and I would argue that most of the discussion of mathematics in the *Republic*, in fact, reflects a disagreement between Plato and the Pythagoreans on the proper role of mathematics. As Kahn emphasizes, it is especially in the *Timaeus* that Plato makes an extended attempt to explain the nature of the physical world in mathematical terms, although even here there are significant differences from the Pythagoreans. To accept Kahn's analysis of Pythagorean influence on Plato, however, is not at all to accept the standard reading of Sentence P, which calls on us to see the Platonic system as for the most part Pythagorean, with a few idiosyncratic developments on Plato's part. Platonic myths, where one cluster of Pythagorean ideas resides, and the *Timaeus*, where the other resides, are undoubtedly important parts of Plato's achievement; indeed in the later tradition the *Timaeus* was the central work of Plato. Nonetheless, the myths are usually presented by Plato himself as subsidiary to his main argument, and the *Timaeus* is probably a late and is certainly in many ways an atypical work. If these are the main areas of Pythagorean influence, we are once again driven to puzzle over Aristotle's apparent assertion that Plato followed the Pythagoreans in most things. A reexamination of Sentence P is in order.

The sentence is difficult, and there are reasonable arguments for the standard reading, but the arguments for an alternative reading are stronger, and that alternative makes better sense both of Aristotle's own presentation of Plato's connection to the Pythagoreans and also of modern analysis of the development of Plato's thought. Here is the text of 987a29–31:

> μετὰ δὲ τὰς εἰρημένας φιλοσοφίας ἡ Πλάτωνος ἐπεγένετο πραγματεία, τὰ μὲν πολλὰ τούτοις ἀκολουθοῦσα, τὰ δὲ καὶ ἴδια παρὰ τὴν τῶν Ἰταλικῶν ἔχουσα φιλοσοφίαν.

> After the philosophies that have been mentioned, the Platonic system came next; on the one hand, it agrees with *these* in most respects, but, on the other hand, it also has some distinctive features in contrast to the philosophy of the Italians.

The traditional reading is that "these" refers to the Pythagoreans, so that Aristotle is saying that Plato's philosophy agrees with the Pythagoreans in most respects. The best argument for this reading is Cherniss's point that "*toutois* [these] . . . *must* [my emphasis] refer to the 'Italians' as the contrast of *men* [on the one hand] . . . *de* [on the other hand] . . . shows."[4] Since it is the Italians (i.e., the Pythagoreans) who are contrasted to Plato in the "on the other hand" clause, it is logical that the "these" of the "on the one hand" clause, with whom Plato is said to agree, should also be Pythagoreans. The only change I would make in Cherniss's point is to remove the word "must." Taken by itself, the "on the one hand similar . . . on the other hand different" structure naturally suggests that Plato is being compared to the same people in each case; he is similar to them in most things but differs in others. This point does not override all other evidence for the meaning of the sentence, however, and there is considerable evidence that the traditional reading cannot be right.

We need to begin by looking at the context of Aristotle's remark at 987a29–31. In book 1 of the *Metaphysics*, Aristotle has identified the knowledge of the causes of things as characteristic of the highest wisdom, that is, metaphysics (983a24). Aristotle's professed goal in the bulk of book 1 of the *Metaphysics* is to examine his predecessors' views on causes to see (1) whether they have identified any other cause besides the four which Aristotle has defined in the *Physics*, and (2) to what extent they have succeeded in correctly analyzing those four causes (983b5, 993a11). It is crucial to recognize that all of Aristotle's remarks on his predecessors' philosophical systems in book 1 of the *Metaphysics* are limited to what they have to say about the basic causes/principles of things. He is thus not talking about Plato's political philosophy, ethics, or psychology or even directly about epistemology. When he compares Plato to the Presocratics in general or to the Pythagoreans in particular, the comparison is in reference to their account of the basic principles/causes that are used to account for the natural world and, more specifically, in reference to the extent to which they anticipated Aristotle's four causes.

From 983b2 to 987a2, Aristotle discusses the principles/causes employed by Presocratics down to and including the Pythagoreans and atomists. Next, in the paragraph immediately preceding Sentence P, he summarizes what can be learned from the discussion of his predecessors that he has so far presented (987a2–987a28). This summary is in turn divided into two parts. In the first part (987a4–9) he says that we have learned from the earliest philosophers that the principle is bodily, although they disagreed as to whether there was just one such principle (e.g., Anaximenes' air) or many (e.g., Empedocles' earth, air, fire, and water). Others of these early philosophers had posited, in addition, a cause that was the source of motion, some making this cause one and others two (e.g., Anaxagoras and Empedocles). He characterizes these early thinkers as being "down to and apart from the Italians" and concludes that they were vague in what they said, although they appear to use two causes (the material cause and the source of motion). The second and longer part of his summary of his predecessors' views deals exclusively with the Pythagoreans (987a13–27). Aristotle emphasizes that the Pythagoreans similarly spoke of two principles/causes but that they added some things that were peculiar to them, for example, they provided some of the first definitions of things. There is much that is obscure in Aristotle's account of the Pythagoreans here, but the general structure of the summary is clear. The Pythagoreans are presented as following, in at least a quasi-chronological fashion, on the first philosophers. The Pythagoreans are treated as the last of the Presocratics and, in some sense, as the culmination of Presocratic thought, accepting from their predecessors that there are two causes but adding some unique features of their own.

It is crucial to recognize that Aristotle then ends his summary of the views of earlier philosophers with a summarizing sentence, which refers to *all* of the early thinkers and not just to the Pythagoreans: "So much can be grasped from others who have lived before us" (παρὰ μὲν οὖν τῶν πρότερον καὶ τῶν ἄλλων τοσαῦτα ἔστι λαβεῖν). Sentence P follows immediately on this summarizing sentence. In this context, the initial words of Sentence P, "after the philosophies that have been mentioned, the Platonic system came next," are most naturally read as referring to all the Presocratics whose views Aristotle has just summarized. The plural "philosophies" also shows that Aristotle is thinking not just of the Pythagoreans but of all the earlier thinkers he has considered. One might object that Aristotle, in an earlier passage, did distinguish two different groups of Pythagoreans (986a22) and that he could thus refer to Pythagorean philosophies in the plural. It seems to me doubtful, however, that Aristotle would regard the distinction he made between groups of Pythagoreans as a distinction between separate philosophies. He calls the second group of Pythagoreans "others of *the same school*." Be that as it may, in the passage immediately preceding Sentence P, Pythagoreanism has been presented as a single system, and, most telling of all, the last words of Sentence P itself refer to "the Italian philosophy" in the singular. Thus, the context overwhelmingly suggests that Aristotle is presenting Plato's philosophy as following on all of the earlier philosophies discussed by Aristotle. In the previous paragraph, he has summarized the views of the Presocratics on causation and now goes on to consider the next major philosophy, that of Plato.

This brings us to the crucial clause of Sentence P. On first reading, the words "on the one hand, it [i.e., the philosophy of Plato] agrees with these in most respects" can only be understood as referring to the Presocratics as a whole, since it was the Presocratics as a whole who were the subject of the summarizing sentence, which immediately precedes Sentence P, and who are referred to in the first clause of Sentence P itself ("philosophies"). "These" (*toutois*) is masculine in Greek and thus refers to the philosophers who put forth the philosophies (feminine in Greek), which Aristotle mentioned in the first part of Sentence P. In his broad survey of previous accounts of causation, Aristotle is arguing that Plato followed the Presocratics for the most part.[5] One might object that it is highly implausible to describe Plato as in most respects a Presocratic, and this objection may in part explain the dominance of the standard reading of Sentence P. Aristotle's assertion is not as problematic as it might appear, however. While it is surely not accurate to describe Plato's philosophy as a whole as following the Presocratics in most things, the description has some plausibility if restricted to Plato's account of the causes that explain the natural world. Plato's only extended and detailed account of such causes is to be found in the *Timaeus*. Although Plato is famously critical of the Presocratic cosmologists for not giving a teleological account of the cosmos (*Phd.* 96a–99d), his own cosmology is full of discussion of the material elements (earth, air, fire, and water) first used by the Presocratics and of topics typical of a Presocratic treatise. Scholars have found the dialogue to show the influence of a wide range of Presocratics, from Milesians such as Anaximenes to Empedocles, to Alcmaeon, to Diogenes of Apollonia, and to Pythagoreans such as Philolaus. Some scholars have even argued that there is little in the *Timaeus* that is original to Plato.[6] Whether or not this is a correct view of the *Timaeus* cannot be debated here, but this trend in scholarship shows the plausibility of Aristotle's remark. Plato's account of the physical world can be viewed as following Presocratic accounts for the most part, with certain distinctive additions of his own. That Aristotle is thinking along these lines becomes clear in the sentence that follows Sentence P in the *Metaphysics*. His first specific assertion about Plato's views focuses on his account of the sensible world. Plato takes over the Presocratic conception of material causation in the form it took in Heracliteanism, that is, the sensible world is viewed as a constant flux of the material elements, earth, air, fire, and water. Aristotle is emphatic that Plato was not only familiar with this view as a young man but actually held the view in his later years (987a32–b1).[7]

The first two clauses of the sentence at 987a29–31 as well as the immediately following sentence thus clearly suggest that Aristotle is comparing Plato to the Presocratics as a whole and is presenting him as firmly in the Presocratic tradition, as following them for the most part, when it comes to explaining causes in the natural world. What then are we to make of the final clause of 987a29–31 with its reference to the philosophy of the Italians, the clause on which the standard interpretation is based? The last clause says, "on the other hand, it [i.e., the philosophy of Plato] also has some distinctive features in contrast to the philosophy of the Italians." The standard view argues that this clause should cause us to jettison the interpretation of the first two clauses of the sentence that follows naturally from the context—that is, that Aristotle is talking about the Presocratics as a group—and recognize that his remarks have been limited to the Pythagoreans all along. It is unreasonable, however, to simply disregard all the clues from the context I have discussed so far and, in defiance of them, assume that Pythagoreans alone have been the focus of the whole sentence. We can do justice both to the last clause and the natural reading of the first two clauses if we recognize that, in his immediately preceding summary of Presocratic views, Aristotle treated the Pythagoreans as the culminating step in the development of Presocratic views on causation. The Pythagoreans agreed with earlier thinkers in positing two causes but added their own distinctive features. His point about Plato is that, in terms of the narrow question of the causes of natural phenomena, Plato agreed with the Presocratics in most things but introduced some distinctive ideas, which went beyond even the most advanced Presocratics, the Pythagoreans. In what follows, it will become clear that Aristotle also finds the comparison between Plato and the Pythagoreans particularly striking in several areas and for this reason as well singles out the Pythagoreans for special contrast with Plato. The sentence at 987a29–31 does not, however, present Plato as agreeing with the Pythagoreans in most things. It presents Plato as agreeing with the Presocratic tradition as a whole and chooses to present Plato's distinctive new ideas in contrast with those of the Pythagoreans.

This reading of 987a29–31 is much more in accord with what Aristotle goes on to say about Plato in the immediately following pages of the *Metaphysics* than the standard reading. In analyzing Aristotle's account of the connections in thought among his predecessors, it is important to distinguish cases where Aristotle is making a historical point and those where he is making an analytical one. In some cases, Aristotle is arguing that there was a historical connection between the thought of philosopher X and philosopher Y, while in other cases he notes similarity in thought without claiming any historical connection. It is not always possible to draw a clear line between historical and analytical points. When he says that Plato followed the Presocratics in most things, he is making a broad analytical generalization and not a historical point.[8] In his account of Plato in the passage following our sentence, however, he pretty clearly starts out with a historical point. He asserts that in his youth Plato associated (ἐκ νέου τε γὰρ συνήθης) first with Cratylus and the Heracliteans before later following Socrates. These historical connections are used to explain Plato's belief in the constantly changing nature of the sensible world and his development of the idea of an intelligible world of forms, which are the true subjects of definitions and in which sensible things participate. Platonic metaphysics in the form in which it appears in middle dialogues, such as the *Republic*, is thus explained totally in terms of the development of Heraclitean and Socratic influences.

It then comes as a jolt when we are told next that, in saying that things participate in forms, Plato "just changed the name," since the Pythagoreans said that things exist by imitation of numbers (987b11). Read as a historical comment, these words seem to be saying that the Pythagoreans had originated the entire theory of forms and that Plato differed from them only in changing the name for the relation between particulars and forms from imitation to participation. This cannot be what Aristotle means, however. He makes it abundantly clear elsewhere that the Pythagoreans did not believe in forms and indeed that they did not believe in the split between the intelligible and sensible, which is at the core of the Platonic system (e.g., 987b27–8 and 989b33–4). Thus Aristotle is not making the historical point that Plato developed his theory of forms from the Pythagoreans; that theory has already been explained historically in terms of the Heracliteans and Socrates, and there is no room for the Pythagoreans. Aristotle is just making a small aside on a specific point. Plato's conception of the relation between things and forms as participation seems similar to the relation between numbers and things in Pythagoreanism. Even this is a problem, since the Pythagoreans do not distinguish the sensible from the intelligible; hence it is hard to see how their notion of imitation can be very similar to Plato's participation, which is precisely designed to link sensible with intelligible. The main point in the comparison may reside in Aristotle's next words, where he emphasizes that neither participation nor imitation was ever explained by its exponents. Aristotle's point then is a narrow one; both the Pythagoreans and Plato use an unexplained term to name the relationship between their fundamental entities (forms in Plato's case and numbers in the Pythagoreans' case) and individual things in the world.

Next, Aristotle argues that Plato, since he makes the forms the causes of everything else, also supposes that the elements of forms are the elements of all things (987b19). The elements of the forms are then identified as the "Great and Small" on the one hand and the "One" on the other. It is with regard to these elements that Aristotle introduces most of the comparisons between Plato and the Pythagoreans. He says that, in treating the one as a substance rather than as a predicate of something else and in treating numbers as the causes of being for other things, Plato's teaching resembles that of the Pythagoreans. Aristotle emphasizes the differences more than the similarities, however. Plato differs from the Pythagoreans in regarding numbers as distinct from sensible things (in Aristotle's formulation, the Pythagoreans think that things *are* numbers)[9] and in positing an intermediate class of mathematicals. Moreover, it is peculiar to Plato to make the unlimited a duality and to call it the great and the small. This is not the place to try to unravel the complexities of Plato's later metaphysics. For the purpose of understanding Aristotle's comparison of Plato and the Pythagoreans, it is striking that most of the points of comparison deal not with the theory of forms as it is found in Plato's middle dialogues but rather with the Platonic metaphysics associated with the so-called unwritten doctrines, which makes its clearest appearance in the *Philebus*. If Aristotle's point is that Plato shows most similarity to the Pythagoreans in his account of the ultimate principles of forms, this point is strikingly confirmed by the Platonic dialogues themselves, since it is precisely in the *Philebus* that Plato invokes the basic metaphysical principles employed by Philolaus, limiters and unlimiteds.[10] Aristotle emphasizes that the significant differences between Plato and the Pythagoreans (i.e., the introduction of the forms and the separation of the one and numbers from things) are the result of Plato's investigations in logic (i.e., his Socratic search for definitions). All of Plato's predecessors are said to have had no share in dialectic.

In concluding his treatment of Plato in this section of the *Metaphysics*, Aristotle says that Plato recognized two causes, the essence and the material cause. The ultimate principles of forms, and hence of all things, are the Great and the Small, as material cause, and the One, as the essence. Aristotle's final remark in this discussion of Plato compares him to earlier Presocratics; in making the One the cause of good and the Great and the Small the cause of evil, Plato is responding to a problem that Empedocles and Anaxagoras had addressed earlier (988a14–17). If we look back over Aristotle's whole treatment of Plato in this chapter of the *Metaphysics*, a treatment that begins with Sentence P, we see that Aristotle begins by assigning the origin of Plato's philosophy to his contact with the Heracliteans and Socrates and ends by noting a connection between Plato and his predecessors Empedocles and Anaxagoras. Aristotle emphasizes that what distinguished Plato from all his predecessors was his study of dialectic under the influence of Socrates, since this was what led to the introduction of forms. The Pythagoreans are introduced primarily in comparison with Plato's later metaphysics, with his introduction not of forms but of the first principles of forms. Aristotle's introductory Sentence P, when read in context, matches what we find in the following chapter very well. Aristotle presents Plato as following the Presocratics in most things but as, in his mature philosophy, going beyond even the most developed of the Presocratics, the Pythagoreans. The Pythagoreans are mentioned in the last clause of Sentence P, because Aristotle is presenting them as the final phase of Presocratic thought and because Plato's later metaphysics does present interesting points of comparison to the Pythagoreans. Aristotle is very quiet about any historical connection between Plato and the Pythagoreans. All of Plato's earlier development is explained independently of them, and it is Plato's work in dialectic under the influence of Socrates that is seen as responsible for the distinctive features of Plato's system. We must firmly banish the notion that Aristotle regarded Plato as following the Pythagoreans in most things and recognize that Aristotle makes no direct historical connections between Plato and the Pythagoreans. Plato's philosophy is presented as largely explicable in complete independence from the Pythagoreans, until we reach the latest phase of Platonic metaphysics, in which he introduces the one and the large and the small as the ultimate principles of forms. Aristotle clearly thinks that it is fruitful to compare these principles with Pythagorean ideas, but he emphasizes the differences as much or more than the similarities, and he presents these similarities as the result of analysis of the two systems, without making any claim about the historical connection of Plato to the Pythagoreans.

2

Who counts as a Pythagorean? The difficulty of answering this question can be highlighted by comparing the answers given to it in the early and late ancient tradition. In the biography of Pythagoras read by Photius in the ninth century CE (Bibl. 249 = 438b16–441b14), Plato is presented as the pupil of Archytas and the ninth successor of Pythagoras. Aristotle is presented as the tenth successor. Later in the biography, both Parmenides and Zeno are also presented as Pythagoreans (439a36–7). On this reckoning, there are going to be few ancient philosophers who are not Pythagorean. If we go back to the fourth century, however, philosophers are much more hesitant about assigning the label "Pythagorean." Plato uses the term only once in all his writings, to refer to Pythagorean harmonic theorists, including Archytas (R. 530d). When Philolaus is mentioned in the *Phaedo*, he is not called a Pythagorean, nor is Archytas called a Pythagorean in the *Seventh Letter*. Aristotle uses the term Pythagorean much more frequently but applies it only to two groups. The first group is philosophers of the fifth century, who are described as living at the same time or a little before the atomists (*Metaph.* 985b23). Their philosophy of limiters and unlimiteds is largely the same as what we find in the fragments of Philolaus, so that Philolaus must have been the foremost figure in this group. The second group is described as "others of the same school" who put forth the table of opposites (986a22–26). On the other hand, Aristotle wrote several books on Archytas (D.L. 5.25) and refers to him several times in his extant writings but never describes him as a Pythagorean.

Part of the difference in the scope of the use of the term "Pythagorean" in the early and late tradition is the emphasis in the later tradition on organizing philosophers according to schools. The life of Pythagoras read by Photius is an extreme case of this emphasis, in which Greek philosophy is virtually limited to a single school, the Pythagorean. One important type of writing in the historiography of philosophy, the *Successions* (*diadochoi*), organized philosophers into schools according to teacher/student relationships. Sotion (200–175 BCE) was an important figure in this tradition, and this sort of tradition particularly flourished in the first and second centuries BCE.[11] Diogenes was undoubtedly influenced by Sotion, but he also shows a "passion for classifications" of his own and discusses different ways of organizing the philosophers.[12] It is almost inevitable that such arrangements of teacher/student relationships far after the fact will introduce some falsification either in the name of "neatness" or to glorify a given school. The earlier tradition was much less interested in such classifications. Thus Aristotle appears to treat Archytas largely as a philosopher in his own right and does not see any value in labeling him a Pythagorean. Some of the same attitude can be observed in Plato's treatment of Philolaus in the *Phaedo*. Aristotle is clearly uncomfortable with the term "Pythagorean" as applied even to Philolaus and usually refers to "the so-called Pythagoreans" as a way of indicating that this is a label commonly given to Philolaus and others, although he has doubts as to what connection they may have had with Pythagoras.[13] In Aristotle's case, the term "Pythagorean" seems to be applied primarily on the basis of doctrine. If a philosopher believed in the limit and the unlimited as first principles and thought that numbers were the essence of things but not separable from things, he was what was called a Pythagorean. Plato, too, may be using doctrine as a criterion, since his one reference to Pythagoreans picks out those who search for numbers in "heard harmonies" (R. 531c), again suggesting that numbers are not separated from things.

If we define Pythagoreanism using Plato's and Aristotle's doctrinal criterion, then those who can be labeled Pythagoreans will be limited to a relatively small circle, including Philolaus, Archytas, and Eurytus. It is part and parcel of Aristotle's and Plato's treatment of Pythagoreanism that Pythagoras himself is not counted as a Pythagorean in this sense. Plato regarded Pythagoras as the founder of a way of life rather than as a systematic philosopher (R. 600a9–b5), and Aristotle's silence about Pythagoras himself suggests the same thing.[14] It is also important to recognize that this characterization of Pythagoreanism in terms of doctrine does not license us to label anyone who works in mathematics a Pythagorean. Neither Plato nor Aristotle calls prominent Greek mathematicians, such as Theodorus, Theaetetus, or Hippocrates of Chios, Pythagoreans. Nor do we have evidence that these thinkers believed in a philosophy of limiters and unlimiteds or discussed the relation between numbers and things in the Pythagorean fashion.

An alternative to this attempt to identify Pythagoreans on doctrinal grounds has been proposed by Leonid Zhmud.[15] He argues that to use the doctrinal criterion is a *petitio principii*. We need to first identify who Pythagoreans were and then examine their beliefs to see the range of beliefs that counted as Pythagorean. Since matters of doctrine are not being used as the criterion of Pythagoreanism, evidently what makes someone a Pythagorean on this approach is that he followed a Pythagorean way of life or was a member of a Pythagorean society. How do we know that a given figure was a Pythagorean in this sense? Zhmud suggests that we should consider as Pythagoreans anyone whom a reliable ancient source calls a Pythagorean. Thus, an ancient source may preserve early evidence that philosopher X lived a Pythagorean life or was a member of a Pythagorean society, and this information is prior to any classification by doctrine.

The difficulty with this approach is in determining what we mean by a reliable source. Zhmud treats Diogenes Laertius and Iamblichus as reliable sources and relies in particular on the catalogue of Pythagoreans in Iamblichus's work *On the Pythagorean Life*, which Zhmud and many scholars believe to be based on the work of Aristoxenus. It is well known, however, that starting as early as the later fourth century Pythagoras came to be regarded in some circles as the philosopher par excellence, to whom the true philosophy had been revealed. In these circles all later Greek philosophy, including the work of Plato and Aristotle, insofar as it is true, is simply a restatement of the revelation received by Pythagoras.[16] This belief is the primary motivation for the large number of pseudo-Pythagorean treatises collected by Thesleff. This is the point of view of the author of the biography of Pythagoras, which Photius read, and which makes Plato and Aristotle the successors of

Pythagoras. This point of view was not limited to a few people, however. Iamblichus believed that the surely spurious works on categories that were forged in Archytas's name were genuine and thus that Archytas had anticipated Aristotle's *Categories* (*CAG* 8.2.9–25). Diogenes Laertius argues vehemently that Pythagoras wrote books (8.6), although modern scholars are almost universally in agreement that he did not. Diogenes also accepts as an accurate summary of early Pythagoreanism the material preserved by Alexander Polyhistor (8.24), most of which must surely be later.[17] Even apart from the tendency of the later Pythagorean tradition to glorify Pythagoras and the early Pythagoreans, Diogenes Laertius is clearly influenced by the desire to arrange philosophers by schools, which leads to some misleading classifications.

Thus, it is very doubtful that we can regard Diogenes Laertius and Iamblichus as reliable sources when it comes to identifying individuals as Pythagoreans. We simply don't know whether their assertions to this effect are based on reliable early tradition or are a result of the later Pythagorean tradition's attempt to claim as much ground as possible for Pythagoreanism. The assertions of Diogenes and Iamblichus are not bedrock, are not reliable starting points, but must be examined in light of other earlier evidence. For example, Diogenes includes Empedocles, Alcmaeon, and Eudoxus among the lives of Pythagoreans in book 8 of his *Lives of the Philosophers*. Apart from Diogenes, there is only one other text in the entire ancient tradition that labels Eudoxus as Pythagorean, and this, not surprisingly, comes from Iamblichus.[18] None of the early sources calls Eudoxus a Pythagorean (e.g., Aristotle and Eudemus). In the later tradition, he is identified by his city, as "the mathematician," or as a Platonist. Diogenes evidently regards Eudoxus as a Pythagorean, because he knows of a report that Eudoxus studied with Archytas (D.L. 8.86).

This is an important case; does the fact that someone studies with a Pythagorean make that person a Pythagorean? If we accept this as a general criterion, Plato should be classified as a Socratic and Aristotle as a Platonist. There is a sense, of course, in which it is right to call Plato a Socratic and Aristotle a Platonist; both philosophers were heavily influenced by their masters and retain in their mature philosophy traits that are clearly owed to their teachers. On the other hand, Plato and Aristotle develop philosophies that differ in such fundamental ways from their teachers' views that we regard them as having developed their own philosophies. We could then call Eudoxus a Pythagorean, in the sense that he studied with the Pythagorean Archytas, but this would be at best equivalent to saying that Plato was a Socratic, and the evidence, in fact, suggests that the connection between Eudoxus and Archytas was not that close. Even Diogenes limits Eudoxus's study with Archytas to the subject of geometry. Certainly Eudoxus's hedonism (Arist. *EN* 1172b9–10) is in accord neither with Archytas's view on pleasure (A9) nor with any suggestion that Eudoxus lived a Pythagorean way of life, which by all accounts avoided pleasure (Aristox. frs. 37-38, Iamb. *VP* 205). His study with Archytas may have formed a good foundation for his work on proportion and astronomy, but all the evidence is that, even in these areas, Eudoxus was highly original. There is no useful sense in which Eudoxus should be labeled a Pythagorean, and we should reject Diogenes' claim that he was.

Alcmaeon is a slightly different case. In addition to Diogenes, four other ancient texts label Alcmaeon a Pythagorean, two of them again deriving from Iamblichus (*VP* 104, 267; the other two are Philoponus *in de An.* p. 88 and the scholia on Plato *Acl.* 121e). The considerable majority of references to Alcmaeon in the ancient tradition do not call him a Pythagorean, however. He is not called a Pythagorean by Aëtius, Clement, Galen, Calcidius, or Censorinus. Nor do our earliest sources, Aristotle and Theophrastus, ever call him a Pythagorean.[19] Even more significantly, in a famous passage Aristotle specifically compares and then contrasts Alcmaeon with the Pythagoreans (*Metaph.* 986a27). Aristotle points out that Alcmaeon, like the Pythagoreans of the table of opposites, posited opposites as basic principles. He stresses, however, that whereas the Pythagoreans presented a clearly defined table of 10 pairs of opposites, Alcmaeon seemed to seize on a chance set of opposites. The crucial point is that Aristotle's contrast between Alcmaeon and the Pythagoreans and his assertion that it is not clear whether Alcmaeon derived his theory from the Pythagoreans or they from him only makes sense if Alcmaeon was not regarded as a Pythagorean.[20] Simplicius reports that some people in the later tradition had regarded Alcmaeon as a Pythagorean but takes just this passage of the *Metaphysics* to show that Aristotle denied this view (*in de An.* 32.3). Certainly there are very few doctrinal grounds on which to classify Alcmaeon as a Pythagorean, since he does not even include the Pythagorean opposition of limit and unlimited among his lists of opposites.

Although up to the middle of the twentieth century most scholars followed Diogenes in calling Alcmaeon a Pythagorean, since about 1950 the overwhelming majority of scholars have recognized that he is not one.[21] In this case, the most likely reason for his classification as a Pythagorean by Diogenes and his sources is that he lived in Croton, where Pythagoras founded his school, and that his book was addressed to individuals who are identified in the later tradition as Pythagoreans. It seems very likely that Alcmaeon knew Pythagoreans, but addressing a book to some of them need not mean that he himself was a Pythagorean or agreed with them on philosophical issues. It is just as likely to be an appeal to them to change their point of view in light of Alcmaeon's arguments.[22] Again there are no reliable grounds for calling Alcmaeon a Pythagorean.

There are better grounds for Diogenes to call Empedocles a Pythagorean. Empedocles believes in transmigration of souls, one of the few doctrines we can confidently assign to Pythagoras himself. In fact, when authors in the later tradition wanted to cite texts to explain the Pythagorean doctrine of metempsychosis, they regularly cited texts from Empedocles, since Pythagoras wrote nothing (Sextus Empiricus, *M.* 9.126–30). Similarly, Empedocles believed that number played a significant role in the structure of the universe and its parts (B96), which is similar to what we find in the fragments of Philolaus and in Aristotle's account of fifth-century Pythagoreanism. Since Empedocles came from Sicily, close to Pythagoras's city of Croton in southern Italy, it seems quite likely that Empedocles did study with some Pythagoreans, although he was born too late to have studied with Pythagoras himself. Yet no early source calls Empedocles a Pythagorean, and few modern scholars would simply label him one. The reason is not far to seek. Empedocles' relationship to Pythagoreanism might profitably be compared to Plato's relationship to Socrates. Empedocles' mature philosophy does show the clear impact of Pythagorean teaching, but he also developed a distinctive view of the cosmos, which is developed in such an original way that few are willing to label the result Pythagoreanism.[23] The four elements and the cosmic cycle in which they engage under the influence of Love and Strife has little to do with Pythagoreanism. Nor does the Pythagorean opposition of limit and unlimited appear prominently in Empedocles. So we should certainly describe Empedocles as heavily influenced by Pythagoreanism, but it makes little sense to call him a Pythagorean, other than in the sense in which we call Plato a Socratic.

Both Parmenides and Melissus are listed along with Empedocles as Pythagoreans in the catalogue of Pythagoreans included at the end of Iamblichus's work *On the Pythagorean Life* (267). Parmenides is also called a Pythagorean in a few other late sources, including the biography of Pythagoras that Photius read (A4, A12). Diogenes, interestingly enough, does not include Parmenides among the Pythagorean lives in book 8 or describe him as a Pythagorean, but he does report the evidence which undoubtedly played a large role in some authors' classification of him as a Pythagorean. According to Diogenes, Sotion (second century BCE) reported that Parmenides was the student of a Pythagorean, Ameinias, and built a shrine to him on his death (D.L. 9.21). We cannot confirm Sotion's story, but there is no particular reason to doubt it. Here again is the familiar situation of someone being labeled a Pythagorean because of his or her teacher. No one in the early tradition thought Parmenides' association with Ameinias sufficient to label him a Pythagorean. Plato, Aristotle, and Theophrastus refer to him numerous times, and there is never any hint that they thought it useful to call him a Pythagorean, nor did the vast majority of authors in the later tradition. It is possible that Parmenides was influenced in important ways by Pythagorean ideas, as was Empedocles, but there is much less evidence in the case of Parmenides, and the reconstructions of such influence are quite speculative.[24] Clearly Parmenides' philosophical system was so distinctive as to leave little doubt that he should not be classified simply as a Pythagorean.

There is not a trace elsewhere than in *VP* 267 that Melissus was considered a Pythagorean, and it is reasonable to suspect that he is included on the list of Pythagoreans in Iamblichus precisely because he in turn was viewed as a pupil of Parmenides. Zeno is not mentioned in Iamblichus's list; the very few references to Zeno as a Pythagorean (DK 28A4 and 12) are also probably inferences from his having been a pupil of Parmenides. Diogenes' treatment of the Eleatics (Parmenides, Zeno, and Melissus) is particularly revealing. He includes none of these figures in book 8, which is devoted to the Pythagoreans and, apart from mentioning the student/teacher relationship between Ameinias and Parmenides, says nothing about Pythagoreans in these three lives. In the proem to his lives, however,

Diogenes includes Parmenides and Zeno in the Italian school as successors to Pythagoras (1.15). Not only that but Xenophanes is there included in the Pythagorean succession as well! This is most easily explained again on the assumption that, once one Eleatic, that is, Parmenides, had been shown to have some connections to the Pythagoreans, then all other figures associated with Parmenides, either as supposed teacher (Xenophanes) or pupils (Melissus and Zeno), become Pythagoreans. In the same section of the proem, Democritus is included in the Pythagorean tradition (undoubtedly because of the tradition that he studied with Philolaus; see D.L. 9.38) and Epicurus (!) is listed as the last Pythagorean (see 1.14). It is thus clear that Diogenes preserves several different, conflicting reconstructions of the successions of early Greek philosophers and that his testimony in itself provides very little firm ground. Doubtful reconstructions of student/teacher relationships in the *Successions* genre lead not just Melissus and Zeno to be included as Pythagoreans but also Xenophanes, Democritus, and Epicurus.

It is now time to discuss explicitly the catalogue of Pythagoreans found in Iamblichus (*VP* 267). Rohde and Diels argued that the catalogue goes back to Aristoxenus, and this view has been supported and buttressed with further argumentation by Timpanaro-Cardini, Burkert, and Zhmud.[25] It does seem most plausible to assume that Aristoxenus is responsible for the core of the catalogue, but it is important to recognize both that the arguments for Aristoxenus's authorship are not ironclad and that, even if the core is assigned to Aristoxenus, this does not mean that the catalogue has not undergone modifications. It is often noted in support of Aristoxenus's authorship that none of the Pythagoreans named in the catalogue about whom we know anything are to be dated later than Aristoxenus.[26] This is not very surprising, however, since it was widely recognized that early Pythagoreanism largely died out in the first half of the fourth century (probably on the evidence of Aristoxenus; see Iamb. *VP* 251 and D.L. 8.46). Anyone writing about Pythagoreanism after 350 BCE, including Iamblichus, would be likely to limit the catalogue to figures from the first part of the fourth century or earlier. This was the golden age of Pythagoreanism, and there simply are not that many figures who could be plausibly named Pythagoreans who lived later. A sign of this focus on Pythagoreanism before 350 BCE is the text of Iamblichus's work *On the Pythagorean Life*, apart from the catalogue. Iamblichus there limits himself to Pythagoreans who lived before Aristoxenus as well. Aristoxenus is likely to be the ultimate source for the core of Iamblichus's catalogue, not because of the dates of the individuals included but because it contains such a large number of names that are attested nowhere else (145 of the 235 names occur only here). Unless we suppose that the names were invented, the author of this list must have been in a position to tap a rich vein of information about Pythagoreanism from its beginnings until its demise in the first half of the fourth century. Aristoxenus (375–c. 300) lived at a time when early Pythagoreanism was dying out, but he was in a uniquely favorable position to uncover information from both oral and written sources, which could go back to the very beginning of the school. He was born in an important Pythagorean center, Tarentum, when the Pythagorean Archytas was at the height of his power, and he would go on to study with the Pythagorean Xenophilus in Athens (fr. 1 = *Suda*). Aristoxenus could also rely on his father, Spintharus, for firsthand reports of Pythagorean activity from an even earlier period (fr. 30 = Iamb. *VP* 197).

Burkert notes that the catalogue cannot be Iamblichus's because it omits 18 names that Iamblichus mentions elsewhere.[27] This argument assumes that Iamblichus is a careful author, who in composing such a catalogue or in making additions to a catalogue accepted from someone else would go methodically through his writings to assure that the catalogue was consistent with his other writings. Iamblichus hardly fits such a description, however, as is shown by numerous contradictions and repetitions in the body of *On the Pythagorean Life*, which leads up to the catalogue (some of these are defended as having a pedagogical purpose by Dillon and Hershbell).[28] Such methodical consistency was not important to him, and he could well have added names to the catalogue, even if all the names he mentions elsewhere are not included. There is also the distinct possibility that names were added to the catalogue in the period between Aristoxenus and Iamblichus. The upshot is that, while we can regard a significant part of the catalogue as likely to be the work of Aristoxenus and thus as preserving reliable early tradition about who was a Pythagorean, we can have no certainty that individual names are not added later.

The catalogue is a relatively conservative document and does not reflect the extremes of the later Pythagorean tradition; for example, it does not include Plato, Aristotle, Zeno, Democritus, and Epicurus. On the other hand, there are difficulties with it that point to additions to the Aristoxenian core or to questionable judgment on Aristoxenus's part. The catalogue lists Pythagoreans by geographical locations, and some of the unusual correlations correspond to fragments of Aristoxenus; for example, Philolaus and Eurytus are assigned to Tarentum as in Aristoxenus fragment 19 (= D.L. 8.46).[29] On the other hand, Aristoxenus's own teacher Xenophilus is described as being from Cyzicus in the catalogue, whereas in the fragments of Aristoxenus he is said to be from the Thracian Chalcidice (frs. 18 and 19). This certainly suggests that the catalogue has not been preserved strictly in the form in which Aristoxenus wrote it. The catalogue lists the legendary figure Abaris as a Pythagorean and even identifies his country as the mythical Hyperborea. Zaleucus and Charondas are also listed as Pythagoreans, although they were active in the seventh century before Pythagoras was born.[30] These mistakes might be attributable to Aristoxenus himself, but it does not seem likely. Aristoxenus shows some tendency to rationalize the Pythagorean tradition,[31] and it would be odd for him to include a figure from myth like Abaris. Fragment 43 is often cited as evidence that Aristoxenus did regard Zaleucus and Charondas as Pythagoreans, but it is not at all clear that the sentence in that fragment that refers to Zaleucus and Charondas should be assigned to Aristoxenus.[32] The inclusion of Parmenides and Melissus in Iamblichus's catalogue, whether due to Aristoxenus or the later tradition, shows a willingness to include figures whose teacher was a

Pythagorean, or whose teacher's teacher was, although, as we have seen, most or all of the early evidence suggests that they were not regarded as Pythagoreans. The catalogue is then a valuable document in general, but by itself, without confirmation by early evidence, it does not constitute definitive evidence that a given figure was a Pythagorean. Given the later tradition's tendency to claim famous figures for Pythagoreanism, it is precisely the famous names on the list, such as Parmenides and Melissus, that are most likely to be additions.

What criteria, then, should we use in identifying someone as a Pythagorean? There are three reliable criteria, any one of which is grounds for calling a given philosopher a Pythagorean. The first and most important criterion is unambiguous evidence from the early tradition, before the end of the fourth century, that the person in question was considered a Pythagorean. The second criterion is unambiguous evidence that the person in question adopted the basic metaphysical scheme of the Pythagoreans as described by Aristotle or as found in the fragments of Philolaus. It is important to emphasize that a figure does not satisfy this criterion by simply mentioning mathematics or number in some regard. There needs to be explicit reference to limiters and unlimiteds as basic principles and to numbers as giving us knowledge of things without being metaphysically separate from them. The third criterion is evidence that the person is embedded in the biographical tradition as living the life of a Pythagorean beyond having had a Pythagorean teacher or having once talked to a Pythagorean. If a figure appears embedded in Iamblichus's or Porphyry's account of the early Pythagorean societies and not just superficially connected to them, there is some likelihood that this is based on fourth-century authors such as Aristoxenus.

The first criterion nets us Philolaus,[33] Eurytus (Aristox. fr. 19), Archytas (Pl. *R.* 530d; Aristox. fr. 18), and the unnamed Pythagoreans whom Aristotle says posited the table of opposites (*Metaph.* 986a22). A number of other Pythagoreans named by Aristoxenus in frs. 18 (Iamb. *VP* 248–51) and 19 (D.L. 8.46) also fit this criterion (Archippus and Lysis, who escaped from the attack on the Pythagorean societies around 450; a group of Pythagoreans from Phlius [Echecrates, Polymnastus, and Diocles]; and Xenophilus of the Thracian Chalcidice, who are described as the last of the Pythagoreans). The famous Pythagorean friends Damon and Phintias would be included by Aristoxenus's testimony, as would Amyclas and Cleinias (fr. 31 = Iamb., *VP* 233–36 and fr. 131 = D.L. 9.40). The second criterion does not, in effect, add anyone to the list, since people who fit this criterion are also included by the first criterion (e.g., Eurytus, 45A2).

The third criterion is a bit more subjective but admits figures who may well never have written anything but who were famous examples of some aspects of the Pythagorean life. The friends Damon and Phintias would be included by this criterion as well as by the first one. Similar figures are Myllias and his wife Timycha, who bit off her tongue rather than reveal Pythagorean secrets (Iamb. *VP* 189–94), and the friends Cleinias and Prorus (Iamb. *VP* 239). Hippasus should be included because of his importance in the split between *acusmatici* and *mathematici.*[34] Diels identifies Cercops, Petron, Bro(n)tinus, Calliphon, Democedes, and Parmeniscus as older Pythagoreans (DK 15–17 and 19–20). Of these only Brontinus, Calliphon, and Parmeniscus appear in Iamblichus's catalogue. Brontinus is presented either as the father or husband of Theano, who in turn is presented either as the wife or student of Pythagoras. Some Orphic poems are also associated with Brontinus (DK 17). He was thus clearly associated with Pythagoras, but in what sense he was a Pythagorean is less clear. There is no reason to deny that Calliphon and Parmeniscus were Pythagoreans, but we know essentially nothing about them. The *Suda* calls Cercops a Pythagorean, and he is reported to have written Orphic poems (DK 15). Zhmud gives good reasons for not regarding Petron, as well as Paron and Xuthus, who are also included in DK (26 and 33), as Pythagoreans.[35] Only one late source calls Democedes a Pythagorean (19A2c). He is likely to have been a rough contemporary of Pythagoras, and Iamblichus does mention a Democedes, with no patronymic, as a Pythagorean who led the younger men to safety during the attack on the Pythagoreans in Croton (*VP* 257–61). Hermippus, without mentioning Democedes, reported that a Calliphon of Croton was an associate of Pythagoras (DK 19A2). On the other hand, Herodotus (3.125 etc.) tells the story of the physician from Croton, Democedes, son of Calliphon, in some detail but never hints that he is a Pythagorean, nor is he found in Iamblichus's catalogue. The early evidence thus suggests that he should not be regarded as a Pythagorean. Some other individual names mentioned in Diogenes Laertius, Iamblichus's work *On the Pythagorean Life*, and Porphyry's *Life of Pythagoras* are likely enough to be Pythagoreans, and surely a large number of the names that are preserved only in Iamblichus's catalogue were genuine Pythagoreans whose names Aristoxenus collected.[36]

On the other hand, there is no reason to include figures who merely conversed with Pythagoreans. Thus, Simmias and Cebes, who heard Philolaus at Thebes could as easily be called Socratics as Pythagoreans, since they also discoursed with Socrates in Athens (they are also not found in Iamblichus's catalogue). There is no more reason to regard Polyarchus, whom Aristoxenus presents as arguing for hedonism in opposition to Archytas (DK 47A9), as a Pythagorean than to regard Callicles as a Socratic because he argues against Socrates in the *Gorgias*. Nor should we regard as Pythagoreans figures who are named in Iamblichus's catalogue but who, although discussed elsewhere, are never called a Pythagorean by anyone else. Thus, a Theodorus of Cyrene is listed as a Pythagorean in Iamblichus's catalogue, but there is no hint in Plato's *Theaetetus* or *Statesman*, in which Theodorus is a character, that he was a Pythagorean, nor does Eudemus call him a Pythagorean in his history of geometry. A Menestor is listed as a Pythagorean from Sybaris in the catalogue, but the botanist Menestor who is discussed by Theophrastus is never described as a Pythagorean or as from Sybaris but rather as one of the old natural philosophers (*CP* 6.3.5). Hippo is a difficult case, because the catalogue lists a Hippo from Samos, and Aristoxenus is given by Censorinus as an authority for assigning Hippo to Samos rather than Metapontum. Censorinus does not say, however, that Aristoxenus called him a Pythagorean. Burkert makes some connections between Hippo and the Pythagoreans on the basis of doctrine,[37] but neither Aristotle nor Theophrastus nor any of the Aristotelian commentators calls him a Pythagorean. There is certainly nothing impossible about Theodorus, Menestor, or Hippo being Pythagoreans; the point is simply that, without some testimony apart from their names appearing in Iamblichus's catalogue, it would be rash to regard them as Pythagoreans, in the face of the silence of earlier authors who do not so much as hint that they are Pythagoreans when discussing them.[38]

Iamblichus and Diogenes cannot be the decisive evidence for regarding someone as a Pythagorean. It is the early evidence, before the growth of the Pythagorean legend, that is crucial. The evidence of Iamblichus and Diogenes can only be accepted if it is positively corroborated by the early evidence. In cases where the early evidence has nothing to say, we can accept what Iamblichus and Diogenes say, but, given the nature of the Pythagorean tradition, we must regard their evidence with caution, even in such cases. One might complain that at least some figures in the early tradition (e.g., Plato, Theophrastus, Aristotle) identify essentially no one as a Pythagorean and that the list of Pythagoreans I have identified by relying on early evidence is in consequence too limited. Yet the list of Pythagoreans I have given is already more extensive than could be given for any other Presocratic tradition.[39] We group Parmenides, Zeno, and Melissus together as Eleatics and join Cratylus to Heraclitus as Heracliteans. Leucippus and Democritus are paired as atomists. These groupings are analogous to what we find in the Pythagorean tradition with Philolaus, Eurytus, and Archytas. The fact that, even by my rigorous criteria, there is a much longer list of Pythagoreans than of any other Presocratic "school" is a reflection of the fact that Pythagoras was famous for leaving behind him a way of life, so that in addition to Pythagoreans of a cosmological and metaphysical bent, such as Philolaus and Archytas, there were a number of other figures who can be called Pythagoreans merely on the basis of the way they lived their lives. The criteria suggested here leave us with a vigorous Pythagorean tradition but also one that is defined in a way that makes "Pythagorean" something other than a hopelessly vague term.

NOTES

1. See, e.g., Cherniss, *Aristotle's Criticism of Plato and the Academy*, 177 n. 100; Burkert, *Lore and Science in Ancient Pythagoreanism*, 30; Ross, *Aristotle's Metaphysics*, 1.158; Kahn, *Pythagoras and the Pythagoreans*, 1; HGP 1.331.
2. Kraut, *The Cambridge Companion to Plato*, 123.
3. Kahn, *Pythagoras and the Pythagoreans*, 3–4.
4. Cherniss, *Aristotle's Criticism of Plato and the Academy*, 177 n. 100.
5. It might be possible to take the phrase τὰ μὲν πολλά literally as meaning just that Plato followed the Presocratics "in many things," but it is more probable that Aristotle

is saying that he followed them "in most things." LSJ gives the standard meaning of both the singular τὸ πολύ and the plural τὰ πολλά as "for the most part" (III. a). In a number of passages in Aristotle, it is simply not possible to determine whether the phrase means "many" or "most," but there are several passages in which the context clearly indicates that the meaning is "most," and I have found none that require the meaning "many." Thus at *Mete.* 360b12–15 the juxtaposition of τὰ πολλά and ἐνίοτε (sometimes) must indicate the contrast between what happens "for the most part" and what happens sometimes. Even clearer is *PA* 663b27–29, where Aristotle equates looking at what happens εἰς τὰ πολλά in nature with what happens in every case (ἐν τῷ παντί) or for the most part (ὡς ἐπὶ τὸ πολύ). In such a context, the translation of εἰς τὰ πολλά as "in many cases" would simply not work, since "many" cannot be equated with "in every case or for the most part." These passages suggest that τὰ πολλά was generally understood to mean "for the most part" rather than "in many cases."

6. Taylor, *A Commentary on Plato's Timaeus*, viii–ix; Bury, *Plato*, 14–15.

7. I would like to thank Myles Burnyeat for pointing out the correct reading of this sentence to me.

8. ἀκολουθοῦσα, "following," could in itself indicate a historical connection, but the verb is also used by Aristotle to indicate simple similarity in thought between two thinkers. See *Poetics* 1449b9–12, where epic is said "to follow" (ἠκολούθησεν) tragedy in being a form of mimesis of elevated matters. Epic developed before tragedy, so it cannot be said to follow tragedy in a historical sense. Aristotle is clearly just analyzing a similarity between the two genres. Cherniss, *Aristotle's Criticism of Plato and the Academy*, 177 n. 100 points to a similar sense for συνηκολουθήκασι at *Physics* 188b26–7.

9. See Huffman, *Philolaus of Croton*, 57–64.

10. Huffman, "The Philolaic Method."

11. Mejer, *Diogenes Laertius and His Hellenistic Background*, 62.

12. Mejer, *Diogenes Laertius and His Hellenistic Background*, 52.

13. Huffman, *Philolaus of Croton*, 31–34.

14. Burkert, *Lore and Science in Ancient Pythagoreanism*, 29–30, 216.

15. Zhmud, *Wissenschaft, Philosophie und Religion im frühen Pythagoreismus*, 67–74.

16. Huffman, "The Pythagorean Tradition," 66–69; O'Meara, *Pythagoras Revived*.

17. Burkert, *Lore and Science in Ancient Pythagoreanism*, 53.

18. *In Nic.* intro., p. 10 Pistelli and Klein, *Iamblichi in Nicomachi Arithmeticam introductionem liber*.

19. I am puzzled by Zhmud's assertion (*Wissenschaft, Philosophie und Religion im frühen Pythagoreismus*, 71) that the tradition treats Alcmaeon as a Pythagorean "without exception" (*ausnahmslos*).

20. Zhmud argues that Aristotle is distinguishing Alcmaeon just from a later group of Pythagoreans, i.e., those who developed the table of opposites, which need not imply that Alcmaeon was not a Pythagorean. Aristotle does not call these Pythagoreans "later," however. He introduces them as "others of this same school" and a few lines later simply calls them *Pythagoreioi* (*Metaph.* 986b2). His careful description of this second group of Pythagoreans as "others of the same school," and his use of the name "Pythagorean" for them shows that Aristotle is perfectly capable of recognizing differences among Pythagoreans and is in strong contrast with his treatment of Alcmaeon. If Alcmaeon, too, was a Pythagorean, Aristotle's remarks are most puzzling.

21. E.g., *HGP* 1, and Lloyd, *Methods and Problems in Greek Science*, 164–93; see Huffman, "Alcmaeon."

22. Vlastos, "Isonomia," 344 n. 25.

23. Huffman, "The Pythagorean Tradition," 76.

24. Coxon, *The Fragments of Parmenides*, 13–19, 38–39.

25. Rohde, "Die Quellen des Iamblichus in seiner Biographie des Pythagoras," 171; Diels, *Antike Technik*, 23; Timpanaro-Cardini, *I Pitagorici*, 3:38–9; Burkert, *Lore and Science in Ancient Pythagoreanism*, 105 n. 40; Zhmud, *Wissenschaft, Philosophie und Religion im frühen Pythagoreismus*, 67–69.

26. Burkert, *Lore and Science in Ancient Pythagoreanism*, 105; Zhmud, *Wissenschaft, Philosophie und Religion im frühen Pythagoreismus*, 67.

27. Burkert, *Lore and Science in Ancient Pythagoreanism*, 105.

28. Dillon and Hershbell, *Iamblichus*, 28–29.

29. See Burkert, *Lore and Science in Ancient Pythagoreanism*, 105.

30. Gagarin, *Early Greek Law*, 130; Dunbabin, *The Greeks in the West*, 68–75.

31. Burkert, *Lore and Science in Ancient Pythagoreanism*, 107.

32. Wehrli (*Die Schule des Aristoteles*, 63) may have assigned too much of the passage of Diogenes Laertius from which Fragment 43 is derived to Aristoxenus. It is more likely that the material derived from Aristoxenus ends with the anecdote about his teacher Xenophilus. The sentence about Zaleucus and Charondas that follows is still in indirect discourse and thus might be a continuation of the report of what Aristoxenus said, but it also introduces a new subject, which suggests that Diogenes might have taken it from a different source.

33. Aristox. fr. 19; the similarity between the content of Philolaus's fragments and Aristotle's reports also shows that Aristotle included him as one of the "so-called Pythagoreans"; see Huffman, *Philolaus of Croton*, 28–35.

34. Burkert, *Lore and Science in Ancient Pythagoreanism*, 192–208.

35. Zhmud, *Wissenschaft, Philosophie und Religion im frühen Pythagoreismus*, 69–70 n. 14.

36. I will not attempt to give a definitive list here. Ecphantus and Hicetas might be included, since they are called Pythagoreans in the doxographical tradition inspired by Theophrastus (DK 50 and 51). One might argue that Empedocles should be classed as a Pythagorean on the basis of the third criterion. Anecdotes about Empedocles are embedded in Iamblichus's account of the Pythagorean life. Such a result would not be completely unreasonable, since, as we have seen, Empedocles clearly was closely connected to Pythagorean ideas such as metempsychosis, and he heaped praise on Pythagoras (B129). On the other hand, the anecdotes told about Empedocles do not in fact present him as engaged with other members of Pythagorean societies but rather show him engaged in activities that are parallel to things done by Pythagoreans, such as soothing the anger of a young man by playing the lyre (Iamblichus, *VP* 113). Empedocles' miraculous abilities are also presented as a parallel phenomenon to Pythagoras's similar abilities (Iamblichus, *VP* 135). It thus still seems better to regard Empedocles as his own man, despite the heavy Pythagorean influence on him.

37. Burkert, *Lore and Science in Ancient Pythagoreanism*, 290.

38. Zhmud regards all the figures mentioned in this paragraph as Pythagoreans (*Wissenschaft, Philosophie und Religion im frühen Pythagoreismus*, 69–74).

39. The list of Pythagoreans I have given in this essay is by no means definitive. There has not been space to discuss a number of problematic cases, including but not limited to Zopyrus, Diodorus of Aspendus, Lycon, and the Pythagorists presented in middle-comedy. For a more detailed treatment of these issues see Huffman, "Pythagoreanism."

BIBLIOGRAPHY

Burkert, Walter. *Lore and Science in Ancient Pythagoreanism*. 1962. Translated by E. L. Minar, Jr. Cambridge, Mass.: Harvard University Press, 1972.

Bury, R. G. *Plato: Timaeus, Critias, Cleitophon, Menexenus, Epistles*. Cambridge, Mass.: Harvard University Press, 1929.

Cherniss, Harold. *Aristotle's Criticism of Plato and the Academy*. Baltimore: Johns Hopkins University Press, 1944.

Coxon, A. H. *The Fragments of Parmenides*. Assen: Van Gorcum, 1986.

Diels, Hermann. *Antike Technik*. 3rd ed. Osnabrück, 1965.

Dillon, John M., and Jackson P. Hershbell. *Iamblichus: On the Pythagorean Way of Life*. Atlanta: Scholars Press, 1991.

Dunbabin, T. J. *The Greeks in the West*. Oxford: Clarendon Press, 1948.

Gagarin, Michael. *Early Greek Law*. Berkeley: University of California Press, 1986.

Huffman, Carl A. "Alcmaeon." *Stanford Encyclopedia of Philosophy* (2003), edited by Edward N. Zalta (http://plato.stanford.edu/archives/sum2003/entries/alcmaeon/).

———. "The Philolaic Method: The Pythagoreanism behind the *Philebus*." In *Before Plato*, vol. 6 of *Essays in Ancient Greek Philosophy*, edited by Anthony Preus, 67-85. Binghamton: State University of New York Press, 2001.

———. *Philolaus of Croton*. Cambridge: Cambridge University Press, 1993.

———. "The Pythagorean Tradition." In *The Cambridge Companion to Early Greek Philosophy*, edited by A. A. Long, 66–87. Cambridge: Cambridge University Press, 1999.

———. "Pythagoreanism." In *The Stanford Encyclopedia of Philosophy (Summer 2006 Edition)*, edited by Edward N. Zalta (http://plato.stanford.edu/archives/sum2006/entries/pythagoreanism/).

Kahn, Charles H. *Pythagoras and the Pythagoreans*. Indianapolis: Hackett, 2001.

Kraut, R. *The Cambridge Companion to Plato*. Cambridge: Cambridge University Press, 1992.

Lloyd, G. E. R. *Methods and Problems in Greek Science*. Cambridge: Cambridge University Press, 1991.

Mejer, Jørgen. *Diogenes Laertius and His Hellenistic Background*. Hermes Einzelschriften, vol. 40. Wiesbaden: Franz Steiner, 1978.

O'Meara, Dominic J. *Pythagoras Revived: Mathematics and Philosophy in Late Antiquity*. Oxford: Clarendon Press, 1989.

Pistelli, H., and U. Klein *Iamblichi in Nicomachi Arithmeticam introductionem liber*. Stuttgart: Teubner, 1975.

Rohde, Erwin. "Die Quellen des Iamblichus in seiner Biographie des Pythagoras." *Rheinisches Museum* 26; 27 (1871): 554–76; 23–61.

Ross, W. D. *Aristotle's Metaphysics*. 2 vols. Oxford: Clarendon Press, 1924.

Taylor, A. E. *A Commentary on Plato's Timaeus*. Oxford: Clarendon Press, 1928.

Timparano Cardini, Maria. *I Pitagorici: Testimonianze e Frammenti*. 3 vols. Florence: La Nuova Italia, 1958–64.

Wehrli, F. *Die Schule des Aristoteles, Vol. II: Aristoxenus*. Basel: Benno Schwabe, 1945.

Vlastos, Gregory. "Isonomia." *American Journal of Philology* 74 (1953): 337–66.

Zhmud, Leonid. *Wissenschaft, Philosophie und Religion im frühen Pythagoreismus*. Berlin: Akademie Verlag, 1997.

CHAPTER 10

ATOMISM'S ELEATIC ROOTS

DAVID SEDLEY

1. ELEATIC ORIGINS?

Some gave in to both arguments: to the argument that everything is one if what-is signifies one thing, by saying that what-is-not is; to the argument from dichotomy, by positing atomic magnitudes. (Aristotle, *Physics* 1.3, 187a1–3)[1]

This is one of the most promising doxographical sentences to have come down to us from the entire ancient tradition, appearing as it does to sum up how two Eleatic stimuli combined to bring fifth-century BCE atomism into being.

First, Parmenides in his poem had discounted not-being as unthinkable, and had further been understood as arguing that what was left, namely being, could not all by itself admit of the differentiation necessary to give rise to the apparent world of change and plurality that we inhabit. The atomists Leucippus and Democritus, Aristotle seems to be telling us, responded by vindicating not-being. Being *can* be differentiated, provided only that it is spatially broken up, and thus suitably textured, by interspersed not-being. Or to reword this essentially metaphysical thesis in physical terms, body can be differentiated into a world such as our senses report to us, provided only that it is separated into discrete and mobile portions by the interspersal of void. Thus atomism, a physicalized dualism of being and not-being, can easily be seen as inspired by a desire to reconcile Parmenides' arguments for the unity of being with cosmic plurality, and possibly also by the dualism that Parmenides had himself in the second half of his poem postulated as the minimum (but, for him at least, unacceptable) condition for the rehabilitation of a pluralized and changing world.[2]

Second, Aristotle cites, alongside his reference to the introduction of not-being, a "dichotomy" paradox that he says inspired in the same people the postulation of atomic magnitudes—to all appearances, a reference to the birth of atomism. The paradox in question is generally agreed to be the handiwork of Parmenides' disciple and champion Zeno of Elea. In principle we might understand the paradox in question as either or both of the following.

Aristotle might, first, be referring to Zeno's critique of motion based on the need for a moving object to traverse an infinite sequence of discrete distances (Arist. *Ph.* 239b9–14)—one of the four celebrated motion paradoxes that have made Zeno's name a household word. No explicit reference to infinity occurs in it as it has come down to us. Its beguilingly simple formulation is that it is impossible to cross the stadium because of the need for what moves "to get half way before it reaches the end." This may mean that, even allowing hypothetically that you begin the journey, you cannot *complete* it, since before arrival at your destination you must first reach the journey's halfway point, followed by the halfway point of the distance remaining between it and the end, followed by the halfway point between *that* halfway point and the end, and so on ad infinitum. The need to complete an infinite sequence of tasks—a sequence, that is, that by definition has no last member— seems to make the prospects of arrival bleak. Alternatively, the paradox may be read as questioning how motion could even begin, since before you can get to the halfway point you must get halfway to *it*, and so on ad infinitum. What is not open to doubt is that the author of this paradox, despite perhaps not mentioning "infinity" (*to apeiron*) in its formulation, was familiar with the mathematical problems of infinity, and was busy exploiting them. Hence the prima facie plausibility of the idea that atomism arose in Zeno's aftermath, as an attempt to rescue motion from his critique. A distance is *not* infinitely divisible, the atomists will have replied to him: division eventually reaches its limit in an indivisible magnitude, which is traversed all at once, not in stages.

I now turn to the second possibility. Aristotle could have in mind a particular subargument from Zeno's complex large–small antinomy (B1–2).[3] Unlike the four motion paradoxes, which I am convinced enjoyed no more than oral circulation in Zeno's day,[4] this argument undoubtedly came from Zeno's celebrated book of antinomies, in which each antinomy was a criticism of plurality in the form "If there are many things, they are both F and G," "F" and "G" being each time contraries (like/unlike, large/small, finite/infinite, etc.). The large–small antinomy, whose materials survive largely intact thanks to Simplicius, can be pieced together as follows.

1. Each of the many has no magnitude, since it is the same as itself and one (Simplicius, *in Ph.* 139.18–19). (I.e., each of the many is an ultimate unit; if it had magnitude, it would have parts, and those parts would have a stronger claim to be units than it itself did; so it must have no magnitude.)

2(a). What has no magnitude, bulk, or mass would not even exist. "For if it were added to some other existing thing it would make it no larger. For, its magnitude being nil, its addition could make no increase in magnitude. Thus it would already follow that that which was being added was nothing. If the other thing, on its subtraction, will be no smaller, and, on its addition, will not be enlarged, clearly that which was added, or subtracted, was nothing" (139.10–15).

(b). "[Therefore] each one, if it does exist, must have some magnitude and bulk, and one part of it must be distinct from the other. And the same argument applies to the bit that protrudes—it too will have magnitude, and some part of it will protrude. It is the same to say this once and to say it forever. For no such part of it will be the last, or be unrelated to a further part (141.2–6). [Hence] each of the many has magnitude, and indeed infinite magnitude" (139.16–17).

3. "Thus, if there are many things, they must be both small and large—[1] so small as to have no magnitude, [2] so large as to be infinite" (141.6–8).

Here 2(b) could well, as Simplicius suggests (140.34), be the "dichotomy" argument that Aristotle has in mind. As formulated by Zeno, it infers the infinite bulk of any given magnitude from the fact that each part of it contains subparts, making the whole the sum of infinitely many parts, and therefore, by inference, itself infinitely large. If it is indeed this dichotomy to which the atomists were responding, Aristotle will presumably mean that they posited indivisible components of a body in order that the body should be the sum of only finitely many parts, thus escaping Zeno's unwelcome consequence.

On either assumption as to what dichotomy argument Aristotle intends, the postulation of atoms—the particles of which Democritus's universe is built—is presented as a response to the absurd consequences that would, if Zeno is right, follow from the harmless-sounding assumption that whatever there is in the world can be divided ad infinitum.

At least two prima facie difficulties stand in the way of these identifications. One applies specifically to the latter. For a competent mathematician, this particular dichotomy argument is one of the easier Zenonian paradoxes to deflect. Although the precise mode of division envisaged by Zeno in step 2(b) of his large–small antinomy is unclear, there is not much doubt that it generates, and sums, a series of diminishing parts, roughly of the form [a half plus a quarter plus an eighth . . .]—a series whose sum is not, mathematically speaking, infinity, but simply converges on 1. How plausible is it that Democritus, famed for his attainments as a mathematician, thought this puzzle sufficiently grave to justify an entire restructuring of physical theory in order to deflect its implications?

The second difficulty, to which I shall return later, applies to both identifications of the "dichotomy." The problem this time is whether Democritean atoms are indivisible in a sense that would provide any kind of protection against Zeno's inferences. Atoms are certainly incapable of being physically separated into their component parts. But Zeno's arguments are about merely *counting* a magnitude's parts, not about breaking it up into them. There is, as we shall see confirmed later, no good reason to think that Democritus conceived his atoms as entities lacking proper parts that one could set about distinguishing and counting.

Worse, we have to ask whether, in my opening quotation, Aristotle is even talking about the atomists at all. None of the ancient commentators on this passage thought that he was,[5] and one by-product of the present chapter will be to suggest that they may have been right. They took its first half to refer to Plato's vindication of not-being in the *Sophist*—and it must be admitted, in their favor, that this is a self-declared response to Parmenides. One might have thought nevertheless that reading it this way would be ruled out by Aristotle's indication in the lemma that the very same people postulated indivisibles: surely Plato didn't do *that*. Perhaps not, but his pupil Xenocrates did, and in fact Aristotle does, as we shall see shortly, tend to retroject the same thesis onto Plato himself. Thus the commentators' idea that Aristotle is here talking about the Platonists is not as far-fetched as it at first might sound.

It does at all events seem a good idea to start with a glance at Xenocrates' atomism.[6] Two of the contributions for which Xenocrates achieved widespread publicity are (1) his deliteralization of Plato's creation story in the *Timaeus*, maintaining that the world is eternal and that Plato had described its creation merely as an expository device (frs. 153-58 Isnardi), and (2) his doctrine of "indivisible lines" (frs. 123-51 Isnardi). I doubt whether the combination of those two theses is accidental. I suggest this on the ground that the thesis of indivisibles, which otherwise looks like a surprising and unmotivated one to emerge from Plato's school, gains immediate point if taken in conjunction with the eternity thesis.

The *Timaeus*, read literally, propounds the notorious asymmetric thesis that the world had a beginning but will have no end. However, it mitigates the asymmetry by observing that the world *is* perishable, but will in fact never perish since only God is capable of destroying it, and God, being good, would not want to do so (32c, 38b, 41a–b, 43d; *cf.* 40b). Xenocrates' deliteralization, I assume, will have included a rereading of this latter thesis as likewise merely expository, the world in fact being not contingently everlasting but essentially both beginningless *and* endless. Now in the Timaean world, destruction at the lowest level of analysis stops with the primary triangles. These are separated and recombined in the inter-transformations of air, fire, and water, but they themselves, although they apparently have *archai* of their own (53d), are never resolved into them. Hence readers of the *Timaeus* since Aristotle have regularly understood that the primary triangles are indivisible and indissoluble.[7] But how indissoluble? Since, so long as the world lasts, a body's resolution into these same triangles marks the lower limit of its destruction, it is a natural inference that the triangles are no less indissoluble than the world is. There is, therefore, every probability that Xenocrates felt impelled to infer, from his thesis of the world's intrinsic indestructibility, that the triangles too are not merely contingently everlasting, thanks to divine protection, but intrinsically indissoluble. And since this indissolubility can hardly derive from the entirely passive and featureless receptacle in which they inhere, it can only belong to the triangles themselves, viewed as formal rather than material objects. That would, it strikes me, be sufficient motivation to set Xenocrates off on his defense of indivisible geometrical entities.[8]

As well as providing a useful point of comparison for Democritean atomism, the case of Xenocrates is a valuable reminder of the need to distinguish the arguments a philosopher invokes in defense of a thesis from his philosophical motivation in advocating it. We may doubt the suggestion of Aristotle (at least as read by the ancient commentators) that in positing indivisible lines Xenocrates "gave in" to Zeno. On the contrary, if I am right, Xenocrates needed indivisible quantities in order to vindicate his reading of the *Timaeus*; and it seems plausible that the Zenonian dichotomy puzzle—if he really did invoke it[9]—conveniently served him as an instrument for achieving this goal.

The early atomists' motive for postulating atoms may on first impression seem utterly unlike Xenocrates'. Their world, after all, is one they happily concede *will* be destroyed, and they are in no need of a physical theory that might help preserve it. But, that difference apart, there is good reason to press a certain parallelism between the motivations of the two theories. Vindicating the eternity of the basic constituents of the universe and, derivatively, that of the universe itself, is a recurrent concern of the generation of philosophers who surfaced in Parmenides' wake, and the evidence implicates the atomists in this aim as much as Empedocles, Anaxagoras, or anyone else. Thus it is a shared feature of both these early forms of atomism, along probably with most later versions, that indivisibility is prized as a key to indestructibility.

When I sketched an interpretation of Xenocrates, it seemed natural—as well as in accordance with the ancient evidence—to speak of "formal" indivisibility, because the objects whose indivisibility he defended were themselves formal and not material. Whatever his reason for the indivisibility of the primary triangles (and, ultimately, lines), it inevitably has to do with their properties qua triangles, and not qua bodies, which indeed they are not. But when we turn to the interpretation of Democritean atomism, there are no such constraints. Atoms are referred to as "indivisible magnitudes" and "indivisible bodies" with roughly equal frequency in our sources, including Aristotle. And in fact much of the debate about the character of early atomism has turned on the precise question whether indivisibility is viewed as a physical attribute, or as a "theoretical," "mathematical," or "conceptual" one—these last three terms representing an overlapping, if not interchangeable, group.[10]

There have been many approaches to this problem. Both physical and theoretical indivisibility have had their defenders,[11] and it has also been argued that the very distinction is anachronistic. I do at least hesitate to accept this last view. While Richard Sorabji is quite right to point out the unlikelihood that as early as the fifth century BCE anyone should have distinguished different kinds or senses of possibility, there are other ways the distinction could be made;[12] for example, one might (as the Epicureans and others later did) contrast the possibility of successfully "cutting" a body (*temnein*, a primarily physical process) with the belief that the body possesses parts.[13]

There is, at all events, a well-known and very powerful reason for doubting that Democritean atoms were meant to satisfy this latter description of partlessness, despite the assertion in one or two deviant sources that they were.[14] For Democritus's atoms famously differ from each other in shape and size, and his theory would be impoverished beyond redemption, thanks to losing most of its power to explain phenomena, if that fundamental tenet were sacrificed at the altar of indivisibility. Yet it takes only a moment's reflection to appreciate that if atom A is larger than atom B, atom A must have at least two parts: the part that corresponds in size to atom B, and a further part by which it exceeds it. A similar inference can be drawn regarding differences in shape.

Both the term "atom"—"uncuttable"—and the insistence that atoms differ in size and shape seem to push us towards an interpretation of them as no more than physically indivisible. But this too appears unsatisfactory, for reasons I have already sketched. If an atom contains parts and is simply too solid to be broken up into them, what kind of answer is that to either of Zeno's dichotomy puzzles? What, for example, will block the inference that the atom contains infinitely many parts, with the consequence that each of these either has magnitude, making the whole atom infinitely large, or has no magnitude, in which case the atom, too, as their sum, will be altogether sizeless? The *motivation* of atomism will still be intact—roughly speaking, the need to account for a changing universe out of basic entities that satisfy the Parmenidean canon of eternal being—but we will be very far from knowing its theoretical justification. The distinguished mathematician Democritus is unlikely to have endorsed the Zenonian arguments without at the very least thinking them through with care, and it becomes a pressing need to see just how he deployed and responded to them. However, in the course of investigating that question, we will find that Zeno's own role recedes considerably.

2. ARISTOTLE, *GC* 1.2

It is at this point that we can usefully turn to what has been widely recognized as our best single item of evidence. This is the very full and uniquely sympathetic discussion of Democritus in Aristotle, *De Generatione et Corruptione* 1.2.[15] The trouble with this passage, as currently read, is that it seems to import all kinds of distinctively Aristotelian considerations into its reconstruction of Democritus's reasoning, thus inviting serious doubt as to whether it has any genuine historical value. I want to argue that, on the contrary, it is an extraordinarily meticulous exercise in historical reconstruction, carefully avoiding anachronistic imports.

In order to see this, we must start with a structural question. Where is the transition between Aristotle's report of Democritus and his own ensuing reply?

The usual impression given by editors and translators is that the break occurs at 316b16, where Aristotle appears to say the time has come to answer Democritus.[16] Unfortunately, however, that is not what happens next. Instead he remarks that the Democritean puzzle needs to be restated from the beginning, which is what he proceeds to do. It is not until 316b34 that Aristotle's answer finally begins, with signposting as explicit as one could ask for: "That, then, is the argument which is thought to make it necessary that there should be atomic magnitudes. Let us now say that, and where, it contains a concealed fallacy."

So what are we to make of the false start back at 316b16? It is important to scrutinize Aristotle's words closely:[17]

ὥστ' εἴπερ ἀδύνατον ἐξ ἀφῶν ἢ στιγμῶν εἶναι τὰ μεγέθη, ἀνάγκη εἶναι σώματα ἀδιαίρετα καὶ μεγέθη. οὐ μὴν ἀλλὰ καὶ ταῦτα θεμένοις οὐχ ἧττον συμβαίνει ἀδύνατα. ἔσκεπται δὲ περὶ αὐτῶν ἐν ἑτέροις. ἀλλὰ ταῦτα πειρατέον λύειν· διὸ πάλιν ἐξ ἀρχῆς τὴν ἀπορίαν λεκτέον. (316b14-19)

> So, if it is impossible for magnitudes to consist of contacts or points, there must be indivisible bodies and magnitudes. On the other hand, for those who posit these too there follow no less impossible consequences. They have been discussed elsewhere. But these are things that we must try to resolve, and hence the puzzle needs to be restated from the beginning.

"But these [tauta] are things that we must try to resolve" (b18). What are "these"? Since Philoponus, the universal assumption of commentators and translators has been that the reference is to Democritus's arguments, or more specifically to the puzzles that underlie them, which Aristotle would be announcing his intention to resolve. But not only does that create the problem with which I started—that Aristotle's own solution does not in fact begin here; it also leaves the anaphoric pronoun without any natural point of reference in the text. There is no suitably located mention of Democritus's puzzles, or of the arguments founded on them, for tauta to pick up. If guided by the immediate context, we might expect the reference to be either to the indivisibles, already designated with the pronoun tauta in the previous sentence, or to the "impossibilities" (adunata), which are said to result from positing those indivisibles. But one cannot make much sense of the idea of "resolving" indivisibles, and equally the idea of resolving impossibilities, as distinct from difficulties, is a surprising one, for which I have found no parallel in Aristotle. Rather than adopt any of these options, then, we should take the reference to be to the impasse that has now come about between two sets of impossibilities—those that arise from the supposition of infinite divisibility and those that arise from the thesis of atomism.[18] It is this stalemate, with equally balanced impossibilities on both sides, that requires resolution: the argument must be taken a step further.

What I propose is the following construal.[19] Aristotle has down to this point presented Democritus's arguments in historical or quasi-historical fashion. The reasoning at 316a14–b16 has in its entirety been meant to capture the way Democritus himself arrived at his atomist thesis (see its introduction at 316a13–14:

"Democritus would appear to hold his view on the basis of appropriate physical arguments. What I mean will be clear when we proceed"). At 316b16, the historical reconstruction ends, but, I suggest, the thinking continues to be in effect that of Democritus. He is made to speak as if he acknowledged the difficulties consequent on his argument for indivisibles—difficulties we as readers are asked to recognize as ones formulated in Aristotle's own writings (ἔσκεπται δὲ περὶ αὐτῶν ἐν ἑτέροις, b17–18). Thus it is still from Democritus's, not Aristotle's, point of view that the text acknowledges the need to resolve the conflict, and proceeds accordingly.

For that, I submit, is how the argument does proceed. Democritus is fictionally permitted to reformulate his argument in terms that acknowledge, and even incorporate into his own defense, the key Aristotelian distinction between potentiality and actuality. This is a distinction that Aristotle had used elsewhere in his refutation of the arguments for atomism, but that he, one may conjecture, knew better than anyone not to have been deployed by the historical Democritus.

There is, I confess, an inaccuracy involved in this, but not one grave enough to put the interpretation in serious doubt. The "impossibilities" to which Democritus is made to respond are not, as we have perhaps been led to expect (καὶ ταῦτα [that is, atoms] θεμένοις οὐχ ἧττον συμβαίνει ἀδύνατα), problems consequent on the actual positing of atoms, such as the conflict with mathematics that Aristotle notoriously alleges at *De Caelo* 3.4, 303a20–24, but rather, as we shall see, ones consequent on the *arguments* used in favor of atomism.

The point of Aristotle's unsolicited gift is, I take it, to enable Democritus to marshal his strongest possible defense, even lending him some weapons from Aristotle's own arsenal, before Aristotle's own refutation begins at 316b34.[20] However unusual this strategy may be for Aristotle, it earns him credit for scrupulous methodology, and it coheres with the overall tenor of the chapter, in which Democritus is built up into the truly professional physicist at the expense of Plato, the latter being made to look like a rank amateur.

In the light of the foregoing sketch, I propose to read the defense of atomism in two separate halves. The first half, 316a14–b16, which I shall call the Democritean argument, I read as a historical reconstruction, consciously free of Aristotelian presuppositions. The second (316b16–34), by contrast, which I shall call the neo-Democritean argument, is added as a fiction—the argument that Democritus might, anachronistically, have used in reply to Aristotle's own criticisms of him, drawing freely on Aristotelian concepts. (My expectation that Aristotelian presuppositions should be *consciously* excluded from the first argument arises simply from the carefully signaled contrast with their presence in the second.)[21] Aristotle's ensuing reply to Democritus (which I do not have space to discuss here) will succeed only if it refutes the neo-Democritean as well as the Democritean version of the argument. However, my own primary aim in this context is to extract the authentic Democritean argument, and I shall discuss its neo-Democritean counterpart only in order to show that they can be separated in the way I propose.

3. THE DEMOCRITEAN ARGUMENT

(D1) A puzzle would arise if one were to posit that some body and magnitude is divisible everywhere, and that this is possible. For what will there be to escape the division? If it is divisible everywhere, and this is possible, it could also be in that divided state simultaneously, even if it has not undergone the division simultaneously;[22] and if this did happen there would be nothing impossible about it. Thus the same applies also at the midpoint, and generally too, if it is by nature divisible everywhere, then if it gets divided nothing impossible will have happened. For not even if it is divided into a hundred million pieces[23] is there any impossibility, although perhaps no one would so divide it. (316a14–23)

It seems clear that for a magnitude to be divided, as distinct from divisible, into *n* parts is for some substantive separation of its parts to occur—certainly more than the merely conceptual operation of someone entertaining the thought that it contains *n* parts, boundaries, or points. Otherwise, there would be little motivation for the closing words of the foregoing excerpt, "although perhaps no one would so divide it," or for the repeated proviso that not only is the magnitude divisible everywhere but also "this is possible," which must in the context mean "and this division can actually be carried out."[24] Thus far, the process might still be a fundamentally mental one, where every division is discretely thought of. But the later speculation about some kind of sawdust being produced by the division process (316a34–b2) confirms that something more than this is envisaged.[25] No one in their right mind would wonder about sawdust being produced by a merely theoretical or mathematical process, such as the bisection of a circle. The entire Democritean argument will prove to be one about the actual decomposition—and not merely the analysis—into its ultimate constituents of a magnitude that is *ex hypothesi* divisible throughout.

Note, too, however, that Aristotle's formulation is just about as vague as it could be as to how the decomposition is achieved. At 316a17–18, "it could also be in that divided state simultaneously, even if it has not undergone the division simultaneously" leaves it open whether the divisions occurred simultaneously, in an ordered sequence,[26] or in an unspecified way over a period of time. This will be important later when we compare the neo-Democritean argument.

(D2) Since, therefore, the body is like this everywhere, let it have been divided. What magnitude will be left, then?[27] There cannot be one, for then there will be something undivided, but it was said to be divisible everywhere. On the other hand, if there is going to be no body or magnitude left, but the division is going to exist, either the body will consist of points and its components be sizeless, or they will be nothing at all, with the consequence that it could come to be and be composed from nothing, and the whole thing would be a mere appearance. Similarly, even if it consists of points, there will be no quantity. For when the points were in contact and there was a single magnitude and they were together, they did not make the whole thing any bigger; for when the magnitude was divided into two or more, the whole was no smaller or bigger than before; hence even if they are all put together, they will produce no magnitude. (316a23–34)

This is perhaps the most lucid part of the argument. If the magnitude is potentially divisible at every point, let that potential division be realized, which, as we have seen, means "Let the magnitude be fully decomposed by separation at every point." The problem is then how you can reassemble it out of the resultant parts. These parts are either nothing at all, Democritus argues, or points. If they are nothing at all, then their sum, the original magnitude, is also nothing at all. If they are points, they are sizeless, and therefore still cannot contribute to its magnitude.

An encouraging sign of Aristotle's attempt to recapture Democritus's original reasoning, and not simply to apply his own presuppositions,[28] is that the inability of points to compose a magnitude is not taken for granted, but is supported by a specific subargument: "when the magnitude was divided into two or more, the whole was no smaller or bigger than before" (316a31–33). Why is this relevant? Because Democritus assumes that the division process would either diminish or increase the number of points in the magnitude, yet fail to alter the magnitude itself. Accounting for the idea of increase here is relatively simple:[29] if a line is separated into two lines by the imposition of a division at point A, point A is replaced by two points, the (formerly united) extremities of the two resultant lines. But why might anyone have thought, alternatively, that division could *diminish* the number of points in the magnitude?[30] I suggest that points are for this purpose equated with contacts, which elsewhere in the argument are several times listed alongside points as if the two notions were somehow interchangeable (esp. 316b6–8): if so, then every division realized means one less contact, and hence one less point. (The dialectical offer of a choice between two conceptions of a point should be read as a hint that Democritus's own positive theory is not built on any specified conception of a point.)

> (D3) (a) But even if during the process of division something is produced like sawdust from the body, and in this way some body is removed from the magnitude, the same applies: *it* is somehow divisible. (b) If on the other hand what has been removed is not body but some separable [or "separate"] aspect or affection, and the magnitude is a set of points or contacts to which the affection belongs, we get the absurdity of a magnitude consisting of nonmagnitudes. (316a34–b5)

Here (a) envisages some of the magnitude not as vanishing into nothing but as somehow leaking out during the division process, like sawdust. The editions at this point print a question, ἐκεῖνο γὰρ πῶς διαιρετόν; (some follow the manuscripts EHJL in omitting the γὰρ): "how is it [the sawdust] divisible?" I propose instead to read it as an assertion, ἐκεῖνο γάρ πως διαιρετόν, and I have accordingly translated it "*it* is somehow divisible." Thus read, Aristotle is making the point that, were we to identify a portion of sawdust that had escaped during the division, there would be some dividing still left to do, namely on the sawdust itself, before we could claim to have divided the original magnitude at every point. (On the interrogative reading, he would seem to be raising a problem about how you *can* divide sawdust, but I fail to see what that problem would be or how it would help his case for atomism; it is atoms, not sawdust, that cannot be divided.)[31]

In (b) we encounter a trickier stretch of argument, too condensed to yield a single clear reading. We are asked to think of the leakage not this time as that of a body, such as sawdust, but as that of a property. For convenience I shall call this hypothesized property "mass," although Democritus's own term for it might well be "continuity," "solidity," or, perhaps best, "fullness" (ναστότης). A body's loss of its mass as a result of the envisaged decomposition into points would be a property-change analogous to the loss of color or shape. The motive for this alternative suggestion is presumably that it offers the advantage of reversibility. Whereas the *exhaustive* decomposition of a magnitude into points offered no components from which it could later be reassembled, on this revised model the recombination of the points would not itself already reconstitute the magnitude, but the bodily mass of the magnitude would be enabled to return in the way that color and shape can return to, say, a piece of chalk that has been pulverized and then reconstituted.

Democritus's objection to this alternative model is the absurdity of a magnitude consisting entirely of nonmagnitudes. His wording (b3–4, καὶ ἔστι τὸ μέγεθος στιγμαὶ ἢ ἁφαὶ τοδὶ παθοῦσαι) makes it clear that these nonmagnitudes are not to be taken as the points *plus* the property, but as the points alone, viewed as that to which the property belongs. Take again the analogy of a reconstituted piece of chalk. Qualitatively it may be white, cylindrical, and so on, but what it is constitutively is a just a collection of grains or particles, in the absence of which the whiteness and cylindrical shape would have nothing to belong to. In the case of division everywhere, the counterpart of the chalk grains is a set of mere points. If they, recombined, cannot constitute a magnitude, there will be nothing for the returned bodily mass to belong to. Thus the model envisaged in (D3) (b) proves to offer no advance on the kind of decomposition already rejected in (D2).

> (D4) (a) Moreover, *where* will the points be, and will they be immobile or moving?
> [b] And a single contact is always between a pair of things, which implies that there is something over and above the contact and the point and the division.
> (316b5–8)

This pair of arguments illustrates an interpretative principle I advocated at the outset. Commentators since antiquity have looked for specifically Aristotelian tenets underlying them. Thus Philoponus, followed by Joachim and Tricot, detects in (a) the Aristotelian doctrine of natural place: if the points allegedly constituting a magnitude were separated out, how could they find natural places, being neither heavy like earth and water nor light like air and fire? In fact, once one sets off on that path, one could raise even more pertinent questions about how a free-standing point can have a place at all, given Aristotle's definition of place as the inner *surface* of the container;[32] and equally one could invoke Aristotle's argument at *Physics* 6.10 to show why something partless could never be in motion.

But this kind of speculation is misdirected. The argument is Democritus's own, and Aristotle is not—at least not yet—offering him any help. The question asked in (a) is an intuitively powerful one even without any special Aristotelian presuppositions. Suppose we watch a body decompose into its constituent points, and I then tell you that these points are now spread all over the table, or alternatively that they are traveling slowly toward the ceiling. You do not need to be an Aristotelian to ask me (1) what are the truth-conditions of such claims, (2) what could, even in theory, cause a free-moving point to acquire a specific location or trajectory, given its total lack of physical properties, and (3) what it would mean for a point, all by itself, to be moving.

Similarly with (b), it is misleading to spell out, with Philoponus, Joachim, Williams, and others, what grounds Aristotle himself might have for insisting that there are always two parties to a contact. The argument is, once again, Democritus's own, and simply trades on the meaning of the word "contact": you cannot exhaust a magnitude by division into "contacts," if that would entail nothing's being left over for the contacts to be between.

> (D5) These are the consequences if someone posits that any body, or a body of any magnitude, is divisible everywhere. [Again, if I divide and put back together a stick, or anything else, it is once more equal and one. Clearly then the same applies whatever point I may cut the stick at. Hence it has been potentially divided everywhere. What then is there over and above the division? For if there is also some affection, how is it dissolved into these and how does it come to be out of these? Or, again, how do these get separated? (316b9–14)] So, if it is impossible for magnitudes to consist of contacts or points, there must be indivisible bodies and magnitudes. (316b8–16)

In bracketing 316b9–14, I am agreeing with the judgment of Prantl and Williams that these lines cannot belong here, both because they interrupt the sense and because they largely repeat points already made, in their proper place, at (D3).[33] At the same time, however, I agree with Joachim that the lines are unmistakably by Aristotle. The correct response, therefore, is surely neither to delete them, with Prantl and Williams, nor to retain them as they stand, with Joachim, but to transpose them. I believe that the distinction between the Democritean and the neo-Democritean argument enables us to see where they must be relocated, and why. These lines do indeed repeat the substance of the earlier argument at (D3), but this time, crucially, with the benefit of an Aristotelian potentiality–actuality distinction. They therefore belong in the neo-Democritean argument. We will meet them there, renamed (ND2), in due course.

Leaving aside the intrusive lines, the remainder of (D5) simply rounds off the Democritean argument, formally stating its atomist conclusion.

4. THE NEO-DEMOCRITEAN ARGUMENT

We can now move on to the restatement of the atomist argument in its neo-Democritean form. I have already in section 2 dealt with Aristotle's transition to it, 316b16–19. We can therefore move directly to its first section.

> (ND1) That every perceptible body is subject to division [*diaireton*] *and* not subject to division [*adiaireton*] at every point is no absurdity: for it will be subject to division in potentiality but not subject to division in actuality. But that it should be simultaneously subject to division everywhere in potentiality would seem to be impossible. For if it is possible, it might happen (not so that it is simultaneously in actuality both not subject to division and divided, but so that it is simultaneously divided at any point whatsoever). Thus there will be nothing left, and the body will have perished into something incorporeal, and would come to be again either out of points or out of nothing at all. And how is that possible? (316b19–27)

I have in this context translated *diaireton* and *adiaireton* as, respectively, "subject to division" and "not subject to division," rather than with the usual "divisible" and "indivisible." This is because Aristotle's distinction between the potentially and the actually *diaireton* does not seem to be one either between first and second potentialities, or between what is divisible merely in theory and what is capable of actually undergoing division. Rather, it looks like his way of distinguishing two senses of the *–ton* termination, "(in)divisible" and "(un)divided."[34] Hence the first sentence serves mainly to focus us on the sense of the word *diaireton* as "having the potentiality to be divided." The second sentence then returns us to the main Democritean argument, as we encountered it at (D1–2), but with the notion of potentiality now firmly in the frame.

By this maneuver, the neo-Democritean is being allowed to acknowledge an Aristotelian countermove to the atomist argument, with a view to rebutting that countermove in the next sentence. The Aristotelian countermove seems to be the one found at *Physics* 8.8, 263a4–b9 (with theoretical foundations laid at *Physics* 3.6–7). Aristotle maintains that paradoxes of infinite division fail because the infinite division they postulate is infinite *only in potentiality*. Very well, the neo-Democritean argument now goes, let us concede that to call a magnitude "simultaneously *diaireton* everywhere" is (in line with the distinction between two senses of the *-ton* termination) no more than to indicate a potentiality, not an actuality. However, the neo-Democritean continues, surely to call a certain state of affairs "potential" is to allow that it could be actual.[35] He therefore proceeds to repeat, in summary, the argument of (D2): this supposedly realizable state of affairs would resolve the magnitude into components that were either sizeless points or altogether nonexistent—leading to consequences with which we are by now all too familiar.

Aristotle need not be read, here or later, as conceding the neo-Democritean objection. In fact, as early as the next chapter (318a20–21) he will be reaffirming his own belief that division is infinite only in potentiality, no doubt relying on the re-mark at *Physics* 3.6, 206a18–21 that the "potential" being of an infinite division is of a kind that does *not* entail realizability.[36] He is, however, in this context acknowledging that a satisfactory refutation of atomism cannot afford to rely on so debatable a premise; and his actual refutation later in the chapter does avoid any such reliance.

It is at this point in the neo-Democritean argument that it seems natural to insert the displaced lines 316b9–14:[37]

> (ND2) (a) <Again, if I divide and put back together a stick, or anything else, it is once more equal and one. Clearly then the same applies whatever point I may cut the stick at. Hence it has been potentially divided everywhere. What then is there over and above the division? For if there is also some affection, how is it dissolved into these and how does it come to be out of these? (b) Or, again, how do these get separated?> Yet that it does, at any rate, get divided into magnitudes that are separ*able*, and into ones that are continually smaller and nonadjacent and sepa-rat*ed*, is clear. Now, neither could gradual division yield infinite fragmentation, nor can it be simultaneously divided at every point (that is impossible), but only within some limit. (c) Therefore it must necessarily contain unseen atomic magnitudes—especially if generation is going to be by aggregation and destruc-tion by disintegration. (316b9–14, plus 316b28–34)

The argument of (a) is too condensed for its meaning to be immediately clear,[38] but I suggest that it expands into the following sequence of ideas. Think first of physically bisecting a stick and then rejoining the two parts. Next try applying the same thought to *every* point on the stick. You have now divided the stick everywhere—not actually, of course, but potentially. That is to say, Aristotle's expression "Hence it has been potentially divided everywhere" (316b11–12, πάντη ἄρα διῄρηται δυνάμει) does not mean merely that it could in the future be divided everywhere,[39] but that this potential division *has now been carried out*.

If the meaning of this expression has gone undetected, it is because editors have failed to notice that the construction used in it, *dunamei* (or *kata dunamin*) plus perfect, is unique in the entire Aristotelian corpus.[40] Aristotle must be struggling to convey something beyond the usual range of his potentiality-talk. Now some modern discussions of Democritean atomism have, as noted earlier, introduced a distinction between physical and theoretical division, debating whether it is to one or both of these that atoms are supposed to be immune. Such a distinction between two kinds of divisibility has never, to my knowledge, been identified in any ancient source. But in this passage, if I am not mistaken, we have encountered the nearest Aristotle can get to expressing the idea of theoretical divisibility. In his terms, when you have run through a purely mental procedure of registering divisions within some magnitude, you have performed a potential division—a *virtual* division, one might say—though not an actual division.

The neo-Democritean argument helps itself to this Aristotelian (or quasi-Aristotelian) notion of a potential division, and maintains that even if no actual division at every point were to be carried out (that is, even if one did not, as in [ND1], insist on the realizability of an exhaustive division), the mere "potential" division carried out in thought, that is, the conceptual analysis of the magnitude into sizeless components, is already enough to replicate exactly the problems that we have already encountered at (D2–3) and that are now briefly summarized at the end of (ND2) (a).

This new twist on the argument would, if accepted, threaten to prove too much, since even within a single atom such potential divisions could arguably be registered in thought, so that the only true indivisibles would be either altogether sizeless or at any rate partless. It is widely recognized that, if atoms were altogether partless, that would clash with the well-attested tenet that they vary in shape and size. It is, then, fortunate for Democritus that this whole extension of the atomist argument turns out to be an openly unhistorical addition on Aristotle's part. By including it only in the neo-Democritean argument, Aristotle is in effect providing testimony that, so far as he is aware, nothing corresponding to theoretical indivisibility featured in Democritus's own atomist thesis.

Moving on to (b), we should assume that its opening question, "Or, again, how do these get separated?" still refers by "these" to the same ultimate components (whether points, or points plus properties) as were yielded by the conceptual, or potential, analysis outlined in (a). But as the argument proceeds, the topic is explicitly extended from these potential components to the actual components yielded by an actual division process: division yields not just separable but actually separated parts. (ND2) (a) has shown us the disastrous consequences of positing divisibility everywhere. Now (b), which directly paves the way to the argument's atomist conclusion, reassures us that, fortunately, division everywhere is not possible. When we are asked how to conceive of the sizeless components as undergoing the actual process of being separated from each other, no answer is forthcoming. Clearly a decomposition process can, for as long as we keep it up, separate the magnitude out into ever smaller parts. But that gets us no nearer to division at every point, which could not be achieved either by progressive or by simultaneous division.

This last appears to be an essentially *Aristotelian* view, on the unrealizability of an infinite sequence, now recruited to the neo-Democritean cause. Previously it seemed to be present in the background as Aristotle's anti-Democritean weapon: recognition of the impossible consequences of an infinite division need not lead to atomism, because there is something other than atomic indivisibility to ensure that those consequences will never arise, namely the impossibility of completing an infinite sequence. Now the two appear to have come together, and according to the neo-Democritean argument it is precisely the existence of atoms that guarantees the uncompletability of an infinite series of divisions. Yet again we see here the phenomenon of Aristotle lending his best weapons to the enemy camp.

It is noteworthy that, whereas the Democritean argument was altogether inexplicit about how the division at every point was to be accomplished, the neo-Democritean argument, at (b), is rather explicit: since simultaneous division everywhere makes no sense, it will have to be progressive, like a Zenonian dichotomy. And a progressive division could never become an exhaustive one. Therefore, there must be some limit to division, and atomism is vindicated. The fact that this description of the attempted exhaustive division process appears in the neo-Democritean but not the original Democritean argument is a clue that we should not expect Democritus himself to have appealed to a Zenonian dichotomy when hypothesizing division at every point.

The conclusion to the entire neo-Democritean argument follows at (c). Since division at every point is impossible (both [a] because of its ruinous consequences and [b] because of its conceptual and actual impossibility of realization), the necessary alternative is that division must eventually reach its limit (see the end of [b]). Wherever that limit may lie, it marks the end of division and thus the threshold of atoms, indivisible magnitudes.

We have witnessed the following progression within the neo-Democritean argument. First, in (ND1), the hypothetical opponent responded to Aristotle's use of potentiality as a weapon in the debate, by showing why it fails to disarm the main atomist argument. Second, in (ND2) (a), Aristotelian potentiality was shown, on the contrary, to offer the neo-Democritean a strengthened version of his own argument, since potential divisions to infinity, unlike actual ones, could, on the hypothesis of infinite divisibility, be successfully performed, thus exposing the unacceptable consequences of that hypothesis. At (ND2) (b) we are shown that not only the potential but also the actual division of a magnitude must be constrained by certain limits, since *no* conceivable process could result in division at literally every point. This finally leads in (c) to the conclusion that there are atoms.

That the atoms are "unseen," and that they underlie generation and destruction, are parts of the conclusion not warranted by the argument itself. The invisibility claim reflects a well-known independent feature of the atomist theory, and one that will become relevant in the light of Aristotle's own stipulation (*GC* 1.4) that in substantial generation, unlike alteration, there should be no perceptible subject that endures. The further point that atoms underlie generation and destruction represents Aristotle's own primary motive for scrutinizing atomism within the context of the present work; to discuss that here would take me too far from my topic.

5. DEMOCRITEAN ATOMS

It is time to take stock. By segregating Aristotle's historicizing reconstruction from his neo-Democritean argument, we have been able to see what he singles out as the considerations invoked by Democritus himself. This offers us a clearer light in which to address two questions: (1) How Zenonian is the inspiration of Democritean atomism? (2) Is Democritean indivisibility physical or mathematical?

First, the Zenonian question. It has to be admitted, I think, that the derivation of Democritus's puzzle from Zeno's dichotomy paradoxes looks a bit shaky. There is no reference at all to the problem of motion across a divisible continuum, and even the problem of magnitude raised by Zeno is not directly involved. Zeno's large–small paradox (B1-2, discussed in section 1) obtains its formal contradiction by showing each of the many to be (1) so small as to have no magnitude, and (2), because composed of infinitely many parts each with some magnitude, infinitely large. Although the arguments for these two conclusions contain materials that could be used to generate Democritus's puzzle, namely how a magnitude can consist of nonmagnitudes, Zeno does not do so here; and Democritus, for his part, does not appeal to any inference from a body's possession of infinitely many parts to its having infinite magnitude. Nor would it even be accurate to apply the term dichotomy—which refers to *progressive* bisection of an original magnitude—to the division puzzle described by Democritus. Democritus's puzzle simply assumes that if a magnitude is divisible everywhere, then one could in principle make sense of an exhaustive division somehow having taken place. As we have seen, the Democritean argument formulated by Aristotle shows no particular interest in how this division might be brought about, and it is only in the neo-Democritean version that the question is seriously addressed. To this extent, the ancient commentators may seem to be on unexpectedly solid ground when they fail to link Democritus to Aristotle's remark that the thesis of indivisibles was a response to the dichotomy.

If one *is* hoping to identify Eleatic inspiration for Democritus's puzzle, there is a much more promising candidate than the dichotomy. The following pair of conjoined arguments is preserved by Simplicius as a reported defense of the Eleatic One:

> (1) For if, he [Parmenides] says, it is divisible, let it be divided in half, and then let each of the two parts be divided in half, and when this has continued for ever it is clear, he says, that either what will be left will be some ultimate minimal and atomic magnitudes, infinite in number, and the whole will consist of a numeri-cally infinite set of minima; or it will vanish and be dissolved into nothing and be constituted from nothing. Both of these are absurd. Therefore it will not be divided, but will remain one. (2) Moreover, since it is alike everywhere, if it is divisible it will be divisible everywhere alike, and not here but not there. Then let it have been divided everywhere. It is clear once again that nothing will be left, but it will have vanished, and if it is going to be recomposed it will be composed out of what is nothing. For if something is going to be left, it will not yet have been divided everywhere. On these grounds too, he says, it is clear that what-is will be indivisible, partless, and one.[41]

Now of these two arguments, the first does indeed owe much of its material to Zeno's large–small antinomy, even if it differs from that antinomy to the extent that it takes the form of a dilemma, not a contradiction. Moreover, it includes as explicit an application of the Zenonian dichotomy as one could ask for.

However, it is not this first argument but the second that recalls Democritus's defense of atomism as reported in *GC* 1.2. Although the second argument is a defense of Eleatic, not Democritean, indivisibility, its resemblance to the Demo-critean one is so close that coincidence looks unlikely.[42] The primary difference is as follows. The Democritean argument starts from the hypothesis that body is divisible *everywhere*, and then, by negating this, defends its conclusion that body is divisible in some places but not others: in a word, atomism. The Eleatic argument, on the other hand, starts one step further back, from the hypothesis that being is divisible *somewhere*, adding the premise that if it were divisible somewhere there would be nothing—given the presumption of its homogeneity—to stop it being divisible everywhere. Thus by showing that being cannot be divisible everywhere, the Eleatic argument is able to make the further move of arguing that it is not divisible at all. This difference in a way corresponds to the fact that Democritus, unlike Parmenides, includes in his ontology a component of not-being, the interspersed void. Hence, while he could have applied the whole of the Parmenidean argument to a single discrete portion of body, proving it to be altogether indivisible, he instead, at least as presented by Aristotle, considers body as a whole, and therefore aims merely to show that while divisible in some places—the void interstices—it is not divisible throughout.

But who is the author of the Eleatic argument? If it is standardly assigned to Zeno, this is for reasons that deserve to be treated with a little caution.[43] Simplicius quotes the linked pair of arguments from Porphyry, who had himself attributed them to Parmenides. Simplicius responds that there is no such argument to be found in Parmenides, and therefore that it might be worth considering whether it is in fact from the pen of Zeno.[44] His ground for the latter suggestion is that the dichotomy argument (with explicit reference both to the motion version of it and to the plurality paradoxes in Zeno B1-3) is well known to be Zeno's. He is clearly on good ground here, to the extent that, although the second argument does not, the first argument does employ a dichotomy—that is, an argument from progressive division.

It seems to me, nevertheless, that in a sense Porphyry was right: these *are* Parmenides' arguments. I say this because the first argument implicitly, and the second explicitly, are inferences from "It [i.e., what-is] is alike everywhere" to "It is indivisible." And that in turn looks like a conscious expansion of Parmenides B8.22, "Nor is it divisible, because it is all alike" (οὐδὲ διαιρετόν ἐστιν, ἐπεὶ πᾶν ἐστιν ὁμοῖεν).[45] I am not suggesting that the expansion is founded on any reasoning present in Parmenides' poem. Moreover, there is an obvious sense in which the expansion could be called Zenonian in spirit. It may very well have originated from Zeno, as one part of his defense of Parmenides, or for that matter from Parmenides himself, who presumably did not give up developing arguments after he had published his poem, and whose thinking could easily have been influenced by that of his pupil Zeno. But what is most important here is that, if we assume this argument to have been known to Democritus and to have led directly to the puzzle from which we have seen him launch his defense of atomism, his starting point was not, strictly speaking, the need to *answer* Zeno. Rather, the direct forebear of his argument may well have been an Eleatic defense—perhaps constructed or at least influenced by Zeno—of the indivisibility of being. This suggests that Democritean atoms originated less as a bulwark against Zeno's paradoxes than as a pluralized set of Parmenidean beings,[46] sharing the indivisibility and eternity of Parmenidean being but differing to the extent that they are, unlike their Parmenidean counterpart, surrounded by not-being, as a result of which they are able to be separated from each other and to move.[47] The difference between the two origins lies in the fact that while the former is overtly anti-Eleatic, the latter could even be a form of neo-Eleaticism.

I now turn to the second question consequent on Aristotle's presentation of Democritus. How do the considerations that Aristotle imputes to Democritus condition our response to the old question, whether we should call Democritean indivisibility physical or theoretical. The answer would have to be that it is a hybrid of the two. The through-and-through division imagined by Democritus is indisputably physical: it involves physically separating the body at every point, in a way that does not in fact generate sawdust, but that might have done. The focal problem is how you could, as a result of such a division, end up with components that can be understood as having jointly composed the original body, or out of which you could *even in theory* imagine reassembling the original body. By "even in theory" I mean, not that the reassembly would take an infinitely long time or make other superhuman demands, but that no coherent mathematical account can be given of what would go on *during* the rebuilding. Yet if you cannot coherently describe the reassembly process, there is no plausible sense in which the parts you have now accumulated are identical to the original body's constituents.

The way to sum up Democritean indivisibility appears to be as follows. Body can be physically separated at some points, namely at the void intervals that punctuate it, but not at others, namely where the body is solid and uninterrupted. If it could be separated at every point, it could in principle be broken up into parts that did not stand in any suitable mathematical relation to each other for reassembly, and this would cast doubt on how they can have been its constituent parts in the first place. Thus it may be a condition of a thing's consisting of certain parts that it should not admit of being physically separated into them. And the reason for this is that the *physical* separation would produce *mathematically* impossible consequences.[48] Neither "physically indivisible" nor "mathematically indivisible" fully captures this kind of impossibility.

6. THE CONE PARADOX

A merit of this way of viewing the matter is the progress it may offer us with placing and understanding Democritus's cone paradox, reported, without so much as a clue as to its original context or purpose, by Plutarch.[49]

> Again, look how he [Chrysippus] responded to Democritus when the latter vividly raised this physical puzzle: "If a cone were cut along a plane parallel to its base, what should we hold the surfaces of the segments to be, equal or unequal? For if they are unequal they will make the cone uneven, with many step-like

indentations and rough edges. But if they are equal, the segments will be equal and the cone will turn out to have the properties of a cylinder, through consisting of equal, not unequal, circles, which is quite absurd."[50]

A cone is sliced along a plane parallel to its base (fig. 1). The puzzle lies in the difficulty of stating the size relation between the lower face of the upper cone and the upper face of the frustrum. If they are equal, then at the height at which it has been cut, the cone does not taper; and since, by reapplication of the same test, we will find that it does not taper at any other height either, we will have the absurd result that the cone is a cylinder.[51] If on the other hand they are unequal, then the cone is stepped (both here and at any other height at which we administer the same test), and hence, once again, not a cone at all.

Now mathematically speaking, the puzzle may appear to be ill posed. For so far as geometry is concerned, there are not two planes at all, just one. The two faces are equal, simply because they are both the same plane.

That response, however, looks a bit too easy, and Democritus, the reputedly eminent mathematician, need not be suspected of so elementary a blunder. There can be virtually no doubt that when he speaks here of "cutting" (*temnein*, from which *atomon* derives) what he is describing is physical cutting, the separation of a body into two discrete parts. And while there is no puzzle to be posed about a geometer's cone, there surely is when it comes to the fragmentation of a physical cone into an upper and a lower part (assuming hypothetically a clean break, without any bits flaking off). For when we try to reassemble the cone, how can it be denied that one of the exposed faces is *above* the other? If the higher one is no smaller than the lower one, it may seem inescapable that, at least at this level, the

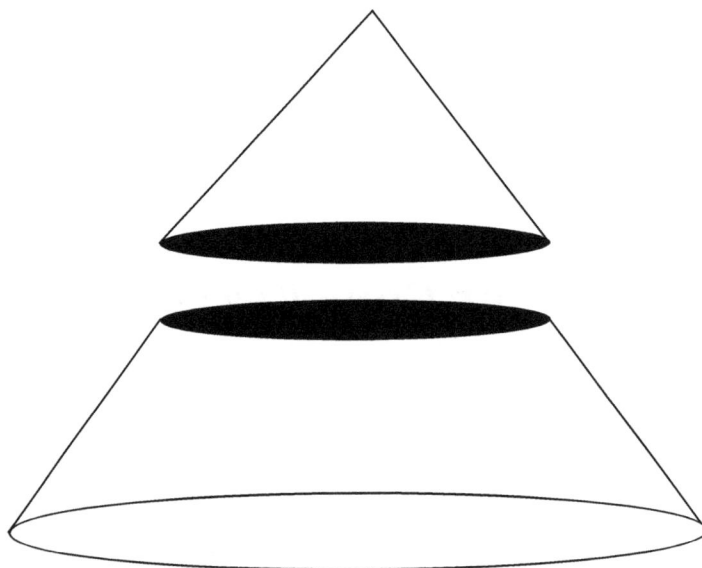

Fig. 1

cone is not tapering, since what is it for a body to taper vertically if not for its horizontal planes to become progressively smaller? And, as I have said, since the same experiment could be repeated at any level with the same result, it follows that the cone does not taper *anywhere*.

The resemblance to the preceding argument for atomism should be obvious. As there, so here we appear to have an impossibility that is generated only when a physical body is actually cut. And once again the impossibility is that of stating a relation between the separated parts that would make it intelligible how the original body can have consisted of them in the first place. For clearly there would be no problem at all if the cutting had not actually taken place: prior to the cutting there were not two distinct surfaces, and therefore no question could be asked about their interrelation.

If Democritus is right, *no* genuine cone could ever be cut parallel to the base. Nor, as a matter of fact, could it be cut in any other way—except, as it happens, into exact halves perpendicularly to the base, an exception to which I shall return shortly—without giving rise to slightly more complicated versions of the same problem: one would every time be confronted with the question, are the two exposed faces equal or unequal? That poses no problem at all for phenomenal cones, since there is absolutely no reason to suppose that these *are* perfect cones, and moreover very good reason—given that they are assemblages of innumerable juxtaposed atoms—to assume that they are no better than approximations to cones. But suppose that a single perfectly continuous body were conical. *It* could not be cut parallel to the base. Hence if there are any conical bodies, they are atomic.

A little further reflection shows that cones do no more than provide a simple example of a truth that will apply to discrete continuous bodies of any shape whatsoever.[52] A sphere cannot be cut, other than into exact hemispheres, without raising the equivalent problem of how the exposed faces compare in size. A pyramid cannot be cut, other than by exact symmetrical bisection, without the same problem arising. No kind of prism could be cut along any plane intersecting with two or more adjacent edges. And so on for all possible geometrical shapes: they will be cuttable, if at all, only along a strictly delimited subset of internal planes. Indeed, many irregular solids will not be cuttable *at all*. And once it has been admitted that, for a genuine physical solid, at most a closely circumscribed range of cuts will avoid falling foul of the paradox, it might seem very odd indeed to insist that even those limited cuts are actually possible. What could it be about the solid—especially given the absolute homogeneity of Democritean body—that enabled it to distinguish in advance which cuts will, when completed, lead to mathematical absurdities, and to respond accordingly to the attempt to cut it? The much more economical response is, it seems, to apply Democritus's favored *ou mallon* principle: given the homogeneity of all being (that is, body) and, consequent on that, its uniform resistance to cutting, there is *no more reason* for it to be indivisible here than anywhere else; but it is indivisible here; therefore it is indivisible everywhere. If so, no genuinely solid body can be cut in any way at all. And that conclusion is, once again, tantamount to atomism.

NOTES

....

My thanks, for helpful comments on an unscripted antecedent of the *GC* part of this chapter, to various members of an audience at the Padua Aristotle Seminar in December 1998 (kindly organized by Enrico Berti), and to an M.Phil. class at the University of Cambridge in January 1999. A subsequent scripted version benefited from a thorough critique at the Symposium Aristotelicum in Deurne, Netherlands, in summer 1999; I am grateful to all participants in that discussion, and to John Cooper, Alan Code, and Geoffrey Lloyd for further correspondence. My resultant article, focused on the interpretation of *GC* 1.2, has now appeared as *"On Generation and Corruption* I.2." The version of the article given here, refocused on Democritus and his background, has benefited from discussions at the University of Michigan, the University of Toronto, the December 2001 ancient philosophy colloquium at Princeton University, the Central European University, Budapest, the University of Oslo, and Tokyo Metropolitan University. At Princeton, Sylvia Berryman, as commentator on the article, deserves particular thanks, and I am also grateful to István Bodnár for discussion and correspondence. Finally, I must mention that Marwan Rashed's fine new edition of *De generatione et corruptione* came out only after I had completed my typescript, and therefore could not be taken into account.

1. ἔνιοι δ' ἐνέδοσαν τοῖς λόγοις ἀμφοτέροις, τῷ μὲν ὅτι πάντα ἓν εἰ τὸ ὂν ἓν σημαίνει, ὅτι ἔστι τὸ μὴ ὄν, τῷ δὲ ἐκ τῆς διχοτομίας ἄτομα ποιήσαντες μεγέθη.

2. I sketch this picture of the origins of atomism in Sedley, "Two Conceptions of Vacuum." Although I believe it to rely on a more or less correct reading of Parmenides, it is not part of my agenda to defend that reading here.

3. Simplicius, *in Ph.* 140.34, commenting on our Aristotelian lemma, explicitly names this as a "dichotomy" argument that Aristotle may have in mind.

4. This palpable fact has remained curiously unrecognized. Simplicius (*in Ph.* 140.21–28), responding to Porphyry's attribution of a version of the dichotomy argument to Parmenides (see section 5 of this chapter), writes "But it is worth pausing to ask whether the argument does belong to Parmenides, and not to Zeno, as Alexander also thinks. For [a] nothing of this kind is found in Parmenides' writings, and [b] the mainstream historical tradition ascribes the dichotomy puzzle to Zeno. Moreover [c] in the arguments about motion it is recorded as being Zeno's. And [d] why speak at length, when it is actually found in Zeno's own book?" Whereupon he proceeds to quote the B1–2 dichotomy argument verbatim. From the contrast between (c) and (d), it could hardly be clearer that Zeno's book, from which Simplicius is directly quoting B1–2, did not also contain the dichotomy argument against motion. The four motion paradoxes are in any case not cast in the form of the plurality antinomies, and are much more naturally read as independent arguments, attacking not plurality as such but motion, which is (1) a concept theoretically separable from plurality (since there might be plurality without motion, as e.g. in the Platonic realm of Forms), and (2) by tradition an independent target of Eleatic criticism, as at Parmenides B8.26–33 and Melissus B7.7–10. It is clear, too, from the ancient commentaries on *Ph.* 6.9, where Aristotle records the four motion paradoxes, that the commentators have virtually no more information about these paradoxes than they have learnt from Aristotle's own text. I see every probability that Aristotle learnt the motion paradoxes from oral sources, and that thereafter he himself became the sole source for their transmission. Zeno was, after all, a dialectician (the founder of dialectic according to Aristotle, fr. 65 Rose, 3rd ed.), so we should not be surprised if not all his arguments were produced

in written form. What may well have been his only book was, according to Plato (*Prm.* 128d6–e1), published against his will when he was very young. Cf. his millet seed paradox (DK A24), preserved only as a record of a dialectical conversation. The purely oral circulation of the motion paradoxes does not exclude them as a possible influence on Democritus, but it does raise additional questions about philosophical contacts around the Mediterranean in the fifth century BCE.

5. Simp. *in Ph.* 133.30–142.27 (citing earlier commentators), Philop. *in Ph.* 83.28–85.2, Themistius, *Par.Phys.* 12.6–18, plus the scholia quoted in Heinze, *Xenokrates*, 177. The commentators' assumption is generally rejected, e.g. Ross, *Aristotle's Physics*, 479–81; Furley, *Two Studies in the Greek Atomists*, 81–82. But as Ross himself admits, the parallelism with *Metaph.* 1089a2-6 could be thought to favor a reference to the Platonists.

6. Cf. chap. 7, "Indivisible Magnitudes in the Academy," in the first study of Furley, *Two Studies.* However, my conclusions about Xenocrates are rather different from his. They are developed more fully in Sedley, "The Origins of Stoic God."

7. E.g. Arist. *GC* 325b26–7, 33, 326a22, and cf. *Metaph.* 1.9, 992a20–22. These triangles should not be confused with the composite triangles making up the faces of the elementary particles, which *are* dissoluble (e.g. *Ti.* 89c).

8. Thus with his theory of indivisible lines Xenocrates is uncovering the *archai* that, according to Plato, make the triangles truly primary. Since these *archai* are known only to "god and, of men, any who is dear to him" (*Ti.* 53d), Xenocrates is making an extravagant claim for himself. His indivisible lines, planes, and solids are *formally* indivisible, although materially and *quantitatively* divisible, according to Porphyry (*ap.* Simp. *in Ph.* 140.6–18). I am far from pretending to understand this theory, but I take part of the point to be to enable the lines to vary in size and thus to constitute an adequate variety of indivisible planes, including triangles.

9. According to [Arist.] *De lineis insecabilibus* 968a19, the Zenonian dichotomy did provide an argument for the thesis of indivisible lines, but it is hard to be sure how much of the jumble of material in the treatise represents Xenocrates, who is never named there. Porphyry (*ap.* Simp. *in Ph.* 140.13–18) explains Aristotle's reference to the dichotomy in terms of Xenocrates' fear that what-is might be dissolved into not-being if there were no indivisibles, and this, while struggling a little to make adequate sense of Aristotle's reference to the dichotomy, seems similar to the cosmological motive I have attributed to Xenocrates (except that in a Timaean context the world's destruction would entail, not reduction to not-being, but the removal from the Receptacle of the *order* whose lower limit the triangles represent). It should be added that if the lines are materially and quantitatively divisible (see previous note), Xenocrates would still have some work to do in explaining how they help defuse Zeno's dichotomy.

10. I discount as probably irrelevant a distinct sense of "conceptually indivisible" discussed by Barnes, *PP* 356, namely "so small that nothing smaller is imaginable." I do not think that this kind of indivisibility is considered by the ancient atomists, including Epicurus, whom Barnes cites for it.

11. For physical indivisibility: Barnes, *PP* 352–60. For mathematical indivisibility under one name or another: *HGP* 2.503–7, Furley, *Two Studies*, study 1, chap. 6.

12. Sorabji, *Time, Creation and the Continuum*, 354–57. For a denial that the distinction is appropriate to Democritus, see Makin, "The Indivisibilty of the Atom."

13. Already in the fifth century, Melissus B9 denies that the One has parts, even though the nature of his argument there is notoriously obscure.

14. Alex. *in Metaph.* 36.25–7, Simp. *in Ph.* 925.13–15.

15. Curd, *The Legacy of Parmenides*, 185–86, with note 17, is perhaps overcautious in saying that Aristotle does not explicitly ascribe the argument to Democritus or the atomists: it is not obvious how else one is to read 316a13–14.

16. Philoponus, *in GC* 34.5–9, *ad* 316b16-18, σημειωτέον οὖν ὅτι νῦν οὐ πρόκειται αὐτῷ προηγουμένως δεῖξαι μὴ εἶναι ἄτομα μεγέθη (ἐν γὰρ τοῖς εἰρημένοις βιβλίοις αὐτὸ καθ' αὑτὸ τὸ δόγμα τοῦτο ὡς ἀδύνατον ἤλεγξεν), ἀλλὰ λῦσαι τοὺς εἰσάγοντας τὰ ἄτομα μεγέθη λόγους. ἀναλαμβάνει οὖν τὸν τοῦ Δημοκρίτου λόγον ἐν συντόμῳ καὶ διαρθροῖ μᾶλλον, καὶ οὕτως τὸν ἔλεγχον ἐπιφέρει; Aquinas, *in GC* 34, "praemissa ratione Democriti, hic procedit ad eius solutionem"; Joachim, *Aristotle, On Coming-to-Be and Passing-Away*, 83 *ad* 316b18–19; Migliori, *La generazione e la corruzione*, 144; Williams, *Aristotle's Generation and Corruption*, 72, *ad* 316b19, "Aristotle begins to expound his own solution of the paradox. It is to rely on the distinction between actuality and potentiality. For the moment, though, it is not worked out in detail, but Democritus' arguments against infinite divisibility are further summarized." An honorable exception is Mugler, *Aristote*, whose marginal headings imply that the reply to Democritus does not begin until 317a2.

17. In this essay, I follow the text of Joachim (apart from minor matters of punctuation) except where indicated.

18. I am grateful to Christian Wildberg for helping me to see this.

19. The bare outline of this construal (although without the proposed way of reading 316b14–19) is already to be found in Luria, "Die Infinitesimallehre der antiken Atomisten," 129–35. If it has gone virtually unnoticed, the reason may be that it appeared to have been successfully refuted by Mau, *Zum Problem des Infinitesimalen bei den antiken Atomisten*, 25–26. However, this was primarily because Luria had failed to account for the presence of Aristotelian-seeming material at 316b9–14, a problem that no longer arises if my proposal for transposition (section 3) is accepted.

20. On this I go beyond Luria, "Die Infinitesimallehre der antiken Atomisten," 135, who does not see the revised argument as different in content, but only in form, from the first version.

21. Cf. Luria, "Die Infinitesimallehre der antiken Atomisten," for a similar observation, although I suspend judgment on the question whether, as Luria believes, the first argument is a direct report of Democritus, or just Aristotle's reconstruction.

22. 316a17–18, κἂν ἅμα εἴη τοῦτο πάντῃ διῃρημένον, καὶ εἰ μὴ ἅμα διῄρηται. One might have expected εἶναι διῃρημένον and διῃρῆσθαι to be synonymous, both referring to the object's present state of division, so that the meaning would be "It *could* be simultaneously in a divided state everywhere, even if it *isn't* simultaneously in that divided state." However, by Aristotle's day the perfect often, perhaps even regularly, has a past temporal designation (Chantraine, *Histoire du parfait grec*; see e.g. *Ph.* 217b34, γέγονε καὶ οὐκ ἔστιν, *Cat.* 5a34–35, εἴρηταί τε καὶ οὐκ ἔστιν ἔτι τοῦτο λαβεῖν, *Poet.* 1457a17–18, τὸ δὲ βαδίζει ἢ βεβάδικε προσσημαίνει τὸ μὲν τὸν παρόντα χρόνον τὸ δὲ τὸν παρεληλυθότα). In the light of this, it makes more sense to follow the regular translation, as I have done. The anomaly that διῄρηται is indicative, where the sense should strictly be "even if it *would not have* undergone the division simultaneously," does not much harm intelligibility.

23. I retain the MS reading at 316a22, well defended by Verdenius and Waszink, *Aristotle on Coming-to-Be and Passing-Away*, 10–11, against Joachim's διῃρημένα <διαιρεθ>ῇ.

24. Another prima facie possibility (which I owe to Brad Inwood) is that the point is to disambiguate διαιρετόν, picking out the sense "divisible" as opposed to "divided" (on which see also section 4). But Democritus has no reason to stress that he means a potential

division *as opposed to* an actual one, since it is precisely the envisaged realization of the division that yields the impossibilities.

25. My remarks on this owe much to Barnes, *PP* 358–59.

26. The reference to the "midpoint" (316a19–20), though obscurely put, does not seem to allude to a Zenonian dichotomy, but simply to assert that what is true at (e.g.) the midpoint is true everywhere else.

27. 316a24, τί οὖν ἔσται λοιπὸν μέγεθος; I cannot see why the editors have preferred the scarcely natural punctuation τί οὖν ἔσται λοιπόν; μέγεθος.

28. Mau, *Zum Problem des Infinitesimalen*, 25–26, argues for Aristotelian contamination, but see my note 19. Migliori, *La generazione e la corruzione*, 151, goes so far as to comment "Per comprendere queste critiche, bisogna ricordare che per Aristotele il punto non è un elemento, ma il limite della linea e della divisione delle parti. Abbiamo quindi un classico caso di rilettura dei presocratici all'interno delle categorie aristoteliche."

29. See Furley, *Two Studies*, 84-85; Migliori, *La generazione e la corruzione*, 151; Williams, *Aristotle's Generation and Corruption*, 70.

30. This half of the argument is usually overlooked. Luria, "Die Infinitesimallehre der antiken Atomisten," 133 n. 71, does, however, attempt an elucidation of it, while Williams, *Aristotle's Generation and Corruption*, 70, notes it in passing, expressing doubt whether it is meant seriously.

31. If, alternatively, the question meant "How *far* can it be divided?" πῶς would be a poor choice of interrogative, where what was meant was e.g. εἰς πόσον.

32. One might also have considered invoking the claim at *Ph.* 4.1 (208b22–25) that mathematical entities have no place, just relative position for an observer. However, that view is contradicted by *GC*, at 1.6, 322b32–323a3.

33. Prantl, *Aristoteles*, 490 n. 15, argues that these lines are an interpolation by a later hand.

34. Cf. *de An.* 3.6, 430b6–11, τὸ δ' ἀδιαίρετον ἐπεὶ διχῶς, ἢ δυνάμει ἢ ἐνεργείᾳ, οὐθὲν κωλύει νοεῖν τὸ <διαιρετὸν ᾗ > ἀδιαίρετον, <οἷον> ὅταν νοῇ τὸ μῆκος (ἀδιαίρετον γὰρ ἐνεργείᾳ), καὶ ἐν χρόνῳ ἀδιαιρέτῳ· ὁμοίως γὰρ ὁ χρόνος διαιρετὸς καὶ ἀδιαίρετος τῷ μήκει. οὔκουν ἔστιν εἰπεῖν ἐν τῷ ἡμίσει τί ἐνόει ἑκατέρῳ· οὐ γὰρ ἔστιν, ἂν μὴ διαιρεθῇ, ἀλλ' ἢ δυνάμει. Although the interpretation is controversial, I believe that by the "potential" sense of *adiaireton* Aristotle must here mean, not e.g. what is potentially indivisible even if actually divisible, but what is *adiaireton* in the sense of that word where the termination expresses potentiality, not actuality—i.e., indivisible rather than undivided. I here agree with, among others, J. A. Smith in Barnes, *The Complete Works of Aristotle*. For a similar case of Aristotle's potentiality-actuality language being used to disambiguate the *–ton* termination, see *Ph.* 8.5, 258a32–b4. If Aristotle feels the need to disambiguate the termination in the present passage too, that is no doubt because he considers its modal sense, on which he here wishes to concentrate, to be a secondary one (*Cael.* 1.12, 282a27–30).

35. Alternatively, one could translate 316b22 "For if it were possible, it would [not just 'might'] happen," in which case the principle of plenitude would be being invoked or assumed. Since versions of that principle have been ascribed both to Aristotle (esp. on the basis of *Cael.* 1.12) and to Democritus (Makin, *Indifference Arguments*, chap. 7), its presence in the neo-Democritean argument would be no surprise.

36. I do not intend to get diverted into discussion of this very problematic concept, on which see esp. Hussey, *Aristotle's Physics, Books III and IV*, xx–xxiii, and Charlton, "Aristotle's Potential Infinites."

37. If the displaced passage belongs within the neo-Democritean argument at all, it cannot stand at the beginning of it, since its opening ἔτι indicates that it follows another argument for the same conclusion; nor can it come any later than here, because by then the atomistic conclusions are already being drawn. Moreover, 316b28–29—if it is read, as I am proposing, as the direct continuation of the passage—appropriately takes up its theme of "separation."

38. Cf. Philoponus' comment on this passage (*in GC* 33.7), διὰ περίνοιαν συντόμως πέφρασται.

39. Even more implausible, but at least a welcome recognition of the expression's oddity, is Aquinas's gloss " 'omnino divisum potestate,' idest in omnia in quae poterat dividi" (*in GC* 33, quoted by Migliori, *La generazione e la corruzione*, 152–53).

40. I say this on the basis of a Thesaurus Linguae Graecae search of the corpus covering all 413 occurrences of δυνάμει and all 52 of κατὰ δύναμιν. Myles Burnyeat points out to me that at *de An* 2.5, 417a31 we may be expected to supply κατὰ δύναμιν with the aorist ἀλλοιωθείς. However, all the editors and translators I have consulted agree that Aristotle is there elliptically (or even explicitly, if one adopts Ross's supplement) describing the actuality corresponding to the potentiality described in his preceding clause. Whether or not they are right, the prevalence of such a reading confirms how strange it is to find "potentially" attached to a past tense.

41. Simp. *in Ph*. 140.1-7: καὶ γὰρ δὴ ἐπεὶ πάντῃ ὅμοιόν ἐστιν, εἴπερ διαιρετὸν ὑπάρχει, πάντῃ ὁμοίως ἔσται διαιρετόν, ἀλλ' οὐ τῇ μέν, τῇ δὲ οὔ. διῃρήσθω δὴ πάντῃ· δῆλον οὖν πάλιν ὡς οὐδὲν ὑπομενεῖ, ἀλλ' ἔσται φροῦδον, καὶ εἴπερ συστήσεται, πάλιν ἐκ τοῦ μηδενὸς συστήσεται. εἰ γὰρ ὑπομενεῖ τι, οὐδέ πω γενήσεται πάντῃ διῃρημένον. ὥστε καὶ ἐκ τούτων φανερόν φησιν, ὡς ἀδιαίρετόν τε καὶ ἀμερὲς καὶ ἓν ἔσται τὸ ὄν. It is a merit of Makin, *Indifference Arguments*, to have brought out the historical and philosophical importance of this argument.

42. The resemblance has already been noted by, among others, Makin, "The Indivisibility of the Atom," and Curd, *The Legacy of Parmenides*, 186 n. 15.

43. See the bibliography reported by Curd, *The Legacy of Parmenides*, 173 n. 119; I am not aware that anyone has defended Porphyry's attribution of it to Parmenides.

44. See note 4.

45. The reading of ὅμοῖον here as adverbial, proposed by Owen, "Eleatic Questions," 92–93 and 97, in order to interpret 22 as picking up 11 and thus as indicating only temporal indivisibility, has had a surprising persistence in subsequent translations. It seems to me linguistically unlikely, and interpretatively unnecessary, since "it is all alike" does not need an antecedent in the poem: it is enough to assume that it is defended in the *following* lines (23–25).

46. For an analogous idea, see Wardy, "Eleatic Pluralism."

47. They are also absolved of necessarily being spherical, an attribute that Parmenides, B8.42-49, infers from the unavailability of any not-being to cause asymmetry by making being larger in one direction than another. Of course I am aware that these lines are most frequently read as not describing literal sphericity, but I know of no evidence that anyone in antiquity took them in any other than the obvious spatial sense (cf. Plato, *Sph*. 244e).

48. I thus tend toward the formulation of Taylor, *The Atomists*, 165: "It is theoretically impossible to divide an atom physically."

49. Plu. *Comm. not.* 1079E = Democr. B155 DK. The literature on this puzzle has focused more on Chrysippus's solution than on Democritus's own intentions: see esp. Hahm, "Chrysippus' Solution to the Democritean Dilemma of the Cone." For discussions

of Democritus's use of the puzzle, see *HGP* 2.487–88; Vlastos, "Minimal Parts in Epicurean Atomism," 128–29; Luria, "Die Infinitesimallehre der antiken Atomisten," 138–41; Mau, *Zum Problem des Infinitesimalen*, 22–23; Taylor, *The Atomists*, 199–200; more bibliography in Hahm, 206 n. 3.

50. ἔτι τοίνυν ὅρα τίνα τρόπον ἀπήντησε Δημοκρίτῳ διαποροῦντι φυσικῶς καὶ ἐπιτυχῶς· εἰ κῶνος τέμνοιτο παρὰ τὴν βάσιν ἐπιπέδῳ, τί χρὴ διανοεῖσθαι τὰς τῶν τμημάτων ἐπιφανείας, ἴσας ἢ ἀνίσους γιγνομένας; ἄνισοι μὲν γὰρ οὖσαι τὸν κῶνον ἀνώμαλον παρέξουσι πολλὰς ἀποχαράξεις λαμβάνοντα βαθμοειδεῖς καὶ τραχύτητας, ἴσων δὲ οὐσῶν ἴσα τμήματα ἔσται καὶ φανεῖται τὸ τοῦ κυλίνδρου πεπονθὼς ὁ κῶνος, ἐξ ἴσων συγκείμενος καὶ οὐκ ἀνίσων κύκλων, ὅπερ ἐστὶν ἀτοπώτατον.

51. This is expressed as "consisting of equal . . . circles," which, if taken to imply that a solid can actually be constituted out of planes, will sit uneasily with Democritus's denial that a magnitude can consist of nonmagnitudes (D2; see section 3). However, he need mean no more than that a cone's or cylinder's shape can be fully mapped by charting the location and size-relation of all the circles parallel to its base.

52. Why then choose a cone? Perhaps because this was a special favorite of Democritus among geometrical solids: he was credited with having known, albeit without proof, the theorem that the volume of a cone is one-third of that of the cylinder on the same base and with the same height (Archimedes, *Eratosth.* 428.26 Heiberg). There is, however, no apparent reason to posit any *direct* link between the theorem and the cone paradox.

BIBLIOGRAPHY

Barnes, Jonathan, ed. *The Complete Works of Aristotle*. 2 vols. Princeton, N.J.: Princeton University Press, 1984.

Chantraine, Pierre. *Histoire du parfait grec*. Paris: Champion, 1926.

Charlton, William. "Aristotle's Potential Infinites." In *Aristotle's Physics*, edited by Lindsay Judson, 129–49. Oxford: Clarendon Press, 1991.

Curd, Patricia. *The Legacy of Parmenides*. Princeton, N.J.: Princeton University Press, 1998.

Furley, David J. *Two Studies in the Greek Atomists*. Princeton, N.J.: Princeton University Press, 1967.

Hahm, D. E. "Chrysippus' Solution to the Democritean Dilemma of the Cone." *Isis* 63 (1972): 205–20.

Heinze, R. *Xenokrates*. Hildesheim: Olms, 1965.

Hussey, Edward L. *Aristotle's Physics, Books III and IV*. Oxford: Clarendon Press, 1983.

Joachim, H. H. *Aristotle, On Coming-to-Be and Passing-Away*. Oxford: Clarendon Press, 1922.

Luria, Salomon. "Die Infinitesimallehre der antiken Atomisten." *Quellen und Studien zur Geschichte der Mathematik*, B2 (1933): 106–85.

Makin, Stephen. *Indifference Arguments*. Oxford: Blackwell, 1993.

———. "The Indivisibility of the Atom." *Archiv für Geschichte der Philosophie* 71 (1989): 125–49.

Mau, J. *Zum Problem des Infinitesimalen bei den antiken Atomisten*. Berlin: Deutsche Akademie der Wissenschaften zu Berlin, 1954.

Migliori, M. *Aristotele: La generazione e la corruzione*. Naples: Loffredo, 1976.

Mugler, Charles. *Aristote: De la Génération et de la corruption*. Paris: Belles Lettres, 1966.

Owen, G. E. L. "Eleatic Questions." *Classical Quarterly*, n.s., 10 (1960): 84–102.

Prantl, C. *Aristoteles: Vier Bücher über das Himmelsgebäude und zwei Bücher über Enstehen und Vergehen*. Leipzig: Englemann, 1857.

Rashed, Marwan. *Aristote, De la génération et de la corruption*. Paris: Belles Lettres, 2005.

Ross, W. D. *Aristotle's Physics*. Oxford: Clarendon Press, 1936.

Sedley, David. "*On Generation and Corruption* I.2." In *Aristotle's On Generation and Corruption I*, edited by Frans de Haas and Jaap Mansfeld, 65–89. Oxford: Clarendon Press, 2004.

———. "The Origins of Stoic God." In *Traditions of Theology*, edited by Dorothea Frede and André Laks, 41-83. Leiden: Brill, 2002.

———. "Two Conceptions of Vacuum." *Phronesis* 27 (1981): 175–93.

Sorabji, Richard. *Time, Creation and the Continuum*. London: Duckworth, 1983.

Taylor, C. C. W. *The Atomists: Leucippus and Democritus*. Toronto: University of Toronto Press, 1999.

Verdenius, W. J., and J. H. Waszink. *Aristotle on Coming-to-Be and Passing-Away: Some Comments*. Leiden: Brill, 1966.

Vlastos, Gregory. "Minimal Parts in Epicurean Atomism." *Isis* 56 (1965): 121–47.

Wardy, R. B. B. "Eleatic Pluralism." *Archiv für Geschichte der Philosophie* 70 (1988): 125–46.

Williams, C. J. F. *Aristotle's Generation and Corruption*. Oxford: Clarendon Press, 1982.

CHAPTER 11

LEUCIPPUS'S ATOMISM

DANIEL W. GRAHAM

THE FOUNDER of atomic theory, according to Aristotle and Theophrastus, is Leucippus. Yet they tell us nothing about Leucippus the man, and thanks to a skeptical remark made by Epicurus, his very existence has been called into question. Three of the best minds of nineteenth-century scholarship were embroiled in a vehement debate on this question, which thereupon became a *cause célèbre*, with scholars weighing in on both sides for the next half century. Ultimately the debate seems to have ended in stalemate and exhaustion rather than in any clear-cut decision. The last 75 years or so have seen no serious contributions to the question; recent scholarship tends to avoid the question as much as possible. Yet the question remains an important one with significant implications for the historical roots of atomism. I believe progress can be made in this question. After (1) briefly reviewing the debate, (2) I shall argue that there are indications of an atomic theory different from Democritus's that can plausibly attributed to Leucippus, (3) consider indications that the atomic theory was known in the mid–fifth century, and then (4) tentatively explore Leucippus's contributions to atomism in a way that will illuminate Democritus's contributions.

1. WITHOUT A TRACE

The problem of Leucippus ("die Leukipp-Frage") can conveniently be divided into three subordinate problems:[1]

P1. Was there a philosopher named Leucippus?

P2. What (if anything) did he write?

P3. What (if anything) did he contribute to atomism?

Obviously a negative answer to the first question renders the following questions otiose. If there was a philosopher named Leucippus, but he wrote nothing, the third question is practically impossible to answer, or at best can be answered by appeal to hearsay from an early source. Even if Leucippus wrote something, but it is indistinguishable in content from the writings of Democritus, the third question will remain difficult or impossible to answer. The first two questions are historical questions; the last a partly philosophical question with immediate implications for the history of philosophy and the history of ideas. It is ultimately the last question that makes all the fuss about the first two questions worthwhile.

Notoriously Aristotle attributes the main doctrines and arguments of atomism to Leucippus and Democritus jointly. He sometimes discusses Leucippus by himself, but in other places attributes virtually the same views to Democritus by himself.[2] Thus we find no clear grounds for distinguishing the two philosophers in Aristotle. We are told that Theophrastus and his followers attributed the work titled *Megas Diakosmos* ("The Great Cosmology") to Leucippus.[3] One doxographical source attributes the *Peri Nou* ("On Mind") to Leucippus.[4] Thus there are two candidates for Leucippus's writings. On the other hand, these two works are included in the corpus of Democritus's works assembled by Thrasyllus, working in Rome in the early first century CE, who apparently made no concessions to Leucippus.[5] There is some evidence that earlier the scholars of Alexandria had not distinguished between Leucippus and Democritus in the corpus.[6] Thus there is already dissension in the ancient scholarly tradition.

The modern debate begins with a revival of Epicurus's challenge. Diogenes Laertius reports Epicurus's response to Leucippus:

> Apollodorus in his *Chronicles* says [Epicurus] was a student of Nausiphanes and Praxiphanes. He himself denies this and says in his *Letter to Eurylochus* that he was self-taught. He claims he does not even know if there was any philosopher named Leucippus, and so says Hermarchus, who some (including Apollodorus the Epicurean) say was the teacher of Democritus. (D.L. 10.13 = DK 67A2)

After pointing out that Aristotle does not distinguish between the contributions of Leucippus and Democritus, Erwin Rohde argues that already in Epicurus's time there must have been no trace left of Leucippus.[7] The possibility of identifying a role for Leucippus depends on the attribution to him of the treatise *Megas Diakosmos*. But a *Megas Diakosmos* presupposes a *Mikros Diakosmos*, which is firmly attributed to Democritus. The later tradition rejects Theophrastus's attribution of the former work to Leucippus. In general, Rohde argues, we should recognize the originality of Democritus and reject any attempt to relegate him to the subordinate status of a disciple of an unknown figure (80; see 74). Paul Natorp challenged the view that Diogenes of Apollonia was influenced by Leucippus, questioning whether

Theophrastus was the source for that claim, and hence became entangled in the debate.[8] Hermann Diels wrote a blistering criticism of both Rohde and Natorp, focusing on chronology and on Theophrastus as a source for the report.[9] But Rohde had already questioned the reliability of Theophrastus, so that a further appeal to him was inadequate. Subsequently the reliability of both Aristotle and Theophrastus in matters historical has been challenged in a systematic way.[10] So a defense based merely on their testimony will no longer do.

The chief difficulty for P1, whether there is a historical Leucippus, is the lack of any biographical information about him. Later sources say he was from Miletus, or Elea, or Abdera.[11] Optimistic scholars have turned this into a travelogue: born in Miletus, Leucippus was educated in Elea under the tutelage of Zeno, and finally settled in Abdera, where he founded a school and taught Democritus.[12] But the very inability to ascribe a secure place of origin to Leucippus tells against this. There are a priori reasons for assigning all three cities to him: Miletus was the birthplace of natural philosophy; Elea the home of Zeno, with whom Aristotle connects him dialectically; and Abdera the home of Leucippus's most famous (and only known) follower. Hence it is quite possible that succession writers, eager to fill in gaps in the story, inferred his place of origin in the absence of any evidence. In any case, there is no piece of biographical information to confirm his city of origin, and we must remain skeptical.

In the absence of biographical information, the question must revolve around P2, the question of authorship. Here skeptics have appealed to the tradition of Alexandria and Rome that did not recognize Leucippus as an author of any works in the Democritean corpus.[13] Furthermore, it has been suggested that the lack of historical evidence for Leucippus can best be explained on the supposition that the name is a pseudonym for Democritus, perhaps to avoid prosecution for impiety.[14] Alternately, he has been seen the character of a dialogue written by Democritus.[15] He has also been seen as an oral teacher like Socrates,[16] or a writer of lectures, which were not meant for publication—much as in the manner of Aristotle's esoteric works; thus he may be the founder of atomism, but all the surviving works were polished literary works composed by Democritus.[17] On the latter two views, there was a Leucippus, but for all practical purposes, his theoretical contributions are indistinguishable from those of Democritus.

On the positive side, there have been two major attempts to distinguish the content of the respective theories of Leucippus and Democritus. Adolf Dyroff reconstructed Leucippus as responding with bold and incisive logic against the Eleatics, as Democritus later responded to the sophists.[18] Citing a number of differences in the respective cosmologies, Dyroff pictured Leucippus as a pure cosmologist, while Democritus was interested in anthropology, psychology, epistemology, ethics, theology, aesthetics, mathematics, and biology.[19] After an inconclusive discussion of theories of weight, Dyroff returned to his distinctions between the two philosophers: Leucippus developed an old-fashioned cosmology, while Democritus dedicated himself to specialized studies.[20] Leucippus was more of a dialectician, Democritus more concerned with experience.[21] Accordingly,

Dyroff vindicated Aristotle and saw Leucippus as the founder of atomism in the mid–fifth century.[22]

Some three decades later, Cyril Bailey attempted a detailed reconstruction of Leucippus in his influential book on the atomists.[23] Rejecting Leucippus's authorship of the *Megas Diakosmos*, Bailey yet saw Aristotle as the key to differentiating the master from the student.[24] Leucippus posited atoms and the void, "introduc[ing] a new conception of reality" in the latter.[25] The cosmogony of the *Megas Diakosmos* was close to that of Leucippus.[26] It included a curious astronomical theory with the sun farthest out, as in Anaximander, and a drum-shaped earth, which overall was "disappointing and lacking in independence."[27] Democritus would take Leucippus's basic theory and "work [it] into something like a universal system."[28]

Dyroff and Bailey offer detailed discussions that are rich in insights, many of which cannot be discussed here. But both are, from a methodological standpoint, inadequate. Dyroff jumps back and forth from argument to reconstruction to a grand vision of the founders of atomism without really laying a foundation for his vision. He seems at times to present his vision as a basis for his reconstruction, before he has told us why we should accept the reconstruction. Bailey, for his part, pulls the rug out from under himself before he gets started. He first rejects Leucippus as an author of the *Megas Diakosmos*, then later tells us that most of what is in that work reflects his views.[29] But what criterion can we now use to tell us what comes from Leucippus and what from Democritus? Aristotle's view, as skeptics have shown, does not clearly distinguish between what comes from the teacher and what from the student. And our evidence for Leucippus's own views comes from Theophrastus, who evidently extracts the Theophrastean theory from the *Megas Diakosmos*. But if Theophrastus is wrong about the authorship of the work, he cannot be relied on to distinguish between the philosophers. It is also unsettling to note that Dyroff and Bailey come to different conclusions as to the contributions of the two philosophers: whereas for Dyroff, Leucippus develops the system and Democritus undertakes specialized scientific and theoretic studies, for Bailey, Leucippus presents the basic arguments and insights, while Democritus systematizes them.

As if these problems were not enough, one more problem arises in connection with Leucippus: the dating of Democritus. Though he is generally thought to have been born about 460, there are some wildly different dating schemes for him, along with the report that he lived to be over one hundred years old.[30] By dating Democritus earlier in the fifth century, skeptics push Leucippus out of the picture; but some date him, or at least his major contributions, into the fourth century, and stress the lack of any visible response to the atomists in the fifth century to call Leucippus into question.[31] Thus questions of Democritus's chronology further complicate the picture.

Let me finish this preliminary survey by sketching broadly the theoretical options that have been advanced, from most skeptical to most optimistic, with important advocates.

1. Leucippus is an invention (Rohde, Tannery, Bokownew, Nestle, Howald, de Ley).[32]
2. The question is undecidable (Brieger).[33]
3. Leucippus is the historical founder of atomism, but is difficult or impossible to distinguish him from Democritus in a systematic way. (Furley, Kirk-Raven-Schofield, Barnes, Salem, Andolfo, C. C. W. Taylor).[34]
4. Leucippus can be distinguished from Democritus in a systematic way (Diels, Dyroff, Bailey, Guthrie, Alfieri).[35]

Most recent contributions fall into the third group. I shall argue for the fourth.

2. FINDING LEUCIPPUS

We have no reliable biographical information about Leucippus. Hence, our access to him can come only through writings of his, or from what Democritus may have said about him in his own writings. But evidently later scholars and philosophers did not find anything significant in what Democritus said that could provide a basis for understanding Leucippus. Theophrastus, however, claimed that the *Megas Diakosmos* was written by Leucippus, and based his exposition of atomism on that assumption. Thus whatever differences there are between Leucippus and Democritus must be found in peculiarities of that one work. As Brieger already saw, the case for Leucippus depends crucially on the authorship of the *Megas Diakosmos*.[36] In other words, it depends on what evidence Theophrastus had for attributing that work to Leucippus rather than Democritus.

It is possible that Theophrastus could rely on school traditions or other external information he had for his information; if that were his only evidence, however, it would not be accessible to us. What would be accessible would be systematic differences between the doctrines of the *Megas Diakosmos* and other works of the Democritean corpus. One report of Aëtius attributes the *Peri Nou* to Leucippus also.[37] But we find no confirmation of that attribution in Diogenes Laertius, who is well informed about Theophrastus's interpretation; since Aëtius is late and derivative, we are best advised to ignore his report in the absence of supporting evidence. Aëtius does, however, reflect Theophrastus's judgments about which doctrines belong to which philosophers, and hence will be useful to us in reporting doxography.

When we compare the doctrines reported for Leucippus and Democritus, respectively, we find systematic differences. I shall concentrate on two areas, which I shall designate crudely as astronomy and geology. A number of these points, I may observe, were recognized by Dyroff and Bailey (and later Guthrie) but were presented in a question-begging way.

Astronomy. According to the doxographical tradition, Leucippus had a curious and unique astronomical arrangement:

> The orbit of the sun is outermost, that of the moon closest to the earth, while
> those of the others lie between these. And all the heavenly bodies are fiery because
> of the speed at which they travel. The sun is also kindled by the stars, but the moon
> has only a small share of fire. (D.L. 9.33 = DK 67A1)

Here the sun is the heavenly body most distant from the earth, while the moon is
the closest, and everything else lies between the two.[38] Apparently the other
heavenly bodies include the fixed stars and any planets Leucippus may have recognized. This arrangement is in part a throwback to Anaximander, whose sun is
the highest body. A clue to Leucippus's reasoning is found in the second sentence:
since heat is caused by something like friction, the hottest body must be traveling
the fastest, and hence be in the highest orbit. (Please note: I here follow Theophrastus in attributing these views to Leucippus, but only in a provisional way. I
take it that all these views are to be found in the *Megas Diakosmos*, whoever the
author was; for now, assume it is Leucippus.)

For Democritus, we get another arrangement:

> In our world the earth came to be before the heavenly bodies, and the moon is
> below, next the sun, then the fixed stars. The planets do not have the same altitude
> either. (Hippol. *Haer.* 1.13.4 = DK 68A40)

> Democritus [says] the fixed stars are first [outermost], after them the planets, after
> them sun, morning star, moon. (Aët. 2.15.3 = DK 68A86)

In this arrangement the moon is the lowest, then Venus, then the sun, then the
other planets, and finally the fixed stars. Democritus makes a clear distinction
between the fixed stars and the planets, as Leucippus does not (at least in the report
we have). It is our good fortune to have an account that gives reasons for Democritus's arrangement:

> [The motion of the sun] may seem most plausibly to occur
> according to the venerable theory proposed by the great Democritus:
> The closer each heavenly body is to earth,
> the less it is able to be borne by the vortex of heaven.
> For the rapid and sharp forces of it vanish
> and decrease in the lower region, and thus gradually
> the sun is left with later constellations
> insofar as it is much lower than the fiery stars.
> And the moon more so: to the degree that her path is lower, far
> from heaven and near the land,
> she is much less able to keep pace with the constellations.
> To the degree that the vortex that bears her
> below the sun is weaker, so much faster do all the constellations
> overtake her and travel on beyond.
> That is why she appears to return
> more quickly to the constellations, because they return to her.
> (Lucr. 5.621–36 = DK 68A88)

The speed of each heavenly body is correlated with its distance from earth. The vortex moves most rapidly toward the circumference of the world. The fixed stars move most swiftly, returning to their place every night. The moon returns to its place (relative to the fixed stars) in a month's time; but in reality that means it travels so slowly that it only takes the stars one month to overtake it. The sun, by contrast, takes a year to be overtaken. The planets all take more than a year, with the exception of Mercury and Venus, which have the same average period as the earth. We are not told about Mercury,[39] but Venus lies below the sun. Perhaps the way it overtakes the sun and then falls behind it suggests it is subject to eddies from the lower regions. In any case, the order of the heavenly bodies is correlated with their respective periods of rotation, which can then serve as a criterion for determining their relative distance from earth. Most important, the order of heavenly bodies is not only different from but *theoretically incompatible with* that of "Leucippus" in the *Megas Diakosmos*. Moreover, insofar as Democritus's heavenly bodies are traveling with the vortex, they cannot be illuminated by friction, as Leucippus's bodies seem to be. An astronomical system is one of the most basic components of a cosmology, and here we seem to have two incompatible systems, one in the *Megas Diakosmos*, another in other works of Democritus.

Geology. Another important component of Presocratic cosmologies is a theory of the shape and physics of the earth. We get two separate images concerning the shape of the earth attributed to Leucippus and Democritus, respectively:

> Leucippus [says the earth] is drum-shaped. Democritus [says it] is disk-shaped in cross-section, but concave in the middle. (Aët. 3.10.4–5)

These images do not necessarily presuppose incompatible theories. Leucippus's image requires us to understand the shape of an ancient drum. Whatever that is, it would have a flat upper surface and a finite depth.[40] Democritus's picture seems to be much like that of Anaximander's column drum.[41] Democritus is sometimes thought to make the earth an elongated circle, that is, an ellipse; but this claim seems to confuse his view on the shape of the landmass with his view on the shape of the heavenly body itself.[42]

We get similar but different accounts concerning the tilting of the earth attributed to the two philosophers:

> [Concerning the inclination of the earth:] Leucippus says the earth tilts toward the south because of the rarity of the southern regions, whereas the north is compacted because it is frozen by frosts, while the contrary regions are fiery. (Aët. 3.12.1 = 67A27)

> Democritus says because the southern part is weaker than its surroundings, as the earth grew it tilted toward the south. For the northern regions are intemperate, the southern temperate; hence this region is heavy, where there is a greater abundance of fruit, as a result of the growth. (Aët. 3.12.2 = 68A96)

Leucippus's account seems to make the earth tilt because the surrounding air is rarified in the south, owing to the warmth of the region. Thus the cushion of air beneath the earth provides less support in the south than in the north. Democritus's account seems to make the south heavier by reason of a greater abundance of living things—a greater biomass. It is unclear what Aëtius means by saying the southern part is weaker—perhaps Democritus pictures the earth itself as sagging under the extra weight. This would make the earth a deformed disk.

In the north countries, according to Leucippus, the earth is always frozen:

> The region toward the north is always snowy, cold, and frozen. (D.L. 9.33 = 67A1)

By contrast, Democritus envisages a significant melting of ice and snow in the summer:

> (1) Democritus of Abdera says that [the Nile floods occur] not because of snowfall in the southern regions, as Anaxagoras and Euripides suppose, but because of snowfall in the north, which is obvious to everyone. (2) The great mass of snow in the northern parts remains frozen around the time of the [winter] solstice, but in summer when the ice is melted by the heat, there is a great runoff. As a result many thick clouds are produced around the higher regions, as the abundant vapors rise aloft. (3) These clouds are driven by the etesian winds until they encounter the highest mountains in the world, which they say are in Ethiopia. Then forcefully crashing into these lofty mountains they create prodigious rains, from which the river is filled, especially in the season of the etesian winds. (D.S. 1.39.1–3) (see 68A99)

In his unique contribution to the problem of the Nile floods, Democritus portrays the northern regions as subject to summer melting. The resulting moisture evaporates and produces clouds, which are then carried south by the etesian winds (the northerly winds that blow in the Mediterranean beginning around the summer solstice), which dump their moisture on lofty mountains in Ethiopia. In fact, the Nile floods are caused by monsoon rains in the Ethiopian highlands—though the moisture comes from the Indian Ocean rather than from northern Europe.[43] What is crucial in this theory is that the northern lands do not always remain frozen, but experience a large amount of thawing and melting. Leucippus's theory, by contrast, requires that the north remains frozen solid; in fact, if it did not, he could not account for the permanent tilt of the earth. Here the two theories are not just different, but incompatible.

The discussion of geology has already brought us into the realm of meteorology. We do not get much information about Leucippus's meteorology, but there is one area in which different theories are recorded:

> Leucippus declares that when fire is trapped in very thick clouds, its violent escape produces thunder. (Aët. 3.3.10 = 67A25)

> Democritus says thunder results from an unbalanced compound forcing its way out on a downward path through the cloud containing it. Lightning is a collision of clouds, by which the bodies that generate fire are filtered through the rare regions full of void, creating friction as they gather into one place. And a thunderbolt occurs when quite pure, fine, even, and "close-fitted" bodies, as he calls

them, that generate fire, force a passageway [namely, through the cloud]. And a fireburst[44] occurs when compounds of fire containing much void are contained in places and regions with much void, so as to create a body with its own membranes, which by its extreme mixture carries the force to the depths. (Aët. 3.3.11 = 68A93)

Here, however, it is possible to say that the theory of Democritus is just an elaboration of that of Leucippus, or, from another point of view, the theory of Leucippus is just a compressed version of that of Democritus. Similarly, in the realm of embryology, there are reports of different theories for the two philosophers, but there is no clear indication that the theories are incompatible.[45] In the end, we are left with just the two conflicting theories, the astronomical and the geological.

Yet we have enough information to establish two different and competing theories in the doxography. The differences do not appear in the realm of foundational principles but in that of cosmology. What are we to make of the differences? We know that Theophrastus identified the *Megas Diakosmos* as the work of Leucippus, and on that basis ascribed theories from that work to the master, theories from other works to his student. We find, however, that there are systematic differences in the theories of the *Megas Diakosmos* and those of other works, as evidenced by the results of surveying the opinions themselves. Note that this is not a question-begging procedure: we hypothesize that work W_1 is by philosopher P_1 and work W_2 is by philosopher P_2. We find that W_1 contains doctrine D_1 and W_2 contains doctrine D_2; D_1 and D_2 purport to explain the same phenomenon or set of phenomena, but D_1 is incompatible with D_2. We are justified in inferring that overall W_1 is incompatible with W_2, and we consequently infer that P_1 is different from P_2. There was no a priori reason why the hypothesis should be confirmed by evidence; we might have found that all doctrines expounded by P_1 were also propounded by P_2. But in fact we found discrepancies and hence at least a preliminary case to confirm the hypothesis.

We do not know whether Theophrastus, or Aristotle before him, went through this chain of reasoning. If so, we may view his differentiation of Leucippus and Democritus as an explanatory hypothesis that is vindicated by his results. It is possible that he had other evidence on the basis of which to differentiate the philosophers. If he did, his differentiation is still supported by the results of his study. Now there is one other hypothesis that can explain the discrepancies between the *Megas Diakosmos* and other works: Democritus changed his mind. After writing his first cosmology, he revised his theories and recorded his new theories in successive works. A developmental hypothesis will account for the discrepancies without recourse to another author. Democritus's alleged long life might give him ample time to revise his thinking on cosmological issues. Indeed, detractors of Leucippus cite Plutarch as providing evidence that Democritus changed his mind on some points.[46]

Here, as in all cases regarding the Leucippus question, evidence is scarce. But one consideration seems to count in favor of Theophrastus's hypothesis and against the developmental hypothesis: we are told that Democritus made his statements about his age and relationship to historical events and persons in the *Mikros Diakosmos*.[47] There has been much debate over the possible differences in content between the *Mikros* and the *Megas Diakosmos*, and much speculation about the significance of the respective titles. Suffice it to say that we do not know how the Little Cosmology differed from the Great in content, and both works were written at a time when prose treatises did not regularly carry titles.[48] Thus the titles may well not be original, and the content of the Little Cosmology (as opposed to the Great, which was retailed by Theophrastus and is partially reported in the tradition) is unknown. Nevertheless, we know that the Great Cosmology was a classic cosmology in the grand style, and we can infer that it contained no statement by Democritus of his relationship to previous writers of the tradition. In the Little Cosmology, by contrast, Democritus located himself in the philosophical tradition (stating his own age in relation to that of Anaxagoras) and even his work in the history of the world (in relation to the fall of Troy). There can be little doubt that Democritus saw this work as his coming-out party—his personal manifesto, *magnum opus*, and individual claim to fame. Had he written the Great Cosmology, he should have put his stamp on that work instead, as his comprehensive statement of the origin and nature of the world.[49] I conclude that he is in all probability not the author of the Great Cosmology; Leucippus is.

Here let me append a point sometimes made by defenders of Leucippus. Aristotle wrote three books on Democritus.[50] Furthermore, he grew up only a short distance from Abdera and spent the middle years of his life in neighboring Macedonia. And we can say there was a school tradition in Abdera that long outlived Democritus: while other early philosophical traditions died out, the atomist theory boasted a number of adherents down to the time of Epicurus.[51] I would not wish to make this possible personal connection a central premise of my argument, but it is difficult to doubt that Aristotle knew more about Democritus and his fellows than he reported in his esoteric works.[52]

3. Pre-Melissean Atomism?

It is perhaps time to confront the problem of Democritus's dates. For all the speculation about how early or late he lived, the one secure piece of evidence is his statement from the *Mikros Diakosmos*:

> As for his time period, he was, as he himself says in the *Mikros Diakosmos*, young when Anaxagoras was old, being 40 years his junior. He says the *Mikros Diakosmos* was composed 730 years after the sack of Troy. (D.L. 9.41 = 68A1)

The phrase "being 40 years his junior" could be an interpolation based on Apollodorus's dating schemes. But even if so, it cannot be far off, given his claim to be young when Anaxagoras was old. Unfortunately, we do not know when

Democritus thought the sack of Troy occurred. In any case, he thought his own work was sufficiently important to be assigned a date in relation to the most important events of the Greek world—as an epoch-making study. Thus Democritus was born around 460, as Apollodorus has it,[53] and we may suppose he wrote his defining work between 430 and 420. This by itself does not solve any major issues. The bone of contention between Diels and Natorp was whether Leucippus had influenced Diogenes of Apollonia or not. Diogenes seems to have been parodied in Aristophanes' *Clouds* in 423. Any atomist influence could still derive from Democritus. In any case, there is no real confirmation in the fragments or detailed testimony of Theophrastus's claim that Diogenes was influenced by atomism.[54] If we could, however, find evidence of atomism earlier than 430, we would have a prima facie case for Leucippus's activity.

A classic article of Hans Diller makes a striking argument: Melissus of Samos in his case against change and plurality makes a series of criticisms of earlier cosmologists.[55] Melissus makes specific attacks on the theories of Anaximenes, Anaxagoras, Empedocles, and Heraclitus, and, Diller argues, on Diogenes as well. But Melissus also rejects the possibility that there is any void into which things could move, and he also criticizes the notion of rearrangement.[56] Here we have a specific argument against a specific cosmological theory, and the obvious target is atomism. Interpreters have often assumed that Melissus was either filling a gap or extending an argument of Parmenides for the fullness of being.[57] Yet Parmenides' arguments against what-is-not do not obviously envisage empty space, but rather something else, either complete nonexistence or some kind of conceptual indeterminacy.[58] Nor is there any sign in Zeno of a conception of the void, even as a foil to reality.[59] Furthermore, neither Anaxagoras nor Empedocles allows a void in his system.[60] In Melissus, by contrast, the notion is fully formed and provides the possibility of motion, just as in the atomists.

It is perhaps significant that Melissus introduces the concept of a void with no theoretical preamble:

> Nor is there any void, for the void is nothing, and what is nothing would not be. Nor does it [what-is] move, for it does not have anywhere to withdraw to, since it is all full. Now if there were void, it [what-is] would withdraw into the void. But since there is no void, it does not have any place to withdraw to. (B7.7)

Melissus does not present the void as a theoretical presupposition of motion, and then refute it; rather, he rejects it, then points out that without void, motion is not possible. But the notion of a void or "empty" (*keneon*) in the abstract is, we must remind ourselves, a strange notion, absent a theory that makes void a basic component of reality. Normally something empty is something not full; an empty space in ordinary parlance is not an absolute vacuum, but just a location that could in principle be filled up, as for example an empty cup. Yet Melissus seems to expect his readers to understand what he is talking about without any further explanation. Furthermore, we must either ascribe to Melissus an uncanny prescience in anticipating future theories or grant that in this argument, Melissus is polemicizing against a specific opponent or set of opponents. Indeed, if Melissus were the first to name, consider, and hypothesize (even *per impossibile*) the void, he would turn out to be, if not the father, at least the stepfather of atomism. For he would be providing, for the first time, all the principles and resources, and in general the theoretical framework, needed for the atomic theory. It is logically possible that he did so; but it is more likely from a historical perspective that he was arguing against a position already articulated. In all other cases in B7-8, we can find a specific philosopher against whom Melissus is arguing in his refutations. It is plausible to think that in his refutation of the void, too, he is targeting a specific philosopher.

Melissus must be writing in the period 445-430, so that his immediate atomist opponent is not Democritus but Leucippus.[61] So again we find reasons for thinking the atomic theory antedates Democritus.

4. ELEATIC ATOMISM

We have seen that the Democritean corpus contained two similar but different, and at points incompatible, cosmologies, one in the *Megas Diakosmos*, one in other works. We have found reasons to think that the author of the first work was different from the author of the others. The author of the other works was Democritus; the author of the *Megas Diakosmos* was Leucippus. There are traces of an atomic theory prior to Melissus and hence prior to Democritus; this must have been the work of Leucippus.

What, then, did Leucippus contribute to atomism? He wrote a single work of cosmology and cosmogony, like most Ionian natural philosophers. That work posited the existence of atoms and the void, and showed how the world arose out of them. When scholars ask what Leucippus contributed, they are usually interested more in the foundations of atomism than in details of cosmology. Were Leucippus's atoms different in any important way from those of Democritus? Did he advance different arguments, or in any other way offer a different ontology or aetiology of atomism? This study does not offer any direct answer to those kinds of questions. So far, we have seen differences not in the foundations of atomism, but only in the cosmological applications of the theory. Yet the picture seems historically coherent: cosmology was the bread and butter of scientific philosophy until Parmenides, and arguably even after. The traditional format for publication was a single treatise on cosmology, *Peri phuseos*, as it would come to be understood, showing how the world arose out of a primitive state through the operation of natural powers of natural bodies. It is, in fact, only with Democritus that Ionian philosophy turns to monographs on special scientific and even ethical topics.

We find, then, a difference in applications and in the scope and content of the research, but not yet any foundational differences. The results of this study may seem disappointing, insofar as many of those who hold that the theories of the master and his student are not distinguishable in a systematic way have allowed for this much differentiation.

There is, however, one area where there may be a significant difference, if not in ontology, then in argumentation. Malcolm Schofield recently pointed out that Simplicius, like Hippolytus, attributes a key argument for atomism only to Democritus.[62] The *ou mallon* argument, according to which what-is is no more than what-is-not, seems to come from Democritus rather than from both Leucippus and Democritus, according to Simplicius's source. And it is likely that Simplicius's source is Theophrastus himself.[63] Thus it turns out that, on this point, Theophrastus corrects Aristotle and makes Democritus alone responsible for what is probably the main dialectical argument for atomism. Insofar as we have found reasons to follow Theophrastus in his account of atomism, we are well advised to take this correction seriously.

What would atomism look like without the *ou mallon* argument? The theory itself is no different: the argument is a polemic directed against those who deny what-is-not. But on the other hand, the whole historical orientation of atomism comes into question. What the *ou mallon* argument does, in effect, is to call into question the foundations of Eleatic theory, specifically the argument presented in Parmenides B2 that what-is-not is to be banished from philosophical theory. To allow what-is-not, as such, is to reject an established theorem of post-Parmenidean thought and to move beyond the *krisis* that divided the objects of inquiry into two kinds, what-is and what-is-not, and rejected one of these kinds. Atomism is famous for its direct challenge to Eleatic principles. But what would Leucippus be doing if he did not formulate the challenge? How could there possibly be atomism without a confrontation between Abderite principles and Eleatic principles?[64]

Here I can make only a tentative suggestion for further consideration. One of the features of the first generation of post-Parmenidean cosmologists is their adherence to certain Eleatic axioms, and most explicitly, that of no-becoming: that what-is cannot arise from what-is-not.[65] Yet, contrary to what most historians of the period would lead one to expect, we find that Anaxagoras and Empedocles make no actual defense against Parmenides' alleged attack on cosmology. I have suggested that we can best understand their failure to combat Parmenides as due to their own more positive reading of Parmenides: they read the *Aletheia* in light of the *Doxa*, rather than vice versa. They see the *Doxa* as providing a positive program for cosmology rather than a negative prognosis.[66]

Is it possible to see Leucippus as sharing that orientation? In some ways, he fits the picture even better than Anaxagoras and Empedocles. Whereas both of them begin their ontology with a plurality of beings, Leucippus begins with a duality— just like the *Doxa*. To cite Parmenides' hypothetical ontology:

> and they distinguished contraries in body and set signs
> apart from each other: to this form the ethereal fire of flame,
> being gentle, very light, everywhere the same as itself,

not the same as the other; but also that one by itself
contrarily unintelligent night, a dense body and heavy.
(B8.55–59)

Parmenides' light and night comprise multiple contrary qualities. But there are
only two forms or types of thing. Parmenides' goddess hints at some sort of
foundational error mortals make (B8.53–54). Suppose this is to attribute positive
qualities to both forms. Ultimately, there must be one "dense body and heavy" and
one "very light" something. The former is completely full, the latter almost
completely empty. By pushing the goddess's analysis to the limit, Leucippus arrives
at an ontology that can account for motion and change, while staying as close as
possible to the theory of the master: dense bodies move in empty space, combine,
separate, and recombine. The *Doxa* is a model for atomic theory: with just a small
modification, night and light become atoms and the void.

There is one piece of evidence that suggests this interpretation may be on the
right track. In several accounts of atomism, we are told that Leucippus (and
Democritus) identify two *elements*. The most authoritative statement, that of
Aristotle, *Metaphysics* 985b4–20 (= 67A6), identifies the two elements (*stoicheia*)
with the full and the void (empty), which he compares with the dense and the rare
of Ionian theory (in the tradition of Anaximenes) (b10–12). Where we would
expect him to say there are infinitely many elements, he identifies only two,
stressing atomism as a dualistic rather than a pluralistic theory. The language of
stoicheia is most likely anachronistic, but earlier Empedocles had proposed the
concept of elements without using the word, when he called his four types of
matter *rhizômata* or "roots" (B6).[67] Leucippus's two elements are the closest an-
alogues to Parmenides' two forms in neo-Ionian philosophy.

On this interpretation, Leucippean atomism is a strict instance of "Eleatic
pluralism."[68] Only with Democritus does atomic theory break with and challenge
the foundations of Eleaticism. Only, that is, in the wake of Melissus's criticism of
atomism with Democritus's defense of atomism. Leucippus provides an elegant
physical theory in which he explains how atoms can become concentrated in
certain regions under conditions that will produce a cosmic storm organizing
atoms into structures within a protective membrane, in a cosmic birthing process.
He goes on to show how the familiar features of the world can result from this
process, and how astronomical, meteorological, and chemical phenomena are to be
accounted for. Presumably, he does not give a detailed theoretical justification for
the existence of atoms and the void, any more than Anaxagoras does for his
innumerable stuffs or Empedocles does for his four elements.

Melissus responds to the Eleatic pluralists—Anaxagoras, Empedocles, and
Leucippus—that their theories are precluded by reason. The axioms of Parmenides
entail that there is only one reality, undivided and undifferentiated. In particular,
the claim that particles of matter can be rearranged presupposes coming to be and
hence is ruled about by the axiom that nothing comes to be. And the concept of
void is ruled out by the rejection of what-is-not. Void is pure nonbeing and hence

impossible. In effect, Melissus understands the *Aletheia* in Parmenides' poem as putting such strict conditions on what-is that the cosmology of the *Doxa* cannot meet them. The *Doxa* is not a model cosmology, but an object lesson in how even the best cosmology must fail. Melissus's reading of Parmenides is consistent with the dominant modern reading. But it goes against that of the Eleatic pluralists, who seem to have taken the *Doxa* as an application of the *Aletheia*.

Subsequently, Democritus had to defend atomism against Melissus and his austere reading of Parmenides' argument. He produced the *ou mallon* argument, which I take to be a substantive reply (not a mere begging of the question).[69] In the court of public opinion, Melissus would win the argument about how to read Parmenides. Henceforth, Melissus would be seen as an Eleatic, and the pluralists as anti-Eleatic; but that is not how they saw themselves, for they thought of themselves as genuine heirs of Parmenides. In the new scheme of things, the atomists would be seen as at least post-Eleatic in some sense; now atoms and the void represented not the dense and the rare of the *Doxa*, but the what-is and what-is-not of the *Aletheia*. Now atomism constituted not an essay in Eleatic cosmology but a rejection of Eleatic metaphysics. Henceforth, cosmology and Eleatic theory were incompatible, and to be a cosmologist was in some sense to renounce Eleatic principles.

If this is right, the difference between Leucippus and Democritus amounts to more than cosmological details and range of applications. It is not precisely a difference of ontology, but rather a difference of foundational assumptions. Leucippus is an Eleatic, working in the framework of a constructive model of cosmology. Democritus is a reformer of Eleatic theory, with a sharp criticism of a defining theorem of Eleatic metaphysics, namely the distinction between what-is and what-is-not—and a deep commitment to the importance of sensory experience as a starting point for philosophical explanation. Melissus's revival of Eleatic theory forces Democritus to explore the metaphysical foundations and epistemological presuppositions of atomism in particular and cosmology in general. What was a relatively naive theory in Leucippus becomes a critical and reflective theory in Democritus.

I have argued that there are signs of two theories of atoms—in particular two cosmological applications of atomic principles. One is found in the *Megas Diakosmos*, one in the other works of the Democritean corpus, including the *Mikros Diakosmos*. It is plausible to follow Theophrastus in attributing the former theory to Leucippus, the latter to Democritus—thus providing an answer for P1 and P2. There are signs of an atomic theory prior to Melissus, which it is reasonable to attribute to Leucippus. There are indications that the theory of Leucippus lacks a key argument and perhaps any polemical reaction to Parmenides' theory. It is possible, accordingly, to suggest in answer to P3 that Leucippus's atomism is formulated as an instance of Eleatic pluralism, and that Leucippus, no less than Anaxagoras and Empedocles, sees himself as a follower of Parmenides. Something needs to be said about the role of Zeno;[70] for now, it is enough to note that on this account Melissus looms ever larger as the figure who reiterated the incompatibility of Eleatic theory with neo-Ionian cosmology and set the terms of the debate for the fourth century. In any case, Leucippus emerges as a figure to be reckoned with in his own right and located in the context of issues peculiar to the mid–fifth century. And Democritus appears as the man who provided a post-Eleatic foundation for atomism in response to a new Eleatic challenge, and to that extent marked a new beginning for cosmology.[71]

NOTES

1. That it has a German title indicates the importance the problem once had, comparable to the Socratic Problem.

2. *Metaph.* 985b4–20; *Ph.* 213a34–b22; *Cael.* 275b29–276a1; *GC* 314a21–24; 315b6–15; 324b35–325a6; 325a23–b11, b24–32. See *GC* 316a13–b16.

3. D.L. 9.46 = DK 68A33.

4. Aëtius 1.25.4 = 67B2.

5. D.L. 9.45–46.

6. *Suda* s.v. Δημόκριτος, with Bokownew, *Die Leukipp-Frage*, 6–7.

7. Rohde, "Ueber Leucipp und Demokrit [1]," 75–76.

8. Natorp, "Diogenes von Apollonia," with Simp. *in Ph.* 25.1–8 = DK 64A5.

9. Diels, "Leukippos und Diogenes von Apollonia"; see replies to (an earlier version) in Rohde, "Ueber Leucipp und Demokrit [2]," and to the article cited in Natorp, "Nochmals Diogenes und Leukippos." Diels cites similarities between Diogenes' and Leucippus's theories of lightning (10–11, with Aëtius 3.3.8, 10) but without advancing any convincing reason to think the former is derived from the latter.

10. Brieger, "Das atomistische System," 167, says, prophetically, "ich es für einen Gewinn halten würde, wenn Aristoteles Autorität auf diesem Gebiete einigermassen erschüttert würde." Subsequently Cherniss, *Aristotle's Criticism of Presocratic Philosophy*, criticized Aristotle as a historian of philosophy, and McDiarmid, "Theophrastus on the Presocratic Causes," similarly criticized Theophrastus.

11. D.L. 9.30 = DK 67A1; Simp. *in Ph.* 28.4–5 = Thphr. *Phys. Op.* fr. 8 Diels = DK 67A8.

12. Kranz, "Empedokles und die Atomistik," 19; Bailey, *The Greek Atomists and Epicurus*, 66–67; Burnet, *Early Greek Philosophy*, 330–32; Alfieri, *Atomos idea*, 22; for a cautious assessment, see *HGP* 2.384.

13. Rohde, "Ueber Leucipp und Demokrit [1]," 85–86, "Ueber Leucipp und Demokrit [2]," 744.

14. Tannery, "Pseudonymes Antiques," 127–29.

15. Howald, "Noch Einmal Leukippos," pushing the *Megas Diakosmos* into the early fourth century, the era of Socratic dialogues.

16. Bokownew, *Die Leukipp-Frage*, 18.

17. Stenzel, "Leukippos."

18. Dyroff, *Demokritstudien*, 11. His monograph on Leucippus in relation to Democritus is found on pp. 3–49.

19. Dyroff, *Demokritstudien*, 12–16; 16–27.

20. Dyroff, *Demokritstudien*, 39.

21. Dyroff, *Demokritstudien*, 44–47.

22. Dyroff, *Demokritstudien*, 49.

23. Bailey, *The Greek Atomists and Epicurus*, 64–214; Barnes, *PP* 628 n. 2, cites Bailey as providing the best attempt to sort out the two philosophers (though probably in vain).

24. Bailey, *The Greek Atomists and Epicurus*, 67–69.

25. Bailey, *The Greek Atomists and Epicurus*, 75.

26. Bailey, *The Greek Atomists and Epicurus*, 90.

27. Bailey, *The Greek Atomists and Epicurus*, 98–100.

28. Bailey, *The Greek Atomists and Epicurus*, 108.

29. Guthrie is in a similar situation: he accepts the distinction between the two philosophers but follows Stenzel in making Leucippus the author of esoteric school writings: *HGP* 2.383. Hence he also makes interesting and, I think, correct observations about differences between Leucippus and Democritus without a methodogical foundation.

30. Lucian, *Macrobii* 18.

31. For an early date, Ley, "Democritus and Leucippus," 621–26; for a late date, Ferguson, "On the Date of Democritus"; Davison, "Protagoras, Democritus, and Anaxagoras," 38–39.

32. Rohde, "Ueber Leucipp und Demokrit [1], [2]"; Tannery, "Pseudonymes antiques," 127–29; Bokownew, *Die Leukipp-Frage*; Nestle (departing from Zeller himself) in ZN 1.1037 n. 5 at 1040-43; Howald, "Noch einmal Leukippos"; Ley, "Democritus and Leucippus."

33. Brieger, "Das atomistische System."

34. Furley, *The Formation of the Atomic Theory*, 115; KRS 403–4; Barnes, *PP* 628 n. 2; Salem, *Démocrite*, 29; Andolfo, *Atomisti antichi*, 87; Taylor, *The Atomists*, 157–58.

35. Diels, "Leukippos und Diogenes von Apollonia"; *Die Fragmente der Vorsokratiker*, 4th ed., 1.vi–xii; Dyroff, *Demokritstudien*, 3–49; Bailey, *The Greek Atomists and Epicurus*, 64-214; *HGP* 2.383-89; Alfieri, *Atomos idea*, 21–37.

36. "Die Frage also, ob Leukippos die Atomistik geschaffen hat, fällt zum Theil mit der andern zusammen, ob der μέγας διάκοσμος ein Werk des Leukippos gewesen ist" (Brieger, "Das atomistische System," 168).

37. Aëtius 1.25.4 = 67B2.

38. Bollack, "L'ordre et la formation des corps célestes chez les atomists," argues that the fixed stars must be at the periphery, *pace* the sources. His argument depends too much on the traditional order of heavenly bodies. There are, however, arguments that might be more convincing: first, the fact that they do not change relative positions, and hence must be literally fixed; second, D.L. 9.33 = 67A1, though not perfectly clear, might suggest that some heavenly bodies are fixed to the membrane that makes up the outer heaven. Even if this correction is right, the order still disagrees with that of Democritus, because the planets and whatever other miscellaneous bodies are present are below the sun in Leucippus, above it in Democritus. On 67A1 see also Bollack, "La cosmogonie des anciens atomists."

39. Indeed, we are told that he did not enumerate the planets: Seneca *NQ* 7.3.2 = 68A92.

40. Panchenko, "The Shape of the Earth in Archelaus, Democritus and Leucippus," has recently given a heterodox account of the earth's shape in Leucippus and Democritus: the earth is convex on top; but this seems problematic.

41. Hippol. *Haer.* 1.6.3 = 12A11; Aët. 3.10.2 = A25.

42. E.g. *HGP* 2.422; Agathemerus 1.1.2 = 68B15 and Eustathius *ad Il.* 8.446 = 68A94 refer to the "inhabited earth" (*oikoumenê*) not the earth *simpliciter*; I understand the reference to be to the continental landmass.

43. See Bonneau, *La crue du Nil*, 16–25.

44. The term is *prestêr*—some sort of fiery and windy storm phenomenon: Arist. *Mete.* 371a15–17, Pliny *HN* 2.133.

45. Aët. 5.7.5a = 67A36; 5.7.6 = 68A143.

46. Plu. *Mor.* 448a, but without specifics, cited by Nestle, ZN 1042 n., following Rohde.

47. D.L. 9.41, quoted later.

48. See Schmalzriedt, *Peri Phuseos.*

49. See Oppermann, "Die Einheit der vorsophistischen Philosophie," 26–27. There is already an argument against a developmental hypothesis in Dyroff, *Demokritstudien,* 47–49.

50. D.L. 5.26, 27: two books on problems of Democritus, and one reply to him.

51. Alfieri, *Atomos idea,* 21–37.

52. Ley, "Democritus and Leucippus," 627–33, uses the supposed order of composition of Aristotle's books to argue that he had less to say about Leucippus as time went on. But first, the order of composition is controversial (and though I have interests in Aristotle's development, I am skeptical of any detailed chronology), and second, in any case the scarcity of references to Leucippus in Aristotle's "later" psychological and biological studies may indicate an absence of material on those topics in Leucippus rather than skepticism in the later Aristotle.

53. The eightieth Olympiad, 460–57 BCE (D.L. 9.41).

54. Of course Natorp questions whether the connection with Leucippus was even part of Theophrastus's testimony. Yet at least Theophrastus was the great champion of Leucippus. See note 3 here.

55. Diller, "Die philosophiegeschichtliche Stellung des Diogenes von Apollonia," 363–67; see Klowski, "Antwortete Leukipp Melissos oder Melissos Leukipp?"

56. Melissus 30B7.3, 7–10.

57. E.g. Burnet, *Early Greek Philosophy,* 179, 181, 325–26, *HGP* 2.36, 104.

58. See Kirk and Stokes, "Parmenides' Refutation of Motion," followed by Tarán, *Parmenides,* 111–12; this view is questioned by Malcolm, "On Avoiding the Void," but only by his calling into question the prevailing interpretations of Parmenides.

59. Unless we credit the alleged cosmology in D.L. 9.29, which DK refers to Empedocles. Zeno's handling of place does not bring in questions of void: DK 29A24.

60. Anaxag.: Arist. *Ph.* 213a22–27 = 59A68; Lucr. 1.843–44 = A44; Hippol. *Haer.* 1.8.3 = A42. Emped.: B13, B14. We do not have Anaxagoras's words on the subject, but Empedocles does use *keneon,* yet not obviously in a technical way. It is in any case possible that Anaxagoras and Empedocles reject a void precisely because they are reacting to Leucippus's theory.

61. See Diller, " Die philosophiegeschichtliche Stellung des Diogenes von Apollonia," 368, on the dates.

62. Schofield, "Leucippus, Democritus and the *ou mallon* Principle."

63. Others attribute the main *ou mallon* argument to Leucippus, following Simplicius 28.4–25: McGibbon, "The Atomists and Melissus," 251–52. But Schofield argues convincingly that Simplicius has transposed his discussion of the *ou mallon* argument from Democritus to Leucippus, as can be seen from parallel accounts, esp. Eusebius *P.E.* 14.3.7–9.

64. Aristotle presents Leucippus as arguing against the Eleatics in his theory: *GC* 325b35 = 67A7.

65. Anaxag. B17; Emp. B8–12.

66. See Graham "Empedocles and Anaxagoras," 166–72 and *Explaining the Cosmos,* ch. 7; see Curd, *The Legacy of Parmenides.* Until now I have not considered the atomists to be part of the Eleatic movement.

67. The first use of the term *stoicheion* to mean element is found in Plato *Tht.* 201e1, according to Eudemus from Simp. *in Ph.* 7.13. For its linguistic use as "letter" see Pl. *Cra.* 424e4.

68. See Wardy, "Eleatic Pluralism," for the term; elsewhere I have reserved it for those who see themselves as followers of, not opponents of, Eleatic theory—and hence for Anaxagoras and Empedocles, but not Democritus.

69. See Graham, *Explaining the Cosmos*, 264–65.

70. Solmsen, "Abdera's Arguments for the Atomic Theory," expounds atomic theory as a direct response to Zeno without the mediation of Melissus; and see David Sedley's chapter here.

71. This essay marks a rethinking of the connections between Eleatic thought and atomism relative to my position in *Explaining the Cosmos*, chap. 9, where I did not seriously explore an Eleatic atomism.

BIBLIOGRAPHY

Alfieri, Vittorio Enzo. *Atomos idea: L'origine del concetto dell'atomo nel pensiero greco.* 1953. 2nd ed. Galatina, Italy: Congedo Editore, 1979.

Andolfo, Matteo. *Atomisti antichi: Testimonianze e frammenti.* Milan: Bompiani, 2001.

Bailey, Cyril. *The Greek Atomists and Epicurus.* Oxford: Clarendon Press, 1928.

Bokownew, P. *Die Leukipp-Frage.* Dorpat: Bergmann, 1911.

Bollack, Jean. "La cosmogonie des anciens atomistes." *Siculorum Gymnasium* 33 (1980): 11–59.

———. "L'ordre et la formation des corps célestes chez les atomistes." *Revue de Philologie, de Litérature et d'Histoire Anciennes* 54 (1980): 276–83.

Bonneau, Danielle. *La crue du Nil: Divinité égyptienne à travers mille ans d'histoire.* Paris: Librairie C. Klincksiek, 1964.

Brieger, A. "Das atomistische System durch Correctur des anaxagoreischen entstanden." *Hermes* 36 (1901): 161–86.

Burnet, John. *Early Greek Philosophy.* 1892. 4th ed. London: Adam & Charles Black, 1930.

Cherniss, Harold. *Aristotle's Criticism of Presocratic Philosophy.* Baltimore: Johns Hopkins University Press, 1935.

Curd, Patricia. *The Legacy of Parmenides.* Princeton, N.J.: Princeton University Press, 1998.

Davison, J. A. "Protagoras, Democritus, and Anaxagoras." *Classical Quarterly, n.s.,* 3 (1953): 33–45.

Diels, Hermann. *Die Fragmente der Vorsokratiker.* 4th ed. Berlin: Weidmann, 1922.

———. "Leukippos und Diogenes von Apollonia." *Rheinisches Museum* 42 (1887): 1–14.

Diller, Hans. "Die philosophiegeschichtliche Stellung des Diogenes von Apollonia." *Hermes* 76 (1941): 359–81.

Dyroff, Adolf. *Demokritstudien.* Leipzig: Dieterich'sche Verlagsbuchhandlung, 1899.

Ferguson, John. "On the Date of Democritus." *Symbolae Osloenses* 40 (1965): 17–26.

Furley, David J. *The Formation of the Atomic Theory and Its Earliest Critics.* Vol. 1 of *The Greek Cosmologists.* Cambridge: Cambridge University Press, 1987.

Graham, Daniel W. "Empedocles and Anaxagoras: Responses to Parmenides." In *The Cambridge Companion to Early Greek Philosphy,* edited by A. A. Long, 159–80. Cambridge: Cambridge University Press, 1999.

———. *Explaining the Cosmos: The Ionian Tradition of Scientific Philosophy*. Princeton, N.J.: Princeton University Press, 2006.

———. "Philosophy on the Nile: Herodotus and Ionian Research." *Apeiron* 36 (2003): 291–310.

Howald, Ernst. "Noch einmal Leukippos." In *Festschrift für Karl Joël*, 159–64. Basel: Helbing & Lichtenhahn, 1934.

Kirk, G. S., and Michael C. Stokes. "Parmenides' Refutation of Motion." *Phronesis* 5 (1960): 1-4.

Klowski, Joachim. "Antwortete Leukipp Melissos oder Melissos Leukipp?" *Museum Helveticum* 28 (1971): 65–71.

Kranz, Walther. "Empedokles und die Atomistik." *Hermes* 47 (1912): 18-42.

Ley, Herman de. "Democritus and Leucippus: Two Notes on Ancient Atomism." *L'Antiquité Classique* 37 (1968): 620–33.

Malcolm, John. "On Avoiding the Void." *Oxford Studies in Ancient Philosophy* 9 (1991): 75–94.

McDiarmid, John B. "Theophrastus on the Presocratic Causes." *Harvard Studies in Classical Philology* 61 (1953): 85–156.

McGibbon, D. "The Atomists and Melissus." *Mnemosyne*, ser. 4, 17 (1964): 249–55.

Natorp, Paul. "Diogenes von Apollonia." *Rheinisches Museum* 41 (1886): 349–63.

———. "Nochmals Diogenes und Leukippos." *Rheinisches Museum* 42 (1887): 374–85.

Oppermann, Hans. "Die Einheit der vorsophistischen Philosophie." In *Xenia Bonnensia: Festschrift zum fünfundsiebzigjährigen Bestehen des Philologischen Vereins und Bonner Kreises*, 5–34. Bonn: Friedrich Cohen, 1929.

Panchenko, Dmitri. "The Shape of the Earth in Archelaus, Democritus and Leucippus." *Hyperboreus* 5 (1999): 22–39.

Rohde, Erwin. "Ueber Leucipp und Demokrit [1]." *Verhandlungen der Philologenversammlung* (1881): 64-89. Reprinted in *Kleine Schriften*, 1:205–45. Tübingen: J. C. B. Mohr, 1901.

———. "Ueber Leucipp und Demokrit [2]." *Jahrbuch für classiche Philologie* (1881): 741–48. Reprinted in *Kleine Schriften*, 1:245–55. Tübingen: J. C. B. Mohr, 1901.

Salem, Jean. *Démocrite: Grains de poussière dans un rayon de soleil*. Paris: J. Vrin, 1996.

Schmalzriedt, Egidius. *Peri Phuseos: Zur Frühgeschichte der Buchtitel*. Munich: Wilhelm Fink, 1970.

Schofield, Malcolm. "Leucippus, Democritus and the *Ou Mallon* Principle: An Examination of Theophrastus *Phys. Op.* Fr. 8." *Phronesis* 48 (2003): 253–63.

Solmsen, Friedrich. "Abdera's Arguments for the Atomic Theory." *Greek, Roman and Byzantine Studies* 29 (1988): 59–73.

Stenzel, Julius. "Leukippos." In *Paulys Realencyclopädie der Classischen Altertumswissenschaft*, edited by Georg Wissowa et al., 12:2266–77. Stuttgart: J. B. Metzler, 1925.

Tannery, Paul. "Pseudonymes antiques." *Revue des Études Grecques* 10 (1897): 127–37.

Tarán, Leonardo. *Parmenides*. Princeton, N.J.: Princeton University Press, 1965.

Taylor, C. C. W. *The Atomists: Leucippus and Democritus*. Toronto: University of Toronto Press, 1999.

Wardy, R. B. B. "Eleatic Pluralism." *Archiv für Geschichte der Philosophie* 70 (1988): 125–46.

CHAPTER 12

....

SPECULATING
ABOUT DIOGENES
OF APOLLONIA

....

ANDRÉ LAKS

TWENTY-FIVE YEARS ago, I made an attempt (in my book *Diogène d'Apollonie*, 1983) to take Diogenes somewhat more seriously than he had usually been taken, at least since Diels's devastating 1881 article in which he portrayed Diogenes as a second-rate eclectic thinker. Diogenes' popularity in the last third of the fifth century, which Diels greatly contributed to establishing through an analysis of Diogenian echoes in Aristophanes' *Clouds* and was confirmed by the discovery in 1962 of the Derveni Papyrus, went along with Diogenes' depreciated intellectual status: Are not serious thinkers ignored by the vulgar?[1]

Has this attempt been successful? The fact that some collections and translations of Presocratic philosophers leave him out may or may not be significant: some publishers obviously think the corpus is too bulky.[2] But Diogenes is certainly still lacking general recognition. Histories of archaic philosophy tend to overlook him, and often offer little more than an implicit justification for his exclusion, the core of which is encapsulated in the term "eclecticism."[3] What makes him visible is his absence, rather than any discussion about him. One complaint made by a reviewer of the *Cambridge Companion to Early Greek Philosophy* was that it nowhere happens even to mention the one achievement Diogenes is credited with, namely his alleged role in the history of teleology, for which he is occasionally praised.[4] It is all the more noteworthy that Graham, in his recent book, has made of Diogenes a landmark in the history of Presocratic philosophy by making him, rather than the older Anaximenes, the real promoter of the doctrine of "material monism."[5]

I personally tend to think that Diogenes' contribution, on this point, is rather to have explicitly stated the implications of Anaximenes' monism, rather than substituting a material monism to an Anaximenean pluralism (Graham's paradoxical point); but Graham's book came out after this contribution was submitted and could not be taken into account.[6] I shall consequently restate in a rather perfunctory manner, without adding much to what I have written before, what seem to be two basic points about Diogenes. The first one concerns what I take to be the center of Diogenes' own thought, namely the relation between his noetics (so I shall call his doctrine of Intelligence) and his teleology; the second is about the reception of Diogenes' thought, and the origin of his reputation as an eclectic.

1

In my 1983 book (*Diogène d'Apollonie*), I both downplayed some extravagant claims about Diogenes' teleology articulated by Theiler in 1925 and supported, against more skeptical views,[7] the claim that teleology remains an important feature of Diogenes' thinking. My proposal, although it has been rightly noticed (and critically assessed) by Kerferd in a review,[8] has drawn little attention—perhaps due to my own timidity about its speculative bent. I would like to restate it here more confidently (though no less speculatively), in the light of some thoughts on Anaxagoras I have developed in the meantime.

Theiler's famous interpretation (also meant to give some importance to Diogenes) made Diogenes the hidden (and for most part lost) source of Socrates' Panglossian teleology that features in two chapters of Xenophon's *Memorabilia*, in which Socrates offers a series of arguments aiming at establishing the existence of divine providence (1.4, arguments from the perfection of man; 4.3, arguments from the perfection of the universe). We may here leave aside the irritation that comes from Theiler's indulgence in the doubtful pleasures (and frequent paralogisms) of the so-called *Quellenforschung* (an approach consisting of reconstructing a lost source from the traces it left in the works that use or are supposed to use them); readers of Xenophon have developed more plausible views about Socrates' teleology.[9] What is important is to understand the kind of question that inspired Theiler's enterprise in the first place.

In a very famous passage of Plato's *Phaedo*, Socrates reports how he was disappointed in his youth when he read Anaxagoras's book after having heard, in the course of a public lecture, that Anaxagoras was taking Intelligence (*Nous*) as the principle of all things.[10] This implied, Socrates thought, that Anaxagoras gave teleological explanations of the universe, by telling his reader *why it is best that* the earth be either flat or spherical, or that it be located at the center, or that the sun, the moon, and the other stars move at the speed they move, follow the paths they follow, and so on—the presupposition being, of course, that intelligence always acts for the best.[11] Socrates' disappointment came from the fact that he found no explanation of this kind in Anaxagoras's writing; instead, when Anaxagoras came to explain how the world came into being, he mobilized traditional kinds of explanation ("airs, aithers, waters, and many more strange things")—alleged "causes" that Socrates refuses in fact to call such, and would rather describe as conditions for causal actions.[12]

Now we do have Diogenes B3 (= F6 Laks), an explicit declaration to the effect that the way air is distributed in the world ensures that the "measures of everything" (*metra panton*) are the most beautiful possible:

> Without intelligence it could not have been so distributed as to preserve the measures of all things—of summer and winter and night and day and rain and wind and good weather; and all other things, if you are willing to apply your intelligence, you will find to be disposed in the finest possible way.[13]

One can understand why Theiler thought Diogenes had in fact fulfilled what Socrates had been looking for in Anaxagoras in vain.

Such a reading of the fragment opens, of course, some further questions, such as why Plato does not mention Diogenes in the *Phaedo*, or for that matter elsewhere. Could it be the same silence as the one he kept about Democritus, to whom he is supposed to owe so much in the *Timaeus*?[14] And what about Socrates himself, to whom Aristophanes lends some distinctively Diogenian tenets in his *Clouds*?[15]

We need not indulge in authorial psychology, however, because there are good reasons to think that Diogenes did not in fact fulfill the lacuna Socrates complained about. To be sure, Diogenes' teleological program is a fairly encompassing one, even if the scope of the term "all," in the formula "the measure of all things," is limited by its being the complement of "measure." As the open list of examples suggests, Diogenes is thinking of a certain kind of phenomenon, namely periodical or cyclical, of which he gives the most obvious examples (whether the shape of earth, to take up Socrates' first example in the *Phaedo*, would qualify as an object of a Diogenian teleological explanation is not clear; the other astronomical explanations would probably qualify more, although Socrates does not present them as of typically cyclical phenomena). We have no reason to think, however, that Socrates or for that matter Plato, if they knew this passage (and we may assume they did), would have recognized that Diogenes went further than Anaxagoras in matter of teleology. Of course, *we* feel that there is an important difference between Anaxagoras's *implicit* promises (as read by the Platonic Socrates) to the effect that *Nous* acted so as to ensure that everything is organized in the most perfect manner and Diogenes' *explicit* pronouncement that a universal set of phenomena, disposed as it is in the most beautiful way, is the work of an intelligence. But Socrates (and Plato) may well not have been as sensitive to this difference as we are; their hermeneutics was not ours. They may well have insisted that both Anaxagoras and Diogenes did promise something that neither implemented. As a matter of fact, we may even read in Diogenes' fragment the intention of *not* implementing the program it sketches. For even if the optative *heuriskoi an* (translated above with the future "one will find," which is correct, although a conditional would also do) does not imply that Diogenes did *not* go on to show in the rest of his writing why such and such phenomenon or sequence of phenomena is structured in the best possible way, it of course does not exclude it either, and we in fact have every reason to doubt that Diogenes was actually interested in the kind of teleological explanations Socrates was supposedly looking for in Anaxagoras, not to mention the kind of teleological explanations Xenophon so generously lends him in his *Memorabilia*.[16] On the basis of B3, what we can say about Diogenes' teleology is that he made an argument of the "most beautiful" regulation of a number of cosmic phenomena in order to attribute intelligence to his principle—pretty much in the way the legislator in Plato's *Laws* wishes people to react to the spectacle of the celestial order, on the face of it, without further argumentation.[17]

Is Diogenes, then, no more than a naive teleological thinker—the perfect Platonic citizen? There are reasons to doubt this conclusion, too. First, it is by no means trivial to have defined the range of phenomena liable to a (virtual) teleological explanation by means of the word *metra* ("measures"). The proper object of teleological explanation is not "everything" but the regularities of things—a position that is interesting in itself, and has also an anti-Heraclitean side. The point is that nature respects measures and hence orders things not in virtue of some cosmic *justice* (Heraclitus's *Erinyes*, who prevent the sun from transgressing his "measures)"[18] but by reference to the working of some cosmic *intelligence*.

But a second, and in my opinion more decisive, point concerns the relationship between the various cosmological cycles on which the life of the universe depends and the encompassing cycle that consists of the world returning to the undifferentiated state from which it stems (that of the principle itself) and that amounts to the destruction of the universe.

A comparison with Anaxagoras is helpful here. For Anaxagoras, the world as it is at the present time is the result of the limited separation, operated by *Nous*, of an indefinite number of quasi-elemental entities that at the beginning were in a much higher state of mixture ("All things were together," 59B1). Mixture is still there, however. Anaxagoras goes so far as to say that even after separating, there is still now a bit of everything in everything, exactly as was the case at the beginning (B6). But the process of separation will go further, or so it seems, for according to B12, the cause of separation is revolution (*perichôrêsis*), and this revolution, which began in a limited place and then began to expand, is continuously expanding. Does not that mean that the world, as it is, is doomed to disappear? In fact, we do know through doxographical reports, that Anaxagoras's world (or worlds) is perishable (*phtharton*).[19] The absence of any other indications concerning the destruction of the world suggests that this is the process doxographers had in view.

Thus the world as it now is, for Anaxagoras, not the ultimate stage in the history of the world (as it is, for example, in Plato's *Timaeus*, where the demiurge warrants the factual indestructibility of an essentially perishable construct).[20] But if that is the case, one can legitimately wonder whether the world as such is *Nous*'s ultimate goal.[21] I have suggested elsewhere that this in fact might not be the case, and that what *Nous* in fact strives for is complete separation of the things that exist, a perfectly respectable project for an intellect, whose function is certainly to "discriminate."[22] The scheme according to which the world is only the trace left, so to speak, by the realization of another, encompassing project is not without parallel within early Greek philosophy. Indeed, it features as one of its favorite patterns. One prominent case would be that of Empedocles: Love makes the world, which is a marvel, but the destruction of this marvel is the price for the coming-to-be of total unification, which is what Love ultimately strives for (the structural parallel goes with a striking inversion, of course: unification is to Empedocles what separation is to Anaxagoras).[23]

Now it seems to me that, *mutatis mutandis*, the same line of argument applies to Diogenes. Of course, the differences between Diogenes and Anaxagoras are no less fundamental than those between Anaxagoras and Empedocles. There can be no separation in Diogenes, for in order for things to be separated, there must be a mixture, and a mixture is only possible if there is a plurality of things to be constituents of that mixture. This of course is not the case with Diogenes, whose single principle cannot be separated, but only differentiated and, as we saw in B3, *distributed* according to certain rules.[24] Accordingly, air cannot be discriminating, at least in Anaxagoras's "critical" sense. What can he be doing, then?

Diogenes' views about the future of the world, again, are relevant here. We know that for Diogenes, too, the world, or more accurately the worlds, are going to perish.[25] We can also fathom how this is to happen, thanks to a report of Theophrastus: Diogenes, like Anaximander, assumed that the ongoing heating of by the sun would ultimately lead to the earth's complete desiccation.[26] Should not this further lead, at least in Diogenes, to a state of fusion, in which air comes back to its original form, which may have been not air simply but "hot air"?[27] If that is so, the ultimate goal of Diogenes' intelligent principle would be not the world either but, rather, the sheer return to the initial state (a scheme Diogenes would have in common with Empedocles, against Anaxagoras, where complete dissociation represents the most extreme departure from the initial stage). This fits well with the pronouncement in B2 (= F4 Laks) according to which "all these things [that is, all that exist in the world, in particular plants and animals] that are modifications from the same thing, transform themselves differently at different moments, and return to the same thing."[28]

In fact, the scheme according to which things as they are will at some point return to the principle they come from is certainly older than both Diogenes and Empedocles. There are some reasons to think that it goes back to Anaximander, even if we grant that this is not what the famous fragment B1 is about.[29] And we have reasons to doubt it constitutes a distinctive mark of natural philosophy as such, as Aristotle suggests it is when he says (*Metaph.* 1.3, 983b8-11, using a formula that is so strikingly similar to the sentence just quoted from Diogenes B2 that I wonder whether the latter could not be its proximate source):[30]

that of which all things that are consist, and from which they first come to be, and into which they are finally resolved (the substance remaining, but changing in its modifications), this they say is the element and the principle of things.[31]

In any case, Diogenes' return of the principle to itself, which does fall under the Aristotelian scheme, is also the only one, in the history of early Greek philosophy, which is linked to a *noetic* activity. This is, in my opinion, a most important point. For it means that Diogenes' intelligence, because it belongs to air, comes back to itself in the same movement as air does, in a sort of reflective process that might be considered as anticipating—in a resolutely cosmological (and thus once more metaphorical) fashion—some later speculation about the nature of intellection, where it appears to be essentially linked with *circularity*: according to Plato, circular movement is the image of intellection, and for Aristotle, the intellect thinks itself.[32] If the interpretation of Anaxagoras that I have sketched here is correct, Diogenes' scheme is plausibly interpreted as a pointed reply to it: what intelligence aims at is not the separation of independently existing things (discriminating them) but the coming back to what it itself is, which amounts, in some sense, to thinking its own identity.

All this is, of course, speculative (which I take to be a virtue) and hence controversial. Less so, I submit, is the idea that between Anaxagoras's *Nous* and Diogenes' *Noesis* there is a significant difference we should not lose, because it is at the core of Diogenes' relationship to Anaxagoras, and hence of his own philosophical project. Anaxagoras's Intellect is a thing among others, even if is the finest thing of all, and enjoys the exceptional status of not being part of any mixture or, for that matter, a mixture of any kind—it is, on the contrary, the only thing constituting is entirely itself and pure: a wholly separated entity (B12) that, for this very reason, is also in a position to cause separation (by means of the cosmic revolution). Diogenes' monism does not allow for any kind of autonomy, neither the relative autonomy of being a thing nor, much less, that of being a separate thing. This, in my opinion, is the reason Diogenes chose to speak of *Noesis*, which, like other Greek substantives ending with the suffix -*sis*, is the name of an action and refers to an activity or a function (grasping, perceiving), not to a "substance" (namely the intellect).[33] In Diogenes' case, understanding is an activity of the principle itself, namely air.

Now if my initial argument about teleology is right, Diogenes did not bother himself with, or was not interested in, showing in what sense the world is organized in the best possible manner; this looked to him as something that happened as a matter of course. What did interest him, on the other hand, was to show what is that thing that exercised intelligence. From this point of view, the emphasis is definitely not on teleology, but rather on noetics. Here, primary textual evidence is available, for the fragments, as well as Simplicius's presentation of them, definitely support the view that the point of Diogenes' argumentation was to show that intelligence is *air's*.[34] This fundamentally monistic, anti-Anaxagorean noetics is interesting enough to make of Diogenes a philosophically most respectable figure, independently of the speculative outlook of his ultimate teleology, which I defended earlier here.

2

....

I now wish to briefly turn to my second point, which bears on the reason Diogenes' status in modern studies of early Greek philosophy is such a low one. This is to be found in a powerful tradition, stemming from the biased exploitation of ancient evidence. It is worthwhile coming back to the question, since this is the main obstacle, I think, to an unprejudiced reading of Diogenes—the one I have suggested here, or any other.

Two sets of negative comments about Diogenes as a philosopher come from antiquity, as follows.[35] (1) In the critical section of his treatise *On the Senses*, Theophrastus twice uses the word *euêthes* (naive) in order to qualify some of Diogenes' claims.[36] There is no doubt that the term is meant to be deprecatory. But two points should be stressed: first, it does not apply to Diogenes' thinking as a whole, but to a definite set of doctrines, and second, one of Empedocles' claims is also rejected as *euethes*.[37] The word hardly characterizes Diogenes' specific philosophical outlook.[38] (2) Interpreters might in fact have been less severe toward Diogenes had there not been another Theophrastean characterization of Diogenes that sounds much harsher than the *De Sensibus* passages, and looks more like a global condemnation of his philosophy (although, as we shall see in a moment, this is not entirely true either). Here is the decisive Theophrastean notice, reported by Simplicius, on which Diels based his judgment:

> Diogenes of Apollonia . . . wrote for the most part in a jumbled way, saying some things in accordance to Anaxagoras, others according to Leucippus; but as for the nature of the whole, he too says that it is unlimited and eternal air. . . . This is what Theophrastus relates about Diogenes.[39]

It is important to understand what this criticism exactly consists in. Diels and most interpreters after him have followed the line that Theophrastus was here characterizing Diogenes' philosophy as an *eclectic* one.[40] Now I need not engage here in the question of eclecticism, of its possible merits, taken as a philosophical attitude, or of its factual universality—for all our thoughts, including philosopher's thoughts, are made of borrowings, are they not? The point is, rather, that the term *eclecticism* does not capture adequately what Theophrastus is telling us about Diogenes. For Theophrastus accuses Diogenes not of eclecticism but of patching together incompatible lines of thought: incoherence, rather than borrowing, is the point at stake, and a most specific kind of incoherence at that.[41] One can be pretty certain, as a matter of fact, that Anaxagoras's name stands for Diogenes' noetico-teleological principle, whereas Leucippus stands for mechanical necessity.[42]

We are back where we started from, for if I am right, Theophrastus, with a language of his own (a doxographical language, as we may put it) is here repeating against Diogenes the criticism Plato leveled against Anaxagoras in the *Phaedo*, namely that he had not been true to his teleological principle. Of course, we must assume that Theophrastus's Anaxagoras is not quite that of the *Phaedo*, since, contrary to the latter, he represents here an accomplished and not a virtual kind of teleology. But then Anaxagoras's own image is a shifting one: Plato's eulogy of Anaxagoras's *Nous*, in *Phaedrus* 270a, contrasts with his treatment of Anaxagoras in the *Phaedo*, and the same is true of Aristotle's treatment of Anaxagoras in two successive chapters of his *Metaphysics*.[43] In Theophrastus's presentation, Anaxagoras is taken to be the "good" Anaxagoras, and Leucippus the "bad" one, opened to Plato's criticism in the *Phaedo*.

NOTES

1. Diels, "Über Leukipp und Demokrit." The latest treatment of Diogenes in the Derveni Papyrus, that of Betegh, *The Derveni Papyrus*, suggests that Diogenes' importance for the Derveni commentator was not that high, when compared to that of Anaxagoras or even more Heraclitus. Even so, the allegorical use of Diogenes' doctrine of air remains obvious. For Diogenes in Aristophanes, see note 15 here.

2. Diogenes does not appear either in Mansfeld, *Die Vorsokratiker*, or Dumont, *Les écoles présocratiques*. He is included in McKirahan, *Philosophy before Socrates*, and Waterfield, *The First Philosophers*.

3. It is significant, for example, that the few lines that Rapp, *Vorsokratiker*, devotes to Diogenes are part of a chapter (the last one) dealing with the "*reception* of Presocratic philosophy" (which implies that Diogenes is no real part of the latter): "Diogenes... berücksichtige in seinem eklektischen Zusammenschnitt der wichstigsten Strömungen bereits die jüngeren Naturphilosophen Anaxagoras und Leukipp" (240). Though putting forward an original (though unconvincing; see note 24 here) interpretation of Diogenes, Barnes is quite disparaging: an "essentially second-rate man" (*PP* 568). I tried to say something about the history of this reputation in *Diogène d'Apollonie*, xxix–xxxi (see also hereafter). McKirahan's moderate praise is double-edged: "though he made some important innovations, he took an essentially conservative approach, exploiting existing ideas and synthesizing them in new and more effective ways.... In the context of the second half of the fifth century, Diogenes' aim to return to the simplicity of the beginnings of the presocratic tradition is breathtaking in its ambition" (*Philosophy before Socrates*, 351.)

4. Robinson, review of *The Cambridge Companion to Early Greek Philosophy*, 175–76 (with Long's response, "Locating Diogenes of Apollonia" 476). Vander Waerdt, "Socrates in the Clouds," is one of the few commentators who thinks fairly highly of Diogenes (see esp. 62) on this ground, although his reasons for thinking so in part differ from mine (as will become apparent).

5. Graham, *Explaining the Cosmos*, chap. 10.

6. I come back to the problem in the revised edition of my *Diogène d'Apollonie*.

7. Theiler, *Zur Geschichte der teleologischen Naturbetrachtung bis auf Aristoteles*; Hüffmeier, "Teleologische Weltbetrachtung bei Diogenes von Apollonia?"

8. Kerferd, review of *Diogène d'Apollonie*.

9. See Dorion, *Xenophon*, 138–40 (note 231). Vander Waerdt, "Socrates in the Clouds," on the other hand, thinks that "the evidence suggests that Diogenes significantly influenced Socratic teleology" (62 n. 50). See also note 16 here.

10. We must suppose either that Socrates left the lecture before the end or that the reading was of an extract, a sort of publicity announcement.

11. *Phd.* 97d8–98e7.

12. *Phd.* 98c, 99a5, 99b6. In *Ti.* 46c7–d3, Plato will call them "concomitant causes," *sunaitia*. Note that Menn, *Plato on God as Nous*, 38–41, thinks that the Socratico-Platonic distinction between *aition* (cause) and *sunaition* (concomitant cause) goes back to Diogenes, whom both *Ti.* 46d4–e6 and the Hippocratic treatise *On Breaths* (esp. chap. 15) would be echoing.

13. Barnes, *Early Greek Philosophy*, 291. The verb *dedasthai*, which is used here, alludes to the Homeric *dasmos*, the division of the universe among Zeus, Poseidon, and Hades in *Il.* 15.189, reinterpreting it in a monistic way.

14. See D.L. 9.40 = Aristoxen. fr. 131 Wehrli. See Bollack, "Un silence de Platon," 242–43.

15. That Socrates in the *Clouds* holds Diogenian tenets had convincingly been argued by Diels (see note 1 here). Vander Waerdt, "Socrates in the Clouds," 61–66, further claims that Aristophanes' Socrates is Diogenian throughout (which implies that his position should not be confounded with those of the other, typical sophists in the Phrontisterion), and that Aristophanes' portrayal pretty much reflects that Socrates had once been in agreement with Pl. *Phd.* 96a6–10). Byl, "La parodie de Diogène d'Apollonie dans les *Nuées*," draws a list of parallels that does not add much; Ronsmans, "L'influence de la pensée de Diogène d'Apollonie," adds nothing, and the two last paragraphs of his article are taken word for word, and without indication of source, from my *Diogène d'Apollonie*, xx–xxi—a fact that obviously escaped the editors.

16. Vander Waerdt, *The Socratic Movement*, 63 n. 55, announces an article (to the best of my knowledge never published) arguing that:"Diogenes undertakes to demonstrate the workings of nature's intelligent design from the orderly succession of the seasons down to the internal working of the human body."

17. *Lg.* 10, 887c. On the sense in which Diogenes is and is not a teleologist, see now Betegh, *The Derveni Papyrus*, 313–18.

18. Heraclit. B94—a fragment whose relationship to B30, which also refers to *measures*, requires interpretation.

19. Stob. *Ecl.* 1.20 = Aët. 2.4.6 = 59A65.

20. *Ti.* 41b. See, however, Simp. *in Ph.* 154.29–31 = 59A64.

21. Although never explicitly stated, it is a natural assumption that rational action is goal-directed. I leave aside the hypothesis, for which I see no support in the available material, that the destruction of the world reveals some kind of limitation in *Nous*'s power (to which the Platonic demiurge would not be submitted).

22. This is the point of my article "Mind's Crisis," in which I developed the idea that Anaxagorean cosmological processes can be read as a metaphor for the critical activity of the intellect. See also my article "Les fonctions de l'intelligence," which is a retraction of the former one.

23. For further reflection on the Empedoclean cycle (or more exactly cycles), see my book *La vide et la haine*.

24. I cannot convince myself that *PP* 574–76 is right in suggesting that air is not the one principle that is common to all things, but some kind of indeterminate substrate, which anticipates Aristotle's prime matter (*hupokeimenon*). It is precisely the whole point of Simplicius's series of quotations, 151.20–153.22 of his commentary on Aristotle's *Physics* (reproduced in Laks, *Diogène d'Apollonie*, app. 1, sec. 4, 245–46) to say that *although* B4 suggests that Diogenes had in mind some Aristotelian substrate, what followed clearly showed that Diogenes' principle was air (see esp. 153.16–17: "in these passages he is manifestly saying that what men call air, is the principle"; see 25.7–8, which makes the same point, before introducing the divergent opinion of Nicolaus of Damascus: not air, but an intermediate between fire and air, i.e., hot air. See also Simplicius's summary of Diogenes' goal: "he undertakes to show through numerous arguments that in the principle he poses [i.e., air], there is an abundant intelligence" (151.28–30). It remains curious that Simplicius cannot come up with a more explicit statement about air being the principle. Skepticism toward Barnes's proposal is also expressed in KRS 439 n.1.

25. Diogenes is associated with Anaxagoras (as well as with Anaximander, Anaximenes, Archelaus, and Leucippus) in the testimony quoted in note 19 here (= T23d Laks, where an error on p. 183 in the translation of the lemma should be corrected: read "impérissable" for "périssable").

26. In Alex.Aphr. *in Mete.* 67.13 = A17 and T32 Laks.

27. This might be a further reason for Nicolaus to think of Diogenes' principle as being "hot air," besides the fact that the principle of *living* beings is warm air (see Laks, *Diogène d'Apollonie*, 9).

28. Admittedly, the coming back to the principle applies here to individual things, not to the cosmos as a whole. But I think we can confidently assume that the pattern is global, too. On cyclical cosmogony in Diogenes, see Simp. *in Ph.* 1121.12–15.

29. Kahn, *Anaximander and the Origins of Greek Cosmology*, 168, clearly shows that the fragment does not claim that things dissolve back into the Boundless, only into the elemental powers, but he also suggests that this might well have been the ultimate scheme (185).

30. Compare Xenoph. B27, Epich. 23B9.

31. The Revised Oxford Translation. Neither Parmenides' cosmology nor Anaxagoras's fit the scheme. A new study of how the world is destructed according to archaic cosmologies would be worthwhile.

32. Pl. *Lg.* 10, 897d–e. See Arist. *Metaph.* 12.7, 1072b19–20 and 9, 1074b34.

33. I see no reason to suspect, as Kerferd does in his review of my *Diogenes of Apollonia* (271), that *noesis* in Simplicius's text (the only one to quote all the relevant fragments) might simply reflect a standardized post-Aristotelian usage. In *Diogène d'Apollonie*, I suggested distinguishing the French "intellection" (for *noesis*) from "intellect" (*nous*). Betegh, *The Derveni Papyrus*, suggests the English pair "intelligence/intellect."

34. See Laks, *Diogène d'Apollonie*, 10.

35. The fact that both of them come from Theophrastus, who wrote a compendium of Diogenes' doctrines (D.L. 5.42) is interesting and is probably no coincidence, but I have not pursued the question and need not do so here.

36. Diogenes' idea, in explaining vision, that it is internal air that sees (sec. 47) and his idea that differences among men are due to the purity of what they inhale, rather than to their nature (sec. 48), are naive. The latter point is exploited in Aristophanes' *Clouds*, 225–34.

37. Sec. 21. Theophrastus may have liked the word. Diels's index indicates an occurrence of the substantive *euêtheia*, to qualify an agument, in the passage of Philo's *De*

aeternitate mundi, which is supposed to be an extract from Theophrastus (= *Phys. op.* fr. 12, 490.25).

38. Even if it did, we should be wary of drawing hasty conclusions about Diogenes' value. Aristotle may have been right to erase Hippo from the history of philosophy by describing his thought as "simple" (διὰ τὴν εὐτέλειαν αὐτοῦ τῆς διανοίας)—but we cannot check. Things are more complicated in the case of Melissus who also is the object of a dismissive remark of Aristotle (his argument is vulgar, *phortikos*; see *Ph.* 1.2, 185a10 and 1.3, 186a8). But although we can see the point of Aristotle's judgment, and may recognize that Melissus is definitely not Parmenides, we would not consider following him blindly, and certainly should not treat him as a negligible philosopher, as is often done in Diogenes' case.

39. Simp. *in Ph.* 25.1 = A5 = T4 Laks.

40. The quotation from Rapp, *Vorsokratiker*, is only one in an impressive series that begins in the *apparatus criticus* of *DG* 477. For reasons explained in Laks, *Diogène d'Apollonie*, 88–90, I do not follow those who (like Natorp, for example) refer to Theophrastus only the second half of the sentence (the point on the nature of the whole).

41. In the few occurrences of the word, or one of its forms derived from *sumphoreô*, in extant Greek literature, the meaning is always "jumbled together." See Pl. *Phdr.* 253e1; *Phlb.* 64e1; *Lg.* 693a4; Epicur. *Nat.* 14, col. 40 Leone, in a passage that is particularly relevant here, because it specifically bears on philosophical systems (which is not the case of the three Platonic texts) and in some sense defines the term *sumpephorêmenos in contrast with* the idea of "eclecticism": "jumbling is not the act of one who unites in the same doctrine an opinion which is dispersed among others which are foreign to it, but of one who puts together opinions which are not compatible between them, whether he draws them from himself, or from others." The important notion is that of incoherence. See Leone, "Epicuro, *Della Natura*, Libro XIV," 99.

42. In my *Diogène d'Apollonie*, xxxv n. 2, I insisted perhaps too much on the idea that Theophrastus linked Leucippus's name to Diogenes' pattern of air circulating through conduits, although I did associate this with mechanism (91). The usual interpretation is that what Diogenes took from Leucippus is the doctrine of infinite worlds (see 64A1, A6, and A10).

43. Compare *Metaph.* 1.3, 984b15–18, where Aristotle takes up the *Phaedo* picture, with *Metaph.* 1.4, 985a18–19, which presents Anaxagoras much more positively, even if a close reading of the passage reveals Aristotle's caution.

BIBLIOGRAPHY

Barnes, Jonathan. *Early Greek Philosophy*. London: Penguin, 1987.
Betegh, Gábor. *The Derveni Papyrus: Cosmology, Theology, and Interpretation*. Cambridge: Cambridge University Press, 2004.
Bollack, Jean. "Un silence de Platon." *Revue de Philologie* 41 (1967): 242–46.
Byl, Simon. "La parodie de Diogène d'Apollonie dans les *Nuées*." *Revue Belge de Philologie et d'Histoire* 72 (1994): 5–9.
Diels, Hermann. "Über Leukipp und Demokrit." 1881. In *Kleine Schriften zur Geschichte der antiken Philosophie*, edited by Walter Burkert, 185–98. Darmstadt: Wissenschaftliche Buchgesellschaft, 1969.

Dorion, Louis-André, ed. *Xenophon: Mémorables*. Collection des Universités de France, vol. 1. Paris: Belles-Lettres, 2000.

Dumont, Jean-Paul. *Les écoles présocratiques*. Paris: Gallimard, 1991.

Graham, Daniel W. *Explaining the Cosmos: The Ionian Tradition of Scientific Philosophy*. Princeton, N.J.: Princeton University Press, 2006.

Hüffmeier, Friedrich. "Teleologische Weltbetrachtung bei Diogenes von Apollonia?" *Philologus* 107 (1963): 131–38.

Kahn, Charles H. *Anaximander and the Origins of Greek Cosmology*. New York: Columbia University Press, 1960.

Kerferd, George B. Review of *Diogène d'Apollonie*, by André Laks. *Ancient Philosophy* 10 (1990): 269–71.

Laks, André. *Diogène d'Apollonie: La dernière cosmologie présocratique*. Lille: Presses Universitaires de Lille, 1983.

———. *Diogène d'Apollonie: Edition, traduction et commentaire des fragments et témoignages. Deuxième édition revue et augmentée*. Saint Augustine: Academia Verlag, 2008.

———. "Mind's Crisis. On Anaxagoras' ΝΟΥΣ." *The Southern Journal of Philosophy*, 31, Supplement (Proceedings of the 1992 Spindel Conference) (1993): 19–38.

———. "Les fonctions de l'intelligence: Derechef à propos du *nous* d'Anaxagore." *Methodos* 2 (2002): 7–31. (Reprinted in A. Laks, *Histoire, doxographie, vérité*, 193–217, Louvain-le-Neuve: Peeters, 2007.)

———. *Le vide et la haine: Eléments pour une histoire archaïque de la négativité*. Paris: Presses Universitaires de France, 2004.

Leone, G. "Epicuro, *Della natura*, Libro XIV." *Cronache Ercolanesi* 14 (1984): 17–107.

Long, Antony. "Locating Diogenes of Apollonia." *Ancient Philosophy* 21 (2001): 476.

Mansfeld, Jaap. *Die Vorsokratiker*. Stuttgart: Philip Reclam Junior, 1987.

McKirahan, Richard D., Jr. *Philosophy Before Socrates*. Indianapolis: Hackett, 1994.

Menn, Stephen. *Plato on God as Nous*. Journal of the History of Philosophy Monograph Series. Carbondale: Southern Illinois University Press, 1995.

Rapp, Christof. *Vorsokratiker*. Munich: C. H. Beck, 1997.

Robinson, Thomas M. Review of *The Cambridge Companion to Early Greek Philosophy*, edited by A. A. Long. *Ancient Philosophy* 21 (2001): 175–78.

Ronsmans, Francis. "L'influence de la pensée de Diogène d'Apollonie." In *Mythe et philosophie dans les Nuées d'Aristophane*, edited by S. Byl and L. Couloubaritsis, 194-215. Brussels: Ousia, 1994.

Theiler, Willy. *Zur Geschichte der teleologischen Naturbetrachtung bis auf Aristoteles*. 1925. 2nd ed. Berlin: de Gruyter, 1965.

Vander Waerdt, Paul A. "Socrates in the Clouds." In *The Socratic Movement*, edited by Paul A. Vander Waerdt, 48-86. Ithaca, N.Y.: Cornell University Press, 1994.

———, ed. *The Socratic Movement*. Ithaca, N.Y.: Cornell University Press, 1994.

Waterfield, Robin. *The First Philosophers*. Oxford: Oxford University Press, 2000.

CHAPTER 13

THE SOPHISTS

MICHAEL GAGARIN AND PAUL WOODRUFF

1. WHO WERE THE SOPHISTS?

The view fostered by Plato of the sophist as a charlatan carries little weight today, though it still underlies some treatments and it lingers in many popular views of the sophists and in the ordinary use of words like "sophistic." Most scholars no longer claim that the sophists formed a "school" in the sense of sharing a body of specific views, as Plato implies in his caricature in the *Sophist*. Instead, since the publication of Kerferd's deservedly influential book, it has become more common to think of the sophists as a movement—better, but perhaps still implying greater doctrinal coherence than in fact was the case.[1] For the authors of this chapter, the sophists were a group of (mostly) itinerant intellectuals from different parts of the Greek world who lived around the second half of the fifth century BCE and shared many interests. Far from being a unified group, they disagreed strongly on many issues and were more likely to compete than to collaborate with one another.

Although the term "sophist" is today generally restricted to a group of fifth-century thinkers, in antiquity the term was more broadly used of poets and other purveyors of wisdom, including Socrates, whom Plato sharply separates from the sophists, and of fourth-century orators and logographers such as Lysias and Demosthenes.[2] Isocrates usually applies the term specifically to litigants who frequent the courts on private business and to their logographers. Even outside Plato and his circle, the term was generally used in a pejorative sense in the fourth century. After that century, the followers of Plato adhered to his sharp distinction between philosophy and the work of the sophists, but other intellectuals, largely under the influence of Isocrates, came to associate the sophists not only with rhetoric and philosophy but also with involvement in public affairs.[3] Thus the term was later revived, and a group of public figures who taught and practiced rhetoric from the late first to the early third centuries CE came to be known as "the Second Sophistic" (a group outside the scope of this essay). A full history of the sophists would thus have to cover many centuries, but for this essay we will confine ourselves to the main figures from the second half of the fifth century: Protagoras, Gorgias, Prodicus, Hippias, Antiphon, Critias, Thrasymachus, and Callicles.[4]

In attempting to differentiate Socrates from the sophists, Plato identifies the latter as teachers who took pay. Before the sophists, there were no established teachers or educational institutions beyond the elementary level, where schoolmasters (*grammatistai*) taught reading, writing, and other subjects.[5] Young men attracted to intellectual pursuits would generally continue their education informally in the company of older friends, but no formal courses of study were offered.[6] Some of the sophists, at least—Protagoras, Gorgias, Prodicus, Hippias, and perhaps others—filled this gap by offering formal courses of study for a fee, but all sophists (and Socrates, too) were probably teachers in the broad sense of attracting young men to their company for the sake of intellectual inquiry and learning.

Plato's objections to the sophists' taking pay are, first, that they could not say exactly what they were selling or show its value; Plato himself believed that knowing the essence of a thing and being able to give an account of it were essential for a philosopher, and he criticizes almost all who came before him for failing to do this. Plato also argues that by accepting pay, the sophists were obligated to sell their knowledge to anyone who could pay for it, whereas he felt that the higher levels of education should be reserved for those with superior intelligence and training.[7] This suggests that the sophists were relatively egalitarian in their teaching, although we must remember that those who studied with them (like those who associated with Socrates) must have led a life of leisure. Another contrast is that the sophists were mostly non-Athenian and itinerant, whereas Socrates famously never left Athens except in his military service. Antiphon and Critias were also Athenian, but their writings indicate an interest in other Greek cities, and both probably traveled abroad often.

General descriptions of the sophists usually begin with a list of their main interests, which included natural philosophy, mathematics, social sciences (history, geography, anthropology), language and literature, morality and religion, and rhetoric and techniques of argument. We will examine some of these issues in the following sections, but a general feature, first noted by Grote, is that the sophists' interests (as opposed to Plato's) tended to be more practical than theoretical.[8] This point should not be overemphasized, however. Many sophistic works are far from practical (e.g., Gorgias's *On Not Being*), and although the sophists attracted young men from prominent families who would normally expect to follow a career in public life, their teaching was not narrowly vocational. Protagoras claims to offer a more practical course of instruction than other sophists, for he will teach Hippocrates "good judgment [*euboulia*] about domestic matters, so that he may best manage his own household, and about political affairs, so that in affairs of the polis he may be most able both in action and in speech" (Pl. *Prt.* 319a). But even students who sought purely practical training from the sophists did not necessarily receive this. In *Clouds*, for instance, Strepsiades wants to learn how to escape his creditors, and after studying with Socrates he does indeed use several specious arguments he has learned in order to send them packing. But such arguments obviously would not be effective in real life. Rather, most of what Strepsiades learns is strikingly impractical, as is much of the rest of the sophists' teaching.

In our view, the sophists are united more by common methods and attitudes than by common interests, and so instead of seeking to identify their interests, it will be more helpful to examine these. All sophists, for example, challenged traditional thinking, often in ways that went far beyond questioning the existence of the gods, or the truth of traditional myths, or customary moral rules, all of which had been questioned before. Gorgias, for example argued that nothing exists; Protagoras found fault with Homer's Greek; and Antiphon presented arguments for the innocence of someone who seems obviously guilty. It is not clear how seriously these and other such arguments were meant to be taken, but each is instructive in the sense that it served to advance people's understanding of important issues, such as the nature of reality, the nature of language, and the relationship between cause and responsibility.

In challenging traditional views, the sophists liked to use deliberately provocative, sometimes paradoxical arguments that seem aimed at capturing the audience's attention rather than enlightening them. Some of them may seem nitpicking, especially when parodied in comedy (as for instance in Strepsiades' learning to measure the length of a flea's jump). But after the initial impression, a more serious purpose usually becomes evident. Thus, beyond any set doctrines or specific theories, the sophists created a climate of intellectual ferment that affected all of Greek culture at the time, including history, drama, philosophy, and oratory. None of the developments in these areas in the late fifth and fourth centuries would have been possible without the sophists, and a full assessment of their influence would require study of Sophocles, Euripides, and Thucydides, in particular, as well as many others.

2. WERE THE SOPHISTS A POLITICAL FORCE?

Although our evidence for the lives of individual sophists is fairly slight, it is clear that most of them were interested in political matters and many also participated in public life in various ways.[9]

Protagoras, from Abdera (in Thrace), was born around 490 and may have died around 420. He apparently visited Athens several times, and one such visit provides the setting for Plato's *Protagoras*, which gives the fullest portrait we have of him. He seems to have become associated with Pericles (as one would expect), and he is reported to have written laws for the new pan-Hellenic colony at Thurii (in southern Italy), in whose foundation in 443 Pericles was probably involved.[10]

Gorgias of Leontini (in Sicily) was probably also born around 490 and by all accounts lived more than a hundred years, dying between 385 and 380. He traveled widely and, like other sophists, frequented international gatherings such as the Olympic festival. He also (like other sophists) represented his own city on public business, most notably in 427 as ambassador to Athens, where a speech he gave drew considerable notice (D.S. 12.53.1–5; see Pl. *Hp.Ma.* 282b).[11]

Hippias of Elis (in the Peloponnesus) and Prodicus of Ceos (an island in the Aegean) were both somewhat younger. Hippias was probably born around 470 and Prodicus a few years later; both lived into the fourth century. Plato (*Hp.Ma.* 281a–b, 282c) represents both as often conducting public business for their home cities, the former especially at Sparta, the latter at Athens.

Thrasymachus of Chalcedon (on the Bosporus) was probably a bit younger than these two, though we have almost no information about his life. But his major surviving fragment is from a speech to the Athenian assembly, which he may well have delivered as an official representative of this city, perhaps in 407.[12]

We know virtually nothing about the involvement (if any) of these figures in domestic politics, but (not surprisingly) we have more information in this regard about the two Athenian sophists, Antiphon and Critias. Antiphon was born around 480 and became an important force behind the scenes in Athenian political and legal affairs.[13] Among other things, he invented the practice of logography, or writing a speech for someone else to deliver in court. The many clients for whom he wrote speeches (and probably gave advice as well) included at least two foreign cities (Lindos and Samothrace), who were contesting the amount of tribute Athens had assigned them. In 411, at the age of about 70, he participated in (some would say masterminded) an oligarchic coup, and when the coup was quickly reversed, he was tried and put to death by the democracy.

Critias was probably born before 450; he came from an aristocratic family (Plato was his cousin). He, too, participated in the oligarchic coup in 411, but left the city after it and later returned. In 404, he was one of the notorious Thirty Tyrants who ruled Athens ruthlessly for a little less than a year. He was killed in the fighting against democratic forces that ended their rule. During his life he seems to have taken a great interest in Sparta, the city primarily responsible for the ascension of the Thirty.

During the second half of the fifth century, most Greek cities were politically divided between democratic and oligarchic forces. Antiphon and Critias clearly stood with the oligarchs, and Protagoras, because of his connection with Pericles and the democratic city of Thurii, is usually assumed to have supported democracy. We can only speculate about the political leanings of the others. It appears that Leontini was a democracy, at least in 427, when it sent Gorgias to Athens to appeal for help, and Ceos and Chalcedon were both tribute-paying allies of Athens, and therefore probably democracies, though the latter was taken over by oligarchs for several years.[14] Elis was an ally of its neighbor Sparta during the Peloponnesian War, but it seems nonetheless to have remained democratic during this period. In sum, all the sophists came from cities that were democratic during most of their lives, and all—except for the Athenians, Antiphon and Critias—represented these democratic cities on official business. To the extent that it is valid to infer political beliefs from these actions, then, it seems likely that the non-Athenian sophists had democratic political views.[15]

This conclusion is not inconsistent with what we know of the sophists' political writings, though our information in this regard leaves much to be desired. The only surviving sophistic text that clearly indicates a political view is Protagoras's Great Speech in *Protagoras* (320c–328d), which is aimed at defending the democratic practice of letting anyone speak in the assembly. This is consistent with Protagoras holding democratic views, but since the speech has been altered to an unknown extent by Plato, it is impossible to arrive at more specific conclusions about his views.[16] The short speech Hippias makes in the *Protagoras* (337c–338b) on the common nature of all mankind may, if it represents the sophist's real views, indicate an egalitarian political view. And the papyrus fragment from Antiphon's *Truth* (DK B44, GW 244–47) used to be restored as presenting an egalitarian view of class differences, and thus as being incompatible with the political activities of Antiphon. But a new find has invalidated this restoration (*POxy.* 3647), and all we can now say is that the criticisms of the Athenian legal system in this text may indicate oligarchic dissatisfaction with this democratic institution, though in what survives Antiphon does not explicitly draw this conclusion. Finally, in some of his poems Critias seems to express admiration for Sparta, which was a common aristocratic view at the time.[17] In sum, the meager remains of the sophists' political writings are not inconsistent with what we know of their political activities, though they provide almost no detailed information about their specific political views.

Considerably more evidence survives for the sophists' views on other topics related to politics, such as justice, rhetoric, or the origins of society (we will treat some of these below), and these might imply or suggest more specific political views. But it is risky to assume that any thinker at the time understood the implications of his ideas in exactly the same way as we might today. A critic of justice is not necessarily a supporter of oligarchy, and a promoter of rhetoric is not necessarily democratic. Thus, we are left with a mixed conclusion. All the major sophists were important public figures in their own cities and participated in the public affairs of their cities, often by officially representing those cities abroad. Such representation was consistent with their penchant for travel, in part as a way of spreading their ideas. They undoubtedly understood that participation in public life would help to make them better known, both at home and abroad, and that their status as public figures would attract more people to their lectures and other activities. But if the surviving texts are any guide (and their survival is to some extent a matter of chance), the sophists seem to have shied away from expressing specific political views, perhaps because they wished to preserve some degree of political neutrality as they traveled among cities with different forms of government. In addition, it seems that here and in other areas they were less interested in specific, political issues than in more general, abstract ideas and arguments.

3. DID THE SOPHISTS TEACH RHETORIC?

"One subject at least they all practiced and taught in common: rhetoric or the art of the *logos*."[18] This common view of the sophists may be misleading, in part because it begs the question of what we mean by "rhetoric" and "art" (*technê*). Cole, and Schiappa have recently denied that any of the sophists taught rhetoric, defined by Cole as "a speaker's or writer's self-conscious manipulation of his medium with a view to ensuring his message as favorable a reception as possible on the part of the particular audience being addressed."[19] The crucial points here are self-consciousness (which leads to the development of a discipline or art of rhetoric), the separation of the medium from the message with the primary focus being on the former, and the practical goal of persuading a specific audience.[20] If we accept Cole's definition, then it does seem likely that the idea of rhetoric as a *technê* was a later creation of Plato and was not part of the teachings of the sophists. If we take a broader view of rhetoric, however, as (say) inquiring into the nature of discourse or *logos*, then we may find that almost all the sophists took an interest in some aspects of this subject.[21]

The leading figure in this area is Gorgias, whose *Encomium to Helen* is particularly notable for its discussion of *logos* (sections 8–14), the earliest such discussion that survives.[22] In a wide-ranging treatment, Gorgias notes the persuasive power of *logos*, its emotional force, its magical and (as it were) pharmaceutical power, and its deceptiveness; he also argues that in view of the limitations of human knowledge, the use of *logos* is inevitable. Gorgias's treatment, however, is discursive and allusive rather than systematic and analytical, and it does not seem to apply to his own practice in writing demonstration speeches, especially *Helen*, which is a virtuoso display of verbal ingenuity with little if any persuasive force. Other remarks of Gorgias seem similarly inclined to provoke a response rather than to persuade, as for example his paradoxical observation that "tragedy produces a deception in which the one who deceives is more just than the one who does not, and the one who is deceived is wiser than the one who is not" (B23, GW 204.10). Gorgias undoubtedly stimulated much thought about many aspects of *logos*, and among his students was Isocrates, who has been a major influence on the study of rhetoric from later antiquity to the present.

Other sophists explored many other aspects of *logos*—from semantics and etymology to style and methods of argument to the relation of words to reality. These interests were undoubtedly stimulated in part by the fact that the sophists regularly performed their *logoi* in public and private settings, and that public speaking was a vital part of the lives of many Athenians and probably of many Greeks outside Athens, too. One broad idea among the sophists was that of speaking on both sides of a subject. This idea is specifically attributed to Protagoras, who said that "on every matter [*pragma*] there are two *logoi* opposed to one another" (B6a, GW 187.24).[23] Following Protagoras's lead, other sophists wrote pairs of opposed speeches,[24] and this practice also found its way into the works of dramatists (especially Euripides and Aristophanes) and historians (notably Thucydides).

The practice of speaking on both sides of an issue led inevitably to the development of arguments that at first sight might seem unlikely or even impossible. This practice was referred to as (in Protagoras's words) "making the weaker [*hêttôn*] *logos* stronger [*kreittôn*]" (B6b, GW 188.27 = Arist. *Rh.* 2.24). This practice was often condemned by others, as for instance, in Plato's *Apology* (19b), where Socrates complains that he has been falsely accused of making the weaker *logos* stronger. This reflects a popular view that "weaker" and "stronger" mean inferior and superior in a moral sense, though the surviving examples indicate that Protagoras and other sophists did not necessarily attach moral implications to "weaker" and "stronger." Nor did they necessarily wish to make the weaker *logos* prevail. In many cases, such as Gorgias's *Helen*, a sophist wants only to make the best case possible for the weaker *logos* (in this case, Helen's innocence), and it is unlikely that in the end he or any of his audience thought that this weaker *logos* had now prevailed. Indeed, in some paired speeches it is difficult to know which of the two *logoi* the author considers superior, even when a decision (or verdict) of sorts is indicated. The Weaker *Logos* wins the debate in the *Clouds*, but it is not clear whether Aristophanes (or his audience) considered his argument weaker or stronger. The point of such debates is not so much in who wins as in the arguments that are made. And in cases where no verdict is indicated, as in Antiphon's *Tetralogies*, a verdict seems unnecessary, for the exercise has other aims, including that of stimulating debate about which side in fact has the stronger *logos*.

In connection with *logos*, another broad focus of interest for the sophists was the term *orthos* ("straight, correct, right"). In its simplest sense, it designates "correct" usage, as for example in Prodicus's insistence on "the correctness of words" (*onomatôn orthotês*), which is parodied by his discourse on near synonyms in Plato's *Protagoras* (337a–c). Protagoras himself taught "correct speech" (*orthoepeia*), which seems to have covered topics as narrow as correct diction and syntax, and as broad as correct argument or the correct composition of prose or poetry.[25] A related attribute of *logos* that became important for the sophists was precision (*akribeia*), in particular the precise differentiation among terms or concepts. The pursuit of *akribeia* was sometimes seen as hairsplitting, and as such is parodied in *Clouds* (e.g., 740–42) and elsewhere. In recognition of this popular attitude, the defendant in Antiphon's Second Tetralogy, whose argument for the weaker *logos* will depend on a detailed and precise set of arguments that some may see as hairsplitting, begins by apologizing to the jurors for being "more precise" than they are accustomed to. But precision was an important goal of the sophists, and also of some who were influenced by them, such as the historian Thucydides (1.22).

Precision was associated particularly with written communication. Writing was a relatively limited practice in the middle of the fifth century, but it expanded rapidly in the following decades and had a substantial, though not well understood, impact on the work and thought of the sophists. Traditional oral performance continued to be an important part of their activity, and many works composed and circulated in writing were primarily communicated to others by being read aloud to small groups. But gradually a more complex written style developed that did not easily lend itself to oral communication. Antiphon's Tetralogies and Thucydides' *History* are notable examples. Alcidamas's fourth-century treatise *On Those Who Write Written Speeches or On the Sophists* (GW 276–83) criticizes written composition and the written style as unsuitable for oral performance. Rather, he says (13), someone who writes for oral delivery should "avoid precision [*akribeia*] and imitate instead the style of extemporaneous speakers." This tension between oral performance and written communication that originated in the sophistic period continued to influence fourth-century thinkers (notably Plato and Isocrates) in various ways.

A more difficult issue that was also part of the sophists' exploration of *logos* is their view of and attitude toward truth. Both Protagoras and Antiphon wrote works entitled *Truth*, though none of the preserved fragments explicitly discusses this subject. Plato attacks many different aspects of the sophists' views of truth, asserting that "Protagoras's *Truth* is true to nobody" (*Tht.* 171c), that rhetoric deals in falsehood (*Grg.* 458e–459c, etc.), and that his predecessors honored likelihood (*eikos*) more highly than truth (*Phdr.* 267a, 272d–273c). But the sophists consistently present truth as a positive value, while at the same time recognizing that it is often not directly accessible. They understand that truth is, in some sense, derived from the real world, but that to be known, it has to be constructed and conveyed by *logoi*, and there is inevitably a distance between these *logoi* and the truth they express. Gorgias maintained that if anything could be known, it could not be communicated to others, and one of Antiphon's speakers (the defendant in his Second Tetralogy) argues that different *logoi* may truthfully represent the same set of facts, in which case it is up to the jurors to decide between these (3.4.1–2). Antiphon's truth thus somehow involves both the facts (or reality) and the *logos* that expresses these facts. Ideas like these led thinkers at the time to expand their consideration of the traditional opposition between the facts (*erga* or *pragmata*) and the world of discourse (*logos*), a duality that assumes major importance in Thucydides' great account of the Peloponnesian War.

In arriving at whatever truth was attainable in practice, the sophists often relied on arguments from reasonableness (*eikos*), that is, the demonstration that a proposition is reasonable though not necessarily certain. Arguments from *eikos* had existed from the earliest times, but in the middle of the fifth century, two Syracusans, Tisias and Corax, explored new methods of arguing according to *eikos*, and Gorgias (in his *Palamedes*) and Antiphon (in his First Tetralogy) continued to explore further variations of this argument. But far from adopting the view ascribed to them by Plato, that probabilities should be more honored than truths (*Phdr.* 267a), the sophists seem always to have recognized that arguments from *eikos* are to be used only when the truth is otherwise unobtainable.

In sum, the sophists explored every possible facet of *logos*, from the most particular, such as the gender of a word, to the most general, such as the correctness and truth of an entire speech. Whether this amounts to the study of rhetoric, as has traditionally been thought, depends largely on what one means by this term. In terms of Cole's definition (mentioned above), sophists like Gorgias may be self-conscious in their reflections on *logos*, but as far as we can see, they do not distinguish between the medium and the message (as Plato does in the *Gorgias*), and they do not normally make persuasion the primary goal of their discourse (though this may often be an objective).

4. Did Sophists Defer to Convention?

Sophists were often interested in convention (*nomos*) and nature (*phusis*), between which some of them drew a sharp dichotomy. We shall ask in this and the following section how widely sophists observed that dichotomy, and with what results. Earlier poetry and philosophy associated *phusis* with unchanging truth, and *nomos* with appearance or with the fluctuations of opinion. On the whole, it is *nomos*—not *phusis*—that sophists treat with disdain.

Had the sophists restricted themselves to the narrow goal of persuasion (as Plato sometimes represented them) then we would expect the sophists to have preferred *nomos* to *phusis*, because appealing to the opinions of an audience would seem to be more persuasive than offering them an unpalatable truth. To use a Platonic example, we would expect a sophist to be like a baker of sweet pastries who appeals to your taste without attention to the truth about nutrition (*Grg.* 464d; see 517d–e). Could it be typical of sophists to prefer *nomos* to *phusis*? The answer must be a firm negative. Deference to convention would have made them relativists, since most thinkers of the period recognized that convention is relative to culture. But most sophists do not appear to have been relativists (see section 5 below).

Gorgias (if he is properly called a sophist) is the one who seems best to fit the pastry cook model, but he does not in general defer to convention The art of speaking may have been his main subject (A21), and he was known for introducing a number of devices that seem to be pleasant but neutral with respect to truth. Although he begins his famous *Encomium of Helen* with the remark that truth is the finest ornament a speech may have, he appears in this to be making a rhetorical ploy. And he includes in his *On Not Being* a striking argument to the effect that nothing, not even the truth, can be communicated. If so, then even persuasion is impossible, as this is normally understood, and the sophist would have to aim at pragmatic agreement.[26]

Even so, Gorgias was not concerned narrowly with securing people's agreement, regardless of subject matter. He showed interest in the study of poetry (A23) and in either metaphysics or the refutation of a metaphysical view (B3). Also, he was said also to have "trained the soul for contests in virtue" (A8b) and to have had some ideas about what virtue amounts to for different categories of people; here he may have been influenced by convention, although he does not appear to appeal to it (B19 = Pl. *Men.* 71e). In the *Helen* and *Palamedes*, he defends unconventional causes using arguments that are deployed according to a system. We will never know for sure how far Gorgias took the quest for truth, but we cannot accuse him, on the basis of the evidence we have, of disdaining it in favor of convention.

Along with Gorgias, many sophists made use of the concept of *eikos* in their arguments. Plato understands this word to mean a deceptive image of the truth, close to our "verisimilitude" (*Phdr.* 273d), but this is not how it was understood by the many speakers and writers who used it freely in the classical period. When the truth is not known, or cannot be known, some opinions about the truth are more reasonable than others, and in those cases the standard of judgment should be what is most reasonable.

"Reasonable" is the best translation for *eikos*, although "probable" is better established.[27] Plato represents sophists as slipping *eikos* into a speech as a substitute for truth (*Phdr.* 272d–e), but this is wrong. The concept of *eikos* is derivative of truth: it is what is reasonable to believe, and to believe something is to believe that this something is true. What many sophists actually did was to appeal to *eikos* as a substitute for knowledge when knowledge was not available. In any case, it should be clear that in using *eikos* the sophists are not deferring to *nomos*, but making a reasonable effort to find the truth.

Protagoras announced that his main teaching concerned *euboulia*, good judgment (Pl. *Prt.* 318d–319a). Probably this was related to the concept of the reasonable. Good judgment is the ability to make useful decisions in circumstances that do not permit deciding on the basis of knowledge, so *euboulia* must be independent of convention for the same reason *eikos* is. Good judgment must include the ability to construct good arguments as to what it is reasonable to expect (*eikos*) when knowledge is not available. An excellent test for what is reasonable is the technique of adversary debate. Protagoras was famous for teaching that, too—the ability to argue on both sides of a question (D.L. 9.51). Only by testing a proposal against the best counter-arguments that can be devised can we reasonably declare that one proposal is more reasonable than another. This method cannot lead to knowledge, of course, but it is a way of getting after the truth.

On the subject of language, Protagoras certainly did not defer to convention, although this would seem to have been easy enough for him to do. Most modern students of language use descriptive rather than prescriptive methods. But Protagoras is clearly a prescriptivist on issues of usage; he seems to have wanted to correct conventional usage in accord with the way things are. He was famous for objecting to the feminine gender of Achilles' wrath in the opening of the *Iliad* (GW 189.32; see GW 188.30). At the same time, Protagoras showed an interest in classifying speech acts (GW 189.33; see Gorgias B27).

Justice was an important topic for many sophists, and it fits well with the interest in forensic rhetoric that was common among them. On this topic, some of them were explicit in favor of nature over conventional justice.[28]

5. WERE SOPHISTS RELATIVISTS OR SKEPTICS?

Protagoras said, "A human being is measure of all things" (B1 = GW 186.15), meaning, apparently, that all human beliefs are true, at least to those who believe them. This looks like relativism.

Gorgias is reported to have said "[a] Anything you might mention[29] is nothing; [b] if it were something, it would be unknowable; and [c] if it were something and knowable, it could not be made evident to others" (B3 = GW 206.18). This looks like a form of skepticism.

In addition, many sophists did or said things that seemed to imply a disregard for the truth. Disregard for truth might spring from relativism or skepticism. In any case, these three—relativism, skepticism, and disregard for the truth—appear to be similar and, although different, are often confused.

We must be clear, to begin with, that relativism and skepticism are not compatible, and that neither is clearly stated by a sophist.

Skepticism after Aristotle is a method for abstaining from dogmatic belief altogether. Gorgias's triple statement is entirely dogmatic (albeit negatively so), unless it is intended as an irony. If it is a precursor of skepticism, it is so in a weak sense. The most we can say about sophists on this score is that Gorgias and those who followed him seem to have been more interested in verbal artistry than in knowledge of any kind (*Grg.* 459d), and this we may set down as a kind of disregard for truth.

Relativism with regard to truth is the doctrine that different things are true for different individuals or for different communities. Plato tells us that this is what Protagoras meant by the human-measure sentence quoted above (B1), but no surviving quotation from Protagoras unequivocally supports this interpretation, and some Protagorean material implies the contrary. We have seen that Protagoras did not systematically defer to convention, as he should have if he were a relativist with regard to communities. If he were a relativist with regard to individuals, it is hard to see what he thought he was teaching (a point Plato makes in the *Theaetetus*, for example at 170b). Most scholars have held that Protagoras was a relativist, but the case is not proved, and there are dissenting voices.[30]

Plato treats Protagoras as a relativist in his *Theaetetus*, where Socrates gives a relativistic interpretation of the man-measure fragment (B4). We do not know enough about the text from which the fragment comes to reject Socrates' reading of the sentence. Still, on the basis of the other evidence we have about Protagoras— his theories of language, his teaching of good judgment, his interest in contradictory arguments—we can say that on the whole Protagoras did not exhibit the sort of relativism that is refuted in *Theaetetus*. His approach to language is prescriptive, as we have seen, his concept of good judgment involves at most relativity to circumstance, and his interest in opposed speeches is not compatible with extreme relativism. The very notion of contradiction goes under (as Aristotle pointed out) on a strong relativisitic hypothesis (*Metaph.* 4.4). Still, it may be that Protagoras was a relativist on issues of justice.

In any case, we must not expect the sophists to have held a common theory on these points. Protagoras's human-measure sentence seems to imply that opposed positions are both true, while Gorgias's doctrine would imply that opposed positions are both false (B3a). If "opposed" means "contradictory," then one must be true and the other false, and on that reading both sophists would violate the law of noncontradiction, but from opposite directions.

Disregard for truth is not a technical notion. We must distinguish an ethical issue from a methodological one. The ethical issue must be further subdivided between deliberate deception and carelessness. Some sophists (according to Plato in the *Phaedrus*) set out to persuade people of blatant falsehoods. Plato's example is a speech designed to talk an assembly into taking a donkey in place of a horse; in order to succeed at such deception, speakers should have to know something about donkeys and horses (*Phdr.* 260b–d). Deliberate deception does not happen by accident or ignorance. Plato's *Gorgias*, on the other hand, considers rhetoric a knack for persuasion whose user simply does not bother to learn the truth about the matters under discussion (462c–466a).

The methodological issue is that on many subjects we must find ways of reasoning that do not depend on knowledge. This applies to deliberative debate on issues such as war, which depend on beliefs about the future that cannot be known to be true or false. It applies also to forensic debate when either the facts are not clearly known or the bearing of the laws is not clearly defined. The ancient Greeks thought that the facts are never clearly known unless a reliable eyewitness has come forward. Even when the facts are known, the bearing of the law may not be clear, as in a case treated in Antiphon's *Tetralogies*—the killing of a boy by accident in javelin practice. Either way, debate will turn not on what is known to be true, but rather on what seems most reasonable (*eikos*) or in accordance with the "most right speech" *(kata ton orthotaton logon*, Protagoras, GW 188.30). Speeches aimed at this sort of success do not aim at the truth, because no speakers in such a case are able to see the truth toward which they wish to aim. The speeches that aim at *eikos* are not therefore guilty of deception or carelessness.

Is there other evidence that sophists practiced deliberate deception or were careless toward the truth? Many sophists taught students how to speak on both sides of an issue, or, at least, to support positions that seem obviously false. Protagoras probably offered to teach the art of opposed speeches (*antikeimenoi logoi*, GW 250.24), and Antiphon published examples of such speeches in his *Tetralogies* (GW 219–44). The thesis of at least one out of every pair of opposed speeches would have to be false, if the two theses are logical contraries. Even if the speaker does not know which speech is false, when he speaks on both sides he ought to know that he will speak falsely at least some of the time. And to do so, some philosophers charged, would be a deliberate deception. This charge would be sound, of course, only if the speaker intended to persuade. But opposed speeches like Antiphon's *Tetralogies* are plainly not intended to persuade.

As for single speeches, Gorgias was famous for a speech composed in defense of Helen against a charge that his audience probably thought to be true. Such evidence led critics to the conclusion that sophists taught their students to engage in deliberate deception. Again, the charge would stick to Gorgias only if he wrote the *Helen* to persuade.

In any case, the charge is based on an error in logic. When opposed speeches concern what is reasonable to believe, both of them may turn out to be reasonable to the same degree, even if they are logically contradictory. That is, the truth of A may imply the falseness of B, and vice versa, but the available evidence may support A as strongly as it supports B, and in that case A and B would be equally reasonable. It does not follow, if A is reasonable, that B is unreasonable. So, in fact, the sophist who argues both sides of such a case is innocent of the charge. From the available evidence, he cannot know that either speech is unreasonable. And therefore he cannot set out to deceive his audience by making them accept as reasonable a position that is not. In the case of a single speech such as the *Helen* of Gorgias, the writer is challenging a common or conventional opinion, as sophists often did, rather than undermining a known truth; and he is doing so in a way that illuminates issues of causation and responsibility.

The sophists taught the art of opposed speeches for two reasons. First, Greeks of this period simply enjoyed adversary debate; it was an entertainment in itself on public occasions and a feature of many plays, both comic and tragic. Entertainment, in itself, does not aim to deceive.[31] Second, ancient Greek cities, whether or not they were democratic, used adversary debate in politics and in the courtroom. Adversary debate is a practical way of bringing arguments on both sides under consideration, and can serve as a defense against bad judgment. Nevertheless, the critics are right to charge that speakers in debates may aim more at winning than on telling the truth. But if adversary debate secures the best result that is humanly possible, then both speakers, however weak the arguments available to them, are working toward the best result for all, when each tries to win.

6. WERE SOPHISTS A THREAT TO RELIGION?

Before the age of the sophists, thinkers had questioned conventional beliefs about the gods. In a polytheistic system like that of the ancient Greeks, stories about gods vary widely from location to location, and even citizens of the same city can disagree about what the gods require of human beings. In Sophocles' *Antigone*, for example, we see that Creon's loyalty to Zeus clashes with Antigone's devotion to gods of the underworld. If there was a consensus of conventional beliefs, it did not extend far beyond the claims that there are gods and that they had better be treated with respect.[32] These claims were probably beyond question in the age of the sophists.

Specific points about the gods, however, had been fair game for some time. On this subject, we will have to depend on writers who were not sophists but who evidently represented the teachings of certain sophists. The philosopher-poet Xenophanes attacked anthropomorphism before the rise of the sophists (B15 = GW 38.2), and even Homer and some of the tragic poets raised questions about the veracity of prophets (e.g., E. *Hel.* 744–57 = GW 66.11; *IT* 570–75 = GW 66.9).

Moral criticism of the gods as represented in myth is voiced in the plays of Euripides (esp. *Ion* 436–51), who wrote under the influence of sophists. Raging over tales about gods raping women, a young servant of Apollo addresses his god in these terms: "How could it be just for you to write the laws for us mortals, and then incur a charge of lawlessness yourselves? . . . It will no longer be just to call men bad if we are only following the 'good' examples set by gods."

The sharpest point against the gods comes in a fragment of a play known as the *Sisyphus*, which some scholars attribute to the oligarch Critias but most now consider to be the work of Euripides (GW 260.5).[33] The speaker in this fragment explains theism as a human invention, designed by some clever person who wanted to frighten people into obeying the laws. The speaker may be an atheist, for he says the story is false (l. 26), but the story would be false if any part of it were false, and the context seems to point the finger at the claim that the god is watching and will punish wrongdoers—a claim easily challenged on the basis of experience. The fragment belongs with other passages in which Euripides' speakers deny the moral attributes of the gods (such as the *Ion* passage cited above). This of course brings into focus the freedom of the gods, according to myth, from conventional moral constraints.

It does more. It explains the origin of religion in human terms. Both before and during the time of the sophists, Greek thinkers were working out explanations for events without reference to the gods. Early Presocratic philosophers had an interest in explaining the origins of the cosmos; some also took on that traditional domain of the gods—the weather. This movement is satirized in Aristophanes' *Clouds*, which depicts Socrates supplanting Zeus with the whorl as an explanation for meteorological events. (In this play, the character Socrates stands as the archetypal intellectual, and probably bears little resemblance to the historical philosopher.) Around this time, too, early anthropologists (possibly led by Democritus) were explaining the development of human culture in such a way that it can no longer be seen simply as a gift of the gods.[34] And medical thinkers challenged traditional explanations of disease. Thucydides noted that the plague in Athens was not ameliorated by religious observances, and treats with scorn the claim that the plague was predicted by an oracle. In his history, moreover, Thucydides explores the human causes of war and peace, victory and defeat, leaving the gods almost entirely out of the picture.

All such theories displace the gods from their traditional place in explanation. And displacement of that sort must have been disturbing to nonintellectuals—just as evolutionary theory is disturbing to many Christians today. Evidence for this comes from Aristophanes' *Clouds*, which seems to have whipped up anger against intellectuals on this score.

Religion in ancient Greece is not separable from political and ethical tradition. In addition to bringing out the displacement of the gods by the new science, *The Clouds* lambastes intellectuals for undermining morality—particularly for undermining the respect in which young people should hold their elders. It does so while also airing criticism of traditional morality, but the burning of the school, with which the play ends, no doubt catered to fear and loathing ordinary people felt in reaction to the new learning.

Generally, then, intellectual movements in the time of the sophists were seen to threaten traditional religion. Most of the guilty scientists and social theorists were not sophists, but a few particular sophists came in for criticism on religious grounds. Prodicus found his way to ancient lists of atheists, but the evidence for his atheism is weak. We are told that Protagoras was exiled from Athens for his views on religion, but the tradition appears to be false, because we are told on better authority that Protagoras's reputation shone brightly to the end of his days (Pl. *R.* 600c–d). Of his views on the gods we know only that he professed a kind of agnosticism, on the grounds that the subject is obscure and human life is short—by which he probably meant that the gods are not known by human observation. If human observation is the standard for what exists and does not exist (as the man-measure fragment suggests) then a shortfall in observation of the gods leaves us with no basis for or against the claim that gods exist.

Traditional religious views and practices were under fire in the time of the sophists, but the there was no concerted antireligious movement, and the sophists were not leaders in such criticism as there was.

NOTES

Initial drafts of sections 1–3 were written by Gagarin, 4–6 by Woodruff. The entire text was read and discussed by both of us. In the designation of sophistic works, GW refers to

Gagarin and Woodruff, *Early Greek Political Thought from Homer to the Sophists*; the page number is sometimes followed by the number of the quotation on that page.

1. Kerferd, *The Sophistic Movement*, is now the standard treatment, along with Guthrie, *The Sophists*.

2. Kerferd, "The First Greek Sophists"; Guthrie, *The Sophists*, 27–54.

3. As Philostratus says at the beginning of his *Lives of the Sophists* (480), "we must consider the old sophistic art [*tên archaian sophistikên*] to be a philosophical rhetoric [*rhêtorikên philosophousan*]."

4. Socrates could legitimately be included in this list, since he shared many of their interests and their methods. But there are practical reasons for leaving him out, including the complexity of the "Socratic Question" and the awkwardness of including him in a collection of essays on the "Presocratics."

5. Beck, *Greek Education 450–350 B.C.*

6. See Meno's claim that "any Athenian gentleman he happens to meet" can teach a young man virtue (*aretê*) better than the sophists (*Men.* 92e; the entire conversation 89e–94e is revealing on the matter of postelementary teaching).

7. The sophists display their wisdom to "all sorts of people" (*en pantodapois anthrôpois*; *Hp.Ma.* 282d). Xenophon uses the analogy of a prostitute who sells himself to all comers (*Mem.* 1.6.13). See Kerferd, *The Sophistic Movement*, 25–26.

8. Grote, 8:158.

9. The most convenient summary of the evidence is Guthrie, *The Sophists*, 262–304.

10. Stadter, "Pericles among the Intellectuals," 114, disputes the involvement of both Protagoras and Pericles in the foundation of Thurii. But the information about the former comes from Heraclides Ponticus (fourth century BCE), who almost certainly had reliable sources (Diodorus's story that the seventh-century lawgiver Charondas wrote laws for Thurii cannot be correct); and since Athenian involvement in the foundation is almost certain, it is hard to imagine that Pericles himself was not involved.

11. For further references to the diplomatic activity of Gorgias and others see White, "Thrasymachus the Diplomat," 314.

12. White, "Thrasymachus the Diplomat," 315–16.

13. We are assuming (as are a growing number of scholars) that the traditional separation of "Antiphon the Sophist" from Antiphon of Rhamnous is wrong and that these were in fact one and the same figure; see Gagarin, *Antiphon the Athenian*, 38–52, and Woodruff, "Antiphons, Sophist and Athenian."

14. Athens regained control of Chalcedon and restored democracy there in 408; if White is correct about the date of Thrasymachus's fragment (see above, n. 12), the sophist was representing this restored democracy.

15. Explicit Athenian defenses of democracy are found scattered through Athenian drama.

16. For an interesting discussion see Farrar, *The Origins of Democratic Thinking*.

17. If a speech attributed to Herodes Atticus was really composed by Critias (see GW xlii), then we have even better evidence of his explicit admiration of Sparta.

18. Guthrie, *The Sophists*, 44.

19. Cole, *The Origins of Rhetoric in Ancient Greece* (the quote is from p. ix); Schiappa, "Did Plato Coin Rhetorike?"

20. Cole does not define "favorable reception," but traditionally this would mean that the audience was persuaded. On persuasion see Gagarin, "Did the Sophists Aim to Persuade?"

21. Only for Critias do we lack specific evidence for an interest in *logos*.

22. Segal, "Gorgias and the Psychology of Logos," is still fundamental. More recent studies include Romilly, "La loi dans la pensée grecque"; Poulakos, *Sophistical Rhetoric in Classical Greece*; Schiappa, *The Beginnings of Rhetoric in Ancient Greece*, esp. 114–32.

23. See Cicero's report (*Brutus* 12.47 = DK 82A25) that Gorgias thought an orator should have the special ability "to amplify a subject with praise and to diminish it with criticism."

24. Antiphon's *Tetralogies* (GW 219–44); Prodicus's "Choice of Heracles" (GW 211–14); *Dissoi Logoi* (GW 296–308).

25. The example of incorrect poetic composition given in *Protagoras* is the error of internal contradiction in a poem of Simonides.

26. Fragment B3, GW 208–9.18c, on which see Mourelatos, "Gorgias on the Function of Language."

27. "Probability" in contemporary usage is mainly reserved for quantifiable probabilities supported by empirical science, and this concept was unknown to the ancient Greeks.

28. Callicles, in Pl. *Grg.* 483b, and perhaps Antiphon B44 = GW 244.7.

29. In Gorgias B3 we have supplied this subject as being the most likely way to complete the open sentence ". . . is" that opens the passage.

30. Bett, "The Sophists and Relativism"; Woodruff, "Rhetoric and Relativism."

31. Gorgias is famous for saying, however, that tragic theater produces a deception in which deceiving is more just than failing to deceive (B23 = GW 204.10).

32. Yunis, *A New Creed*.

33. See Kahn, "Greek Religion and Philosophy in the *Sisyphus* Fragment."

34. Guthrie, *The Sophists*, 79–84. On the origins and character of early Greek anthropology, see Cole, *Democritus and the Sources of Greek Anthropology*.

BIBLIOGRAPHY

Beck, Frederick A. G. *Greek Education 450–350 B.C.* New York: Barnes & Noble, 1964.

Bett, Richard. "The Sophists and Relativism." *Phronesis* 34 (1989): 139–69.

Cole, Thomas. *Democritus and the Sources of Greek Anthroplogy*. Chapel Hill, N.C.: Press of Western Reserve University, 1967. Reprint, Atlanta: Scholars Press, 1990.

———. *The Origins of Rhetoric in Ancient Greece*. Baltimore: Johns Hopkins University Press, 1991.

de Romilly, Jacqueline. *La loi dans la pensée grecque: Des origins à Aristote*. Paris: Les Belles Lettres, 1971.

Farrar, Cynthia. *The Origins of Democratic Thinking: The Invention of Politics in Classical Athens*. Cambridge: Cambridge University Press, 1988.

Gagarin, Michael. *Antiphon the Athenian: Oratory, Law, and Justice in the Age of the Sophists*. Austin: University of Texas Press, 2002.

———. "Did the Sophists Aim to Persuade?" *Rhetorica* 19 (2001): 275–91.

Gagarin, Michael, and Paul Woodruff, eds. *Early Greek Political Thought from Homer to the Sophists*. Cambridge: Cambridge University Press, 1995.

Grote, George. *A History of Greece*. London, 1869.

Guthrie, W. K. C. *The Sophists*. Cambridge: Cambridge University Press, 1971.

Kahn, Charles H. "Greek Religion and Philosophy in the *Sisyphus* Fragment." *Phronesis* 42(1997): 247–62.

Kerferd, George B. "The First Greek Sophists." *Classical Review* 64 (1950): 8–10.

———. *The Sophistic Movement*. Cambridge: Cambridge University Press, 1981.

Mourelatos, Alexander P. D. "Gorgias on the Function of Language." *Philosophical Topics* 15 (1987): 135–70.

Poulakos, John. *Sophistical Rhetoric in Classical Greece*. Columbia: University of South Carolina Press, 1995.

Schiappa, Edward. *The Beginnings of Rhetoric in Ancient Greece*. New Haven, Conn.: Yale University Press, 1999.

———. "Did Plato Coin *Rhetorikê*?" *American Journal of Philology* 111 (1990): 457–70.

Segal, Charles P. "Gorgias and the Psychology of Logos." *Harvard Studies in Classical Philology* 66 (1962): 99–155.

Stadter, Philip A. "Pericles among the Intellectuals." *Illinois Classical Studies* 16 (1991): 111–24.

White, Stephen A. "Thrasymachus the Diplomat." *Classical Philology* 90 (1995): 307–27.

Woodruff, Paul. "Antiphons, Sophist and Athenian: A Discussion of Michael Gagarin, *Antiphon the Athenian*, and Gerard J. Pendrick, *Antiphon the Sophist*." *Oxford Studies in Ancient Philosophy* 26 (2004): 323–36.

———. "Rhetoric and Relativism: Protagoras and Gorgias." In *The Cambridge Companion to Early Greek Philosophy*, edited by A. A. Long, 290–310. Cambridge: Cambridge University Press, 1999.

Yunis, Harvey. *A New Creed: Fundamental Religious Beliefs in the Athenian Polis and Euripidean Drama*. Göttingen: Vandenhoeck & Ruprecht, 1988.

PART III

TOPICS

CHAPTER 14

THE ROLE OF MEDICINE IN THE FORMATION OF EARLY GREEK THOUGHT

PHILIP VAN DER EIJK

INTRODUCTION: "MEDICINE" AND "PHILOSOPHY"

A chapter on Greek medicine in a handbook of Presocratic philosophy needs perhaps less justification today than would have been the case 20 or 30 years ago. The philosophical aspects of Greek medicine are now more widely appreciated, not only by historians of science and medicine but also by students of philosophy in a more narrow sense. There has also been a greater appreciation of the fact that Greek medical writers not only reflect a derivative awareness of developments in philosophy—something that led to the longstanding qualification of philosophy as the "mother" of medicine—but also actively contributed to the formation of philosophical thought more strictly defined, for instance by developing concepts and methodologies for the acquisition of knowledge and understanding. Yet the consequences of this for a renewed study of the formation of Greek philosophy have yet to be drawn; and disciplinary boundaries between historians of medicine (and science) on the one hand and philosophers and historians of philosophy on the other still pose obstacles to an integrated account of Greek thought that takes on board the contributions by the medical writers. Some preliminary remarks may therefore be in order.

1. MEDICAL INTERESTS OF "PHILOSOPHERS"

First of all, "philosophy" and "medicine" are headings that, although not entirely inappropriate to the early Greek period, may easily conceal the very substantial overlap that existed between the various areas of activity. Making too rigid a use of these concepts presents a serious danger of misrepresenting the views the main protagonists in early Greek thought themselves had about the disciplines or intellectual contexts in which they positioned themselves. Moreover, it would be quite misleading to present the relationship between doctors and philosophers solely in terms of interaction between science and philosophy, the empirical and the theoretical, the practical and the systematical, or observation and speculation; for this would ignore the philosophical, speculative, theoretical, or systematizing aspects of Greek medicine and science, as well as the extent to which empirical research and observation was part of the activities of people whom we have come to regard as philosophers. Thus Empedocles, Democritus, Parmenides, Pythagoras, Alcmaeon, Philolaus, Diogenes of Apollonia, Plato, Aristotle, and Theophrastus took an active interest in subjects we commonly associate with medicine, such as the anatomy and the physiology of the human body, embryology and reproduction, youth and old age, respiration, the causes of disease and of the effects of food, drink, and drugs on the body. Indeed, according to one major, authoritative ancient source, the Roman author Celsus (first century CE), it was under the umbrella of philosophy (*studium sapientiae*) that a theoretical, scientific interest in health and disease first started, and it was only when the physician Hippocrates "separated" the art of healing from this theoretical study of nature that medicine was turned into a domain of its own for the first time—yet without fully abandoning the link with "the study of the nature of things," as Celsus himself recognizes when reflecting on developments in dietetics during the fourth century BCE (*On Medicine*, proem, secs. 8–11).

This perception of the early development of medicine and its overlap with philosophy was more widely shared in antiquity, both by medical writers and by philosophers. Thus authors such as Galen and the so-called Anonymus Londiniensis (the author in the first century CE of a medico-doxographical work preserved on papyrus) treated Plato's views on the human body and on the origins of diseases as expounded in the *Timaeus* (as well as the views of the Pythagorean philosophers Philolaus and Hippo) on a par with the doctrines of major Greek medical writers, and Aristotle and Theophrastus continued to be regarded as authorities in medicine by medical writers of later antiquity such as Oribasius and Caelius Aurelianus. Conversely, philosophers such as Aristotle commented favorably on the contributions by "the more distinguished doctors" to the area of natural philosophy; and in the later doxographical tradition of Aëtius, in the context of physics or natural philosophy, a number of medical writers such as Diocles, Herophilus, Erasistratus, and Asclepiades are cited alongside philosophers such as Plato, Aristotle, and the Stoics for their views on such topics as change, the soul, the ruling part, dreams, respiration, monstrosities, fertility and sterility, twins and triplets, the status of the embryo, mules, seventh-month children, embryonic development, and the causes of old age, disease, and fever.

It would be quite wrong to regard this perception as just a later, anachronistic distortion or to believe that these medical interests of philosophers were nothing more than eccentric curiosity. To the Greek thinkers, these areas represented aspects of natural and human reality just as interesting and significant as the movements of the celestial bodies or the origins of earthquakes, and at least equally revealing of the underlying universal principles of stability and change. And it would be equally wrong to retroject the Aristotelian distinction between theoretical and practical sciences to the earlier period and to imply that while doctors were primarily concerned with practical application, philosophers' interests in the medical area were limited to theoretical study or the pursuit of knowledge for its own sake without extending to clinical or therapeutic practice. Some are known to have put their ideas into practice, for example, Empedocles, who seems to have been engaged in considerable therapeutic activity, or Democritus, who seems to have carried out anatomical experiments on a significant scale.

Such connections between theory and practical application are, of course, in accordance with the fact that in the early Greek period philosophy itself was hardly ever pursued entirely for its own sake and was deemed of considerable practical relevance, be it in the field of ethics and politics, in the technical mastery of natural things and processes, or in the provision of health and healing. We may rightly feel hesitant to call people such as Empedocles, Democritus, Pythagoras, and Alcmaeon doctors, but this is largely because that term conjures up associations with types of professional organization and indeed specialization that only developed later, but are inappropriate to the actual practice of the care for the human body in the archaic and early classical period. The evidence for specialization in this period is scanty, for doctors as well as mathematicians and other scientists, and there is good reason to believe that disciplinary boundaries, if they existed at all, were fluid and flexible.

2. PHILOSOPHICAL INTERESTS OF MEDICAL WRITERS

Conversely, it is no exaggeration to say that what a number of Greek people whom we regard as medical thinkers were up to is very similar to, or at least coterminous with, the activities and pursuits of philosophers. The fact that these writers and their works have, in the later tradition, been associated with Hippocrates and placed under the rubric of medicine tends to make us forget that they may have had rather different conceptions of the disciplines or contexts in which they were working. Thus the authors of such Hippocratic works as *On the Nature of Man, On Fleshes, On the Nature of the Child, On Places in Man,* and *On Regimen,* as well as the Pythagorean writer Alcmaeon of Croton,[1] emphatically put their investigations of the human body in a physicist and cosmological framework. Some of them may have had very few clinical or therapeutic interests; for others, the study of the human body and its reactions to disease and treatment was just one of several areas of research. Thus it has repeatedly been claimed (though this view has been disputed) that the Hippocratic works *On the Art* and *On Breaths* were not written by doctors or medical people at all, but by sophists writing on *technai* ("disciplines," fields of systematic study with practical application) for whom medicine was just one of several intellectual pursuits. Be that as it may, the authors of *On Regimen* and *On Fleshes,* for instance, certainly display interests and methods that correspond very neatly to the agendas of people such as Anaxagoras and Heraclitus, and the difference is of degree rather than kind.

A further relevant point here is that what counted as medicine in the fifth and fourth centuries BCE was still a relatively fluid field, for which rival definitions were continuously being offered. And medicine (*iatrikê*), just as philosophy, was not a monolithic entity. There was very considerable diversity among Greek medical people, not only between the "rational," philosophically inspired physicians we find in the Hippocratic writings on the one hand and practitioners of what is sometimes called "folk medicine" (drugsellers, rootcutters, etc.) on the other but even among more intellectual, elite physicians themselves. Indeed, one of the crucial points they were divided on was precisely the philosophical nature of medicine—the question to what extent medicine should be built on the foundation of a comprehensive theory of nature, the world, and the universe. It is interesting in this connection that one of the first attestations of the word *philosophia* in Greek literature occurs in a medical context—the Hippocratic work *On Ancient Medicine*—where it is suggested that this is not an area with which medicine should engage itself too much. It is clear from the context that what the author has in mind are approaches to medicine that take as their point of departure a general theory about nature (*phusis*), and in particular theories that reduce all physical phenomena to unproven postulates (*hupotheseis*), such as the elementary qualities hot, cold, dry, and wet— theories that the author associates with the practice of Empedocles, who reduced natural phenomena to the interaction and combinations of the four elements earth, fire, water, and air. The polemical tone of the treatise suggests that such philo-sophical approaches to medicine were becoming rather popular, and this is borne out by the extant evidence such as that provided by the Hippocratic treatises mentioned earlier. There were a number of medical authors of whose project what we call philosophy was an essential part—regardless of whether they knew and used the term—and obviously such authors will appear more relevant to this volume than their more practical-minded colleagues.

3. DIVERSITY IN MEDICINE AND IN THE HIPPOCRATIC WRITINGS

The diversity noted here is to be found even among the writings attributed to Hippocrates and assembled, at some time long after they were written, under the heading of the "Hippocratic Corpus." As has been recognized ever since antiquity, these Hippocratic writings are not the work of one author; rather, they constitute a heterogeneous group of over 60 treatises, which display great differences in con-tents and style. None of these writings mentions the name of its author, and none provides secure internal evidence as to date and geographical or intellectual provenance. Whether any of these works was written by the historical Hippocrates himself and if so, which, has been the object of centuries of scholarly debate, but none of the proposed candidates have found widespread acceptance, and the question (usually referred to as "the Hippocratic question") has proved unan-swerable. More recently, even the assumption that these works, regardless of the question of their authorship, all derive directly or indirectly from a Hippocratic medical "school" or "community" on the island of Cos has been exposed as the product of wishful thinking by scholars (and of anachronistic extrapolation of early twentieth-century models of medical institutional organization). The upshot of all this is that there is no secure basis for regarding and studying the Hippocratic writings as a "collection" and individual writings as part of such a collection, even though this has been the norm for many centuries. There is no intrinsic tie that connects these writings more closely with each other than with the works of other authors, both medical and philosophical, of the same period that did not have the good fortune of being preserved. It is true that some Hippocratic writings clearly refer or react to each other, or display such great similarities in doctrine and style that it is likely that they derive from a common background (and in some cases even from a common author). Yet similarly close connections can be perceived between some of these works and the fragments of some Presocratic philosophers (e.g., between the author of the Hippocratic *On Regimen* and philosophers such as Anaxagoras and Heraclitus), or indeed of non-Hippocratic medical writers such as

Philistion of Locri and Alcmaeon of Croton. To suggest otherwise—a suggestion still implicitly present in most talk of Hippocratic medicine, Hippocratic thought, and so on—is to run the risk of making seriously misleading use of traditional labels. In fact, one has to say that it is very unlikely that all these treatises were conceived and written with a view to the collection the later tradition grouped them in (and there are good reasons to believe that the constitution of a Hippocratic "Corpus" happened several centuries after they were written). The only thing the Hippocratic writings have in common is that they are written in the Ionic dialect and that they were, at some stage of their tradition, attributed to, or associated with, Hippocrates—the latter on grounds that in most cases we do not know and that may have been different from one case to another. This fact of their being associated with Hippocrates may well have been the reason they have been preserved, whereas the works of other medical authors and, as we are painfully aware, philosophical writers only survive in fragments. Their attribution to Hippocrates may also have been the reason why the names of their original authors were suppressed—their anonymity, once stripped of their Hippocratic label, standing in marked contrast to the confidence with which contemporaneous prose authors such as Herodotus and Hecataeus put their names at the beginning of their works. Yet whatever the answer to these questions may be, there is no intrinsic reason to look for a unified doctrine in these works, and the fact that two treatises have been handed down as part of the Hippocratic collection does not provide any conclusion regarding their intellectual affinity.

In spite of the aforementioned uncertainties, though, there is a scholarly consensus that the earliest group or "layer" of the Hippocratic writings dates from the latter half of the fifth century, and a second group from the beginning of the fourth century. It is these writings I shall primarily be concerned with (thereby slightly stretching the chronological boundaries of this book). One of the major advantages of the Hippocratic writings compared to the doctrines of the Presocratics is that, as said, the former have been preserved as complete writings and are thus much more accessible to interpretation and much less prone to speculation than the fragmentary remains of many a philosopher of the same period.

4. THE CONCEPT OF NATURE AND ITS RELATION TO THE DIVINE

As the Presocratics inquired into nature (*phusis*) as the origin, source of growth, and identifying structure of things, Hippocratic writers in their examination of the body and its affections and processes were seeking to find the nature of things— bodily processes and changes, illnesses, conditions, affections, symptoms, but also substances like food, drinks, drugs, and poisons and the effects they produced on the bodies of human beings. The clearest articulation of this is found in the treatise

On the Sacred Disease, the author of which presents a parallel to the Presocratics in two respects. Just like the Ionian philosophers Anaximenes and Anaxagoras in their explanations of earthquakes, solar eclipses, thunderstorms, and other marvelous phenomena, he produces a natural explanation for a phenomenon—in his case "the so-called sacred disease," epilepsy—that used to be seen as the manifestation of immediate divine agency. Furthermore, in so doing he is primarily focusing on the nature of individual things rather than Nature as an all-embracing, comprehensive force or principle in its own right. His claim is that epilepsy, like all other diseases (and, one may add, like all other phenomena), has its own nature, that is, its determined, normal, stable, and self-contained identity. Knowledge of this identity, and of the regularity that results from this, will allow one to recognize and understand individual instances of the phenomenon, to predict its future occurrence and by medical intervention influence it or even prevent it from happening or spreading. The emphasis with which the author makes this point suggests that to say that epilepsy "has a nature" (*phusin echein*) was a novel, revolutionary thing to do. He polemicizes against what he calls "magicians, quacks, charlatans," and so on who regard the disease as a form of whimsical, unpredictable divine intervention or even demonic possession and whose therapeutic practice is determined by magical beliefs and procedures. He attacks their views and practices with a range of arguments, and then reiterates his point:

> This disease seems to me to be not in any respect more divine than the others. Rather, it seems to me that, just as other diseases have a nature out of which each originates, this one, too, has a nature and a cause, and it derives its divinity from the same things as the others and is no less curable than others. (2.1, 6.364 L.)

It is clear that in using the word *phusis*, the author stays very close to the fundamental meaning of "origin, that out of which something comes into being." Elsewhere in the text, he uses the similarly organic phrase "originate and come to fruition" (*ginesthai kai thallein*), as if the disease comes into being and grows like a plant according to a definite, intrinsic pattern (13.13, 6.386 L.). He describes this development from its earliest, prenatal and indeed ancestral stages. The disease is genetic in that it is passed on from one generation to another, and only with people (and animals) of a particular physiological constitution (which is also inherited): using a division between constitution types that was common in his days, the author claims that the disease affects individuals who have a phlegmatic constitution but not those of the bilious type. Why this is so emerges from his explanation of the formation of the disease during embryonic development. Whereas in healthy cases, the brain of the fetus is purged from an excessive amount of phlegm before the child is born, people prone to epilepsy are born with a potentially harmful amount of phlegm gathering in the region of the brain. This phlegm spreads over the vessels connecting the brain with other parts of the body, thus causing blockage to the transmission of air (*pneuma*) from the brain to the sense-organs and the limbs through these vessels. Since this air is the carrier of consciousness, intelligence, and voluntary motion, its obstruction accounts for the spasms, the loss of control over muscular movement, and eventually the loss of consciousness that are characteristic of epileptic seizure. The author describes in great detail the various stages of such seizure, relating each of the various manifestations to its underlying patho-physiological cause, thus giving a good illustration of what "having a nature" involves, and what the grasping of this nature by the medical scientist means.

A further interesting thing to observe, however, is that the author's emphasis on the naturalness of diseases rules out neither their divinity nor the possibility of divine intervention as such. Toward the end of the treatise, the author says:

> This disease that is called sacred arises from the same causes as the others, from the things that come and go away and from cold and sun and winds that change and never rest. In this respect they are divine, so that one ought not to separate this disease and regard it as being more divine than the others; it is rather that all are divine and all are human, and each of them has a nature and a power of its own, and none is hopeless or impossible to deal with. (18.1, 6.394 L.)

Interpreters of this passage have wavered between two different ways of reading it, some regarding it as an essentially negative statement amounting to something like "all that is divine in this disease is its being caused by . . ." (i.e., nothing is left of the divine), others reading it as a positive statement reflecting something of the author's "theology," or at least his concept of the divine. Within the latter strand, there has in turn been a division between adherents of two different interpretations, as follows. One says that the author relates the genuine divine character of the disease to its supposedly divine causes—climatic factors such as the sun, the winds, cold, but presumably also foods and drinks, as well as their excretions. The other says that the author's point is that the divinity of the disease—and of any disease, and indeed of any phenomenon—lies in its having a nature, that is, its having a constant, never-changing pattern of cause and effect, origin and development, and thus displaying a "constancy" similar to that of the gods or divine beings of traditional Greek religious belief. Along the lines of the latter interpretation, the author of *On the Sacred Disease* (and, one may add, of *On Airs Waters Places*, which expresses a very similar view on the naturalness of diseases and on the role of the divine) is at the same time providing evidence of a "rationalized" or "naturalized" theology and can in this respect be compared with some of the Presocratics (such as Anaximander or Anaxagoras) when they apply the word "divine" (*theios*) to their first principles, on account of such characteristics as being "eternal," "unchanging," "all-pervading," which were traditionally attributed to the gods of Homeric Greek mythology.

It should be noted, though, that this does not mean that in the author's worldview there is no room for gods in a more traditional sense. He speaks on several occasions about the gods, their nature, and the way they reveal themselves in human experience. At one stage, he even says:

> But I hold that the body of a man is not polluted by a god, that which is most corruptible by that which is most holy, but that even when it happens to be

polluted or affected by something else, it is more likely to be cleansed from this by the god and sanctified than to be polluted by him. Concerning the greatest and most impious of our transgressions it is the divine that purifies and sanctifies us and washes them away from us; and we ourselves mark the boundaries of the sanctuaries and the precincts of the gods, lest anyone who is not pure would transgress them, and when we enter the temple we sprinkle ourselves, not as polluting ourselves thereby, but in order to be cleansed from an earlier pollution we might have contracted. Such is my opinion about the purifications. (1.44–46, 6.362–64 L.)

The purpose of this passage is not simply rhetorical point-scoring. What he is trying to do here is to distinguish between an appropriate appeal to the gods for purification from the pollution (*miasma*) that was brought about by moral transgressions (*hamartêmata*) and that has disturbed the relationship between man and the gods, and an inappropriate appeal to the gods for the purification of the alleged pollution allegedly brought about by the so-called sacred disease. Inappropriate, he says, for diseases are not sent by a god—to say this would be blasphemy, he insists— rather, they are natural phenomena that can be cured by natural means, and they do not constitute a pollution in the religious sense. The text has often been read as if the author ruled out divine intervention *as such*. But in fact, there is no evidence that he does—indeed, he does not even rule out the possibility that gods may cure diseases, if approached in the proper way and on the basis of appropriate premises. Such negative readings of the text attributing to the author the ruling out of all forms of divine intervention have presumably been inspired by a wishful belief among interpreters from the second half of the twentieth century to rationalize or secularize Hippocratic medicine—a belief no doubt inspired by the desire to see Hippocratic medicine as the forerunner of modern biomedicine, which can be paralleled with interpretative tendencies to demythologize philosophers such as Parmenides, Pythagoras, and Empedocles. Yet recently, there has been a renewed appreciation of the mythic or religious aspects of early Greek thought, and a readiness to take documents such as the Derveni Papyrus, the introduction of Parmenides' poem, and the *Purifications* of Empedocles more seriously. Similar paradigm shifts have taken place in the study of Hippocratic medicine, and there is now a much greater willingness among interpreters to accept the religious and rational elements as coexistent and—at least in their authors' conception— compatible. The question is not so much to disengage from their mythical context those elements that we, or some of us, regard as philosophically interesting from a contemporary perspective, but rather to try to see how those elements fit into that context. Within this approach, the author of *On the Sacred Disease* can be regarded as an exponent of a modified or purified position on traditional religious beliefs without abandoning those beliefs altogether; and as such, he can be said to have contributed also to the development of Greek religious or theological thought. For his arguments closely resemble those found in Plato's outlines of theology in the second book of the *Republic*, or Aristotle's arguments against the traditional belief that dreams are sent by the gods in his *On Divination in Sleep*.

Further clear evidence for the compatibility of religion and naturalism in the Hippocratic writings is provided by the work *On Regimen*. I will have occasion to dwell on the worldview of this author later. What is relevant here is that in the final part of his work he deals with dreams and their significance for medical diagnosis. Now dreams in the Greek world (as in other ancient Mediterranean civilizations) were traditionally regarded as forms of divine intervention, or at least as channels for divine revelation. Similarly to the author of *On the Sacred Disease*, the author of *On Regimen* makes an interesting distinction between two types of dreams: (1) dreams that are sent by the gods and that contain messages that are relevant to "cities and individuals" but that have no medical significance, and (2) dreams that arise from the body of the dreamer and that contain important clues about his or her present and future physical condition, if correctly interpreted. While leaving the interpretation of the first category of dreams to professional diviners (whose competence he does not question), the author claims expertise in the interpretation of the second category. This claim is based on his understanding of the mechanism of dreams and of the relationship between soul and body during sleep. Whereas in the waking state, he says, the soul is the "servant" of the body and distributes itself over the body in order to execute the various bodily functions, in sleep, the body is inactive, but the soul remains active and concentrates itself in a central part of the body and is "on its own" and carries out "itself" the activities normally associated with the body, such as thinking, perceiving, feeling, walking, and so on. These experiences are the dreams he is concerned with, and they reveal information about bodily states not normally available to the medical examiner during the waking state—bodily states that may develop into disease if no preventative action is taken. On the basis of this information, the doctor and the patient can try to remedy the condition of the body in order to prevent an imminent illness from actually occurring. All this is set out in the rest of the treatise: the author provides a number of interpretations of specific dream images and explains their medical significance, and he gives instructions as to how an imminent illness announced by the dream image can be averted by means of various measures. Now the interesting point here is that whereas the author presents an entirely natural and rational account of the origin and formation of the medically significant dreams, he does not rule out divine intervention. First, (1) he allows the existence of other types of dreams that are divine and in which the gods reveal themselves or the future to cities and individuals, even though the interpretation of such dreams is not his business, and (2) in recommending his own prophylactic measures for the treatment of people whose dreams he has interpreted as indicating potentially harmful bodily conditions, he does not rule out divine intervention either, for on several occasions he includes prayer to the gods alongside dietetic measures. Thus at some stage, he prescribes various dietetic precautionary measures about eating, emetics, walking, and voice exercises, and then concludes by saying that one should "pray to the gods . . . and then the turbulence will come to a halt" (4.88, 6.644 L.). At chapter 89, again toward the end, he sums up his discussion of dreams pertaining to "celestial signs" and says that one should take precautions and adopt a certain regimen "and pray to the gods, in good cases to Helios, Zeus Ouranios, Zeus Ktesios, Athena Ktesie, Hermes, Apollo, in opposite cases to the gods that avert this, and to Gê (Earth) and the heroes, that all difficulties will be averted" (6.652 L.). Finally, at chapter 90, he says, again in addition to dietetic measures, that "one should pray to Earth, Hermes and the heroes" (6.656–58 L.).

This combination of prayer with dietetic treatment is succinctly summarized in his statement that "Prayer is a good thing, but while calling on the gods one should oneself also help" (89, 6.642 L.). This statement has sometimes been quoted and interpreted by twentieth-century scholarship as if the author, perhaps under the pressure of social convention, is paying lip-service to traditional religious customs. However, this is not what his actual practice in the following chapters suggests, nor does it explain why he mentions these particular gods and not others, or why he mentions them in some contexts but not in others. It is preferable to conclude that the author regards his own, avowedly innovative ability to interpret the signs of the body correctly and to deal with them properly as entirely compatible with traditional beliefs in the gods of the Greek pantheon and in their various modes of activity within the human sphere.

5. THE NOTIONS OF CAUSE AND POWER

A further major contribution to philosophical thinking the Hippocratic authors made was their articulation of the notion of cause, in its various terminological manifestations (*aitiê, aition, archê, prophasis*) and as distinct from related concepts such as sign (*sêmeion*), indication (*tekmêrion*), or affection (*pathos*). Moreover, the Hippocratic writers not only insisted on the use of causal explanations as a condition for a truly technical, that is, scientific discipline but also had views on the requirements that causal explanations themselves had to fulfill and on their varying degrees of appropriateness in different contexts. This search for causes was conducted in two areas: the causes of disease, and the causes of the effects of substances such as foods, drinks, and drugs on the body to which they were administered. In the first area, the medical authors often went far beyond the observable and engaged in sometimes wide-ranging speculation about internal patho-physiological states and processes. I will have occasion to dwell on the empirical basis of their explanation later on. Greater opportunities for empirical verification were available in the other area, that of the effects of substances such as food and drink taken in by the body. Here, there was at least a visible agent, namely the substance, or at any rate a visible carrier of agency bringing about a change in the state of the body of the patient. It is especially the dietetic treatises in the Hippocratic writings such as *On Regimen* and *On Ancient Medicine* that are concerned with this aspect, trying to account for the efficacy of foods and drinks by reference to the power (*dunamis*) of the substance in question and the way in interacts with its environment. An example:

> Beans are nutritious, astringent and flatulent. They are flatulent, because the passages (in the body) do not admit the abundant nourishment which is brought in, astringent because it has only a small residue left over from its nourishment. (*On Regimen* 2.45, 6.542 L.)

The concept of *dunamis*, often translated as "power," "faculty," or "function," was to have a long influence in the history of philosophy and science. It refers primarily to the power to produce a certain effect in the environment of the entity in which the power inheres: something which has the *dunamis* cold has the ability to exercise a cooling effect on its environment, and the realization of that ability depends on the environment as much as on the substance itself. But *dunamis* also refers, more generally, to an active property or characterizing force—a usage of the term already present in *On Ancient Medicine* and of considerable influence on later thought, for instance on Plato's doctrine of material objects participating in the forms as "clusters of *dunameis*."

Yet the question how exactly the *dunamis* of a substance works, and why it works in some cases but apparently not in others, raises further questions about causal efficacy, modus operandi, side-effects, interference, and so on. These questions are addressed in *On Ancient Medicine*, a treatise primarily concerned with dietetics and the ways humankind has learned by trial and error to cope with the influence of food and drinks on the body. As we have seen, the author of this work is polemicizing against those who apply philosophical postulates such as warm or cold to the area of medicine, and instead he offers an account that is based on facts of experience. Yet at the same time, he is very keen on causal explanation; he defines cause (*aition*) as "that as a result of whose presence something happens necessarily in this particular way and by whose change into a different mixture it stops" (19.3, 1.616–18 L.). And he insists that one should state the cause of such influences, yet in a proper way and while taking care to distinguish between cause and "accompanying phenomena." Thus he insists that a doctor should know about the nature of things and not just say "cheese is bad, for it causes trouble to those who eat much of it" but also say "what kind of trouble, what it is caused by, and which parts of the body it is particularly inappropriate to" (20.3, 1.622 L.). And he goes so far as to insist that fever is not just a matter of heat, but of the cooperation of a number of factors and their interaction with the bodily condition of the patient:

> I hold this [i.e., the fact that people who as a result of certain diseases suffer from fever are not easily released from their fever] to be a most important indication of the fact that it is not just by heat alone that people get fever, and that heat is not the only cause of the disease; rather, it is the combination of heat with bitterness, and the combination of pungency with heat, and the combination of saltiness with heat, and so on, and the same goes for the combination of cold with other qualifying properties [*dunameis*]. (17.2, 1.612 L.)

Likewise, the author of *On the Sacred Disease* in his discussion of epilepsy frequently uses terminology referring to causal connections, such as *aitios* and *prophasis*. There has been some discussion as to whether early Greek writers intended a difference in meaning between these two terms, with *prophasis* being used in the specific senses of "external, observable, apparent, preceding, and/or exciting cause or catalyst," as opposed to *aitios*, referring to the "intrinsic, internal, or structural cause," thus anticipating the later Hellenistic distinction between antecedent and "contentive" causes that one finds for example in Galen. In addition, it is sometimes claimed that early Greek thought differentiated between *to aition* as "the causing factor" versus *hê aitia* as "the cause" or even "the explanation" attributed to a sequence of events. As to *prophasis*, it is certainly striking that the author of *On the Sacred Disease* uses the term with particular reference to specific external factors, such as wind, rain, air, food, and so on, which play the role of initiating, catalyzing factors without themselves being involved in the nosological process they lead up to. A distinction with *aitios* seems intended in chapter 3, where he first says that the brain is "causally responsible" (*aitios*) for the disease, after which he is going to explain "through what cause" (*prophasis*) the disease comes into being. But in other Hippocratic writings it is less clear whether a difference in meaning is really intended. Similarly inconclusive is the question regarding possible distinctions between *aitios* and *aitia* (or, in Ionic Greek, *aitiê*), and it seems preferable simply to regard them as being related to each other as "responsible" to "responsibility," with *to aition* being the substantivized adjective "the responsible factor."

Further contributions by the Hippocratic authors to the development of thought on causes are the idea that one and the same phenomenon can have different causes and that identification of the actual cause in question is important not only for diagnosis but also for treatment. Thus the author of *On Regimen in Acute Diseases* criticizes other doctors for their lack of awareness of this issue:

> I perceive that doctors do not have any experience as to the manner in which to distinguish in cases of illness the different kinds of weakness, for example whether the patient is weak because of emptiness of the vessels, or because of some other irritation, or because of pain, or because of the acuteness of the disease, and which sufferings are brought about by our constitution or our condition and what kinds of all these there are; if one knows about these things, it will bring security, but if not, they can be lethal. (11, 2.314–16 L.)

The connection between therapy and causal explanation is also stressed by the author of *On Breaths*, even when these causes are not plainly visible:

> The judgment regarding the least visible and most unclear diseases is a matter of opinion rather than art; and in these things there is great difference between competence and incompetence. One of these points is the following: What is the cause of diseases, what is their starting point and what is the source of harmful things going on in the body? For if one knows the cause of disease, one's knowledge of what is harmful to the body enables one to administer what is beneficial to the body. For that is the natural way of healing. (1.4, 6.90–92 L.)

6. OBSERVATION, EXPERIENCE, EXPERIMENT, INFERENCE, SPECULATION

The medical writers were, for obvious reasons, very much concerned with the question of how one can obtain knowledge of the body, especially of things supposedly hidden within the body; and how claims to this sort of knowledge can be verified, modified, or expanded. The constraints here were immediately obvious: opportunities for systematic dissection, even of animal bodies, were limited, partly by practical, partly by moral considerations, and this meant that information about internal bodily processes had to be gained from, or elicited through, external appearances that served as a basis for inferential reasoning.

The Hippocratic writers were the first to develop elaborate and systematic techniques for meticulous examination and recording of observations. They stressed the importance of autopsy and focused observation. This is expressed most clearly in the so-called *Epidemics*, a collection of clinical case histories of individual patients, whose symptoms are recorded by reference to the day in which they manifested themselves. However, this is not naive, uninformed observation—the Hippocratic writers were aware that their observations were guided by presuppositions concerning what to look for, as expressed in questions. A revealing passage is *Epidemics* 1.23:

> The circumstances accompanying the diseases on which we built our judgments we know from the common nature of all (diseases) and the particular nature of the individual: from the disease, the patient, from what has been administered, and from the person who has administered it (for it depends on these things whether a diagnosis is favorable or not); from the constitution of the weather, both as a whole and with respect to particular parts, and of each region; from the patient, his custom, mode of life, activities and age, from his words, his manner, silence, thoughts, sleep or sleeplessness, his dreams, their nature and time of appearance, pluckings, scratchings, tears; from the exacerbations, excrements, urine, sputa, vomit, the antecedents and the sequence in which each of these things manifest themselves in the successions of diseases, the abscessions leading to a fatal outcome or a crisis, sweat, rigor, chill, coughing, sneezing, hiccoughs, breathing, belchings, flatulence, silent or noisy, hemorrhages, and hemorrhoids. On the basis of these things we must consider what their results will be. (1.23; 2.668–70 L.)

This passage looks like a questionnaire, perhaps even a checklist for a medical examination, on the basis of which the doctor could proceed in his diagnosis of individual patients. Inevitably, however, it is restricted to external appearances and provides no direct information on what is hidden inside the body, which had to be inferred. This did not prevent medical authors from making bold claims about internal anatomy and physiology. The basis for such claims was formed either by animal dissection, inference from external signs and symptoms, inference from analogy, mere speculation, or, as often, a combination of these. A well-known example of a reference to animal dissection is, again, a passage from *On the Sacred Disease*, where the author says that if one were to open the skull of a goat that has died of an epileptic seizure, one will find that the brain is soaked with foul-smelling moisture (11.5, 6.382 L.). The author explains this observation as a further piece of evidence that the disease is not due to a god or demonic power, but to natural causes, and that his particular version of these causes—in terms of a failure of the brain to get rid of harmful moisture—is correct. It is unclear from the text, however, whether the author himself carried out this anatomical experiment or had heard of it by word of mouth.

The use of the word "experiment" reminds us of that old question as to whether the Greeks had a concept of experiment and carried out experiments at any scale. Early medical writers certainly had no elaborate theory of experimentation; they did, however, clearly realize that deliberate, focused manipulation of natural things or states of affairs could provide information not readily available to passive observation. An interesting example is provided by the author of the embryological Hippocratic work *On the Nature of the Child*. At some point in his discussion, he argues that the human fetus is surrounded by a kind of skin or membrane that has an umbilicus in the middle, through which the fetus breathes; the fetus's growth takes place in stages that are comparable to the growth stages of plants. He then supports his statement with a reference to the following experiment.

> If one wishes to take 20 eggs, or more, and to put them to hatch under two hens or more, and if each day, beginning on the second day and continuing until the time when the egg hatches, one takes one egg, breaks it open, and examines it, one will find that it is exactly as I have described it—with due consideration, of course, of the extent to which the growth of a chicken can be compared to that of a man. Thus one will discover that it contains membranes that proceed from the umbilicus—indeed, all things I have described in relation to the growth of a human child can also be found in a chicken's egg. (29.2–3; 7.530 L.)

It is, again, unclear from the context whether the author has carried out this experiment himself or has heard about it from others. Yet the passage is of great interest for the history of experimental research and the use of analogy as a mode of thinking. Evidently, the author has used the observation of chicken eggs as a basis for inferring a similar process in the human domain. He is aware that this inference cannot be made without difficulty, yet at the same time he seems to assume that in this case it is justified. This assumption may be based on an observation the author has made in an earlier stage of his discussion, when he advised a woman who wanted to abort her pregnancy to jump up and down and at each leap to strike her feet against her buttocks; the effect was, he says, that after more than seven times she aborted the fetus, which according to the author resembled a raw egg without shell, so that the moisture contained within it shone through the membrane:

> It was round and red, and within the membrane one could see thick, white fibers, surrounded by red serum, while on the outside of the membrane there were clots

of blood. In the middle of the membrane there was a small growth, which looked like an umbilicus, and it seemed as if the fetus was breathing through this. Proceeding from this umbilicus, the membrane extended and encompassed the whole fetus. This is what the six-days embryo looked like. (13.3; 7.490 L.)

What the author actually observed (if anything) is difficult to reconstruct. Yet the passage is very revealing of his method—and its limitations. On the one hand, he uses this observation as a starting point for his own argument later on; at the same time, the limitations of his procedure are painfully obvious. In his interpretation of the observation, he is clearly influenced by what he expects to find, while at the same time he does not proceed to an analysis of the aborted fetus.

Further reflection on inference from the visible to the invisible can be found in the Hippocratic treatise *On the Art of Medicine*:

> None of these things (i.e., parts and states hidden within the body) can be known by visual observation; this is why they are called invisible, and this is what the art of medicine has judged them to be.... For everything that escapes being seen by the eyes is known by the vision of the mind.... Although the art of medicine cannot view by visual observation the suppurations, the diseases surrounding the liver and the kidneys and all illnesses that occur within the cavities of the body... it has other means at its disposal: the clarity or hoarseness of the voice, the speed or slowness of breathing, or the smell, or color, or narrowness or density of the fluxes that normally go through the body along their appropriate ways provide clues as to whether they are indications of parts that are already ill or parts that are potentially ill. And when nature does not yield this information spontaneously, the art has discovered forceful ways to control unpunished nature and to make it release this information; and when this is released, it makes the experts clear what they have to do. (11.1–12.3, 6.18–24 L.)

Again, the articulation of the principle here is more important and more impressive than its actual application—which is often haphazard and poorly executed. The principle found its expression in the formula *opsis adêlôn ta phainomena*, "the things that manifest themselves provide a view of what is invisible," which was quoted by a number of philosophers (Democritus, Anaxagoras) as well as doctors (Diocles of Carystus).

7. THE NATURE OF THE HUMAN BEING: ELEMENTS, PRINCIPLES, QUALITIES, HUMORS

In the field of elemental physiology and embryology, the Hippocratic writers, again, pursued very similar issues to the Presocratics by trying to reduce the variety of phenomena to a small number of elemental entities, forces, or powers—in short, doing what the author of *On Ancient Medicine* described as "narrowing down the primary cause" of health and disease. Three treatises stand out here: *On Regimen*, *On Fleshes*, and *On the Nature of Man*. The first, which I have already mentioned, is a work apparently written by a trainer or supervisor of athletes who is promulgating a new doctrine about *diaita*, a "life-style" or "way of life" that ensures the most balanced physical condition and allows the trainer to monitor the athlete's bodily condition on a day-to-day basis. Yet he puts his dietary recommendations in an extremely wide-ranging cosmological framework, in which the primary active forces are fire (*pur*) and water (*hudôr*). These two elements are the basic constituents of everything that exists, organic and inorganic, and their interaction and quantitative and qualitative relationships permeate the whole universe, the human body, and the human soul in their development from their earliest embyonic stage to full maturity and old age; and their various and variable purity and proportion determines health and disease, sanity and insanity. In addition, the author perceives, in an almost Heraclitean manner, contrast and reciprocity as present and active both in the natural world but also in all areas of human action and craft, which "imitate" (*mimêsis*) the natural order; his views on "pangenesis"—the idea that all parts of the body contain ingredients from all other parts—show interesting similarities with Anaxagoras; and supervising all these cosmological processes are the gods and fate.

Similarly, the author of *On Fleshes*, in spite of its misleading title, is concerned with what could best be described as "the nature of man"—the anatomy, physiology, pathology, and reproduction of the human body. But again, like the author of *On Regimen*, he feels that this can only be understood properly within the wider context of the cosmos and the forces working in it. He identifies heat (*to thermon*) as the fundamental principle of everything; and in a cosmogonic and anthropogonic narrative, he describes how under the action of heat the four fundamental cosmic principles earth, water, air, and aether have come into being. This is followed by an account of the origin of the human body, its various solid and soft parts and the fluids it contains, again through the agency of heat acting on two active principles within the human domain, the fatty (*to liparon*) and the glutinous (*to kollôdes*), in a process that is compared to the cooking of food. Moreover, the author provides a discussion of the five senses and their respective organs and concludes by discussing the numerical relationships between things by showing the omnipresence of the number 7 in a whole range of fields.

A third example of a universal system providing the explanatory context of health and disease of the human body is offered by the author of *On the Nature of Man*. In his case, the overriding force seems to be the number four—there are four elementary qualities (hot, cold, dry, wet), four humors (blood, phlegm, yellow bile, black bile), four types of disease, four seasons, and so on. It is peculiar to this author, and of great influence on later generations of thinkers, that while in other medical writers of the same period these humors are primarily seen as causes or manifestations of disease, in his view they are natural, indeed they "make up the nature of man," as he puts it; disease consists in the excess or default of one of these humors over the others, or in the segregation of one humor in particular parts of the body. We find here the notion of balance, of the right proportion, the just mean articulated for the first time.

For all their individual variations, what these authors have emphatically in common is the idea that human nature is closely related to the nature of the universe. This relationship can be one of correspondence, analogy, or imitation (as the author of *On Regimen* puts it), but often it goes further: the same forces and the same material constituents that underlie the structures and processes in the body are also operative in the universe at large, and the one cannot be comprehended, let alone therapeutically influenced, without reference to the other. A variant of this idea is the belief that the elements and forces that are at work in the universe have a major influence on the state of the body. This explains another characteristic feature of Hippocratic medicine, namely its focus on the environment and on the climatic and meteorological forces that determine human health and disease. This idea is expressed most clearly in the treatise *On Airs, Waters, Places*, which describes a variety of geographical regions and their differing conditions not only environmental and climatic but also ethnographic, with a view to their impact on the human bodily condition. Like the author of *On the Nature of Man*, the author of this treatise thinks in strongly schematized polar patterns, by contrasting regions, climatic factors such as winds, and features of the human body in pairs of opposites.

8. ANATOMY AND PHYSIOLOGY: THE HEART, THE BRAIN, AND THE VASCULAR SYSTEM

Views on the anatomical structure of the human body and its constituents differed widely among the writers of the Hippocratic Corpus, partly as a result of the varying availability of unambiguous evidence. On the one hand, knowledge of surface anatomy, as displayed especially in the surgical writings (such as *On Joints*), and knowledge of skeletal anatomy was relatively well advanced and uncontroversial. Yet internal parts, which were not readily accessible to dissection, were the subject of conflicting views and of sometimes wild speculation. Thus the author of *On the Art* in his discussion of invisible diseases distinguishes between those that are present "in the region of the bones" and those that are present "in the cavities," of which, he adds, there are many in the body (10, 6.16 L.). The author of *On Ancient Medicine* in his account of internal anatomy distinguishes between faculties (*dunameis*) and structures (*schêmata*) (22, 1.626 L.), while the author of *On Generation* identifies as the internal parts of the body "the solid parts, the soft parts, and the fluids" (3, 7.474 L.).

To generalize, we can say that the Hippocratic writers in their discussion of the structure of the body distinguished parts (organs and tissues, for example, the brain, the heart, the blood vessels, the spleen), substances (blood, water, phlegm, etc.), properties (hot, cold, dry, wet, but also secondary qualities such as sweet, salt, bitter, etc.), relationships (e.g., balance, imbalance, proportion), processes (e.g., heating, cooling, concoction), and functions (e.g., sense perception, thinking, digestion, etc.). The structure that united most of these categories and attracted most attention was the vascular system, of which we find many different descriptions—and again, this was a topic that attracted attention from philosophers just as much as from doctors, as is testified by Aristotle's report of several theories about the vascular system in *Historia animalium* 4. Views on the structure and ramifications of the vascular system differed considerably, and even on such apparently crucial points as the role of the heart, agreement was by no means reached. Thus the authors of *On the Sacred Disease* and *On the Nature of Man* posit the starting point of the vascular system in the head rather than in the heart.

9. SOUL AND BODY

Similar variations can be found in views concerning the cognitive function of the heart, the blood, and the brain and, more specifically, on the question of the location of the mind. This was a question that later attracted great interest in Hellenistic philosophy, where medical evidence played a major (though by no means decisive) role in the discussion, but the way for this debate was already paved in the medical writings of the fifth century, though in a slightly different context. For in their discussions of disease, the Hippocratic writers frequently also discussed mental illness and other disturbances of the mental, cognitive, behavioral, or motor functions of the body. What is striking here is that in many of these cases, the authors do not make a categorical distinction between mind and body: all mental affections are presented as being of a physical nature and having a physical cause. And even those authors who speak about soul (*psuchê*) as distinct from the body, such as the author of *On Regimen*, still conceive of the soul as something physical, whose workings and failings can be described in material terms—for example, a particular blend of fire and water—and influenced by dietary measures (e.g., in 1.35–36, 6.512–14 L., or in 4.86, 6.640 L.).

The question about the location of this soul or mind was already disputed in the times of the Hippocratic writings. The author of *On the Sacred Disease* in his discussion of the brain as the center of consciousness alludes to this controversy:

> For these reasons I believe that the brain is the most powerful part in a human being. So long as it is healthy, it is the interpreter of what comes to the body from

the air. Consciousness is provided by the air. The eyes, ears, tongue, hands, and feet carry out what the brain knows, for throughout the body there is a degree of consciousness proportionate to the amount of air that it receives. As far as intelligence is concerned, the brain is also the part that transmits this, for when a man draws in a breath it first arrives at the brain, and from there it is distributed over the rest of the body, having left behind in the brain its best portion and whatever contains consciousness and intelligence. For if the air went first to the body and subsequently to the brain, the power of discernment would be left to the flesh and to the blood-vessels; it would reach the brain in a hot and no longer pure state but mixed with moisture from the flesh and from the blood so that it would no longer be accurate. I therefore state that the brain is the interpreter of intelligence.

The diaphragm (*phrenes*), however, does not have the right name, but it has got this by chance and through convention. I do not know in virtue of what the diaphragm can think and be conscious (*phronein*), except that if a man suddenly feels pleasure or pain, the diaphragm leaps up and causes throbbing, because it is thin and under greater tension than any other part of the body, and it has no cavity into which it might receive anything good or bad that comes upon it, but because of the weakness of its structure it is subject to disturbance by either of these forces, since it does not perceive faster than any other part of the body. Rather, it has its name and reputation for no good reason, just as parts of the heart are called auricles though they make no contribution to hearing.

Some say that we owe our consciousness to our hearts and that it is the heart that suffers pain and feels anxiety. But this is not the case; rather, it is torn just like the diaphragm, and even more than that for the same reasons: for blood-vessels from all parts of the body run to the heart, and it encapsulates these, so that it can feel if any pain or tension occurs in a human being. Moreover, it is necessary for the body to shudder and to contract when it feels pain, and when it is overwhelmed by joy it experiences the same. This is why the heart and the diaphragm are particularly sensitive. Yet neither of these parts has any share in consciousness; rather, it is the brain that is responsible for all these. (16–17, 6.390–94 L.)

According to the author, the brain—which he had earlier designated as the cause of epilepsy, and indeed of most major diseases—is the point from which physical and mental faculties are coordinated, but it is also particularly sensitive to harmful influences from the environment, such as climate, season and so on. These influences can therefore be additional factors that contribute to the course the disease takes. The author emphasizes this crucial role of the brain as part of his polemic against two rival groups that consider the diaphragm or the heart to be the central source of consciousness. He rejects the etymological argument of the first group (who relates the term *phrenes*, "*diaphragm*," to the term *phronêsis*, "*intelligence*") and accommodates the empirical fact that both groups put forward—the heart's leaping in cases of sudden gladness or sadness—into his own theory, which is also based on empirical observations (the delicacy of the diaphragm and the vessels extending to the heart). What is particularly striking is his distinction between consciousness (*phronêsis*) and intelligence (*sunesis*): the latter is apparently related to the discernment (*diagnôsis*) that is mentioned later in the text, and which requires a certain degree of purity and precision that is adversely affected by contact with organs and tissues. In this context, *phronêsis* clearly means more than "thinking" or "intelligence," as the word is commonly translated. It refers to a universal force by which a living being can focus on its surroundings and can undertake activities; it also implies perception and movement. *Phronêsis* can be found throughout the body, whereas "intelligence" is restricted to the brain. A further striking element is the author's opinion that the brain is also the source of feeling— though he admits that the heart and diaphragm take part in this as well.

Yet with equal confidence, the author of another Hippocratic work, *On Breaths*, uses the example of epilepsy to advocate his position that it is the blood that is the center of consciousness:

> In my view, the same cause is also responsible for the disease called sacred. . . . I believe that none of the parts of the body that contribute to consciousness in anyone is more important than blood. So long as this remains in a stable condition, consciousness, too, remains stable; but when the blood undergoes change, consciousness also changes. There are many things that testify that this is the case. First of all, an affection which is common to all living beings, namely sleep, testifies to what has just been said. When sleep comes upon the body, the blood is chilled, for it is the nature of sleep to cause chill. When the blood is chilled, its passages become more sluggish. This is evident; the body leans and gets heavy . . . the eyes close, and consciousness is changed, and certain other thoughts remain present, which are called dreams. . . . So if all of the blood is brought in a state of complete turmoil, consciousness is completely destroyed. . . . I state that the sacred disease is caused in the following way. When much wind has been mixed throughout the body with all the blood, many obstructions arise in many places in the blood-vessels. . . . At this moment the patients are unconscious of everything—deaf to what is spoken, blind to what is happening, and insensible to pain. (14.1–4, 6.110–12 L.)

The reference to sleep and dreams in this passage reminds us of the discussion of the soul–body relationship in the waking state and in sleep in *On Regimen* discussed earlier, where again the soul is conceived as something material that moves around in the body.

10. EMBRYOLOGY AND THE THEORY OF THE ORIGIN OF THE HUMAN SEED

A final, major example of the common ground that connected doctors and philosophers was provided by the question of the origins of life, the mechanisms of reproduction, and the ways inherited characteristics were passed on from one generation to another; and, as we can see from an author such as Aristotle (in his *Generation of Animals*) but also from the later doxographical tradition of Aëtius, interaction between the two domains is particularly likely to have taken place here.

Again, however, it would be misleading to present this relationship in terms of interaction between science and philosophy—as if doctors were just doing the empirical research that provided the facts, while philosophers were theorizing on these and systematizing them. In fact, the medical writers were pursuing very much the same questions as people like Anaxagoras, Empedocles, Democritus, or Aristotle, and their methods and theoretical concepts were very similar. The chief issues here were threefold: (1) the question of the male and female contribution to the reproductive process; (2) the question of the origin of the semen; (3) the question of inherited characteristics. Related to this were questions of fertility and infertility, stages of embryonic development, the way the embryo is nourished, twins and triplets, and so on.

As to the first question, there was a widespread belief in the Hippocratic writings but also beyond these that both the male and the female contribute "seed" to the reproductive process, and that conception consists in the union or mixing of these two seeds; failure to conceive was held to be due either to deficiencies of either seed or to unfavorable circumstances (such as irregularities in the structure, position, or condition of the uterus). In spite of Aristotle's resistance, this theory was authoritative until well into the sixteenth century.

The second question had to do with the transmission of life. How can a complete human being, with a full-grown body and a developed mind, find his origin in such a small and apparently unsophisticated substance as seed? Theories here differed according to the part of the body from which the seed was believed to be drawn, with some advocating the brain and spinal marrow (e.g., the author of *On Airs, Waters, Places* and, a generation or two later, Plato and Diocles), others the blood (such as Aristotle), and yet others the body as a whole (the pangenesis theory), in particular the moistures bile, phlegm, blood, and water. The latter theory is expounded in the Hippocratic treatise *On Generation/On the Nature of the Child/On Diseases* 4. This author provides the most extensive discussion not only of reproduction and embryological development but also of the question of the sex of the offspring and of inherited features. He assumes that both the male and the female seed are, as it were, doubly characterized and contain both male and female elements. Again, he substantiates this claim with an appeal to experiential evidence by pointing out that while a particular combination of two partners produces only girls or only boys, a different combination of either of these two partners with a new partner produces also offspring of the opposite sex, respectively. And he says that although the male seed is more powerful than the female, the question which of these in a particular case "gains the upper hand" (*epikrateein*, a notion later adopted by Aristotle in his *Generation of Animals*) depends on the respective quantity in which either is present. Inherited properties deriving either from the father's side or the mother's side come about as a result of a similar mechanism, he argues: the seed comes from all parts of the body, but when, for instance, the female element in seed deriving from a particular part of the body is present in greater quantity than the male, the offspring will in this particular part resemble the mother rather than the father.

Similar explanations are advanced for the transmission of secondary, acquired properties and of constitutions and diseases. For instance, the author of *On Airs, Waters, Places* explains the occurrence of "long-headed" people (*makrokephaloi*) among particular communities as a result of the custom held in these communities to mould the head of the newborn child while it is still soft, and to force it to grow more in length than width; this, he argues, has gradually led to the emergence of a natural type of long-headedness, which in turn came to be passed on to the next generation. Likewise, constitutions like "bilious" or "phlegmatic" were believed to be inherited, and the corresponding diseases that were believed to be associated with these constitutions. Once again, the author of *On the Sacred Disease* makes this point in relation to epilepsy:

> This disease, like all others, has its origin in its genetic background. For if a person with a phlegmatic constitution produces another phlegmatic person, and a choleric another choleric, and a consumptive another consumptive, and a spleen-type another spleen-type, what then prevents one of the offspring of a father or mother who had the disease from having it himself? For the seed comes from all parts of the body, both the healthy parts and the unhealthy ones. (2.4, 6.364 L.)

11. ETHICS

Finally, while most of the contributions by the Hippocratic authors to the formation of philosophical thought discussed so far pertain to the fields of natural philosophy and epistemology, their relevance to moral thinking should not be left unmentioned. To us, it may seem inevitable that medical practice raises questions of an ethical nature, but a comparison with other ancient medical traditions suggests that this is by no means to be taken for granted. The Hippocratic writings, and especially the famous *Oath*, first of all reflect on the duties and responsibilities the doctor has in relation to the patient, for instance in articulating such famous principles as "to do no harm," not to cause death; or in advocating confidentiality, self-restraint, discretion, gentleness, and acting without fear or favor. Yet, interestingly, they also emphasize the need for moral and religious integrity of the practitioner and for correspondence between theory and practice—thus anticipating a question that became particularly prominent in Hellenistic moral philosophy. Furthermore, in the field of dietetics, the Hippocratics' development of the notions of moderation, "the mean," and the right balance between opposites provided concepts and modes of thinking that found their way into ethical discussions as we find them in Plato and Aristotle; and, paradoxically, their tendency to naturalize aspects of human life-style such as sexual behavior, physical exercise, and eating and drinking patterns by presenting these in terms of healthy or harmful provided arguments to those participants in ethical debates stressing the naturalness or unnaturalness of certain forms of human behavior.

CONCLUSION

The foregoing discussion will, I hope, have sufficiently highlighted some of the more striking philosophical elements in the Hippocratic writings, and indicated in what respects these writings influenced both contemporaneous thinkers and later generations such as Plato and Aristotle. Interaction between medicine and philosophy continued to be fruitful in the fourth century, with medical writers such as Diocles of Carystus, Mnesitheus of Athens, and Praxagoras of Cos contributing to the formation and articulation of philosophical ideas. This development continued also during the Hellenistic period and found its culmination in Galen—according to whom the best doctor is a philosopher—whose contributions to areas such as logic and epistemology have been of major philosophical significance. That, however, is a story that exceeds the chronological boundaries of this book.

NOTES

The material covered in the first four sections of this chapter is further elaborated in my *Medicine and Philosophy* and in my "Between the Hippocratics and the Alexandrians." Sections 5 and following are based on material published earlier in German in my "Hippokratische Beiträge zur antiken Biologie."

1. But this identification of Alcmaeon as a Pythagorean is disputed by Huffman in this volume.

BIBLIOGRAPHICAL NOTES

Primary Sources

References to the Hippocratic writings (e.g., 2.346 L.) pertain to the relevant volume and page number in the edition of the Hippocratic writings by Emile Littré, *Œuvres Complètes d'Hippocrate*, 10 Vols. (1839–1861), which prints the Greek text with facing French translation. A more recent but incomplete edition of the Hippocratic writings is Hugo Kühlewein, *Hippocratis opera quae feruntur omnia*, 2 Vols. (1894–1902). Critical editions of individual Hippocratic writings with translation and notes have come out in the series Corpus Medicorum Graecorum (CMG) (9 vols. so far) (Berlin: Akademie Verlag), and in the *Collection des Universités de France* (Budé collection, 13 vols. so far; Paris: Belles Lettres). Most Hippocratic writings are now also accessible in the Loeb Classical Library, text with English translation (Cambridge, Mass.: Harvard University Press; 8 vols. so far). A selection of Hippocratic works in English translation is included in Lloyd, *Hippocratic Writings*. A very useful survey of all the Hippocratic writings, their dates, contents, and style, is in Jouanna, *Hippocrates*, app. 2.

SECONDARY LITERATURE

Older discussions of the relationship between medicine and philosophy in the early and classical Greek period can be found in Schumacher, *Antike Medizin*, Burnet, *Early Greek Philosophy*, and Edelstein, "Greek Medicine in Its Relation to Religion and Magic"; for more recent discussions see Longrigg, *Greek Rational Medicine*, Frede, "Philosophy and Medicine in Antiquity," and van der Eijk, *Medicine and Philosophy*.

On the "Hippocratic question" see Joly, "Phèdre et Hippocrate"; Lloyd, *Methods and Problems in Greek Science*; Mansfeld, "Plato and the Method of Hippocrates"; and Smith, *The Hippocratic Tradition*.

For a survey of the interpretive debate on *On the Sacred Disease* see van der Eijk,"The 'Theology' of the Hippocratic Treatise *On the Sacred Disease*"; for *On Regimen* see van der Eijk, "Divination, Prognosis, Prophylaxis."

Useful indices to the Hippocratic Corpus are Kühn and Fleischer, *Index Hippocraticus*, and Maloney and Frohn, *Concordantia in Corpus Hippocraticum.*

Bibliographical surveys can be found in Maloney and Savoie, *Cinq cents ans de bibliographie hippocatique*; Byl, Les dix dernières années (1983–1992) de la recherche hippocratique; and Bruni Celli, *Bibliografica hipocrática.*

BIBLIOGRAPHY

Abel, K. "Die Lehre vom Blutkreislauf im Corpus hippocraticum." *Hermes* 86 (1958): 192–219.

Baader, G., and R. Winau, eds. *Die hippokratischen Epidemien: Theorie—Praxis—Tradition.* Akten des 5. Colloque international hippocratique in Berlin, Stuttgart 1988. Sudhoffs Archiv, Beiheft 27.

Balss, H. "Die Zeugungslehre und Embryologie in der Antike. Eine Übersicht." *Quellen und Studien zur Geschichte der Naturwissenschaft und der Medizin* 5 (1936): 1–82.

Bourgey, L., and J. Jouanna, eds. *La collection hippocratique et son rôle dans l'histoire de la médecine.* Actes du Colloque hippocratique de Strasbourg. Leiden: Brill 1975.

Bruni Celli, B. *Bibliografica hipocrática.* Caracas, 1984.

Burnet, J. *Early Greek Philosophy.* Oxford: Oxford University Press, 1945.

Byl, S. "Les dix dernières années (1983–92) de la recherche hippocratique." *Lettre d'Informations Centre Jean Palerne* 22 (1993): 1–39.

Deichgraeber, K. "Die Stellung des griechischen Arztes zur Natur." *Die Antike* 15 (1939): 116–38.

———. *Medicus gratiosus. Untersuchungen zu einem griechischen Arztbild.* Akademie der Wissenschaften und der Literatur Mainz, Abhandlungen der Geistes- und Sozialwissenschaftlichen Klasse, 1970.3.

Diller, H. "Hippokratische Medizin und attische Philosophie." *Hermes* 80 (1952): 385–409.

———. "ὄψις ἀδήλων τὰ φαινόμενα." *Hermes* 67 (1932): 14–42.

———. "Das Selbstverständnis der griechischen Medizin in der Zeit des Hippokrates." In *La Collection hippocratique et son rôle dans l'histoire de la médecine*, edited by L. Bourgey and J. Jouanna, Actes du Colloque hippocratique de Strasbourg, 85–87. Leiden, 1975.

Dittmer, H. L. "Konstitutionstypen im Corpus hippocraticum. Würzburg." 1940.

Ducatillon, J. *Polémiques dans la Collection Hippocratique*. Paris, 1977.

Duminil, M. P. "Le sang, les vaisseaux, le cœur dans la Collection Hippocratique: Anatomie et physiologie." Paris: Belles Lettres, 1983.

Edelstein, L. "Greek Medicine in Its Relation to Religion and Magic." In *Ancient Medicine. Selected Papers by Ludwig Edelstein*, edited by O. Temkin and C. L. Temkin, 205–46. Baltimore, 1967. First published in *Bulletin of the History of Medicine* 5 (1937): 201–46.

———. "The History of Anatomy in Antiquity." In *Ancient Medicine. Selected Papers by Ludwig Edelstein*, edited by O. Temkin and C. L. Temkin, 247–301. Baltimore, 1967. First published in *Quellen und Studien zur Geschichte der Naturwissenschaften und der Medizin* 3 (1933): 1–50.

Eijk, P.J. van der. "The 'Theology' of the Hippocratic Treatise *On the Sacred Disease*." *Apeiron* 23 (1990): 87–119 (reprinted in *Medicine and Philosophy*, 45–73).

———. "Hippokratische Beiträge zur antiken Biologie." In *Geschichte der Mathematik und der Naturwissenschaften in der Antike*, edited by G. Wöhrle. 1, *Biologie*, 50–73. Stuttgart: Steiner Verlag, 1999.

———. "Divination, Prognosis, Prophylaxis: The Hippocratic work 'On Dreams' (*De victu* 4) and Its 'Near Eastern Background.'" In *Rethinking the History of Medicine: "Rationality" and Magic in the Graeco-Roman World and in Ancient Mesopotamia*, edited by H. F. J. Horstmanshoff and M. Stol, 187–218. Leiden: Brill, 2008.

———. *Medicine and Philosophy in Classical Antiquity*. Cambridge: Cambridge University Press, 2005

———. "Between the Hippocratics and the Alexandrians: Medicine, Philosophy and Science in the Fourth Century BCE." In *Philosophy and the Sciences in Antiquity*, edited by R.W. Sharples, 72–109. Aldershot: Ashgate, 2005.

Fichtner, G. *Corpus Hippocraticum. Verzeichnis aller hippokratischen Schriften*. 6th ed. Tübingen: Institut für Geschichte der Medizin, 1996.

Flashar, H. *Melancholie und Melancholiker in den medizinischen Theorien der Antike*. Berlin: De Gruyter, 1966.

Frede, M. "Philosophy and Medicine in Antiquity." In id., *Essays in Ancient philosophy*. Oxford (1987): 225–42.

Grensemann, H. *Die hippokratische Schrift Ueber die heilige Krankheit*. Berlin: De Gruyter, 1968.

Grmek, M. D., ed. *Hippocratica*. Actes du Colloque hippocratique de Paris. Paris, 1980.

Gundert, B. "Soma and Psyche in Hippocratic medicine." In *Psyche and Soma: Physicians and Metaphysicians on the Mind-Body Problem from Antiquity to the Enlightenment*, edited by J. P. Wright and P. Potter, 13–36. Oxford: Oxford University Press, 2000.

Harris, C. R. S. *The Heart and the Vascular System in Ancient Greek Medicine*. Oxford: Oxford University Press, 1973.

Hüffmeier, F. "*Phronesis* in den Schriften des Corpus Hippocraticum." *Hermes* 89 (1961): 51–84.

Joly, J. Platon. "Phèdre et Hippocrate vingt ans après." In Lasserre–Mudry, 407–22.

Joly, R., ed. *Corpus hippocraticum*. Actes du Colloque hippocratique de Mons (22–26 septembre 1975), Mons, 1975.

Jouanna, J. *Hippocrates*. Paris, 1999.

Keus, A. *Über philosophische Begriffe und Theorien in den hippokratischen Schriften*, Diss. Bonn: 1914.

Kudlien, F. "Antike Anatomie und menschlicher Leichnam." *Hermes* 97 (1969): 78–94.

Kühlewein, H. *Hippocratis opera quae feruntur omnia*. 2 Vols. Leipzig: Teubner Verlag, 1894–1902.

Kühn, J. *System- und Methodenprobleme im Corpus hippocraticum*. Wiesbaden: Steiner Verlag, 1956 (Hermes Einzelschriften 11).

Kühn, J.–H., and U. Fleischer. *Index hippocraticus*. 5 vols., Göttingen: Vandenhoeck & Rupprecht, 1986–89.

Langholf, V. *Medical Theories in Hippocrates: Early Texts and the "Epidemics."* Berlin and New York: De Gruyter, 1990.

Lasserre, F., and P. Mudry, eds. *Formes de pensée dans la collection hippocratique*. Actes du IVme Colloque international hippocratique de Lausanne (21–26 Septembre 1981), Geneva, 1983.

Lesky, E. *Die Zeugungs- und Vererbungslehren der Antike und ihr Nachwirken*. Abhandlungen der Geistes- und Sozialwissenschaftlichen Klasse der Akademie der Wissenschaften und der Literatur in Mainz, 1950, vol. 19.

Littré, E. *Œuvres Complètes d'Hippocrate*. 10 Vols. Paris, 1839–61.

Lloyd, G. E. R. "Who is Attacked in On Ancient Medicine?" *Phronesis* 8 (1963): 108–26 [reprinted in Lloyd (1991): 49–69].

———. "The Hippocratic Question." *Classical Quarterly* 25 (1975): 171–92 [reprinted in Lloyd (1991): 194–223].

———. *Magic, Reason and Experience*. Cambridge: Cambridge University Press, 1979.

———. *Methods and Problems in Greek Science*. Cambridge: Cambridge University Press, 1991.

———. "Experiment in Early Greek Philosophy and Medicine." *Proceedings of the Cambridge Philological Society* 190 (1964): 50–72.

———, ed. *Hippocratic Writings*. Harmondsworth: Penguin Classics, 1987.

Longrigg, J. *Greek Rational Medicine*. London: Routledge, 1993.

———. *Greek Medicine from the Heroic to the Hellenistic Age*. London: Duckworth 1998.

Lonie, I. M. *The Hippocratic Treatises On Generation, On the Nature of the Child, Diseases IV*. Berlin: De Gruyter, 1981.

López Férez, J. A., ed. *Tratados hipocráticos*. Actas del VIIe Colloque international hippocratique (Madrid, 24–29 de Septiembre de 1990), Madrid, 1992.

Maloney, G., and R. Savoie. *Cinq cents ans de bibliographie hippocatique, 1473–1982*. Québec, 1982.

Maloney, G., and W. Frohn. *Concordantia in Corpus Hippocraticum*, 6 vols., Hildesheim, Zürich, New York: 1986–89.

Manetti, D. "Valore semantico e risonanze culturali della parola φύσις." *La Parola del Passato* 28 (1973): 426–44.

Mansfeld, J. "Plato and the Method of Hippocrates." *Greek, Roman and Byzantine Studies* 21 (1980): 341–62.

———. "Theoretical and Empirical Attitudes in Early Greek Scientific Medicine." In Grmek (1980): 393–408.

Miller, H. W. "A Medical Theory of Cognition." *Transactions and Proceedings of the American Philological Association* 79 (1948): 168–83.

———. "*Dynamis* and *Physis* in *On Ancient Medicine*." *Transactions and Proceedings of the American Philological Association* 83 (1952): 184–97.

————. "The Concept of *Dynamis* in *De victu*." *Transactions and Proceedings of the American Philological Association* 90 (1959): 147–64.

Plambóck, G. *Dynamis im Corpus hippocraticum*. Wiesbaden, 1964.

Pohlenz, M. "Nomos und Physis." *Hermes* 81 (1953): 418–38.

Potter, P., G. Maloney, and J. Desautels, eds. *La maladie et les maladies dans la Collection hippocratique*. Actes du Vme Colloque international hippocratique de Québec (28 Septembre–3 Octobre 1987). Québec, 1990.

Regenbogen, O. "Eine Forschungsmethode antiker Naturwissenschaft." In *Quellen und Studien zur Geschichte der Mathematik*, B, 1, 130–82, 1929–30. Reprinted in *Kleine Schriften*, 141–94. Munich, 1961.

Rüsche, F. *Blut, Leben, Seele*. Paderborn, 1930.

Schiefsky, M. *Hippocrates: On Ancient Medicine*. Leiden: Brill, 2005.

Schöner, E. *Das Viererschema in der antiken Humoralpathologie*. Sudhoffs Archiv für die Geschichte der Medizin und der Naturwissenschaften, 4, 1964.

Schumacher, J. *Antike Medizin. Die naturphilosophischen Grundlagen der Medizin in der griechischen Antike*. Berlin, 1940.

Senn, G. "Über Herkunft und Stil der Beschreibungen von Experimenten im Corpus Hippocraticum." *Archiv für die Geschichte der Medizin und der Naturwissenschaften* 22 (1929): 217–89.

————. *Die Entwicklung der biologischen Forschungsmethode in der Antike und ihre grundsätzliche Förderung durch Theophrast von Eresos*. Veröffentlichungen der Schweizerischen Gesellschaft für Geschichte der Medizin und der Naturwissenschaft. Leipzig, 1933.

Smith, W. D. *The Hippocratic Tradition*. Baltimore: Johns Hopkins University Press, 1979.

Thivel, A. "Le 'divin' dans la Collection hippocratique." In *La Collection hippocratique et son rôle dans l'histoire de la médecine*, edited by L. Bourgey and J. Jouanna, Actes du Colloque hippocratique de Strasbourg, 57–76. Leiden: Brill, 1975.

Wittern, R., and P. Pellegrin, eds. *Hippokratische Medizin und antike Philosophie*. Verhandlungen des VIII. internationalen Hippokrates-Kolloquiums in Kloster Banz/Staffelstein. Medizin der Antike 1. Hildesheim: Olms, 1996.

Zhmud, L. *Wissenschaft, Philosophie und Religion im frühen Pythagoreismus*. Berlin: Akademie Verlag, 1997.

CHAPTER 15

PRESOCRATIC
COSMOLOGIES

M. R. WRIGHT

I have witnessed a widespread yearning to understand what current research says about the fundamental laws of the universe, how these laws require a monumental restructuring of our conception of the universe, and what challenges lie ahead in the quest for the ultimate theory.

Brian Greene, *The Elegant Universe*

A SUITABLE SUBJECT FOR TREATMENT

The origins of the stimulus to find a "theory of everything" may be traced to the first Presocratics. With extraordinary optimism, they set out to explain "the whole thing," the nature of what there is, the formation and present structure of the universe, and the role and function of its parts.[1] It was thought that the bewildering array of phenomena could be pared down to an explanation in terms of unity and order, that the explanation was accessible to human reason, and that the subject was worthy of the effort required to reach an understanding of it.

This new approach to the world around us, which marks the beginnings of cosmology, started in the Ionian city of Miletus in the early sixth century BCE. There are many explanations suggested for its beginnings there and then: the expansion of trade and the exchange of ideas as well as goods, contact with non-Greek cultures, political movements, and the resulting foundations of city-state democracies, which fostered independent argument, reflection, and decision-making. In the drafting of laws and the writing of constitutions, but also in medicine and other emerging professions, it became important to generalize, to abstract universal principles from individual instances, and to deal with complex problems. This combination of generalization and abstraction, along with natural curiosity, lifted the subject from the mere collection of data that characterized Babylonian astronomy and the practical uses of geometry found in Egypt. Effective verbal expression became crucial, and, with the adaptation of the Phoenician alphabet and the spread of literacy, what was said and thought in the language could be written down, and was available to be studied at leisure, published abroad, and criticized.

The spirit of competition was rife in the Greek world, not only in politics and athletics[2] but also in rival events in music and poetry, and Greek tragedies were produced not so much for the glory of literature as to win prizes, and the first cosmologists were in a similar competitive mood. For the Greeks, to be best was a way of life, and this self-awareness of what they were doing, and the desire to be better at it than anyone else, stimulated their speculation and gave it a sharp edge. "I'm telling you this," said Parmenides' goddess to the young man as she introduced a new (albeit false) cosmology, "so that no one's thinking shall outpace you."[3] Plato reports that Zeno used his puzzles to defend the counter-intuitive argument of Parmenides' *Aletheia*, and to give back to his critics "as good or better than they gave."[4] Most of the other Presocratics, and in particular Anaximenes, Heraclitus, Melissus, Empedocles, Anaxagoras, and Democritus, saw themselves in a competitive tradition, knowledgeable about previous work in "physics" (which, in its original sense of the study of nature, was concerned in particular with cosmology)[5] and ready to defend or criticize, develop, modify, or reject their predecessors' achievements.

The Milesians were the first to be concerned with the basic nature and structure of the world around them, as they attempted to simplify the range of perceived phenomena. Because of the singularity of the subject and the paucity of observational evidence, theory and counter-theory advanced initially through assumptions of homogeneity, balance, and order, expressed by the imaginative use of analogies, models, and metaphors. These first philosophers set out to go beyond observational evidence in their search for unity in plurality, order in difference, and permanence through change. Free of later Socratic constraints to be relevant to human living, the early Presocratics realized that there were laws controlling the natural world, and that these were discoverable, so that the whole cosmic structure became the subject of research (*historia*) and rational analysis. To explain meteorological phenomena within this structure, they progressed from myths that provided answers that were external and unpredictable (a lightning flash due to the anger of Zeus, the rainbow as a messenger from Olympus) to explanations that were internal, self-consistent, intelligible in natural terms, and predictable. They recognized, moreover, that all such explanations require arguments and evidence to support the conclusions reached, both in criticizing the old and furthering the new. And, by means of a methodology that provided a framework for both rational and imaginative solutions, advances were made as a cumulative process, resulting from stimulus and provocation. As Xenophanes said: "in time by searching we find a better answer."[6]

In the exposition of competitive cosmologies, there are three questions still unresolved: we do not know the form of most of the matter in the universe; we do not know how the universe began; and we do not know for sure whether the universe is finite or infinite.[7] Presocratic solutions to these problems, still perplexing to our contemporaries, will be tackled here under the headings "Cosmic Matter" (section 1) and "Cosmic Beginnings and Limits" (section 2), with the addition of a note on what is called the anthropic principle, which addresses the place of human life and human observation in the whole.

1. COSMIC MATTER

The first cosmological problem, therefore, is to define what there is in its most basic form—what *is* the ultimate material? Such a principle unifying the variety of phenomena became known as the *archê*,[8] covering what has always been in the past and continues to exist in a fundamental form. Leaving aside Thales, who appears to have given primacy to water as essential to life, a main constituent in the structure of things, and providing support for the earth, we find Anaximander offering a solution:

> Anaximander said that the limitless [*to apeiron*] is both *archê* and *stoicheion*[9] of what there is, being the first to use the word *archê*. And he says that it is neither water nor any other of the so-called elements, but some other unlimited nature [*physis*], from which come to be all the heavens and the *kosmoi* in them.[10]

Aristotle provides the supportive argument (which may well be original to Anaximander), with the implied criticism of other views, that if one of the opposites were the *archê* and limitless, then it eventually would destroy the rest, so it must be separate from them. What Anaximander has done is to make up a neuter noun, "the limitless thing," from the adjective *apeiros* and apply it to his fundamental principle. This would show that it had no fixed spatial limit, and, being separate from any entity with definite characteristics, was suitable to be the origin of everything. Lack of limit also applied temporally, so that it was eternal, being immortal and indestructible,[11] but also without beginning; Aristotle reports the argument: "There is no beginning to the limitless, for then there would be a limit to it."[12] For the first time, there is an understanding that eternity works both ways: logically either there should be a beginning and end (which characterizes the mortal) or neither. Yet, whereas the *apeiron* ever exists, it is the source of a kind of seed (*gonimon*) from which opposite qualities viewed as things emerge and so form a cosmos: the cold compresses to form the earth, the hot surrounds it as fire, and then this breaks up into circles to form sun, moon, and stars.

Anaximander's successors Anaximenes and Heraclitus returned to the concept of a characterized substance for their basic principle, *aêr* for Anaximenes and "ever-living fire" for Heraclitus. *Aêr* followed Anaximander's *apeiron* in being fundamental, all-pervading, and without beginning or end, but Anaximenes could argue against his predecessor's need for a neutral origin by claiming the obvious preponderance of air and the necessity of air as breath of life. His solution was simpler, in that the one substance could produce observed variations in temperature and density as the result of *quantitative* change. The report is from Theophrastus:

> Anaximenes, a colleague of Anaximander, says that there is one underlying natural principle, and he calls it *apeiron* like him, but not indefinite as he did, but defined, naming it air. It varies in thinness and thickness according to a variety of substances, becoming fire when it is thinner, and wind when thicker, then cloud, and water when further condensed, then earth, then stones, and everything else from these.[13]

An additional note explains that the air is in continual motion, and the changes occur as a result of this movement. And, just as Anaximander had *apeiron* extending beyond the structured world, so for Anaximenes "breath and air surround the whole *kosmos*."[14]

Heraclitus of Ephesus was very much aware of his predecessors in the tradition of tackling problems in the natural world, and criticized many of them, but not the Milesians, his neighbors further down the coast. He was on the same track as they were in aiming to explain the world in terms of one principle underlying its diversity, itself without beginning or end but responsible in some way for all else that is generated and destroyed. And, like that of Anaximenes, this principle would need to be in constant movement (for everything is constantly changing), and to be active at both the macroscopic and microscopic levels. Just as the air we breathe was for Anaximenes a principle within the individual as *psychê* and also that which surrounds the whole, so Heraclitus related the substance of the *kosmos* to that of the individual *psychê*, but as ever-living and all-controlling fire:

> This *kosmos*, the same for all, no one of men or gods has made, but it ever was and is and will be ever-living fire, kindling in measures and being quenched in measures.[15]

Fire keeps a local identity, but in itself can never be still, since its preservation depends on the continual intake and transformation of fuel. It is both the paradigmatic example and the complete instantiation of the perpetual mobility that was summarized in the tag *panta rhei*, "everything is in a state of flux."[16] So fire, in the cosmos and the *psychê*, "turns," taking its place in the cycle of the changes of the world masses, from fire to water to earth and back through water to fire. Three fragments are relevant: "the turnings of fire: first sea and from sea half earth, half *prêstêr*" (B31); "it is death to souls to become water, and death to water to become earth, and from earth comes water, and from water soul" (B36); and "all things are an exchange for fire and fire for all things, as goods for gold and gold for goods" (B90).[17] Water is the first exchange and then earth, the antithesis of fire, but earth in turn dissolves into water, and water rises to feed fire and be absorbed in it. On the cosmic scale, the sun plays a crucial part as a primary concentration of fire, controlling the lengths of the days and the seasons, and the distances of the solstices. The proportion or *logos* according to which all these amounts are measured and balanced at different times and places maintains the equilibrium of the cosmos, and the continual movement of the parts ensures the permanence of the whole: "changing it rests" (B84a).

Aristotle reports that Xenophanes used to look up at the night sky and "one-ify," making up a word for "finding a theory of everything."[18] But the search by early Presocratics for a single entity (such as water, air, fire, or *apeiron*) to explain diversity and change received a blow from Parmenides' *Aletheia* from which it never recovered. Merely giving an explanation of the possible composition of things was not enough—a justification of plurality and change was needed to meet the "hard-hitting challenge" of the Eleatics. Yet in Parmenides' own *Doxa*, the "Way of Opinion" (provocatively labeled deceptive and untrue), lay the origin of an explanation that was to dominate future science—the concept of an element. In this part of his poem he reduced everything to two principles, light (also called fire) and night, and proposed two rather than one as the minimum required for interaction. They are described as follows:

> on the one hand aithereal flame of fire, gentle, tenuous, *the same as itself in every direction and not the same as the other, but the other is on its own as its opposite—* dark night, thick in form and heavy.[19]

Struggling with the limitations of the language available as he set out the ground rules for a theory of elements, Parmenides adds:

> since all things have been named light and night and their powers assigned to each, the whole is full of light and unclear night, *both equal, since nothing is without either*.[20]

If this basic pair were taken as permanent and unchanging entities, with inherent and separate characteristics, together comprising all that there is, and if each phenomenon consisted only of a mixture of the two, then there might be a way, mistaken but plausible, of accounting for plurality and change throughout the cosmos. The proportions of the two in any particular compound would give that compound its particular character, and a preponderance of one or the other would be particularly noticeable, for example in the sun and moon on the cosmic scale, and the composition of *nous* for humans.

Empedocles of Acragas, in nearby Sicily, reacted to Parmenides on two fronts. He accepted the conclusions from the *Aletheia* that there could be no absolute generation or destruction, since these would introduce the banned Is-not before and after, nor could Is-not be allowed to exist spatially as *kenon*, "the empty," to produce gaps in the continuity and homogeneity of being.[21] Furthermore. there could be no additions or subtractions from the sum of things—"birth" and "death" are merely names mistakenly used in human speech for the mixing and separating of eternal, unchanging substances.[22] Despite appearances, everything is reducible to a proportionate mixture of basic ingredients:

> These are the only real things, but, as they run through each other, they become different objects at different times, yet are throughout forever the same.[23]

As Empedocles thought through the implications of a theory of elements, he realized that two were insufficient and four was the economical minimum, the first square number, allowing for complex mutual activity and reaction within a structure of balance and equilibrium. And so he proclaimed:

> Hear first the four roots of all things: bright Zeus, life-bringing Hera, Aidoneus, and Nestis, whose tears are the source of mortal streams.[24]

The "roots" are listed as divinities, two male and two female, two from Olympus (Zeus and Hera) and two of the earth (Aidoneus and Nestis), the divinities recast as the four elements—permanent, unchanging, equally powerful, and corresponding to the four natural masses of earth below, water at its edge, the sky above, and (obvious to a Sicilian) fire from the bright sun and volcanic rocks. As he says:

> All these—sun and earth and sky and sea—are one with the parts of themselves that have been separated off and born in mortal things.[25]

Constructions ranging from the smallest organisms to the vast cosmic masses are all to be explained in terms of just four basic, unchanging, corporeal entities, forming temporary arrangements (or "births") as their parts come together in compounds, and separations (or "deaths") as the compounds disintegrate into their different elements, which are again recycled.[26] To give an explanation or *cause* for the mixings and dissolutions (and after Parmenides' arguments against change, such an explanation was now *de rigueur*), Empedocles posited opposed principles of attraction and repulsion (which he called *Philia*, "Love," and *Neikos*, "Strife") according to which the elements come together or separate. The tensions of such attraction and repulsion, allied to the most powerful of human drives, are found at various levels: in the repeated movements and arrangements of elemental masses within the cosmos, in the genesis and destruction of successive generations of mortal life, and, for individuals, in their friendships and enmities.

Where previous Presocratics had attempted to pare down plurality and diversity and attribute them to the manifestation of one, two, or four basic substances, Anaxagoras embraced them all. Maximum plurality and diversity are there in his first blunt statement: "all things were together."[27] This would seem to mean that there was a complete and uniform fusion of all the components of the cosmos. His enigmatic denials of an ultimate small or large show in effect the irrelevance of size to the complexity of the material, for any part of the original homogeneity, whatever the size and however small, contains "all things":

> Since there are equal shares in quantity of the large and small, so too there would be everything in everything; for these are not separate but everything has a portion of everything . . . for how could hair come from what is not hair or flesh from what is not flesh? (B6, B10)

Scorning a theory of elements or variations on a basic substance to explain the vast variety of phenomena, Anaxagoras claimed that *everything* is in everything and was there all together at the beginning, a claim that is remarkably similar to modern theories of the cosmos being contained in miniature in the microdot, followed by a separating out in a continually expanding universe.[28] As with other Presocratics, Anaxagoras agreed that the common parlance of birth and death is incorrect,[29] and should be replaced by terms involving "mixing" and "separating," meaning not a repositioning of parts of a limited number of elements but the emergence and dissolution of new arrangements of a preponderance of ingredients that had always been present. All the other ingredients are still there but imperceptible, and any are likely to become accessible to the senses when a different grouping brings different ingredients to the fore. In some unexplained way, the only unmixed substance, *Nous* ("mind"), "knows" and has power over everything; it caused the initial rotation, controls the consequent separatings, and arranges the order of the whole; but there are no details and no *moral* aspect to its activity was given.[30]

Although roughly contemporary with Socrates and the sophists, the atomists are included among the Presocratics because they produced a physical theory that brought to a logical conclusion the investigation of the material and structure of the cosmos that began with the Milesians. Direct evidence for the Presocratic atomists is scanty, and Epicurus, who took over the atomic theory with some modifications, gives no credit for his borrowings. From the doxography, it seems that Leucippus initiated the theory, using a rather exotic vocabulary, and further details and supporting arguments were provided by Democritus, but the two are usually taken together. Like Empedocles and Anaxagoras, they followed Parmenides' *Aletheia* in denying absolute generation and destruction but posited a limitless plurality as the only way of explaining phenomena. For Leucippus and Democritus, what there is consists of *atoma*, unlimited numbers of uncuttable units that are solid and immutable, without parts, and of different shapes and sizes, but all too minute to be visible to the eye.[31] What we do see are atomic compounds, and for these to be able to move, and so account for perceptible change, scope for movement is required. Here what is not—denied by Parmenides and identified in its spatial aspect as *kenon*, "the empty," by Empedocles—was given a paradoxical existence: for the atomists no-thing (*to mêden*) is as real as thing (*to den*). Such a breakdown of spatial boundaries resulted in the assumption of limitless material in the form of an infinite number of atoms moving at random through a limitless expanse of space, the final answer to Presocratic theories of matter and elements.

The movement of atoms through space was according to their nature, and here Leucippus and Democritus went back to their Ionian roots, requiring no further explanation (such as Love and Strife in Empedocles and Nous in Anaxagoras) as the cause of motion. Zeno had supported Parmenides with his various paradoxes, showing how the assumption of movement and plurality, contrary to Eleatic argument, resulted in conclusions even more bizarre than those of Parmenides seemed to be.[32] If such simple questions are asked of the pluralists as (1) how many are the many? (2) how big are they? (3) do they move? then the respondent will find that his many turn out to be (1) none at all and an unlimited number, (2) of no size at all and infinitely big, and (3) both moving and at rest. To counter the first and second dilemmas, Anaxagoras came down firmly on one side, that matter is infinitely divisible, and the atomists just as firmly on the other side, that there are absolute minima. All the pluralists followed Parmenides and the earlier Presocratics in agreeing that what there is is for ever, with no time, in past or future, when the basic material of the cosmos is not in existence, but, *pace* Zeno, there has to be movement to explain the known world.

2. COSMIC BEGINNINGS AND LIMITS

The search for an explanation of matter and movement leads to the further questions that initiated the study of cosmology: how did the universe begin? and the related problem: does this world, this cosmic order inhabited by us humans, have a limit, even if the material of which it is made does not?

To start at the end with the atomists: if they suppose that there is an infinite amount of material and an infinite extent of space, then it is likely that there will be innumerable worlds at any one time, and an infinity of worlds through eternity.[33] And this was indeed the claim, as reported by Diogenes Laertius:[34] "Leucippus says that the whole is infinite... and infinite worlds [*kosmoi*] arise and disintegrate again into [the full and the empty]." Through the void some *kosmoi* are increasing in size, others are at their peak, and others disintegrating. Some have human, animal, and plant life, and some, where there is no water, are barren,[35] but the formation of the world-structures is basically similar, as Diogenes continues:

> The *kosmoi* have their genesis as follows: many bodies of all sorts of shapes are "cut off" from the infinite and move into a great emptiness. There they come together and produce a whirling [*dinē*], in which they collide with one another and revolve in different ways and begin to separate out, like to like. But when there are so many that they can no longer rotate in equilibrium, those that are fine [*lepta*] go to the surrounding void as if "sifted," while the rest stay together and become entangled so that they move together and form a spherical structure. This is like having a "membrane" that contains all sorts of bodies, and, as they whirl around, the surrounding membrane becomes thin because of the resistance of the center as

contiguous atoms keep flowing round together in the whirl. So the earth is formed when the atoms that had been brought to the middle stay together there, while the surrounding membrane expands as it attracts bodies from outside, drawing in whatever it touches as it swirls around. Some that get entangled form a structure that is at first moist and muddy, but, as they revolve with the whirling of the whole, they dry out and ignite to form the substance of the heavenly bodies.[36]

This extraordinary account marks the culmination of Presocratic cosmogony. It has a modern ring, with the concepts of "whirls" starting up randomly in space and attracting more and more matter, of initial density and a cooling from great heat, and of cosmic clumps being transformed into galaxies.[37]

Atomic cosmogony had its roots in early Milesian reasoning, and especially in the breakthrough of Anaximander. The earlier *Chaos* of Hesiod's *Theogony*, the "gap" that came into existence before anything else, was subjected to scrutiny, and recast by Anaximander into *to apeiron*, neutral and limitless, from which a "seed" of hot and cold emerged.[38] *Apeiron*, by definition, had no temporal or spatial limit, but this particular *kosmos* had a beginning within it. The hot part formed a flame that broke off into the circles[39] of sun, moon, and stars, and the cold concentrated into the earth within, with *aêr* between the two. This set the pattern for future cosmogonies, in which the dense and cold formed earth, the less dense and cold formed moisture and mist, and the fine and hot the surrounding *ouranos*, containing the heavenly bodies. And Anaximander also had an answer to the question "Why does the earth not fall down?" It is because it is at equal distance from the extremities, and, if there is no reason for it to move in one direction rather than another, it will stay immobile at the center.[40] He further supposed that the shape of the earth was cylindrical, like the section of a column, with a world-structure comparable to ours in the antipodes.[41] The depth of the earth was given as a third of its diameter, equal in size to the sun; the sun ring, however, was 27 times the circumference of the earth, the moon ring 18 times, and the ring of the stars 9 times. So Anaximander supposed first that our world-structure grew like an organism from a seed, but, when established, followed mathematical laws connected with the powers of 3.

This combination of a biological model—of a cosmos living and breathing ("the whole heaven analogous to an animal") within the constraints of a mathematical structure—later characterized Pythagorean cosmology. According to Philolaus, earth was one of the body's "limbs," no longer at the key position in the middle but encircling the hearth of the central fire there, and requiring a dark "counter-earth" both to explain eclipses and also to bring the number of heavenly bodies to the mystical number of 10.[42] Anaximenes, between Anaximander and Pythagoras, identified the universal principle with air, breath in eternal motion, so that his cosmos was a living, breathing organism, directly analogous to a human being, but his cosmogony brings in a new process, that of quantitative chemical change. Air is neutral and invisible, but if thinned it takes on the aspect of fire, and if condensed becomes visible as moisture, then as degrees of solid bodies.[43] In Anaximenes' cosmogony, the earth appears first, from a condensation of air (which makes the mass colder and denser); its shape reverts to being quite flat, closely covering the air beneath it "like a lid." Moon, sun, and stars (now in the right order) are also flat, and emerge through the exhalations that rise from the earth, which become hotter and fiery as they thin out. The stars then are fixed to the crystalline sky vault; the planets float like leaves below; and the sun encircles the flat earth by going not under but around it, like a cap twisting on the head, and causing darkness on the earth when it moves behind the high mountains in the north.[44] This basic theory further allowed Anaximenes to explain a range of meteorological phenomena, such as clouds, wind, rain, hail, snow, thunder, and lightning, by the movement of air and its changes in density and temperature. In the doxography, the rainbow's appearance is attributed to the reflection of sunbeams, and we have Xenophanes' own words for the thrust of this type of explanation:

> The one they call Iris, this too is a cloud by nature, seen as purple, red, and yellow.[45]

Homer's golden-winged goddess, bringer of signs, portents, and messages from immortals to mortals, is now accounted for in naturalistic terms; the tone, rather than being sarcastic or deflationary, expresses pride in the proclamation of the new physics.

So far in the first explorations for a beginning for the cosmos we have had one ever-existing fundamental principle (*archê*) and an explanation, handed down in the doxographical tradition, of the formation or emergence of this particular inhabited world order, with observable plurality, and change deriving from the *archê*. With Heraclitus and Empedocles, we move into more complex thought, grounded in the Ionians, but with evidence, argument, and aetiology elaborated in their own extant words. When the Eleatic guest in Plato's *Sophist* gives a generalized and somewhat ironic account of Presocratic thinking, he contrasts these two in the guise of Ionian and Sicilian Muses.[46] They claim that there is both many and one, the stricter Ionic (i.e., Heraclitean) that they exist simultaneously, and the more relaxed Sicilian (i.e., Empedoclean) that one and many alternate. It has been shown that for Heraclitus the basic principle is ever-living fire, and for Empedocles the four roots of earth, air, fire, and water. How could Plato's comment be interpreted in the light of their respective cosmologies?

In the case of Heraclitus, Plato may well be thinking of sayings that have two opposites copresent, as in B10—"taken together wholes and not wholes, coming together and moving apart, singing together and separately, from all things one, and one from all things"—or B88: "the same in one, living and dead, waking and sleeping, young and old." There are also the well-known quotations that have two opposites united in the one god, as B67—"God: day night, winter summer, war peace, satiety hunger"—and B102: "to god all things are good and just, but men suppose some unjust, others just." More generally, there are B51, "What is different agrees with itself"; B54, "Unseen harmonia is stronger than seen"; and B50, "listening not to me but to the *logos* it is wise to agree that all things are one."[47]

Specifically, in cosmology, Heraclitus posited one and many simultaneously, in that ever-living fire, the physical instantiation of the "one wise," steers all things, but also takes on the different forms as it goes through the unending processes of "igniting in measures and being quenched in measures." In these turnings, fire is transformed into sea and "poured again in the same ratio" to become earth, and from earth it returns to sea, and the exhalations arising from the sea ignite again as fire and serve as its fuel. The one principle, in some parts of the cosmos, becomes other world masses as they, in other parts, are returning to fire. Fire is part of the exchange and yet governs the amount of the exchange as coinage is involved in trade, and also sets the standard for the value of goods traded.[48]

Plato's contrast between simultaneous unity and plurality in Heraclitus and successive states in Empedocles also tells against the supposition that the Stoic doctrine of *ekpurôsis* (a periodic cosmic burn-up) should be read back into Heraclitus. And the fragments cited make it clear that fire is part of an ongoing exchange—the gold does not buy up all the goods and bring the present world to a close. The cosmic turnings are according to measure and proportion and follow natural laws: "cold things warm up, the warm cools down, the moist dries and the parched gets moist."[49] Everything is in a state of flux,[50] and fire is a stage in the universal flowing, but also, like the river, a paradigm of the process, with new material constantly being taken in and then given off. For everything to become fire would contravene Heraclitus's fundamental principles and Plato's interpretation of them, and there is an explicit rejection of such a concept in B94: "Sun will not overstep its measures, otherwise Erinyes, executors of Justice, will find out." As the sun may not go beyond its limits but turns at the tropics to maintain the regularity of the seasons, so cosmic fire is restrained, like opposites in Anaximander, by cosmic law.[51]

So for Heraclitus there was no cosmogony; ever-living fire was, is, and will be, and the processes of its transformations have neither beginning nor end. The fragments contain little in the way of meteorology or astronomy, apart from B3 "[the size of the sun]: width of a man's foot" and B6: "the sun is new every day." These are provocative statements, perhaps connected with the unreliability of sense-perception, perhaps to be understood in the context of a complicated account of the heavenly bodies as bowls of fire ignited daily,[52] but they could well indicate a rejection of the careful, detailed Milesian cosmogony. Such an attitude is supported by the dismissive tone of B124: "the fairest *kosmos* is like a pile of sweepings."[53]

In the passage quoted earlier from the *Sophist*, Plato contrasts the simultaneous one and many of Heraclitus with the "more relaxed" assumption of their succession in Empedocles, where in turn the whole is one under Aphrodite and then many through Strife. Empedocles' original words are found in B17.7–13:

> And these things[54] never cease their continual exchange of position, at one time all coming together through Love, and at another again being borne away by Strife's repulsion. So, insofar as one is accustomed to arise from many and many are produced from one as it is again being divided, to this extent they are born and have no abiding life; but, insofar as they never cease their continual exchange, so far they are forever unaltered in the cycle.[55]

This alternation of one and many is to be regarded as a process on both cosmic and human scales. Empedocles appears to have started his exposition with an account of the many, namely earth, air, fire, and water, as eternal, unchanging entities.[56] These are brought together by the spirit of attraction, named Philia or Aphrodite, until their minute particles are so mingled that it is impossible to pick out any distinguishing characteristic. The whole cosmos then "is held fast in the close covering of harmony, a rounded sphere, rejoicing in encircling stillness" (B27). The natural movement of elements, however, is toward their like,[57] and, when the unity of the sphere is broken by the entry of Strife, this tendency reasserts itself. The present state is thought of as a battlefield between the forces of attraction and repulsion, and, in this turmoil, first the world masses of earth, sea, air, and fire begin to separate, and then individual compounds take on the different forms of mortal life. Eventually the many will dominate, until Love again begins to take control. In the mirror world of many-to-one, it seems a place was found for unattached limbs and various monstrous formations, but the present generation arose in the one-to-many stage from "whole-nature forms" as like tended to like. When these whole-nature forms became fully articulated, they took on the shapes of men and women and were able to reproduce themselves, but this generation, too, will pass away in the inevitable advance of Strife. Whether there would ever be either a stage of complete separation of elements, with earth surrounded in order by water, air, and fire, or a temporary vibration of the four masses as they turn is uncertain, and there is continuing controversy over the details. But on the reading of the fragments themselves and the evidence of Plato and Aristotle, it is clear that the pattern of balance and antithesis of the many-to-one and the one-to-many is continuous and self-repeating, fixed according to a broad oath that ensures the invariance of the stages of transition.[58]

In the one-to-many stage, the structure of the present world takes shape, and Empedocles gives notice of the details of a complete cosmogony (B38):

> Come now, I shall tell you from what sources, in the beginning, the sun and all those others which we now see became distinct—earth and swelling sea, moist air and Titan sky, whose circle binds all things fast.

In the first activity, under the principle of repulsion, when the parts of the elements began to separate out away from the center, fire moved "swiftly upward" along with air. The sea was then sweated out from the earth, and air continued to move haphazardly until the masses increased their bulk by further separation, and it settled as a misty layer above the level of earth and sea and below the fire at the circumference. Even so, this structure is only part of the whole, for beyond it lies "inactive matter,"[59] and the separation is not complete; for example many fires still burn beneath the earth's surface, shown particularly in the volcanoes of Sicily and south Italy.[60] The sun is explained as a kind of lens that draws the fire from the upper sky to its top surface and then through the lower surface transmits heat and light during the day to the earth below. It is now recognized that the earth is spherical, the sun and moon travel around it, the moon gets its light from the sun, and the true cause of solar and lunar eclipses is understood.[61]

Empedocles' scheme did not rule out variations in human life in the recurring cycles,[62] and indeed there are strong suggestions that a change of attitude, of following love rather than hate, is up to the individual, who can so secure a better life now and hold back for a time the forces of evil. The Pythagoreans first made explicit the implied assumptions in cyclic time to give a theory, adopted later by the Stoics, of the exact recurrence of events. So, according to Porphyry, Pythagoras says that "events recur periodically, and that nothing is absolutely new." The theory provided an opportunity for black humor in the lecture hall:

> If you believe what the Pythagoreans say, everything comes back in the same numerical order, and I shall deliver this lecture again to you with the pointer in my hand as you sit there in the same way as now, and everything will be the same.[63]

In positing one or more principles existing without beginning or end, all the Presocratics could agree with the answer to the questions put by Parmenides' goddess:

> What creation will you seek for [what is]? How did it grow? and from what source? I will not allow you to say or to think "from what is not," for it is not possible to say or to think what is not.[64]

But the problem comes with the next question: "if it did come from nothing, what compulsion was there for it to arise later rather than earlier?" Where Anaximander had applied the "principle of sufficient reason" spatially to show that the earth stays where it is if there is no cause for it to move in one direction rather than another, here Parmenides has a temporal application: if there were no cause for there to be generation at one time rather than another, then it would never happen.[65] The question was not faced by those before Parmenides, and the atomists, after him, were happy to accept that the swirlings and subsequent world-structures were just chance happenings that would arise naturally from the movements and collisions of atoms in void, and there was no further cause or need for one. Empedocles, as has been shown, assigned to principles of attraction and repulsion the stimuli for the formation of alternating *kosmoi*;[66] Anaxagoras attributed his cosmogony to universal Mind.

The Mind (*Nous*) of Anaxagoras is not divine or moral or teleological,[67] but it does have knowledge and power, and ensures an ordered *kosmos*. In some way it is aware of everything and has control over it, and this control was shown most obviously when it caused an initial rotation:[68]

> All that has life, whether larger or smaller, Mind controls, and Mind controlled the rotation of the whole, so as to make it rotate from the beginning. First it began the rotation from a small area, but now rotates over a wider area *and will continue to rotate ever more widely.*

There is here an expanding universe with no limit imposed either in the time available or in the area covered. "All things were together" at the beginning, and then at some indefinite moment and for no given reason, the omniscient and omnipotent Mind caused a vortex to start in the cosmic mixture, and this began a separating out of traditional opposites:[69]

> All that was going to be, all that was but is no longer, and all that is now and will be Mind arranged in order, and this rotation too, in which now rotate the stars and sun and moon and air and aether, as they are being separated off. And it was the rotation that caused the separation. The dense was being separated from the rare, and the hot from the cold, the bright from the dark and the dry from the wet.

After the initial separating out, the force of the vortex (and it is tempting to see this as a gravitational pull) compacted the dense, the wet, the cold, and the dark together and formed clouds, water, earth, and rocks, whereas the (mainly) rare, hot, and dry moved out toward the aether. But Anaxagoras also recognized that the vortex would have a counter-tendency to swing some heavy bodies outward, so that he was ready to say that sun, moon, and stars are red-hot stones hurled from the center and are now carried around in the revolutions of the outer aether. This denial of the divinity of the heavenly bodies was made the basis for the charge of impiety and resulted in his exile from Athens.

We are now in a position to summarize Presocratic answers to the related problem posed by modern cosmologists: in addition to ignorance on the form of most of the matter in the universe and problems with its beginning, we do not know for sure whether the universe is finite or infinite. In temporal terms, Anaximander's *apeiron* and Anaximenes' air had neither beginning nor end, but from these origins the present world was generated and will continue indefinitely. Heraclitus was more explicit: ever-living fire has no birth and is indestructible, but the endless series of its turnings produce the masses and details of the known world, and with this theory comes the first expression of the concept of a self-generating and self-regulating universe. Empedocles' elements are eternal—in Eleatic language, what beginning or end could there be?—but the forces of attraction and repulsion working on them cause a series of generations and destructions of a mortal world in ever-recurring cycles. For Anaxagoras, "everything in everything" is, was, and will be ever true, but from the initial microdot and subsequent rotation the present cosmos had its beginning and will continue indefinitely. Leucippus and Democritus allowed neither beginning nor end for their atoms and void. These have always existed, and, given the solidity of atoms and the intangibility of void, there is no way they could be destroyed, although individual world-structures, composed of them, have their life span of birth, maturity, increasing weakness, and eventual disintegration.

In all cosmologies, matter, time, and space are interconnected, so what about spatial infinity? Anaxamander's *apeiron* by definition has no external edges, and Anaximander took over this characteristic for air; for these Milesians and for Heraclitus, there is a limited world-structure set in a limitless *archê*. The atomists on the other hand show how, given no restrictions on matter or void, innumerable world-structures in the infinity of space are likely. Anaxagoras took up a mid-position, in that "everything in everything" appears to have been an initially enclosed microsystem, but, as matter separated out from it, there would be an ever-continuing, indefinite expansion; he was the only known ancient philosopher to anticipate an inflationary universe. Parmenides' false cosmos described in the *Doxa* broke with the principles set out in the *Aletheia* to produce the model of an enclosed sphere that contains and maintains a complex structure of fiery rings to explain astronomical phenomena and movements. What is interesting here is that the laws of the physical structure, based on the twin elements of fire and night, are bound by the same necessity that guaranteed the validity of the earlier metaphysical arguments:

> You shall know also of the surrounding *ouranos*,
> from where it grew and how necessity led and bound it
> to hold the limits of the stars. (B9)

The Pythagoreans before and after Parmenides again had an enclosed cosmos, with the planets in order, emitting the harmony of the spheres, and some, the most important being Philolaus, replacing the geocentric system with a central fire.[70] The evidence is obscure, but it would seem that in one Pythagorean version, the cosmos would be generated from the imposition of limit on unlimited, with the result that "unlimited" extends beyond the boundaries of the cosmos, and this is reinforced by the assumption that the cosmos is a living organism and rhythmically "inhales" the external, limitless space.[71] Empedocles seems to have been in line with this general Presocratic tendency of setting an enclosed cosmos within indefinite outer space, but the only direct evidence is an enigmatic line from Aëtius: "Empedocles posits one cosmos; the cosmos however is not the whole [*to pan*] but a small part of the whole, and the rest is inert matter [ἀργὴ ὕλη]."[72]

3. THE ANTHROPIC PRINCIPLE

Finally, it is pertinent to report briefly early views on the "anthropic principle"— that is, the connection between life, especially human life, and the cosmos, and the role of human intelligences as (possibly) unique observers of it.[73] For most of the Presocratics, humans were considered an integral part of the cosmology, occupying a central position as creatures of the central earth, but also, as detached observers, having the mental resources to study the whole, and their own place within it. In addition, humans were linked to the cosmos in the material of which both were composed. The analogy is first drawn by Anaximenes in the one surviving fragment:

> As our *psychê*, which is air, maintains us, so breath and air surround the whole cosmos.

The air we breathe, invisible but essential for life, is easily accepted as the source of that life, and, if the cosmos is a living organism, then air will have a similar role as a vital principle, but also surrounding and maintaining the whole. Similarly for Heraclitus, ever-living fire maintains and controls the cosmos and is part of it, and in the individual in the same turnings it provides the material for life and *logos*. In Parmenides' *Doxa*, light and night make up all that there is, and the level of human reasoning depends on which of the two preponderates. Anaxagoras adopted the concept more explicitly, having Nous as all-controlling principle, which is also present in humans as rational mind. Empedocles identified the four elements as cosmic masses and showed that they constitute the physical bodies that inhabit them (B22.1–3):

> for all these—sun and earth and sky and sea—are one with the parts of themselves that have been separated and born in mortal things.

Conversely, the most powerful stimuli in human activity, love and hate, were projected on to the universe as motive forces of attraction and repulsion.[74] Plants, fish, birds, animals, humans, and "long-lived gods" all had the same origins, were subject to the same forces, and went through the same life-cycle of generation, maturity, and disintegration as the cosmos itself. The concept of limitless matter and void allowed the atomists to posit innumerable *kosmoi* scattered randomly through space at different stages of their life-cycles, while individual humans were viewed as similar random grouping of atoms making up a working whole on a smaller scale; Democritus therefore coined the term for a human as a *microcosm*.[75]

It is not overzealous to see the Presocratic attitude to the cosmos and man's place in it continuing into present-day thinking:

> Just why *homo sapiens* should carry the spark of rationality that provides the key to the universe is a deep enigma. We, who are children of the universe—animated stardust—can nevertheless reflect on the nature of that same universe, even to the extent of glimpsing the rules on which it runs. How we have become linked into this cosmic dimension is a mystery. Yet the linkage cannot be denied.[76]

NOTES

1. For the references for *panta* ("all things"), *to pan* ("the all"), *to holon* ("the whole thing") as the subject of study of the first Presocratics see Hussey, "Ionian Inquiries," 430–31. "Universe" is derived from Latin, the neuter of *universus* "turned into one," "all taken together," used as a noun; the Greeks spoke of *kosmos*, meaning order or "whole ordered structure"; adding *logos* gives the word "cosmology," with the sense of "a reasoned account of the total arrangement and structure of things"; see Wright, *Cosmology in Antiquity*, 3–4.

2. Pan-Hellenic competitive games were an annual event on a rota of Isthmian, Nemean, Pythian, and Olympic.

3. B. 8.60-61: τόν σοι ἐγὼ διάκοσμον ἐοικότα πάντα φατίζω, / ὡς οὐ μή ποτέ τίς σε βροτῶν γνώμη παρελάσσῃ.

4. *Prm.* 128d: ἀντιλέγει δὴ οὖν τοῦτο τὸ γράμμα πρὸς τοὺς τὰ πολλὰ λέγοντας, καὶ ἀνταποδίδωσι ταὐτὰ καὶ πλείω.

5. See note 1 here. *Peri phuseôs (On Nature)*, even if not original to the Presocratics, was the title by which their work was generally known, and Aristotle called them *hoi phusikoi* or *phusiologoi* (physicists); see Plato's gloss on Presocratic aims in their *peri phuseôs historia* at *Phd.* 96a: "to understand the causes of each thing, why it has a beginning and an end, and why it exists."

6. B18: χρόνῳ ζητοῦντες ἐφευρίσκουσιν ἄμεινον. See Hawking, *Black Holes and Baby Universes*, ix: "I have written in the belief that the universe is governed by an order that we can perceive partially now, and that we may understand fully in the not-too-distant future."

7. From the epilogue to Coles, *Cosmology*, 129.

8. *Archê* (from *archô*, "I begin, I rule") was Aristotle's term, but may well go back to Anaximander. Its dual sense is as with the English "first," first in time and first in importance.

9. *Stoicheion*, the Aristotelian word for element, was also used for letters of the alphabet forming syllables.

10. A9, Simp. *in Ph.* 24.13–16.

11. B3: ἀθάνατον καὶ ἀνώλεθρον. οἱ ἀθάνατοι, lit. "the deathless," was the usual Homeric word for the gods, who were born, but then lived for ever.

12. A15 from *Ph.* 203b6.

13. A5 from Simp. *in Ph.* 24.26, quoting Theophrastus, and see A7, from Hippol. 7.3: "When air is uniform it is invisible . . . but when its consistency is thinner it becomes fire, but wind is air condensing, and cloud comes from air that is 'felted.' When packed further, water results, then earth, and, at its most condensed, stones." When thinner, air is warmer; when more condensed, colder.

14. ὅλον τὸν κόσμον πνεῦμα καὶ ἀὴρ περιέχει from B2, probably Anaximenes' only extant fragment (see Alt, "Zum Satz des Anaximenes über die Seel").

15. B30: κόσμον τόνδε, τὸν αὐτὸν ἁπάντων, οὔτε τις θεῶν οὔτε ἀνθρώπων ἐποίησεν, ἀλλ᾽ ἦν ἀεὶ καὶ ἔστιν καὶ ἔσται πῦρ ἀείζωον, ἁπτόμενον μέτρα καὶ ἀποσβεννύμενον μέτρα. The *metra* here could be both temporal and spatial—at different times and in different places, fire is kindling and being quenched, but it never completely dominates, nor is it ever completely quenched; see the discussion below, p. 423, on the denial of *ekpurôsis*.

16. The tag *panta rhei* is is not in the extant fragments, but that everything is in flux was attributed to Heraclitus by Plato (see *Cra.* 402a4, *Tht.* 152d–e) and Aristotle (*Cael.* 279b16, 298b30, *Metaph.* 987a31). Some version of the related maxim "It is impossible to step into the same river twice" does go back to Heraclitus, see B91 and B12: the unceasing movement and continual replenishment of its waters are the means whereby the river's identity is maintained. (But see Graham's chapter on Heraclitus here.)

17. Heraclitus seems to have dismissed Anaximenes' *aêr*, presenting water and earth as the primary derivatives from fire. *Prêstêr* is a stage between fire and water when the two appear simultaneously, as in a storm with rain and lightning, see note 48 here.

18. *Metaph.* 986b21: ἐνίσας . . . εἰς τὸν ὅλον οὐρανὸν ἀποβλέψας τὸ ἓν εἶναί φησι τὸν θεόν.

19. B8.56–59; the key phrases (italicized) for the purity and independence of the elements are ἑωυτῷ πάντοσε τωὐτόν, / τῷ δ' ἑτέρῳ μὴ τωὐτόν... / τἀντία.

20. B9; the last line is ἴσον ἀμφοτέρων, ἐπεὶ οὐδετέρῳ μέτα μηδέν.

21. For the content and argument of the *Aletheia* see McKirahan's chapter 6 on Parmenides here.

22. See Empedocles B8, 9, 13, 17.30–35, 26.

23. B.17.34–35: ἀλλ' αὐτ' ἔστιν ταῦτα, δι' ἀλλήλων δὲ θέοντα / γίγνεται ἄλλοτε ἄλλα καὶ ἠνεκὲς αἰὲν ὁμοῖα.

24. B6; the assignment of the names to the "roots" is disputed, but most obviously Zeus is fire, Hera air, Aidoneus earth, and Nestis (an obscure Sicilian goddess of springs) water; see Wright, *Empedocles*, 165. Alternative pairings of divinities and elements are discussed by Kingsley, "Empedocles and His Interpreters."

25. B22; see also B21: "take note of the witnesses to what I have said," indicating sun as fire, sky as air, rain as water, and earth as the fourth "root."

26. There are parallels for a basic quartet in the contemporary four-color map theory, and also the four-letter alphabet of DNA strings—A, T, G and C—that make up the units of protein.

27. B1: ὁμοῦ χρήματα πάντα ἦν.

28. See Greene, *The Elegant Universe*, 83: "Extrapolating all the way back to 'the beginning' the universe would appear to have begun as a *point* in which all matter and energy is squeezed together to unimaginable density and temperature. It is believed that a cosmic fireball erupted from this volatile mixture spewing forth the seeds from which the universe as we know it evolved." On seeds see Anaxagoras B4(3): σπερμάτων ἀπείρων πλῆθος ("a vast amount of limitless seeds").

29. See B17: τὸ δὲ γίνεσθαι καὶ ἀπόλλυσθαι οὐκ ὀρθῶς νομίζουσιν οἱ Ἕλληνες.

30. As Socrates complained in the biography of his philosophical journey given by Plato at *Phd.* 97b–99b.

31. The term *atomon* is a negative derivation from *temnô, I cut.*

32. See Pl. *Prm.* 127a.

33. Philoponus gives the argument: "What selection would cause one part of the void to be filled with a world and another not? So if there is a world in any part of the void, there will be one in all the void. And since the void is infinite, the worlds too will be infinitely many," *in Ph.* 405.23–27; see Taylor, *The Atomists*, 97.

34. D.L. 9.31–33.

35. See Hippol. *Haer.* 1.13 (68A40).

36. Leucippus was known for his exotic vocabulary, and many of the instances in this passage suggest that the summary is close to Leucippus's original text. Diels highlights κατὰ ἐπιτομὴν ἐκ τῆς ἀπείρου εἰς μέγα κενόν ("according to a cutting-off from the unlimited to a great emptiness"), ὑμήν ("membrane," which has Orphic connotations, see DK 1A12), and συμμένειν ("stay together," as a technical term).

37. See Greene, "The Standard Model of Cosmology," in *The Elegant Universe*, 346–47; Harrison, "The Early Universe," in *Cosmology*, 346–52.

38. See the discussion on pp. 415–16 earlier; Vlastos, "Equality and Justice in Early Greek Cosmologies," 171, suggested that the *gonimon* was a process rather than a seed, even a "whirl," which would bring it closer to atomic theory.

39. Sun, moon, and stars, in that order, from outer to inner, according to Anaximander, were formed from rings of fire encased by air, with the light from sun, moon, and stars shining through "breathing holes" (*ekpnoai*) in the dark coverings, comparable to the nozzle of a pair of bellows; Hippol. *Haer.* 1.6.4–5 (A11), Aët. 2.16, 5, 20.1, 21.1 (A18, 21).

40. From Arist. *Cael.* 295b12 (A26). This principle of sufficient reason was an important innovation in logic, and was to be used by Parmenides to show that there would be no start to the cosmos at one time rather than another. But see McKirahan's chapter.

41. "Antipodes" of course means "with feet opposite,"a world like ours, but upside-down. This is surely the meaning of the "world like ours," rather than another world in the *apeiron*, an anachronism read back into Anaximander from the atomists, see KRS 122–26; Schofield, "The Ionians," 62.

42. See Pythagoras on "all things are like numbers," Aët. 1.3.8, S.E. *M.* 7.94 (58A15), and, for Philolaus, Arist. *Cael.* 293a (58B37) and Aët. 2.7.7 (44A16).

43. Theophrastus in Simp. *in Ph.* 24.26 (A5), Hippol. 1.7 (A7), Plu. *Prim.frig.* 947f (B1).

44. Arist. *Mete.* 354a38 (A21), *Cael.* 294b13 (A20), Hippol. 1.7. (A 7), Aët. 2.2.4, 11.1, 13.10 (A12-14). The earth was supposed to be tilted to the north whereas the sun circled along a horizontal path; a similar explanation was already given in Homer for the Great Bear constellation not setting in the west, see *Il.* 18.487.

45. See Hippol. 1.7 (A7), Aët. 3.3.2 (A17), Xenoph. B32.

46. *Sph.* 242d (22A10); the philosophers are not named, but the references are clearly to Heraclitus (from Ephesus in Ionia) and Empedocles (from Acragas in Sicily).

47. ... ὁμολογεῖν σοφόν ἐστιν ἓν πάντα εἶναι is deliberately ambiguous between "all things are one" and "one is all things," or even "one and many are identical."

48. See B30, B31 and B90. In B31, *prêstêr* is evidence for the copresence of water and fire as in a lightning-storm where rain does not put out the fire of lightning; Kirk, *Heraclitus*, 331, understands the term as "burner" or "blazer," and a synonym of fire; see *keraunos* in B64.

49. B126.

50. On *panta rhei*, see note 16 here.

51. The most comprehensive survey (and refutation) of the evidence for *ekpurôsis*, from Aristotle and Theophrastus onward, is still Kirk, *Heraclitus*, 319-24, 335–38.

52. The main account is from D.L. 9.9–10 (22A1); see Kirk, *Heraclitus*, 264–83.

53. εἰκῇ κεχυμένων ὁ κάλλιστος κόσμος. For the most competent commentary on this fragment see Conche, *Héraclite*, 276–78.

54. The reference is given variously as *panta, polla, pleona*; it is spelled out in line 18 as fire, water, earth, and air.

55. The lines are from Simp. *in Ph.* 157.29, and repeated in B26.8–12 from *in Ph.* 33.26 and Arist. *Ph.* 250b30. B17.9 is reinstated from 26.8.

56. See B6: "Hear *first* the four roots of all things."

57. See B110.4-5: αὐτὰ γὰρ αὔξει / ταῦτ' εἰς ἦθος ἕκαστον, ὅπη φύσις ἐστὶν ἑκάστῳ.

58. See B27, 36, 30, 31, 38, 35, 62; Wright, *Empedocles*, 40-54, supported by *PP*; Inwood, *The Poem of Empedocles*; and Graham, "Symmetry in the Empedoclean Cycle" among others; a contrary view was first put forward by Bollack, *Empédocle*, and Hölscher, "Weltzeiten und Lebenskyklus," and adopted more recently by Long, "Empedocles' Cosmic Cycle in the 'Sixties," and Osborne, "Rethinking Early Greek Philosophy." On the effect of the Strasbourg papyri on the debate see Primavesi's contribution in this volume, as well as Martin and Primavesi, *L'Empédocle de Strasbourg*. Empedoclean-type "cycles of creation" have received a recent boost from research at Cambridge and Princeton; see Chown, "Cycles of Creation," 26–30.

59. ἀργὴ ὕλη, Aët. 1.5.2 (A47).

60. See B51, 53-55, 37, 52, Aët. 2.6.3 (A49), Arist. *Mete.* 357a24, *GC* 334a1.

61. See B40-48 and Wright, *Empedocles*, 198–204. Some of these astronomical details may not originate with Empedocles (Parmenides, for example has the moon as reflected light, *allotrion phôs*, B14, and a spherical earth is probably Pythagorean), but Empedocles' pattern of central earth, surrounding sea, air, and fire/aither (which contains the encircling planets) became the norm, carried over into Plato's *Timaeus* and beyond.

62. "Just because the cycles repeat does not mean that the events in each cycle are identical"; Neil Turok, quoted by Chown, "Cycles of Creation," 30.

63. Porph. *VP* 19 (14A8a), Eudem. *Ph.* fr. 51 (58B34).

64. B8.6–9; see Emped. B12, 17.33–4, Meliss. B1–2.

65. Parmenides does however allow a (false) cosmogony in the *Doxa*, see B8.55–61, B10 and B11

66. The concept of "dark energy" again gives a modern ring to Empedocles' theory. There is a counter-energy that repels as well as the energy that attracts, according to the pull of gravity: "the universe is a battleground between the two tendencies, and repulsive gravity is winnning"; see J. P. Ostriker and P. J. Steinhardt, "The Once and Future Cosmos," *Scientific American*, 2002, 42.

67. See Socrates' famous complaint, Pl. *Ap.* 26d, *Phd.* 97b–99b, and the explanation in Sider, *The Fragments of Anaxagoras*, 96, 104.

68. The term used is *perichôrêsis* or *periphora*, obviously a "swirling" similar to the *dinê* in Empedocles and the atomists; see Anaxagoras B12, Sider, *The Fragments of Anaxagoras*, 100–102.

69. The quotations are from B12, B15, and B16; the opposites are never completely separated out (unlike Empedocles' elements or Democritean atoms), for "everything has a portion of everything" (B9) and "the contents of the cosmos are not separated from each other or cut off by an axe—not the hot from the cold nor the cold from the hot" (B8).

70. But see Huffman, *Philolaus of Croton*, 240–60 on the attributions to Philolaus.

71. See Arist. *Cael.* 293a18–b8 (58B36), *Metaph.* 1019a5, Philol. B7 and B17, and the discussions by KRS 326–27, Huffman, *Philolaus of Croton*, 202–15.

72. Aët. 1.5.2 (A47).

73. This is taking "anthropic principle" as median between the strong form "man is at the center of all and the purpose of all" and the denial of any special status to the human race; see Coles, *Cosmology*, 125-26; Davies, *The Mind of God*, 21–22, 148–50, who quotes Einstein: "the only incomprehensible thing about the universe is that it is comprehensible."

74. On love and hate see B22.4–9, 17.6–8, 20.1–5; note too B62, B79, and B82 on analogous parts for animals, trees, birds, and fish, and B109, "with earth we perceive earth," on perception through affinity of subject and object.

75. ἄνθρωπος μικρὸς κόσμος, B34.

76. Davies, *The Mind of God*, 232.

BIBLIOGRAPHY

Alt, Karin. "Zum Satz des Anaximenes über die Seele: Untersuchung von Aetios *Peri archôn*." *Hermes* 101 (1973): 129–64.

Bollack, Jean. *Empédocle*. 3 vols. Paris: Les Éditions de Minuit, 1965–69.

Chown, Marcus. "Cycles of Creation." *New Scientist*, March 16, 2002, pp. 26–30.

Coles, Peter. *Cosmology: A Very Short Introduction*. Oxford: Oxford University Press, 2001.

Conche, Marcel. *Héraclite: Fragments*. Paris: Presses Universitaires de France, 1986.

Davies, Paul. *The Mind of God*. New York: Simon and Schuster, 1992.

Graham, Daniel W. "Symmetry in the Empedoclean Cycle." *Classical Quarterly* 38 (1988): 297–312.

Greene, Brian. *The Elegant Universe*. London: Random House, 2000.

Harrison, Edward R. *Cosmology: The Science of the Universe*. Cambridge: Cambridge University Press, 1981.

Hawking, Stephen W. *Black Holes and Baby Universes*. London: Bantam Press, 1993.

Hölscher, Uvo. "Weltzeiten und Lebenskyklus." *Hermes* 93 (1965): 7–33.

Huffman, Carl A. *Philolaus of Croton*. Cambridge: Cambridge University Press, 1993.

Hussey, Edward. "Ionian Inquiries: On Understanding the Presocratic Beginnings of Science." In *The Greek World*, edited by Anton Powell, 530–49. London: Routledge, 1995.

Inwood, Brad. *The Poem of Empedocles*. 1992. 2nd ed. Toronto: University of Toronto Press, 2001.

Kingsley, Peter. "Empedocles and His Interpreters: The Four-Element Doxography." *Phronesis* 39 (1994): 235–54.

Kirk, G. S. *Heraclitus: The Cosmic Fragments*. Cambridge: Cambridge University Press, 1954.

Long, A. A. "Empedocles' Cosmic Cycle in the 'Sixties." In *The Pre-socratics*, edited by A. P. D. Mourelatos, 397–425. Garden City, N.Y.: Doubleday, 1974.

Osborne, Catherine. *Rethinking Early Greek Philosophy: Hippolytus of Rome and the Pre-socratics*. New York: Cornell University Press, 1987.

Schofield, Malcolm. "The Ionians." In *Routledge History of Philosophy*, vol. 1, *From the Beginning to Plato*, edited by C. C. W. Taylor, 47–87. London: Routledge, 1997.

Sider, David. *The Fragments of Anaxagoras*. Meisenheim am Glan: Verlag Anton Hain, 1981.

Taylor, C. C. W. *The Atomists: Leucippus and Democritus*. Toronto: University of Toronto Press, 1999.

Vlastos, Gregory. "Equality and Justice in Early Greek Cosmologies." *Classical Philology* 42 (1947): 156–78.

Wright, M. R. *Cosmology in Antiquity*. London: Routledge, 1995.

———. *Empedocles: The Extant Fragments*. New Haven, Conn.: Yale University Press, 1981.

CHAPTER 16

REASON, CAUSE, AND EXPLANATION IN PRESOCRATIC PHILOSOPHY

R. J. HANKINSON

IN THE ARCHAIC Greek world of epic poetry (and indeed in the numinous world of classical tragedy), the causes of things are shrouded in divine mystery; the gods intervene in human affairs, and bring about events, in a cruel and capricious fashion, according to their whims (albeit ultimately under the command of the unalterable will of Zeus); Apollo visits the devastating plague of *Iliad* 1 on the Greek host to avenge Agamemnon's ill-treatment of one of his priests; Poseidon shakes the earth and angers the sea, bringing to destruction those who have incurred his ire, as does Zeus himself with his thunderbolts. The gods take on human shape and intervene in battle with devastating effect (apart from Aphrodite—her devastations are of a different order). In tragedy, the houses of Atreus and of Laius are brought low when men offend against the gods. Explanations of a sort are offered for all of these, mostly ghastly, eventuations—but they are ex post facto (except in the case of seers like Calchas, Cassandra, and Teiresias, whose advice is usually ignored or misinterpreted until it is too late), arriving too late to be of any use. Fate is ineluctable, but often surprising, and not usually in a good way. As flies to wanton boys...

1. MATERIAL PRINCIPLES

But the Greek world is not uniformly dark and terrifying, under the sway of powerful but opaque supernatural forces. For the Greeks also invented the concept of the *natural* world, a world of orderly and regular processes, both physical and biological, whose structure was at bottom rational, and hence could be plumbed by the rational mind; and amid all the superstition and religious flummery, they were also capable of manifesting supremely critical, evaluative, imaginative, and creative processes of thought. The first serious stirrings of this new way of seeking to understand the world and our place in it have since Aristotle usually been attributed to the Presocratics.

In Aristotle's view, the original manifestation of the philosophical and scientific spirit in the Greek world took the form, appropriately enough, of the search for origins or principles, *archai*:

> there must be either [A] one principle [*archê*] or [B] many; and if [A] one, it must either [i] unchanging [as Parmenides and Melissus say) or [ii] changeable, as the natural scientists say, some declaring [a] air, and others [b] water, to be the first principle. But if [B] there are many, they must be either [i] finite or [ii] infinite in number; and if [i] finite but more than one, then either [a] two or [b] three or [c] four or [d] some other number; and if [ii] they are infinite, they must either [a] be, as Democritus says, different in form although the same in generic substance, or [b] the opposite. (1: Arist. *Ph.* 1.2, 184b15–21)[1]

Aristotle limns an exhaustive division of the types of physical theory he discovers in his predecessors. Thus Parmenides and his Eleatic disciples fall into category (Ai): there is only one thing, and it is unalterable and unaffectible. Material monists such as Anaximenes and (on Aristotle's view at least) Thales slot into (Aii). The pluralists, too, divide into distinct classes, the finitists among them such as Xenophanes (Bia) and Empedocles (Bic) believing, respectively, in two and four elements, the infinitists being distinguished according to whether they think their infinity of elements differ only in shape (Democritus: Biia) or in substance as well (Anaxagoras: Biib). Some of Aristotle's divisions are included simply for completeness's sake (we know of no three-element theorist,[2] and hence (Aiib) is an empty category), and in some cases assignment is difficult: Heraclitus apparently held that there were four material, intertransmuting elements, but also seems to make fire (or on some accounts air) primary.

Aristotle might usefully have added further distinctions: in addition to the question of whether the elements are finite or infinite in number, he might also have noted the dispute between those (preeminently the atomists) who held that the total quantity of stuff in the universe was infinite and those who supposed by contrast that the sum of the material components of the cosmos was limited; and he might also have distinguished between those for whom matter was continuous and infinitely divisible and those (again the atomists) who supposed that it was not—although the main battles between the proponents of continuous and discontinuous physics belong to a later period. But at all events, a wide variety of different candidates for fundamental physical theory were available on the Greek market of ideas in the two centuries or so of its history that we conventionally label Presocratic. The centrality of the search for principles of things is affirmed by another passage from Aristotle:

> most of the earliest philosophers thought that the principles [*archai*] of all things were merely material in form. For they say that the element [*stoicheion*] and principle of things is that from which they all are and from which they first are generated and into which they are finally destroyed, its substance [*ousia*] persisting while its properties are altered. . . . Hence they believe that nothing is either generated or destroyed, since this nature is always preserved . . . since there is some one entity (or more than one) which always exists and from which all other things are generated. However, as to the number and form of this sort of principle, they do not say the same thing. (2: *Metaph.* 1.3, 983b6–20 = DK 11A12 [part])

That passage is couched in Aristotle's own distinctive technical vocabulary; yet there is no reason to impugn the general veracity of the picture here offered. The predilection for material (as opposed to formal or kinetic) principles is indeed to be found in the extant remains of the earliest Presocratics, Thales, Anaximander, and Anaximenes; and indeed a concern with isolating the structural elements of things persists throughout the period, along with a growing acceptance of some sort of principle of material conservation (see section 5). But, as Aristotle says, at the level of particulars the agreement ends; and the Presocratic period is notable not only for the variety of types of theory, as attested by the first passage, but also for the proliferation of different tokens of those types.

2. MATERIAL PRINCIPLES OF THE MILESIANS

The word translated as "principle" is the word *archê*. It has a variety of meanings in Greek (beginning, origin, source, axiom, government); but there is no hint of its existing in the sense of "material principle" in archaic Greek—indeed the only usage known to Homer is its fundamental sense, that of a beginning (see, e.g., *Il.* 22.112). But it is relatively easy to see how the semantic field of the word spread from the sense of a temporal beginning to that of a causal origin, and finally to that of something in control or fundamental, a sense it has both in politics and axiomatized science.

But the sense in which Aristotle is using *archê* here, and that he is attributing to the earliest Presocratics, is closer to that suggested by the word "element," or *stoicheion*, another word not used at the time in this sense (or indeed apparently in any other); its original meaning was that of the elements of speech; it then takes on the sense of letters of the alphabet; and finally (in Democritus and Plato) by transference comes to refer to any basic building-block, and attains its physical sense.

Aristotle continues:

> Thales, the initiator of this type of philosophy, says it [namely the *archê*] is water (this is why he says that the earth rests on water), perhaps deriving this assumption from seeing that the nourishment of everything is moist and that heat itself is generated from moisture and depends on it for its existence (and that from which something is generated is always its origin [*archê*]). For this reason, then, he acquired this belief; and also from the fact that the seeds of everything are moist, and water is the origin of the nature of moist things. (3: *Metaph.* 1.3, 983b20–27 = DK 11A12 [part])

Aristotle, in common with other Greek thinkers and historians (and most modern commentators), considered Thales of Miletus (fl. 585 BCE) to mark a radical new turn in Greek thought, indeed perhaps even the beginning of Greek thought itself. But there is no reason to think that Thales himself used the word *archê* to describe his water (although his successor Anaximander may have thus referred to his own indefinite element: passage 4); indeed Aristotle may be wrong to ascribe to him any very developed theory of a material principle as such at all. In order to pursue this question further, we need to specify more clearly just what material principles are supposed to be.

The basic idea, expressed in passage 2, is that a material principle (MP) is the fundamental stuff of the physical world, out of which everything else is generated and into which it is resolved. In this sense, the MP (or MPs) "underlie" everything else; and the physical constitutions of all the derived materials are in some sense to be referred to and reduced to them. If Thales' water is an MP in this sense, then it will be the case that absolutely everything in the universe will be made of (or at any rate from)[3] water. All the various types of stuff will simply be water in modified form (if they are made *of* it) or elaborations of water (if they are made *from* it). Aristotle certainly seems to ascribe some such view to Thales in passage 3; but the only doctrine he actually refers to is that of the earth's being supported by water—and there surely the support is physical rather than metaphysical.[4] On the other hand, he offers (albeit cautiously) several reasons why Thales might have considered water to be his MP, at least in the sense of an originative principle, something everything is made from; and he knew more (although perhaps not much more) about Thales than we do. At all events, we do not know how Thales conceived of his water: whether it really was an MP, or whether it was merely a prerequisite of (but not necessarily the only constituent of or ingredient in) things.[5]

But whatever we may make of this, it seems clear enough that Thales aimed at generality in his account—and generality is the hallmark of scientific explanation. Moreover, in contrast with his mythographic predecessors, he apparently sought to give reasons in favor of his views. If Homer really did, as Plato thought, conceive of the heavens as a brazen bowl, he gave no reason for so doing; and there was no conceivable justification, geographical, hydrodynamical, or zoogonical, for the supposition that the inhabited earth was surrounded by a great river, Ocean, which was somehow responsible for replenishing all life (*Iliad* 14.200, 244).[6] Even so, the watery nature of this and other early mythographic essays in cosmology has moved some scholars to suppose that Thales was simply one of a long line of aqueous archologists, influenced ultimately by the cosmologies of the ancient Near East,[7] and there may be something to that—but the tenor of his attitude to his theory, whatever its origins, was surely distinctive and novel.[8]

Thus (on any interpretation) the new style of account involves generality and naturalism (the avoidance of inherently untestable appeals to the desires of supernatural agents in explanation); and it also both hypothesizes general causes, and offers reasons to commend them. Thus, although he no doubt did not employ the terminology, he makes use of *aitiai*, causes, explanations, and reasons, in all three of their standard later Greek senses.

Thales did not have everything his own way, however. His immediate successor and fellow citizen of Miletus[9] Anaximander (fl. c. 560 BCE) rejected the primacy not merely of water but of any determinate candidate for element-status as such:

> He said that some certain unlimited nature is the origin of things, from which are generated the heavens and the world in them. It is eternal and ageless, and encloses all the worlds. He speaks of time, generation, and existence and destruction being determinate. He said that the unlimited [*apeiron*] is the origin and element of things, and was the first to call it *archê*. (4: Hippol. *Haer.* 1.6.1–2 = 12A11)

It is unclear whether Anaximander really did coin this technical sense of *archê*;[10] although that matters little. He certainly did call his basic stuff *apeiron*, unlimited, indeterminate, or infinite. Again, scholars have argued over which of those translations (all perfectly well attested for later Greek) is appropriate;[11] and again that need not detain us. His basic stuff was clearly no particular thing or element— and there was an awful lot of it. He needs the first, apparently,[12] since he accepts that ordinary elements can turn into one another (this was to be a basic feature of most later Greek element-theories, including those of Aristotle and the Stoics).[13] But if that is the case, no one of them is more basic than any other, and moreover there must be something that underlies all of them, that persists through the changes (otherwise they won't change as such—one will simply be annihilated, and another spring into existence: see section 5). According to Simplicius,

> he creates generation not from the alteration of the elements, but from the separating off of the opposites as a result of the eternal motion. (5: *in Ph.* 24.22–23)

I will have more to say about the "eternal motion" later (in section 4); but if this report is remotely accurate (and there is no reason to suppose that it is radically misguided), Anaximander conceived of the generation of things (perhaps including the usual candidates for elements, earth, water, air, and fire) from his *apeiron* by a process of physical separation: and he may well have appealed (as later thinkers were to do) to homely examples of such mixture and separation to support his general picture of things.

His *apeiron* was indefinitely big in order to underwrite the apparent continuity of generation; so at any rate Aristotle argues at *Ph.* 3.4, 203b15–20; but Aristotle himself pointed out that the assumption of an indefinitely large background material was not necessary if generation was not to fail, provided only that "it is possible that the destruction of one thing is the generation of another" (*Ph.* 3.8, 208a9–10). But it is plausible to suppose that Anaximander did not see that, or thought that such reciprocal generation and destruction was for some other reason impossible; and the development of the notion of conservation principles needed to wait on later generations of thinkers.

Anaximander's own successor, Anaximenes, changed the direction of elemental explanation once again. He rejected Anaximander's *apeiron*, opting to make his basic element one of the ordinary stuffs of experience:

> Anaximenes . . . an associate of Anaximander, also says . . . that the underlying nature is one and unlimited, but not undefined [*aoriston*] as Anaximander said, but definite, saying that it is air. And it differs in respect of its substance [*ousia*] in rarefaction and density. Being rarified fire is generated, being thickened wind, then cloud, then water, then earth, then stone, and the other things from these. He too makes motion eternal, through which change comes to be. (6: Thphr. from Simp. *in Ph.* 24.26–25.1 = 13A5)

Anaximenes' air, then, is unlimited in extent (presumably for reasons similar to those that motivated Anaximander: see passage 7), but is still determinate. Air becomes everything else by way of processes of rarefaction and condensation,[14] and these processes are somehow themselves maintained by an eternal motion.[15] His retreat to a familiar stuff after the boldness of Anaximander's move to a theoretical postulate has been castigated as intellectual cowardice;[16] but it has something to be said for it. Air is, after all, one of the empirically discernible stuffs; and it is also, as Anaximenes notes,

> close to the incorporeal; and because we come into being by an outpouring of air, it is necessary that it be both unlimited and rich on account of its never giving out. (B3) (7: ps.-Olympiodorus, *On the Sacred Art of the Philosopher's Stone*, 25)[17]

It is "close to the incorporeal" in that of all the ordinary stuffs around us, it impinges least on our senses—hence it has fewest sensible qualities. Anaximenes then presumably inferred that air (in its airy form) was the most basic form of matter, since it was the least elaborated and most inert. Thus he manages implicitly to answer the Anaximandrean argument that no ordinary stuff should be denominated *the* basic stuff any more than any other, if all of them are capable of intertransmutation. One further text is worth quoting:

> Anaximenes held that air is the origin [*archê*] of existing things; for from it everything comes to be, and into it everything is resolved; "just as our souls," he says, "being air, hold us together, so breath [*pneuma*] and air contain the whole world." (B2) (8: Aët. 1.3.4)[18]

Again, passage 8 does not explicitly attribute the use of the *term archê* to Anaximenes; but again that doesn't matter. And here the imputation that air really is a material principle is inescapable. We shall hear more of souls later on.

3. LATER THEORISTS

The broad outlines of what Aristotle meant in passage 2 by saying that the early Greek philosophers concentrated on the material principles of things should be now be clear enough, although as we shall see Aristotle is perhaps less than entirely fair to the explanatory resources at their command. Later theorists added to the list: Xenophanes made earth and water foundational (21B29, 30, 33), although B27 seems unequivocally to make the earth basic: "since from earth everything [comes] and into earth everything ends." The earth we stand on is the flat upper limit of a pillar extending indefinitely far down (B28), and thus Xenophanes anticipates and answers Aristotle's objection to Thales' hypothesis that the earth rests on water (see note 4): it rests on itself, infinitely.[19]

For Heraclitus, the basic stuff is fire; the world is "an ever-living fire" (22B30), while "everything is exchanged in return for fire and fire in return for everything, as goods are for gold and gold for goods" (B90); although he also recognizes earth and water as being (at some level) basic as well:

> turnings of fire: first of all sea, and of sea, half is earth and half fire; earth is scattered as sea, and is measured in the same proportion as it was before it became earth. (9: Clem.Al. *Strom.* 5.104.3 = B31)

That is couched in obscure language (and Heraclitus's name was an ancient byword for obscurity) but it is clear that he advocated a physics of transmutation from fire, and one that involved proportional elements (measure and proportion are important recurring concepts in Heraclitus's remains: see section 5).

The idea of proportion recurs in Empedocles (31B17, B22, B98). The ordinary stuffs around us are determinate combinations of the four elements (or "roots" as he called them; B6):

> And gracious earth received in her broad hollows
> Two parts of the eight of the gleam of Nestis [i.e., water],
> Four of Hephaestus [i.e., fire]; and white bones came to be
> Wondrously joined by the bonds of harmony.
> (10: Simp. *in Ph.* 300.21–4 = B96)

> And earth happened in roughly equal quantity on these,
> Hephaestus, rain, and all-flashing *aithêr* [here-air]
> Anchored in the perfect harbors of Love,
> Either a little more or less in more of them,
> And from them came blood and the other forms of flesh.
> (11: Simp. *in Ph.* 32.6–10 = B98)

Thus bone is (apparently: Empedocles' lucidity is not aided by the fact that he wrote in verse) two parts earth, two parts water, and four parts fire; while the organic compounds are formed by mixing roughly equal quantities of all four of them: earth, water, air, and fire. Here, for the first time, we have a fully developed element-theory, in which the stuffs of the world are supposed to be reducible to specific compounds of the fundamental elements. Moreover, these really *are* elements—unlike the entities of Anaximander, Heraclitus, Aristotle, and the Stoics, they do not intertransmute, but remain intact in the compounds, and serve to explain, reductively, the nature of those compounds (see B23).

Empedocles' rough contemporary Anaxagoras[20] developed a physics of an altogether different and idiosyncratic kind. Starting from a smooth primeval mixture (59B1, B4, DK = 467–68 KRS), things were gradually separated off; but never totally. Anaxagoras held that "in everything there is everything" (B6, B11), and not just in the preliminary stages of cosmic development. The only exception to this, the only pure and unmixed substance, is mind (B12), which controls everything (control is also attributed in B1 to air and fire). The "everything in everything" principle appears to be both literal and (for stuffs at least) exceptionless: every sample m of stuff S contains admixtures of every other stuff. What is more, this is apparently true ad infinitum; any proper part p of m will also contain such admixtures. Thus matter is uniform.[21] This means that any ordinary sample of a given (ordinary-language) stuff, oil, say, will not be *pure* oil, but only predominantly so—it will also contain a certain amount of water. This makes pure oil (and pure water for that matter) a theoretical postulate—but there is nothing incoherent about that.[22] It is a further question why anyone should have developed such a bizarre doctrine; and it found few adherents.

Finally, in this context, let us glance at the physical views of the atomists, Leucippus and Democritus. About the former very little is known, although to him is ascribed the postulate of atoms and the void (67A6, 68A37). Much more survives of Democritus (c. 450–c. 360 BCE); and we are able to reconstruct his physical doctrine with some degree of assurance. Crucially, matter for the atomists is discontinuous, and only finitely divisible. All of the atomists' predecessors (so far as we can tell) were continuum theorists, as Aristotle and the Stoics were to be: there are no smallest divisions of matter or space. The atomists reject this. There are things into which you can divide ordinary stuffs, but that cannot themselves be divided: the atoms, the adamantine, irrefragible, unaltering, sempiternal building-blocks of material stuffs. The emergence of all macroscopic structure is to be explained as a result of the interconnection and interreaction of the atoms, in virtue of their particular shapes (smooth round atoms form fluids; hooked rough ones aggregate into solids (68A37, 14). The number of atomic types, and the number of tokens of each type, were infinite (67A8, 68A14); and so, too, is space, and the number of worlds (*kosmoi*: large-scale organized structures of matter): 67A1, 68A40. For the first time clearly there is the postulate of universe infinite in extent. But how does it get to be the way that it is? And what are the dynamical forces at work to create and preserve it and the processes within it? These questions had preoccupied other Presocratics, too; and to them we now turn.

4. DYNAMICAL PRINCIPLES

Aristotle thought that the early thinkers concentrated too exclusively on material causes (passage 2); and indeed he applies his own division of explanatory types (the "four causes": see *Ph.* 2.3) to his analysis of his predecessors' shortcomings (*Metaph.* 1.3). Most of them (a few negligible thinkers like Hippo aside: *Metaph.* 1.3, 984a3–5) managed to get something right—but they fail to account for the total picture, since they fail to give a complete set of explanations, in all the categories, of the facts of things.

Aristotle clearly thought that the absence of any clearly expressed dynamical principles vitiated the early accounts: they might (in a sense) be able to explain what things are, but not how they came to be that way (analogously, they fail to give complete formal or structural specifications of things, and to account for natural necessity: these questions will be dealt with in sections 6–7). But (with the exception of Thales) nods to the importance of dynamic explanation are to be found throughout Presocratic philosophy.

To Anaximander is attributed[23] an "eternal motion in which it comes about that the heavens are generated" (A11), and he held that the opposites are "separated off" from the *apeiron*, presumably as a result of it (A9). Anaximenes, too, seems to have postulated an eternal motive principle to inject dynamism into the system: his air is always in motion (A7), and it is by condensation and rarefaction that it becomes all other things. Anaximenes does not specify that the air is responsible for its own motion, however; and A7 suggests that "the most important factors in coming into being are hot and cold." But this, too, is inexplicit: the text does not state directly that hot and cold are *responsible* for the changes, as opposed to simply being most directly implicated in them; and another text (B1) suggests rather that hot and cold are derivative of rarefaction and condensation.

At all events, all these reports are vague; and if Aristotle is harsh to suggest that the Milesians ignored dynamical explanation altogether, it is surely the case that their attempts at it were jejune. But there is another possible source of motion in the universe: the postulation of an autonomous motion-generating principle, or what the Greeks called a *psuchê* (traditionally Englished as "soul"). To ascribe motion (or more accurately the ability to cause motion) to souls is for the Greeks a truism, with no immediate metaphysical connotations: souls just are what makes the difference between things being alive and not being alive, and one of the features of (animal) life is the ability to cause and direct movement (indeed our word "animal" is derived from the Latin for *soul*). As such, such a postulate is not explanatorily very helpful—but in the case of natural explanation it is not (as it perhaps is in the case of animal motion) entirely trivial either.

Thales held that magnets possessed souls because they have the ability to move iron (A22). The idea seems to be that magnets are not merely recipients of motive force: they are able actually to induce it, both in other things and in themselves; but that is precisely the characteristic of something animate, and so magnets have souls (in this sense: nothing of course commits Thales to the view that they are sentient, although he may have noted the fact that they exhibit a marked preference for iron over any other material). Thales is also said to have held that "everything is full of gods" (A22), and that presumably because of the dynamism in the world; and here is where the thesis becomes nontrivial, since this sort of pan-psychism (if such it is) rests on the idea that the explanation of motion-causing ought to be the same in all cases. If apparently highly various things can all generate spontaneous movement, than that must be because, first appearances notwithstanding, they are similar in fundamental ways. And that hypothesis, mistaken though it may be (and the fact that it *is* mistaken of course shows it to be nontrivial), is a paradigm of a certain sort of (naive) scientific theory-building (in this context it is worth noting that Anaximenes too assimilates soul to air: passage 8).

Another early argument involving the concept of the soul is attributed to Alcmaeon of Croton (fl. c. 480 BCE). He was a medical man as well as a philosopher (he was associated with the Pythagoreans of southern Italy), and he elaborated an account of health as a balance among opposing forces, thus inaugurating (in the West at least) a medical tradition of extraordinary longevity (24B4). He also remarked, enigmatically, that "human beings die because they cannot join the beginning to the end" (B2): the idea seems to be that the progress of a human life is a linear one, and hence one that must come to an end—it does not have the infinite character of a circle. This is not the case, however, with the soul:

> Alcmaeon takes the soul to have a self-moved nature in eternal motion, and for this reason it is immortal and similar to the gods. (12: Aët. 4.2.2 = A12)

Here, apparently, we have an argument for the immortality of the soul. Souls are immortal because they are self-movers; and because they are self-movers, they cannot fail to move. That argument can be interpreted in different ways;[24] I prefer to see it as going somewhat as follows. The soul is an autonomous cause of motion (this is a piece of conceptual analysis); what is autonomous cannot be interfered with by outside agency; therefore, nothing can interfere with the soul's autonomous motility; hence (since what it is to be a soul is to be such a motion-causer) nothing can prevent the soul from moving—so it does so for ever. The argument also apparently assumes that what causes motion must itself be in motion (an assumption later rejected by Aristotle, *Ph.* 8.10); and so the soul, like the heavenly bodies, is in continuous, circular motion; and so it is immortal. That argument is not of course sound—in particular, it need be no part of the concept of an autonomous mover that its capacity to move is unaffectible by external causes—but neither is it negligible, and Plato was moved to appropriate it (without acknowledgment) for himself (*Phaedrus* 245c–46a).

Heraclitus made the world "an ever-living fire"; and fire was consequently associated with the soul. Indeed, "for souls it is death to become water" (B36), while "a dry soul is wisest and best" (B118), and drunkenness is a moistening of the soul (B117); but none of this really offers much in the way of a dynamic theory. Heraclitus evidently believed in a cyclical movement between the elements (passage

9), and the view that the universe is periodically resolved into pure fire in a great conflagration is attributed to him by some sources; it was certainly later held by the Stoics, who saw themselves in some ways as Heraclitus's heirs, but it seems inconsistent with B30, which says that this world has always existed and will always do so (thus Heraclitus has no need of the sort of cosmogony earlier thinkers felt it incumbent on them to supply). But there is remarkably little in the way of any account of dynamic principles. Perhaps the closest we get is in the enigmatic B64: "Thunderbolt steers everything," where Thunderbolt is presumably particularly pure fire, and seems to be assimilated to God.

The problem of the source of energy (as well as that of cosmogony) is comprehensively sidestepped by Parmenides (c. 510–440 BCE) and his Eleatic followers Zeno and Melissus, since in their world there isn't any motion in any case. But the post-Eleatic physicists Anaxagoras, Empedocles, and Democritus, each of whom is usually and plausibly seen as attempting to rehabilitate physical inquiry and explanation in the wake of the Eleatic assault on the very coherence of such an enterprise, all seek to address that issue.

Anaxagoras's favored principle is his Mind—and in this he follows in the footsteps of Anaximenes and Heraclitus. In the course of his cosmogony, according to Diogenes Laertius (2.8, 59A1) he held that "Mind is the source of motion; heavy bodies occupy the lower place and light ones the upper" (cf. B16), although (as noted in section 1) he also ascribes control to air and fire. But both Plato and Aristotle were dismissive of the explanatory usefulness of Anaxagoras's Mind ("he wheels it in like a stage device whenever he gets into difficulties," Aristotle said: *Metaph.* 1.4, 985a18–20; cf. Pl. *Phd.* 98b). Given the fragmentary nature of our sources, it is difficult to assess its status as an explanatory principle; but certainly one cannot dismiss the view of Plato and Aristotle that it was simply a convenient ad hoc device.

Empedocles also offered a cosmogony for the present world (although its elements were eternal and not subject to intertransmutation): first *aither* (bright air) was separated off, and then fire, followed by water and earth (A30, 49). But he also views the history of the universe as cyclical, consisting of a constant dynamic interaction between two cosmic forces, Love and Strife, in which first one and then the other gains the upper hand. Love is conceived as a sort of entropic principle, smoothing out the differences between things, and eventually at the moment of its triumph uniting the four elements into a smooth, harmonious, spherical whole (B27, 29, 31). But as soon as that stage is reached, Strife, the discriminating principle, begins to break things down once again (B30). Conversely, as soon as maximum segregation has been achieved, Love once again goes to work, and the resulting partial reunification gives rise to living things (B35).[25] Aristotle complains that no reason is given why this should be so "other than that things are naturally like this" (*Metaph.* 3.4, 1000b12–13; cf. *GC* 2.6, 333b30–34); and apparently Empedocles conceived of this as a fundamental, irreducible feature of the natural order of things.

Empedocles refers, in B35, to the action of a vortex, as apparently does Anaxagoras—and vortices also do a good deal of work for the atomists (as they were to do two millennia later for Descartes and his followers). For Democritus and Leucippus, too, the universe has no beginning and will have no end; but within it, from time to time, as a result of the chance aggregation of atoms, pockets of order emerge—and these are the various *cosmoi*, or worlds. They do so under the influence of vortical action; but quite how this was supposed to happen is obscure, and Simplicius for one thought that no answer was given:

> when Democritus says that "a vortex of all types of shape was separated off from the whole" [B167], he does not say how or for what reason, and he seems to generate it on the basis of spontaneity or chance. (13: *in Ph.* 327.24–6; see further section 5)

The other great atomist kinetic principle is that of the rebounding of the atoms. The atoms are constantly moving in the void, not apparently "downward" under the influence of their weight, as they were to do for Epicurus (the Democritean texts are equivocal on the question of atomic weight: 68A61, 47),[26] but simply as a result of their momentum, and the fact that they have always done so. The fundamental atomic properties, along with their shape and size, are solidity, resistivity, and (probably) weight; and these together account for the facts of their motion. But while it is clear that the atomists had some primitive (and no doubt qualitative) notion of momentum, it is a mistake to attribute to them, as some have done, an inkling of the great principle of inertia.

5. METAPHYSICAL PRINCIPLES

Aristotle's view that the early philosophers concentrated excessively on material causes is partially borne out by those aspects of the history I have examined so far; certainly their treatment of dynamics seems sketchy and naive. But even so, we must not lose sight of the other explanatory principles the Presocratics deployed. Let us begin with a famous doctrine of Anaximander:

> some say that it [namely the earth] remains where it is on account of similarity, like Anaximander . . . for it is no more fitting for what is stationed in the center and similarly disposed towards the extremes to move either upward or downward, or laterally; and since it is impossible to move in opposite directions at the same time, necessarily it remains where it is. (14: Arist. *Cael.* 2.13, 295b10–16 = A26)

Thales had supposed that the earth rested on water (passage 3); Xenophanes made it a pillar stretching infinitely downward (B28); for Anaximenes it floated on the air like a saucepan lid (A20), and in this he was followed by Anaxagoras and perhaps Democritus (although it seems unlikely that his world would require any such support). For Anaximander, the world's stability is secured by logic alone—there is no reason for it to move in any one direction rather than any other. This is the first recorded application of the principle of sufficient reason (PSR), and it constitutes a revolution in explanation: what previously was thought to demand positive explanation is now seen to require none; and what looks at first sight surprising turns out to be, given the appropriate conceptual machinery, only what one would expect.

In one of its forms, PSR later came to be expressed by way of the phrase *ou mallon*, "no more," that is, no more this way than that, and deployed epistemologically it was later to become a formidable weapon in the skeptical armory (see e.g., Sextus Empiricus, *Outlines of Pyrrhonism*, 1.188–91). Democritus also made extensive use of it, sometimes also to skeptical ends, but more often in support of physical principles, in particular that of infinity: there will be atoms of all shapes and sizes, since there is no reason for there not to be (67A8), while for similar reasons both matter and void will be infinite (KRS 559).

But its most celebrated and influential appearance occurs in the works of someone who has barely figured in the account so far, and that for the reason that, as Aristotle says, he could not be accounted a physicist (*Ph.* 1.2–3): Parmenides. Parmenides argued (quite how is controversial, but that controversy need not detain us) that motion and change were impossible, since they imply nonbeing (what comes to be *F* does so from having *not been F*), and nonbeing cannot be referred to or do any explanatory work. Part of his argument seems to turn on linguistic considerations; but part of it is metaphysical: if something did come to be from nothing, why should it do so earlier rather than later (B8.5–21)?

The idea that nothing can come to be from nothing, NN, thus rests on PSR. It also had a long philosophical history, and has often been taken for an a priori truth. Parmenides' physicist successors sought to rehabilitate the notions of change and motion, but they did so conscious of the need to accommodate what they, too, saw as a compelling principle of physical explanation, namely NN. But what precisely is it? At first sight, it seems plausible to take it materially, as asserting that there must always be some preexisting stuff out of which generation can take place. In the words of Empedocles:

> there is no birth of any mortal thing, nor any end in destructive death; but there is only mixture and exchange of the mixing things, which is called birth by men. (15: Plutarch, *Against Colotes* 1111f = 31B8; see B9–11)

Moreover

> it is impossible for anything to come to be from what is not, and it cannot be brought about or believed that what is should be utterly destroyed. (16: ps.-Arist. *MXG* 2, 975b1–2 = 31B12)

Passage 16 explicitly asserts the converse corollary of NN: there can be no complete annihilation either. NN also underlies Anaxagoras's strange physics; it is partly because he thinks that Parmenides is in a sense right that he has everything mixed in everything and makes generation merely a winnowing out and rearrangement: "nothing is generated or destroyed, but rather is compounded and discriminated out of things that are" (B17).

But there is also implicit in Parmenides' argument the idea that nothing can come from nothing in the sense of without any preceding cause: spontaneous *ex nihilo* generation would, he argues, be causeless generation—and that is unintelligible. Whether the latter claim is true is of course controversial, and indeed controverted by the standard accounts of quantum physics; but it commanded an enormous degree of philosophical support for a very long time (witness the derision incurred by Epicurus's positing of an uncaused atomic swerve). The trick is to define change in such a way that it does not involve coming to be from nothing at all, or for no reason, but still makes sense of the idea that if something comes to be *F* it does so from not-*F*.[27]

In rehabilitating the idea of change, Parmenides' successors all point to the fact that in every change there is something that persists through the change, but that undergoes some alteration; moreover, that alteration is externally caused, perhaps typically by something that has (in some sense) the altered property.[28] Thus the refrigerator cools my beer because it is already cold; there is a transfer of an existent property from one thing that has it to another that gains it—but the latter (in this case the beer) persists through the change. Aristotle made this account canonical (*Ph.* 1.6–8); but there are already hints of it in the Presocratics.

A related strand in Presocratic thought about the intelligibility of the universe concerns the notion of conservation. In one form or another, conservation principles are absolutely central to modern physics: inertial motion, angular momentum, mass, energy, mass and energy, the lepton number—all have been or are supposed to be subject to a conservation of the relevant physical quantities. Indeed, at a stretch, one might say that conservation principles are the residual kernel of the Parmenidean idea; and even Heraclitus, who held that everything in the universe was in a constant state of flux (A6, B12, 91)[29] still supposed that there was stability in his continual change (see B49a, 51, 54, 91, 123, 125).

And one might see such concerns adumbrated as early as Anaximander, indeed in the one surviving fragment of his actual words:

> the things from which existing things are generated are also the those into which they are destroyed, in accordance with necessity, "for they give justice [*dikê*] and restitution to each other in accordance with the arrangement of time." (B1) (17: Simp. *in Ph.* 24.19–21 = A9)

That fragment certainly suggests some sort of overall stability in the form of a repeating cycle—at one time one "element" gains the upper hand, but it pays for it in the end by becoming comparatively diminished. As such, this prefigures the continual interchange between Empedocles' Love and Strife (see section 4), and similar ideas are to be found in Heraclitus. The metaphor of justice was to become hugely influential (it lingers on in our concept of a law of nature); and the thought that anyone or anything overstepping the limits would make recompense in due course by being brought low was extremely congenial to the Greek mind (it underpins classical tragedy). But it is unlikely that Anaximander thought in terms of the overall conservation of physical quantities; indeed, one of the motivations for making his *apeiron* indefinitely large was probably in order for it never to give out as a source of generative material (A12, A17; see Arist. *Ph.* 3.4, 203b15–17; the same may also be true of Anaximenes' infinite air).[30]

It is the idea of a natural balance, an overall order, that is crucial here—and crucially it is a metaphysical principle of natural explanation: this is the way the world, fundamentally, is. A similar metaphor was deployed by Alcmaeon in the context of medicine: health is an egalitarianism (*isonomia*) of the opposing powers (B4). There is no surviving suggestion that imbalances will be corrected by balances in a cyclical fashion, although Alcmaeon did believe in the fundamental cyclicality of nature, while the idea that nature strives to restore the proper balance of things (and relatedly that the doctor's job is to help nature on its way), was to become central to Hippocratic medicine, and persisted until the nineteenth century.

Metaphors of judgment and justice are also common in Heraclitus, and in more relevant contexts: "fire will come and judge and convict all things" (B66); "war is universal, strife is just" (B80); while

> this world was made neither by gods nor men, but always was and is and will be, an ever living fire kindled in measures and extinguished in measures; (18: Clem.Al. *Strom.* 5.104.1 = B30; see passage 9)

> everything is a reciprocal exchange for fire and fire for everything else, as goods are for gold and gold for goods. (19: Plutarch, *On the "E" at Delphi* 388d = B90; see B31a–b)

Here again the idea seems to be one of the maintenance, over a long period of time, of some sort of cosmic balance. And although Heraclitus uses religious language (he speaks of Zeus and the gods as well as of the Thunderbolt), it seems that it describes not a set of Homeric supernatural agents, but rather personifications of the natural order of things (see B67).[31] This is also suggested by the fact that the sun apparently has a central role to play (presumably in its determination of day and night and of the seasons) of the natural cycles of things, in another fragment full of judicial imagery:

> the sun will not overstep his measures, or else the Furies, the ministers of justice, will seek him out. (20: Plutarch, *On Exile* 604a = B94; see B99)

6. CHANCE AND NECESSITY

The great explanatory shortcoming of the Presocratics, according to Aristotle, was their innocence of the final cause, of teleological explanation. Almost all of them, he thought, were mechanists of one sort or another, who might on occasion invoke the purposes of the gods, but in a metaphoric vein, and in any case missed the essentially goal-directed nature of nature itself. For Aristotle, the natural world is a kingdom of ends, of individuals striving to realize their species-forms in processes whose structures and stability cannot be made comprehensible (or so at any rate Aristotle believed) solely in terms of material necessity and antecedent causation.

Most clearly in his sights in such polemics are the atomists, but he also takes Empedocles to task for assigning primary roles to the forces of chance and necessity at the expense of immanent purpose, while Anaxagoras's Mind is a gesture in the direction of teleological explanation but one that, as we have seen (section 4), Aristotle stigmatizes for its timidity and ad hoc character; moreover, he castigates Anaxagoras for thinking that human beings are the most intelligent animals because they have hands, rather than the other way around (*PA* 4.10, 687a19–23). From a modern viewpoint, the refusal to ascribe intentionality to nature, and the tendency to explain things, particularly in the animal kingdom, in terms of random interaction plus the necessities of natural law may seem altogether more appealing.

And this is what Empedocles apparently did. In his curious "evolutionary" zoogony, he describes how at first separate limbs and organs arose, which then became attached to bodies, which then contrived (fairly ineffectually at first) to procreate, before finally resulting in settled species (A72, B57–62). What matters from our point of view is that the initial conjunctures seem to be random (this seems true in the case of the formation of blood as well: see passage 11). Aristotle describes it as follows.

> when everything turned out just as if it were coming to be for the sake of something, these things survived, being put together by chance, but in a suitable fashion. But those that were not like this perished and are still perishing, as Empedocles says of his "man-faced ox-offspring." (21: Arist. *Ph.* 2.8, 198b29–32 = B61)

Aristotle thought that merely mimicking purpose was not good enough (see *PA* 1.1, 640a18–19: generation is for the sake of being, not vice versa, as Empedocles held: B97); nowadays we may reasonably see Empedocles as adumbrating, albeit in a vague and remote fashion, the great principles of natural selection.

Even more hostile to purpose in nature were the atomists. The view that "nothing comes to be for no reason, but everything for a reason and as a result of necessity" is attributed to Leucippus (67B2); and this is associated with Democritus's vorticism: "everything comes to be in accordance with necessity, and the vortex, which he calls necessity, is the cause of the generation of everything" (KRS 566); but another report has him assimilate necessity to the fundamental properties of the atoms, resistance, motion, and rebounds (KRS 567).

But as in the case of Empedocles, such a notion of necessity is perfectly compatible with the operation of chance—and Democritus comes in for Aristotelian criticism on this score, too:

> there are some who make chance the cause of this heaven and all of the worlds; for from chance came the vortex and the motion, which, by discriminating things established the current ordering of the universe. (22: *Ph.* 2.4, 196a24–28)

The mechanisms postulated for such discrimination are various. For Empedocles, it is (as we saw: section 4) the result of a fundamental force, Strife, whose role it is to yield this result. For Democritus, the principle rather is that like tends toward like under the influence of motion: the vortex acts rather like a sieve, organizing things according to type (68B164); and this, too, is supposed to be a result of motion and the fundamental atomic properties. Democritus's explanatory apparatus is thus simpler and more all-embracing—it is another question whether it is plausibly adequate.

7. FORMAL PRINCIPLES

Aristotle's last explanatory category is that of the formal cause; and since it is closely related to the final cause, we may deal with it briefly. The issue here has to do with structure: form is the organizational arrangement of things. Form is also essence—what things really are, and what explains their specificity. The problem with a highly reductive system of explanation, such as that of the atomists (or, at any rate on Aristotle's view, of the Milesians), is to account for the emergence not only of structure, but of stable and repeatable structure. One alternative (that of Aristotle, and in a sense of Heraclitus and Empedocles as well, and perhaps also of Anaxagoras) is simply to make form, or a form-producing principle, basic.

Heraclitus is (and was) legendarily obscure: but central to his metaphysics is the concept of the *logos* (B1–2, B50); *logos* originally means "word"; it comes to mean "account" (in any of several senses), "proportion," and finally (in Aristotle) "formula" or structural principle. It is usually supposed to have the third sense (as well as some of the second) in Heraclitus, and that may well be right, although it is too obscure to be readily assessible (after all, it is something of which "men forever prove uncomprehending": B1); but it is clearly linked with Heraclitus's other metaphysical contentions that at bottom everything is one (B50), and that in all things opposites are intrinsically intermingled (see, e.g., B60–61).

In fact, the general issue of form and its emergence only emerges explicitly in Melissus (fl. c. 440 BCE). After rehearsing a familiar Parmenidean veto on generation (30B1–2), he writes:

> nor can it change in arrangement. For the previously existing arrangement [*kosmos*] is not destroyed, nor does a nonexistent arrangement come into being. (23: Simp. *in Ph.* 1.2, 111.24–26 = B7 [3])

In other words, NN is supposed to apply to form and arrangement as well as to material: the form cannot simply pop into existence. At this point, one might reply, "Why not?"—if form is just arrangement, and to be an arrangement is to be matter ordered in a certain way, there is no pressing reason to suppose that the order itself must have been there beforehand. But that is too quick—and there may still be a serious explanatory gap here. Once again, it will not be the organization as such that requires accounting for, but the fact that it is this *particular* organization, at any rate in a stable and formally repeating world.

One group of Presocratics who did accept the necessity for formal explanations, albeit in the form of their bizarre numerological metaphysics, were the fifth-century Pythagoreans, notably Philolaus, a rough contemporary of Socrates. His first fragment exhibits a typical Presocratic ambitiousness:

> Nature in the cosmos is fitted together out of the unlimited and the limiters, both the cosmos as a whole and everything in it. (24: D.L. 8.85 = 44B1)

And fragments DK 44B2–3 offer an argument of sorts for this. Everything must be either limited or unlimited (or both—albeit presumably not in the same way); but if everything were unlimited, then nothing could know or be known (presumably because in order for something to be known, it has to be a distinct thing, and in such a universe there would be no differentiation), so there must be limiters, but equally there must be unformed stuff to limit. Philolaus thus sketched the distinction between the material and the formal cause; but it is only a sketch, and we do not know how, if at all, it was filled out (and interpretations of it are multiple and various). We do know from other fragments (B4–5) that he made number fundamental to things in the standard Pythagorean fashion; and he certainly connected number with knowability: presumably because for things to be known they must be individual, and if individual denumerable—and again presumably such particulars will be compounds of limiter and unlimited. The idea of their being fitted together (or harmonized) recurs in B6, which argues that none of the objects of knowledge (particulars in the universe) could have come to be unless from a harmony of the two great principles, namely form and what is informed. And if what survives (and there isn't much) of Philolaus does not suggest much if any physical fleshing out of that formal skeleton, nonetheless his thought represents a conceptual breakthrough of huge proportions, one also no doubt influenced by Parmenides' challenge: satisfying explanations of the world and its contents must be able to account for the emergence and stability of their form and structure.

One further fragment bears quoting in this context, from Empedocles:

> As when painters skillfully craft votive tablets...
> When they grasp many-colored pigments in their hands
> And mix them with harmony, some more, some less,
> They create from them forms alike to everything,
> Crafting trees and men and women.
> (25: Simp. *in Ph.* 160.1–5 = B23)

The mixtures of the elements in some way give rise to new properties, as do the mixtures of colors on a painter's palette: nothing comes to be literally from nothing, but such properties are emergent on combinations of the elements—they are not preceded by something that possesses and transfers them. This is an ingenious suggestion;[32] and if one is left with the feeling that it is more of a placeholder for an explanation than an explanation proper, it fares no worse than many similar modern accounts in this regard.

8. SENSATION AND EVIDENCE

Any attempt to distinguish between appearance and reality, and to account for the former in terms of some metaphysical theory of the latter, as the accounts I have been examining all, to a greater or lesser extent, seek to do, raises serious issues regarding the nature of perception and knowledge, and of the security of our access to the world we seek to explain. The problem is particularly acute for the atomists, since if, as they hold, the real properties of things are the basic properties of their atomic constituents, how do we account for the multiplicity of apparent perceptual properties? The atomists' answer is uncompromising: the only things that are real are atoms, everything else is mere appearance or convention (68B125); and a number of fragments suggest a certain skepticism with regard to the senses (68B6–10).

On the other hand, for Democritus, following Anaxagoras, "the apparent is a glimpse of the hidden" (59B21a); and it is clear that he thought that, although perceptual properties depended on the structure of the perceiver, they nonetheless would allow the perceiver to infer to the way things really are. This was a controversial thesis, and Democritus himself explored it in a dialogue between reason and the senses, in which he has the senses say: "wretched mind! Relying on our evidence, do you then seek to overthrow us? Our overthrow is your downfall too" (B125). What Democritus had reason reply is lost; but no doubt it would have taken the form of affirming that even if sense-reports can be shown to be literally untrustworthy, still the mind can construct on the basis of those reports what the world must be like in reality in order to produce them; and elsewhere he contrasts the genuine knowledge of the understanding with its "dark" perceptual sibling (68B11a).

Skeptical reflections are as old as Xenophanes:

> The clear truth no-one has ever known, nor will know,
> Concerning the gods and all the things of which I speak;
> For if he should happen in fact to utter the whole truth,
> He himself will yet not know: belief reigns over all.
> (26: S.E. *M.* 7.49.110 = B34)

And other fragments (B18, 38) seem equally pessimistic. Yet he, too, thought that, with care, progress could be made:

> The gods did not at first reveal everything to mortals
> But by seeking over time they make better discoveries.
> (27: Stob. 1.8.2 = B18)

And in general the Presocratics realistically supposed knowledge to be hard to come by rather than pessimistically thinking it to be impossible—thus Heraclitus has a Xenophanean contempt for the delusions of the multitude (B17, 19, 22, 86, 104), and he also dismisses Xenophanes' own claims to know, along with those of other philosophers (B40); but he himself thought he had penetrated to the true heart of things, the genuine structure of reality, or the *logos* (B1–2, B50).

Xenophanes' caution was perhaps motivated by his realization that the different Milesian physical explanations were incompatible with one another, but there seemed to be no obvious or principled way of deciding which (if any) of them was correct; but even so he held, like Democritus and Heraclitus (and Parmenides, in his own idiosyncratic way) that reason, properly deployed, could make good some of the deficiencies in our understanding.

Xenophanes' rationalism is perhaps most clearly displayed in his attack on traditional religion. He rejected Homer's portrayal of brawling, bickering, back-biting, adulterous Olympians as impious (B11–12), and thought that anthropo-morphism was a vulgar inanity (B14). Everybody builds gods in his own image—and if cows and horses had gods, they would look like cows and horses (B15). In contrast, he advocated a purely rationalistic, monotheistic theology, constructed on the basis of conceptual analysis of the intrinsic properties of the divine (B23–26; cf. A28, A31);[33] this is an intellectual world away from the religion of myth.

9. Natural Explanation

This leads neatly into the final strand in the fabric. At the outset we saw that the archaic world-picture was one in which humankind found itself helpless in the face of a world run by terrifying and unpredictable occult forces, at whose whim we may be raised up only to be cast low again. The best we can do is tread carefully, and try to propitiate the capricious and cruel divinities (to be sure, the Homeric poems speak of the justice of Zeus—but it is a flinty, uncompromising, draconian justice). Large-scale, indiscriminately destructive phenomena such as earthquakes and lightning-strikes, as well as portentous if not directly harmful events such as eclipses, all fall into this numinous category. One of the great advances made by the early Greek rationalists was the concerted attempt to demythologize the expla-nation of such phenomena, and to integrate them into a general picture of the causal functioning of the natural world. Such an integration will not rob them of all their terrors—but they will terrify only for what they are and do, not for what they supposedly signify and portend.

The cool, rational temper of the Presocratics manifested itself in their attempts to provide purely naturalistic accounts of such things; moreover, they sought to do so from within the framework of their particular physical accounts. Thus Thales deployed his notion of the earth's riding on water to account for the occasional quake (KRS 88); while Anaximenes likened the interior of the earth to an old building, full of hollows that might collapse without warning and as a result of a minimal initial cause (A7, 21; cf. Sen. *Q Nat.* 6.10). Anaximander thought that lightning was caused by wind rupturing the clouds (Hippol. *Haer.* 1.6.7), a view shared by Anaximenes (Hippol. *Haer.* 1.7.8), although characteristically he added an illustrative analogy—it is like what happens when oars part the sea (only presumably on a larger scale: Aët. 3.3.2). Anaximenes' fondness for analogy is well attested: the sun is "flat like a leaf" (Aët. 2.22.1), while the stars "are fixed in the crystalline like nails" ([Plu.] *On the Scientific Beliefs of the Philosophers* 890d, 889a); and in some cases they are clearly intended as more than merely poetical flourishes. The flatness of the sun may explain why it rides on the air, as leaves do (Hippol. *Haer.* 1.7.4; its flatness also account for the stability of the earth, supported on air like a saucepan lid: Arist, *Cael.* 2.13, 294b13-19); stars do not fall because, although they have no visible means of support, they are nonetheless somehow supported. In the case of lightning, comparison with a more familiar, and less awe-inspiring natural phenomenon may serve to help convince us that it, too, is natural and capable of explanation without recourse to the caprices of the divine. Eclipses, which are also a perennial source of fear, start to receive physical explanations— even more surprising, they are sometimes even the correct ones.[34] Anaximander probably deployed his bizarre account of the heavens as consisting of fire-filled hollow tires through holes in which the light escaped (Hippol. *Haer.* 1.6.4-5) to account for eclipses in terms of the physical interposition of dark objects between us and luminous ones, and so did Anaximenes, populating his heaven with "some earthy substances" (Aët. 2.13.10). Indeed eclipses and their prediction and explanation take us right back to the very beginning—Thales is said to have predicted the solar eclipse of 585 BCE (Herodotus 1.74; D.L. 1.23), and while most scholars think that if he did so it must have been a lucky guess, the important thing is that later generations thought that he might have done.

And this, in sum, is the Presocratics' achievement in the field of cause and explanation. They matter not because for the most part they really did understand the causes of things, or because their explanations were the correct ones. They are important, even crucial, in the history of ideas simply because they tried to explain things in the way they did. Looking for general, repeatable patterns of physical behavior to underlie and unify apparently disparate phenomena (lightning and the gleam of the sea cut by oars), their explanations were reductive, attempting to show how at bottom everything was a manifestation of the fundamental physical natures of things. And while no Presocratic philosopher (as far as we know at least) made a serious attempt to subject the notions of cause and explanation themselves to second-order philosophical scrutiny (the Hippocratic doctors went further in this regard, as in a different way did fifth-century forensic rhetoricians such as Antiphon), at least they laid the foundations for the great enterprise of natural science, an enterprise that seeks at once to understand and render familiar the strange and numinous phenomena of the world. Eclipses are no longer the random outcomes of divine whim, but the regular results of regular (albeit hugely complex) natural motions. And to render the world thus amenable, at least in principle, to prediction, even if they failed for the most part actually to make the predictions (that would have to wait on later generations), is the great achievement of the Presocratics, in all their disparate panoply. In the world of myth, human beings are alienated interlopers. The Presocratics began to create a world we could all be at home in.

NOTES

1. This and subsequent quotations are numbered for ease of reference.

2. At any rate, before the Paracelsan salt, sulphur, and mercury; Aristotle may have had Heraclitus in mind: 22B31, B36; and see section 3 (passage 9); but this is very unlikely.

3. On this useful if slippery distinction, see Barnes, *PP* 39–44.

4. Compare the following report from Aristotle: "some say that it [i.e., the earth] rests on water . . . and they say it was advanced by Thales of Miletus who thought that the earth rests because it can float like a log or something else of such a kind (for none of these things can rest on air, but they can rest on water) as if the same must not hold of the water as holds of the earth itself" (*Cael.* 2.13, 294a28–34 = 11A14). Aristotle is obviously unimpressed with the explanation (it recalls Locke's Indian "who, saying that the world was supported by a great elephant, was asked, what the elephant rested on? to which his answer was, a great tortoise: but being again pressed to know what gave support to the broad-backed tortoise, replied, something, he knew not what": *Essay* 2.23.2); but it is worth noting that Thales supplies a reason (of sorts) as to why the heavy earth might be stable—other heavy things can be seen to float stably (on this style of analogical explanation, see further section 9).

5. See also Heraclitus Homericus: "the moist nature is readily molded into each thing, and is accustomed to change in subtle ways; for the exhaled part of it becomes air, and the lightest part is kindled from the air into fire, while water, when it is compressed, also changes into slime and becomes earth; for this reason Thales averred that water was the element that was most causal, as it were, of the quartet of elements" (*All.* 22 = KRS 87).

6. This explanatory failure was noted by Herodotus (4.8 = 5 KRS).

7. See KRS 92-94, and the scholars cited there.

8. So, effectively, Barnes, *Early Greek Philosophy*, 60.

9. Hence the generic term 'Milesian', used to refer to Thales, Anaximander and Anaximenes.

10. The claim is also made in Simplicius (*in Ph.* 24.13–17), but that is evidentially worthless, since both Simplicius and Hippolytus are clearly relying on the same doxographical source. For discussion, see KRS 108–9; Kahn, *Anaximander and the Origins of Greek Cosmology*, 29–32.

11. See KRS 109-11; Barnes, *PP* 29, 36.

12. Barnes, *PP* 29-35, offers a skeptical assessment of our evidence for attributing to Anaximander any of the following considerations, which are admittedly only attested in much later texts—but I think the skepticism is overdone. See also Kahn, *Anaximander and the Origins of Greek Cosmology*, 44–46, 231–39; KRS 129–30.

13. This account is given by Simplicius, *in Ph.* 24.21–24; see Arist. *Ph.* 1.4, 187a20–23.

14. Compare the view attributed to Thales, note 4 here.

15. It is not necessary to ascribe to Anaximenes, as some have done, a two-level account of physical processes, in which the elements are phase-states of the basic air, and everything else mixtures and compounds of elements: see Hankinson, *Cause and Explanation in Ancient Greek Thought*, 19.

16. An exception is Barnes, *PP*, ch. 3, who in a refreshingly, if not wholly convincingly, contrarian manner sees Anaximenes as superior to his predecessor in almost every way.

17. The words in quotation marks probably closely approximate Anaximenes' actual words, although most scholars do not accept them as *ipsissima verba*.

18. This is usually regarded as a genuine fragment; but both the vocabulary and the style seem late, Stoic even (see KRS 159; on the other hand, there is no reason to doubt the ascription of the doctrine itself to Anaximenes).

19. Aristotle did not appreciate the answer: at *Cael.* 2.13, 294a21–24, he censures Xenophanes on this score for intellectual idleness: "he did this in order not to look for an explanation of the matter."

20. His dates and his chronological relation to Empedocles are both controversial (for some forthright views, see Kahn, *Anaximander and the Origins of Greek Cosmology*, 163-65); but fortunately we need not be any more precise than this.

21. This at any rate seems to the obvious way to interpret the physics—some, however, have thought Anaxagoras to be a sort of corpuscularian. For an excellent discussion of the issues, see Barnes, *PP* ch. 16.

22. *Pace* Cornford, "Anaxagoras' Theory of Matter," 14.

23. However see KRS 127–28 for a skeptical assessment: they make Anaximander's *apeiron* itself simply (and unanalyzedly) a source for movement.

24. See Barnes, *PP* 114–20; Hankinson, "Greek Medical Models of the Mind"; Hankinson, *Cause and Explanation in Ancient Greek Thought*, 30-33.

25. I do not have space to discuss Empedocles' curious account of the development and selection of animals (see B57–62); or his prescient understanding of biological analogy and homology (B79, B82–83).

26. See KRS 421–23.

27. I assume that the best way to understand Parmenides' argument involves this sort of formulation; but this is controversial, and some prefer to interpret coming-to-be as coming into existence as such.

28. This is the "Principle of Causal Synonymy" (see Arist. *Ph.* 8.5, 257b9–14): what makes something *F* must itself be *F*; the principle is clearly not universally applicable, but nor is it as negligible as is sometimes supposed; see Barnes, *PP* 88–89, 118–19; Hankinson, *Cause and Explanation in Ancient Greek Thought*, 31–32, 346–48, 449.

29. But see KRS 194–97.

30. But see KRS 113–15.

31. Some fragments may be more literalist in tone, however: see B32; but Heraclitus is unremittingly hostile to ordinary religious practice: B5, B14–15, B93.

32. For an interesting development of it, see Mourelatos, "Quality, Structure, and Emergence in Later Pre-Socratic Philosophy."

33. See Barnes, *PP*, ch. 5, for a rigorous discussion of Xenophanes' theology.

34. It is not clear when the first genuine explanation of lunar eclipse in terms of the interposition of the earth between sun and moon was given—but for Aristotle it is already old hat, and Parmenides knew that the moon shone by reflected light: 28B14.

BIBLIOGRAPHY

Barnes, Jonathan. *Early Greek Philosophy*. London: Penguin, 1987.

Cornford, F. M. "Anaxagoras' Theory of Matter." *Classical Quarterly* 24 (1930): 14–30, 83–95.

Hankinson, R. J. *Cause and Explanation in Ancient Greek Thought*. Oxford: Clarendon Press, 1998.

———. "Greek Medical Models of the Mind." In *Psychology*, edited by Stephen Everson, Companions to Ancient Thought, vol. 2, 194–217. Cambridge: Cambridge University Press, 1991.

Kahn, Charles H. *Anaximander and the Origins of Greek Cosmology*. New York: Columbia University Press, 1960.

Mourelatos, Alexander P. D. "Quality, Structure, and Emergence in Later Pre-Socratic Philosophy." *Proceedings of the Boston Area Colloquium in Ancient Philosophy* 2 (1987): 127–94.

CHAPTER 17

THE HUMANIZING OF KNOWLEDGE IN PRESOCRATIC THOUGHT

J. H. LESHER

1. THE OLDER PESSIMISTIC OUTLOOK

Near the outset of the *Metaphysics*, Aristotle briefly considers the possibility that knowledge of the ultimate principles of explanation might exceed human capacities. Perhaps, as the poet Simonides had declared, "only God can have this privilege" (1.1, 982b28–30). Although Aristotle dismisses the idea (insofar as "jealousy would be unfitting for the divine" and "poets tell many a lie"), the poets of archaic Greece had often disparaged the intellectual capacities of mortal beings.[1] The only exceptions to this broad indictment were seers, prophets, and the poets themselves, who claimed a share in divine wisdom.[2] As Guthrie summed up the general outlook: "It was already a commonplace of poetry, expressed in invocations to the Muses and elsewhere, that mankind had no sure knowledge unless the gods chose to reveal it."[3] The motivating impulse behind this view was probably more religious than epistemological: with respect to wisdom and intelligence, as with all other things worth having, the gods have everything while mortals have nothing.

Traces of the traditional piety, however, can be seen in the writings of a number of Presocratic philosophers. In his famous fragment B34, Xenophanes proclaimed that "no man has known or ever will know the clear and certain

truth ... but opinion is allotted to all." One later commentator summed up Xenophanes' message in these terms: "It is for god to know and humans to opine."[4]
Heraclitus also affirmed that "Human nature does not have intelligent insights
[gnômas], but the divine does" (B78),[5] and so in similar terms said Alcmaeon,
Parmenides, Empedocles, and Philolaus.[6] Parmenides framed his account of the
nature of what is as an insight imparted to him by a goddess, both Pythagoras and
Empedocles appear to have claimed divine status, and disparaging references to
"know-nothing mortals" continue to be made.[7] In these respects, at least, the
Presocratic philosophers appear to have taken the mantle of the divinely inspired
poet or seer and wrapped it around themselves.

In what follows, however, I will argue that while some aspects of the older
outlook remained, it would be a mistake to see the Presocratic philosophers,
including those just mentioned, as perpetuating the "pious pessimism" of an
earlier period. A review of the relevant fragments and *testimonia* will show
that Xenophanes, Alcmaeon, Heraclitus, and Parmenides—even Pythagoras and
Empedocles—all moved some distance away from the older "god-oriented" view
of knowledge toward a more secular and optimistic outlook.[8] But to get some sense
of the dynamics at work in this transition we must begin, as virtually every account
of early Greek thought must begin, with Homer and Hesiod.

2. KNOWLEDGE AND IGNORANCE IN EARLY GREEK POETRY

One passage often considered the *locus classicus* for Homer's view of the cognitive
powers of mortal beings is the well-known "second invocation" of the Muses in
Iliad 2. As the singer prepares to launch into his listing of "the captains of all those
who sailed to Troy," he calls on divine powers for assistance:

> Tell me now Muses who have dwellings on Olympus—
> For you are goddesses, you are present, and know [iste] all things,
> Whereas we hear only a report and know [idmen] nothing—
> Who were the captains of the Danaans and their lords.
> But the vast number I could neither tell nor name,
> Not if I had ten tongues, and ten mouths,
> A voice unwearying, and a heart of bronze within me,
> Did not the Muses of Olympus, daughters of Zeus who bears the aegis,
> Call to my mind [mnêsaiath'] those who came beneath Ilios.
> And now I will tell the leaders and their ships ... (484–93)

These words have often been thought to show that during this early period,
"knowing" was regarded as essentially synonymous with "having seen" (insofar as

the knowledge credited to the Muses is linked to their omnipresence), that the "we" referred to in the second line means "mortal beings" generally, and that the "nothing" in the third line means "no information on any subject whatsoever."[9] In defense of this reading, it must be granted that the knowledge claimed by or granted to the figures who appear in the Homeric poems is often grounded in their direct observation of an event or state of affairs. As Menelaus comments at one point to Antilochus:

> Since you have observed it for yourself [auton eisoroônta], I think you
> Already know [gignôskein] that a god has rolled destruction on the
>   Danaans
> And given victory to the Trojans. (Il. 17.687–88)[10]

But while individuals do often come to know the truth on the basis of what they directly witness, it would be a mistake to identify "Homeric knowing" with eyewitness experience or "having seen," and to read the prayer to the Muses as the opening salvo in a campaign of philosophical skepticism. Even here, in the context of a comparison of divine and mortal forms of awareness, it is clear that the poet offers an account based not on autopsy or direct personal experience but on reliable information provided by others who were themselves eyewitnesses to the original event.[11] Moreover, in Iliad 20 Aeneas says to Achilles:

> We know [idmen] each other's lineage and know [idmen] each
>   other's parents,
> Having heard words of mortal men handed down by tradition
>   [epea prokluta],
> But not by sight [opsei] have you seen my parents, nor I yours. (203–5)[12]

And knowledge in the form of special "skills" or "expertise" is often linked with the promptings or instruction given by others. Homer speaks of a carpenter "well skilled in all manner of craft by the promptings of Athena" (Il. 15.411–12); of "Calchas . . . who had guided the ships of the Achaeans to Ilios by the soothsaying that Phoebus Apollo had bestowed upon him" (Il. 1.69–72); and of the Sirens who promised Odysseus that he would "know more" since they themselves "knew all things that come to pass" (Od. 12.188).

What a person learns may also be a general truth or principle acquired through extensive experience rather than a single truth based on direct observation of a particular situation:

> For I know [oida] that cowards shrink from battle
> Whereas he who would excel in battle must steadfastly stand his ground.
> (Il. 11.408–9)

Similarly, knowledge can be gained not though simple observation but through the use of an instructive trial or testing procedure. When Zeus threatens to hurl into

Tartarus any god he catches giving aid to either side of the conflict, he boasts that such an act will confirm the magnitude of his powers:

Then you shall know [gnôsete] just how mighty among the gods I am.
But come, gods, make trial [peirêsasthe] so you will all know [eidete].
    (Il. 8.18)

In the Iliad, the relevant testing is quite often a "trial by arms" in order to determine the superior warrior:

But come, make trial [peirêsai], so that these too may know [gnôôsi].
Straightway, I tell you, your dark blood will flow around my spear.
    (Il. 1. 302–3)[13]

In the Odyssey, though, the testing often takes the form of an athletic competition:

Of the rest, if any man's heart and spirit bid him,
Let him come here and be put to a trial [peirêthêtô] . . .
But of the others I will refuse none and make light of none,
But I wish to know [idmen] and try them [peirêthêmenai] face to face.
    (Od. 8.204–5, 212–13)

When, in book 6, Odysseus awakens to the sound of the voices of Nausicaa and her companions, his response sets the tone for his conduct throughout the poem:

But, come, I will make trial [peirêsomai], and see for myself.
    (Od. 6.126)

Each of these three "routes to knowledge"—direct observation, the reliable testimony of others, and the setting of a test or trial—appears in Homer's account of Odysseus's reception by the members of his household. Telemachus discovers the stranger's true identity when he is told the truth (Od. 6.188); the old hound Argos knows his master the moment he spots him (hôs enoêsen, 17.301); and Eurycleia and the shepherds recognize Odysseus by touching (19.468) and seeing (21.217–25) the identifying scar on his leg. Penelope, however, discovers the stranger's identity neither from visual indicators nor on the basis of assurances given to her, but by putting the stranger to a trial or test (see peirômenê at 23.181). When a seemingly casual suggestion to relocate the marital bed provokes an involuntary flash of anger from Odysseus (23.181–204), Penelope gets the telltale indicator (sêma) she has been waiting for.

There are also many references in both poems to knowledge in the form of physical expertise gained through extensive experience:

I know [oida] how to wield to the right and left a shield of
    seasoned hide . . .

I know [*oida*] also how to charge into the battles of swift mares,
And I know [*oida*] how to do the dance of Ares one-on-one. (*Il.* 7.238–41)

We hear of warriors who are *epistamenoi polemizein*—"skilled in fighting" (*Il.* 2.611), of others who are *toxôn eu eidôs*—"well skilled with bows" (*Il.* 2.718), as well as those who are *êpia pharmaka eidôs*—"skilled in soothing drugs" (*Il.* 4.218). In the *Odyssey*, there are fewer references to skill in the arts of war and medicine and more to individuals such as Odysseus who "know all manner of devices and tricks" (*eidotes . . . kerdea, Od.* 13.296–97).[14]

Thus, the somber tone of "the second invocation of the Muses" notwithstanding, the figures who appear in Homer's stories enjoy access to an extensive body of factual knowledge and performative expertise acquired from a variety of different sources. In general, an individual may assert *autos oida* or "I know for myself"[15] on the basis of what he or she has directly perceived, or established through some form of testing or learned over time, and one may also discover a good many facts or truths through information or testimony supplied by others.[16]

Nevertheless, two broadly pessimistic themes relating to knowledge emerge over the course of both epics. The first, more characteristic of the *Odyssey* than the *Iliad*, is that mortals do not always immediately grasp the full significance of what they experience. While many are able to observe Odysseus when he appears in disguise among the Trojans, only Helen recognizes who he really is (*anegnôn, Od.* 4.250). And although there are many signs of impending disaster, only the seer Theoclymenus is able to "take note of" (*noeô*) the evil about to befall the suitors (*Od.* 20.351). The ability to "see through" or "see beyond" what appears or is directly apparent to the senses is in some respects a hallmark of intelligence. So frequent and central to Homer's story are these moments of discovery, or failures in discovery, that Aristotle identified "recognition" (*anagnôrisis*) as the poem's main theme (*Poetics* 1459b15).

Second, one particular body of knowledge that is consistently regarded as the special prerogative of the gods and the select few mortals with whom they choose to share it is knowledge of events or conditions in distant places and times. Virtually by definition, the gods and goddesses live forever and enjoy a synoptic view of events as they look down from their superior vantage points.[17] Being able to comprehend the larger course of events spread out over time—"knowing how to look before and after" as the idea is commonly expressed—is also the characteristic excellence of those rare specimens of human wisdom.[18] By contrast, the characteristic failure of "foolish morals" is an inability to look beyond their actions and present circumstances in order to appreciate the long-term consequences. Achilles famously faults Agamemnon in just these terms:

> Nor does he know how to think of what lies before and after
>   [*noêsai prossô kai opissô*]
> So the Achaeans might safely wage war beside their ships. (*Il.* 1.343–44)

Similarly, the failure of Penelope's suitors to sense the disaster that lies ahead of them marks them all as *nêpioi*—"fools who did not know that over them one and all the cords of destruction had been made fast."[19] In his speech to Amphinomus, Odysseus identifies the inability to "see ahead" as a defining characteristic of the human race:

> Nothing feebler does earth nurture than man,
> Of all the things that move and breath on the earth.
> For he thinks that he will never suffer evil in the time to come [opissô],
> So long as the gods give him prosperity and his knees are quick;
> But when again the gods decree him sorrow;
> This too he bears with a steadfast heart.
> For such is the mind [noos] of man upon the earth,
> Like the day the father of gods and men brings to him. (Od. 18.130–37)

About the larger dimensions of events—how long health and prosperity will last, or what kind of fate awaits each individual—these matters must remain dark to a race of beings who can think of things only in terms of what they have "met with" or directly experienced for themselves.[20] "Wisdom," in such cases, consists in seeking the kind of truth that befits our mortal nature and avoiding "aiming too high."

Typically, however, the poet who gives expression to these pessimistic sentiments regards himself as a happy exception to the general rule. Hesiod proclaims that

> the mind of Zeus who holds the aegis is different at different times,
> and it is hard for men to conceive it [argaleos . . . noêsai]. (Op. 483–84)

Yet the Muses have selected him to sing "beautiful song" (Th. 22), "tell of realities" (Op. 10), and "celebrate the things that will be and were before" (Th. 32, 38). As he undertakes to relate "the mind of Zeus" (more specifically, the cycles of sea winds and weather) Hesiod invokes the Muses as his authorities, claiming that his poetic prowess more than makes up for a lack of experience:

> I will show you the measures of the loud-resounding sea,
> Although I am skilled [sesophismenos] in neither ships nor sea-faring;
> For never yet have I sailed by ship over a broad sea . . .
> So much is my experience [pepeirêmai] of many-pegged ships.
> Nevertheless, I will tell you the mind of Zeus who holds the aegis,
> For the Muses have taught me to sing in marvelous song.
>   (Op. 648–50, 660–62)[21]

Theognis and Pindar also present themselves to their audiences as individuals endowed with a knowledge that sets them apart from the general run of humankind:

> And from whence the strife of immortals arose,
> concerning these things the gods are able to prompt wise poets,

though it is impossible for mortal men to find it out.
But since you maiden Muses know all things, you are permitted this,
along with Memory and the cloud-wrapped father,
so listen now, for my tongue loves to pour forth
the choicest and sweetest bloom of song...(Pi. *Pae.* 6.51–58)

A servant and messenger of the Muses, if preeminent in knowledge (*perisson eideiê*), should not be begrudging of his expertise (*sophia*), but should seek out these, point out those, invent other things, for to whom is he useful if he alone is knowledgeable (*epistamenos*)? (Thgn. 769–72).

The poetic verdict on "the *noos* of mortals" was, therefore, decidedly mixed. Human beings can discover truth and develop expertise in many different areas—either through their own efforts and devices or with the assistance of others. Direct observation, the testimony of a reliable source, and the setting of a trial or test can all provide a suitable basis for gaining insight or understanding. Nevertheless, whatever the character of its achievements, the *noos* of mortals is still constrained to operate within a narrow set of circumstances. Most people are unable to expand their understanding beyond the immediate environment in which they find themselves, and no one—without some form of divine assistance—can possibly know anything about events or states of affairs in distant realms and periods.[22] There is, then, a consistent if somewhat mixed "folk epistemology" that runs through the earliest period of Greek literature. And there is good reason to believe that the first philosophers knew and responded to it.

3. PRESOCRATIC VARIATIONS ON THE TRADITIONAL THEME

Our knowledge of the teachings of the Presocratics is of course incomplete and subject to conflicting interpretations, but enough remains to support a view of the members of this group as gradually moving away from the older, essentially religious perspective on knowledge and toward a more secular and optimistic outlook. In the case of the earliest figures known to us, the Milesian philosopher-scientists Thales, Anaximander, and Anaximenes, we can only infer a more optimistic outlook on the basis of their wide-ranging investigations and theories; we have no comments concerning the sources or limits of knowledge from any member of this group.[23] For a number of other Presocratic thinkers, however, there is a good deal more to go on.

3.1. Pythagoras and Empedocles

If there is anything we can be reasonably sure of in connection with the semi-legendary figure of Pythagoras of Samos, it is that he was widely credited with a special body of knowledge. In one of the earliest ancient *testimonia*, Xenophanes of

Colophon reports that Pythagoras claimed to recognize (*egnôn*) the soul of a departed friend from the cries of a yelping puppy (B7). Similarly, Heraclitus B40 cites Pythagoras as one of those who prove that "much learning" (*polumathiê*) does not teach "an intelligent understanding" (*noos*), and Heraclitus B81a and 129 castigate Pythagoras as a "prince of swindlers" who "trained himself the most of all human beings in inquiry [*historiên*] and, having selected from these writings, constructed a wisdom [*sophiên*] of his own—a "much learning" [*polumathiên*] that was also a piece of skullduggery [*kakotechniê*]." Clearly, some claim to a special body of "expertise" or "learning" must have prompted these attacks.

Other ancient writers appear to have viewed Pythagoras's "creative borrowings" in a more positive light. Diogenes Laertius (1.120) quotes the fifth-century poet Ion of Chios: "if indeed Pythagoras was really wise [*sophos*], who above all others knew and learned [*eide kai exemathen*] the opinions of men." By far the most enthusiastic assessment is found in Empedocles' fragment B129:

> And there was among them a man of surpassing knowledge [*periôsia eidôs*],
> master especially of all kinds of wise works, who had acquired the utmost wealth
> of understanding [*prapidôn ... plouton*]: for whenever he reached out with all his
> understanding, easily he saw the things that are in ten and even twenty generations
> of men.

Other accounts credit Pythagoras with attributes characteristic of supermortal status: having lived a number of different lives,[24] being seen at widely separated locations at the same time,[25] and possessing a golden thigh (a sign, as Burkert explained, of being authorized to travel to the underworld).[26] Other sources credit him with performing miracles and predicting the future (an impending earthquake, that a ship would sink, that Sybaris would be conquered, etc.).[27]

Before Pythagoras's time, the two miracle workers and "servants of Apollo" Aristeas and Abaris had been hailed in similar terms. Within Pythagoras's own lifetime, there were the miracle worker Epimenides of Crete and the theologian and proto-cosmologist Pherecydes from the Cyclades. The "Pythagoras legend" is richly interwoven with references to all of these individuals.[28] Diogenes Laertius says that Pythagoras "studied with Pherecydes ... and went down into a cave on Ida in Crete with Epimenides ... and entered the sanctuaries in Egypt and learned the ineffable mysteries of the gods" (2.3). Thus, whether or not the model can be traced back to the shamans of central Asia, as some have believed,[29] there is a sizable body of evidence that Pythagoras presented himself to others, and perhaps even saw himself,[30] as one who had been raised above mortal status, endowed with a superhuman grasp of the nature of things, and authorized to impart this special wisdom to others.

A generation later, Empedocles presents himself to his audience in much the same terms:

> O friends, who dwell in the great city of the yellow Acragas ...
> Hail! I, in your eyes a deathless god, no longer mortal,
> go among all, honored, just as I seem. ... And they follow at once,

in their ten thousands, asking where is the path to gain,
some in need of divinations, others in all sorts of diseases
sought to hear a healing oracle,
having been pierced about by harsh pains for too long a time. (B112)[31]

In this way let not deception overcome your thought organ
[by convincing you] that the source of mortal things,
as many as have become obvious—countless—is anything else,
but know these things clearly, having heard the story from a god. (B23)

For I have already become a boy and a girl
and a bush and a bird and a fish [corrupt text] from the sea. (B117)

And finally they become prophets and singers and doctors
and leaders among men who dwell on earth;
thence they sprout up as gods, first in their prerogatives. (B146)[32]

But while both Pythagoras and Empedocles presented themselves to their audiences or followers as divinely inspired individuals, neither appears to have regarded his special status as a precondition for all knowledge, or knowledge in general. The evidence for Pythagorean doctrines is of course late, fragmentary, and highly suspect, but a number of Pythagoras's associates appear to have regarded him as one who had passed down to others the key to understanding the nature of all things. In the *Philebus*, Plato may be describing Pythagoras's legacy to humankind when he relates:

> There is a gift—so it seems to me— that the gods let fall from their abode, and it was through Prometheus, or someone like him, that it reached mankind, together with a fire exceeding bright. The men of old, who were better than we are, passed on this gift in the form of a saying. All things, so it ran, that are ever said to be consist of a one and many, and have in their nature a conjunction of limit and unlimited. This then being the ordering of things we ought, they said, whatever it be that we are dealing with, to assume a single form . . . then we must go from one form to look for two, if the case admits of there being two, otherwise for three or some other number of forms. (16d)

Testimonials to the sacred powers of the *tetraktys* reinforce this view of Pythagoras as one who imparted to humankind the important insight that the study of numbers held the key to understanding the real natures of things.[33]

To the extent to which the fragments ascribed to Philolaus afford some insight into the nature of fifth-century Pythagorean thinking,[34] we can conclude that at least one strain in the Pythagorean tradition focused on understanding numerical relationships as the key to grasping the nature of all things. Philolaus B3 speaks of the possession or imposition of a limit as a precondition for knowledge,[35] and B4 restricts the knowable to the numerable.[36] Fragment B6 makes a broader epistemological claim concerning the natural order as well as the eternal reality from which it has been derived:

> Concerning nature and harmony the situation is this: the being of things, which is eternal, and nature in itself admit of divine and not human knowledge, except [plan ga] that it was impossible for any of the things that are and are known by us to have come to be, if the being of the things from which the world-order came together, both the limiting and the unlimited things, did not preexist. But since these beginnings preexisted and were neither alike nor even related, it would have been impossible for them to be ordered, if a harmony had not come upon them, in whatever way it came to be. (trans. Huffman, *Philolaus of Croton*)

In other words, phenomena that occur within the natural realm are knowable to the extent they are numerable, and "that which exists eternally" or "nature in itself" can also be known insofar as it must satisfy certain general conditions. What exists eternally could not have given rise to the natural order we are familiar with (and understand through the study of numbers) unless there existed: (1) something unlimited, (2) one or more limits to impose on what was unlimited, and (3) some harmonizing force with the power to impose the latter on the former. In short, Philolaus regards what can be determined to be the case through philosophical reflection (here, the necessary conditions for things existing as they do) as representing an important exception to the standard denial of knowledge to mortal beings.

Similarly, even though Empedocles claims divine status and powers for himself, he encourages those in his audience to seek knowledge of each thing "in the way it is clear":

> But come, consider, by every device, how each thing is clear,
> neither holding any sight more trustworthy than hearing
> nor resounding hearing above the clarities of tongue,
> nor withholding trust in any degree from the other faculties,
> in whatever way a pathway is available for understanding.
> But understand each thing in the way in which it is clear. (B3.4–8)

Although Empedocles subscribes to the traditional notion that "we think what we meet with" (see B2 quoted in n.6) he gives the ancient maxim a positive spin: since the thoughts of mortals are determined by what they happen to experience, they must take care to expose themselves to what is worthy of being learned:

> For if, thrusting them down in your crowded sense thinking organs,
> you gaze on them in kindly fashion, with pure meditations,
> absolutely all these things will be with you throughout your life...
> But if you reach out for different things, such as
> the ten thousand wretched things, which are among men and
> blunt their meditations,
> truly they will abandon you quickly, as time circles round,
> desiring to arrive at their own dear kind [lit. birth or generation].
> For know that all have thought and a share of understanding. (B110)

Pythagoras and Empedocles may have claimed divine status or divine insights for themselves but both encouraged their students or followers to gain a proper understanding of the cosmos by directing their own thoughts along certain specific lines.

3.2. Xenophanes and Alcmaeon

As noted, the ancient doxographer Arius Didymus credited Xenophanes of Colophon with a pious view of the cognitive capacities of mortals:

> There was a respectable tradition among the Greeks concerning Xenophanes
> that he rebuked in jest the audacity of others and demonstrated his own piety (in
> holding that) God therefore knows the truth, while "opinion is fashioned for all."[37]

The concluding phrase placed within quotation marks is taken from Xenophanes' B34:

> And indeed no man has been nor will there be one
> Who knows [*eidôs*] what is clear and certain [*to saphes*]
> About the gods and such things as I say about all things.
> For even if at best one were to succeed in speaking of what is brought
>   to pass
> Still he himself would not know. But opinion [*dokos*] is fashioned
>   for all.[38]

Since the fragment begins *to men oun*—"and indeed"—it is entirely possible that we do not have the whole of Xenophanes' remark, or all the considerations from which its main conclusion was meant to follow. But the use of the term *saphês* by his Ionian contemporary the historian Herodotus provides a helpful clue. At several points in his *History* Herodotus speaks of what is *saphes*, or what can be known in a *sapheôs* manner, as what can be confirmed to be the case on the basis of firsthand observation.[39] Since the gods were thought to inhabit a realm far removed from that of mortal beings, it would be natural for Xenophanes to have thought that no account of their nature and activities could ever be established as correct on the basis of first-hand observation, hence known for certain to be correct.[40] And since the pioneering cosmological accounts put forward by his Milesian predecessors had asserted that a single material substance underlay *all* phenomena (past, present, and future), it would be equally impossible for any individual to confirm on the basis of firsthand observation the truth of so universal a claim, hence know for certain that it was correct—even if in fact it was correct.[41] The sentiments expressed in lines 3 and 4 might then be seen as reinforcing this cautionary sentiment. The point would be that no one (moreover) should be credited with knowledge (of the certain truth concerning the gods or the nature of all things) simply on the basis of having correctly spoken of individual events as they take place (perhaps an implicit reference to self-styled paragons of wisdom who were also famous predictors of events—including the same Pythagoras whom Xenophanes ridiculed for his special knowledge). The primary message of B34, from its opening reference to "no man" to its concluding phrase "fashioned for all" would have been that there never has been and never will be anyone who can possess certain knowledge concerning all these important but ultimately unobservable matters. Fragment B34, then, repeats the familiar refrain that while mortals may discover much about matters lying within the circle of their daily experiences, knowledge concerning events or circumstances in distant places and times must exceed their grasp.

Nevertheless, Xenophanes' allocation of human awareness to the category of "opinion" or "conjecture" (dokos) is not an inherently dismissive characterization. By Platonic standards, certainly, "opinion"—even when correct—would still be considered inferior to knowledge, but there is no reason to assume that Xenophanes viewed dokos in the same light. Xenophanes B35, for example, quoted by Plutarch to encourage a bashful speaker, speaks of "opinion" in a positive vein: "Let these be believed [dedoxasthô] as like the realities." The similarity between the verbal imperative dedoxasthô of B35 and the nominative dokos of B34 suggest a somewhat moderated pessimism: there never was nor will be anyone who knows the deepest truths, but dokos—opinion or conjecture—has been "fashioned" or made available for all mortal beings. Certainly a more positive view of the prospects for knowledge emerges from the well-known B18:

> Not indeed from the outset did gods reveal all things to mortals,
> But, in time, by seeking they discover something better.

The full resonance of these remarks has been much debated, but it is impossible not to sense some degree of opposition between the divine revelation or "intimation" (upodeixan) mentioned in line 1 and the "inquiry" or "seeking" (zêtountes) in line 2. Whether discovery takes place with divine assistance or without it, and whether the subject matter is the workings of the cosmos or "progress" in the conditions of life generally, there is an unmistakably upbeat quality to B18. Taken together, B18, B34, and B35 signal a departure the older poetic outlook: the poets claim that the limitations inherent in human existence will forever prevent mortals from discovering the most basic truths about the cosmos and the nature of the gods themselves, yet "something better," and "opinion" about these and other matters, still lies within our reach.[42]

Fragment B1 of Alcmaeon of Croton reaffirms the familiar distinction between divine and mortals, but here, too, there is at least a suggestion of a partial change in outlook:

The gods possess certainty [sapheneian] concerning nonevident matters, but [it is given to] men to conjecture from signs [tekmairesthai]. (B1)[43]

It is possible that Alcmaeon was just repeating the familiar divine-human refrain—the gods have certain knowledge and mortals must make do with mere conjecture. Yet a less traditional reading is also possible: the gods have knowledge about matters that are far removed from human observation (*ta aphanea*), yet mortals have the capacity to learn at least some things on their own by "inferring from signs."[44]

3.3. Heraclitus

Heraclitus B78 holds that "The human nature (*êthos anthôpeion*) does not possess insight, but the divine does," and B32 speaks in a similar vein of a divine being as the "one, the only wise thing." Yet when Heraclitus goes on to state that this "one wise thing is both willing and unwilling to be called by the name of Zeus" (B32), we begin to sense some movement away from the traditional identification of wisdom with the gods of Greek popular religion. The power that rules the cosmos, and is the one truly wise or intelligent being, is in some ways like Zeus, but in other ways it is not. As B53 explains, the epithet traditionally ascribed to Zeus, "father of all and king of all," is now ascribed to *Polemos*—"war" or "conflict." Fragment B41 helps to fill out the new point of view when it identifies "the one wise thing" not as Zeus but as "knowing the intelligent understanding [*epistasthai gnômên*], how all things are steered through all," thereby suggesting that wisdom may exist *in us*, insofar as we align our thoughts with the Zeus-like power that rules and orders the cosmos. Taken in isolation, B78 sounds like the standard indictment of mortal intelligence, but seen in its context, it is rather Heraclitus's way of claiming that insight and wisdom come to mortal beings not as part of their natural endowment but to the extent to which they learn how to think and speak about the cosmos.

Exactly how those who heard Heraclitus's teachings were to escape from their benighted condition to achieve some understanding of cosmic truths has never been entirely clear.[45] On some accounts, Heraclitus called for the acquisition of extensive information through sense perception—the testimony of "eye and ear" or "fact-finding travel and direct observation" (i.e., Ionian-style *historiê*)—as a preliminary first stage of inquiry. But not only is the textual basis for this reading inconclusive at a crucial point, there is no indication that Heraclitus himself ever practiced *historiê*—as there is clear evidence that his Ionian predecessors sought to gather information on conditions in other regions. On the contrary, he announces "I inquired into myself" (B101). We should see Heraclitus as urging those in his audience not to focus their attention on the appearances of things, but to try to get beyond appearances to the unifying force or forces lying behind apparently discordant phenomena.

In various ways Heraclitus makes it clear that one key feature of "this *logos*" (as well as his *logos*) is "the hidden unity of opposites"—the way many if not all natural phenomena embody an internal "tension" or "strife" among opposite qualities and forces, a conflict symbolized, perhaps also epitomized, by fire. Under the general heading "unity in opposition," Heraclitus observes (1) that things that are the same can also be different—for example, that one and the same road can be both the road down and the road up—depending on the direction one is headed, or that seawater can be both pure and polluted—depending on whether it is fish or people who are drinking it; or that the same river contains ever-changing waters, and so on; (2) that things that are different can also be the same, for example, that classic opposites like day and night, high and low notes, and male and female can also be understood as closely linked with one another, both conceptually, and as causally related phenomena; and (3) that many entities work to sustain the existence and proper functioning of their opposite numbers— for example, that "disease makes health pleasant and good, as hunger does satiety, and weariness does rest" (B111). And because tension or conflict between the opposites is seen as a positive, creative force at work throughout the cosmos, Heraclitus concludes that "war is father and king of all" and that "all things happen by strife and necessity" (B80).

The mention in B40 of Xenophanes and the Milesian geographer Hecataeus— both exponents of *historia*—suggests that no amount of inquiry in the tradition of the Ionian philosopher-scientists can bring one to a proper appreciation of the *logos*:

> The learning of many things does not teach understanding (*noos*); or else it would have taught Hesiod and Pythagoras, and again Xenophanes and Hecataeus.

As stated in B1, "even men of experience are like men of no experience" when it comes to grasping the *logos*. The inclusion of Hesiod and Pythagoras in this indictment would suggest that poets and seers who claim to have gained truth from divine sources have done no better than those who travel about the world observing things for themselves. Fragment B107 reinforces the point that a proper understanding of the real nature of things cannot be extracted from the information supplied by the senses: "Bad witnesses are eyes and ears of those having barbarian souls." Our sensory faculties provide false or misleading testimony to those not already attuned to the hidden principle of unity. In strictly sensory terms, no two things could be more different, more "at opposite ends of the spectrum" than light and dark—or, as we might say, "as different as night and day." So if our aim is to discover how things that differ can also be the same, we must move beyond mere sensory content and into the realm of thought and reflection.

A second element in the traditional view of human *noos*, the notion that mortals "think such things as they meet with"—that their thoughts reflect only their own (extremely limited) personal circumstances[46]—also undergoes a transformation in Heraclitus's hands when he complains (B17): "The many do not think such things as they meet with, nor, having learned, do they know, though each thinks he has." Although "the *logos* is common" (B2) and mortals are in "continuously in contact with it" (B72), they fail to notice it, or understand how it works in all things. Through a series of juxtapositions of opposing qualities— experienced but still inexperienced, having heard the word but not gotten the message, being in contact but still isolated, and being awake but still asleep— Heraclitus seeks to provoke his audience into considering the possibility that their usual sources of information may have failed them in some crucial respects, and that what they confidently regard as knowledge is really only a kind of ignorance.

But if neither the "much learning" of the sages nor the "much experience" provided by eyes and ears can "teach understanding," what can? One instructive simile appears in B51:

> They do not understand [*xuniasin*] how, while differing from itself, it is in agreement with itself. There is a back-stretched connection, like that of a bow or lyre.

Grasping the nature of the "back-stretched connection" in the case of the bow and lyre presumably requires coming to understand (Heraclitus's term here and often elsewhere is *xunienai*, "to come together with" or "understand") how each of the physical parts—the string and wooden frame—contributes to the effective operation of the whole, either the whole weapon or the whole musical instrument. The string must be pulled taut against the frame in order for either device to function properly—where there is no antecedent tension, there can be no subsequent action either. At least part of the message here is that we must go through the same processes of analysis and synthesis if we are to understand how the *logos* is at work in the cosmos as a whole. So, in general, understanding how "things that differ" are also "in agreement" requires mastering the principles of "unity in opposition" just mentioned—understanding how each of two opposing qualities has a place and essential role to play within a single larger entity; and conversely, how one entity can happily accommodate two qualities that are fiercely opposed to one another; and how bitter enemies can also mutually support and sustain one another's existence and operation. Thus, while much that Heraclitus proclaimed bore a superficial resemblance to the usual poetic indictment of human intelligence, his message was actually quite different: most people have no clear sense of how things really are, but those who can be provoked by Heraclitus's paradoxical remarks into considering how things that are opposed are actually in agreement are at least embarked on a path to understanding.

3.4. Parmenides

In fragment B1, Parmenides of Elea describes how an unnamed "youth" (presumably Parmenides himself at some earlier time) was transported by special powers along an exotic "roadway of a goddess":

> The mares that carry me, as far as mind might reach,
> Were escorting me, when leading me they set me on a roadway
>   rich in song
> Of the goddess that bears the knowing man down to every town.
> On that way I was carried; for on it much-revealing mares carried me
> Straining to pull the chariot, and maidens were leading the way (ll. 1–5)

Escorted by "maidens, Daughters of the Sun," the youth journeys to where the paths of Night and Day converge. There the maidens persuade a "much-avenging"

Justice to open a set of heavenly gates. Proceeding along a broad roadway, the youth arrives at the house of a goddess who greets him with these words:

> Youth attended by immortal charioteers
> Who reaches our house accompanied by the mares that carry you,
> Welcome, since no evil fate has sent you forth to journey on
> This road (for it is far indeed from the beaten path of men),
> But right and justice. And it is proper that you should learn all things,
> Both an unshaking heart of well-rounded truth
> And opinions of mortals in which there is no true trust.
> But nevertheless you shall also learn these things: how the things
>   that seem
> Had to genuinely be, all passing through all.[47]

While the full significance of many of the details in these lines may never be known, it seems likely that Parmenides intended for these introductory comments to mark the account to follow as a set of truths revealed to him by a divine power.

Should we conclude then that in these lines Parmenides expressed his personal conviction that knowledge, at least on this topic, comes to mortal beings through divine revelation? Many have thought just this, in part because Parmenides elected to cast his account in verse, the traditional language of prophetic revelation;[48] in part because some aspects of the proemium call to mind the earlier figure of the shaman who could travel to distant realms to acquire knowledge;[49] and in part because some form of superhuman authentication might be regarded as essential, given the supersensible character of the account Parmenides is about to present.[50]

Nevertheless, a better case can be made that Parmenides actually rejected the traditional idea of divinely revealed knowledge in favor of an alternative view of the route to knowledge. One passage often cited in support of a more "rationalist" or "humanistic" reading is B7.5–6. There the goddess urges the youth to "decide by reasoning" (*krinai de logôi*) the "much-contested testing spoken by her." Here, too, translators have opted for different renderings, but the goddess's injunction appears to mean something along the lines of "decide on the basis of the various considerations put forward in this poem which of the possible ways of speaking and thinking about 'what is' is correct."[51]

In a related remark in the opening lines of B8, the goddess alludes to the many "signs" or "indicators" (*sêmata*) that necessitate a particular way of thinking about what is:

> ... still single remains the account of the road
> That it is, and on this road are signs,
> Very many in number, that insofar as it is, it is generated and
>   imperishable,
> Whole, single in kind, steadfast, and complete (1–4)

And in lines 15–18 she announces what appears to be the outcome of these deliberations:

the decision on these matters consists in this:
It is or it is not. But it has been decided as is necessary,
To let go the one as unthinkable and unnameable (for it is no true
Road), and to allow the other as genuine and real.

In the remaining lines of B8, the goddess lays out a series of carefully reasoned arguments whose conclusions seem to reinforce the thesis that one must say and think of what is only that it is: what is cannot come into being nor be destroyed, be divided into parts, move about from place to place, or develop over time in any respect.[52] While here, too, much remains unclear, the general message must be something like "decide the correct view of the nature of what is on the basis of the well-reasoned arguments provided to you." What the goddess does not say is anything like "accept this account as true because you have heard it from a goddess."

Other features of Parmenides' poem lend support to the view that the learning forecast by the goddess in B1 will involve an active effort on the part of the youth (and indirectly those in Parmenides' audience) to determine where the truth lies. While B1.31 speaks in terms of what happened to the youth (or was done to him by special powers) at some point in the past, from B1.31 onward the goddess consistently speaks in terms of what the youth must do for himself. Employing a series of imperatives and both active and middle indicative forms, she asserts that he will or must "learn" (mathêseai, B1.31), "look upon things" (leusse, B4.1) "ponder" (phrazesthai, B6.2), "restrain your thought" (eirge, B7.2), "not permit custom to force you" (biasthô, B7.3), "judge" (krinai, B7.5), "learn mortal beliefs" (manthane, B8.52), "know the nature of the aither" (eisêi, B10.1), "learn the wandering works of the moon" (peusêi, B10.4), and "know the surrounding sky" (B10.5).

Parmenides also ties his discovery of the truth about what is to a set of powers that are available, both to him and to others, on a continuing basis. The contrast between the present tense employed in line 1 of B1—"The mares who carry me as far as mind might reach"—and the imperfect of line 2—"Were escorting me, when leading me they set me on a roadway rich in song" indicates that the set of powers that direct Parmenides' thinking do so on a continuing basis, as opposed to having given him a "one-shot" revelation. And while the goddess and guiding maidens are clearly immortals, the "horses" or powers that convey Parmenides (or his thumos) are never so designated. The path of thought along which Parmenides travels is, moreover, described as one "that bears the knowing man down to every town," suggesting that Parmenides saw himself as drawing on sources available to others on both previous and future occasions.

Finally, in B4 Parmenides asserts and argues for a thesis that has a direct bearing on the traditional indictment of the powers of human intelligence:

Look upon things which, though far off, are yet firmly present to
    [or by] the mind [noôi];
For you [or it] shall not cut off what-is from holding fast to what is,

> For it neither disperses itself in every way everywhere in order,
> Nor gathers itself together. (B4.1–4, Gallop trans.)

Many have sensed in these lines a subtle response to the river mentioned by Heraclitus that "disperses and gathers" (B91), but B4 has a broader target in its sights: the connection between knowledge and "presence." Coxon usefully places the fragment in its broader historical context:

> It is reasonable to believe that fr. [4] is part of [Parmenides'] answer to Xeno-phanes himself. Xenophanes had borrowed from Homer (B485–6) the equation of knowing with present perception and concluded that, with regard to the gods and other matters beyond the range of the senses, human beings can have no knowledge but only belief. [Parmenides] answers that the mind not only may have an immediate awareness of "absent things" but that its vision of Being is "steady," as the apprehensions of the dense and rare manifestation of a physical substance cannot be.[53]

Parmenides here rejects the traditional assumption that the only possible objects of human knowledge are the events or conditions mortals can directly experience through use of their sense faculties. Since what is "all alike" (B8.22), to know the nature of what is at some place and time is to know the nature of what is at all places and times. And once the essential link between knowledge and presence has been broken, with the human mind declared capable of knowing truths that pertain to all times and places, the rationale behind the traditional indictment of the *noos* of mortals disappears. In short, Parmenides not only suggests at different points, and in various ways, that human beings have the capacity to reason their way toward a correct understanding of the nature of what is; he also directly attacks the underlying view of the conditions of knowledge on which the traditional indictment of human intelligence had been based.

Yet if Parmenides sought to "humanize knowing"—that is, bring those in his audience to a fuller appreciation of their capacity to understand the nature of things through the exercise of their own rational faculties—why would he choose to frame his account in the traditional language of poetic inspiration and fashion a prologue rich in the imagery and language of divine revelation? Here, too, there are many possible alterative explanations. On some accounts, Parmenides' decision to versify should be seen, in effect, as a selection of the default mode for discourse on any serious subject. Others have suggested that Parmenides cast his account in verse form in order to plant it securely in the minds of his audiences. It has also been thought that versification might have made his difficult doctrines more palatable, as well as prevented inaccurate and incomplete summaries of the ar-gument. Perhaps presenting his account to his audience as the fruits of divine inspiration would help secure its acceptance; and framing his discovery in the language Homer had used to describe a famous journey might have enhanced the perceived aesthetic merit of his composition. While there may well be some truth in many of these suggestions, I suspect there was something more pointed in Parmenides' choice of format. In early Greek philosophy, as in other aspects of early Greek life, it is useful to remember the agonistic dimension of creative activity, as new ways of speaking and thinking emerged alongside, and often in conflict with, older and well-entrenched points of view. In this instance, we should consider the possibility that Parmenides adopted the traditional way of speaking, with its attendant assumptions and commitments, precisely in order to move beyond it.[54] If, as seems virtually certain, Parmenides came to appreciate the ability of the human mind to reason its way to insights about the nature of what there is, he would have had good reason to try to find an effective way to subvert the dominant paradigm, that is, to show that the traditional disparagement of the powers of human intelligence was in error. What more convincing proof of mastery over a competing way of speaking and thinking could Parmenides have given than to use that mode of expression in order to present a doctrine antithetical to its main assumptions?[55] And what more fitting way to signal the transition from a god-centered to a human reason–centered understanding of the route to knowledge than to have a goddess declare that what can be known about the nature of what is is what can be established through the use of reasoned argument?

To sum up: over a period of several centuries a number of Presocratic thinkers declared and defended views of human knowledge that departed from the pessimistic outlook characteristic of earlier Greek poetry. Although the philosophers retained some trappings of the older outlook, and generally endorsed the basic contrast of divine and human capacities, they often encouraged those in their audiences to seek an understanding of the natural realm, near and far, by means of inquiry and reflection. Pythagoras and Empedocles presented themselves to their audiences as divine—or at least divinely inspired—beings, but they also explained how those who listened to their inspired words could achieve some measure of knowledge on their own. Xenophanes, Heraclitus, Alcmaeon, Parmenides, and Philolaus all described ways of thinking or inquiry that could lead to useful results, even in circumstances in which a completely secure grasp of the truth was not possible. The gods have not been declared entirely otiose, but they no longer work alone.

NOTES

1. See *h.Cer.* 256–57: "Unknowing [*nêides*] are humans and foolish not foreseeing the good or evil that comes upon them"; *h.Ap.* (189–93): "Humans . . . live foolish and helpless, nor are they able to find healing for death or defense against old age"; Archil. fr. 70: "Of such a sort, Glaucus, is the mind [*thumos*] of mortal man, whatever Zeus may bring him for the day, for he thinks such things as he meets with"; Semon. fr. 1: "There is no mind [*noos*] in men, but we live each day like grazing cattle, not knowing [*ouden eidotes*] how God shall end it"; Thgn. 141–42: "Mortals think vain things, knowing nothing, while the gods accomplish all to their intentions"; Simon. fr. 22: "You who are a human being, never say what tomorrow will bring, nor when you see someone prosper,

how long this will last. For change is swifter than the changing course of the wide-winged fly"; Sol. fr. 13: "We mortal men, good and bad, think in this way: each holds his opinion before something happens to him, and then he grieves, but before that we rejoice open-mouthed in vain expectations"; fr. 1: "All that we do is fraught with danger; no one can ever know where a thing may end, when it has once begun . . . for us no visible limit of wealth is appointed; those blessed beyond others with wealth hunger for double the sum"; and fr. 16: "This, the hardest part of knowledge [gnômosunês], to grasp in thought [noêsai] the invisible measure that alone holds the limits of all things"; Pi. *O.* 7.25–26: "Around the spirit of man drift endless errors; helpless to find out what now or at the last will be best for him"; *N.* 6.6–7: "We know not where, according to what the day or night brings to us, fate has appointed as the end toward which we hasten"; *N.* 7.23–24: "But the heart of the mass of men is blind indeed"; *N.* 11.43–47: "What comes from Zeus is not accompanied by any sure sign [saphes tekmar]. We embark on bold endeavors, yearning after many exploits, for our limbs are fettered by importunate hope. But streams of foreknowledge [promatheias] lie far from us."

2. The connection between poets and seers in early Greek thought is well documented. See Detienne, *The Masters of Truth in Archaic Greece*: "The prehistory of the philosophical *Alêtheia* leads us to the system of thought of the diviner, the poet, and the king of justice, three figures for whom a certain type of speech is defined by *Alêtheia*" (37). See also Cornford, *Principium Sapientiae*; Dodds, *The Greeks and the Irrational*, and Chadwick, *Poetry and Prophecy*, who comments: "The fundamental elements of the prophetic function seem to have everywhere been the same. Everywhere the gift of poetry is inseparable from divine inspiration. Everywhere this inspiration carries with it knowledge—whether of the past, in the form of history and genealogy; of the hidden present, in the form commonly of scientific information; or of the future, in the form of prophetic utterance in the narrower sense. . . . The lofty claims of the poet and seer are universally admitted, and he himself holds a high status wherever he is found" (14).

3. *HGP* 1, 398.

4. Varro in August. *De civ. D.* 7.17: "scribam . . . ut Xenophanes Colophonius scriptsit . . . hominis est enim haec opinari, Dei scire." Similarly Arius Didymus (A24): "God therefore knows the truth, while opinion is allotted to all." It is not certain that the *pasi* of Xenophanes' conclusion actually meant "all men" rather than "all things," but that is how Varro and Arius Didymus understood it.

5. Heraclitus B78: ἦθος γὰρ ἀνθρώπειον μὲν οὐκ ἔχει γνώμας, θεῖον δὲ ἔχει. The precise meaning of the remark is contested, but clearly some contrast of divine and mortal capacities is intended. My translation follows that of DK ("Einsichten"), but the wide range of meanings of *gnômê* allows for multiple translations—"discerning judgments," "opinions," "decisions," "intentions," "purposes," etc. The root sense of *gnômê* is "means of knowing"—either an identifying mark on an object or the faculty of intelligence. The various secondary meanings of the term relate back to its core meaning as so many products of the capacity. The particular choice of "insight" is warranted by Heraclitus's evident interest in the degree to which human beings have either failed or succeeded in grasping the *logos* (B1, 50, 114) or in achieving some degree of *xunesis* (B2, 17, 34, 51), *phronesis* (B17), or *noos* (B40, 104). The same range of choices applies to the *gnômên peri pantos* that Anaxagoras credits to the *nous* and that orders or controls the cosmos (B12).

6. Alcmaeon B1: "The gods possess certainty [sapheneian] concerning non-evident matters, but [it is given to] men to conjecture from signs [tekmairesthai]"; Philolaus B6: "Concerning nature and harmony the situation is this: the being of things, which is eternal, and nature in itself admit of divine and not human knowledge." Similarly, Parmenides

contrasts the reliable account given by the goddess with the unreliable beliefs of mortals (B1.29–30 and B8.50–52). In B2, Empedocles echoes Homer's characterization of mortal *noos* as dictated by external circumstances:

> having seen only a small portion of life in their experience
> [mortals] soar and fly off like smoke, swift to their dooms,
> each one convinced of only that very thing which he has chanced to meet,
> as they are driven in all directions. But each boasts of having seen the whole.
> In this way, these things are neither seen nor heard by men
> nor grasped with understanding. (Based on the Greek text in DK and following the
> translation in Inwood, *The Poem of Empedocles*, B2.3–8.)

7. See Xenophanes' disparaging reference to what "mortals think" about the gods (B14) and "however many things they have made evident for mortals to look upon" (B36); Heraclitus's references to those who have heard the *logos* but failed to understand it and who base their beliefs on the accounts given by supposed experts (B1, 17, 34, 51, 56, 86, and 104); Parmenides' reference to *brotoi eidotes ouden* (B6.4) and the "beliefs of mortals in which there is no true trust" (B1.30 and B8.51–54); and Empedocles' reference to "fools [*nêpioi*] for their meditations are not long lasting" (B11), etc.

8. This account differs from several alternative ways of understanding early Greek ways of thinking about knowledge: (1) the view defended in Snell, *The Discovery of the Mind*, and elsewhere, that the meaning of the Greek expressions for "knowing" evolved from the time of the Homeric poems down to Parmenides; (2) the view defended by Barnes in *PP* that Xenophanes introduced a modified form of skepticism that continued unabated through the course of Presocratic philosophy; and (3) the view defended in Cornford, *Principium Sapientiae*, Most, "The Poetics of Early Greek Philosophy," Kingsley, "Empedocles for the New Millennium," and elsewhere that Parmenides and Empedocles conceived of knowledge as divinely revealed truth.

9. Snell, *The Discovery of the Mind*, among others, claimed that over the space of several centuries the main Greek expressions for "knowing" (*noein*, *gignôskein*, and *eidenai*) showed clear evidence of semantic development, away from an early identification with eyewitness experience and toward a more "reason-based" or "intuitive" conception of knowing. For a critique of the different versions of "the developmental thesis," see Lesher, "Parmenides' Critique of Thinking"; Lesher, "The Emergence of Philosophical Interest in Cognition."

10. See also *Od.* 16.470: "And I know [*oida*] at least one other thing, for I saw it with my own eyes [*idon ophthalmoisin*]; similarly *Il.* 11.741; 14.153–54; 17.84–86, 115–16; *Od.* 5.77–78, 215; 8.560; 15.532; 16.470–71, among many others.

11. Cornford, *Principium Sapientiae*, comments: "As a man among men, the poet depends on hearsay; but as divinely inspired, he has access to the knowledge of an eyewitness, 'present' at the feats he illustrates. The Muses are, in fact, credited with the same mantic powers as the seer, transcending the limitations of time" (76–77). It has been recently argued by Zellner, "Scepticism in Homer," that the prayer in *Iliad* 2 should be read not as an expression of a "folk epistemology" or "Homeric skepticism" but as a pious contrast of divine and human powers. But, as I argue in what follows, there are additional reasons to believe that Homer reflected on the narrowness of human experience and the consequent difficulty of knowing about matters far removed in space and time. The Muse prayer taken by itself expresses neither pessimism nor skepticism (since the poet is able to present a reliable account of events that took place in an earlier time), but it does reflect the view that on at least some occasions, mortal beings are able to discover the truth only with the assistance of divine powers of inspiration.

12. Among many other instances: Aegisthus learns his fate when the gods "spoke to him, sending keen-sighted Hermes" (*Od.* 1.38); Echenor the Corinthian learns his from the expert seer Polyidus (*Il.* 13.666); and Odysseus learns what the future holds for him from the words of the ghost of the seer Teiresias (*Od.* 11.100).

13. For other examples of "peirastic knowledge" see *Il.* 13.448–49, 457; 16.243; 18.269–70; and 21.226.

14. As has often been noted, Homer also speaks of "knowing" where we might speak of experiencing certain feelings and desires, or harboring certain dispositions. Menelaus says of Patroclus *pasin gar epistato meilichos einai*—"for he knew gentleness to all," while Nestor and Menelaus are described as sailing home from Troy *phila eidotes allêloisin*—"knowing friendliness to one another" (*Od.* 3.277). For a detailed discussion of this aspect of early Greek thought, and its relationship to classical accounts of the relationship between thought and action, see O'Brien, *The Socratic Paradoxes and the Greek Mind*, and Warden, "The Mind of Zeus."

15. For this use of *autos* meaning "of one's own accord" or "by oneself," see Smyth, *Greek Grammar*, sec. 1209a, and *Od.* 16.470; *Od.* 5.215: "I know for myself [*oida kai autos*] that in appearance and stature wise Penelope fails to compete with you"; *Od.* 1.216: "For never yet did any man know for himself [*autos anegnô*] his own parentage"; and *Od.* 3.26, where the goddess explains to Telemachus that in part he will devise an effective strategy "by himself" [*alla men autos eni phresi sêisi noêseis*) and in part a god will prompt him [*de kai daimôn hupothêseai*]. See also *Il.* 13.729; 17.686–88; *Od.* 6.188.

16. See also the common expression "tell me so that I/we may know" (as in *Il.* 1.363 and elsewhere). So natural is the idea of learning from the words of others that the verb *peuthomai/punthanomai* commonly means "to learn about some matter from another person." Similarly, *akouô*, "hear," can mean "learn of or come to know about by hearing," as at *Il.* 24.543: *to prin akouomen olbion einai*—"we hear/know that earlier you had been prosperous." The same attitude is reflected in the odd remark at *Od.* 6.185 that when two like-minded people become husband and wife, "they become a great sorrow for their enemies and a joy to their friends, but they *hear* this best themselves—*malista de t' ekluon autoi*" (see also *Il.* 13.734: *malista de kautos anegnô*—"but he knows this best himself").

17. See *Il.* 8.51–52: "And [Zeus] himself sat on the mountain peaks exulting in his glory, looking upon both the city of the Trojans and the ships of the Achaeans"; Hesiod, *Op.* 267: "the eye of Zeus, seeing all things and noting all things," among many similar remarks.

18. See the description of Calchas in *Il.* 1.69–72: "who knew what was, what had been before, and what was yet to be." Similarly, at *Il.* 3.109, Menelaus comments: "Always unsteady are the wits of the younger generation, but in whatever an old man takes part, he looks both before and after, that the results may be far the best for either side." Both Polydamus and Halitherses are praised for being able to "see *prossô kai opissô*" (*Il.* 18.250; *Od.* 24.452).

19. The fact that *nêpiê* means both "foolish" and "childish" makes it a natural foil for *noos*, the quality of mind associated with the extensive experience characteristic of those who have achieved an advanced age.

20. See the passages quoted in note 1 here.

21. Similar testimonials to the powers of the Muses appear in Ibycus 3.23; Solon, 1.49; Bacchylides 19.1, 5.31, 9.3; Pindar *Pae.* 7.5–8.

22. This aspect of early Greek poetry is summarized in Heath, *The Poetics of Greek Tragedy*: "Poetry was an important channel through which stories of the gods and heroic ancestors were transmitted and disseminated in Greek society; in so far as these myths embodied the religious traditions and moral norms of the community, the poets could be

seen as having a crucial formative influence on the beliefs and values of the Greeks at large" (39). I would add only that the advice provided by Hesiod in the *Works and Days* concerned not simply religious traditions and moral norms but also a range of practical matters.

23. Barnes, in *PP*, for example, speaks of "the pantological knowledge" of Anaximander simply on the basis of what other ancient writers tell us about the breadth of his cosmological interests (20).

24. Heracl. Pont. fr. 89 = D.L. 8.4.

25. Ael. *V.H.* 2.26 and elsewhere.

26. See Burkert, *Lore and Science in Ancient Pythagoreanism*, 160.

27. Similar achievements were credited to Phercydes. For the references and a discussion of the larger significance of these stories, see Burkert, *Lore and Science in Early Pythagoreanism*, 144–47.

28. For a detailed description of these individuals and their association with Pythagoras, see Burkert, *Lore and Science in Ancient Pythagoreanism*, 120–65.

29. See Cornford, *Principium Sapientiae*, and Burkert, *Lore and Science in Ancient Pythagoreanism*, 120–65.

30. It would be wrong, I think, to dismiss out of hand these claims to a divine connection as mere pretense or pose. As Dodds and others have explained, during this early period it was natural to think and speak of virtually any abnormal occurrence as the work or manifestation of a divine power. Achieving an intellectual breakthrough, experiencing a sudden flash of insight, solving a difficult puzzle, remembering a long-forgotten fact—each of these would naturally be regarded as something "given" or "revealed" by a superior power. See Dodds, *The Greeks and the Irrational*, esp. chap. 3, "The Blessings of Madness"; see also the discussion of the nature of a divinity in Whitman, *Homer and the Homeric Tradition*, esp. ch. 10, "Fate, Time, and the Gods."

31. Following the text and translation in Inwood, *The Poem of Empedocles*.

32. See A1.57, 60, 68–70; A2, A13, A14, and A21.

33. See "And so the Pythagoreans used to invoke the tetrad as their most binding oath: 'Nay, by him that gave to our generation the *tetraktys*, which contains the fount and root of eternal nature'" (Aëtius 1.3.8); "For 1 is the point, 2 is the line, 3 the triangle, and 4 the pyramid . . . and the same holds in generation too, for the first principle in magnitude is the point, the second the line, the third surface, and the fourth the solid" (Speusippus in *Theol.Ar.* 84.10 de Falco); "The sixth *tetraktys* is of things that grow. The seed is analogous to the unit and point, growth in length to the dyad and the line, growth in breadth to the triad and the plane, growth in depth to the tetrad and the solid" (Theo Sm. 97.17 Hiller).

34. For a recent defense of this view of the Philolaus material see Huffman, *Philolaus of Croton*.

35. "For there is not going to be anything that is going to know at all, if everything is unlimited." For a defense of this translation, see Huffman, *Philolaus of Croton*, 116 Ff.

36. "And indeed all the things that are known have number. For it is not possible that anything whatsoever be conceived or known without this."

37. In Stob. 2.1 (DK 21A24). Similarly, Varro in August. *De civ. D.* 7.17.

38. Following Hussey, "The Beginnings of Epistemology," and others, I adopt the *geneto* of Plutarch's text of the fragment rather than the *iden* in Sextus's version (as defended by Fränkel). The dates of Xenophanes' birth and death are uncertain, but he is reported to have visited the court of Hieron, tyrant of Syracuse, who ruled from 478 to 467 BCE. Since B34 probably refers back to what Xenophanes himself has said about the nature of "all things," it seems reasonable to assign this remark to a later stage of his career.

39. See Hdt. 2.44: "And wishing to gain sure knowledge of these things [*thelôn de toutôn peri saphes ti eidenai*] from a point where this was possible, I took ship to Tyre in Phoenicia, where I heard there was a very holy temple of Heracles. There I saw it [*eidon*] richly equipped. . . . Then I went to Thasos where I also found a temple of Heracles. . . . Therefore what I have discovered by inquiry clearly shows [*ta men nun historêmena dêloi sapheôs*] that Heracles is an ancient god."

40. In a set of well-known remarks, Xenophanes relates "what mortals think or suppose" (*dokeousi*) about their gods (B14) and suggests that mortals have an inherent tendency to conceive of the gods as endowed with features very much like their own (see B15 and B16).

41. This view of the significance of B34 is defended by Hussey, "The Beginnings of Epistemology," 22–23, and by Lesher, *Xenophanes of Colophon*, 166–69.

42. Additional support for this view is provided by Xenophanes' remarks about natural phenomena traditionally regarded as having religious significance—the sun, clouds, rainbow, meteors, eclipses, etc. Perhaps nowhere does the Ionian spirit of inquiry come out more clearly than in the *testimonium* of Hippolytus (A33) that reports the discovery of fossilized remains of ancient sea creatures at inland locations, as evidence for a broader theory of cosmic flooding and drought. The extent of Xenophanes' engagement in natural science is discussed in Lesher, *Xenophanes of Colophon*.

43. The text in DK runs *peri tôn apheneôn, peri tôn thnêtôn, saphêneian men theoi echonti, hôs de anthôpois tehmairesthai*, but others omit the phrase *peri tôn thnêtôn* ("concerning things mortal"). I follow LSJ in supplying *dedotai* ("it is given").

44. A methodological remark made by Thucydides near the outset of his history makes it clear that *tekmeresthai* can represent a significant addition to information obtained through firsthand observation: "As to the events of the period just preceding this one, and those of a still earlier date, it was impossible to get clear information [*saphôs . . . heurien*] on account of the lapse of time; but from evidence [*ek de tekmêriôn*] that in pushing my inquiries to the furthest point I find that I can trust [*moi pisteusai*], I think they were not really great events, either as regards the wars then waged or in other particulars"(Th. 1.1.1).

45. Pritzl, "On the Way to Wisdom in Heraclitus," sees Heraclitus as championing the empirical route to knowledge. Lesher, "The Emergence of Philosophical Interest in Cognition," finds the emphasis placed on interpretation and reflection. Barnes, in *PP*, denies that Heraclitus has a view on this topic.

46. See Archil. fr. 70: "Of such a sort, Glaucus, is the consciousness [*thumos*] of mortal man, whatever Zeus may bring him for the day, for he thinks such things as he meets with." See also Semon. fr. 1; Thgn. 141–42; Sol. frs. 1, 13, 16; Pi. *O.* 7.25–26; *N.* 6.6–7; 7.23–24; 11.43–47; etc.

47. Translation mine, based on the text in DK. Lines 1–30 of B1 were quoted by S.E. *M.* 7.111; ll. 28–32 were quoted by Simp. *in Cael.* 557.20.

48. "In archaic Greece, the language in which gods speak through human voices is in general that of metrical verse. . . . Whatever other purposes it served in archaic Greece, then, the dactylic hexameter also seems to have functioned as an unmistakable sign that the ultimate source of the text it articulated was not human but divine" (Most, "The Poetics of Early Greek Philosophy," 353). But this seems to me most unlikely. Parmenides almost certainly knew of Hesiod's poetically framed claim that "Truly, first of all Chaos came into being [*geneto*], and next Broad-bosomed Earth, the ever-sure foundation of all" (*Th.* 116–17) and rejected it at B8.7, 9–10, and 26–28. Xenophanes had already repudiated the accounts of the gods given (in verse form) by Homer and Hesiod, as both socially destructive and false to the true nature of the divine. Even in the *doxa* section of Parmenides'

poem, doctrines are expressed in metrical form that Parmenides could not possibly have thought were correct. Among those mortal errors was the decision to conceive of light and dark as "opposites in body [with] signs apart from one another" (B8.55–59) rather than thinking of things (as explained in B9) as "full of light and obscure night together, of both equally." Not only does the goddess express these erroneous mortal beliefs in verse form, she even describes the presentation of these errors as a "deceitful ordering" (kosmon . . . apatêlon) and "seemly arrangement" (diakosmon eoikota), phrases that high-light the poetic character of her presentation.

49. "However the tradition may have come to him, his journey to, or round the heavens recalls the heaven-journey of the shaman's ritual drama. He travels on a chariot, attended by the daughters of the Sun, on the way of divinity, which conducts the man who knows (eidota phôta) 'as far as his heart desires' and 'far from the beaten track of men' " (Cornford, Principium Sapientiae, 117; similarly, Kingsley, "Empedocles for the New Mil-lennium"). But others have found equally convincing indications that the youth is des-cending into a lower realm, or traveling to various cities in the manner of Odysseus. It is also been suggested (by Mourelatos) that Parmenides deliberately kept the references vague in order to avoid any such identifications.

50. "For Parmenides and Empedocles the choice of poetic form seems designed to resolve a crucial philosophical problem: given that all human beings are subject to the delusion of appearance, how can the philosopher know the truth of what he claims to know? For them, only a god could possibly be the source of a set of transcendent truths to which a mere mortal, if left to his own devices would have had no access" (Most, "The Poetics of Early Greek Philosophy," 353). Similarly Cornford: "Parmenides' originality lies in his perception that that there is a gulf, which cannot be bridged, between that realm of timeless, metaphysical truth and the welter of changing qualities which the senses, and the opinions of mortals founded on the senses, falsely mistake for realities. Henceforth the immortal and divine element in man is no longer merely the spirit which, when it leaves the sleeping body, communes with gods in prophetic dreams and visions and discerns the course of past, present, and future time; it has become the faculty of which thinks and give a rational account of metaphysical reality beyond the boundaries of time and change" (120). This line of thought might carry some weight if Parmenides had adopted the tra-ditional understanding of human knowledge as grounded in direct experience. But it is clear from B4 that he believed that noos has the capacity to discover the nature of what is as it must be at all times and places.

51. A view endorsed by Vlastos, review of Principium Sapientiae, and Curd, "The Presocratics as Philosophers." For a discussion of the various alternative translations of poudêrin elenchon see Lesher, "Parmenides' Critique of Thinking."

52. I follow the general analysis of the structure of the arguments as explained in Coxon, "The Philosophy of Parmenides."

53. Coxon, "The Fragments of Parmenides," 187.

54. This view of the significance of Parmenides' decision to present his account in verse, and to borrow heavily from his poetic predecessors, is put forward in Wright, "Philosopher Poets," although not with respect to Parmenides' view of the nature and sources of knowledge.

55. Plato appears to follow Parmenides' lead in adopting the language and techniques of an opposing approach in order to demonstrate his mastery over it. In the Symposium, for example, Plato demonstrates his complete mastery of the encomium speech in order to reveal its inadequacies as a means for expressing the truth. And, as Rachel Barney, Names and Nature in Plato's Cratylus, has shown, in the Cratylus Plato gives the etymological

approach to knowledge a thorough run for its money in order to reveal its inferiority to philosophical dialectic.

BIBLIOGRAPHY

Barney, Rachel. *Names and Nature in Plato's Cratylus.* New York: Routledge, 2001.

Burkert, Walter. *Lore and Science in Ancient Pythagoreanism.* 1962. Translated by E. L. Minar, Jr. Cambridge, Mass.: Harvard University Press, 1972.

Chadwick, N. K. *Poetry and Prophecy.* Cambridge: Cambridge University Press, 1942.

Cornford, F. M. *Principium Sapientiae.* Cambridge: Cambridge University Press, 1952.

Coxon, A. H. *The Fragments of Parmenides.* Assen: Van Gorcum, 1986.

———. "The Philosophy of Parmenides." *Classical Quarterly* 28 (1934): 134–44.

Curd, Patricia. "The Presocratics as Philosophers." In *Qu'est-ce que la philosophie présocratique?* edited by André Laks and Claire Louguet, 115–38. Lille: Presses Universitaires du Septentrion, 2002.

Detienne, Marcel. *The Masters of Truth in Archaic Greece.* 1965. Translated by Janet Lloyd. New York, 1996.

Dodds, E. R. *The Greeks and the Irrational.* Berkeley: University of California Press, 1951.

Fränkel, H. "Xenophanes' Empiricism and His Critique of Knowledge." In Mourelatos *The Pre-Socratics*, 118–31; trans. M. R. Cosgrove from "Xenophanesstudien," *Hermes* 60 (1925): 174–92.

Gallop, D. *Parmenides of Elea.* Toronto: University of Toronto Press, 1984.

Heath, Malcolm. *The Poetics of Greek Tragedy.* London: Duckworth, 1987.

Huffman, Carl A. *Philolaus of Croton.* Cambridge: Cambridge University Press, 1993.

Hussey, Edward. "The Beginnings of Epistemology: From Homer to Philolaus." In *Epistemology*, edited by Stephen Everson, Companions to Ancient Thought, vol. 1, 11–38. Cambridge: Cambridge University Press, 1990.

Inwood, Brad. *The Poem of Empedocles.* 1992. 2nd ed. Toronto: University of Toronto Press, 2001.

Kingsley, Peter. "Empedocles for the New Millennium." *Ancient Philosophy* 22 (2002): 333–413.

Lesher, James H. "The Emergence of Philosophical Interest in Cognition." *Oxford Studies in Ancient Philosophy* 12 (1994): 1–34.

———. "Parmenides' Critique of Thinking: The *Poludêris Elenchos* of Fragment 7." *Oxford Studies in Ancient Philosophy* 2 (1984): 1–30.

———. *Xenophanes of Colophon: Fragments.* Toronto: University of Toronto Press, 1992.

Most, Glenn W. "The Poetics of Early Greek Philosophy." In *The Cambridge Companion to Early Greek Philosophy*, edited by A. A. Long, 332–62. Cambridge: Cambridge University Press, 1999.

Mourelatos, A. P. D. *The Pre-Socratics.* Garden City, NY: Anchor Books/Doubleday, 1974.

O'Brien, M. J. *The Socratic Paradoxes and the Greek Mind.* Chapel Hill: University of North Carolina Press, 1967.

Pritzl, Kurt. "On the Way to Wisdom in Heraclitus." *Phoenix* 39 (1985): 303–16.

Smyth, Herbert Weir. *Greek Grammar.* Edited by Gordon M. Messing. Cambridge, Mass.: Harvard University Press, 1956.

Snell, Bruno. *The Discovery of the Mind: The Greek Origins of European Thought.* 1948. Translated by T. G. Rosenmeyer. 2nd ed. New York: Harper, 1960.

Vlastos, Gregory. Review of *Principium Sapientiae*, by F. M. Cornford. *Gnomon* 27 (1955): 65–76.

Warden, J. R. "The Mind of Zeus." *Journal of the History of Ideas* 32 (1971): 3–14.

Whitman, Cedric Hubbell. *Homer and the Homeric Tradition.* Cambridge, Mass.: Harvard University Press, 1958.

Wright, M. R. "Philosopher Poets: Parmenides and Empedocles." In *Form and Content in Didactic Poetry*, edited by C. Atherton. Bari: Levante Editori, 1998.

Zellner, H. M. "Scepticism in Homer?" *Classical Quarterly* 44 (1994): 308–15.

CHAPTER 18

PRESOCRATIC
THEOLOGY

T. M. ROBINSON

IF, IN the context of early and classical Greek thought, we take the term "theology" to mean "a notion (however precisely or imprecisely systematized) of God/gods/ the gods and his/their putative relationship, causal and directive, to the world and its operations, and to ourselves within that world," or something of that order, the first ascription of such a notion to a Presocratic philosopher is to be found in Aristotle's comment that "Thales thought that all things are full of gods" (*de An.* 411a8).[1] The statement as it stands is tantalizing, since we have no means of knowing for sure whether Thales ever used the exact spoken or written words "all things are full of gods," but it seems safe to infer from their trenchancy and premodernity of locution that Thales could well have thought or said something like that if by "god" he meant something such as "powerful life-principle." The evidence for this, though still coming to us at very tentative second hand and without formal as-severation, is to be found in Aristotle's earlier statement that "Thales, too, from what they tell us, seems to have thought that the soul was something that causes motion, if indeed he did say that the [Magnesian] stone possesses soul because it moves iron" (*de An.* 405a19–22).

The cautious inference one can draw from this, as Kirk has pointed out, is that for Thales there were a great number of forces in nature, possibly many more than most people assumed, and manifested most strikingly in the qualities of magnetic stone, that suggest not just the presence of life but a degree of life, and a power to bring about change/motion (*kinesis*), that one might wish to call divine. As such, the view is not in itself strikingly different from other animistic theories of nature, except perhaps in the boldness of it extension, if the Magnesian stone really were included in Thales' roster of "gods." But lack of evidence allows us to venture little further than this on the matter; one can merely speculate on whether "water," for example, would have been included among what he called gods.

That such speculation would not be entirely groundless, however, is suggested by a view Aristotle attributes to the second of the Milesian philosophers, Anaximander. Anaximander's principle of things, the "boundless" or "indefinite" (*apeiron*), is, Aristotle says, "the divine; for it is immortal and indestructible, as Anaximander says and most of the philosophers of nature" (*Ph.* 203b13–15). In the same passage, Aristotle says that the *apeiron* "seems to be the beginning of the other things, and to surround all things and to steer everything, as all those say who do not posit other causes, like mind or love, over and beyond the *apeiron*." It is clear from this statement that, for Aristotle at any rate, the beginning point (*arche*) for all three Milesian philosophers—water for Thales, the *apeiron* for Anaximander, and air for Anaximenes—possesses basic characteristics of divinity: each is immortal and indestructible. In the case of Anaximander, however, however, he goes further, saying of the *apeiron* that it "surrounds all things and steers everything." Of these two verbs, the latter is precisely the terminology used ordinarily of Zeus, and would, one can safely assume, have been deliberately chosen because of this, had Anaximander himself used the word in question or some word closely analogous to it. It also seems very possible that in using the phrase "immortal and indestructible" Aristotle is using his own more formal wording for the formulaic phrase "eternal and ageless," which Anaximander may well have used, along with the words "steering everything," to make clear his equation of the significant characteristics and operation of the *apeiron* with those of Zeus. As for its "surrounding" all things, this characteristic Aristotle also attributes elsewhere to the water of Thales, the air of Anaximenes, and the fire of Heraclitus (*Cael.* 303b10). While this may be intended as a reference to the *arche* of things as being in some way protective, as the womb protects a fetus, it may also be simply a description of its locus in the scheme of things. So the reference to "steering"—if that or something similar was the term Anaximander used—is probably a securer guide in the matter to how Anaximander expected to be understood.

It is also tempting to see the use of a word such as "steering" as a piece of demythologization on Anaximander's part: what most people characterize as the works of Zeus are simply features of the natural world. But this would be premature, given the way the terms are used in the one undoubted fragment of Anaximander we possess. In this statement, he says that the same *apeiron* is both the source of the coming to existence of things and the end point into which they are destroyed, all of this happening "according to necessity; for they pay penalty and retribution to one another according to the assessment of time" (B1 = Simp. *in Ph.* 24.17). If, as Kirk has argued, it is the *apeiron* itself that is being credited with injustice, such that it needs to make periodic amends, this is an unexpected piece of anthropomorphism from one who is supposedly setting out to demythologize. On the other hand, the referent of "they" in the fragment is sufficiently unclear as to leave doubtful whether what is in question are the two temporal poles of the *apeiron* or the two basic "opposites" of his system that later came to be called the hot and the cold.

The question of possible demythologization recurs when we turn to Anaximenes, the third member of the Milesian triad. For Anaximenes, the beginning point of things was air, which he may possibly have called "God." Aëtius says without qualification that he did (Aëtius 1.7.13). According to Hippolytus (*Haer.* 1.7.1), drawing on Theophrastus, he said that air was the beginning-point of all things, including "the gods and things divine." Both accounts, as Kirk points out, could be offering us parts of his overall view if he held that one god (in this case air) was supreme and all the other gods (i.e., the gods of popular religion) the product of this one god and subsidiary to him. This could perhaps be construed as demythologization, but if so it is demythologization of a very attenuated nature, since the gods of popular religion are apparently left intact, a point to which Augustine draws attention (*De civ. D.* 8.2). Unless, of course, for Anaximenes air is in fact the equivalent of Zeus, in which case the demythologization is much more broad-ranging, and greatly more significant in its implications; if the supreme Olympian has been demythologized, what remains of the others? On this crucial point, however, our sources are silent, and we are in the end left in the same state of doubt about Anaximenes' stance in the matter as we were over Anaximander's.

If a major physical discovery (the properties of the Magnesian stone) was, as it seems, of some significance for at least one of the Milesian philosophers, stories being brought back to Greece about beliefs and social customs beyond its boundaries had major influence on these philosophers' immediate successor, Xenophanes. Writing in verse, he talked of how

> Ethiopians say that <their gods> are snub-nosed and black,
> Thracians that theirs have blue eyes and blond hair. (B16)

While we have no context for these two lines, a natural inference that it is meant to underpin a generalization about a human tendency to anthropomorphize when discussing the gods seems to be corroborated by B15, in which he says:

> But if cattle and horses or lions had hands, or were able to draw with their hands and fashion the things that men can, horses would draw the forms of gods like horses and cattle like cattle, and they would make their bodies like the body each of them had.

That such anthropomorphization was something he wanted to criticize with some severity seems clear from the tone of *reductio ad absurdum* that permeates the sentence, and a similar mood seems to characterize B11, in which Greek poets of distinction are attacked for attributing shameful moral attributes to the gods ("Homer and Hesiod have attributed to the gods everything that is a shame and reproach among men, stealing and committing adultery and deceiving one another") and, more generally (B14), for simply making the gods like ourselves ("But mortals consider that gods are born, and that they have clothes and speech and bodies like their own").

Given the general reverence at this time for poets, especially Homer, this stance looks courageous as well as being new, and cannot but have caused surprise, if not consternation, among many of its first hearers—and, had nothing of Xenophanes survived but these lines, would have guaranteed him a place of importance in the history of theological speculation. Because from them we could have legitimately inferred that for him the gods—if there were any—were by definition (1) good and only good, (2) immortal, and (3) in no way human in appearance in form or activities—three attributes of divinity that would become axiomatic in future Western theological thinking.

Famously, however, he went much further than this, and talked of

> one god, greatest among gods and men,
> in no way similar to mortals either in body or in understanding
>   (B23)

The sentence is as it stands incomplete,[2] but no amount of conjectural reconstruction to make it complete would turn Xenophanes into the monotheist that, since Aristotle, he has often been made out to be. The "god" in question is clearly meant to be the head of a hierarchy of gods, whom we can assume to be the Olympians familiar to his hearers. This supreme god, whom we can safely conjecture from the reference to "shaking" (see *Il.* 1.530) to be Xenophanes' nonanthropomorphic substitute for the anthropomorphic Zeus, is further described as follows.

> Always he remains in the same place, in no way in motion;
> nor does it make sense[3] that he go to different places at different
>   times,
> but without toil he shakes all things by the thought of his mind.
>   (B26, 25)

And the manner of his cognition is spelled out as follows.

> All of him sees, all of him apprehends, and all of him hears

or perhaps

> He sees as a totality, he apprehends as a totality, and he hears as a totality. (B24)

Statements of this order led Aristotle to believe that the supreme god of whom Xenophanes speaks is in fact the world (*Metaph.* 986b21), and this may be right. However, it is not necessarily right. Once the decision has been made by Xenophanes to make his supreme god "in no way similar to mortals either in body or in understanding" (B23), any sense of fixed locus for cognitive activities vanishes, and it makes sense to credit the totality with apprehension rather than a supposed part. But to claim that such a totality is coextensive with that totality that is the universe is a further move altogether, and the evidence of the fragments does not, as Lesher convincingly shows, allow us to make that step.[4]

Whether Xenophanes made such a further move or not (and Aristotle, who clearly thought he did, may well have had access to much more of Xenophanes' poem than we now have), even the little that has survived of his poem allows us to conclude that he is a significant figure in the history of theological speculation, whose arguments, negative and positive, will serve as a *terminus a quo* for a line of major investigators over the next two millennia. Among these fragments is a major statement of caution about what can be known about the gods (including, one must assume, his Zeus-like "one god"):

> No man know, or will ever know, the truth
> About the gods and everything I speak of. . . (B34)

What we seem to be confined to is opinion:

> Let these things be opined as resembling the truth. (B35)

Yet there does appear to be partial access to the truth, an access that grows with the passage of time, and this access is provided by direct revelation:

> Yet the gods have not revealed all things to men from the beginning,
> but by seeking men find out better in time. (B18)

This is, on the face of it, a remarkable new role for the gods, as the indispensable, firm, and incontrovertible underpinning for rational enquiry about the world, and a clear and simple response to uncertainty that will be picked up by Xenophanes' immediate successors Heraclitus and Parmenides.

Whether Heraclitus knew of or heard Xenophanes' poem we do not know, but we have reason to believe that he himself was pantheistic in belief. In a famous series of fragments, he talks of a "statement" or "account" (*logos*) of things that is "common" or "universal," even though most people fail to appreciate this, and live as though they had a private understanding (B1, B2). On the assumption that accounts and statements are uttered by rational agents for the hearing and understanding of other rational agents, Heraclitus makes it clear (B50) that the account or statement is not his own, except as conduit; he is not to be listened to qua Heraclitus, but qua bearer of the account. Which rational agent, in that case, *is* the utterer of the account? "That which is wise," he answers, which "is both unwilling and willing to be called Zeus" (B41).

Like Xenophanes, Heraclitus has clearly set up a supreme god of some sort that has at any rate some affinities with Olympian Zeus (in B64 he is called "thunderbolt"), but his nature, and the nature and import of his account, are still to be investigated. And Heraclitus does not disappoint us in the matter, even if what he says is puzzling. "God," he says, "is day night, winter summer, war peace, satiety hunger (all the opposites, this is the meaning); he changes in the way that <fire?>, when it is mixed with spices, is named in accordance with the scent of each of them" (B67). On the assumption that the bracketed words are the explication of Hippolytus, our source for the fragment, what remains can be taken as a reference either to God or to "God." To put it differently, Heraclitus could, on the face of it, be either describing here what he takes God to be, or demythologizing what he takes most people to *think* God is (where "God" is in effect another locution for "what people call God"). On the latter presupposition, he is a nonbeliever in what most people take God to be, God either not existing at all or being something quite other than these opposites. On the former presupposition, he is affirming his belief in God, but describing him in way dramatically different from the way most people would describe him. Either interpretation would fit the fragment if read on its own, but the evidence of other fragments suggests that the first presupposition is the more likely of the two. The utterer of the account of the real (B1, 2) is in effect the world, or at any rate the world qua rational, and, this world being characterized by opposing states and features, he, too, is said to be in some sense those opposing states and features.

This is, on the face of it, a hard saying, which, in conjunction with others even more paradoxical-looking (e g., B57, B88, B126), led Aristotle to accuse Heraclitus of breaking the law of noncontradiction. But this is to misunderstand Heraclitus in a very severe way, since he makes it clear in B88 that his talk of the supposed "sameness" of opposites is to be taken as a reference to the essential connectedness of opposites rather than their absolute identity. As though facing Aristotle's later objection head-on, he writes:

> And as the same thing there exists in us living and dead and the waking and the
> sleeping and young and old: for the latter things, having changed around are
> the former, and the former, having changed around are <back again to being>
> the latter. (B88)

In Kirk's words, Heraclitus is here offering us an example of things essentially connected, in the sense that "they succeed, and are succeeded by, each other and nothing else."

What Heraclitus takes God to be is this world, characterized by apparent polar opposites that are in fact essentially connected, and the ordered process (*kosmos*) of which is described, either really or metaphorically or possibly both, as "an ever-living fire, kindling in measures and going out in measures" (B30).

But if so much has been apparently clarified, it remains to be investigated just what Heraclitus can have meant by crediting this God/world with rational utterance, and what exactly such utterance amounts to. That it does indeed engage in rational utterance, and that such utterance can be heard and understood by us, even if only through the conduit that is Heraclitus, seems clear enough from B50, as does one of the major things, if not *the* major thing, that is affirmed:

> Listening not to me but to the account, it is wise to agree that all things are one.

What "that which is wise" is everlastingly affirming (for the world is for Heraclitus indeed something without beginning or end; B30) is in fact a set of basic truths about itself, which are there for us to hear and understand, either by listening to Heraclitus or, better, by learning for ourselves the language it speaks. In addition to these basic truths, which we might call the laws of physics, and which constitute God's/the world's descriptive self-utterance, there are also a set of universal prescriptive injunctions, which Heraclitus calls "the divine law":

> Those who speak with sense must rely on what is common to all, as a city must rely on its law, and with much greater reliance. For all the laws of men are nourished by one law, the divine <law>; for it has as much power as it wishes and is sufficient for all and is still left over. (B114)

That the world is some sort of book, on the pages of which we see we see the plan of God for the operations of the universe and, in some respect, for the conduct of humans within it, has become a commonplace in a number of systems of natural philosophy. But Heraclitus (followed by Plato, in the *Timaeus*) seems to be offering us an image considerably more dynamic than this, and something, as it happens, readily intelligible to a world that has grown used to visual and radio telescopes. If for everlasting self-utterance we substitute the notion of radio waves everlastingly emitted by objects, like planets, or systems of objects, like galaxies, in circular motion, we have an equally striking picture of a universe that is forever describing itself, so to speak, to those who have the equipment and expertise to understand the language of the description. The operation of the radio waves can be seen, on a Heraclitean interpretation, as the ultimate in rational procedure, since they themselves never err in what they describe; it is merely ourselves who will on occasion err over the interpretation of that description.

If, to the modern mind, it seems more than a little bizarre to interpret the large-scale predictability of the operations of the macrocosmos as a sure sign of the presence of intelligence, one need only, to understand the driving force behind it, see it as yet another piece of that extrapolation from particular to general that is such a pivotal feature of early Greek philosophy. In this instance, all that is needed for the argument to seem prima facie plausible to many, if not a majority, of its Greek hearers is that it be seen as a reasonable extrapolation from the truism that a sign of rationality in the human individual is precisely a large-scale predictability in his or her speech and conduct; large-scale *un*predictability is precise evidence, for most people, that what we are up against, in such an instance, is *irrational* speech and conduct.

However, nothing in this vision of things could have prepared Heraclitus's first hearers (or, for that matter, many readers up to and including our own times) for some further claims he makes about his God/world. For example:

> To God all things are beautiful and good and just, but men have supposed some things to be unjust, others just. (B102)

Or, in overt demythologization, apparently, of the popular notion of the existence and activity of demigods (*daemones*):

> One's character is one's *daemon*. (B119)

However, the demythologization of popular religious belief is not total. As we have already seen,

> One thing, the only truly wise thing, is unwilling and willing to be called by the name Zeus. (B32)

And his clear irritation at much popular belief seems to be directed more at practices he considers nonsensical than at popular religion as such. In B63, for example (though its interpretation is notoriously obscure), he may be suggesting that, whatever his beliefs about *character* being one's *daemon*, he also feels it to be the case that certain souls—those of those who die bravely?—could in fact achieve the status of demigod (*daemon*) as a reward for this. Likewise, when he says (B14) "The secret rites practiced among men are celebrated in an unholy manner," he seems to be alluding to the fact that secrecy is often a cover for inappropriate conduct; what the rites are actually celebrating is not itself necessarily under attack.

The same can be said for his comments on blood-purification and prayer to statues:

> They vainly purify themselves of blood-guilt by defiling themselves with blood, as though one who had stepped into mud were to wash with mud; he would seem mad, if any person noticed him doing this. Further, they pray to these statues, as if one were to carry on a conversation with houses, not recognizing the true nature of the gods or demigods [*heroas*]. (B5)

In a tradition initiated by Xenophanes, Heraclitus uses a tone of biting *reductio ad absurdum*, but what clearly survives his strictures is the fact that he himself believes, in some serious way, in the gods and demigods that most people believe in; his disagreement is not over their existence, but how they are to be understood. So the phallic hymns, he says, sung during the procession to Dionysus are in themselves a shameful spectacle, but saved by the fact that they are a hymn to a god, Dionysus (whom he goes on to equate with Hades) (B15).

Along lines that Aristotle, too, will defend later (*Metaph.* 1074b1–14), Heraclitus is clearly satisfied that whatever the deeper truth of the pantheism he himself professes and proposes, popular religion, in its more commendable practices, can and often does point to truths about the divine, even if the detail of what is said is something less than the most complete and accurate account. This seems to be at least the partial import of one of the most famous of all his sayings:

The lord whose oracle is in Delphi neither speaks out nor conceals, but gives a sign. (B93)

By general consent the most influential of all philosophers antedating Socrates, Heraclitus's contemporary Parmenides of Elea shares with Heraclitus and, earlier, Xenophanes, a commitment to some sort of divine revelation as the source of serious understanding of the world, a revelation underpinning any efforts we ourselves must make to investigate the real with all techniques at our disposal. The source of the revelation—which was the world qua rational in Heraclitus, but the clear counterpart of Zeus in the Olympian pantheon in terms of popular religion—is in analogous fashion understood by Parmenides as another deity the Greeks would have recognized: Justice or Necessity (Aët. 2.7.1). This deity's name is reminiscent of the Fate of the Homeric poems to whom even Zeus was subject, but Parmenides' description of her as "the goddess that steers all" (Aët. 2.7.1) would seem to make her the equivalent of Zeus. (A similar reference to Justice occurs in Heraclitus [B94], where he says "Sun will not overstep his measures; otherwise, the Furies, ministers of Justice, will find him out.") However, the reference to steering is from a secondary source, and may be an interpretation of Aëtius's own, rather than anything to be found specifically in Parmenides' poem, so the matter remains in doubt.

Apart from the foregoing, nothing is known of Parmenides' views on the divine, except that it forms part of the Way of Opinion, and to that degree is never the subject of knowledge, which treats uniquely (B8) of the one real universe qua real (*eon*) and as a totality (*pan, oulon*), never in its particular manifestations, including particular divine manifestations. But it would be unwise to equate the term *opinion* here with an asseveration of major skepticism, since so much of the poem-as-revelation turns on the stability and pivotal nature of his belief in the existence of a particular goddess; while Parmenides may not have wished, perhaps, to propose, as Plato was later to propose, that there is such a thing as a *true* opinion, he almost certainly, to make sense of the role of the goddess Necessity/Justice in his scheme of things and the details about the world he propounds in the Way of Opinion, wished to affirm that, in a world of opinion, including a world of opinions about the role and status of the gods, some opinions are more defensible than others.

Whether Parmenides' one universe was seen by him as also divine, like that, apparently, of Heraclitus, we cannot know, since no evidence on the matter has survived, but the fact that his immediate successor Empedocles, who adopts so much from him in his description of his own one, real, spheroid universe, also refers to it as "God" (B31) may suggest that this, too, was something his predecessor said. However this may be, the claim on Empedocles' part that the cosmos is God puts him firmly in the pantheistic tradition of Heraclitus. As for his further understanding of the world, we cannot be sure whether it is simply his poetic sense or his own deep personal belief that, in some more than just metaphorical sense, the world is indeed, in the phrase attributed to Thales, not just itself a god but also full of gods, since he apparently refers (B6) to the four "roots" of things (earth, air, fire, water) as Zeus, Hera, Aidoneus, and Nestis (though of these, it must be said only Nestis can be confidently equated with water; the precise identifications of the rest are in doubt). And a similar divine status appears to characterize his two motive forces accounting for change, Love and Strife (B17.6–8).

Certainly, Empedocles imagines that gods can appear on earth, live a series of lives here, and return to the state of godhead, since he himself, he seems to say, is on the verge of such a return (B112.4–5). In this, as in his general belief in transmigration, where he has much in common with Orphico-Pythagoreanism, he may be close in his thinking to Heraclitus, though the details of this are obscure. A pair of fragments of Heraclitus, for example, may well be interpreted as expressing a similar belief in transmigration (B25, B62), and another pair of fragments (B36 and B63), despite what may be the counter-evidence of B119—"One's character is one's *daemon*"—can be reasonably interpreted to mean that a brave or noble death (as exemplified in particular by death in battle) is the point of departure for transformation into a *daemon*. If this is the case, Heraclitus appears to be fairly close in his beliefs on the matter to Empedocles, who sees himself, along with others, as a fallen *daemon*, who, for his sins, is compelled to wander through various lives for a period of 30,000 years till he returns to his primeval divine state (B115). It is also striking how he describes the law of such expulsion and return in terms of an oracle of (the goddess) Necessity (B115.1), analogously to the way the same goddess (in her appellation as Justice) formulates and controls the real in Heraclitus (B94), and the way she also does (in her appellations as both Necessity and Justice) in the poem of Parmenides (see Aët. 2.7.1).

Despite these similarities in view, Empedocles' generally Orphico-Pythagorean stance in the matter of primeval sin and transmigration seems to represent a move back in the direction of religious belief as a guide to understanding—though a belief, as it happens, recently imported into Greece rather than a belief in the standard Olympian pantheon—and away from that trust in reason and (with due caution) sense perception as a guide to understanding the world that had characterized the writings of Xenophanes, Heraclitus, and Parmenides. However, a judgment of this order would probably be premature, given his clear parallel interest in careful observation of the world as well, as exemplified by his observation of what happens with the clepsydra (B100), and the implication one could reasonably draw from this that air is corporeal. The same interest is evident in the many fragments dealing with plant physiology and embryology, and in the bold evolutionary cast of his thought on the stages through which life forms develop by a process that appears to be random, in its detail if not its broader structure (B57, B59, B60–62)—to the dissatisfaction of Aristotle, for whom an explanation in terms of internal finality is more plausible (*Ph.* 198b29).

In view of this, it is natural enough to assume (as the young Socrates seems, for example, to have assumed; Pl. *Phd.* 97c–99d) that, in introducing the notion of Intelligence (*Nous*) as the motive force for things, rather than Empedocles' Love and Strife (what we would now likely call centripetal and centrifugal force),

Anaxagoras was actively setting out to counter an Empedoclean theory of randomness with some sort of teleological account of things. Notoriously, however, Socrates was greatly disappointed, in that *Nous* was given no such role. Far from giving *goals* to the real, it simply "initiated motion" (B13) and "controlled" (B12) the rotation of the universe from its first beginnings. In Aristotelian terms, it remained, like Empedocles' Love and Strife, a simple efficient cause of how the world was and is; it is never credited by Anaxagoras with the role of either goal-setter or final cause in the scheme of things.

As far as its ontological status is concerned, Anaxagoras has the following to say.

> All other things have a portion of everything, but Intelligence is boundless [*apeiron*] and self-ruled, and is mixed with nothing but is all alone by itself. For if it were not by itself, but was mixed with anything else, it would have a share of all things, if it were mixed with any. For in everything there is a portion of everything, as I said earlier; and the things that were mingled with it would hinder it so that it could control nothing in the same way as it does now being alone by itself. For it is the finest of all things and the purest, it has all knowledge about everything and the greatest power; and Intelligence controls all things, both the greater and the smaller, that have life. Intelligence controlled also the whole rotation <of the universe>, so that it began to rotate in the beginning. (B12, opening lines)

On the face of it, this looks like another instance of a demythologized Zeus, which exercises a power of control (*kratos*) over the universe. In saying it is unmixed with anything physical, and the finest and purest of things, Anaxagoras may also have been reaching toward the notion of Intelligence as an immaterial substance. The same inference might be drawn from his calling it boundless or infinite. But too much should not be made of this. We cannot be sure whether Anaxagoras had any clear notion of a supposed locus for Intelligence, other than that it is not coextensive with the physical universe; in this it would clearly differ from Xenophanes' one god, if Xenophanes had in fact thought that such a god was coextensive with the universe (a supposition, as we have seen, however, very much open to question). And to infer from the adjective "boundless" that it was actually infinite in extent is hazardous, since the term *boundless*, as evidenced by its employment to portray the boundless Stream of Ocean in the Homeric poems, can simply mean "extremely large."

The matter is not clarified by a comment toward the end of B12 in which Anaxagoras informs us that "Intelligence is all alike, both the greater and the smaller <quantities of it?>." If this means, as it seems to mean, that cosmic Intelligence and intelligence as found in humans are of the same order, we are still no further forward as to his understanding of the parameters of cosmic Intelligence, except that they very broadly transcend the boundaries of the spheroid, rotating, and still expanding universe (B12) but cannot themselves be said to involve a physical boundary we could recognize.

If this aspect of Anaxagoras's doctrine of cosmic Intelligence has to remain somewhat obscure, the reference to Intelligence's specific control over "all things, both the greater and the smaller, that *have life*" (B12) might be thought to be illuminating in another respect. Because the area of life is precisely the area in which being controlled by Intelligence could possibly be thought to mean being "goal-directed" by Intelligence. But here, too, we have no independent evidence to suggest that this was what Anaxagoras had in mind, even though he could well have been edging his way toward such a notion, in the way he might have been edging toward the notion of Intelligence's immateriality. And this in itself might well have proved enough to make Socrates and Plato accept both ideas as foundational in their system of natural philosophy/theology. But as it happens, they had a more immediate precursor, in the matter of teleology at any rate.

Diogenes of Apollonia, a contemporary of Socrates, is most widely known for his return to a Anaximean doctrine of air as the basic material of things. Like that of Anaximenes, Diogenes' air is also thought of as eternal, divine, intelligent, and controlling the operations of things (B4, B5, B7). By contrast with the *Nous* of Anaxagoras, however, it pervades everything, and is coextensive with the cosmos (B5). But even more important is the *manner* of its control of things, which is now for the first time set out in clearly teleological terms. Divine air, Diogenes says (B5), "seems to me to have reached everywhere and to dispose [*diatithenai*] all things," and later in the fragment, talking of living creatures, he says that "all live and see and hear by the same thing, and have the rest of their understanding from the same thing" (namely divine air). Taking note of the regularity and predictability of such things as seasonal change, night and day, and the like, he also writes that

> it would not be possible without Intellection [*Noêsios*] for it [namely the basic stuff of things] so to be divided up that it has the measures of all things—of winter and summer and night and day and rains and winds and fair weather. The other things, too, if one wishes to consider them, *one would find disposed in the best possible way.* (B3; italics added)

The statement is remarkable, and rich in implications, on two counts. Unlike anything we find in the extant fragments of Anaxagoras, it is, for the first (and as, it happens, last) time in Presocratic thought a clear and unambiguous use of teleological explanation. And it employs, again for the first (and last) time in Presocratic thought, the dynamic word "Intellection" (*Noesis*) rather than Anaxagoras's more static word "Intelligence" (*Nous*) to account for what he sees as the best possible disposition of things. With the first move, he makes himself the immediate precursor of Socratic/Platonic teleological explanation in natural philosophy/theology; with the second he makes himself the precursor of one of the most astonishing claims of Aristotle, that the Prime Mover is *Noesis Noeseos* ("apprehension of apprehension, intellection of intellection, discovery of discovery"; *Metaph.* 1074b34).

But the Presocratic period ends with no such neat causal sequence. If one train of thinking was moving in the direction of a divinely guided, teleologically explicable universe, another was moving in exactly the opposite direction. For the atomists Democritus and Leucippus, the ever-changing universe is an infinity of space in which, across eternity, chance agglomerations of ever-moving atoms produce and will forever go on producing those contents of the universe that we call realities, from gazelles to galaxies. All is total chance, without guidance and without goal; if there is any "necessity" to it all (a word Leucippus is prepared to use, B2), it is simply the necessity of physical causality.

Fifth-century Greece came to an end with the dramatic battle between opposing political systems that Thucydides described. At the same time, a great battle began in the realm of natural philosophy/theology that is still with us—and still employs parameters little different from those first set out by Presocratic philosophers.

NOTES

1. Translations of fragments of the Presocratics and of the various ancient *testimonia*, as found in DK, are basically those to be found in KRS, with occasional variants of my own. References to "Kirk" are to points made by him in his discussion of particular philosophers in the same volume.

2. For useful comments on the text of this fragment see the notes of Lesher, *Xenophanes of Colophon.*

3. I owe the translation to David Guetter, who has argued convincingly that this is very frequently the correct interpretation of *prep*-root usage in classical Greek. See also Guetter, "The Cognitive Sense of PREP- and PROSHK-."

4. See Lesher, *Xenophanes of Colophon*, 100–101.

BIBLIOGRAPHY

Adoménas, Mantas. "Heraclitus on Religion." *Phronesis* 44 (1999): 87–113.

Babut, D. "Le divin et les dieux dans la pensée d'Anaximandre." *Revue des Études Grecques* 85 (1972): 1–32.

Betegh, Gábor. *The Derveni Papyrus: Cosmology, Theology, and Interpretation.* Cambridge: Cambridge University Press, 2004.

Burkert, Walter. "Apokalyptik im frühen Griechentum: Impulse und Transformationen." In *Apocalypticism in the Mediterranean World and the Near East*, 235–54. Tübingen, 1983.

———. *Greek Religion.* Cambridge, Mass.: Harvard University Press, 1985.

Clarke, Michael. "The Wisdom of Thales and the Problem of the Word *Hieros*." *Classical Quarterly* 45 (1995): 296–317.

Cornford, F. M. *From Religion to Philosophy.* London: Edward Arnold, 1912.

Darcus, S. M. "Daimon Parallels the Holy *Phrên* in Empedocles." *Phronesis* 22 (1977): 175–90.

Deichgräber, Karl. "Hymnische Elemente in der philosophischen Prosa der Vorsokratiker." *Philologus* 42 (1933): 347–61.

Detienne, Marcel. "La démonologie d'Empédocle." *Revue des Études Grecques* 72 (1959): 1–17.

Drozdek, Adam. "Protagoras and the Instrumentality of Religion." *L'Antiquité Classique* 74 (2005): 41–50.

Finkelberg, Aryeh. "On the Unity of Orphic and Milesian Thought." *Harvard Theological Review* 79 (1986): 321–35.

François, G. *Le polytheisme et l'emploi au singulier des mots Theos, Daimon dans la littérature grecque d'Homère à Platon.* Paris, 1957.

Fränkel, Hermann. "Heraclitus on God and the Phenomenal World." *Transactions and Proceedings of the American Philological Association* 69 (1938): 230–44.

Gemelli Marciano, Laura. "Indovini, *magoi* e *meteorologoi*: Interazioni e definizioni nell'ultimo terzo del V secolo a.C." In *La costruzione del discorso filosofico nell'età dei presocratici*, edited by Maria Michela Sassi, 203–35. Pisa: Edizioni della Normale, 2006.

Gerson, Lloyd P. *God and Greek Philosophy: Studies in the Early History of Natural Theology.* London: Routledge, 1990.

Guetter, David. "The Cognitive sense of ΠΡΕΠ- and ΠΡΟΣΗΚ-." *Phoenix* 60 (2006): 329–45.

Hourcade, Annie. "Protagoras et Démocrite: Le feu divin entre mythe et raison." *Revue de philosophie ancienne* 18 (2000): 87-113.

Jaeger, Werner. *The Theology of the Early Greek Philosophers.* London: Oxford University Press, 1947.

Laks, André, and Glenn W. Most, eds. *Studies on the Derveni Papyrus.* Oxford: Clarendon Press, 1997.

Lesher, James H. *Xenophanes of Colophon: Fragments.* Toronto: University of Toronto Press, 1992.

Nestle, Wilhelm. *Vom Mythos zum Logos.* 2nd edn. Stuttgart: Alfred Kröner Verlag.

Palmer, John. "Aristotle on the Ancient Theologians." *Apeiron* 33 (2000): 181–205.

Pépin, Jean. *Théologie cosmique et théologie chrétienne (Ambroise, Exam. I 1, 1-4).* Paris, 1964.

Primavesi, Oliver. "Apollo and Other Gods in Empedocles." In *La costruzione del discorso filosofico nell'età dei presocratici*, edited by Maria Michela Sassi, 51–77. Pisa: Edizioni della Normale, 2006.

Vlastos, Gregory. "Theology and Philosophy in Early Greek Thought." *Philosophical Quarterly* 2 (1952): 97–123.

West, M. L. *The Orphic Poems.* Oxford: Clarendon Press, 1983.

Yunis, Harvey. *A New Creed: Fundamental Religious Beliefs in the Athenian Polis and Euripidean Drama.* Göttingen: Vandenhoeck & Ruprecht, 1988.

Zuntz, Günther. *Persephone: Three Essays on Religion and Thought in Magna Graecia.* Oxford: Clarendon Press, 1971.

PART IV

RECEPTION

....

CHAPTER 19

ARISTOTLE'S ACCOUNT OF THE ORIGINS OF PHILOSOPHY

....

MICHAEL FREDE

IF ONE wants to have an adequate understanding of the history of philosophy or, for that matter, more modestly, just of the ancient part of this history, it obviously greatly matters that one have a reasonable grasp of the beginnings of philosophy and of its early development.

Needless to say, we will have to know who the first philosophers were so that we can start our history with them. But it takes little to see the difficulties involved even in just finding out who the first philosophers were and how they themselves conceived of what they were doing. It seems unreasonable to assume that philosophy appeared all of a sudden out of the blue, out of nothing. We will rather expect that the first philosophers had predecessors of some kind, that their mode of thinking was rooted in, or evolved out of, earlier modes of thinking about things. We will have to identify these earlier modes of thinking, but then will also have to explain in which way the mode of thinking of the first philosophers significantly differed from the earlier modes of thinking, as a result of which we are prepared to call them, but not their predecessors, "philosophers." We will also have to find out why older patterns of thinking no longer seemed adequate and how the dissatisfaction with them led to the emergence of a new way of thinking, namely the way of thinking which characterizes the philosophers as philosophy emerges. But we will not just expect that philosophy did not appear all of a sudden out of nowhere in the mind of some ingenious Greek. We will also not expect that when philosophy did make its first appearance, it did appear fully developed, the way Pallas Athena sprang from the head of Zeus, fully grown, in full armor, brandishing her spear. We will rather assume that it took philosophy, once born, some time to develop a shape and form under which we readily recognize it as such. In fact, it is clear that one only came to think of the origins of philosophy and to call Thales or Anaximander "philosophers," once philosophy had become a reasonably well defined and readily recognizable enterprise. It was then that with hind-sight one could see that the enterprise had started with figures like them. They must have thought of themselves as doing something in a new way, but this does not mean that they thought of themselves as philosophers, let alone as the first philosophers. Nor is there any sign that their contemporaries or near-contemporaries recognized them as having started a new enterprise to which they could put a distinctive name. The terms "philosophy" and "philosopher" in the now familiar sense are of much later origin.

Hence, to get our history off to the right start, what we need is an account along the lines indicated, however difficult this may be, of the origin of Greek philosophy and of its early evolution up to the point at which it has turned into the sort of enterprise we recognize as philosophy, for instance in Aristotle.

But it is not my ambition here to provide such an account. What instead I will try to do is to give an account of how Aristotle seeks to determine and to explain the origin of philosophy and to account for its early development. I will in particular focus on his account of the history of philosophy from its beginnings down to his own time in *Metaphysics* 1.3–10, in particular 1.3–6. For a careful study of Aristotle's account seems to me to be a prerequisite for any reasonable attempt to explain the origin of philosophy. This is so for quite a number of reasons which are familiar to students of early Greek philosophy. Hence I will here just briefly mention those which are particularly relevant to our purposes. We derive a good deal of our knowledge about early Greek philosophy directly from Aristotle. A great deal of the information provided by later ancient sources itself is derived from Aristotle and his students, like Theophrastus or Eudemus. The evidential value of this information is rather high. For Aristotle took great interest in the thought of earlier philosophers, and he taught students to take a systematic interest in them. And obviously Aristotle and his students had sources of information, in particular some of the works themselves of some of their predecessors, still available to them which later authors no longer had access to. But it also is clear that Aristotle had his own particular perspective on the history of early Greek philosophy, and that his students largely shared his general view of the early history of Greek philosophy. Thus much, if not most, of our information about the beginnings of philosophy in Greece has the imprint of a typically Aristotelian perspective. Thus to be able to use this evidence without being misled by the Aristotelian perspective of the sources from which it was drawn, we have to get clear about Aristotle's own view of the origin of philosophy and its early development. But, this said, it needs to be emphasized that the interest in Aristotle's account should not just, and not even primarily, be this negative interest of enabling us to be on guard against an Aristotelian bias in much of our evidence concerning early Greek philosophy. We should appreciate Aristotle's account for what it is worth positively as a guide to our understanding of the beginnings of philosophy, given that Aristotle was in a much better position than we are to form a view about early philosophy.

Now, of particular importance among the many passages in which Aristotle discusses earlier Greek philosophers is the text I want to focus on, *Metaphysics* 1.3–10, in particular 3–6. What makes this text particularly important for our purposes is that in these chapters we, for the first time in history, do get an account of the origin of philosophy and of its early development, down to Aristotle's time. It, moreover, is an account which does at least address the questions I raised at the outset as questions we need to have an answer to if we are to understand the beginnings of philosophy, even if we may feel frustrated by the brevity and vagueness of Aristotle's answers. Aristotle in *Metaphysics* 1, for instance, lets philosophy begin with Thales, drawing a clear line between Thales and whatever predecessors he may have had, and offers a reason for this. It is ultimately due to this text that we traditionally let philosophy begin with Thales. But it also takes, or at least suggests, the view that philosophy only really came into its own in Plato's and Aristotle's days.

Before we turn to some of the crucial details of this text, though, we need to consider its context. Obviously, it is not Aristotle's aim to provide an account of the origin of philosophy and its evolution for its own sake, to satisfy his and his readers' historical interests. After all, the account just forms a part, though a very substantial part, of book 1 of the *Metaphysics*, which constitutes some kind of introduction to a treatise on metaphysics. Hence we would like to know which function this account is supposed to have within the overall line of thought of *Metaphysics* 1. Not much attention seems to have been given to this question. Thus, for instance, A. E. Taylor in 1907 published a translation (with introduction and notes) of *Metaphysics* 1 under the title *Aristotle on His Predecessors* with the subtitle *Being the First Book of his Metaphysics*. But in giving the text this title and subtitle Taylor clearly gets things the wrong way round. It is not that the first book of the *Metaphysics* happens to be an account Aristotle gives of the thought of his predecessors; it rather must be the case that because *Metaphysics* 1 is supposed to be an introduction to Aristotle's metaphysics, it also deals, and this at considerable length, namely for most of the book, with the thought of his predecessors. The question is why this introduction to metaphysics should involve such a detailed historical account. Ross thinks that "Aristotle's object is not to write a history of philosophy but to confirm by reference to earlier philosophers his own account of the primary causes," that is the famous four Aristotelian causes, the formal, the material, the moving, and the final cause: "the four causes the progressive recognition of which, by earlier thinkers, forms the subject of Book A."[1] Ross no doubt is right that one prominent role the historical account plays in the overall argument of *Metaphysics* 1 is to confirm Aristotle's claim that there are four types of causes or explanatory factors in terms of which we can explain things. Aristotle himself explicitly says so. *Metaphysics* 1.3 begins with the claim that we have to come to have knowledge of the first principles or causes (983a24–26). Aristotle then rather dogmatically states that there are four types of cause or principle which he briefly identifies (983a26–32). He goes on to explain the rather categorical tone of his statement by saying that we have considered this matter sufficiently in the *Physics*, but that it still might be worthwhile to look at the earlier philosophers who also have appealed to causes and principles. For, if we see that they have resorted to the same few types of explanation and have not appealed to any other type, we will have more confidence in the claim that there are precisely these four types of cause (983a33–b6). At this point, 983b6ff, the historical account follows. Clearly, then, the immediate point of the historical account in *Metaphysics* 1.3, 983b6 to the end of 1.6 is to reassure us that all principles or causes are of one or another of the four types indicated. That this is at least part of the point of the account is repeated in 1.5, 986a13–15. Hence at the beginning of 1.7, 988a18–23, Aristotle thinks he can say that this brief and summary account shows that none of his predecessors could think of yet a further type of explanation. This claim is repeated at the end of chapter 7 (988b16–19). The final chapter of the book, 1.10, begins with the remark that it should now be clear that all previous philosophers have been looking for the types of explanation identified in the *Physics*, and that we do not seem to have over-looked yet another kind of cause or explanation (993a11–13).

Now it is perfectly true, as commentators repeatedly have pointed out, that Aristotle never provides a systematic argument to show that there are just four types of causes or explanations, and hence it is also true that Aristotle's listeners or readers presumably would like some reassurance on this point. But it does not seem plausible that Aristotle in his introduction to metaphysics would go on for chapters 3 to 7, let alone for chapters 3 to 10, just to make the point that we can be confident that there are precisely these four kinds of causes. For though this no doubt is an important point also in the context of Aristotelian metaphysics, an introduction to this discipline hardly is the appropriate place to dwell on this point at this length. And this is especially so, if we assume that Aristotle is trying to introduce us to a new discipline or at least a new conception of a certain type of inquiry which Aristotle thinks should be distinguished from natural philosophy. Ross himself acknowledges this by saying in one place (1:126 ad 983a26) more cautiously that "it is the main object of Book A to show" that there are just these four causes.[2]

What else, then, is the point of the historical account, of Aristotle's discussion of the thought of his predecessors in 1.3–10? There are two ways to get clearer about this. One is to just look at chapters 3 to 10 to see which points are made, or at least suggested, which are relevant to the metaphysical enterprise. A point explicitly and quite conspicuously made is that his predecessors only had a rather inadequate, dim grasp of the four kinds of causes (see 1.7, 988a22–23 and 1.10, 993a13–15). We are supposed to see this, for instance, when we, in chapters 8 and 9, look at the difficulties they get into in trying to explain things, which in part reveal their confusion about the nature of these causes or principles. There are various aspects of this point which are relevant for our purposes. One aspect is this. In claiming that his predecessors only had such an imperfect grasp of these kinds of causes that one might even say that they had not yet grasped them (see 1.10, 993a 14–15), Aristotle gives himself considerable leeway in interpreting his predecessors. He, for instance, can present Thales as somebody who wanted to claim that water is the ultimate principle of things, because it is the ultimate matter of everything. But clearly Thales did not have a notion of matter, let alone Aristotle's notion of matter. And Aristotle is perfectly aware of this. But he thinks that he can justify his interpretation of Thales, because what Thales actually seems to have said is best understood, Aristotle thinks, if we assume that Thales was thinking of water as something like the matter of things, though he did not yet have a clear conception of what it is for something to be the matter of something. In fact, Aristotle himself still has considerable difficulties in explaining what matter is supposed to be. Commentators to the present day are in disagreement as to what Aristotle's own view was. Another aspect of the point is this. It allows Aristotle to present the early history of philosophy as being driven by the need to introduce, in addition to matter, the further explanatory kinds of principles, and to get clearer about the nature of these explanatory factors, which, Aristotle seems to think, naturally leads us to the sort of position he himself espouses. Whatever we think about Aristotle's confidence in this, it allows Aristotle to construct a real narrative, to give us the sense of an almost natural historical development, rather than to present us with a mere collection of historical facts about his predecessors, more or less chrono-logically ordered.

Yet another aspect of this point is that it allows for the possibility that, though we can trace back the origins of philosophy to, say, Thales, "real" philosophy, philosophy as we are familiar with it, only emerged much later. Yet a further aspect is the following: it is clear from Aristotle's discussion of his predecessors that a crucial task of philosophy will be to get clear about the four types of causes or explanations, for instance about matter and form, which in fact are a main topic in the *Metaphysics*.

An altogether different point which emerges from Aristotle's discussion, and which also is relevant to his metaphysics, is the following. Though from the very beginning philosophers in the first instance were concerned to give an account of the sensible, natural, material world and its prominent features, a review of the earlier history of philosophy shows that a number of important philosophers thought that some of the principles we have to appeal to in order to account for the physical world are not themselves perceptible or material. And in Aristotle's view they were right, though at least partly mistaken in their identification of these principles, for instance as Platonic ideas. This "discovery" of immaterial principles was part of the quasi natural evolution of philosophy.

Aristotle's discussion of his predecessors in 1.3–10 then clearly does not just serve the point to assure us that all principles are of one of the four types identified in the *Physics*. But there is another and more important way to get clearer about the purpose of Aristotle's discussion of his predecessors. We have to see how 1.3–10 connects with 1.1–2. Superficially, the connection between the two sections is clear.

Very roughly speaking, Aristotle in 1.1–2 tells us that we all naturally want to know, even quite independently from any practical benefit we may draw from this knowledge. But the highest form of knowledge is wisdom, that is, knowledge of first principles and causes. Hence we naturally will want to acquire this knowledge of first principles. Chapter 1.3 then begins with the claim that we have to obtain knowledge of first causes or principles and that there are four kinds of causes or principles—matter, form, moving and final cause. Thus the assumption underlying the connection between 1.1–2 and 1.3–10 seems to be that the principles which we are looking for when we try to acquire wisdom will be principles of the four kinds spelled out.

But I think that there is a great deal more to the connection between 1.1–2 and 1.3–10 which also is relevant to the historical account. Aristotle in 1.1–2 is concerned to spell out in considerable detail a certain conception of wisdom. The relevance of this seems to me to be obvious. We expect Aristotle's view of the origin of philosophy to depend on his view of philosophy, and his view of philosophy, in turn, on his conception of wisdom. After all, philosophers are called "philosophers" because they have a particular concern of wisdom (*sophia*). And this is something which Aristotle in our context clearly is aware of. For when Aristotle in 1.2, 982b11–21 argues that wisdom, the knowledge of first principles and causes, is not productive, that it does not aim at some practical benefit, he claims that we can see this also by looking at those who first engaged in philosophy, that is, those who first concerned themselves with wisdom. They were driven to philosophy by their desire to get rid of their ignorance and were looking for knowledge for the sake of knowledge itself rather than for any practical benefit they might derive from it. Similarly in *Metaphysics* 4.3, when Aristotle discusses whether it is the task of the philosopher to inquire not just into substance but also into what in mathematics are called "axioms," principles which hold of beings quite generally, his answer is that this, too, is the task of the philosopher. Neither geometers, nor arithmeticians discuss these principles, though they rely on them. Some physicists (*phusikoi*) have discussed them, quite reasonably so. For they believed that they were dealing with the whole of nature and thus with the whole of what there is. But they were mistaken (1005a29–33). For physics (*hê phusikê*) is a kind of wisdom, but not the primary one (*ou prôtê*, 1005b1–2). Here, again, it is the philosopher, rather than the physicist, who is concerned with such principles, because it is part of wisdom to know about them. We will have to return to this passage later. What matters for the moment is that both in 1.2 and in 4.3 Aristotle for his argument draws on the assumption that, as the very name indicates, philosophy is concerned with wisdom.

If, then, the question of what wisdom is and of its desirability takes up the whole of the first two chapters of the *Metaphysics*, we well may wonder whether the issue is not the nature, scope, and aim of philosophy and the attractiveness of the knowledge to be gained by it. At this point it is relevant to note that in Aristotle's day there was by no means general agreement as to what wisdom consists in, and, as a result of this, no agreement as to what philosophy is, as to how one goes about acquiring wisdom. Plato, at the beginning of the *Sophist* (217a4–b4), describes a state of affairs, at least at the dramatic date of the dialogue, namely in 399 BC, if not at the time of its writing, in which there is general confusion about what it is to be a philosopher and how to distinguish him, for instance, from sophists and from statesmen. One issue, indicated by the question how the philosopher differs from the statesman, was whether wisdom was essentially practical, a matter of knowing how to deal with the affairs of the state, but also one's own private affairs, or whether wisdom, at least in the first instance, was theoretical, something cherished for its own sake. There were quite different versions of the former view. On the one hand there were those who, like Socrates and some of his followers, had a stringent conception of knowledge, but concerned themselves exclusively with ethical knowledge, refusing to engage in any study of nature (see 1.6, 987b1–4). But there were also those, like Isocrates and his followers, for instance Cephisodorus, who thought of wisdom and hence philosophy as a matter of experience and reflection concerning matters of state and private affairs, yielding sound opinion rather than proof, which is unattainable in such matters of real importance.

We know that there was a debate between Isocrates and his followers and Plato and his followers, including Aristotle, about the nature and task of philosophy, reflected by Isocrates' *Against the Sophists* and the *Antidosis*. It also has been argued, for instance by Jaeger and by Düring, *Aristotle's Protrepticus*, that Aristotle wrote the *Protrepticus* to attack the sort of conception of wisdom and hence of philosophy which underlies, for instance, Isocrates' *Ad Nicoclem*.[3] It has been noted, by Jaeger and, following him, by Ross, that there are close parallels between the argument of 1.1–2 and some fragments of the *Protrepticus*.[4] In any case, as we will see, the notion of wisdom Aristotle advocates in 1.1–2 is markedly theoretical. But there also was a disagreement among those who thought of philosophy as primarily a theoretical enterprise. There were those who thought that reality was exhausted by the realm of nature and that thus theory amounted to physical theory or science, whereas others, among them Aristotle, believed that we had to assume the existence of non-material substances to fully understand the natural world. They in turn disagreed as to the nature of these intelligible, as opposed to sensible, entities or substances. Plato and Platonists postulated ideas or mathematical entities of various kinds. Aristotle agreed that there had to be immaterial, non-sensible substances. But they were not of the kind the Platonists assumed, but separate intellects, in particular God (see 7.16, 1040b27–32; 12.6–10). In any case, Aristotle thought that how we conceive of wisdom and hence of philosophy also depends on whether we think that the physical realm is all that there is to reality. And this, too, is reflected in 1.1–2 in that Aristotle hints at a distinction between wisdom in a wider sense in which it covers theoretical knowledge in general and wisdom in its highest form in which it is a form of knowledge which deserves to be called "divine," since it involves knowledge of God, principle of everything, and since perhaps only a god can have this knowledge (1.2, 983a5–10).

So there is reason to think that Aristotle in 1.1–2 also tries to advocate a certain conception of wisdom and thereby of philosophy, that his account of the beginnings and early history of philosophy reflects this conception, and that this conception itself also is influenced by reflection on this history and supposed to be borne out by it. But before we pursue this further, we need to look more closely at what sort of notion of wisdom Aristotle aims at, and at how he arrives at it, at a certain ambiguity in this notion alluded to above, and whether there is any justification for Aristotle's claim that his conception of wisdom as theoretical is supported by common intuitions about who is wise.

The difficulty of Aristotle's task in advocating a specific notion of wisdom, in particular one on which wisdom is theoretical, lies in the fact that the use of the words *sophos* and *sophia* in ancient Greek is somewhat diffuse. It starts from a use in which somebody is called "wise," if he has mastered a certain practical skill or craft, widens, but for the most part clearly retains a practical aspect. As it widens, it takes on a more elevated sense, or even a very elevated, but still rather vague, sense. When the Athenians in 582/1 BC under the archonship of Damasias passed a decree honouring Thales as a *sophos* (D.L., 1.22 referring to Demetrius of Phaleron's "List of Archons"), they must have had in mind such a highly elevated sense, but also must have been thinking, at least in part, of Thales' practical achievements. For even Herodotus, almost 150 years later, when he talks about Thales, thinks of him not just as having predicted an eclipse (1.74), but also as having diverted the river Halys (1.75), and as having advised the Ionians to form a federation with its capital on Teos (1.170).

The way Aristotle proceeds in 1.1 is by constructing a hierarchy of crafts and arts according to the degree and kind of wisdom they involve, appealing to intuitions we are supposed to have about this. The *Metaphysics* famously begin with the claim that all human beings naturally desire to know. He explains that a sign of this is that we like to perceive things, in particular to see things, which contributes most to our knowledge of the world, independently of the practical use we derive from perceiving things (980a20). We get an account of how perception, through memory, gives rise to experience and thus is the basis of skills and crafts like that of the healer, and ultimately of art and science (980a27–981a5). He does not think that ordinary perception as such constitutes wisdom (981b10–11). But he takes note of the basic old use of "wisdom" in the sense of a simple skill or craft in the following way (981b13–17). He says that it is likely that the person who was the first to develop a special skill or craft which allowed him to do something which goes beyond what everybody could do on the basis of what we all have perceived or observed, greatly impressed people (was greatly marveled at, *thaumazesthai*), not just because of the usefulness of the invention, but as somebody wise and standing out from the rest. Thus Aristotle suggests that already the basis for singling out the originators of simple skills and crafts as wise involved an appreciation of non-utilitarian elements in their invention, for instance the cleverness or inventiveness displayed. In any case, they knew something the rest of us did not know, namely what one had to do to achieve a certain result. Now in 981a5–30 Aristotle takes such a craft, that of the healer, and compares it to that of a physician who has some theoretical understanding of what is involved in what he is doing, who knows the causes. The healer, on the basis of mere experience, in some sense knows that a certain remedy does benefit the patient. But he does not know, and hence does not understand, why this is so (981a28–30). This is why we think that the physician is wiser or more properly speaking wise, as if wisdom rather was a matter of knowing, properly speaking (981a24–27). The healer, for all practical purposes, may be as efficacious as the physician. Indeed, the physician, for lack of experience, may be less successful. Nevertheless, we judge him wiser because he not only knows that something is the case, but also the cause or reason why it is so (981a12–24). This is also borne out by the fact that we regard the master-builder or architect as more deserving of respect and as wiser than the carpenter or other craftsmen involved in building. The carpenter knows what to do, but the architect knows why this has to be done. This suggests that wisdom is not so much a matter of efficacy as of knowledge and understanding, of knowing the reason or cause why (981b5–6). Now a physician is able to some extent to explain why a patient benefits from a certain treatment. But once all the crafts and arts have been developed which serve either our vital needs (like the need for health or for shelter) or our comfort, we can turn to the pursuit of knowledge just for the sake of knowledge, that is, knowledge which does not aim at any practical purpose or need, theoretical knowledge (981b2–23; see 1.2, 982b22–24). And such bodies of theoretical knowledge will more fully deserve the name "wisdom" than the productive arts, the arts of the physician or the architect. Wisdom in this sense will involve the grasp or knowledge of first causes and principles (981b27–982a3).

It cannot be said that the line of thought in 1.1 is crystal-clear. It may be due to this that Aristotle himself is saying in 1.1, towards the end, namely in 981b27–29, that the point which is to emerge from his present account is that we all (implicitly) assume that what is called "wisdom" is knowledge about the first causes and the principles. Here lies the ambiguity which I alluded to earlier. It was noticed by Bonitz, *Aristotelis Metaphysica* in his comments on 1.2, 983a20.[5] Bonitz pointed out that it is not altogether clear whether in 1.1–2 Aristotle is trying to characterize the wisdom science or philosophy generally aims at, or specifically the wisdom first philosophy is concerned with. But as Ross notes in his comments on 1.2, 983a21–23, in response to Bonitz, it is clear from 1.2 that Aristotle is concerned to specifically characterize the wisdom of concern to the metaphysician.[6] But this does not fully answer Bonitz's query. For one might think that though 1.2 clearly is trying to characterize a special kind of wisdom, namely the one of concern to the first philosopher, it is not clear that 1.1 is concerned to specifically characterize this special kind of wisdom. It rather ends up giving a characterization of wisdom in general which characterizes all theoretical disciplines, that is, also physics and the mathematical disciplines. They all try to understand something in terms of genuine principles and causes, in a sense they all aim at knowledge of first causes and principles, namely in the sense that the nature of a line is a first cause of facts about geometrical objects. I will later try to give an explanation of this unclarity or ambiguity about what Aristotle is trying to characterize.

In 1.2, as I said, Aristotle clearly is concerned with a special kind of wisdom, wisdom to the highest degree or in the fullest sense. By now it is assumed that wisdom involves the grasp of principles and causes, in terms of which we can explain things. And the question is what sort of principles and causes wisdom is knowledge of (982a4–6). Again we appeal to intuitions about the wise person. The first of them is that the wise person somehow knows everything, to the extent that this is possible, though not necessarily in every detail (982a8–10). There are further intuitions, but in the end they all point to the same body of knowledge, wisdom in the fullest sense of the word (982b7–8). The requirement that the wise person somehow knows everything is met by somebody who has the most universal knowledge of things. Such knowledge is most difficult to obtain, because it is farthest removed from perception. It is most accurate, because it deals with absolutely primary or basic things. These by nature also are the most intelligible things, in terms of which one will understand the less basic things (982a21–b4). In short this knowledge or wisdom is knowledge of the first principles and causes of things quite generally, including the good (982b9–10). It thus includes knowledge of God, and is divine, both in the sense that it deals with the divine, and in the sense that perhaps only a god has this sort of knowledge (983a5–10).

Aristotle argues that wisdom, unlike, say, medicine and the art of building, is not productive knowledge, as one can see from those who first engaged in philosophy. They began to do so being puzzled (*aporôn*, 982b17) and wondering (*thaumasantes*, 982b12, 14, 17) about things, and trying to get rid of their ignorance were looking for knowledge, not for the sake of some practical benefit (982b11–21). In passing Aristotle implicitly also deals with the suggestion that ultimate wisdom might be practical. Already in 1.1 he had claimed that master-builders (*architektones*) are thought to be wiser than the various types of craftsmen subordinated to them (981a30–b1). In 1.2 he again lists as an intuition that a master-discipline is more properly speaking wisdom than its subordinate discipline or disciplines (982a16–19). This is taken up again in 982b4ff. The most authoritative knowledge is knowledge of the good, of that for the sake of which each thing has to be done. Now one might think that this is practical knowledge in the narrow sense, as opposed to theoretical or productive knowledge. In fact one might think that this must be the art of politics, including ethics, which Aristotle in *Nicomachean Ethics* 1.2 characterizes as authoritative (κυριωτάτη καὶ μάλιστα ἀρχιτεκτονική, 1094a26–28), because it is concerned with the good and with what is best. But Aristotle here avoids this conclusion by making the good and the first cause itself a principle of reality as a whole, and thus an object of theoretical wisdom.

Now what is striking about the way Aristotle argues in 1.1–2 is that he presents his conclusion that wisdom, properly speaking, is entirely theoretical, desired for its own sake, rather than for the practical benefit one may derive from it, as being supported by the use of the word "wise" and ordinary intuitions about wisdom. One might think that, though this is Aristotle's view, he hardly is entitled to claim that it is supported by the way the Greeks thought about wisdom. But that Aristotle's conclusion is not entirely at odds with the ordinary Greek view we can see from two well-known passages in Greek literature.

The first is from the "Funeral Oration" which Thucydides attributes to Pericles. Thucydides lets Pericles say (2.40.1): "φιλοσοφοῦμεν ἄνευ μαλακίας."

Pericles clearly does not want to say that the Athenians are philosophers. As, I hope, will become apparent later, if it is not already clear here from the language itself, Pericles also does not mean to say that the Athenians love philosophy. He rather is thinking of wisdom in the more elated, but vague sense I have referred to earlier which Aristotle is trying to clarify and to make more precise. The vague "we cherish wisdom" here gets clarified by the addition "ἄνευ μαλακίας": the Athenians cherish and pursue wisdom to a remarkable degree without, though, thereby getting soft and ineffectual, that is to say without losing sight of, and interest in, what needs to be done, one's affairs, one's own affairs, but in particular the affairs of the city. What Pericles has in mind seems to me to be this: the Athenians take a remarkable interest in general questions, go to great length discussing and arguing about them, though these questions are of no immediate relevance to their current affairs, private or public, indeed may have no bearing on them at all. They are interested in these questions for their own sake. But this does not make them in the least ineffective when it comes to practical matters.

I am fairly confident that this is what Thucydides' Pericles has in mind against the background of a large number of passages in Greek literature which refer to a certain kind of philistinism, the sentiment that education, the discussion of large questions, of questions, for instance, which we might think of as philosophical, that all this, maybe, is fine for the young, but not appropriate or fitting for grown-up persons, because it distracts from the real problems, the concrete issues one has to face energetically in practical life, both private and public. Indulging in the pursuit of such questions will lead to inexperience and weakness in practical life which might ruin one, for instance if one is dragged into a law-court. I am thinking of Callicles's advice to Socrates in Plato's *Gorgias* (484c–485e), of the anecdote about Thales who observing the stars falls into a well and is ridiculed by a Thracian slave-girl which we find in Plato's *Theaetetus* (174a ff.) in the context of the digression about philosophers and men of practice or action (172c–177c), or the story of Chion of Heraclea.

This last story in its very language seems to pick up the "ἄνευ μαλακίας" of Pericles' speech. The story comes from a novel, consisting entirely of 17 letters purportedly written by Chion who is supposed to have been a student of Plato's. His father sends him to Athens to study with Plato. But the son is hesitant. He wants to become involved in public affairs in Heraclea which at the time is ruled by Clearchus, a tyrant. Chion's fear is that "philosophy . . . dissolves the ability to act to a considerable degree and softens it up" (*Ep.* 3.5). The verb used here is *mal-thassein*. The corresponding noun *maltha* is glossed in Hesychius by *malakia*. But, To continue the story, on his way to Athens Chion in Byzantium witnesses how Xenophon returning from Persia puts down a mutiny of his troops by the mere force of his words. He realizes in the example of Xenophon that philosophy does not at all make one unfit for a life of action, and now he is eager to go and study with Plato. In fact, when his father tells him after some years that surely five years of philosophy with Plato is enough, he insists on staying. In the end he will return to Heraclea to mortally wound the infamous tyrant, paying, though, with his own life for it. Against the background of these and other texts it seems clear to me that the claim in the "Funeral Oration" must be that the Athenians do indeed pursue wisdom to a remarkable extent, without, though, thereby, as feared by philistines, becoming unable to deal with the concrete issues at hand, for instance those posed by their being at war.

With this we can turn to the other famous passage I referred to, namely Herodotus's account of Solon's visit to Croesus in Sardis (1.30.2). The verb *philosopheô* which Thucydides used was a relatively new word. Before Thucydides it is only attested once, namely in our passage in Herodotus. Thucydides may well have borrowed the word from Herodotus. In any case Herodotus' use of it sheds light on its meaning in Thucydides and thus on the conception of wisdom both seem to presuppose. Herodotus tells us that Sardis under Croesus was so attractive and interesting that all the Greek "sophists" (*sophistai*) of the time came to visit Sardis, and so also did Solon (1.29.1). Presumably Herodotus is thinking of Thales (see 1.75) and of Bios of Priene or Pittacus (see 1.27.2). All four came to be counted as belonging to the so-called Seven Sages (*sophoi*). Solon, to follow Herodotus' account, having given the Athenians new laws, decided to go traveling for ten years, for the sake of *theoria*, as he said (1.29.2). For the sake of *theoria*, as Herodotus himself now says (1.30.1) he first went to Egypt and then came to Sardis. There Croesus greeted him with the remark that he had heard about Solon's wisdom and his travel, of how he had traveled many lands for the sake of theoria *philosopheôn* (1.30.2). Again, Herodotus does not mean to say that Croesus addressed Solon as a philosopher. The idea rather is that Solon is not traveling in pursuit of any practical affairs, not as a merchant or an ambassador for instance, but for the sheer love of wisdom, and that in pursuit of wisdom he, quite literally, goes to extraordinary lengths. Again the notion of wisdom involved is rather vague. Presumably we are supposed to think that Solon wants to get to know different parts of the world, different nations, the way they think about things, the way they are organized, and the laws they are governed by, in the first instance just to have a better understanding of things, rather than in pursuit of the solution to a practical issue. But, the way Herodotus tells the story, it is Croesus, a barbarian, who finds it remarkable that somebody would engage in this pursuit of wisdom for no identifiable practical purpose.

Hence perhaps Aristotle was not so entirely mistaken after all about the intuitions Greeks had about wisdom. They seem to have cherished a certain general knowledge and understanding of things for its own sake, and to have taken pride in doing so. But even if Aristotle for his notion of wisdom could rely on certain aspects of how the Greeks thought about wisdom, there is no doubt that he is pushing for a notion of wisdom as the one we should accept, rather than one which his contemporaries generally do accept. As we will see, it is a notion in important regards not that different from Plato's. But it will be rejected not much later by Hellenistic philosophers.

In any case, this is the conception of wisdom which Aristotle has, and accordingly he conceives of philosophy. Wisdom is theoretical. In its generic sense it is knowledge of principles and first causes. But in its fullest sense, in its highest form, the one we are concerned with in the *Metaphysics*, it is universal, knowledge of the ultimate causes and principles of things, of what there is, quite generally. This is the knowledge, Aristotle says (1.2, 983a21), we are looking for in the treatise to which *Metaphysics* 1 is an introduction, knowledge that is the ultimate fulfillment of the natural human desire to know.

But if we look at what this means for Aristotle's conception of philosophy, we run into two problems: (1) we wonder where this leaves practical philosophy, that is, ethics and politics (2) when we come to *Metaphysics* 6.1, we see that Aristotle, all of a sudden, instead of talking of theoretical philosophy, talks of three theoretical philosophies in the plural, namely what he calls *prôtê philosophia*, standardly rendered "first philosophy," physics, and mathematics. I will have to be brief and somewhat dogmatic in explaining this.

First practical philosophy. It is noteworthy that Aristotle hardly ever talks of ethics or practical philosophy as "philosophy." One place in which he does so is at the very end of *Nicomachean Ethics* 10.9, 1181b15, where he speaks of "the philosophy concerning human affairs" (*ta anthrôpeia*). Thus he implicitly contrasts it with first philosophy which is concerned with wisdom which is divine and of matters divine, for instance God. It is wisdom which affords us the contemplation of truth, of which Aristotle earlier in *EN* 10 tells us that it makes our life like that of gods, to the extent that this is humanly possible. But first philosophy is concerned with the good or with what is best, and its concern is a theoretical concern, a concern aimed at satisfying our need to know and understand what is the most important thing to understand, namely God, a principle of all things. By contrast, ethics is just concerned with the human good, and this concern is not theoretical, but a practical concern. It is aimed at being good and living well. In Aristotle's terms it is a mistake to think of Aristotle's ethics as a theory. A comparison to medicine may help. To begin with, though, we should note that Aristotle in 1.1–2 carefully avoids claiming that one does not benefit from theoretical knowledge. He is emphatic that wisdom is not productive, that it does not aim at productive benefit. But this leaves it completely open that one may derive productive or practical (in the narrow sense of "moral") benefit from theoretical knowledge. Medicine, according to Aristotle, relies on theoretical knowledge in that it draws on physics. But this theoretical knowledge, from a theoretical point of view either is rather low grade theoretical knowledge or applied knowledge. And in any case, from Aristotle's point of view, the physician's concern is not theoretical when he studies what we would call "medical theory". Similarly with ethics. There is nothing in what Aristotle says which prevents one from availing oneself of theoretical knowledge for moral purposes. Aristotle's ethics in various ways clearly does rely on theoretical knowledge in Aristotle's sense. It, for instance, is a matter of Aristotelian physics that it is the end of animals to live a life appropriate for their kind. It is also a matter of Aristotelian physics that for some kinds of animal a life appropriate to their kind is something like a good life. It is not clear whether physics tells us what the end specifically of human beings is or whether that is a matter of applying our general theoretical knowledge to the case of human beings. What is clear is that the knowledge of what the end of human beings is which we need in ethics is a practical, rather than a theoretical understanding of the end. Something similar holds for the psychology presupposed by ethics. In any case, ethics in Aristotle's view only marginally is a philosophical enterprise, namely to the extent that it draws on theoretical knowledge.

As to the three theoretical philosophies, or kinds of philosophy, of *Metaphysics* 6.1, it is clear that the first one, first philosophy, corresponds to the ultimate wisdom we are supposed to be after in the *Metaphysics* according to *Metaphysics* 1, whereas physics and mathematics correspond to the other theoretical sciences mentioned in *Metaphysics* 1.1–2. They all deal with a specific domain of reality. First philosophy deals with unchanging and hence immaterial divine beings, in particular God; hence it is also called "theology" (6.1, 1026a19). Physics deals with natural things subject to change, and mathematics with mathematical entities. But it is a crucial characteristic of ultimate wisdom as it is described in 1.2 that it somehow is universal, constitutes knowledge of all there is, of the ultimate principles of whatever there is, for instance God. Hence theology, though it has a specific subject matter, at the same time is universal, since its principles are universal, namely are principles also of physical substances and mathematical objects. If there were no immaterial unchanging substances, then physics would be first philosophy and hence universal, assuming, as Aristotle does, that the principles of physical substances also are principles of mathematical objects, rather than the other way round, in that the principles of substances thereby also are the principles of quanta. But if there are separate immaterial substances, then the knowledge of theology is the most desirable and highest form of knowledge, and theology is first philosophy (*Metaph.* 6.1, 1026a19–31).

If, with this in mind, we return to 1.1–2, it becomes clearer, I think, what Aristotle is trying to do at the beginning of the *Metaphysics*, but also why there is a certain ambiguity in the two initial chapters. In characterizing wisdom in a certain way, Aristotle is arguing that we should conceive of philosophy in a certain way. Generically wisdom is a matter of knowing and understanding things in terms of their principles and causes, and hence of knowing the relevant principles. In this sense any body of theoretical knowledge counts as wisdom, and any enterprise aimed at acquiring such knowledge counts as philosophy. But Aristotle also believes that there is a highest form of wisdom which involves knowledge of the ultimate principles of what there is quite generally and which thus is universal, and not just knowledge, say, of the specific principles of geometry. And Aristotle himself also believes that there are immaterial unchanging substances which, because they are ultimate principles, are universal principles, principles of all there is. Hence he thinks that it is first philosophy which aims at this elevated form of wisdom. Thus it seems to me that the way to understand "first" here is the following. Philosophy is concerned with theoretical wisdom, but what philosophy primarily is is metaphysics, an enterprise to understand the ultimate principles of what there is. It is this sense of "first" in which, for instance, Aristotle in the

Categories talks of "first" and "second substances" (*Cat.* 5, 2a11–14). First substances are substances in the primary sense of the word, substances most strictly speaking. That this is the sense required here seems to me to be clear from a remark in *Metaphysics* 5.3, 1005b1–2: "Physics, too, is some kind of wisdom, but not first wisdom." Ross correctly glosses this "Physics is a form of philosophy, but not the primary form."[7] The context is this. Aristotle asks at the beginning of the chapter whether it falls to the philosopher not just to inquire into substance, but also into general or even universal principles of the kind one calls axioms in mathematics, or whether the latter is the task of some other enterprise (1105a19–22). He notes that some of those engaged in physics have tried to discuss such principles, and that this is entirely reasonable, given that they thought of themselves as being concerned with the whole of nature and thus with what is quite generally. But given that reality is not exhausted by the realm of physical substances, because there is a prior kind of substance, namely immaterial unchanging substance, there also is a prior and higher discipline which deals both with this primary kind of substance and with general or universal principles, namely philosophy (1005a22–b1 in conjunction with 1005a21–22). And then comes the remark that physics, too, is some kind of wisdom, but not the primary kind (namely, we have to add, the one that philosophy is concerned with).

In the light of this it seems to me to be clear that 1.1–2 is an introduction, and protreptic, to philosophy in general, but at the same time an introduction to metaphysics, because what philosophy primarily is is metaphysics. What the philosopher primarily is concerned with is not wisdom in the general sense, theoretical knowledge in general, but the highest form of theoretical knowledge, wisdom in the primary sense, knowledge of immaterial non-physical substances like God who is a universal principle, but also of other general or universal principles. If this is not clear already from 1.1–2, it is because this is an introduction to philosophy which, in the face of considerable opposition, tries to emphasize the theoretical character of philosophy, and which cannot afford, without losing much of the audience immediately, to insist not only that philosophy is theoretical, rather than practical or productive, but in the first instance concerned with a non-physical realm of entities like God. This is to emerge as the inquiry progresses. Even in 6.1, 1026a27–28, it is presented as still hypothetical whether there are substances prior to the material substances dealt with by physics. And the same is true, for instance, of 7.11, 1037a10–13. In 1.1–2 we are still at the beginning of an inquiry, at which it is left open what wisdom in its full sense is, some kind of knowledge of physics, perhaps even of some kind of mathematics, or of something else. But it is suggested, as it is assumed by 6.1, 1026a18–19, that physics and mathematics, being theoretical, are philosophical disciplines, though perhaps not primary philosophy, philosophy in its primary sense.

This, then, is the background against which we have to look at Aristotle's account of the origin and the early history of philosophy. As I said above, Aristotle surveys the thought of his predecessors to confirm that all principles or causes, indeed, are of one or another of the four types he had identified in the *Physics*.

From the survey we are supposed to see that they universally tried to explain things in terms of one or more of these types of principle, and that nobody appealed to any other form of explanation. Aristotle's survey takes the form of a history, because Aristotle thinks that the history of philosophy in a way is the history of the discovery of these four kinds of explanation. Philosophers naturally started out to try to explain things in terms of the material components of these things and the properties of these components. But since this, in Aristotle's view, does not yield a satisfactory explanation of everything, especially given their inadequate grasp of what an explanation in terms of matter is, they after some time were driven to resort, in addition, to moving causes, and with time they, or at least some of them, also realized that there are formal explanations and teleological explanations which we have to have recourse to, if we want to fully understand things.

Aristotle lets philosophy begin with Thales. He does not explicitly say that Thales was the first philosopher. He talks of Thales as the originator of this sort of philosophy (1.3, 983b20–21), but it seems clear from the context (see 983b6–7 and 984a16–17) that Aristotle thinks that Thales in being the first to engage in this sort of philosophy was the first philosopher. And it appears to be on the basis of this text that tradition, beginning with Theophrastus (ap. Simp. *in Ph.* 23.29 ff.), has let Greek philosophy start with Thales, from a certain point onwards almost as a matter of convention and often without further thought. The question is why Aristotle would regard Thales as a philosopher at all, and why, if he regarded Thales as a philosopher, he would refuse to regard Thales' predecessors as such. There does not seem to be anything philosophical about Thales' views, at least the way we understand philosophy, for instance about the two views Aristotle ascribes to Thales in our text (983b21–22), namely the view that everything comes from water, and the view that this is why the earth floats on water. Aristotle ventures two conjectures of a physiological or biological kind as to why Thales identified water as the origin of all things: (1) he saw that all things nourish themselves from what is wet and (2) even the hot comes from this and stays alive in this way (983b26). This does not sound particularly philosophical. And Aristotle certainly cannot have been impressed by it. For the second conjectured reason sounds very much like the view he ascribes to Hippon, a philosopher of the late fifth century, in the *De Anima* (1.2, 405b1–5) as a reason for saying that the soul, at least originally, is water, namely that the sperm of all things is wet. Also the first conjectured reason reminds one of a view ascribed to Hippon by Hippolytus (*Haer.* 1.16, DK 38A3), namely that there are two principles, fire, that is, the hot, and water, that is, the cold, but that the hot itself is generated from the wet. But in the *De Anima* Aristotle characterizes Hippon as a less refined thinker, and in our passage in *Metaphysics* 1.3 (984a3–5) he explicitly refuses to discuss him as not being worthy of being mentioned along with figures like Thales, Anaximenes, Hippasus, Heraclitus and others because of the cheapness (*euteleia*) of his thought.

So why did Aristotle take Thales to be a philosopher, indeed the first philosopher? Aristotle explains this in two ways. He says something, though very little, positively about Thales, and then, negatively, makes some remarks about those who might be thought, and indeed had been thought, to be precursors of Thales, but who in Aristotle's view were not philosophers.

Aristotle obviously knows very little about Thales. It is very doubtful whether Thales had left any writings. In any case Aristotle in his works shows no trace of having read anything by Thales. He, as here in 1.3, relies on reports (see 984a2). He has to make conjectures as why Thales made water the origin of everything. It, plausibly, has been suggested that for the reasons which Aristotle very tentatively (see 983b22) ascribes to Thales for positing water as the origin he relied on Hippon who, too, had made water the origin of things, and that this is why Hippon gets mentioned at all in 1.3. It seems that for Aristotle Thales' claim to be counted as a philosopher primarily is based on the mere fact that Thales tried to account for the whole of the sensible world in terms of an ultimate matter. Thales identified this with water. But the general approach of trying to account for the whole of the sensible world in terms of the ultimate material constituents of reality, whether it be just one sort of constituent, like water, or a number of them (987b17–20), Thales had in common with the other early philosophers (see 983b6ff.), except that Thales was the first to engage in "this sort of philosophy" (983b20–21). When Aristotle says "this sort of philosophy" he does not mean "physics" or "natural philosophy." Though he often talks of the early philosophers as *phusikoi* (see *Metaphysics* 4.3, 1005b31), he here means "philosophy as pursued by those who try to account for reality in terms of its ultimate material constituents." He counts this as philosophy, indeed in a sense as primary philosophy, since Thales and others took the sensible world to be the whole of reality, and thus were trying to give an account of what there is quite generally.

There are three ways in which, I take it, Aristotle thought that Thales' approach was philosophical. The first is simply this. For Aristotle explanation in terms of matter is a genuine form of explanation. Matter is a principle and cause of the sensible world. Hence, even if Thales was wrong in his identification of matter with water, and even though, on Aristotle's view, matter only provides a partial explanation of the sensible world, Thales had resorted to the right sort of explanation. Secondly, according to Aristotle, Thales had been trying to do something more ambitious in trying to identify an ultimate matter of things. Its existence would be eternal (983b12–13, 17–18), and thus questions would not arise, as they do, for instance, in the case of Hesiod's Chaos (*Th.* 116), namely where it did come from, a view Aristotle refers to in 1.4, 984b27–28, quoting Hesiod. Water always had been there, just undergoing different transformations. Thirdly, Thales had at least the ambition to account in this way for all there is (983b8), rather than just trying to account for isolated particular phenomena in a piecemeal fashion. One further detail Aristotle has to offer about Thales' views in 1.3 in a way confirms this. The ancients were concerned to understand why the earth does not fall, but seems to stay in place. Hesiod had explained this by claiming that the earth is firmly rooted in Tartarus, which itself is enclosed from below by a wall of bronze (*Th.* 726–29). Thales, according to Aristotle (983b21–22), offered the explanation that the earth floats on water like a log, and took this to be some kind of confirmation of the claim that everything has its ultimate origin in water.

The way Aristotle sees the difference between Thales' account and the sort of account we find, for instance, in Hesiod will become clearer, if we turn to the negative side of Aristotle's belief that Thales was the first philosopher, namely his view of those who might be thought to have preceded Thales. Aristotle refers to some unnamed persons (983b28) who claimed that Thales' view that everything comes from water was nothing new, that this already had been said in very ancient times by those who first engaged in *theologia* in the sense of giving an account of the gods in the form of a narrative. Aristotle in any case will say in *Metaphysics* 3.4, 1000a9–19, that Hesiod and all these "theologians" proceeded *muthikôs*, by telling a story. As evidence for their claim these unnamed persons pointed out that the ancient theologians made Oceanus and Tethys the parents of everything, and that they made the gods swear by Styx. The latter needs some explanation, and so they explain that by "Styx" the ancient theologians meant water, and that these theologians made the gods swear by water, because they attached enormous importance to the oath of the gods and thought that water, being the oldest, was the most important, and hence the thing to swear by. It seems that the *anonymi* are thinking of Homer (for the oath of the gods see *Il.* 14.271; 15.37–38; for Oceanus and Tethys *Il.* 14.201 and 246). But Oceanus and Tethys also play a role in Orphic thought (see Pl. *Cra.* 402b).

To understand Aristotle's response to this, and its importance, we will have to say something about the person or persons who, according to Aristotle, are referring to these ancient views. But to start with, let us look at what Aristotle himself says here, and how he elaborates on this in a later passage in the *Metaphysics*, namely in 3.4. Here in 1.3 (983b33–984a2) Aristotle contents himself with calling into question whether the view that everything has its origin in water actually was held by ancient theologians, but perhaps also whether, if they held the view, it was part of an attempt to give an account of nature, of the sensible world. In any case, he is unwilling to recognize Thales' supposed predecessors as philosophers. More about his reasons for this we find out from *Metaphysics* 3.4. There Aristotle discusses the question whether things which pass away and things which do not pass away do have the same principles. If they do have the same principles, an explanation is needed why, given the same principles, some things pass away and others do not. And he remarks that there is no point in expecting an answer of any help from Hesiod and others who are engaged in this sort of theology (1000a9 and 18–19). These theologians make gods the principles of things from which things have come to be. They then claim that beings do not pass away, if they drink nectar and eat ambrosia, but do pass away, if they do not. This, Aristotle claims, makes no sense, even if we understood what they were saying. For if the beings which consume nectar and ambrosia do so just for pleasure, then nectar and ambrosia cannot be the cause of their everlasting being; and if they consume nectar and ambrosia as food to maintain themselves, they cannot be everlasting, since all beings which require nutrition are subject to generation and corruption. But we do not even understand what they are saying. For we do not know what the words "nectar" and "ambrosia" are supposed to refer to. These theologians did not take us seriously (*hêmôn ôligôrêsan*, 1000a10–11), they talked over our heads (*huper hêmas eirêkasin*, 1000a15). In their accounts they only were concerned with what seemed plausible to themselves (1000a10), not with what might make sense to us, persuade us. A few lines further down, in 1000a18–19, they are characterized as persons who craftily fabricate stories (*muthikôs sophizomenoi*), and they are contrasted with those (namely the philosophers) who give accounts by means of proof (*di' apodeixeôs*). In the light of these remarks we see better why Aristotle in 1.3 wants to draw a sharp line between Thales and his real or supposed precursors. They talked about "Oceanus" and "Tethys," as if we knew what they were referring to. They made no effort to give an account which in principle could persuade or even convince us, let alone tried to give a proof for what they were saying. By contrast, when Thales talks about water, we know what he is talking about. He tries to provide arguments which might persuade us of what he is saying. Most importantly he offers explanations which are at least of the right form in that they appeal to matter.

Now we might be able to get some further insight into Aristotle's decision to draw a line between Thales and earlier figures, if we are able to identify the person or persons who refuse to draw the line. Ross (commentary on 983b27) suggests that Aristotle may have Plato in mind, in particular the *Theaetetus*.[8] Plato there does in fact quote Homer's line in *Iliad* 14.201 as evidence that all wise persons from Homer onwards, except for Parmenides, believed that everything is the product of flux (*rhoê*) and motion, indeed is in motion, as for instance Heraclitus did (152e2– 8; see also 160d6–8; *Cra.* 402b1–5). Later in the *Theaetetus* he again alludes to the Homeric line (180d1–2). According to Ross Aristotle took Plato's humorous remarks about the Homeric origin of the doctrine of flux seriously, and thus set out to counter them. Now, as we will see later, there is a connection between Plato's *Theaetetus* and *Sophist* and the chapters of the *Metaphysics* which concern us. But it does not seem likely that Aristotle here is responding to Plato's *Theaetetus*. For Plato, neither in the *Theaetetus* nor elsewhere, is the source for the fanciful explanation of the oath of the gods which Aristotle refers to. And, of course, Plato does not say anything about Thales' view that water is the origin of things. Much more attractive seems to be the view, first suggested by Bruno Snell and now widely accepted, that both Aristotle and Plato drew on a common source, namely a writing by Hippias of Elis, of which Clement in the *Stromateis*, 6.15 (DK 86B6) preserves a fragment, presumably from the preface of Hippias' work.[9] Hippias says that he is going to produce a new kind of writing in which he will juxtapose brief remarks by various authors on the same topic, be it by Orpheus or Musaeus, Hesiod or Homer, poets or prose authors, Greeks or barbarians. We know that Hippias did talk about Thales. For Diogenes Laertius, 1.24, for instance, reports that Aristotle and Hippias claim that Thales attributed a soul to lifeless things, referring to the magnet and to amber. The suggestion now is that Plato, *Cratylus* 402b is drawn from Hippias who juxtaposed Thales' view that everything has its origin in water with Homer's *Iliad* (14.201) about Oceanus and Tethys, perhaps a line from Hesiod, and two lines from Orpheus mentioning Oceanus and Tethys, except that Plato replaces Thales with Heraclitus, because in this context he is trying to argue for the view that etymology reflects the Heraclitean flux doctrine. Aristotle, by contrast, preserves the original juxtaposition of Thales and the early theologians. The suggestion gains further plausibility, if we accept C. J. Classen's view, "Bemerkungen zu Zwei Griechischen 'Philosophiehistorikern'" that a comparison between Plato's *Symposium*, 178a9–c3 and Aristotle's *Metaphysics* 1.4, 984b23–29 suggests that they rely not only on the same source—given that they both quote, though in reverse order, part of Hesiod, *Theogony* 116–17 and 120, and Parmenides B13—but on Hippias, given that the *Symposium* passage appeals to the same connection between age and importance or worthiness as the Styx passage in 1.3, 983b32–33.[10] If we assume that Aristotle in fact is responding to Hippias, or at least a source like Hippias, it is clear that Aristotle is much more uncompromising about what counts as philosophy than many later authors: he against Hippias and others draws a clear line between Thales and possible precursors, whether Greek or barbarian. By making a clear cut, Aristotle prevents the origins of philosophy from disappearing in the remote legendary past of Greece or even of the Near East. And the cut which Aristotle makes is not at all arbitrary; it is based on his conception of philosophy.

Aristotle and later historians of philosophy had the good luck that after Thales came two other Milesians, Anaximander and Anaximenes, the first only slightly younger than Thales, and the second presumably still born in Thales' life-time. Both of them seem to engage in the same enterprise as Thales, to some extent to respond to him. And so, given Thales as a starting point, we easily get a narrative going which will take us down to the time of Plato and Aristotle.

But not only in *Metaphysics* 1 does Aristotle not mention Anaximander; his narrative, as already indicated, is structured in a way quite different from that which we find in modern histories from the end of the 18th century onwards. This is due to the fact that Aristotle's narrative is subordinated to the aim of *Metaphysics* 1 to serve as a protreptic to, and introduction into, primary philosophy, and more specifically to the aim of assuring us that philosophy is a matter of explaining things in terms of principles or causes of which there are four types. The narrative is a story of the progressive discovery of these four types of explanation, beginning with Thales' use of explanation in terms of matter. But Aristotle's story-line right from the beginning in 1.3, 983b6 is far from transparent. In 1.3, 983b6–984a16, he talks about the first philosophers, who appealed to ultimate material principles, first to one, like Thales' water or Anaximenes' air (984a5), but then to a plurality, like Empedocles' four elements or Anaxagoras' *panspermia* (984a7, a11–13). But at least once we come to Empedocles and Anaxagoras, it is no longer true that they just appealed to material causes. And, indeed, Aristotle had only said at the beginning, in 983b6–8, that most of the first philosophers appealed exclusively to material principles. In 1.3, 984a16ff., Aristotle tries to advance the story by pointing out that philosophers could not fail to realize that matter, being passive, cannot give rise to anything, but requires a moving cause which turns it into something. And so they came to look for the moving cause (984a25–27). It takes us down to the end of chapter 4 to discuss attempts to account for things in terms of these two types of explanation, material cause and moving cause (see 985b20–22). Inserted into this discussion (984a16–985b22) of how the Presocratics were forced to recognize a moving cause and to get clearer about its nature we get a section, (984b8ff.) in which Aristotle explains how philosophers like Anaxagoras or Empedocles incidentally touched on the final cause in introducing moving causes aiming at a good effect, without though clearly recognizing explanation in terms of the final cause as a distinct kind of explanation (see 1.7, 988b8–11). Chapter 5 deals with the Pythagoreans (985b23–986b8) in a way which at first looks as if we had lost the thread, but which some twenty-two lines into the text (986a13ff.) explains that they regarded number as a principle, both as matter and as accounting for properties and states. Aristotle then turns to the Eleatics (986b8–987a9), before he returns to the Pythagoreans, and here the thread is taken up again in 987a19: the Pythagoreans began to talk about the essences of things and tried to define them, though very primitively. So here we have the formal cause. This becomes prominent in chapter 6 on Plato. Socrates was serious about definitions (987b1–4). Plato took this up, but given his Heraclitean or Cratylean background (987a32–33) took the definition to be of non-sensible items, the forms (987b4–7), in terms of which he tried to account for sensible objects. The good, or the final cause, Plato just identified with the ultimate formal cause, the One (988a14–17). Chapter 7 is a résumé, followed in chapter 8 and 9 by a critical discussion of the views of his predecessors and a conclusion in chapter 10.

Rather than going deeper into various details of this account, I want to focus on one aspect of it. If Aristotle's narrative is far from clear and transparent, this is not just because, as Aristotle would see it, his predecessors were rather confused about the different types of explanation available to the philosopher. The account also is supposed to bring out that, though everybody is agreed that those who show concern for wisdom are concerned to understand the sensible world (1.9, 992a24–25), some came to think that this involves an appeal to non-corporeal entities, and that reality is not exhausted by sensible reality. This is what Aristotle himself believes. For Aristotle the formal cause or form—for instance, in the case of living beings, the soul—is not itself a physical, perceptible entity. And, what is crucial for primary philosophy, as he understands it, is that there are immaterial substances like God which are not part of nature at all, but which we have to appeal to in order to understand the sensible world. Finally he thinks that there are the objects of mathematics, for instance of arithmetic or of geometry, which have principles of their own, and cannot be explained in terms of physics. So when we seem to lose the thread of the narrative in chapter 5, it is because we introduce the Pythagoreans who concerned themselves with mathematics and believed that the principles of mathematics, to begin with, numbers, were the principles of the whole of reality (985b23–27). When we turn to Plato, we are told that he, in addition to perceptible objects, introduces not just ideas, but also mathematical objects (1.6, 987b15–18). In 1.9, 992d32–33, we hear that for some of Aristotle's contemporaries, clearly some Platonists, philosophy has become mathematics. But there are not just the objects of mathematics; there also are, in addition to them, incorporeal or immaterial things or substances. Notoriously Plato claimed that the real beings or substances were what he called "ideas" (1.6, 987b4–8), which he distinguished both from perceptible things and the objects of mathematics (1.6, 987b14–18). Aristotle does not accept Platonic forms. But it is difficult to believe that Aristotle does not realize that with forms as conceived of by Plato we for the first time clearly have the idea of immaterial beings, beings which exist separately from, and independently of, physical objects. And this idea Aristotle himself espouses, as is already apparent in several places in his historical account. In his critical review of his predecessors, for instance, in 1.8, 989b21–29, he distinguishes between those who have only inquired into the principles and causes of perceptible beings subject to generation and corruption or change, and those who inquire into all there is, both perceptible and imperceptible beings. And he explicitly says that for our present project it would seem more appropriate to pay heed to what the latter have to say. He then (989b29–990a34) goes on to talk about the Pythagoreans, criticizing them, though, for the fact that they use their non-perceptible principles exclusively to explain the sensible world and what it contains, as if reality were exhausted by what is perceptible (989b33–990a5). But, having discussed them, he (1.9, 990a34ff.) turns to the Platonists who posit ideas. Obviously the existence of non-perceptible, immaterial substances which are principles of the sensible world is crucial to the enterprise of metaphysics or primary philosophy, as Aristotle conceives of it in the *Metaphysics*. They are the special domain of primary philosophy.

It is obvious then that Aristotle's historical account is highly retrospective. It is an account given from the perspective of Aristotle's conception of philosophy, an account based on Aristotle's assumption that proper explanation, and thus understanding, takes the form of one or more of the four types he has identified in the *Physics*, and the assumption, though less prominently so, that the domain of physics does not exhaust reality. But it is not just that the account is based on this conception and these assumptions, it also in turn, especially in conjunction with 1.1–2, is supposed to support this conception. Yet how can it do so, given that even Aristotle cannot believe that his Presocratic predecessors had his conception of philosophy, had any idea of a domain outside that of physics, or had much of a grip on the four types of explanation available? There is something confused about the debate whether Aristotle anachronistically ascribed to Thales his notion of *archê* in the sense of matter. It seems fairly clear from 1.3 that Aristotle does not believe that Thales had properly understood what an *arche* in the sense of matter is. For otherwise Thales would not have thought that water by itself can take on the shape of the world we live in (see 984a21–25). What Aristotle does believe is that Thales somehow was aiming at the notion of matter. In 1.10 he compares philosophy with a young child which has not yet learned to speak properly and which we hence find difficult to understand (*psellizomenê*, 993a15; see 985a5); we on the basis of our knowledge have to conjecture what it is trying to say, what it is trying to get at. Aristotle repeatedly in *Metaphysics* 1 says that his predecessors only had a confused (*amudrôs*, 985a13; 988a23; 993a13) grasp of the four types of principles. He almost presents the history of philosophy as philosophy's finally coming of age in his day in the form Aristotle himself does philosophy. This view might seem rather preposterous to us, but we have to keep in mind Aristotle's considered conviction that we need to respect the so-called *endoxa*, the shared opinion of people, or the views of intelligent and informed persons who have seriously put their mind to a question. Aristotle as part of his method assumes that there must be something to what these persons are saying, that they must be getting at something which is true, even if what they are saying cannot stand as it is. In *Metaphysics* 1, he repeatedly claims that the subject-matter itself, truth or reality, keeps people on the right track, if they give thought to things (see, e.g., 1.3, 984a18–19; see also *Ph.* 1.5, 188b29–30). Hence it is not surprising that Aristotle supposes that his predecessors, once they had started doing philosophy, seriously putting their mind to the matter and to what others had said about it, would make progress, including progress in the very understanding of the task of philosophy.

In any case Aristotle in his account of the origin and the early history of philosophy presupposes a highly specific view as to what philosophy is, a view in particular suited to the *Metaphysics*. This raises the question what Thales himself or, for that matter, the Presocratics quite generally, thought they were doing. It does not sound plausible at all that Thales was trying to do philosophy the way Aristotle conceived of this, except that he had not yet quite understood what this involved. This is a question which we are hardly able to answer. But I think we may get closer about what sort of answer might be appropriate, if we look at the history of the word *philosophos* and its cognates *philosophia* and *philosophizein* down to around 400 BCE.

It will help, if we immediately set aside a story found in later ancient sources according to which Pythagoras introduced the terms *philosophos* and *philosophia* to reflect the fact that human beings can at best aspire to wisdom, as only God is wise. It is clear from Diogenes Laertius (prooem. 1.12) that this story goes back to Heraclides Ponticus' work *On the Woman Who Had Lost Her Breath*, and is part of the growing legend about Pythagoras. The word *philosophos* is first attested in a fragment of Heraclitus (B35 DK) as an adjective in the phrase *philosophos anêr*. But this early use of the word seems to be completely isolated. There seems to be no other occurrence of it in the fifth century. What is more, there is no reason to think that Heraclitus means to refer specifically to philosophers. All he is saying is that a person who aspires to wisdom must be an inquirer (*histôr*) into a great many things. And some light on what he means by this is shed by fragment B40. Heraclitus says "Knowing a lot [*polumathiê*] does not yet teach you to have understanding. For otherwise it would have taught Hesiod and Pythagoras, Xenophanes and Hecataeus." Clearly Heraclitus thinks that wisdom is a matter of understanding of a certain kind, and that this presupposes the study of a great many things, but goes crucially beyond just knowing lots of different things. But there does not seem to be a clear and articulate conception of what this understanding and hence this wisdom would consist in and how it would be acquired.

There are two attested uses of the verb *philosopheô* in the fifth century, namely those in Herodotus and Thucydides, which we discussed earlier. Neither case involves a reference to philosophers or philosophy as some kind of discipline. There is an occurrence of the word *philosophia* in *On Ancient Medicine*, a text which dates from the end of the fifth century. Here it does seem to mean something like "philosophy" in the sense we are looking for. For the author is discussing natural philosophers and explicitly refers to Empedocles (chap. 20).

Now this evidence seems to me to be quite surprising, but also relevant for our purposes. For if there had been a distinct group of persons pursuing a distinct enterprise since the beginning of the sixth century, we would expect the Greeks to have taken note of this and to have had a word to specifically refer to philosophers. But obviously *philosophos*, in any case, was not this word. One used the word *sophos* for those, like Thales, whom one later came to call "philosophers." One also used the word *sophistês*, but as Diogenes Laertius (prooem. 1.12) tells us, this word was also used for poets, like Homer and Hesiod, for instance by Cratinus. Similarly, *sophos* was used equally of poets, lawgivers like Solon, or statesmen. Thus it seems that the Greeks till late in the fifth century did not have a word to specifically refer to philosophers. And this suggests that the Greek public up to this time did not recognize philosophers as forming a clearly distinct group engaged in a distinct enterprise. If we look at the philosophers themselves, they similarly, till rather late, show no clear signs of thinking of themselves as a distinct group. For, when they refer to others to whom they compare themselves with or with whom they think they will be compared to, they, of course do refer to persons who later came to be called "philosophers," but also, often in one breath, to poets or lawgivers or statesmen, that is to those who were taken to have a reputation for wisdom in some elevated, but still quite vague sense. It is only in the latter part of the fifth century, it seems to me, for instance in Democritus, that we find some awareness of a tradition of natural philosophy as a distinct enterprise.

The most plausible account of this evidence seems to me to be this. The early Greek philosophers beginning with Thales did not think of themselves specifically as philosophers, but as being concerned with wisdom in the elevated, but vague, sense in which Herodotus talks of Solon as wise. And one way in which one could be concerned with wisdom in this elevated, but not clearly articulated sense, was by developing a remarkable and enlightening view about the constitution of the world we live in. This as such would not commit one to the view that wisdom just was a matter of having a theoretical understanding of the world. One's concern for a theoretical understanding of the world could be perfectly compatible with assuming that there are other, for instance practical, aspects of wisdom, with recognizing that there were other ways of pursuing wisdom, and hence even with one's own engaging in such other ways of pursuing wisdom. But the quest for a satisfactory overall view of the constitution of the world would lead one to raise, and to try to answer, questions in a way which, with the benefit of hindsight, would be regarded as philosophical. It would lead to a tradition of dealing with such questions in which later authors respond to and build on the work of earlier authors. And from this a distinctive enterprise will emerge which will be recognized as such and called "philosophy." This is how Thales and the other Presocratics later came to be thought of as philosophers.

When we come to the fourth century, the situation has radically changed in that we now find an ample use of the word *philosophia* and its cognates. It surely is not an accident that it is amply used by the followers of Socrates, by as disparate figures as Xenophon and Plato. We get groupings of philosophers which turn into what came to be called much later "schools." I cannot pursue this here in detail. But one significant fact is that we not only now find an ample use of the word *philosophia*, but various uses of the term. These, to some extent, reflect different understandings of what wisdom, or at least human wisdom, consists in, like for instance Xenophon's or Isocrates' understanding. But since I am here concerned with Aristotle's conception of philosophy, I will focus on Plato's uses of the term and its cognates. For it seems to me that Aristotle is very much indebted to Plato in his conception of philosophy, but also in his way of looking at the history of philosophy. In Plato we find three uses of the term *philosophia* and its cognates. One is relatively unproblematic. It is the use which roughly corresponds to the use of the verb *philosophein* in Herodotus and Thucydides which we discussed earlier. In this sense "philosophy" refers quite generally to an eagerness to learn and know about things. Thus Socrates (Pl. *Ly.* 213d7) says that he enjoyed Lysis' "philosophy," that is, his curiosity and inquisitiveness. We see roughly the same use in a passage in the *Republic* (5, 475c2 and 8). The "philosopher" here is somebody who is insatiable in his desire to learn and find out about anything whatsoever. But this sort of person now is contrasted (475e2–476b2) with the philosopher in a narrower sense, the person concerned to know the truth about justice and injustice, good and bad, and generally Platonic forms (476a5–6), rather than practical matters (476a11). So here we have "philosophy" in the narrow, technical sense of a special discipline, namely dialectic.

But then, in the *Theaetetus*, we also find the use of the term as a generic term for a variety of disciplines, apparently dialectic and the mathematical disciplines. Thus Socrates in *Theaetetus* 143d1–2 says to Theodorus that he is not going to ask whether some young people in Cyrene show particular concern for geometry or some other kind of philosophy (*tina allên philosophian*). Now one might want to discount this use as a piece of flattery of Theodorus, an older mathematician, who feels uncomfortable getting involved in a dialectical discussion (see e.g., 169a6ff.) and says that he has long given up such abstract discussion (*psiloi logoi*, 165a1) to focus on geometry. But this clearly is not right. For in the *Timaeus*, too, Plato talks of "harmonics and every kind of philosophy" (*mousikê kai pasa philosophia*, 88c5). Moreover, there are other passages in the *Theaetetus* which group the mathematical disciplines with philosophy under the heading of "philosophy." Of particular interest is the famous digression in *Theaetetus* 172c3–177c5, which usually is taken to contrast the philosopher with the man of the world. But the contrast rather is, in Plato's own terms, between those who have spent a great deal of time in the various kinds of philosophy (*en tais philosophiais*, 172c4–5) and those involved in public affairs. A few lines later (172c9–d2) Plato refers to the same group of persons as "those who have been raised in philosophy and this sort of study." It is in this context that we get the famous anecdote about Thales falling into a well–not about Thales as a philosopher in the narrow sense, but about Thales because he is an astronomer (174a4) and thus engaged in philosophy in a wider sense (174b1). And Plato does not just talk about *philosophiai* in the plural (172c4–5), as Aristotle will do in *Metaphysics* 6.1, 1026a18; he also correspondingly talks of "wisdoms" (forms or kinds of wisdom, 176c6). Surely, this is not all just due to Socrates' trying to humor Theodorus and his two young mathematics students, Theaetetus and Socrates the Younger.

What, then, are we to make of this? For a reader of the *Republic* or the *Sophist* it will be clear that philosophy in the narrow sense is Platonic dialectic. But then Plato also seems to think that mathematics is a philosophical discipline. And there seem to be two reasons for this, as follows.

1. In *Theaetetus* 162d4–163a2 Socrates remarks that just as in geometry one does not content oneself with more or less plausible considerations, but expects stringent proofs, so we also should not accept merely plausible arguments in the discussion we are engaged in in the *Theaetetus*. Now our evidence concerning Plato's views about mathematical proofs is rather meagre, and somewhat confusing. But it seems reasonable to suppose that Plato demands not only that in a mathematical proof the conclusion follows from the premises but also that it follows ultimately from a set of basic assumptions or hypotheses which all engaged in a particular mathematical discipline agree on and take for granted. Plato seems to allude to this in the simile of the line (*R.* 6, 509d6–511e5), when he talks of the different sets of basic assumptions or hypotheses as the principles of the different mathematical disciplines (511c6–7). Hence mathematics is philosophical in that it provides knowledge and understanding of a domain of reality, certain kinds of intelligible non-physical objects, in terms of principles governing this domain.

2. As Aristotle emphasizes in his historical account, and as we see also elsewhere in the *Metaphysics* (see e.g. 3.5 and 7.2), Plato and various Platonists think that we have to resort to mathematical entities to explain the objects in the sensible world. In Plato's case we might gather this from the simile of the line in the *Republic*, but also from the *Timaeus*, if we think, for instance, of the role triangles of two types which are constitutive of the regular solids with which Plato identifies the four elements play in its account. Hence, since everybody agrees that it is the task of philosophy to give an account of the sensible world, it will, according to Plato and to Platonists, also be the task of the philosopher to acquire the knowledge of the mathematical disciplines which deal with a domain of reality which is antecedent or prior to sensible reality, and in terms of which the sensible world has to be understood.

In this way we get a hierarchy of philosophical disciplines. There is dialectic which deals with the form of the good and the Platonic forms in general. It also provides us with a full understanding of the principles which the mathematical disciplines take for granted (see *R.* 6, 510c2–d3; 511b2–d5; τῆι τοῦ διαλέγεσθαι δυνάμει, 511b3; τῆς τοῦ διαλέγεσθαι ἐπιστήμης, 511c5). Then there are the mathematical disciplines which deal with intelligible objects sui generis. And, finally, there is a discipline which tries to explain the sensible world which owes its intelligibility to its being an image of the intelligible world. This is not the point to discuss Plato's conception of physics. This would require, for instance, a discussion of the *Timaeus* and the question whether, for Plato, the sensible world is a proper object of theoretical science at all. It suffices for our purposes that Plato and Platonists in Aristotle's time do try to account for the sensible world in terms of forms and/or mathematical objects of various kinds.

I will note just in passing that Aristotle, too, has his own views about the limits of physics as a scientific discipline, reflected, for instance, in *Parts of Animals* 1.1, 640a1–2, by his distinction between physics and the theoretical sciences, or in 1.5, 644b22ff., by his remarks about our inability to gain firm knowledge about eternal sensible substances.

If this is correct, it turns out that Aristotle's conception of philosophy is remarkably similar to that of Plato and Aristotle's Platonist contemporaries. And this would further help to explain why Aristotle can feel so confident about his conception of philosophy. It is not just a matter of self-confidence. Aristotle can justifiably think that *mutatis mutandis* he is just following Plato in distinguishing three sorts of philosophy. Arguably Aristotle takes his primary philosophy to be the counterpart of Plato's dialectic. As is clear from *Metaphysics* 7.16, 1040b27–1041a3 (see also 7.14, 1039b18–19), Aristotle thinks that in a way Plato was right in postulating immaterial separate forms, except that he went wrong in the way he identified them, namely as Platonic ideas, rather than as eternal substances, namely immaterial intellects of the kind Aristotle discusses in *Metaphysics* 12. The place of the idea of the good will be taken by the first unmoved mover (see 1.2, 982b4–7; 983a8–9; 12.7, 1072b30–34; 12.10, 1075a11–25). Moreover, Aristotle in arguing that, and trying to show how, primary philosophy is universal—somehow deals with whatever there is quite generally, though it has a specific domain, namely unchanging separate substances— is just mirroring the Platonic assumption that dialectic, though concerned specifically with the forms, provides universal knowledge, given that the forms are principles of everything. Aristotle seems to go out of his way, for instance in *Metaphysics* 4.2, to show that primary philosophy, as he understands it, will deal with the questions which are central to Platonic dialectic, being, unity, identity, difference, contrariety, and the like. Also, first philosophy, like Platonic dialectic, is supposed to provide the understanding which is needed to fully understand the principles of the particular sciences, including the mathematical sciences.

Aristotle also has a different view from Plato about the status of mathematics. Whereas for Plato and Platonists physics is subordinated to mathematics, because the objects of mathematics are prior to and principles of the objects of physics, Aristotle notoriously reverses the order. For Aristotle, very roughly speaking, there only are numbers and magnitudes because there are physical objects which come in numbers of a kind of object and in sizes. They thus presuppose physical objects. But given that mathematical objects constitute a domain with principles of its own, they can be studied independently of the objects of physics. But in spite of these differences, it seems clear that Aristotle's talk of three theoretical "philosophies" (6.1, 1026a18–19), namely mathematics, physics, and primary philosophy, and correspondingly his conception of philosophy reflected by the historical account, are very much indebted to Plato, in particular his talk in the *Theaetetus* of "philosophies" (172c5) and kinds of wisdom (176c6) including not just dialectic, but also the mathematical sciences.

But, finally, we should also briefly note that Aristotle's historical account in *Metaphysics* 1 and his view of the history of philosophy in the early books of the *Metaphysics* (i.e. 1, 3, 4) quite generally, betray the influence of Plato in yet other ways, for instance the following. Let us briefly return to the passage in 3.4, 1000a9–19, which we discussed earlier as evidence as to why Aristotle in 1.3 rejected the suggestion that there were philosophers before Thales. The passage down to its wording is highly reminiscent of Plato's *Sophist*, 242c4–243c1. There Socrates has explained how, to get out of our difficulties to define the sophist, we have to show against Parmenides that what is not somehow is (241d5–7) and that to do so we have to scrutinize what now seems obvious to us, namely what we are talking about when we talk about being, as opposed to not being (242b10–c2). And then Socrates starts an attack on Parmenides and all those who have talked about what is. They did so in a rather complacent manner (242c4). They have each been telling us a story (*muthos*) as if we were children (242c8–9). They speak of friendship, marriages, childbirth and the bringing up of children (242d1–2) and the like. In all this Plato is clearly talking about the Presocratics. He then (243a2–5) remarks that it is perhaps unfair to criticize persons of old and of such reputation, but that it is fair enough to make the following observation. And this is where the verbal similarities with Aristotle become striking. They showed little consideration for us (ὑμῶν...ὠλιγώρησαν, 243a7; ὑμῶν...ὠλιγώρησαν, 1000a10–11), they overlooked us (ὑπεριδόντες, 243a7; ὑπεριδόντες, 1000a15), they did not care at all whether we understand (οὐδὲν φροντίσαντες, 243a8; μόνον ἐφρόντισαν, 1000a10). They just each pursued their own agenda (243a9–b1, 1000a10). They talked in a way, as if we understood what they were talking about (243a5–7, 1000a13–14). This is a fairly severe judgment on Plato's part of his Presocratic predecessors. It is striking that Aristotle, down to the very language, applies this judgment to Thales' predecessors, to disqualify them as philosophers, and to justify his view that Thales was the first philosopher. But this should not make us overlook that Aristotle himself did not think much of early Greek philosophy. He himself says (1.10, 993a15–17), as we have seen, that it was like a child which cannot yet properly articulate what it says.

Of relevance here also is a passage in Cicero, *Tusculan Disputations* 3.28.69. It reports a view Aristotle held about the history of philosophy. Since we do not know the context in which the view originally had been expressed, the report has to be treated with caution. But Aristotle seems to have said two things. He accused the ancient philosophers who thought that they had perfected philosophy by their own efforts of being either stupid or vainglorious. But he also noted that philosophy in a short time had made enormous progress and thus could or would attain its final shape in little time. It is tempting to think that Aristotle is referring to the short time in which philosophy under Plato and his followers (like Aristotle himself) made such progress as to make the work of earlier philosophers appear as somehow juvenile.

To conclude, Aristotle's account of the origin and the early history of philosophy in *Metaphysics* 1, for the reasons given at the outset, is a basic source of literally fundamental importance. But in order to be able to use this text, we have to see how firmly embedded it is in Aristotle's *Metaphysics*. It relies on a certain conception of philosophy which it itself is supposed to support. According to this conception philosophy in the first instance is metaphysics, "primary philosophy." It is remarkably close to Plato's conception, at least how Aristotle understands it. It is part of an effort in which Aristotle joins Plato to clarify what philosophy is or should be at a time when this was far from clear and controversial. It is against this background that we have to understand Aristotle's historical account.

NOTES

This essay originally appeared in *Rhizai: A Journal for Ancient Philosophy and Science* vol. 1 (2004): 9–44. We are grateful that Professor Frede allowed us to reprint his essay, and we thank Professor Katerina Ierodiakonou and the other editors of *Rhizai* for their help.

1. Ross, *Aristotle's Metaphysics*, 1:128 and 983a5–6; 1:lxxvii.
2. Ross, *Aristotle's Metaphysics*, 1:126 and 983a26.
3. Jaeger, *Aristoteles*, 55–60 and Düring, *Aristotle's Protrepticus*, 19–24.
4. Jaeger, 68–73; Ross, 1:115.
5. Bonitz, *Aristotelis Metaphysica*, 2:57–58.
6. Ross, *Aristotle's Metaphysics*.
7. Ross, *Aristotle's Metaphysics*, commentary on 1005b1–2, 1:262, ll. 4–5.
8. Ross, commentary on 983b27, 1:130.
9. Snell, "Die Nachrichten über die Lehren des Thales."
10. Classen, "Bemerkungen zu zwei griechischen 'Philosophiehistorikern,' " 175–78.

BIBLIOGRAPHY

Bonitz, Hermann. *Aristotelis Metaphysica*. 1848. 2 vols. Reprint, Hildesheim: Olms, 1960.
Classen, C. Joachim. "Bemerkungen zu zwei griechischen 'Philosophiehistorikern.' " *Philologus* 109 (1965): 175–81.
Düring, Ingemar. *Aristotle's Protrepticus: An Attempt at Reconstruction*. Göteborg: Institute of Classical Studies, 1961–62.
Jaeger, Werner. *Aristoteles: Grundlegung einer Geschichte seiner Entwicklung*. Berlin: Weidmann, 1923.
Ross, W. D. *Aristotle's Metaphysics*. 2 vols. Oxford: Clarendon Press, 1924.
Snell, Bruno. "Die Nachrichten über die Lehren des Thales und die Anfänge der griechischen Philosophie- und Literaturgeschichte." *Philologus* 96 (1944): 170–82.
Taylor, A. E. *Aristotle on His Predecessors: Being the First Book of the Metaphysics*. Chicago: Open Court, 1907.

CHAPTER 20

....

CLASSICAL REPRESENTATIONS AND USES OF THE PRESOCRATICS

....

JOHN PALMER

ANYONE INTERESTED in the influence of Presocratic thought may be tempted to begin with Plato and Aristotle. There is, however, sufficient evidence of Presocratic influence among the sophists to make it clear that this temptation should be resisted. Some traces of this earlier influence may be found in Plato and Aristotle themselves, and this fact should serve as a reminder that their own involvement with Presocratic philosophy did not take place in a vacuum but will have been conditioned or mediated by previous developments. We are in a better position to appreciate how this was so thanks to a series of important studies by Jaap Mansfeld that has made it abundantly clear that the historiography of Greek philosophy began during the sophistic period.[1] While Mansfeld properly acknowledges that this thesis is not new with him, his work has synthesized, corrected, and extended the piecemeal work of earlier scholars so as to yield a more synoptic view of the initial phase of Greek philosophical historiography. Although Mansfeld modestly describes his work on this topic as providing directions for further research, thanks to his efforts we are in a good position to appreciate, as he himself puts it, "that this early historiography is a much more solid phenomenon than has been acknowledged so far, and that its impact upon Plato and Aristotle was decisive."[2] Sophistic representations and developments of Presocratic ideas in other ways also had their

impact on Plato and Aristotle. This is perhaps most apparent in Cratylus's influence on Plato's representation of Heraclitus, and elsewhere I have tried to
show that Plato's uses of Parmenides reflect an effort to recover his thought from
various sophistic appropriations to which it had been subjected.[3] Here I wish to
pursue some of the directions opened up by Mansfeld's fundamental work and to
explore the sometimes unfortunate influence of sophistic philosophical historiography on both Plato's and Aristotle's representations and understanding of the
Presocratics.

The Christian philosopher Clement of Alexandria (second–third century CE),
supporting his claim that the Greeks were inveterate appropriators of others'
ideas, preserves the following tantalizing quotation from the preface of a lost
treatise by the sophist Hippias of Elis: "Some of these things have in like wise been
said by Orpheus, some by Musaeus, summarily in one place or another, some by
Hesiod, some by Homer, some by other poets, some in books composed by
Greeks, some in books by foreigners; but I, collecting from all these sources the
most important related elements, shall produce this fresh and multifaceted work"
(Clem.Al. *Strom.* 6.2.15.2 = 86B6). It would seem, then, that one product of
Hippias's self-avowed polymathy was an anthology of sorts in which various
pronouncements by those noted among the Greeks for their wisdom were arranged so as to bring out what Hippias judged to be their common ideas. Since
Clement's excerpt mentions no philosopher by name, some scholarly detective
work was required before the true nature and importance of Hippias's anthology
would be recognized.

In the first book of his *Metaphysics*, Aristotle notes that there are some (*tines*)
who think the ancient theologians shared Thales' view that water is the principle of
all things: "For they made both Okeanos and Tethys the parents of creation [*cf.*
Hom. *Il.* 14.201], and they made water, called by them 'Styx,' what the gods swear
by [*cf.* Hom. *Il.* 15.36–37], since one swears by what is most revered, and what is
eldest is what is most revered [*cf.* Hes. *Th.* 337, 361, 776–7]" (*Metaph.* 1.3.983b30–33).
Bruno Snell, in a pioneering article, noted that none of the passages in Plato to
which commentators had commonly assumed Aristotle to be referring actually
mentions or otherwise alludes to Thales.[4] Snell thus proposed that Aristotle was
referring to Hippias, whose anthology presumably connected whatever Thales
actually said about the fundamental role of water with comparable elements in the
theogonies of Homer, Hesiod, and Orpheus. Snell went on to propose that Hippias's compilation is likewise reflected in the passage in the *Cratylus* where Plato
has Socrates introduce the Heraclitean theory of universal flux and trace its affiliations to the much older "theories" found in the earliest poets:

> SOCRATES: I seem to behold Heraclitus uttering certain ancient words of wisdom,
> dating right back to the time of Kronos and Rhea, which Homer also
> uttered.

HERMOGENES: What do you mean?

soc: Heraclitus says somewhere that all things give way and nothing abides [πάντα χωρεῖ καὶ οὐδὲν μένει], and, likening the things that are [*ta onta*] to the flow of a river, he says that you could not step twice into the same river.

herm: That's so.

soc: So what of it? Does it seem to you that one assigning the names "Rhea" and "Kronos" to the progenitors of the other gods thinks anything different from Heraclitus? Do you suppose he assigned names of streams to them both just on the spur of the moment? Just so Homer also says, "Okeanos the origin of gods and mother Tethys" [*Il*. 14. 201], and Hesiod too, I think. And Orpheus too says somewhere that "Beautifully flowing Okeanos first made a beginning of marriage, / he who took as wife his sister Tethys born of the same mother" [fr. 156 Kern = 1B2]. Mark, then, how these statements both agree with one another and all tend toward the views of Heraclitus. (*Cra.* 402a4–c3)

Clement's excerpt from the preface to Hippias's anthology makes tracing such lines of affiliation between the statements of a philosopher such as Heraclitus and various verses selected from the poets Homer, Hesiod, and Orpheus seem just the sort of thing Hippias did to produce his "fresh and multifaceted work." On the basis of the connections Snell was able to draw between these passages in Aristotle and Plato, he concluded that this lost work by Hippias played a seminal role in the development of Greek philosophical historiography. Although certain details of Snell's argument have proved to need correction, this principal conclusion has continued to be endorsed ever since and enabled others to discern the influence of Hippias's anthology in other passages of Plato and Aristotle.[5]

Arguably the more important representative of sophistic philosophical historiography, however, was the doxographical schema introducing the first division of Gorgias of Leontini's treatise *On Nature or On What Is Not*.[6] In this work, Gorgias notoriously argues that (1) nothing is; (2) even if something is, it is inapprehensible; and (3) even if something is and is apprehensible, it cannot be communicated to others (ps.-Arist. *De Melisso Xenophane Gorgia* [*MXG*] 979a12–13; *cf.* S.E. *M.* 7.65). Although the first thesis has often been misunderstood as equivalent to the proposition that nothing exists at all, a clear indication of its target, and thus its sense, comes in the lines immediately following: "And to show that it is not, *he collects what has been said by others who spoke about Beings [peri tôn ontôn]* and made, so it appears, statements in contradiction of one another—some demonstrating that these things [namely *ta onta*] are one and not many, others that they are many and not one, and some that they are ungenerated, others that they are generated—and he draws conclusions against each party" (*MXG* 979a13–18). Here the class of *ta onta* or "Beings" does not include all entities without discrimination but only and specifically whatever entities are somehow fundamental to or responsible for the being of all other entities.[7] Gorgias identifies a philosophical concern shared by all the major Presocratics with the real, as opposed to the phenomenal, nature of things—with what would come to be spoken of in the philosophical tradition as "substance." The neuter definite article and participle of *einai* yield the substantive *to on*, which functions in numerous philosophical contexts as the forerunner of the abstract noun *ousia* (literally "being" but standardly rendered in English as "substance"), a term that would not emerge into philosophical currency until the fourth century.

The *Antidosis* of Gorgias's pupil Isocrates features this use of *to on* in a passage presenting a comparable though more rudimentary classification of earlier metaphysical views. Isocrates advises his audience that while some time devoted to astronomy, geometry, and similar theoretical pursuits may be worthwhile, one should avoid becoming too involved in the barren speculations to which they are prone to lead. He likewise warns against getting lost "in the theories of the ancient thinkers with a reputation for wisdom, of whom one declared the number of things-that-are [τὸ πλῆθος . . . τῶν ὄντων] to be unlimited, but Empedocles that they are four with love and strife among them, and Ion that they are not more than three, and Alcmeon only two, and Parmenides and Melissus one, and Gorgias none at all" (Isoc. *Orat.* 15. 268). Here Isocrates employs a classification of previous views regarding the number of Beings, in much the same way Gorgias had done, to justify abandoning the kind of metaphysical inquiries conducted among the Presocratics. The classification mainly serves to point up the inability of the "experts" to reach any agreement, which in Isocrates' opinion is enough to indicate that the layman need not trouble himself with such questions.

Gorgias goes further than this in advocating a dogmatic skepticism on the question, arguing that either there is no such thing as Being or the "real" nature of things, or that it is beyond human capacity to comprehend. Compare how in the *Helen* he dismisses the *meteôrologoi* or "those who speak of lofty matters" as merely substituting one opinion for another as they present their audiences with "things unbelievable and nonapparent [τὰ ἄπιστα καὶ ἄδηλα]" (*Hel.* 13). In *On Nature or On What Is Not*, Gorgias's particular classificatory schema provides a programmatic framework for the demonstrations of its first division. In a manner reminiscent of Zeno, he deploys arguments against each possible view as to the character of Being identified in the series of apparently exhaustive dichotomies on which his schema is based. For example: if there is such a thing as the philosophers' Being, it must be either one or many; but, Gorgias argues, it can be neither one nor many; therefore, there is no such thing as the philosophers' Being. The schema's generated versus ungenerated dichotomy is taken up in the arguments at *De Melisso Xenophane Gorgia* 979b20–34 (*cf.* S.E. *M.* 7.68–72), and the one-versus-many dichotomy in those at 979b35–38 (*cf.* S.E. *M.* 7.73–74), at which point the text of the *De Melisso Xenophane Gorgia* becomes corrupt. There follows at 980a1–8 an argument against Being's possibly being in motion, suggesting that a corresponding argument against its being at rest has been lost in the lacuna and consequently that Gorgias's doxographical classification may have originally included an additional dichotomy, in motion versus at rest. We shall, at any rate, see such a dichotomy reflected in later classifications influenced by Gorgias.

Gorgias's treatise constitutes a cornerstone document of the sophistic movement, in that it provides theoretical justification for the sophists' retreat from the

Presocratic project of attempting to gain access by rational means to the substantial causes of phenomena. Despite its negative purpose, the treatise's doxographical preface played the important role of identifying perhaps for the first time a general philosophical preoccupation shared by all the thinkers we now refer to as the Presocratics. Although Gorgias rejected their metaphysical project, this did not diminish the influence of this view of the Presocratics, especially upon thinkers such as Plato and Aristotle who sought to continue the project Gorgias and other members of sophistic movement would have terminated.

That Gorgias's influence on Socrates was even more immediate is signaled by an unmistakable echo of Gorgias's doxographical schema in Xenophon's explanation of why Socrates avoided natural philosophy. In the course of defending him against accusations of sacrilege and impiety, Xenophon relates some of the reasons Socrates considered it folly to concern oneself with the nature of all things and with the origins and operation of the cosmos (*Mem.* 1.1.11–15). Chief among these reasons is that it should be clear that humans are incapable of apprehending these things from the fact that even those who have thought most about such questions differ from each other in their opinions, leading to harsh disagreement among them (1.1.13). This already suggests some survey of Presocratic views and reminds one of the *Phaedo*'s report of Socrates' early interest in Presocratic ideas. There then follows in Xenophon a passage that bears a striking resemblance to the schema employed by Gorgias in the doxographical preface of *On Nature or On What Is Not*: "Of those pondering the nature of all things, some are of the opinion that Being [*to on*] is one only, while others think there are Beings unlimited in number, and some think all things are ever changing, while others think nothing ever changes, and some think all things come to be and pass away, while others think nothing has ever come to be or will ever pass away" (*Mem.* 1.1.14). The one-versus-many and the generated-versus-ungenerated dichotomies utilized by Gorgias are both reflected here, and so is something that is analogous to the dichotomy in-motion-versus-at-rest that may also have figured in Gorgias's classification. Whereas Gorgias, however, had employed the classificatory schema to facilitate his systematic refutation of all previous claims to have identified the real or underlying nature of things, Socrates, by contrast, deploys the Gorgianic schema to a more cautiously skeptical end in an early instance of what would become a stock strategy of skeptical doxography. The schema developed by Gorgias was easily adaptable by Socrates to the purpose of justifying his turning away from the type of inquiry characteristic of the Presocratics.

   A rather different justification of this decision figures prominently in the famous "intellectual autobiography" related by the Socrates of Plato's *Phaedo*. There Socrates tells of how as a young man he was wonderfully enthusiastic about the type of wisdom that had come to be known as the inquiry concerning nature. He even presents a rudimentary survey of the diverse opinions he encountered regarding the source of cognition, opinions between which he says he kept shifting back and forth, as an example of one kind of experience that convinced him to abandon this type of inquiry (*Phd.* 96b4–9). Yet the most significant complaint the

Phaedo's Socrates levels against the Presocratics is not that their inquiries led them to widely divergent views regarding the nature and operation of things but, rather, that they exclusively employed a material conception of cause that proves inadequate to the *explananda* and that they thereby failed altogether to offer teleological explanations of natural phenomena.[8] Although Socrates directs this complaint at the Presocratics generally, Anaxagoras is singled out for special criticism because his writings were responsible for inspiring a vision of this more adequate mode of explanation.[9] What initially piqued the interest of Plato's Socrates was Anaxagoras's assertion that Reason is the determinant and cause of all things (νοῦς ἐστιν ὁ διακοσμῶν τε καὶ πάντων αἴτιος, 97c1–2; *cf.* Anaxag. B12). The significance of this thesis lies in its suggesting the possibility of employing a type of explanation of natural phenomena at the macrocosmic level that mirrors the type of explanation humans naturally employ at the microcosmic level in accounting for their own actions. Thus Socrates says one might try to explain why he is sitting in prison awaiting execution by referring to such features of his physiognomy as the mechanism of his joints and sinews, that is, in terms of material causes alone; but this would, he goes on to say, be to overlook completely the real reason he is sitting in prison, namely his *decision* that the best course of action is for him to accept the penalty imposed by the Athenian jury, for his joints and sinews could not keep him in prison if he had judged some other course of action, such as escape into exile, best (98c–99a). Plato accordingly calls the decision as to what is best "the cause in reality" (τὸ αἴτιον τῷ ὄντι) and the material conditions merely "that without which the cause could never be a cause" (99b3–4), thus identifying the latter as merely hypothetically necessary rather than necessitating conditions. The hope encouraged in Plato's Socrates by Anaxagoras is that this mode of explanation, which is perfectly natural and appropriate in the area of human action, might be extended throughout the domain of natural philosophy more generally if there were some rational principle governing the changes in the body of the cosmos in a manner analogous to that by which our reason governs the activity of our bodies. In particular, just as human actions need to be explained by reference to the good an agent judges to be achieved by his or her action, so processes of growth and development in nature need to be explained by reference to the good they are designed by cosmic Reason to achieve (see 97c3–d1; *cf.* X. *Mem.* 1.4.8).

However, Plato famously has Socrates relate how the hopes inspired in him by Anaxagoras's claim that Reason is the determinant and cause of all things were soon disappointed: "I thought . . . he would tell me first whether the earth is flat or round, and then he would go on to explain also the necessary cause of its being so, saying what was better—that it was better for it to be such; and if he should say the earth is in the center of the cosmos, I expected him to explain also why it was better for it to be in the center" (97d6–e4). Plato's Socrates had, in effect, hoped to gain access to the reasoning underlying the cosmos's creation. For if the cosmos is the product of the activity of a rational principle that, like our own, causes what it can to be done to achieve what it judges or recognizes as good, then it theoretically should be possible to explain the nature and behavior of each thing in the cosmos by reference to the good that Reason had determined it to fulfill. Plato will continue to adhere to this guiding idea as a fundamental principle of natural science when he comes to present the cosmological theories of the *Timaeus* (see especially 29d7–30a2). In the *Phaedo*, however, Plato complains that Anaxagoras's actual explanations of natural phenomena made no use of the intelligence he had earlier introduced but instead cited only material factors—"things such as air, aether, water, and many other absurd things"—as the causes supposedly determining the nature and order of things (*Phd.* 98b7–c2).[10] He subsequently has Socrates extend this complaint to the majority of earlier thinkers on the basis of their likewise having referred only to material principles in their purported explanations of natural phenomena: "Thus one person, placing a whirl around the earth, makes it remain in place because of the heavens, while someone else props it up on a base of air as if it were a flat-bottomed trough" (99b6–8).[11] In the *Phaedo*, then, Plato treats the Presocratics as thoroughgoing materialists who sought to explain natural phenomena solely in terms of physical principles.

Aristotle displays a similar attitude toward the Presocratics in *Physics* 1, the central argument of which gives every appearance of having been worked out while Aristotle was still a member of the Academy. There are, however, a number of identifiable reasons for his doing so that should make one wary of taking this to be Aristotle's considered view of the Presocratics. In the first instance, it must be recognized that Aristotle is by no means presenting a general history or overview of Presocratic philosophy. He is, instead, engaged in an inquiry into a specific question, the foundational nature of which makes it useful if not necessary to consider such views on the question as can be discerned among earlier thinkers. Aristotle is attempting to isolate the *archai* or ultimate explanatory principles of natural science (*Ph.* 1.1.184a10–16; *cf.* 1.7.190b17–19). He is particularly concerned with isolating the principles of *change*, since entities within the domain of natural science are distinguished from other entities primarily by their being subject to change (*Metaph.* 6.1.1025b19–21, 26–27, 1026a2–3). In some ways, the object of Aristotle's inquiry here is not so different from the question motivating the glance back at Presocratic natural philosophy in the *Phaedo*: "It is necessary," Socrates was made to say in response to Cebes' lingering worries, "to conduct a thorough investigation at a general level into the reason [*aitia*] for coming-to-be and ceasing-to-be in general" (*Phd.* 95e10–96a1; *cf.* 96a8–10). It is significant, and somewhat surprising, that Aristotle nowhere in *Physics* 1 adduces the type of principles or causes of change Socrates was made to indicate are necessary for adequate accounts of these phenomena.

As emerges by the end of *Physics* 1.7, Aristotle's own view in this treatise is that natural change needs to be explained in terms of three principles: a pair of opposites, namely a form or character and its privation, and what underlies them (see in particular 191a3–5, 12–14, 20–22). Now, Aristotle's method for determining that these are the principles required for explanations in the domain of natural science is of necessity dialectical or inductive. For it is not possible for one conducting an inquiry within a science to demonstrate what the principles of the science are, since they are themselves the starting points of all demonstrations within that science. Much of the *Physics* is in fact devoted to such dialectical clarification of the fundamental concepts of natural science, including change and its principles, matter and form, nature, cause, chance and necessity, infinity, place, void, time, continuity, and so on. This methodological point is clearly stated in an important passage at the beginning of the *Topics* (another product of Aristotle's time in the Academy) that characterizes the work's investigation of dialectical practice as useful for, among other things, the pursuit of philosophical knowledge, especially "in relation to the first elements of each branch of knowledge. For starting from the particular principles pertaining to the proffered science, it is impossible to say anything about the principles themselves, since the principles of everything come first, but it is necessary to arrive at these via the reputable opinions relevant to each field. This is peculiar to, or especially characteristic of, dialectic; for, as the art of inquiry, it provides a path to the first principles of all fields" (*Top.* 1.2.101a36–b4). This passage furnishes a clear statement of Aristotle's view that the principles of the sciences can be determined by methods that accord a central role to *ta endoxa* or "reputable opinions," defined previously in the *Topics* as "opinions held by everyone or by the majority or by the wise, and by either all the wise or by the majority of them or by those especially well-known and reputable" (*Top.* 1.1.100b21–23).[12] This methodological prescription makes it unsurprising, then, that Aristotle should devote so much of his inquiry into the principles of natural change in *Physics* 1 to the views of earlier thinkers. In fact, while just the first half of *Physics* 1.7 considers the universally held *endoxa* reflected in how people tend to speak about change, Aristotle devotes the bulk of the treatise (chapters 2 to 6) to teasing out and examining such views on the question as may be found among those earlier thinkers most noted for their own inquiries in the field.[13]

Aristotle's survey of previous views on the principles of natural change is not conducted in a vacuum. On the contrary, it takes as its point of departure a classification of the possible positions that is influenced by the doxographical preface in Gorgias's *On Nature or On What Is Not.* As Aristotle would come to realize, however, this type of classificatory schema purchases its exhaustiveness at the price of a reductive simplicity that obscures important elements in the Presocratic systems germane to his own inquiries. The schema Aristotle sets out at *Physics* 1.2.184b15–22 may be represented as follows.

(I) Single *archê*:
    (A) Immutable;
    (B) Mutable: (i) air, (ii) water.
(II) A plurality of *archai*:
    (A) Numerically limited: (i) two, (ii) three, (iii) four, (iv) some other number;
    (B) Numerically unlimited: (i) of a single kind, (ii) different or opposite in kind.

The only thinkers initially assigned by Aristotle to a position in this schema are Parmenides and Melissus, who are assigned to position I.A (184b16), and Democritus, who is assigned to II.B.i (184b20–1). Which figures should be assigned to the remaining positions has occasioned speculation since antiquity, though in some instances, and in part due to Aristotle's own remarks elsewhere, the assignments seem straightforward enough: for example, Anaximenes to I.B.i, Thales to I.B.ii, Empedocles to II.A.iii, and Anaxagoras to II.B.ii. Furthermore, when Aristotle takes up division I.B at the beginning of *Physics* 1.4, he adds two further options, namely that the single mutable principle might be (iii) fire or (iv) "something else that is more dense than fire but lighter than air" (187a12–15). Heraclitus thus finds a place in the schema at I.B.iii, and perhaps Diogenes of Apollonia is the figure meant to occupy I.B.iv.

Determining just who might occupy positions II.A.i and ii, representing the possibilities that there are two or three principles of change, presents a problem paralleled in Plato's classification of views regarding the number and nature of Beings in the *Sophist*.[14] Since this passage has frequently been identified as the inspiration for Aristotle's own classification, and since it is otherwise important for us, it will be worth quoting at length. The speaker is the Visitor from Elea:

> Each one seems to me to tell us some story [*muthos*], as if we were children, one saying that there are three Beings [*ta onta*], and that at times some of them somehow war with one another, while indeed at other times they become friendly, have weddings and children, and raise their offspring; and another one, saying that there are two Beings, wet and dry or hot and cold, marries them off and has them set up house together. But the Eleatic tribe that issues from us, beginning with Xenophanes and even earlier, go through their tales on the ground that what is called "all things" is one.[15] Later, certain Ionian and Sicilian Muses both had the idea that it is safest to weave both together and to say that what-is [*to on*] is both many and one, and it is encompassed by hatred and love. For though borne apart it is always brought together, say the more severe Muses; but the gentler ones relaxed the requirement that these things always be so, and they say that, in turn, the universe is at one time one and loving under the sway of Aphrodite, while at another time it is many and hostile to itself because of a certain strife (*Sph.* 242c8–243a2).

The Being (*to on*) or Beings (*ta onta*) represented in this classification consist only of that subset of entities somehow basic to the being of other entities. The views represented here fall into three main groups: (1) there is a plurality of such entities; (2) there is a single such entity; and, combining the first two options, (3) Being is both many and one. The account here of the first view within (1), according to which there are three fundamental entities, calls to mind Pherecydes of Syros, who wrote what Aristotle would properly describe as a "mixed" theogony combining mythical and more rational features (*Metaph.* 14.4.1091b8–9), in the beginning of which he identified three entities as having always existed: "Zas and Chronos and Chthoniê were always…" (7B1 from D.L. 1.119). The Sicilian Muse is clearly Empedocles, while the Ionian Muse would seem to be Heraclitus, since the phrase "though borne apart it is always brought together" (διαφερόμενον γὰρ ἀεὶ συμφέρεται) incorporates part of a fragment of Heraclitus that might seem a clear enough statement that Being is both many and one: "collections are wholes and not wholes, brought together borne apart [συμφερόμενον διαφερόμενον], concordant discordant: from all things one and from one all things [ἐκ πάντων ἓν καὶ ἐξ ἑνὸς πάντα]" (B10). We seem to be left, however, with no plausible candidate for the view that there are two fundamental entities as here described, a difficulty paralleled in Aristotle's classification and subsequently in his reference to some who make hot and cold, and others who make wet and dry, their elements or principles (*Ph.* 1.5.188b33; *cf. Metaph.* 1.3.984b5–8).

Now, it may seem a puzzling feature of the *Sophist* passage that Heraclitus is introduced as having come along later than the Eleatics, for the thinker normally considered the prime representative of that group—Parmenides—was active after Heraclitus. This apparent anomaly is easily accounted for once one appreciates that Plato is not here attempting to present an exhaustive survey of previous positions. Instead, he is introducing just those often very early thinkers whose views on the question, to the extent that they can be discerned, tend to be expressed in mythical or otherwise symbolic language: thus Pherecydes, Xenophanes, Heraclitus, and Empedocles are the main figures Plato introduces here, rather than such important figures as Anaxagoras and Democritus, whom one might otherwise have expected to encounter. For this and other reasons, this passage is far less likely to have been the model for Aristotle's classification in *Physics* 1.2, as for a long time it was standardly assumed to be. A much more plausible candidate is Gorgias's classification. Aristotle might seem to indicate as much when, immediately after laying out the classification of possible positions regarding the principles of change, he announces: "Those inquiring into how many Beings there are [οἱ τὰ ὄντα ζητοῦντες πόσα] conduct their inquiries in the same way; for they first inquire whether what things come from is one or many, and if many, whether they are limited or unlimited, so that they are actually inquiring whether the first principle and element is single or plural" (*Ph.* 1.2.184b22–25). The earlier figures Aristotle is referring to here should certainly include Gorgias, even if Aristotle also has in mind others who followed his lead, for Aristotle's own classificatory schema incorporates into its more complex structure some of the basic dichotomies Gorgias had deployed *seriatim*. It is noteworthy, however, that the dichotomy limited-versus-unlimited, which Aristotle mentions here as having been employed by these earlier inquirers and which he deploys in his own schema, features neither in the *Sophist* doxography nor in what we know of Gorgias's doxographical preface. It would not be surprising if Gorgias did actually employ a dichotomy of this type in a portion of his treatise no longer reflected in our sources, since he is reported to have argued that what is ungenerated must be unlimited (*MXG* 979b22–23). It is also possible, though, that Aristotle here reflects an otherwise unknown classification within the genre of philosophical historiography instituted by Gorgias.

Whomever exactly Aristotle may be referring to, his adaptation of the ontological classification for the purpose of cataloguing earlier views regarding the principles of change is not without its problems and unfortunate consequences. Although Aristotle attempts to justify adapting an *onta*-classification à la Gorgias to serve as a classification of views regarding the *archai* or principles of natural change, the one cannot properly be treated as equivalent to the other. The *onta*-classification, in fact, better represents the Presocratics' concerns than Aristotle's *archai*-classification, since virtually all the Presocratics were concerned in one way or another with advancing candidates to occupy a privileged ontological position, regardless of whether these entities might function as principles of change. Moreover, Aristotle's own inquiry in *Physics* 1 is not well served by this kind of schema. Almost immediately, he finds it necessary to qualify or abandon its too simple and restrictive categories when he turns to discussing in earnest the Presocratic principles of change. Furthermore, the inherited schema seems partially responsible for obscuring from Aristotle's view the presence in the Presocratic systems of principles of change other than ones identifiable as the material substrate and the opposite characters qualifying it. The point being made is rather different from the one so persistently pursued by Harold Cherniss—that Aristotle can often be seen to distort the views and concerns of the Presocratics by foisting on them the problem of isolating the principles of natural change and by being determined to find in them confirmation of his own position.[16] Cherniss's worthy aim was to caution the historian who would employ Aristotle as a source for Presocratic philosophy by systematically demonstrating the ways Aristotle misunderstands, distorts, and even willfully misrepresents Presocratic views either for the particular purpose of some specific argument or more generally to support his "apparently sincere belief . . . that each of his predecessors was aiming at the goal represented by his own system."[17] It seems, however, that Aristotle himself was confronted with a problem not unlike the one Cherniss identified as confronting modern historians of Presocratic thought, namely having to account for the potentially distortive perspective imposed by representations of the Presocratics in the previous philosophical tradition.

Toward the beginning of *Physics* 1.4, for example, Aristotle characterizes Anaximander, Empedocles, and Anaxagoras as all having explained the generation of the world's manifold population in terms of the separating out of oppositions present within the one (187a20–21). Empedocles and Anaxagoras are then described, in a manner reminiscent of the *Sophist* doxography's representation of Empedocles, as having alike held the principle to be both one *and* many in so far as they separate out from a primordial mixture the so-called elements (earth, air, fire, and water) and the homoeomeries and opposites, respectively (187a21–26). This is effectively to assign Empedocles and Anaxagoras to *two* places in the initial *archê*-classification: Empedocles to a place in I.B as well as II.A.iii, and Anaxagoras (as well as Anaximander) to a place in I.B as well as II.B.ii. Likewise at the beginning of the next chapter, Aristotle finds it necessary to qualify Parmenides' and Democritus's positions as initially represented within the adapted schema: "Everyone, indeed, makes the opposites principles, those who say that the universe is one and immutable (for even Parmenides makes hot and cold principles, though he calls these fire and earth),[18] those who talk of rare and dense, and Democritus who talks of the full and the void, the former of which he speaks of as being and the latter as nonbeing" (188a19–23). Thus Parmenides becomes a representative of position II.A.i in addition to I.A; and the more generic perspective on Democritus's principles has him also fitting into II.A.i, while the initial classification of his view at *Physics* 1.2.184b20–21 as a representative of position II.B.i is made possible by focusing on the innumerable species of the first genus. These qualifications to the representations dictated by the classification with which Aristotle begins are not made simply to "remold" the ideas of the thinkers under consideration so as better to fit Aristotle's preconceived analysis, but reflect a genuine need to take account of significant elements within their systems that are glossed over or suppressed by the Gorgianic schema Aristotle has chosen to adapt.

Perhaps the most long-lived oversimplification resulting from the Gorgianic schema and reflected in Aristotle is the grouping of Melissus and Parmenides as having held Being to be single and immutable. To this schema one can trace the tags "Being is one" (*hen to on*) and "everything is one" (*hen to pan*), so commonly employed in the subsequent tradition from Plato onward as ways of characterizing the Eleatic position. Parmenides and Melissus are already grouped together under such a rubric in Plato at *Theaetetus* 180e and 183c–184a, though in the latter passage Plato deliberately has Socrates express his reservations about treating their thought as so readily assimilable.[19] Clearly, there are significant differences between Parmenides and Melissus that are obscured by the Gorgianic grouping. Unprejudiced examination of what remains of their respective works reveals that both the attributes and arguments featuring in Melissus's account of Being diverge from those in Parmenides' account rather more substantially than this now standard pairing would suggest.[20] Perhaps the major difference between the two, however, is that Melissus makes no effort to present a cosmological account as Parmenides does in the so-called Way of Mortal Opinion. Melissus in fragment B8 goes so far as to reject outright the enterprise of offering naturalistic explanations of the world of ordinary experience, for the obvious reason that Melissus's characterization of Being explicitly rules out the existence of the phenomenal world. Parmenides, by contrast, did not think his own central argument militated against providing such an account, however one eventually decides the relation between the two accounts should be understood.

One can, in fact, see Aristotle increasingly straining against the confusion engendered by the Gorgianic classification's simplistic collocation of Parmenides and Melissus. At the beginning of their treatment in *Physics* 1.2–3, he dismisses the view that Being is one and unchanging as largely irrelevant to the inquiry into nature, in part since "examining whether it is one in this sense is like arguing against any other *thesis*[21] propounded for the sake of argument . . . or like refuting an eristic account, which in fact both these arguments are, both that of Melissus and that of Parmenides. For they assume false premises and their reasoning does not follow. Or rather, the argument of Melissus is crude and provides no difficulty, but once a single absurdity is granted, the rest follows. But this is nothing difficult to deal with" (*Ph.* 1.2.185a5–12). Aristotle's hesitation here about branding Parmenides an eristic on the level of Melissus is reminiscent of the reservations Socrates expressed in the *Theaetetus*. In particular, Aristotle's labeling of Melissus's argument as "crude" (*phortikos*) seems to echo Socrates' expressed unwillingness to examine Melissus "crudely" (*phortikôs*) and does so in a way that suggests its apparent irony. Aristotle sees the *hen to on* label, under which Parmenides and Melissus have been ranged, as subject to multiple interpretations, given the fact that "being" is employed in several ways (*Ph.* 1.2.185a21–22; *cf.* Pl. *Sph.* 244b6–7). Some of the confusions about being engendered by Parmenides' pioneering work are here acknowledged by Aristotle (185b25–186a3). His treatment of the Eleatic thesis in *Physics* 1.2–3 may be seen as an attempt to dispel some of this confusion by getting clearer about this fundamental concept, not unlike the way Plato does in the *Sophist*. In fact, a fully adequate account of Aristotle's treatment of Parmenides and Melissus in these chapters of the *Physics* would need to trace its affiliations with the treatment of the Eleatic thesis in that dialogue.

Although Aristotle in *Physics* 1.2–3 seems not to have escaped entirely the confusion between Parmenides and Melissus occasioned by the doxographical schema he has adopted, by the time of *Metaphysics* 1 he appears less sanguine about the view of Parmenides implied by the inherited association with Melissus. In *Metaphysics* 1.5 he dismisses Xenophanes, Parmenides, and Melissus from that book's inquiry into principles since their position that Being is one is only superficially similar to claims by some of the early natural scientists (986b12–17).[22] But when Aristotle says here that the Eleatics speak of Being as one "in a different way" than do the *phusikoi*, he is not, as he was at *Physics* 1.2.184b25–185a5, dismissing the Eleatics for having advocated a strict monism that leaves nothing for any principle to be a principle *of*; instead, he is signaling here that the Eleatic position belongs to a higher science. The point is clearer in *De caelo* 3.1, where he says that in denying change, Parmenides did not speak *phusikôs* or "in the manner of natural science" but nevertheless *kalôs* or "finely"—"for the existence of certain ungenerated and generally unchanging entities belongs rather to another inquiry prior to natural science" (298b18–21),[23] that is, to theology or first philosophy. Despite their initial dismissal in *Metaphysics* 1, the Eleatics are readmitted into that treatise's inquiry at three points. First, Aristotle says that their views are relevant to the inquiry into principles, since in Parmenides' conception of the One there seems to be some grasp of the formal cause, and in Melissus's conception, some grasp of the material cause (986b17–20). Parmenides alone is granted further indulgence, since he posited two material principles, having been forced, so Aristotle says, to follow the phenomena and to suppose that Being is one in account but plural with respect to perception (986b27–34, *cf. Ph.* 1.5.188a19–22).[24] Parmenides is likewise admitted into the inquiry in *Metaphysics* 1.4 because he introduced Eros as an efficient-*cum*-final cause (984b23–32). In making these exceptions for Parmenides, Aristotle seems to be moving beyond the limitations of the doxographical schema employed in *Physics* 1, particularly in the attribution to him of the position that Being is one in account but plural with respect to perception. This description is free from any lingering confusion of Parmenides' monism with the strict monism of Melissus. Between the composition of *Physics* 1 and *Metaphysics* 1, Aristotle seems to have had increased reservations about his somewhat unreflective use of this schema, at least vis-à-vis Parmenides, and to have revised his view of Parmenides on further study and reflection.[25]

As the opening of *Physics* 1 echoed the *Phaedo*'s call for an investigation into the causes of natural change, so *Metaphysics* 1.1–2 expands on the idea that knowledge and understanding depend on the apprehension of causes, first principles, and elements and thereby promotes a specific conception of wisdom and of philosophy itself.[26] Here Aristotle appears to be adapting material from his lost *Protrepticus*, written while he was still a member of the Academy. The remainder of *Metaphysics* 1 presents a richer and more nuanced view of the Presocratics, one made possible by its deployment of the theory of the four causes, which Aristotle apparently had yet to develop when he wrote *Physics* 1. Yet the same caveat applies about treating this treatise as if it represented Aristotle at work as a historian of philosophy. Here, too, Aristotle remains in the first instance a philosopher arguing for a specific philosophical thesis—that his identification of the formal, final, efficient, and material causes exhausts the types of explanatory principles—a thesis that, since it concerns ultimate explanatory principles, necessitates a review of *ta endoxa* or reputable opinions on the question. The treatise's final chapter provides both a clear statement of its main thesis and a touchstone for appreciating the general character of Aristotle's treatment of the Presocratics:

> That they all seem [*eoikasi*] to be seeking the explanatory principles spoken of in the *Physics*, and that there is no explanatory principle we might speak of apart from these, is clear also from the previous discussion. But they seem to have spoken of these principles opaquely, and in one way they have all been spoken of before, while in another way they have not been spoken of before at all. For philosophy at first is on all subjects like an inarticulate speaker, seeing as it is young and at the beginning. (*Metaph.* 1.10.993a11–15)[27]

While the historian hoping to employ Aristotle as a source of evidence on which to base the reconstruction of Presocratic thought will find this immensely frustrating, any charge of bad faith leveled against Aristotle needs to be tempered by an appreciation of how conscious he is throughout of the degree of interpretative reconstruction, of both positions and arguments, required to bring the Presocratics into the discussion of philosophical problems. Some of the clearest examples are to be found in his discussions of Thales' view that water is the *archê* (*Metaph.* 1.3.983b20–27), of Empedocles' view in fragment B96 regarding the composition of bone (10.993a17–24), and in the remarkable discussion of how Anaxagoras can be understood as a two-element theorist (8.989a30–b21). Throughout the treatise, moreover, Aristotle does not disguise the interpretative difficulties he has encountered in trying to discern the types of causes operative in the Presocratic systems. He seems to have found it particularly difficult to assimilate the explanatory principles employed among the Pythagoreans so as to support his general thesis, although at 1.5.986b4–6 he rather petulantly places the blame for this on them rather than allowing it to undermine his conclusion. All these difficulties lead him to be somewhat more tentative in stating that conclusion than one might have imagined. This tentativeness is evident not only in the lines already quoted from *Metaphysics* 1.10 but also in 1.7, where Aristotle summarizes the results of the inquiry conducted in the foregoing chapters and states his main conclusion before turning to some of the difficulties (*aporiai*) raised by earlier views: "Therefore," he says, "that a correct determination has been made with regard to the number and nature of causes all of these figures indeed seem to us to bear witness [μαρτυρεῖν ἐοίκασιν ἡμῖν], seeing that they are not able to touch upon another cause" (988b16–18).

Aristotle's comments on the discernibility of some conception of the final cause in the Presocratic systems repay particular attention. For at the same time that he echoes the *Phaedo*'s treatment of Anaxagoras, he sees that Anaxagoras was not alone in satisfying the crucial condition Plato identified as making teleological explanation possible. It was only natural, Aristotle supposes, that at a certain point philosophers should seek to explain why the development and constitution of living things are so well and even beautifully ordered. Eventually, someone had to realize that the intricate adaptations of means to ends and apparent purposefulness evident throughout nature could not be explained solely by reference to material elements and their chance interactions, and thus someone had to have taken the great step of endowing the efficient cause with intelligence. "Indeed," Aristotle says, "when someone said that Reason [*nous*] is present, *even as it is in living creatures*, in nature also, as the cause of the cosmos and its entire order, he seemed like a sober man in comparison with his predecessors' random ramblings" (*Metaph.* 1.3.984b15–18). Aristotle is naturally disposed to see whoever first made this intuitive leap as a philosophical hero, for he himself endorses the central elements of the view here expressed. Socrates' intellectual autobiography in the *Phaedo* would suggest crediting Anaxagoras with the innovation, and Aristotle here immediately mentions Anaxagoras as plainly (*phaneros*) having held this view (984b18–19).

But he goes on to adduce evidence suggesting that there were others earlier than Anaxagoras who pointed to the operation of a rational or directive principle within the cosmos. He mentions that Hermotimos of Clazomenae is credited with such a view, though he does not indicate (and we are otherwise unable to determine) the basis for this attribution. He does, however, quote verses from Hesiod and Parmenides in which each assigns a prominent cosmogonic role to Eros (Hes. *Th.* 116–17, 20; Parm. B13) and on the basis of which, as he tentatively suggests, "one might suppose" (ὑποπτεύσειε δ' ἄν τις) that they were the first to seek a type of cause for things that is at once the source of their beauty and their movement (*Metaph.* 1.3.984b20–4.984b31).[28] Here Aristotle seems to have found Hippias's doxographical compendium a useful tool in his research into the proto-history of the efficient-*cum*-final cause, just as he had in his researches into that of the material cause earlier in chapter 3. For, as noted, the similarities between this passage and the beginning of Phaedrus's speech in Plato's *Symposium* suggest that Hippias's treatise contained a section collecting and comparing the similar statements made by the poets and philosophers on the cosmogonic function of Eros.[29] The *Symposium* passage also mentions Acusilaus alongside Hesiod and Parmenides, and the particular manner in which Aristotle introduces Parmenides alongside Hesiod—"One might suppose Hesiod first sought this kind of cause, or anyone else who located love or desire among the things that are as a first principle, as for instance Parmenides too does" (984b23–25)—suggests that Aristotle was selecting from an even lengthier list. A wealth of *comparanda* would have been available to Hippias, given the widespread employment of marital union and subsequent procreation as a cosmogonic device in mythical sources.

Empedocles may also have made his way onto Hippias's list for his employment of *Philotês* or Love as a cosmic principle. Aristotle, at any rate, includes Empedocles among those in whose systems he discerns a conception of the efficient-*cum*-final cause, on the basis of the roles assigned in his system to Love and Strife as the respective causes of good and bad. As so often with Empedocles, though, Aristotle thinks it here necessary to engage in some interpretative reconstruction so as to understand the intention (λαμβάνοι πρὸς τὴν διάνοιαν) behind Empedocles' inarticulate expression (*Metaph.* 1.4.984b32–985a10).[30] This is perhaps less of a distortion than it may first appear. Empedocles does, at any rate, make the connection between the causes operative at the macrocosmic and microcosmic levels in describing the roles of Strife and, especially, Love:

> I shall tell a twofold tale: at one time they grew to be one alone out of many, at another again they grew apart to be many out of one—fire and water and earth and the immense height of air, and cursed Strife apart from them, equal in every direction, and Love [*Philotês*] among them, equal in length and breadth. *Her must you contemplate with your mind, and not sit with eyes dazed: she it is who is thought innate even in mortal limbs,* because of her they think friendly thoughts, and accomplish harmonious deeds, calling her Joy by name and Aphrodite. *She is perceived by no mortal man as she circles among them: but you must listen to the undeceitful ordering of my discourse.* (B17.16–26, trans. KRS)

The final injunction here, with its echo of Parmenides B8.52, has too often been taken out of context to support the familiar story of Empedocles' largely negative and critical response to Parmenides. But the phrase in Empedocles thought to echo Parmenides has a specific use within this fragment that undermines this detail of that story. What Empedocles here refers to as undeceitful is not the entirety of his cosmological account but his bold claim that Love is a force operating in the cosmos as a whole just as we experience her operating in our own bodies. On this point, Empedocles seems to be essentially in agreement with Parmenides. Likewise, in marking as undeceptive what cannot be directly experienced in perception but must instead be grasped by the mind, Empedocles' perspective again seems in line with Parmenides'.

Despite Aristotle's feeling that the role played by Love in some of the pre-Anaxagorean cosmologies is suggestive of the efficient-*cum*-final cause, Love does not quite seem capable of playing the role of *nous* or Reason. Although it may be thought of in its macrocosmic role as a cause of harmony, it hardly seems to satisfy the crucial condition on teleological explanation—identified by Plato in the *Phaedo* and echoed in Aristotle's praise of the heroic figure who first recognized the presence of *nous* in nature generally—that events at the macrocosmic level ultimately be the products of a directive and purposeful intelligence just as our own actions are at the microcosmic level. Aristotle does not, significantly, bring on stage any figure prior to Anaxagoras who might be thought to have satisfied this condition. Not that there wasn't material he could have drawn on. He might, for instance, easily have seen Xenophanes' description of the greatest god's omnipotence as suggesting an intelligent efficient cause: "but without effort it makes all things tremble with its reason's mind [ἀλλ' ἀπάνευθε πόνοιο νόου φρενὶ πάντα κραδαίνει]" (B25 = Simp. *in Ph.* 23.19). Something similar might have been suggested by Empedocles' description of the *phrên hierê*, or "sacred mind" that "darts throughout the entire cosmos with its swift thoughts" (B134.4–5). Some responsibility for this odd absence should probably be attributed to Aristotle's excessive reliance on Hippias in researching the early history of the efficient-*cum*-final cause. A philosophical explanation is perhaps to be found as well in the fact that Aristotle's own natural teleology does not postulate the activity of a directive and purposeful intelligence within the cosmos.

On this point Aristotle contrasts with Plato. It is thus appropriate that Plato draws on Xenophanes' and Empedocles' divinities in the *Timaeus*'s account of the intelligible living creature and the visible cosmos modeled on it. Timaeus argues that the demiurge created the cosmic living creature with neither eyes nor hearing, since there was nothing visible or audible outside it, and with no organs of respiration or digestion, since there was no air or nourishment outside it (*Ti.* 33b7–d2). The rejection of anthropomorphic conceptions of divinity is generally reminiscent of Xenophanes; and there appears to be a specific use of Xenophanes' view, as reported by Diogenes Laertius, that the greatest god "sees as a whole, hears as a whole, and does not breathe" (ὅλον δὲ ὁρᾶν καὶ ὅλον ἀκούειν, μὴ μέντοι ἀναπνεῖν) (D.L. 9.19). The first two phrases here clearly reflect Xenophanes B24: "it sees as a whole, it thinks as a whole, and it hears as a whole" (οὖλος ὁρᾷ, οὖλος δὲ νοεῖ, οὖλος δέ τ' ἀκούει); and the third phrase may well derive from the close of a lost Xenophanean hexameter known to Plato. Timaeus's denial that the cosmic living creature has specific organs of perception also seems to reflect Xenophanes' conception of divine cognitive activity. Timaeus goes on to argue that it has neither hands nor feet, as these were not required to maintain the rotating motion appropriate to its spherical shape and to the activity of its *nous* (33d2–34a7); here he seems to be drawing on Empedocles' declarations—with respect to both the spherical universe under the rule of Love and subsequently the sacred mind whose thoughts spread effortlessly throughout the cosmos—that "from its back two branches do not spring, no feet, nor swift knees" (B29.1–2, nearly repeated in B134.2–3).[31] The *Timaeus*'s incorporation of these Xenophanean and Empedoclean elements in its description of the animate cosmos suggests that one result of Plato's deepening engagement with the philosophy of southern Italy after writing the *Phaedo* was a greater appreciation for the fact that there were others before Anaxagoras who fulfilled one of the necessary conditions on teleological explanation by recognizing the presence of reason within the cosmos itself.[32] This new awareness also comes through in the *Philebus*, where Plato has Socrates declare that "our predecessors" used to hold that reason and a directive intelligence govern the entire universe (28d5–9, cf. 28c6–8, 30e4–7), though he gives no hint of what earlier figures he has in mind.[33] Still, Socrates' complaint in the *Phaedo* that although Anaxagoras posits Reason as a cause, his actual explanations of natural phenomena make no real use of it (*Phd.* 98b7-c2, cf. Arist. *Metaph.* 1.4.985a17–21)—in other words, that he failed to provide accounts that make clear the rational order underlying and governing natural phenomena—could equally well be leveled against Xenophanes and Empedocles. It is one thing to claim that that there is a governing principle present within the whole cosmos as within each of us, but it is quite another thing to describe its actual operation, as Plato makes some effort to do in the *Timaeus*.

Some now argue that Anaxagorean *nous* fares better as a teleological principle than Plato or Aristotle allows.[34] One might be more inclined to think that the Presocratic philosopher who describes most systematically the natural world's rational order and accounts for it as the product of a governing divine intelligence is Heraclitus, given his conception of the underlying *logos* or rational principle governing the interplay between opposites in all natural change, and given his apparent identification of this *logos* with an intelligent divinity present throughout and governing the cosmos as fire.[35] The Stoics would find in this network of ideas anticipations of their own conception of *pneuma*, the intelligent and creative divine fire present throughout the cosmos and rationally governing all its changes, and would so come to see Heraclitus as their most important Presocratic predecessor.[36] It is striking, however, that virtually none of the elements that would make Heraclitus important for the Stoics feature in Plato and Aristotle.[37] Here the mediating influence of sophistic representations of the Presocratics seems clear. *Cratylus* 402a4–c3 (quoted earlier) shows that the representation of Heraclitus's philosophy under the rubrics "everything flows" (*panta rhei*) and "everything changes" (*panta kineitai*) can be traced back to Hippias's anthology. Moreover, if Gorgias's doxographical preface did in fact include a section classifying views of Being based on the dichotomy in motion versus at rest, its influence would seem to be reflected in this passage's immediate context, wherein these two broad types of view are figured in two variant etymologies of *ousia*. There are some, Socrates says, who call it *essia*, indicating their identification of reality with being and the stability of the hearth because of the morphological similarity with *estin* ("it is") and Hestia (the goddess of the hearth); whereas there are others who call it *ôsia*, indicating a view of reality as essentially dynamic because of the term's connection to *ôthoun* ("to push") (*Cra.* 401c–d). The same basic opposition features again at *Theaetetus* 180c7–e4, where Plato contrasts the Heraclitean thesis that everything changes (*panta kineitai*) with the Eleatic position of the "Melissans and Parmenideans" that all things are one (*hen panta esti*) and unchanging. The representation of Heraclitus summed up in the tag "everything changes," which can be traced back to the sophists, appears to have been promulgated in a more extreme form by Cratylus, the self-styled Heraclitean and contemporary of Socrates whom Aristotle famously identifies as having had a major influence on Plato's view of the sensible world. "From an early age," Aristotle says, "he [Plato] first became familiar with Cratylus and the Heraclitean views, that all perceptibles are always in flux and that there is no knowledge about them, and he held these views later too."[38] The Heraclitean theses ascribed to Cratylus here are precisely those that make up the Heraclitean "secret doctrine" presented by Plato in the *Theaetetus*, and there is thus every good reason to see the representation of Heraclitus in that dialogue as suffused with the Cratylean appropriation.

In turn, the Cratylean representation of Heraclitus in the *Theaetetus* evidently influenced the young Aristotle of the *Topics* and *Physics* 1, where Heraclitus figures as a trader in deliberate paradox. The Heraclitean view that everything changes is cited in the *Topics* as an example of a *thesis*, which Aristotle defines as "a conception contrary to general opinion but propounded by someone famous as a philosopher" (*Top.* 1.11.104b19–22). In the *Theaetetus*, the Heraclitean doctrine of constant change is from its introduction presented as entailing that nothing has a property, *F*, without also having the opposite property, not-*F*: "If you call a thing large, it will reveal itself as small, and if you call it heavy, it is liable to appear as light, and so on with everything, because nothing is one thing or any kind of thing. What is really true, is this: the things of which we naturally say that they 'are,' are in process of coming to be, as the result of movement and change and blending with one another" (152d4–e1)[39]. The identification of the Heraclitean doctrine of constant change as having this particular entailment provides the basis for the other *thesis* Aristotle attributed to Heraclitus in the *Topics* and again in the *Physics*, namely that the same thing can be both *F* and not-*F* (*Top.* 8.5.159b30–35, *Ph.* 1.2.185b19–25; *cf.* 185a5–7). Such is the background of Aristotle's notorious characterization of Heraclitus as denying the law of noncontradiction: "It is impossible for the same thing to both belong and not belong simultaneously to the same thing in the same respect... indeed this is the most secure of all principles.... For it is impossible for anyone to suppose the same thing is and is not, as indeed some think Heraclitus says [καθάπερ τινὲς οἴονται λέγειν Ἡράκλειτον]" (*Metaph.* 4.3.1005b23–25; *cf.* 7.1012a24–26). It is noteworthy, however, that Aristotle is here rather more tentative in ascribing the view in question to Heraclitus than he had been in the *Topics* and *Physics* 1. Despite this note of hesitation, the effect on Aristotle of the sophistic representations of Heraclitus can be seen in his nearly complete absence from *Physics* 1 and *Metaphysics* 1. He figures in these treatises' review of reputable opinions just once, at *Metaphysics* 1.3.984a7–8, where he is mentioned along with Hippasus of Metapontum as having identified fire as the material cause.

Other texts show Aristotle had something more than the passing acquaintance with Heraclitus this suggests. He quotes the first sentence of his book in the

Rhetoric, and either quotes or paraphrases some minor fragments in other texts.[40] Perhaps most significant, however, is Aristotle's attribution to Heraclitus at both *Physics* 3.5.205a3–4 and *De Caelo* 1.10.279b13–17 of the view that the cosmos periodically resolves itself into a state of pure fire, for this indicates some degree of emancipation from the sophistic representation and anticipates an important element in the Stoic use of Heraclitus. Furthermore, the mention of Heraclitus in the *De Caelo* passage alongside Empedocles, as representing with him the view that the generation and destruction of the cosmos recur periodically without end, is reminiscent of the grouping of these two thinkers in Plato's *Sophist* as having held that Being is both many and one.[41] Here, too, there is an incipient move away from the sophistic representation of Heraclitus. Still, there is no real indication that Plato or Aristotle ever recognized the central role Heraclitus attributed to the divine *logos*. Although both Plato and Aristotle seem to have recognized that the schematic representation of Parmenides as the proponent of a single unchanging reality offered too restrictive and reductive a view of him,[42] they never seem to have made a similar leap with Heraclitus and to have acknowledged that there is a single unchanging Being in his system as well, whose presence and activity must be apprehended by reason rather than the senses.

The Presocratics' influence on Plato and Aristotle is so profound, complex, and multifaceted that it is impossible even to begin doing justice to the subject within the compass of a single essay. The primary aim here has therefore been to reinforce in various ways a point that must be appreciated to avoid confusion, namely that Plato and Aristotle's engagement with the Presocratics was conditioned from the outset by representations of their thought stemming from the sophistic period, primarily, though not solely, from the tradition of philosophical historiography that had begun then. Although the true nature and extent of work in the genre during its earliest phase will never be known, enough of its features may still be pieced together to make apparent its influence on Plato and Aristotle, as well as their progressive emancipation from some, if not all, of the misrepresentations it encouraged.[43]

NOTES

1. See especially Mansfeld, "*Cratylus* 402a–c"; "Historical and Philosophical Aspects of Gorgias' *On What Is Not*"; and "Aristotle, Plato, and the Preplatonic Doxography and Chronography"; all are reprinted in Mansfeld, *Studies in the Historiography of Greek Philosophy*, 84–96, 97–125, and 22–83, respectively.

2. Mansfeld, "Aristotle, Plato, and the Preplatonic Doxography and Chronography," 3.

3. Palmer, *Plato's Reception of Parmenides*, especially pt. 2. Failure to take account either of the sophistic appropriations of Parmenides reflected in Plato or of the Parme-

nidean presence in dialogues other than the *Sophist* vitiates the treatment of Parmenides in McCabe, *Plato and His Predecessors*, which is otherwise important for its intricately structured argument aiming to demonstrate how Plato dramatizes fundamental issues of rationality and personhood via representations of earlier philosophers.

4. Snell, "Die Nachrichten über die Lehren des Thales und die Anfänge der griechischen Philosophie- und Literaturgeschichte."

5. Mansfeld, "*Cratylus* 402a-c," reexamines Snell's analysis of the relevant passages in Plato and Aristotle and corrects Snell's conjecture that only Thales, and not Heraclitus, figured originally among Hippias's *comparanda*. Indeed, it makes perfect sense for Thales' identification of water as the origin of all things to have been cited by Hippias alongside the similar identifications to be found among Homer, Hesiod, and Orpheus as all expressing a view related or comparable to Heraclitus's that the things that are (*ta onta*) are like a river and all subject to change. Classen, "Bemerkungen zu zwei griechischen 'Philosophiehistorikern,'" 175–78, detected Hippias's influence in the successive citation by Phaedrus at Pl. *Smp.* 178a9–c1 of Hes. *Th.* 116–18 and 120, Acusilaus, and Parmenides 28B13 as confirmation that Eros is one of the most ancient divinities, the citations from Hesiod and Parmenides being reproduced in Arist. *Metaph.* 1.4. 984b25–8. On Hippias's role in the early development of philosophical historiography, see now also Patzer, *Der Sophist Hippias als Philosophiehistoriker*.

6. Indirect access to Gorgias's original treatise is provided by epitomes preserved in two sources, ps.-Arist. *De Melisso Xenophane Gorgia* [*MXG*] 979a10–980b21 and S.E. *M.* 7.65–87. Although DK failed to print the *MXG* epitome in their collection, it has nonetheless come to be recognized as the more faithful and thus more important source. For the text of the treatise, see Buchheim, *Gorgias von Leontini*.

7. See Mansfeld, "Historical and Philosophical Aspects of Gorgias' *On What Is Not*," 248–49, where he argues that *ta onta* here "are not in the first place the phenomenal things, but the speculative theoretical constructs of the Presocratic philosophers." Guthrie, *The Sophists*, 194, draws a similar conclusion on the basis of the treatise's alternative title, *Peri phuseôs* or *On Nature*.

8. See further Furley, *The Formation of the Atomic Theory and Its Earliest Critics*, ch. 2.

9. For an overview of Plato's, as well as Aristotle's, treatment of Anaxagoras, see Gigon, "Anaxagoras bei Platon und Aristoteles."

10. The *Phaedo*'s dismissive attitude toward Anaxagoras has tended to obscure the fact that he can be seen as influencing Plato's theory of forms. See the final section of Furley, "Anaxagoras in Response to Parmenides"; Kutash, "Anaxagoras and the Rhetoric of Plato's Middle Dialogue Theory of Forms"; Furley, "Anaxagoras, Plato, and the Naming of Parts."

11. Comparison with Arist. *Cael.* 3.2. 300b2–3 and 2.13. 294b13–17 indicates that the first explanation here belongs to Empedocles and the second variously to Anaximenes, Anaxagoras, and Democritus.

12. The seminal study of the role of *ta endoxa* in Artistotelian dialectic is Owen, "Tithenai ta phainomena" (see especially 91–92). See also Barnes, "Aristotle and the Methods of Ethics"; Nussbaum, "Saving Aristotle's Appearances"; Irwin, "Aristotle's Method of Ethics"; Cleary, "*Phainomena* in Aristotle's Methodology."

13. See further Bolton, "Aristotle's Method in Natural Science: *Physics* I."

14. *Sph.* 242c5-6: τὰ ὄντα . . . πόσα τε καὶ ποῖά ἐστιν.

15. This summation of the Eleatic position is a variation on Plato's standard formulation of the Eleatic thesis as *hen to pan* or its equivalent (see *Sph.* 244b6, 245a3, 252a6–7; *Prm.* 128a8–b1; *Tht.* 183e3–4).

16. Cherniss, *Aristotle's Criticism of Presocratic Philosophy*, chs. 1 and 7.

17. Cherniss, *Aristotle's Criticism of Presocratic Philosophy*, 356. One form response to Cherniss's momentous study has taken has been to attempt to defend Aristotle's qualifications as a historian of philosophy; see Guthrie, "Aristotle as a Historian of Philosophy"; Stevenson, "Aristotle as Historian of Philosophy." However, if the proper focus is maintained on the dialectical function of Aristotle's reviews of previous opinions, something Cherniss rightly emphasized throughout his study, then the question of whether Aristotle can properly be regarded as a historian of philosophy seems immaterial. See further Mansion, "Le rôle de l'exposé et de la critique des philosophies antérieures chez Aristote"; Berti, "Sul carattere dialettico della storiografia filosofica di Aristotele"; Collobert, "Aristotle's Review of the Presocratics." See also Schofield, "APXH," for discussion of how Aristotle attempts to cast Presocratic philosophy as a debate about *archai* and for an overview of the use of the term prior to Aristotle.

18. See *Metaph.* 1.5. 986b33–4.

19. See further Palmer, *Plato's Reception of Parmenides*, 93–94.

20. The points of this and the next two paragaphs are developed in greater detail in Palmer, "Melissus and Parmenides."

21. See *Top.* 1.11. 104b19–22: "A *thesis* is a conception contrary to general opinion but propounded by someone famous as a philosopher; for example, 'Contradiction is impossible,' as Antisthenes said, or the opinion of Heraclitus that 'All things are changing,' or 'Being is one,' as Melissus says; for to pay any attention when an ordinary person sets forth views that are contrary to received opinions is foolish."

22. Compare the absence of Parmenides from the contrast between physical monists and pluralists in *GC* 1.1.

23. On this passage and its context, see Kerferd, "Aristotle's Treatment of the Doctrine of Parmenides."

24. Reading τὸ ὂν ἓν μὲν at 986b31–32, as per Alexander's paraphrase.

25. See Mansfeld, "Aristotle, Plato, and the Preplatonic Doxography and Chronography," 5.

26. For development of this point, see Michael Frede's chapter here.

27. Cf. *Metaph.* 1.3. 983a33–b6, 4. 985a10–15, 5. 986a13–15, 7. 988a18–23, 988b16–18.

28. One should not allow the artificially imposed chapter break here to obscure the fact that Aristotle is continuing to discuss the earlier traces of the efficient-*cum*-final cause when he turns to Hesiod and Parmenides. τὸ τοιοῦτον at 1.4.984b23–24 immediately picks up τοῦ καλῶς... τοῖς οὖσιν at 1.4. 984b21–22, and when Aristotle identifies the explanation for the central role of Eros in their cosmogonies as the need for "some cause that will move things and bring them together" (τιν' αἰτίαν ἥτις κινήσει καὶ συνάξει τὰ πράγματα) (984b29–31), he is referring to the role naturally played by Eros as both an efficient cause and the cause of harmony and order.

29. See note 5 here.

30. For a sustained study of Aristotle's representation of Empedocles, see Giannantoni, "L'interpretazione aristotelica di Empedocle." For an examination of Aristotle's extended discussion of Empedocles in *Metaph.* 3.4. 1000a18–b19 in light of the recently discovered papyrus fragments of Empedocles' poem (*P. Strasb. gr.* inv. 1665–1666), see Primavesi, "Neues zur aristotelischen Vorsokratiker-Doxographie."

31. For a sustained examination of other aspects of Plato's engagement with Empedocles, emphasizing Plato's rejection of the Empedoclean idea that a divine power be the cause of evil, see O'Brien, "L'Empédocle de Platon."

32. On the understanding of Xenophanes reflected in Plato (and Aristotle), see further Palmer, "Xenophanes' Ouranian God in the Fourth Century."

33. For an illuminating account of the nature and role of *nous* in Plato that touches upon its presence in earlier thinkers as well, see Menn, *Plato on God as Nous*.

34. See Laks, "Mind's Crisis"; Lesher, "Mind's Knowledge and Powers of Control in Anaxagoras DK B12."

35. Heraclit. B41 in conjunction with B32 in particular indicates that Heraclitus conceived of it as an intelligent principle directing the operation of all things according to a rational plan; see also B1, B30, B31, B32, B41, B64, B67, B78, B114, etc. On the intelligent and directive aspect of Heraclitus's divine principle, see Sullivan, "*To sophon* as an Aspect of the Divine in Heraclitus"; Mitevski, "Heraclitus' *Logos* as a Principle of Change."

36. See further Long, "Heraclitus and Stoicism"; Sharples, "On Fire in Heraclitus and in Zeno of Citium"; Bels, "Le thème de la grande année."

37. On the representation of Heraclitus in Plato and Aristotle, see Kahn, "Plato and Heraclitus"; Viano, "Aristotele e l'arché-fuoco di Eraclito"; Viano, "Héraclite dans la doxographie d'Aristote"; Moyal, "Did Plato Misunderstand Heraclitus?" O'Brien, "Héraclite et l'unité des opposés"; and Adoménas, "The Fluctuating Fortunes of Heraclitus in Plato."

38. Arist. *Metaph.* 1.6. 987a32–b1, closely paralleled by 13.4. 1078b12–15; on Cratylus's Heracliteanizing, see also *Metaph.* 6.5.1010a7–15.

39. Translation by Levett and Burnyeat in Cooper, ed., *Plato: Complete Works*.

40. See *Rh.* 3.5. 1407b11–18, as well as 22B6 *apud Mete.* 2.2. 355a13–14, 22B7 *apud Sens.* 5. 443a23–24, 22B8 *apud EN* 8.1. 1155b4–6, 22B9 *apud EN* 10.5. 1176a6–7, the paraphrases of 22B5 at *EN* 2.3. 1105a8–9 and of 22B85 at *EE* 2.7. 1223b22–24 and *Pol.* 5.11. 1315a30–31, and the anecdotes recorded at *PA* 2.5. 645a17–21 and *EE* 7.1. 1235a25–27.

41. On Aristotle's citation of Empedocles here, see Viano, "Aristotele, *De coel.* I 10: Empédocle, l'alternance et le mythe du *Politique*," calling into question the accuracy of this representation of Empedocles, one anticipated in the myth of Plato's *Statesman*.

42. See earlier regarding Aristotle's view of Parmenides on this point; regarding Plato's, see Palmer, *Plato's Reception of Parmenides*, esp. chs. 4, 6, 7, and 9.

43. In the course of developing this point, some effort has also been made to steer discussion away from the question, which tends to dominate discussion of the subject, regarding the value of Plato and Aristotle as sources in the reconstruction of Presocratic thought, and toward discussion of the philosophical uses they made of their predecessors, partially because this is an interesting topic in its own right but also in the belief that further and more detailed inquiry into the topic can still be the source of new perspectives on the Presocratics themselves.

BIBLIOGRAPHY

Adoménas, Mantas. "The Fluctuating Fortunes of Heraclitus in Plato." In *Qu'est-ce que la philosophie présocratique?* edited by André Laks and Claire Louguet, 419–47. Lille: Presses Universitaires du Septentrion, 2002.

Barnes, Jonathan. "Aristotle and the Methods of Ethics." *Revue Internationale de Philosophie* 34 (1980): 490–511.

Bels, J. "Le thème de la grande année: d'Héraclite aux Stoïciens." *Revue de Philosophie Ancienne* 7 (1989): 169–83.

Berti, Enrico. "Sul carattere dialettico della storiografia filosofica di Aristotele." In *Storiografia e dossografia nella filosofia antica*, edited by G. Cambiano, 101–25. Turin: Tirrenia Stampatori, 1986.

Bolton, Robert. "Aristotle's Method in Natural Science: *Physics* I." In *Aristotle's Physics: A Collection of Essays*, edited by Lindsay Judson, 1–29. Oxford: Oxford University Press, 1991.

Buchheim, T. *Gorgias von Leontini: Reden, Fragmente und Testimonien*. Hamburg: Felix Meiner, 1989.

Cherniss, Harold. *Aristotle's Criticism of Presocratic Philosophy*. Baltimore: Johns Hopkins University Press, 1935.

Classen, C. Joachim. "Bemerkungen zu zwei griechischen 'Philosophiehistorikern.'" *Philologus* 109 (1965): 175–81.

Cleary, J. J. "*Phainomena* in Aristotle's Methodology." *International Journal of Philosophical Studies* 2 (1994): 61–97.

Collobert, Catherine. "Aristotle's Review of the Presocratics: Is Aristotle Finally a Historian of Philosophy?" *Journal of the History of Philosophy* 40 (2002): 281–95.

Cooper, John, ed. *Plato: Complete Works*. Indianapolis: Hackett, 1997.

Furley, David J. "Anaxagoras in Response to Parmenides." *Canadian Journal of Philosophy*, supp. vol. 2 (1976): 61–85.

———. "Anaxagoras, Plato, and the Naming of Parts." In *Presocratic Philosophy: Essays in Honor of A. P. D. Mourelatos*, edited by Victor Caston and Daniel W. Graham, 119–26. Aldershot, England: Ashgate, 2002.

———. *The Formation of the Atomic Theory and Its Earliest Critics*. Vol. 1 of *The Greek Cosmologists*. Cambridge: Cambridge University Press, 1987.

Giannantoni, Gabriele. "L'interpretazione aristotelica di Empedocle." *Elenchos* 19 (1998): 361–411.

Gigon, Olof. "Anaxagoras bei Platon und Aristoteles." In *Ionian Philosophy*, edited by K. J. Boudouris, 142–64. Athens: Kardamitsa, 1989.

Guthrie, W. K. C. "Aristotle as a Historian of Philosophy: Some Preliminaries." *Journal of Hellenic Studies* 77 (1957): 35–41.

———. *The Sophists*. Cambridge: Cambridge University Press, 1971.

Irwin, Terence H. "Aristotle's Method of Ethics." In *Studies in Aristotle*, edited by Dominic O'Meara, 193–223. Washington, D.C.: Catholic University of America Press, 1981.

Kahn, Charles H. "Plato and Heraclitus." *Proceedings of the Boston Area Colloquium in Ancient Philosophy* 1 (1985): 241–58.

Kerferd, George B. "Aristotle's Treatment of the Doctrine of Parmenides." *Oxford Studies in Ancient Philosophy*, supp. vol. (1991): 1–7.

Kutash, E. "Anaxagoras and the Rhetoric of Plato's Middle Dialogue Theory of Forms." *Philosophy and Rhetoric* 26 (1993): 134–52.

Laks, André. "Mind's Crisis: On Anaxagoras' Nous." *Southern Journal of Philosophy*, supp., 31 (1993): 19–38.

Lesher, James H. "Mind's Knowledge and Powers of Control in Anaxagoras DK B12." *Phronesis* 40 (1995): 125–42.

Long, A. A. "Heraclitus and Stoicism." *Philosophia* 5–6 (1975–76): 133–56. Reprinted in *Stoic Studies*, edited by A. A. Long, 35–57. Cambridge: Cambridge University Press, 1996.

Mansfeld, Jaap. "*Cratylus* 402a–c: Plato or Hippias?" In *Studi*, vol. 1 of *Atti del Symposium Heracliteum 1981*, edited by Livio Rossetti, 43–55. Rome: Ateneo, 1983.

————. "Aristotle, Plato, and the Preplatonic Doxography and Chronography." In *Storiografia e dossografia nella filosofia antica*, edited by G. Cambiano, 1–59. Turin: Terrenia Stampatoria, 1986.

————. "Historical and Philosophical Aspects of Gorgias' *On What Is Not*." In *Gorgia e la sofistica*, vol. 38 of *Siculorum Gymnasium*, edited by L. Monteneri and F. Romano, 243–71. Catania: Facoltà di Lettere e Filosofia, Università di Catania, 1985.

————. *Studies in the Historiography of Greek Philosophy*. Assen: Van Gorcum, 1990.

Mansion, Suzanne. "Le rôle de l'exposé et de la critique des philosophies antérieures chez Aristote." In *Aristote et les problèmes de méthode*, edited by Suzanne Mansion, 35–56. Louvain: Presses Universitaires de Louvain, 1961.

McCabe, Mary Margaret. *Plato and His Predecessors*. Cambridge: Cambridge University Press, 2000.

Menn, Stephen. *Plato on God as Nous*. Journal of the History of Philosophy monograph series. Carbondale: Southern Illinois University Press, 1995.

Mitevski, V. "Heraclitus' *Logos* as a Principle of Change." *Ziva Antica* 44 (1994): 45–64.

Moyal, G. J. D. "Did Plato Misunderstand Heraclitus?" *Revue des Études Anciennes* 90 (1988): 89–98.

Nussbaum, Martha C. "Saving Aristotle's Appearances." In *Language and Logos*, edited by M. Schofield and M. C. Nussbaum, 267–93. Cambridge: Cambridge University Press, 1982.

O'Brien, Denis. "Héraclite et l'unité des opposés." *Revue de Métaphysique et de Morale* 95 (1990): 147–71.

————. "L'Empédocle de Platon." *Revue des Études Grecques* 110 (1997): 381–98.

Owen, G. E. L. "Tithenai ta phainomena." In *Aristote et les problèmes de la méthode*, edited by S. Mansion, 83–103. Louvain: Publications Universitaires de Louvain, 1961.

Palmer, John. "Melissus and Parmenides." *Oxford Studies in Ancient Philosophy* 26 (2004): 19–54.

————. *Plato's Reception of Parmenides*. Oxford: Clarendon Press, 1999.

————. "Xenophanes' Ouranian God in the Fourth Century." *Oxford Studies in Ancient Philosophy* 16 (1998): 1–34.

Patzer, Andreas. *Der Sophist Hippias als Philosophiehistoriker*. Freiburg: Karl Alber, 1986.

Primavesi, Oliver. "Neues zur aristotelischen Vorsokratiker-Doxographie." In *Antike Naturwissenschaft und ihre Rezeption 8*, edited by K. Döring, B. Herzhoff, and G. Wöhrle, 25–41. Trier: Wissenschaftlicher Verlag, 1998.

Schofield, Malcolm. "APXH." *Hyperboreus* 3 (1997): 218–35.

Sharples, R. W. "On Fire in Heraclitus and in Zeno of Citium." *Classical Quarterly* 34 (1984): 231–32.

Snell, Bruno. "Die Nachrichten über die Lehren des Thales und die Anfänge der griechischen Philosophie- und Literaturgeschichte." *Philologus* 96 (1944): 170–82.

Stevenson, J. G. "Aristotle as Historian of Philosophy." *Journal of Hellenic Studies* 94 (1974): 138–43.

Sullivan, S. D. "*To sophon* as an Aspect of the Divine in Heraclitus." In *Greek Poetry and Philosophy: Studies in Honour of Leonard Woodbury*, edited by D. E. Gerber, 285–301. Chico, Calif.: Scholars Press, 1984.

Viano, C. "Aristotele, *De coel*. I 10: Empédocle, l'alternance et le mythe du *Politique*." *Revue des Études Grecques* 107 (1994): 400–13.

————. "Aristotele e l'arché-fuoco di Eraclito." *Archives Internationales d'Histoire des Sciences* 37 (1987): 207–21.

————. "Héraclite dans la doxographie d'Aristote." *Les Études Classiques* 57 (1989): 193–207.

Index Locorum

General Index

Acusilaus of Argos, 58
Aëtius, 12, 139
   Diels reconstruction of, 135
   doxai of, 35–36
   on pyrhogenous theory, 144
   pyridia as understood by, 144–45
   reconstructed work of, 30, 36
   sun/moon in work of, 136–37
   zoogonical stages attested by, 260
air
   Anaximenes on, 113–14, 116–17, 439
   as basis for animate/inanimate properties and
      processes, 120–21
   as common principle, 362n24
   differentiation of, 119–20
   Diogenes of Apollonia on, 495
   Diogenes of Apollonia's theory based on, 7–8
   as god, 487
   light in, 130n93
   Plato on, 118
   priority of, 129n86
   Simplicius on, 115
   in theory of change, 116
   vapors v., 118–19
Alcaeus, 135
Alcmaeon of Croton, 33, 388, 390
   on divine/mortals distinction, 469–70
   as Pythagorean, 295, 302n20
   on souls, 443
alphabetic writing, 75n5
   as easy to learn, 58
   Greek adoption of, 57
   success of, 57
   in Syria, 63–64
anatomy, Hippocratic writings on, 402–3
Anaxagoras of Clazomenae, 7, 38, 71
   background assumptions about, 231–33
   cosmic intelligence doctrine of, 495–96
   cosmogony of, 444
   Diogenes of Apollonia v., 355–57, 358
   Eleatic credentials of view of, 232
   Eleatic principles and, 234
   on generation/corruption, 234
   on human perception, 235
   ingredients/natural artifacts and, 233–38
   as intelligence as motive force, 494–95
   on marvelous phenomena, 391

medical tradition and, 231, 244n2
metaphysical analysis of, 233
metatheoretical influence on, 231
Milesians influence on, 231
on mind, 236–39, 425–26, 441, 444
on mind's character/powers, 242
on mixture changes producing world, 233–34
multiple worlds v. world-within-worlds view
   and, 240–41
on original mixture, 235–37, 245n16
original works of, 31
in *Phaedo*, 544, 550n10
physics of, 441, 446
on plants, 238
on plurality/diversity, 418–19
principle of everything-in-everything of, 232–33
principle of homoiometeity in work of, 244n6
principle of unlimited largeness and smallness
   of, 232–33
on range of real things, 234–35
rejection of reality of what-is-not by, 233
on rotation of mixture, 234
scientific theorizing of, 239–40
seeds as referenced by, 238, 246n23
on separation mixture, 237–38
on soul, 237
theory of everything by, 230–43
on world as is, 356–57
on worlds here/elsewhere, 239–41
Anaximander, 43, 65, 520
   Anaximenes v., 112–13
   on *apeiron*, 486–87
   astronomical calendar compiled by, 96
   astronomy and, 103–12
   atomic cosmogony's roots in, 421
   basic principle of, 416–17
   cosmogony of, 107–11
   cosmology of, 112
   on cosmos, 105–7
   cosmos model postulated by, 111
   on cosmos' physical structure, 90, 103
   on cycles of time for change throughout
      cosmos, 112–13
   demythologization by, 486
   determinate boundaries for terrestrial/celestial
      realms proposed by, 103

Sextus' contribution to knowledge of, 41
shortcomings of, 448–49
Simplicius and information on, 43
as term, 3–4
theology, 18
theory of everything for, 413
topics of study by, 3–4
tradition as recorded by, 30
transmission strands for, 31–43
as viewed by themselves, 524–25
The Presocratic Philosopher (Barnes), 20
Presocratic philosophy
analytical philosophy and, 20
causation as viewed in, 289
cause in, 434–55
chance and necessity in, 448–50
cosmologies in, 413–328
epistemology and, 8
explanation in, 434–55
formal principles of, 450–52
historiography of, 9–21
justice in, 447–48
moving cause recognized by, 521
notion of conservation in, 447
orientalizing context of, 55–75
physicians influenced by, 4
Plutarch's information on, 41
reason in, 434–55
sensation and evidence in, 452–53
texts of, 4–5
traditional histories of, 6–7
traditional piety in writings of, 458–59
variations of traditional theme in, 464–76
Presocratics
Aristotle's view of, 8–9
Plato's view of, 8–9
Primavesi, Olivier, 31
Prodicus, as Sophist, 366
Pros Demonikon (Isocrates), 66
Protagoras
Athens visited by, 367–68
democratic views of, 369
on good judgment, 374
on language, 375
language as approached by, 376
Plato's treatment of, 370
as relativist, 375–76
as Sophist, 366
Protagoras (Plato), 368
Protrepticus (Aristotle), 507
Ptolemy, 64
Pyrhogenous theory, 143, 144
pyridia, 144–45, 163n52
Pythagoras, 38
as attributed with supermortal characteristics, 465
body of knowledge credited to, 464–68
character of, 292
Diogenes Laertius on, 294

Egypt associated with, 60
Empedocles on, 464–68
Heraclitus on, 465
miracles by, 465
numerical relationships focused on by, 466–67
preservation of work of, 41
on wisdom as aspired to by humans, 523
Pythagoreanism
Aristotle's account of fifth-century, 284–91
defining, 293
early, 294
as philosophical movement, 41
Plato as influenced by, 284–91
problems in, 284–301
term as used, 292–93
Pythagoreans, 6–7
catalogue of, 297–98
criteria for identifying personas for, 299–301
explanatory principle employed by, 544
formal explanations' necessity for, 451
identifying individuals as, 294–301
on number as principle, 521
in Presocratic views in causation's development, 289
role in early thought, 19
theory of forms and, 290–91, 522
Pythagorean theorem, 64

rainbows, 135–36, 151
pre-classical Greeks use of, 150, 164n72
reincarnation, 265–66
Reinhardt, Karl, 61
Reitzenstein, Richard, 61
relativism, as defined, 375
religion
in ancient Greece, 379
demythologization of popular beliefs from, 492
Heraclitus on, 492–93
naturalism's compatibility of, 394
origin of, 378
philosophy's emergence from, 18
popular, 492–93
Presocratic philosophers and belief in, 8
Sophists as threat to, 378–79
for twentieth century scholars, 18
Republic (Plato), mathematics in, 285
research
on Greek philosophy, 60–62
methods of Aristotle, 34
Research in Astronomy (Eudemus), 111
rhetoric
defining, 370
Sophists as teaching, 370–73
river fragments, 172–74, 179–81, 185n10
as experience, 181
as whole, 181

Lightning Source UK Ltd.
Milton Keynes UK
UKHW04f0957020718
325038UK00013B/609/P

9 780199 837557